THE ANCIENT MESSENIANS

Early in the archaic period of Greek history, Messenia was annexed and partially settled by its powerful neighbor, Sparta. Achieving independence in the fourth century BC, the inhabitants of Messenia set about trying to forge an identity for themselves separate from their previous identity as Spartan subjects, refunctionalizing or simply erasing their Spartan heritage. Luraghi provides a thorough examination of the history of Messenian identity and consequently addresses a range of questions and issues whose interest and importance have only been widely recognized by ancient historians during the last decade. By a detailed scrutiny of the ancient written sources and the archaeological evidence, the book reconstructs how the Messenians perceived and constructed their own ethnicity at different points in time, by applying to Messenian ethnicity insights developed by anthropologists and early medieval historians.

NINO LURAGHI is Professor of Classics at Harvard University, and has published widely on Greek history and historiography. Recent works include an edited volume entitled *The Politics of Ethnicity and the Crisis of the Peloponnesian League* (forthcoming) and *Helots and their Masters in Laconia and Messenia* (coedited with S. Alcock, 2003).

THE ANCIENT MESSENIANS

Constructions of Ethnicity and Memory

NINO LURAGHI

Harvard University

CAMBRIDGE
UNIVERSITY PRESS

CAMBRIDGE UNIVERSITY PRESS
Cambridge, New York, Melbourne, Madrid, Cape Town, Singapore, São Paulo

Cambridge University Press
The Edinburgh Building, Cambridge CB2 8RU, UK

Published in the United States of America by Cambridge University Press, New York

www.cambridge.org
Information on this title: www.cambridge.org/9780521855877

First published 2008

Printed in the United Kingdom at the University Press, Cambridge

A catalogue record for this publication is available from the British Library

Library of Congress Cataloguing in Publication data
Luraghi, Nino.
The ancient Messenians : constructions of ethnicity and memory / Nino Luraghi.
p.   cm.
Includes bibliographical references and index.
ISBN 978-0-521-85587-7 (hardback : alk. paper)
1. Messenia (Greece)–History.   I. Title.
DF261.M45L87 2008
938'.9–dc22
2008004761

ISBN 978-0-521-85587-7 hardback

Μὲ τί καρδιά, μὲ τί πνοή,
τί πόθους καὶ τί πάθος
πήραμε τὴ ζωή μας· λάθος!
κι ἀλλάξαμε ζωή.

For M. K. B.

Contents

Acknowledgments

This book has had a long and somewhat peculiar history. Some fifteen years ago, while studying the foundation legends of the Greek cities of Southern Italy, my attention was caught by the recurrent presence of the Messenian Wars in those of Rhegion, Taras and Lokroi Epizephyrioi. At that time I was trying to understand the evolution of foundation legends in time, and since the ancient tradition on the Messenian Wars had been investigated in some detail, it seemed a promising place to look for a clear and well-defined stratigraphy that could maybe function as a template for the stratigraphy of the foundation legends I was investigating. For various reasons, including the fact that this did not look like a good topic for a doctoral dissertation, my Messenian escapade remained almost without consequences, except that it helped me to make sense of the political culture of the regime led by the tyrant Anaxilaos of Rhegion. Years later, in 1997, I was induced to revive my Messenian interests by the invitation to join a research group on identity and otherness in ancient Greece, led by Hans-Joachim Gehrke at the University of Freiburg, in the framework of the *Sonderforschungsbereich* 541. The academic environment of the Institute of Ancient History at Freiburg, which housed a stunning amount of brainpower, has influenced this work, and in general my way of practicing ancient history, in more ways than I can acknowledge. Two years of work, almost free from other commitments although with quite a lot of constructive side-tracking, made it possible to lay the theoretical groundwork for the project and to make significant inroads in the topic. The move to Harvard as a full-time teacher in the summer of 1999 severely curtailed the time available for this project, but also introduced a number of new and important influences. Besides the exciting scholarly atmosphere of Harvard, the presence of Sue Alcock as visiting professor for one term helped to focus my thoughts on the nature of Helotic dependency, an interest also encouraged by the inspiring proximity of Orlando Patterson. On more than one occasion, the famously searching questions of Albert Henrichs helped me to decide what I thought on some issues that I was trying to avoid. An invitation by Peter Funke in the fall of 2001 compelled me to think seriously about Hellenistic Messenia. In my fourth year at Harvard, a sabbatical, half of it spent at the Institute for Advanced Study, that scholar's paradise, made it possible to fine-tune various parts of the project, taking advantage of Christian Habicht's erudition and wisdom. My time in the Department of Classics of the University of Toronto, where my friend John Magee was unlimitedly liberal with his time and provided abundant advice and encouragement, allowed me to mull over many portions of the book. One sabbatical semester granted by Harvard University in the fall of 2006 made it possible to bring the project to completion. At Harvard, my colleague Christopher Jones generously read the final version of the manuscript, saving me from many infelicities of style and content and offering many helpful comments and suggestions.

Over the years, I have had occasion to discuss and publish various articles that dealt with parts of my general project. Most of them have become parts of this book, usually in a completely revised form. They are listed in the bibliography, but I should alert the reader that, except in the cases where I make explicit reference to any of those previous works, I intend for this book to supersede them.

My project has received generous financial support from a number of sources, including the *Sonderforschungsbereich* 541 "Identitäten und Alteritäten" of the Albert-Ludwigs-Universität Freiburg, the Loeb Fund of the Department of the Classics and the Clarke Fund of the Faculty of Arts and Sciences, Harvard University, and the Connaught Fund of the University of Toronto. To all of them goes my heartfelt gratitude.

On the occasion of my visits to Messenia, the team of the Mavromati Excavations has been friendly, hospitable, and liberal with information and discussions. I want to mention in particular Vanda Papaephthimiou, Kleanthis Sidiropoulos, and Liza Sioumpara. Above all, my gratitude goes to Petros Themelis, the new Aristomenes, director of the excavations and greatest expert in all things Messenian.

Among the many scholars who discussed Messenian problems with me and provided me with their own works, published or not, my thanks go especially to Damiana Baldassarra, Pieter Broucke, Nadine Deshours, Catherine Grandjean, Juko Ito, Moritz Kiderlen, Silke Müth, Daniel Ogden, Yanis Pikoulas, and Maddalena Zunino.

C. Scott Walker, digital cartographer of the Harvard Maps Collection, provided templates for the maps of Messenia and the Peloponnese. The readers of this book will certainly be grateful to him, but their gratitude will scarcely equal the author's.

Susanne Ebbinghaus has liberally put her archaeological expertise at my disposal, shared and discussed thoughts and ideas, twice visited Messenia with me, and offered support over the many years during which this project has kept me busy. I will never be able to thank her enough.

None of the people who generously shared their thoughts and their knowledge with me is in any way responsible for the errors and shortcomings of this book.

Torino, December 2006

Abbreviations

Ager	S. L. Ager, ed. *Interstate Arbitrations in the Greek World, 337–90* BC, Berkeley, Los Angeles and London 1996.
CEG	P. A. Hansen, ed. *Carmina epigraphica Graeca saeculorum VIII–V a.Chr.n.*, Berlin and New York 1983.
CID	*Corpus des inscriptions de Delphes*, Paris 1977–.
CIL	*Corpus inscriptionum Latinarum consilio et auctoritate Academiae Scientiarum Berolinensis et Brandenburgensis editum*, Berlin 1881–.
DAA	A. E. Raubitschek, ed. *Dedications from the Athenian Akropolis: A Catalogue of the Inscriptions of the Sixth and Fifth Centuries* BC., Cambridge, Mass. 1949.
Deltion	Ἀρχαϊολογικὸν δελτίον, Athens 1915–.
Ergon	Τὸ ἔργον τῆς ἀρχαϊολογικῆς ἑταιρείας, Athens 1954–.
FD III	*Fouilles de Delphes*, III: *Les Inscriptions*, Paris 1909–.
FgrHist	F. Jacoby, ed. *Fragmente der griechischen Historiker*, Berlin, then Leiden, 1923–64.
Fowler	R. L. Fowler, ed. *Early Greek Mythography*, I: *Text and Introduction*, Oxford 2000.
IG	*Inscriptiones Graecae consilio et auctoritate Academiae Scientiarum Berolinensis et Brandenburgensis editae*, Berlin 1873–.
IGDS	L. Dubois, ed. *Inscriptions grecques dialectales de Sicile: contribution à l'étude du vocabulaire grec colonial*, Rome 1989.
IGDGG	L. Dubois, ed. *Inscriptions grecques dialectales de grande Grèce*. Geneva 1995–.
ISE	L. Moretti, ed. *Iscrizioni storiche ellenistiche*, Florence 1967–.
IvM	O. Kern, ed. *Die Inschriften von Magnesia am Maeander*, Berlin 1910.

IvO	W. Dittenberger and K. Purgold, eds. *Inschriften von Olympia*, Berlin 1896.
LIMC	*Lexicon iconographicum mythologiae classicae*, Zurich 1981–99.
LSAM	F. Sokolowski, ed. *Lois sacrées de l'Asie Mineure*, Paris 1955.
Magnetto	A. Magnetto, ed. *Gli arbitrati interstatali greci*, II: *Dal 337 al 196 a.C.*, Pisa 1997.
ML	R. Meiggs and D. Lewis, eds. *A Selection of Greek Historical Inscriptions to the End of the Fifth Century* BC, revised edition, Oxford 1988.
Moretti	L. Moretti, *Olympionikai, i vincitori negli antichi agoni olimpici, Memorie dell'Accademia nazionale dei Lincei. Classe di scienze morali, storiche e filologiche*, ser. 8, vol. 8, fasc. 2, Rome 1957.
POxy.	*The Oxyrhinchus Papyri*, London 1898–.
Praktika	Πρακτικὰ τῆς ἐν Ἀθήναις ἀρχαϊολογικῆς ἑταιρείας, Athens 1871–.
Rigsby	K. J. Rigsby, ed. *Asylia: Territorial Inviolability in the Hellenistic World*, Berkeley, Los Angeles, and London 1996.
RO	P. Rhodes and R. Osborne, eds. *Greek Historical Inscriptions, 404–323* BC, Oxford 2003.
SEG	*Supplementum epigraphicum Graecum*, Amsterdam 1923–.
SGDI	F. Collitz and H. Bechtel, eds. *Sammlung der griechischen Dialekt-Inschriften*, Göttingen 1884–1915.
*Syll.*³	W. Dittenberger, ed. *Sylloge inscriptionum Graecarum*, third edition revised by F. Hiller von Gaertringen, Leipzig 1915–24.
Staatsverträge	*Die Staatsverträge des Altertums*, Munich 1969–.
TrGF	B. Snell, S. Radt and R. Kannicht eds. *Tragicorum Graecorum fragmenta*, Göttingen 1971–.

Illustrations

Plates

Figures

CHAPTER I

Introduction

From the point of view of the early twenty-first century, any book on the history of ancient Greece is, or at least pretends to be, a book about the past. However, the present book is not only a book about the past from the point of view of the modern or post-modern reader. Rather, it is mostly a book about the past from the point of view of the Greeks themselves. More precisely, it is a book about the ways in which, at different points in time, Greeks living in Messenia in the southwestern Peloponnese, and Greeks elsewhere who identified themselves as Messenians, construed, interpreted and transmitted, by ways of stories, rituals, and other symbolic practices, representations of their shared past, of what made of them a specific and recognizable group inside the greater community of the Greeks – and also, about how other Greeks reacted to those ideas and contributed, for various reasons, to their shaping. Even though, in order to investigate these issues, it is necessary also to devote some attention to what is from our point of view the history of the Messenians, this will be done in a succinct way and with the purpose of creating a framework in which to investigate how ideas about the past and symbolic practices that articulated such ideas developed over time. For this reason, even events that most modern scholars would not necessarily consider historical, such as the return of the Heraclids, will be discussed in detail – not in order to determine whether or not a Dorian invasion of the Peloponnese ever happened, but in order to try and understand the logic of the development of stories about these foundational events.

The study of how groups of human beings articulate and transmit notions of what makes them essentially different from other groups of human beings, that is, the study of collective memory and ethnic identity, has traditionally been the purview of sociologists and anthropologists, and only more recently, relatively speaking, have historians started to take an interest in such issues. This means that the goals and methods of this field of study are to a large extent the product of a creative blurring of

Figure 1 Map of Messenia

disciplinary boundaries, with all the advantages and problems involved. This book is an attempt at applying such methods to the field of ancient Greek history, undertaken trusting in the possibility of formulating questions based on an interdisciplinary approach and finding answers in a painstaking study of the ancient evidence. The scrutiny of the evidence is informed by the principle that any cultural artifact, be it a story, a building, or an inscription, even though it may ostensibly refer to earlier times, should be seen in the first place as evidence for the individuals or groups that generated it and for their historical circumstances.

The choice of the Messenians as the object of an investigation thus oriented is easily explained. The Messenians are a special case in Greek history – a special case, not really a privileged one, except from the cold viewpoint of the enquirer. During the archaic and early classical ages, the region that later came to be known as Messenia, roughly the southwestern corner of the Peloponnese, west of the imposing Taygetos range and south of the river Neda, was simply a part of what was then called Lakedaimon, the Spartan state. In other words, during the periods commonly associated with the birth and development of the Greek city-state, no independent political entity existed in this extensive region. This changed all of a sudden in 369 BC, when the western part of the Spartan state was once and for all transformed into an independent Messenian polity following Epaminondas' invasion of Laconia. In due course, the new Messenian polity emerged with a mythic and historical heritage of its own, spanning the whole archaic period, during which it had actually not existed. This was an impressive effort in the reshaping of the past if there ever was one. Because of this peculiar situation, the Messenians are an ideal case for investigating issues such as the construction and negotiation of ethnic identity and that kind of creative engagement with the past that is often called, somewhat imprecisely, "invention of tradition." Or, reversing the viewpoint, the history of the Messenians can benefit more than most other subchapters of Greek history from the methods and insights gained by current research on such issues in others fields of history and in the social sciences.

Given the peculiar historical circumstances that characterize the history of the Messenians, it is not surprising that modern scholars have not been the first to perceive Messenian tradition as a problem. The scanty sources of the fourth century – as we will see in more detail further on – show clearly that the identity of the citizens of the newly founded Messenian polity was the object of a fierce dispute. Centuries later the greatest admirer of the Messenians among ancient writers, Pausanias, on the one hand complained about the intrisical feebleness of Messenian memory, weakened by centuries of exile (3.13.2), and on the other enthusiastically praised their ability to preserve their identity notwithstanding all the catastrophes which befell them. Commenting on their return from exile that followed Epaminondas' rallying call, he observes that, although the wanderings of the Messenians outside the Peloponnese had lasted almost three hundred years, during that long period they had not departed in any way from their ancestral customs, and had not lost their Doric dialect, so that even in Pausanias' time they allegedly retained the purest Doric in the Peloponnese (4.27.11). Pausanias' eulogy of the Messenians' cultural and linguistic purism stands in a stark contrast to Thucydides' statement (4.3.3; 41.2) that during the Peloponnesian War the Messenians from Naupaktos were able to produce great damage with their incursions in the Peloponnese because they were *homophonoi* with the Lakedaimonians, and therefore linguistically unrecognizable by them. The juxtaposition of Thucydides' and Pausanias' statements epitomizes the central problem for the study of Messenian tradition, and also anticipates the ways in which that problem has been treated by modern scholars. The Dorian identity of the Messenians, which could make them indistinguishable from the Spartans, has been seen either as the survival of ancestral traits, going back to a time in the Iron Age when Messenians and Laconians were still little differentiated from each other,[1] or as a result of the uprooting of Messenian culture by the Spartan invaders. Accordingly, scholarship on the problem of Messenian tradition can be neatly divided into two parties: the continuists and the discontinuists.[2] The first maintain that in Messenia some sort of continuity in religious cults and historical memory was kept alive from the time before the Spartan conquest in the eighth–seventh centuries BC. According to the continuist school, the Spartan occupation was not able to quench every spark of Messenian identity, so that in fact some continuity existed between the newly founded Messene of the fourth century and the old Messenians who had fought against Sparta many centuries before. The second party, the discontinuists, maintains that the Spartan conquest produced a total interruption of the

---

[1] Zunino 1997 speaks of an original "Messenian–Laconian *koinē*."
[2] For a crisp introduction to this longstanding debate and its huge bibliography see Alcock 1999: 333–5 and 2001: 142–53.

flow of tradition and memory in Messenia, so that on the occasion of the liberation it was necessary to more or less invent a past for the new political community, in both a historical and a religious sense.

In order to understand the development of the debate on Messenian tradition, it is important to note that it is in fact a continuation of an older discussion on the credibility of the sources of the historical narrative in Pausanias' fourth book, devoted to the history and monuments of Messenia. Pausanias' very detailed account of the Spartan conquest of Messenia and of the subsequent struggle of the Messenians to recover their freedom is by far the fullest treatment of the archaic history of Messenia that has been preserved from antiquity, many times longer than all the remaining textual evidence taken together. The discontinuist position builds upon German scholarship from the late nineteenth and early twentieth centuries, consolidated in Felix Jacoby's work. The upshot of this work, conducted according to the most rigorous standards of German source criticism, was that Pausanias' narrative of the Messenian Wars went back to sources no earlier than the fourth century BC, and mostly later. The only certainly genuine materials available to fourth-century historians were some scanty allusions contained in a few verses of the seventh-century Spartan poet Tyrtaeus.[3] The continuist response consisted of shifting the debate away from source criticism, bringing into play notions such as popular oral tradition, memory connected with cult places or surviving among Messenians of the diaspora and so forth. But in spite of this change on the surface, the real nature of the debate remained the same: what the neo-continuists tried to do was to find new arguments to vindicate the use of Pausanias as a reliable source for the archaic history of Messenia.[4]

The reciprocal conditioning that may be observed between continuists and discontinuists explains the fact that both have failed to question some assumptions that are in fact far from obvious, like the idea that Messenia as a unity pre-existed the Spartan conquest. Both continuists and dis-continuists have been rather ready to accept the notion that between the eighth and seventh centuries the Spartans conquered this independent and somehow unified land, and threw its free inhabitants into slavery, turning them into Helots. Of course, the continuists think that these Helotized Messenians were able to preserve some knowledge of their

---

[3] Jacoby 1943. For a summary of the debate, see Pearson 1966.
[4] This is particularly clear in the two most substantial post-Jacobian contributions on the continuist side, Zunino 1997 and Ogden 2004.

shared past as free Messenians, while the discontinuists think that they were not. Neither party doubts that the revolt after the earthquake, in the 460s, was primarily an enterprise of these Helotized Messenians, or that they formed the bulk of the citizen body of Epaminondas' Messene. In other words, both parties have reduced the problem of Messenian identity to the polarity between Spartiates and Helots, and in so doing, have oversimplified it, almost as if Messenia under Sparta could have been a huge slave camp, some sort of Jamaica of ancient Greece where thousands of Helotized Messenians, held under control – nobody knows exactly how[5] – by the Spartiates, would have tilled the land that once had been theirs.

The present book is an attempt at changing the terms of the problem in various ways. First of all, it questions the assumption that any significant level of political or cultural integration existed in Messenia before the Spartan conquest. This of course entails entertaining the possibility that the very idea of Messenia as a regional unit may have been a result of the Spartan conquest. Second, it advocates a broader approach to the evidence, incorporating the results of archaeological research in Messenia in a more systematic way than has been so far the case. Third, it tries to offer a more contextual reading of the evidence itself, which means that especially the literary sources have to be interpreted in the first place in relation to the historical contexts from which they originated. It follows from this that it is necessary to pay attention to the whole historical span in which Messenian tradition developed, taking the investigation into the Hellenistic age and the early Empire. And finally, since what is at stake is the ways in which human groups articulate a sense of relatedness and transmit their notions of their shared past, it is necessary to recur to methods appropriate to deal with this kind of problem.

ETHNICITY AND MEMORY

The division of human beings, above the level of kinship groups, into larger units whose members perceive themselves as connected to each other by primordial ties, which typically go beyond political structures and often also run deeper than such fundamental cultural traits as religion or language, is probably a universal phenomenon.[6] In spite of much research

---

[5] See Hodkinson 2003, a landmark contribution that offers the first sustained attempt at a realistic understanding of the situation on the ground.

[6] The following remarks are intentionally concise and avoid describing and discussing in detail approaches that are normally grouped under headings such as "primordialism," "intrumentalism," and the like. Among the many recent and excellent discussions available, see especially Hall 1997: 17–33;

devoted to proving the opposite, especially during the first half of the last century, today probably not many scholars think that such a notion is based on actual biological relatedness. However, even though it is not a natural fact from a biological perspective, the subdivision of humankind into ethnic groups is not a product of scholarly observation either, but rather a case of "spontaneous anthropology" practiced by the historical actors themselves.[7]

Ultimately, this kind of perceived primordial relatedness is based on putative blood ties, regardless of how far back in the past the roots of those ties are assumed by the actors to lie. In other words, primordial relatedness is based on notional kinship. Groups whose members entertain a subjective belief in their common descent are called ethnic groups.[8] Even though from the point of view of its members the ultimate foundation of the ethnic group and the ultimate criterion for belonging is usually blood ties, members of an ethnic group normally recognize each other and members of other ethnic groups on the basis of ritual practices, speech patterns, styles of clothing and other cultural traits, and in some cases, physical appearance.[9]

Although the essentially social and cultural nature of ethnic groups had been observed already by Max Weber in the early twentieth century, the ramifications of abandoning an emic view of ethnic identity entered the scholars' agenda only later, after the Second World War, one of whose results was the final discrediting of the concept of race. In the field of anthropology, the initial demarche, consisting in replacing racial difference with cultural difference,[10] unexpectedly brought to scholars' attention the apparent paradox that the sense of ethnic distinctness of the actors did not map in a satisfactory way onto the cultural differences observed by the researchers. Circumventing the impasse by framing the discussion in terms of subjective and objective elements in the definition of an ethnic group would only blur the issue.[11] This situation induced the Norwegian anthropologist Fredrik Barth to shift the perspective, focusing attention away from the cultural contents of ethnic identities and onto the

Fabietti 1998: 14–16; Ruby 2006. For a succinct review of the development of the study of ethnicity, see Kohl 1998.

[7] See Fabietti 1998: 25, 39, Barth 1969b: 10. [8] Weber 1972: 237.

[9] See Horowitz 1975: 119–20 for the distinction between criteria and indicia of ethnic identity; see also Ruby 2006: 35. Such a distinction seems to be more fruitful and clearer that Barth's (1969b: 14) between the signals or signs that make members of an ethnic group recognizable and the basic value orientations that apply to the members of the ethnic group. Ultimately, this is one aspect of Barth's strictly synchronic approach, on which more below.

[10] See Barth 1969b: 10–11, Jones 1997: 52. [11] Eriksen 1991: 143 n. 1.

boundaries that separate ethnic groups, understood not so much as territorial borders, but rather as the actors' perception of what distinguishes an ethnic group from another.[12] Barth concluded that the ethnic group should be seen as a form of social organization that makes use of cultural difference in order to articulate the boundaries that separate it from other groups of the same order, but is not dependent on the nature or ultimately even on the very existence of cultural difference. From the point of view of the observer, the relation between cultural discontinuities of any sort and ethnic boundaries is arbitrary. Ethnic groups are essentially defined by self-ascription and ascription by others, a sheer mechanism of inclusion and exclusion, and all that is really necessary for an ethnic group to exist is the boundary itself, regardless of any cultural traits or patterns of behavior that may from time to time be seen as characteristic for the members of the group. On the other hand, the constraints that ethnic identities put on individuals tend to be superordinate to those deriving from other aspects of an individual's identity, such as social status or rank. Ethnic imperatives tend to be absolute.[13]

Independently of Barth, similar results were reached in the same years by the medieval historian Reinhard Wenskus in his research on the origins of the early Germanic peoples. Combining the scrutiny of the evidence with the use of sociological and anthropological models, Wenksus concluded that the early Germanic peoples, as they appear in the sources, were actually the product of processes of ethnic fusion and fission that he called "ethnogenesis." In such processes, cultural or biological relatedness was secondary. Ethnic consciousness and self-ascription were the only ultimate criteria for belonging.[14] In practice, Wenskus thought that processes of ethnic fusion consisted in the aggregation of a larger human group around a smaller core, in some cases an extended kinship group or a group of families, which was the repository of myths of descent that the whole group came to accept and share. The core group was called by Wenskus *Traditionskern* or "tradition kernel." It is fascinating to observe

[12] For a condensed statement of Barth's position, see Barth 1969b. Fabietti 1998: 95–104 offers a very perceptive discussion of Barth's approach. See also the discussion in Vermeulen and Govers 1994, including Barth's own reappraisal, Barth 1994.
[13] Barth 1969b: 17; on the absoluteness of ethnic imperatives, which is of course crucial to an understanding of ethnic conflicts, see also Kohl 1998: 286.
[14] Wenskus 1961: 81: "das ethnische Bewußtsein einer Gruppe und ihre Selbstabgrenzung kann allein das Kriterium für ihre jeweilige, vielleicht wechselnde Zugehörigkeit sein." For a discussion of Wenskus' approach, see Daim 1982: 60–4. For the development of this approach in the study of Late Antiquity and the early Middle Ages, see especially Pohl 1994: 9–19, Pohl and Reimitz 1998. On ethnic fusion and fission, see Horowitz 1975: 115–16.

how Barth and Wenskus, operating on the basis of rather different methodological tenets and certainly without knowledge of each other's work, converged on some very basic points. Apart from the centrality of ascription for the constitution of an ethnic group, which in mutated form is still crucial to current definitions of the ethnic group, both Barth and Wenskus agreed that ethnicity is often an instrument employed by leaders or elites to mobilize larger groups of people towards specific goals.[15] Admittedly Barth and Wenskus had two fundamentally different perceptions of the dynamics of ethnicity. Wenkus' "tradition kernel" involves looking at ethnogenesis essentially from within, as a process of aggregation, while Barth insisted that ethnic groups exist only by way of opposition to other ethnic groups, and ethnic identities are defined as much by what they are not as by what they are. However, their respective perspectives can be seen as complementing each other rather than as being mutually exclusive.

Barth's conclusions have been often criticized, but mostly, it seems, for not doing what he did not intend to do, that is, investigate the logic according to which cultural traits are seen as relevant or irrelevant to ethnic identities in specific historical contexts.[16] In abstract sociological terms, the arbitrariness of the criteria that underpin ethnic boundaries and the primacy of ascription cannot be seriously called into question.[17] This, of course, does not mean that, in concrete historical terms, ethnic groups define themselves by randomly choosing criteria, but simply that there does not seem to be any universal and trans-cultural regularity that allows to predict what kind of cultural traits will be activated as ethnic markers in a specific historical context.[18] Still, in order for a meaningful comparison of phenomena to be possible, it is necessary to focus on isolating and categorizing the kinds of elements that are seen by the actors as constitutive of an ethnic group. A decisive impulse in this direction came from the field of social history. In his influential study of the ethnic roots of modern nationalism, Anthony Smith developed a set of characteristics that, based on empirical observation, he considered typical of an ethnic

---

[15] See the retrospective statement of Barth 1994: 12: "... I emphasized the entrepreneurial role in ethnic politics: how the mobilization of ethnic groups in collective action is effected by leaders who pursue a political enterprise, and is not a direct expression of the group's cultural ideology, or the popular will."

[16] For a particularly thoughtful discussion, see Eriksen 1991: esp. 127–9; on the lack of historical depth in Barth's approach, see also below.

[17] See e.g. Patterson 1975: 306, Orywal and Hackstein 1993: 598–600. See also Barth 1994.

[18] One telling example of the essential instability of the relationship between cultural traits and ethnic identity is offered by language differentiation; see e.g. Smith 1986: 27, Pohl 1998: 22–7.

group.[19] Smith's typology has been further refined by Carlo Tullio-Altan, who lists the following five symbolic complexes as constitutive of the ethnic group as an ideal type: *epos*, the celebration of what the group regards as its shared past; *ethos*, the complex of cultural norms and institutions, religious and social, that regulate the life of the group; *logos*, the group's characteristic speech pattern; *genos*, the kinship and lineage structure that is perceived as underpinning the group's integration; *topos*, a symbolic fatherland of the group, regardless whether it is to any extent identical with the territory occupied by the group in the present or is the lost fatherland of a diaspora.[20] Each and any of these complexes may be more or less prominent in any historical ethnic configuration, and different members of the ethnic group may feel varying levels of connection to any one of the symbolic complexes, often depending on their belonging to different subgroups within the ethnic group, such as status groups or social classes.[21] And of course, a constant and necessary component of an ethnic group is a collective name.[22]

In discussing the application of Smith's approach, Jonathan Hall observed that two components more than others seem to be distinctive of ethnic groups, a myth of common descent and the connection with a specific territory,[23] that is, in Tullio-Altan's terms, *genos* and *topos*. Irad Malkin criticized Hall's position, observing on the one hand that, while assumed blood ties are central to ethnic identity, the explicit formulation of a myth of common descent in the form of a genealogy is not necessary, a general feeling of relatedness being in practice sufficient.[24] On the other

---

[19] Smith 1986: 22–30. Smith calls a group characterized by these components an *ethnie*.

[20] See Tullio-Altan 1995: 19–32. Tullio-Altan correctly points out that Smith is somewhat less than explicit when it comes to defining the historical foundations, from the investigator's point of view, of the components of *ethnie*. Tullio-Altan insists that, on the one hand, regardless of the objective nature and form of any element of the first three components, their symbolic value has to be activated for them to acquire an ethnic meaning in any given context (which is essentially a restatement of Barth's principle of the arbitrary relation of cultural traits to ethnic boundaries), and on the other, that belief in the reality of any of the elements does not correspond to the historicity of any of them from the point of view of the investigator. More on this below.

[21] See Tullio-Altan 1995: 29 on the stronger appeal of *epos*, *ethos* and *logos* on cultural and social elites, and of *topos* and *genos* on subordinate groups – which of course explains why *topos* and *genos* are most often the components of ethnic rallying cries.

[22] As emphasized by Smith 1986: 22–4. On the importance of ethnic names, see also Ruby 2006: 44.

[23] Hall 1997: 25–6.

[24] Malkin 2001: 10–12; it is important to notice that, more than the general notion of the centrality of common descent, what Malkin really criticizes is the emphasis in Hall's book on the importance of texts such as the genealogy of Hellen in the Hesiodic *Catalogue* (Hall 1997: 42–4). In other words, the issue at stake is to what extent notional kinship needs to be articulated in an explicit genealogical narrative, known to and accepted by a sufficiently large portion of the ethnic group. To this extent, Malkin has a point.

hand, Malkin insisted that a shared territory was never really central to any definition of Greekness.[25] From the present perspective, one interesting aspect of these debates is that they essentially come full circle and join, from a more nuanced and significantly more differentiated position to be sure, Barth's fundamental conclusion that ascription and self-ascription are the only really necessary foundation of ethnicity.

However, the apparent gap between Hall's myth of common descent and Barth's ethnic ascription brings to our attention another important and potentially problematic aspect of Barth's approach. Because Barth was observing the interaction of living ethnic groups, and because he was interested in explaining how they functioned in social practice, his approach was definitely ahistorical.[26] His strategic choice has had a powerful impact in setting the agenda for the study of ethnic phenomena, especially within anthropology, and one of its consequences has been to delay the emergence of the problem of the relationship of ethnicity and collective memory.[27]

The lack of interest on the part of scholars following the instrumentalist approach to ethnicity in the temporal depth of ethnic consciousness is one of the main points of criticism that has been leveled against instrumentalists. As long as the ethnic group is observed in a strictly synchronic way, this problem is not necessarily obvious. However, in empirical terms the members of any ethnic group will tend to locate the roots of the group in the past, and most often in the distant past. Ethnic discourse is primordial by nature, which means that it has an implicit temporal dimension.[28] This simple observation seems to sit uneasily with the instrumentalist view that ethnic groups are created for the pursuit of practical goals.[29] On the other hand, in reacting to the lack of historical depth that seems to characterize the instrumentalist approach, scholars seem to have occasionally lapsed into accepting ethnic discourse on its terms, as if documented existence over a long period of time were objectively

---

[25] Malkin 2001: 13–14.

[26] And of course, because he was observing horizontal relations between ethnic groups that to some extent coexisted in the same territory, he was not very interested in the relationship of ethnic and political borders and in general in the importance of territory for ethnic symbolism.

[27] It is telling that both Fabietti 1998, a general introduction to ethnic identity, and Anderson 1991, a highly influential study of the mechanisms that make it possible for members of modern nations to perceive themselves as a community, felt a need to add a chapter on memory to the second editions of their books (the first editions had appeared in 1995 and 1983 respectively).

[28] Malkin 2001: 15–16.

[29] The traditional objection has been that this view cannot explain the fact that people stick to their ethnic identity even in situations in which this goes against their interests; see e.g. Jones 1997: 68.

necessary for an ethnic group.[30] If this were the case, of course, it would be difficult to account for the emergence of new ethnic groups and for the transformation of the way in which a group defines itself, which are both empirically attested phenomena.[31] Rather than jettisoning the instrumentalist perspective, therefore, what seems to be necessary is an approach that makes it possible to integrate the function of the past in ethnic identity. Current historical and anthropological research offers a conceptual framework for such an approach.

In 1983, Eric Hobsbawm and Terence Ranger edited a very influential book called *The Invention of Tradition*. The intentional oxymoron in the title points to the key thesis articulated in different ways by the contributors, that is, that cultural traits, patterns of behavior, social institutions and narratives of the past are often accepted as traditional in spite of having originated in the rather recent past. The authors thought that the phenomenon was characteristic of the modern age, but as soon as their approach became more widely known, historians of earlier periods immediately observed cases of the same kind of phenomena. If the notion that the present creates the past was a traditional tenet of historicist doctrines, this new approach showed that the past was being creatively dealt with not only in the closets of historians and philosophers. However, insistence on the very possibility of creating tradition has somewhat diverted attention from the constraints that affect the process.[32]

The reshaping of the past by a society in order to keep it in touch with the present, as it were, had been on the agenda of anthropologists and historians of pre-colonial Africa since after the Second World War.[33] Originally, this phenomenon had been thought to be characteristic of cultures that do not use writing, and therefore cannot create a rigid and immutable record of their past. However, it soon became clear that the technological divide between literate and illiterate cultures, while certainly very important, was not a sufficiently general explanation for a phenomenon that occurs, if in different forms, in literate societies as well.

---

[30] For a similar problem in diaspora studies, see below, p. 168.
[31] For the transformation of ethnic groups, see the telling example of the Iranian Shahsevan in Fabietti 1998: 46–9.
[32] It is important to underline that Hobsbawm and Ranger were perfectly aware of the fact that the processes they were investigating were indeed "normally governed by overtly or tacitly accepted rules" (Hobsbawm and Ranger 1983: 1). Their choice of the term "invention" seems to be ultimately political, but the title of their book, which turned into a sort of scholarly slogan, may have misleading implications, as pointed out by Østergård 1992: 34.
[33] See especially the groundbreaking article of Goody and Watt 1963, and Vansina 1985.

What at first sight seemed to be a universal difference between societies that use writing to record their past and societies that do not turned out to be a much more complex system of culturally specific practices and institutions that make it possible, in any given society, to generate versions of the past and traditions that could be both plausible and functional, the existence of written records being but one often-recurring element of various sets of criteria that apply in different ways in different historical contexts. The latent tension between these two concerns, that is, plausibility and functionality, is the crucial point and ultimately the very foundation of the reality-effect of tradition. Each culture has its own set of practices and criteria that authorize tradition and set a framework for the kind of phenomena subsumed under the heading of "invention of tradition,"[34] effectively making such phenomena possible.

Along these lines, it seems feasible to find a more satisfactory framework for an instrumentalist approach that at the same time is in a position to deal adequately with the development of ethnicity over time. Ethnic discourse is constrained precisely by the fact that it needs to be believed. For this to be possible, it has to come to terms with the criteria that obtain in any given cultural context. This does not mean that some sort of authentic and immutable past lies completely beyond the reach of an ethnic group, but certainly means that no group can write its primordial past arbitrarily. This is true both within the group itself, where multiple ways of viewing and construing the past are normally found, and in the relations between ethnic groups. In a multi-ethnic context, where the pasts of different groups overlap and interact, we typically observe competition and convergence in the articulation of the pasts of the several groups. Superiority in terms of number, control of resources, solidity of social and political institutions, cultural continuity, will often put one group in a position to impose its own version of the past, and other groups will react either by developing oppositional narratives, which will then tend rarely to go beyond the boundaries of the group, or by adapting their views of the past to those of a dominant group. In this case, the memory of the dominant group will function as a sort of pace-setter, also in chronological terms, for instance in setting standards for the depth of an acceptable ethnic past.[35]

* * *

[34] See e.g. Appadurai 1981, Peel 1984 with further references.
[35] Smith 1986: 178. See also Henningsen 2000: 178.

This is the methodological framework for the present investigation. In the next chapters, the articulation, redefinition, and reaffirmation of Messenian ethnicity will be followed over an extremely long span of time, some seven centuries, and attention will be devoted also to the cultural and historical context from which it emerged, and to the pre-existing patrimony of stories and cultural practices that were available for its articulation. As a framework of sorts for the rest of the book, chapter 2 will outline this historical trajectory almost for its full length, looking at the issue of the boundaries that separated the Messenians from other ethnic groups and starting from the most crucial of all, the political and ethnic border between Messenians and Spartans. The other chapters will follow in an ostensibly chronological order. However, the particular perspective of the book, largely focused on changing perceptions of the past, will complicate this apparently straightforward sequence. Chapters 3 and 4 will deal with events, the return of the Heraclids and the Messenian Wars, that were seen as historical by the Greeks, and address them in the order in which the Greeks themselves thought the events had taken place. However, the extent to which these complexes of events can be regarded as historical, let alone reconstructed in detail based on ancient literary evidence, is controversial, and both chapters will concentrate on offering a reconstruction of how the Greeks themselves narrated them, from as early as we can tell, and of how their narratives changed through the centuries. This means that both chapters will actually extend almost over the full chronological span of the book. Then, in chapter 5, attention will turn to archaeological evidence from archaic and early classical Messenia, and from there on, the sequence of the chapters will become chronological in a stricter sense, moving from the first appearance of an independent political community called "the Messenians," in early fifth-century Sicily, to the revolt in Messenia in the early 460s, to continue with the liberation of Messenia by Epaminondas in 369 BC and the history of the Messenian identity in the Hellenistic age and under the Roman Empire. The conclusion will outline a tentative history of the Messenian identity and discuss its main structural elements and their historical logic.

CHAPTER 2

Delimiting the Messenians

In more senses than one, ethnicity is about borders. Land, understood as the ancestral property of the ethnic group or as its divinely sanctioned share that has to be won back, is a decisive factor of ethnic self-consciousness.[1] Therefore the border, ideally understood as the specific place where the territory of one ethnic group ends and that of another ethnic group begins, and in reality most often an ambiguous zone of shifting allegiances, is a privileged point from which to observe and analyze the emergence, development, and reaffirmation of ethnicity. Marking and patrolling the border is a vital symbolic function for any ethnic group, while the inherent instability of the border is an endless creator of ethnic renegotiation.[2] However, the importance of borders and boundaries for the definition of ethnic communities goes beyond their territorial dimension. Ever since the pathbreaking studies of Fredrik Barth it has been clear that ethnic boundaries should not be understood simply as imaginary lines that delimit a territory. On a deeper level, they are complex systems of norms and expectations that make it possible to identify the people who belong to the ethnic community and to exclude those who do not.

In Barth's view, the boundaries themselves are what really defines the group, more than any characteristics that may be associated with its members.[3] A border between two polities is not necessarily an ethnic border, unless, that is, people living on either side of it think of themselves as ethnically distinct, in which case it will be the mechanisms of ethnic ascription that support the border. For this reason, it seems appropriate to start our investigation of the ethnic identity of the Messenians by looking at the borders that separate the Messenian land from alien lands, and considering how these borders contributed to a definition of the group

---

[1] See e.g. Smith 1986: 28–9, Tullio-Altan 1995: 27–8.
[2] The dynamics of ethnic ascription associated with borders are most compellingly investigated in the works of Peter Sahlins. See Sahlins 1989, much of which is summarized in Sahlins 1995.
[3] See Barth 1969a and above, p. 7–8. For the notion of ethnic boundary, see also Fabietti 1998: 95–115.

that considered itself Messenian. After looking at how the border was articulated and defended, we will move on to consider how it could become problematic and allow alternative constructions and interpretations. Finally, we will consider the case of ethnic borders within the Messenian land itself, observing how preexisting ethnic definitions can react to the drawing of new boundaries.

MARKING THE BORDER: ARTEMIS LIMNATIS

In the year 25 AD, two embassies, one coming from Messene, the other from Sparta, appeared before the Senate in Rome, in the presence of the emperor Tiberius, to request an arbitration. According to Tacitus, our source on the episode (*Ann.* 4.43.1–3), the bone of contention between the two cities was the temple of Artemis Limnatis and the surrounding territory, on the western side of the Taygetos, northeast of Pharai, modern Kalamata. The Spartans maintained that the temple had been built by their ancestors in their own land, and should therefore belong to them. They buttressed their ancestral claim referring to *memoria annalium* and *carmina vatum*, that is, works of historiography and poetry. Only thanks to Philip the Second's violent intervention – they said – had the Messenians gained possession of the temple. However, Gaius Caesar and Marcus Antonius had given it back to the Spartans. The Messenians on their part argued that the temple was in the region called Dentheliatis, which belonged to the territory that had been granted to their king Kresphontes at the time of the division of the Peloponnese among the Heraclids. Monuments in stone and bronze confirmed this. As for the historians and poets, they had more and better than the Spartans to sustain their claim. Philip had acted according to justice and his decision had been confirmed by king Antigonus, by Mummius, by the Milesians and lastly by the praetor Atidius Geminus. The Senate (and Tiberius) ruled in favor of the Messenians.[4]

---

[4] Tac. *Ann.* 4.43.1–3: Auditae dehinc Lacedaemoniorum et Messeniorum legationes de iure templi Dianae Limnatidis, quod suis a maioribus suaque in terra dicatum Lacedaemonii firmabant annalium memoria vatumque carminibus, sed Macedonis Philippi, cum quo bellassent, armis ademptum ac post C. Caesaris et M. Antonii sententia redditum. Contra Messenii veterem inter Herculis posteros divisionem Peloponnesi protulere, suoque regi Dentheliatem agrum, in quo id delubrum, cessisse; monimentaque eius rei sculpta saxis et aere prisco manere. Quod si vatum, annalium ad testimonia vocentur, plures sibi ac locupletiores esse; neque Philippus potentia, sed ex vero statuisse. Idem regis Antigoni, idem imperatoris Mummii iudicium; sic Milesios permisso publice arbitrio, postremo Atidium Geminum praetorem Achaiae decrevisse. Ita secundum Messenios datum.

Both embassies argued on two different levels and using two different sorts of evidence. For the distant past they seem to have used mainly literary works, although the Messenians appear to have been able to refer to monuments, too: one wonders if inscriptions might be meant. For the period after the fourth century, both referred directly to events and decisions, as if knowledge of those could be presupposed; however, as we will see, a closer scrutiny shows that both sides had a rather peculiar way of interpreting those decisions. The recourse to literature, particularly but not only historiography, in order to underpin territorial claims by anchoring them in the distant past is documented in other cases in the Hellenistic and Imperial periods, most famously the controversy between Samos and Priene for the control of parts of the territory of Melia. In this case, the extensive use of historical works by the two parties is documented by the inscriptions that record the arbitrations, which show that the judges considered carefully the authority of the authors, taking account of possible local biases.[5] How precisely the authors were weighed against one another in our case is unclear; Tacitus mentions general criteria such as their number and reliability.

By evoking the division of the Peloponnese among the Heraclids, the Messenians based their claim on what was commonly seen as a sort of foundational moment in the myth-history of the Peloponnese. It was probably not the first time that the return of the Heraclids was recalled in connection with the Dentheliatis, and frequent reference to mythic events in territorial controversies and in general in international politics in the Greek world shows clearly that this part of the Messenians' claim was not as trivial as we might think (see below, pp. 55–65). However, if we want to understand the meaning of the controversy, its post-mythic stages are most revealing.

The Dentheliatis had become Messenian for the first time in the fourth century, thanks to the intervention of Philip the Second. The friendly relations between Philip and the Messenians went back to the mid 340s,[6] but it was only later that the Macedonian king intervened directly in the Peloponnese. Sparta had kept itself aloof from the anti-Macedonian coalition that had been defeated at Chaeronea in 338 BC. Nevertheless, immediately after the battle Philip marched into the Peloponnese

---

[5] For recent editions of the relevant inscriptions, with full commentary and references, see Ager 26 = Magnetto 20 and Ager 74. On the use of literary evidence in territorial controversies in the Hellenistic age, see Curty 1989: 26–35.

[6] See Isocr. *Letter to Philip* [5].74, 346 BC, with Roebuck 1941: 48–52. On the position of the Messenians in international politics of this period, see also below, pp. 253–5.

and announced an ultimatum to king Agis, who had just succeeded Archidamus the Second on the Eurypontid throne at Sparta. The terms of the ultimatum are not documented directly, but it probably compelled the Spartans to renounce some frontier territories to their neighbors and longtime enemies, Argos, Tegea, Megalopolis and Messene.[7] According to a recent and attractive suggestion, the new borders that were being imposed on Sparta were construed as going back to the division of the Peloponnese among the Heraclids.[8] Since the Spartans refused to comply, the Macedonian army invaded Laconia. The region was plundered and the frontier territories changed hands. Later on in the same year Philip had his decision confirmed by a Panhellenic jury, perhaps in the framework of the newly founded League of Corinth[9] – a detail that unsurprisingly does not appear in Tacitus' account of the Spartan allusion to the episode. It is not difficult to understand the goal of Philip's measures. Before embarking on his expedition against the Persian Empire, he wanted to make sure that no trouble could arise in Greece. Once Athens and Thebes had been defeated, Sparta was the only potential threat, and had to be neutralized. To achieve this, Philip revived Epaminondas' strategy of mobilizing Sparta's neighbors.[10]

Interestingly, the second judgment seems to have taken place in similar circumstances. Although Tacitus does not specify which Antigonus he means, Antigonus the Third Doson is by far the best candidate.[11] The new decision in favor of the Messenians almost certainly dates to immediately after the battle of Sellasia in 222, which marked the end of king Cleomenes' dream of reviving the ancient power of Sparta.[12] Messene was not yet a member of the Achaean League and it is doubtful that Messenians had

---

[7] On the terms of the ultimatum, see Hamilton 1982: 81 and n. 88.

[8] Piérart 2001: 30–7. Piérart's suggestion may receive some support from the observation that, according to Polybius (18.14.7), Philip had given back to Argives, Messenians, Tegeans and Megalopolitans land that had originally belonged to them but that had been taken away from them by the Spartans over the centuries. It may be less than accidental that the little-known Little Pamisos river became the new border between Messenians and Spartans in the Mani peninsula (Strab. 8.4.6), while according to Euripides (*TrGF* 727e) the Pamisos was the border between Messenian and Laconian land at the time of the Heraclids; see below, p. 31.

[9] A detailed discussion of the procedure is offered by Jehne 1994: 139–65 and Magnetto 1994, with comprehensive bibliography. See also Piérart 2001: 28, who suggests that Philip invaded Laconia after the judgment by the League of Corinth, rather than before.

[10] On Philip's strategy and its analogies to Epaminondas', see Ryder 1994: 238–41, Grandjean 2003: 69. See also Hamilton 1982, who argues, based on a close scrutiny of the diplomatic relations between Philip and Archidamus, that the Spartan king almost compelled Philip to revive the Theban strategy.

[11] Discussion in Ager 48 and Magnetto 50, both with comprehensive references; see also Piérart 2001: 33.

[12] See e.g. Cartledge, in Cartledge and Spawforth 2002: 53–8.

taken part in Doson's campaign, as Pausanias claims (4.27.7–9).[13] Although they had helped the Achaeans by harboring the fugitives from Megalopolis when Cleomenes destroyed it,[14] there is no evidence for their involvement in the Cleomenic War, and it looks as if Doson's measure was intended to punish and humiliate the Spartans at least as much as to reward the Messenians, especially considering that apparently on the same occasion the Spartans had to give up land to the Arcadians and to the Argives, too. Again, as in Philip's time, the new frontiers seem to have been defined with reference to the division of the Peloponnese among the Heraclids.[15] It should not go unnoticed that Doson's decision implies that at some point between Philip's campaign in 338 and the battle of Sellasia in 222 the Spartans had reconquered the Dentheliatis.[16] Interestingly, the Spartan envoys in Rome failed to mention this detail, too.

The third judgment mentioned by the Messenians poses a number of problems. The *imperator* Mummius mentioned by Tacitus is obviously Lucius Mummius Achaicus, and it is generally assumed that his decision must have been part of the measures taken after the war between Rome and the Achaean League.[17] However, this assumption has some paradoxical implications. The Achaean War had been brought about by the Achaeans' declaration of war against Sparta, at a time when Messene was a member, however grudging, of the Achaean League.[18] One could hardly think of a less appropriate moment for a decision by a Roman magistrate in favor of Messene and against Sparta. At a closer look, perplexities increase. According to the Messenians, says Tacitus, Mummius' judgment had been confirmed by the Milesians, chosen as arbitrators by the Roman Senate. As it happens, the arbitration of the Milesians is preserved in a long inscription from Olympia, which includes three documents: the decision by the Eleans to allow the Messenians to have the text of the arbitration put on display at Olympia, the text of a letter from the Milesians vouching for the genuineness of the record of the arbitration, and finally the minutes of the

---

[13] On the Messenians and the Achaean League in the late third and early second centuries BC, see below, pp. 258–60. Pausanias' views of this may reflect the agenda of his second-century AD informants, see below, pp. 325–6.

[14] Polyb. 2.62.10; Paus. 4.29.8; 8.49.4; Plut. *Cleom.* 24; *Phil.* 5.

[15] See the discussion of *IvO* 47 = Ager 137 = Magnetto 22 by Piérart 2001: 30–3; see also the comprehensive commentary on the inscription by Harter-Uibopuu 1998: 80–97.

[16] Roebuck 1941: 62 suggests that the Dentheliatis may have been conquered by king Areus in the early 270s.

[17] On the measures taken by Mummius and the senatorial commission in 145, documented directly only by Pausanias (7.16.9–10), see Kallet-Marx 1995: 57–96.

[18] On Messene and the Achaean League, see below, pp. 262–4.

arbitration itself, with a lively and detailed description of the procedure.[19] The inscription can be approximately dated on the basis of the name of the Roman magistrate who had been entrusted by the Senate with communicating its decision to the Milesians: the praetor Quintus Calpurnius, son of Gaius. The only possible candidate to be identified with this man is a Q. Calpurnius Gai f. Piso, who was consul in 135 BC.[20] He may have been praetor in 138 at the latest, perhaps some years earlier. The inscription confirms Tacitus in mentioning a senatorial decree: apparently the Messenians and the Spartans had turned to the Senate, and the Senate, as it did on other occasions, designated a Greek arbitrator, in this case the Milesians.[21]

The inscription throws an ambiguous light on Tacitus' passage. If Mummius had decided in favor of the Messenians in 146 or 145, as they maintained according to Tacitus, how could the Spartans expect, just a few years later, to obtain from the Senate what had not been granted to them immediately after the war? After all, they had been on the side of the Romans, and had been rewarded for this,[22] while the Messenians, although they did not really take part in the war, were in theory with the Achaeans. But if we take a closer look at the inscription, in particular at the passages that mention Mummius, we may start seeing hints that point to a rather different reconstruction of the events. The question on which the Milesians had to decide, under request of the Senate, was, who controlled the Dentheliatis when Mummius was consul or proconsul. It is hard to see how this question could be construed as an allusion to a decision taken by Mummius, even one consisting in a simple *uti possidetis*.[23] Clearly, in the decree of the Senate that turned the decision over to the Milesians, Mummius' consulate or proconsulate was mentioned as a mere chronological parameter. If Mummius had previously taken any decision on the matter, surely the Senate would have referred to this fact in some way, rather than adopt the vague formulation "whoever owned the land when Mummius was consul or proconsul." The most natural interpretation of the evidence seems to be that Mummius had not intervened in the controversy at all. Apparently, the Senate simply took

---

[19] *IvO* 52 = *Syll.*[3] 683 = Ager 159.   [20] Broughton 1984: I.483.

[21] See Gruen 1984: 107–8. Based on the context, the initiative to turn to the Senate for an arbitration was most likely taken by the Messenians, see below, p. 21.

[22] According to Paus. 7.16.10, Mummius had condemned the Achaeans to pay 200 talents to the Spartans; however, the fine was later remitted by the Romans. See Schwertfeger 1974: 69 and Kallet-Marx 1995: 92.

[23] As suggested by Dittenberger, *Syll.*[3] 683; see also Kallet-Marx 1995: 82–3 and Ager 412.

the situation of 146–145 as a benchmark, stating that whoever controlled the Dentheliatis then, had a right to it.[24]

The fact that this point needed to be ascertained suggests that immediately after the war, probably after the Roman troops had evacuated Greece, the Spartans reoccupied the territory, assuming in all likelihood that the Romans would turn a blind eye. Also conceivable is that the Spartans tried to regain possession of the Dentheliatis in a purely diplomatic way; but this scenario is less likely, because in this case the reply of the Senate would have been rather awkward, and furthermore, it would have made much better sense for the Spartans to address Mummius directly, instead of waiting for some years before coming out with their grievance. Against this background, the initiative to turn to the Senate must have been taken by the Messenians. It is not too difficult to reconcile Tacitus' version with this reconstruction. Interpreting the senatorial decree in a somewhat loose way, the Messenians must have decided retrospectively to take Mummius' measures as an implicit confirmation of their rights.

Rome features prominently in the next episode of the story, too. After Caesar's death, the Spartans took the side of Octavian and Antony, and 2,000 Spartan infantrymen were torn to pieces rather ingloriously by Brutus' troops at Philippi.[25] One would expect the winner to have rewarded the Spartans for this, and in all likelihood this is what Tacitus is talking about. Octavian apparently took the *praenomen* Imperator, which had been granted to his father, only after 39 BC; right after Philippi, his name would still have been C. Iulius Caesar, and with that name he would have signed any decision taken together with Antony.[26]

After the civil war between Augustus and Antony, Sparta suddenly became very visible in the political arena of Roman Greece: the Spartan Eurykles, later Gaius Iulius Euycles, fought in the battle of Actium and Sparta was entrusted by Augustus with the *prostasia* of the Actia, the penteteric games established to celebrate his victory.[27] Once again, the Messenians had chosen the wrong side. The territorial reward for Sparta was significant. Probably on the occasion of his visit to Sparta in 21 BC, Augustus assigned a number of settlements in southeastern Messenia,

[24] See Grandjean 2003: 230.
[25] Plut. *Brut.* 41.8; see Spawforth, in Cartledge and Spawforth 2002: 95–6.
[26] On Octavian's names, see Simpson 1998: 421–5. There does not seem to be any satisfactory historical context in which Julius Caesar could have taken the decision; cf. Spawforth, in Cartledge and Spawforth 2002: 138 and n. 21, with further references.
[27] See Bowersock 1961 and Spawforth, in Cartledge and Spawforth 2002: 97–101.

Pharai, Thouria, Kardamyle and Gerenia, to the Spartans or to the Eleutherolaconians.[28] This was obviously not a favorable moment for the Messenians to recover the ever-fought-over sanctuary. The judgment of the *praetor Achaiae* Atidius Geminus, the last stage of the controversy in Tacitus' narrative, must be dated later. How much later, it is difficult to tell precisely, since Atidius Geminus is not otherwise documented and it is not easy to reconstruct the historical context in which his judgment took place. Rome's relationships with Messenians and Spartans do not offer unambiguous guidance. Messene may have improved its relations with Augustus by the first years of the first century AD,[29] while Eurykles fell into disgrace around 7 BC, but was rehabilitated soon after his death, which happened sometime before 2 BC, and his son Gaius Iulius Laco apparently recovered the privileged position held by his father.[30] All in all, the first years of the reign of Tiberius may be the most likely date – after all, if no special factor inhibited them, we would expect the Spartans not to wait too long with their complaint.[31] As for the fact that Tiberius and the Senate did not overturn Geminus' decision, it is true that Tacitus

[28] On Augustus' decisions as reported by Pausanias, see Le Roy 2001: 232–7. On their occasion, Migeotte 1985: 604 and Cassius Dio 54.7. On the Eleutherolaconians, the league formed by the former *perioikoi* of Sparta, see Kennell 1999. Kardamyle (Paus. 3.26.7) and Thouria (Paus. 4.31.1, where the Messenians' siding with Antony is mentioned) were given to Sparta, Gerenia to the Eleutherolaconians (3.26.8 and 4.1.1). Pharai, according to Pausanias, was given by Augustus to the Λακωνικόν (4.30.2), which certainly means to the Eleutherolaconians, cf. ἐς τὸν Λακωνικόν in Paus. 4.1.1. Pharai does not appear in the list of the Eleutherolaconians in Paus. 3.21.7, but the list refers to Pausanias' own times, and Pausanias says explicitly that earlier there had been more Eleutherolaconian cities. IG V 1, 1431, line 39, where the Choireios River is called the border between Messene and the Eleutherolaconians, suggests indeed that by AD 78 Pharai was Messenian again. See Kahrstedt 1950a: 235–42, Musti, in Musti and Torelli 1991: 262–5 and 283–4, id., in Musti and Torelli 1994: 248–9 and 250–1, and Lafond 1996: 184. While it is clear that Augustus was rewarding Spartans and Eleutherolaconians, it is not equally clear who was the real target of his punishment. Abia, Thouria and Pharai had become autonomous members of the Achaean League in 181 (Polyb. 23.17.2) and it is unclear what their status vis-à-vis Messene was after the Achaean War. Pharai was apparently reconquered by the Messenians during the Mithridatic war. On the whole problem, see below, pp. 264–5.

[29] See Bowersock 1985: 174; notice, however, that his interpretation of *SEG* 23.207, lines 36–7, is probably wrong, which somewhat weakens his arguments (cf. the translation of this text in Migeotte 1985: 601).

[30] See Bowersock 1961: 116–17, Spawforth, in Cartledge and Spawforth 2002: 101–2; it may be relevant that apparently Laco was himself exiled by Tiberius early in the 30s AD, soon after the adjudication of the controversy over the Dentheliatis. Notice that there may be evidence for influence of the Euryclid family at Messene, probably still under Augustus: see *SEG* 50.426 (cf. Themelis 2000: 62–3), from the architrave of the propylon of the gymnasium at Messene, recording the dedication of 10,000 *denarii* by a member of the family for use in the imperial cult and for the purchase of oil for the gymnasia, and the numismatic evidence discussed in Grandjean 1997: 120–1. This would further reinforce the conclusion that Geminus' judgment belongs in the early years of Tiberius.

[31] See Kolbe 1904: 377; cf., however, Spawforth, in Cartledge and Spawforth 2002: 138–9.

assigns more space to the Messenians, giving the impression that the part that had the best arguments carried the day, but obviously other factors may have played a part, such as patronage connections in Rome and Tiberius' and the Senate's unwillingness to disavow a Roman magistrate.[32]

Summing up this long story, we notice that the Dentheliatis changed hands mostly in connection with turning points in the history of the Peloponnese. Particularly the interventions of Philip, Antigonus and Augustus and Antony show that shifting this territory between Messenians and Spartans was an almost traditional way to punish or reward them. At first sight, it is rather odd that this border territory, somewhere up in the mountains and without any obvious attraction, might have been so important to Spartans and Messenians. Surely the importance of the Dentheliatis has something to do with its position, close to the border between Laconia and Messenia and astride one of the roads that crossed the Taygetos.[33] More generally, however, disputes over borderlands, lasting sometimes for centuries, were an endemic phenomenon in the world of the poleis. In many cases, as in the one at hand, it is not at all clear that the disputed territory had a real value in proportion to the fierceness of the dispute. It rather seems as if staking controversial claims over borderlands was a symbolic way for the political community of the polis to reaffirm its cohesiveness and its overarching right to its own land, as if these territorial disputes transformed the concrete border that separated two political communities into a component of the ethnic boundary that delimited and identified each of them. In our case, the symbolic aspects of the dispute can be grasped very clearly. Without exaggeration, we can say that the sanctuary of Artemis Limnatis was a true icon of Spartan power and Messenian freedom.

The cult of Artemis Limnatis, or Artemis of the Swamp, appears almost exclusively in the southern Peloponnese, especially in Laconia and on its borders. In most cases, its locations have nothing to do with swamps, which strongly suggests that the epithet Limnatis should be interpreted as referring to the most famous sanctuary of Artemis at Sparta, the sanctuary of Artemis Orthia, built in a swampy area called Limnai or Limnaion

---

[32] The episode narrated by Tacitus may not have been the last word on the controversy; see Spawforth, in Cartledge and Spawforth 2002: 139, and Grandjean 2003: 250–1, who suggest that *IG* V 1, 1361, possibly recording a territorial arbitration between Pharai and Sparta in the reign of Marcus Aurelius and Commodus, might imply that at some point, maybe under Marcus Aurelius, the Dentheliatis had been returned to Sparta.

[33] On the importance of the Dentheliatis in relation to the routes across the Taygetos, see Christien 1989: 30–4 and Pikoulas 1991: 280–1.

(Paus. 3.16.7).[34] Although the sanctuary in the Dentheliatis has never been thoroughly investigated, it was certainly located in the area of the chapel of the Panayia Volimiotissa, in the mountains northeast of Kalamata. Stray finds document a cult probably starting in the mid eighth century, making of this one of the earliest sanctuaries in Messenia.[35] Inscriptions of Imperial date reemployed in the walls of the chapel attest to its enduring importance, showing that the Messenians held games in honor of Artemis Limnatis[36] – certainly not up in the mountains. But what made this sanctuary indispensable for Spartans and Messenians alike was its role in the tradition on the Messenian Wars. According to a story found in various ancient authors from the fourth century onwards, the sanctuary had been the backdrop for the *casus belli* of the so-called First Messenian War. Pausanias, who gives the fullest account of this episode, has a Spartan and a Messenian version of it. According to the Spartans (Paus. 4.4.2), Spartan maidens who had come to the sanctuary for a religious festival had been assaulted by the Messenians, who even went so far as to kill the Spartan king Teleklos who had rushed to their rescue. However, the Messenians (Paus. 4.4.3) maintained that the Spartans had sent to the sanctuary a band of beardless youths in women's clothes, in order to assault the most prominent Messenians, who had come to take part in a religious festival. The Messenians then fought back and killed the youths and king Teleklos, who led them. Strabo and Diodorus, writing in the first century BC, were clearly familiar with the Spartan version, which they probably found in the work of the fourth-century historian Ephorus of Cumae. It is impossible to tell with certainty how old the story really is,

---

[34] Sanctuaries of Artemis Limnatis are documented in Messene (*IG* V 1, 1442, 1458, 1470; *SEG* 39.384; see Zunino 1997: 61–5; see also below, pp. 275–6), on the Choireios river, not far from Gerenia (*IG* V 1, 1431, lines 37–9), in Epidauros Limera in Laconia (Paus. 3.23.10), in Tegean territory on the road to Sparta (Paus. 8.53.11), in Sikyon (Paus. 2.7.6, epithet Limnaia) and in Patrai (7.20.7–8; the cult-statue had been allegedly stolen from Sparta). In the sanctuary of Artemis at Kombothekra in Triphylia a late archaic mirror was dedicated to Artemis Limnatis with an inscription that on the basis of the letter-forms could be Laconian or Arcadian; see Sinn 1981: 31–3 and *SEG* 31.356, and note that Kombothekra was on the route from Sparta to Olympia (Taita 2001: 110). On the cult of Artemis Limnatis see Calame 2001: 142–9 and Zunino 1997: 48–55, the latter emphasizing the essential equivalence of Artemis Limnatis and Artemis Orthia (in *IG* V 1, 1376, an early Imperial inscription from Volimos, the site of the sanctuary in the Dentheliatis, Artemis is called "Bortheia," that is, Orthia, according to the spelling that was used at Sparta at that time, cf. e.g. *IG* V 1, 303 etc.). Strabo (8.4.9) says that the Limnaion of Sparta took its name from Limnai on the Taygetos, but this is clearly an attempt at reversing the connection between the two sanctuaries.

[35] The area where the sanctuary was located is called Volimnos in the literature, and Volimos on the map of the Hellenic Military Geographical Service. The early archaeological evidence from the Panayia Volimiotissa is discussed below, pp. 123–4.

[36] *IG* V 1, 1375–6 and *SEG* 39.388bis.

but one can easily imagine how the affair of Limnai, in the Spartan version, may have been adduced, since the mid fourth century, to justify the Spartan conquest of Messenia and to buttress the enduring Spartan claim on that region after its liberation by the Thebans in 369 BC.[37]

In any case, it is clear that by the second half of the fourth century at the latest the sanctuary of Artemis Limnatis at Volimos had become a symbol of the age-old conflict between Spartans and Messenians. Tellingly, the text of the arbitration of the Milesians was inscribed at Olympia on the pillar that supported the famous statue of Victory by the sculptor Paionios of Mende, the most prominent Messenian dedication in the sanctuary, commemorating a victory against the Spartans (below, pp. 191–4 and fig. 4). For the Spartans, who were never able to bring themselves to accept the loss of Messenia, controlling the sanctuary of Volimos meant keeping alive a dream of power that had become more and more unrealistic with time. This explains the meaning of Philip's and Antigonus' measures: by awarding the Dentheliatis to the Messenians, they were not strategically or economically weakening Sparta in any significant way, but symbolically articulating a retrospective judgment on the Messenian Wars and, in concrete terms, making clear to the Spartans that their role as a hegemonic power belonged irreparably to the past. As for the Messenians, the sanctuary of Artemis Limnatis was indissolubly connected with avenging the oppression of their forefathers. Since the third century, if not earlier, the story of their heroic and unlucky struggle against the Spartans back in the archaic age had become the *epos* of the Messenians, a shared history that functioned as the foundation myth of the ethnic community.[38] Affirming their right to the sanctuary was necessary in order to uphold their version of the struggle – a ruthless and lawless aggression by the Spartans.

But there is another important aspect of the meaning of the sanctuary of Artemis Limnatis for the Messenians, one that becomes clear once we consider an aspect that has not yet been discussed. Thus far we have spoken of "the Messenians" and "the Spartans" as the actors in this conflict, as if these denominations were unproblematic and the two parties in the age-old strife had remained the same all along. Surely, this is what Tacitus seems to assume, but this was far from being the case. The

---

[37] For a detailed discussion of the Limnai story in its various versions, see below, pp. 80–3. The terminus ante of the mid fourth century may have to be pushed back to the late fifth in light of the considerations presented below, pp. 158–60.

[38] On the definition of *epos*, see Tullio-Altan 1995: 22–3 and above, p. 10.

political communities that began the conflict in the late fourth century BC were radically different from those that were still struggling against one another in the first century AD.

Beginning with Flamininus' campaign against king Nabis in 192 BC, Sparta had gradually lost control over most of the perioikic settlements of Laconia, which finally formed the League of the Eleutherolaconians, or Free Laconians.[39] By the age of Augustus, only a torso remained of the old Lakedaimonian state. The Spartans, however, had at least preserved a direct route to the Taygetos. As for the Messenians, the changes they had undergone were hardly less radical. The Messenian polity that received the Dentheliatis from Philip the Second comprised the whole region south of the river Neda and west of the Taygetos. But the cohesion of this Messenian polity soon proved to be problematic, and already in the second half of the third century some peripheral towns such as Asine and Pylos appear to have been controlled by the Achaean League. In the first decades of the second century, as the Achaean League progressively took control of Messenia, more and more Messenian towns became independent, until in 182, after the defeat of the Messenians in the war against the Achaeans, the towns of Abia, Pharai and Thouria became independent members of the Achaean League (below, pp. 262–4).

The falling apart of the Messenian polity had a paradoxical consequence for the conflict over the Dentheliatis. In the age of Tiberius, with the cities east of the Pamisos belonging either to Sparta or to the Eleutherolaconians, the Dentheliatis was probably a territorial enclave.[40] On the other hand, the inscriptions of early imperial date from Volimos show beyond doubt that the sanctuary itself belonged to the city of Messene, not to any of the neighboring cities, such as Pharai or Thouria.[41] This strange situation may have begun even earlier. Since it is far from certain that the old Messenian polity had been recomposed after the sack of Corinth in 146 BC, it is quite possible that by the time of the Milesian arbitration the Dentheliatis was already an enclave. At any rate, the party

[39] On the fate of the former *perioikoi* of Laconia, see Kennell 1999.

[40] It is unclear when and if Pharai ceased to be part of the League of the Eleutherolaconians. If it really returned to Messenia before 78 BC (see above, n. 28), there might have been an uninterrupted stretch of Messenian land going from Messene to the Dentheliatis, but only if we assume that the territory of Thouria did not reach the Messenian Gulf (see below, p. 29).

[41] The point was made forcefully by Kahrstedt 1950a: 234–5. Add that Nikeratos, son of Theon, and Straton, son of Straton, mentioned together in an inscription from Volimos (*IG* V 1, 1374), appear again together as *epimelētai* of Oupesia – that is, interestingly, in connection with the cult of Artemis Orthia – in an inscription from Messene dated to AD 42, *SEG* 23.208.

to which the Eleans granted permission to inscribe the Milesian arbitration in Olympia is called in the inscription 'the polis of the Messenians.'[42]

In other words, from the second half of the second century BC the war of memory between Sparta and the Messenians over the Dentheliatis was actually waged single-handedly by the citizens of Messene, the city at the foot of Mount Ithome. This situation was the result of a historical process of which other signs can be identified in the evidence. In the course of the third century BC, the polis of Messene increasingly appropriated the heroic history of Messenian resistance against the Spartans (below, pp. 85–6 and 288–9). This process of exclusive appropriation and concentration of the Messenian identity has left traces even in the toponymy. The name "Messene," which in the fifth and fourth centuries designed the whole region and then the Messenian polity, came to indicate the city at the foot of Mount Ithome, while the name "Messenia" became the common way to designate the region that had formed the Messenian state that came to life in 369 (below, pp. 266–9). In this framework, controlling the sanctuary of Artemis Limatis must have become a way for the polis of Messene to stake its exclusive claim to the cultural heritage of the Messenians and by extension to supremacy over the whole region.

Thus, the symbolic meaning of the borderland between Sparta and Messenia emerges in all its complexity. For the Spartans, refusing to accept the Taygetos as a border must have been a way of keeping alive the memory of their ancestral claim to hegemony over the Peloponnese, of which domination over Messenia had been a crucial component. For the Messenians the situation was more complex, in that the border had a double meaning, in terms of whom it excluded and whom it included. The story of the shifting ethnic definition of Thouria fleshes this situation out in a striking way.

STRADDLING THE BORDER: THOURIAN ETHNICITY

Located on a steep and elongated hill, today called Ellinika, that runs north–south and overlooks from the east the valley of the Pamisos (plates 1–2), Thouria was in antiquity one of the most important centers of Messenia. Settlements going back to the Early and Late Helladic and a number of very impressive Late Helladic chamber tombs dug into the sides of the southern part of the Ellinika hill, not far from its top, and

---

[42] See *IvO* 52, lines 3–4, 10, 17, 20, 22, from the decree of the Eleans. The letter of the Milesians and the arbitration itself simply speak of "the Messenians."

Plate 1 The view from the Ellinika Hill towards Mount Ithome, across the northern
Messenian plain

provided with extremely rich grave goods, have suggested that this place
should be identified with reu-ko-to-ro, the most important center of the
"Further province" of the kingdom of Pylos, second in rank only to Pylos
itself.[43] Written sources and inscriptions testify to the prominence of
Thouria even in the historical period, and the archaeological evidence, in
spite of being still underexploited, confirms the picture. Travelers in the
mid nineteenth century could still recognize the traces of a number of
buildings on the site, including apparently a rather large theatre,[44] and
even now that the hill is covered by an olive grove the remains of its
massive fortification walls are still visible (see plate 3). The fact that the
northeastern part of the gulf of Messenia was called the "Gulf of Thouria"

[43] Early and Late Helladic pottery: Hope Simpson 1966: 123. Mycenaean tombs, including one *tholos*:
Koumouzelis 1996; Chatzi-Spiliopoulou 1998: 539–44; 2001 with further references. Some of the
very rich materials from these tombs, including three gold signet rings, are on display in the Benaki
Museum at Kalamata. Identification of Thouria with reu-ko-to-ro: Hope Simpson 1981: 149,
Bennet 1994.

[44] The reports of early travelers are summarized by Bölte 1936: 635. Architectural remains such as
small column shafts are still to be seen scattered around under the olives on the hill. On the site of
Thouria, see Valmin 1930: 56–63.

Plate 2 The Gulf of Messenia from the Ellinika Hill

further underlines the importance of this city, whose territory must have included a good portion of the southern Messenian plain towards the sea.[45] There can be no doubt that Thouria existed during the Spartan domination of Messenia, and of course it continued to exist once Messenia became independent. This makes it particularly interesting to observe how the Thourians classified themselves, or how they were classified, in ethnic terms. The story of the Thourians' identity in a borderland between Laconia and Messenia offers a perspective that complements in an interesting way the one resulting from the story of the conflict for the Dentheliatis.

Thouria's first appearance in the sources coincides with a turning point in the history of the Messenian identity. Following an earthquake that devastated the southern Peloponnese in the 460s, a revolt erupted in the Spartan territory west of the Taygetos. Among the sources closest in time to the event itself, Thucydides alone furnishes a reasonably detailed description of the rebels: according to him (1.101.2), they were Helots and the *perioikoi* from Thouria and Aithaia. Since most of the Helots who

---

[45] See Strab. 8.4.5 and Roebuck 1941: 16–17.

revolted were descendants of the "old Messenians" – says Thucydides – all the rebels came to be called "the Messenians." As we shall see in greater detail later on, Thucydides' explanation helps to make sense of some more scattered early references to the revolt, where the rebels are simply called 'Messenians,' without further specification, and most importantly, of two inscriptions recording the dedication of booty by "the Messenians" at Olympia and in the sanctuary of Apollo Kory(n)thos at Longà/Ayios Andhreas, on the western coast of the Messenian gulf, just north of the perioikic settlement of Asine.[46] "Messenians" remained the collective name of the rebels once they had to leave the Peloponnese, after a long and hard war against the Spartans, supported by their allies, had come to a standstill. As Messenians they made highly conspicuous dedications in the Panhellenic sanctuaries of Olympia and Delphi (below, pp. 199–200).

Later sources tend to ignore perioikic participation in the revolt, in the framework of a general narrative of Messenian history in which the Messenians had either left their region at the time of the Spartan conquest, or had been reduced to the condition of Helots, then revolted against the Spartans after the earthquake, and finally left the Peloponnese when the revolt was put down. But since there is no reason to assume that such general narrative had started emerging before the fourth century, it seems preferable to take Thucydides at his own word and conclude that the Messenian identity was a feasible rallying cry both for (some) *perioikoi* and for (some) Helots in the western part of the Spartan territory. At least during the revolt the Thourians were identified, and judging by the dedications from Longà/Ayios Andhreas and Olympia probably also identified themselves, as Messenians. It is extremely likely that this Messenian identity implied some more specific ideas about genealogy and origins, and very possibly some sort of narrative that explained how they had come to be Lakedaimonian *perioikoi*, but no trace of this has been preserved in the sources. Rather, Thucydides' narrative of the revolt and later references to the Messenian rebels suggest that the Messenian identity of the rebel *perioikoi* was seen from the outside, and *ex post facto*, as a mere extension of that of (some of) the Helots living west of the Taygetos – a view that was very compatible with the interests of the Spartans.

Even more puzzling than the Thourians' 'Messenian moment' is how they came out of it. There can be no doubt that Thouria existed in the second half of the fifth century: it was not erased from the map, and it still

---

[46] On the identity of the rebels, see below, pp. 195–7; on the sanctuary of Apollo Kory(n)thos, below, pp. 117–21.

held, probably at the sanctuary of Akovitika, close to the coast, its festival in honor of Poseidon, with competitions in which members of the Spartiate elite participated.[47] In all likelihood, not all Thourians left the Peloponnese at the end of the revolt; perhaps not all of them had taken arms against the Spartans in the first place. Clearly, there must be here a number of processes of ascription and redefinition going on, about which we have no direct evidence. Interestingly, though, the question of the ethnic origin of Thouria, and of the whole perioikic district east of the river Pamisos, has left a faint trace in a text from the second half of the fifth century. Some verses from Euripides' lost tragedy *Temenos*[48] quoted by Strabo (8.5.6 = Eur. *TrGF* 727e) include a description of the respective merits of Laconia and Messenia – or rather, praise of the attractiveness of Messenia – that clearly belonged in the context of the division of the southern Peloponnese among the Heraclids. Here, the river Pamisos is called the border between Laconia and Messenia. Strabo protested against this delimitation, which clearly flew in the face of every other source he was familiar with. In modern research, Euripides' idiosyncratic geography is sometimes brought in line with more normal conceptions by pointing to the so-called "Little Pamisos," a small river that flows into the Messenian gulf somewhere on its eastern coast, also mentioned by Strabo (8.4.6).[49] However, it would be rather odd that Euripides should have referred to this small and little-known river, without further explanation and in a way that induced Strabo, who knew of the existence of the "Little Pamisos," to believe that Euripides meant the famous Pamisos. It seems more likely that Euripides reflected a modified description of the borders of Laconia and Messenia, a description in which Thouria had come to be part of ancestral Laconia. Although we cannot tell for sure, it is rather unlikely that this strange way of delimiting the two regions was an original component of the myth; more probably, the ascription of the southern Messenian plain east of the Pamisos to the lot of Eurysthenes and Procles

---

[47] On the sanctuary of Akovitika, see below, pp. 121–3. The Spartiate Damonon lists eight victories in the chariot race in the Pohoidaia of Thouria, *IG* V 1, 213, lines 19–21. The chronology of the inscription is uncertain, but a date in the late fifth century is most likely; Jeffery initially dated it c. 450–431 with question mark (Jeffery 1990: 201), but successively opted for a later date, after 403, see Jeffery 1990: 448 and Jeffery 1988; the years between 431 and 403 are ruled out because none of the ephors that appear in the inscription (lines 66–95) is found in the list given by Xen. *Hell.* 2.3.10. On the stele see also Hodkinson 2000: 303–7.

[48] Or, less likely, from the *Temenids*. See below, p. 50 n. 12. The common attribution of these verses to Euripides' *Kresphontes* should be rejected; see Harder 1985: 278–9 and 1991: 134 and Luppe 1987: 200.

[49] See Bölte 1949: 293–5.

may have been part of a conscious attempt at redefining the ethnic allegiance of the *perioikoi* living there, and this redefinition may well have been a kind of response to Thouria's Messenian moment.

In due course, however, the Thourians became Messenian again. An inscription from Delphi, tentatively dated to 322, records the grant of proxeny by the Delphians to Pancrates son of Pasiteles, "a Messenian from Thouria."[50] The Messenicity of Hellenistic Thouria is further confirmed by the fact that by the second century BC its citizen body appears to have been divided into the five Messenian tribes, Kresphontis, Daiphontis, Aristomachis, Hyllis and Kleolaia.[51] What is not clear is when exactly the Thourians became Messenian again. Of course, this cannot have happened before the liberation of Messenia by Epaminondas, in 369 BC, but in theory, since the earliest datable evidence, the inscription from Delphi, refers to the late 320s, Thouria could have joined the new Messenian state not immediately upon its foundation but at a later stage, presumably in 338 BC, as a consequence of Philip's intervention in the Peloponnese. However, the common assumption that the southern Messenian plain east of the river Pamisos became Messenian thanks to Philip[52] is far from certain. A closer look at the relevant sources, and some general observations, tend to suggest a rather different scenario.

To be sure, the extension of the original Messenian polity created by Epaminondas is never described precisely in the sources, and in particular, no direct evidence exists regarding the position of the perioikic settlements east of the Pamisos. However, the sources on Philip's intervention give the impression that it had to do with portions of land farther to the east and south: the Dentheliatis, in the mountains, and the Little Pamisos river, south of Leuktron.[53] This, of course, does not exclude that also the east bank of the Pamisos belonged to the Spartan land that Philip gave the Messenians, but the silence of the sources is somewhat more significant in view of their mentioning the border districts. More generally, it is difficult to believe that the Pamisos, hardly a natural obstacle, might have functioned for three decades as a frontier between two polities that were so

[50] *FD* III.iv.5; date according to Sánchez 2001: 519. [51] *IG* V 1, 1386; see Jones 1987: 148–9.

[52] See e.g. Roebuck 1941: 39 and recently Shipley 2000: 385, and Grandjean 2003: 69 and 91–2, based exclusively on arguments from silence.

[53] According to Strab. 8.4.6, there was a judgment by Philip in a controversy between Messenians and Spartans regarding the river. It seems obvious to assume that Strabo meant that the river was the border claimed by one of the parties, presumably the Messenians; see Roebuck 1941: 56 n. 132 and above n. 8.

fiercely hostile to each other. Thouria, at that time certainly unfortified,[54] would have been within easy reach of Epaminondas' army in 369, and obviously no match for it. Moreover, all sources concur in giving the impression that, throughout the fourth century and until Philip finally put an end to their hopes, the Spartans had been longing to recover Messene.[55] Their failure to attack it directly would be really strange, if we assume that they had kept control of the eastern portion of the southern Messenian plain and with it the possibility to move troops across the Taygetos at leisure. By contrast, Messenian control of Thouria, Pharai and surroundings would explain the complete absence of Spartan military activity west of the Taygetos during the 350s and 340s.[56]

But quite apart from the inherent probability that Thouria, together with Pharai and with more perioikic settlements in the area, was part of the free Messenian state created in 369 BC, archaeological evidence from the site seems to point in this direction, too. The ancient wall circuit of Thouria, preserved to a height of five meters in some points, was built in isodomic ashlar masonry with the *emplekton* technique (see plate 3), the same technique used in the famous circuit that enclosed Mount Ithome and the new city founded there (see plate 4). All early examples of this highly sophisticated and easily recognizable building technique are connected in one way or another with the Theban hegemony in the early fourth century, and recent scholarship has established that it was developed by Theban military engineers. In all likelihood, the walls of Thouria belong, together with those of Megalopolis and Ithome itself, to the chain of fortifications built under Theban initiative in the framework of Epaminondas' activity in the Peloponnese.[57]

Recent archaeological research in the Bronze Age graves from Thouria has brought to light some evidence that might also point to Thouria's having joined the free Messenian polity from the outset. Most of the many Mycenaean chamber tombs located on the eastern side of the

---

[54] On the chronology of the walls of Thouria see below, n. 57. Located deep in Spartan territory and rather far from its borders, it is unthinkable that Thouria may have been fortified before Epaminondas' campaign.

[55] See e.g. Dem. *For the Megalopolitans* [16].8 and 16–20, from 353 BC, and below, p. 229.

[56] On the territorial extension of the Messenian state founded by Epaminondas, see also below, pp. 228–30.

[57] For a precise description of the fortification walls of Thouria, see Hope Simpson 1966: 123–4; compare with Karlsson 1992: 73–8. Valmin 1930: 58 observed mason marks on some of the blocks, and suggested a dating in the late fifth to early fourth century. On the walls of Messene, see below, pp. 217–18. A new campaign of research on the fortifications of Thouria has been started in 2005 by the Scuola Archeologica Italiana di Atene.

Plate 3 Masonry chains in the walls of Thouria

Plate 4 Masonry chains in the walls of Messene, near the Arcadian Gate

Ellinika ridge had been already looted once archaeologists found them, but some have been found untouched and could be properly excavated. One of them, the only one published in some detail, has brought new evidence for the custom of Dark Age Messenians of burying their dead in the entrances of Bronze Age graves.[58] It also adds one more case to the growing number of Bronze Age graves that show traces of what may be generally called cultic activity beginning in the fourth century. The connection between such activity and the assertion of Messenian identity is an extremely likely hypothesis, one which will be discussed in detail further on (pp. 239–45). If the hypothesis is accepted, then it should be stressed that in the case of the chamber tomb at Thouria the finds start in the early fourth century, well before the age of Philip.[59]

The evidence of early fourth-century cultic activity in the Mycenaean necropolis of Thouria, while supporting indirectly the conclusion that Thouria was part of the free Messenian polity from the latter's foundation, has implications that go beyond the level of political allegiance. It suggests that the Thourians, or at least some of them, upon becoming officially Messenian – for the second time, if we consider the fifth-century revolt – also started to think of themselves as Messenians and to engage in patterns of ritual behavior that marked them as such. Together with the evidence for the introduction of the Messenian tribes in Thouria, the dedications in the Bronze Age tombs are the scanty surviving documents of the Thourians' reviving their old Messenian identity that had surfaced at the time of the revolt in the fifth century. This revival probably involved the reinterpretation of cultural traits that had previously been components of Thouria's Lakedaimonian identity. The competitions in honor of Poseidon, in which the Spartiate Damonon had participated in the late fifth or early fourth century, were apparently still held during the

---

[58] See Chatzi-Spiliopoulou 2001: 293; as she observes, this find suggests that the small assemblage of Dark Age II vases from Ellinika, many whole, allegedly found in a grave, that were given to the Kalamata Museum in 1965 (P. Themelis, *Deltion* 20 (1965) B' 2: 207; on the vases see Coulson 1986: 31–5 and Eder, 1998: 172–3), probably came from a Mycenaean tomb, too.

[59] Chatzi-Spiliopoulou 2001: 293–4. Notice, however, that the fragments of roof tiles mentioned in the first short notice about the excavation of this tomb, *Deltion* 47 (1992), B' 122, do not feature in the later, more comprehensive publication. The most important evidence for cult at a Bronze Age tomb in Thouria actually refers to the *tholos* tomb on the southwestern side of the hill, but is virtually unpublished. Korres 1988: 325 refers to terracotta plaques found there, to be compared to those from Voidokoilia and from the omega-omega sanctuary in Mavromati/Messene (see below, pp. 242 and 125–6), but he gives no indication as to their quantity and date; cf., however, Chatzi-Spiliopoulou 1998: 543 n. 27, who implies that their quantity is comparable to that of the plaques from Voidokoilia (something more than 400).

third, although not any more at Akovitika. In all likelihood, the cult was now seen as ancestrally Messenian.[60]

Needless to say, what to an external observer looks like a series of sudden changes in the ethnic definition of the Thourians was probably experienced by them as so many restorations of their original and true identity. And each change will certainly have had its discontents. Perhaps some Thourians kept alive the memory of their Messenicity from the revolt in the fifth century to the liberation in the fourth, and perhaps some were not at all convinced of being Messenian on either occasion.

In any case, Thouria's recovered Messenian identity was not going to remain uncontroversial for the next centuries. For the Thourians, being Messenian in the mid fourth century was probably not the same thing as being Messenian in the mid third. As we have noted in connection with the controversy over the Dentheliatis, and will discuss more in detail in relation to Hellenistic Messenia, starting during the third century the city by Mount Ithome increasingly assumed a dominant position in the Messenian polity, and, possibly as a reaction to this development, some of the smaller Messenian poleis seem to have begun to break loose already by the last decades of the century.[61] The conflicts that pitted the Messenians against the Achaean League in the first decades of the second century resulted in the vast majority of the minor poleis of Messenia becoming independent members of the League. This happened to Thouria in 182 BC, after the Messenians' attempt to secede from the Achaean League had brought upon them war and defeat.[62] Political independence does not seem to have implied a radical revision of how the Thourians understood their ethnic heritage: the inscription from Thouria bearing the Messenian tribal names is almost certainly later than Thouria's autonomous membership in the Achaean League. The inscription, an ephebic list, mentions a category of ephebes called *tritirenes*, a term found elsewhere only on ephebic catalogues from Messene, offering further evidence of shared institutions.[63] On the other hand, the introduction, possibly in the late

---

[60] For the parallel cases of Artemis Orthia and the Dioscuri, see below, pp. 233–8. The competitions in honor of Poseidon may be documented by a fragmentary third-century inscription from Thouria, *IG* V 1, 1387; see Mylonopoulos 2003: 251. The sanctuary of Akovitika was abandoned at the end of the fifth century because the rising soil level exposed it to floods (Moritz Kiderlen, personal communication).

[61] See below, p. 42 on Asine, and pp. 258–61.   [62] Polyb. 23.17.2.

[63] *IG* V 1, 1386. Inscriptions from Messene: *SEG* 43.145, dated to AD 3, 11 or 20, has *trietirenes*, and *SEG* 51.472, dated AD 70, has *trieteirenes*. The name has a vaguely Spartan sound, reminding of the Spartan age class of the *eirenes* (Xen., *Lac. pol.* 2.11, Plut. *Lyc.* 17.3-4, *IG* V 1, 279). As always when Spartan or Laconizing cultural traits are found in Messenia, the possibility should not be

third or early second century, of the cult of the Syrian Goddess Atargatis, which became the most prominent cult in Hellenistic Thouria, could point to an attempt at shaping a Thourian identity distinguishable from the Messenian one by introducing a new cult, one that had no counterpart in the Messenian pantheon.[64] Of course, the relation between these hypothetical processes of redefinition and the changing political situation of Thouria has to remain essentially indeterminate: it is perfectly possible that the Achaean League, besides punishing the Messenians, also acknowledged a process of estrangement that had been emerging already among the Thourians.

It is generally assumed that some links between Thouria and Messene survived the political separation of 182, or more likely were reinstated after the Achaean War.[65] This seems to be implied by the fact that Augustus after Actium turned Thouria over to the Spartans to punish the Messenians, who had sided with Antony. In so doing, he was logically continuing the trend he and Antony had set after Philippi, by granting the Spartans the Dentheliatis – which should alert us to the fact that Augustus was in all likelihood as interested in rewarding the Spartans as he was in punishing the Messenians. Pausanias, who mentions Augustus' decision, does not say if in his day that same situation still obtained, and this question cannot be decided in a conclusive way. However, two inscriptions from Thouria suggest at least a likely answer, besides fleshing out in interesting ways the relations between Thouria and Sparta – and by implication, between Thouria and the Messenians.

---

excluded that they might have been remains of the period of Spartan domination, possibly reinterpreted as ancestrally Messenian, as is the case with some post-liberation Messenian cults. However, Kennell 1995: 118–19 after a detailed discussion concludes that the institution itself, far from being archaic, was not even necessarily modeled on a corresponding Spartan institution; probably only the name was borrowed from Sparta or fashioned in such a way as to sound Spartan.

[64] On the cult of Atargatis, which spread in the Greek world from the late third century BC, see now Gehrke forthcoming. For an overview, see also Hörig 1984. At Thouria, the cult is documented for the first time in the second quarter of the second century BC (*SEG* 11.972 = Ager 145), and was peculiar in that only here, at least from the late first century BC, the Syrian Goddess was honored with the celebration of mysteries (*SEG* 11.974 and Zunino 1997: 246–7). Lambrechts and Noyen 1954: 269–70 very plausibly suggest that the mysteries of Atargatis at Thouria may have originated under the influence of the prominent mystery cult of the Great Gods of Andania, as a Thourian counterpart of sorts (the conclusion is tentatively accepted by Hörig 1984: 1566; on the mysteries of Andania, see below, pp. 236–7 and 294–9). In this case, the Thourians' intention to detach themselves symbolically from Messene would be even more explicit.

[65] See below, pp. 264–5. Grandjean 2002: 559 discusses numismatic evidence possibly relevant to the relations between Messene and Thouria in this period.

In a fascinating document from the second half of the first century BC,[66] the Thourians honor the Spartan Damocharis son of Timoxenos, who had helped Thourian ambassadors in Sparta and Thourians who were facing trial there, and later moved to Thouria and prevented an outburst of civil strife, thus bringing about a reconciliation among the citizens. As a reward, he was granted citizenship, proxeny and further honors in connection with the celebration of the mysteries of the Syrian Goddess. Moreover, since he had promised to supply the oil for the mysteries for the rest of his life, a painted portrait of him was to be dedicated in the sanctuary of the goddess. There is nothing, in the wording of the inscription, that directly suggests political dependence on the side of Thouria: the polis seems to be alive and well, taking its own decisions autonomously, with all its magistrates acting in their capacities. One would be tempted to date the document to the period before Augustus gave Thouria to Sparta: after all, the fact that Thourians were tried in Sparta could simply be a consequence of their committing crimes in Sparta.[67]

However, a closer scrutiny may suggest a different scenario. Damocharis was an old friend of the Thourians, with links going back generations, and his activities at Sparta on behalf of the Thourians suggest a wealthy and influential citizen. As a matter of fact, a Damocharis son of Timoxenos appears in a list of *patronomoi* from Sparta, dated to the second half of the first century BC.[68] One wonders why such a citizen would move to Thouria, given especially that the offer to pay for the oil for the mysteries suggests that Damocharis was there to stay. Probably the correct conclusion to be drawn from this inscription is that Thouria was now under Spartan control, but the Spartans were exerting that control with considerable discretion. This is confirmed by an inscription coming from the other Messenian city that had been given by Augustus to the Spartans, Kardamyle (*SEG* 11.948). Dating to the first century AD, it records honors, one of which is tax exemption, for a Posidippus son of Attalus, granted by the demos, the polis and the ephors. Again, Kardamyle seems to act as an independent entity, but Pausanias is explicit that Spartan control was still effective in his times (3.26.7). A consequence of subordination to

---

[66] *SEG* 11.974, published with extensive commentary in Valmin 1928–29: 123–37.

[67] There is evidence for the continuing administration of justice in Greek cities, both *liberae* and not, under Rome: see Nörr 1969: 30–4, Horstkott 1999: 303–18, esp. 307, 313, and now Fournier 2005: esp. 124. The borderline between Roman and local justice was obviously a very blurred one; see the new document from Aphrodisia published in Reynolds 2000: 10–15.

[68] *IG* V 1, 48 lines 9–10. For the interpretation of the inscription as a catalogue, see Kennell 1991; on the office of the *patronomoi*, Kennell 1995: 44–5. Compare the case of the Spartan Iunius Chariteles, living in Kalamai (*IG* V 1, 1369, from Kalamai).

Sparta could be the fact that in Thouria, as in Kardamyle, the executive magistrates appear to be ephors rather than the Achaean-style polemarchs attested in earlier documents.[69] Even if this suggestion is correct, by and large the inscription shows that subordination to Sparta did not cause, at least on a formal level, any thoroughgoing loss of institutional structure for Thouria. What it really meant for the Thourians to have been given to the Spartans remains hard to tell.

A second inscription from Thouria, on what was originally the base of a statue of the emperor Trajan, dedicated between 102 and 114 AD,[70] has often been taken as evidence that Thouria, unlike Kardamyle, was at that point autonomous again and had not remained under Spartan control very long.[71] However, if Thouria preserved its own political institutions after being given to the Spartans by Augustus, as the inscription for Damocharis shows, there is no serious reason why it could not have dedicated the statue while still being under Spartan control.[72] More importantly from our point of view, the same inscription also offers a precious insight into how at this point in time the Thourians reconstructed their early history. In the text, Trajan is called savior of the Thourians and of "our metropolis Lakedaimon." In all likelihood, at this time the Thourians thought of themselves as a Spartan foundation, presumably reviving their identity as Spartan *perioikoi*. In the same spirit, Thourian coins of the age of the Severi bore the legend Θουριατῶν Λα(κεδαιμωνίων).[73] The story of the Thourians had come full circle.

NOTHING TO DO WITH MESSENIA: THE OAK-PEOPLE

Although the Spartan domination in the archaic and early classical periods remains the most fundamental fact around which people living in Messenia even centuries after the liberation constructed a sense of their shared past and of their identity, the alternative between being Messenian and being Lakedaimonian does not exhaust all the possibilities of ethnic self-definition in ancient Messenia. We will now turn our attention briefly

---

[69] Polemarchs at Thouria: *IG* V 1, 1379. Cf. below p. 260 on ephors and polemarchs at Messene before 219 BC.

[70] *IG* V 1, 1381.

[71] E.g. by Kahrstedt 1950a: 235, Spawforth, in Cartledge and Spawforth 2002: 139, and Lafond 1996: 184 n. 50.

[72] See Bölte 1936: 637, Ehrenberg 1929: 1449. I am very grateful to Christian Habicht and Nigel Kennel for advice on this point. The latter, however, tends to share the views of the scholars quoted in the previous note.

[73] Head 1911: 433.

to one of the cities of Messenia that shows an extremely original and creative approach to these problems.

After listing the Peloponnesians who defended the Isthmus of Corinth against the Persians just before the battle of Salamis, Herodotus sketches an ethnic map of the Peloponnese, mentioning seven different ethnic groups; one of them were the Dryopians, who inhabited Hermione in the Argolis and Asine, opposite Kardamyle, across the Messenian gulf (Hdt. 8.73). The Dryopians had a peculiar history – or rather, a myth-history. In a way, they belong together with the Lapiths or the Pelasgians to a group of mythical pre-Greek peoples, mentioned in Greek sources as inhabitants of districts of Greece before the current occupants of such districts moved in; strictly speaking, they could be regarded as barbarians.[74] The Dryopians, whose name means "oak-people" or "woodpeckers,"[75] originated in northern Greece, according to some accounts from Doris, the putative homeland of the Dorians of the Peloponnese.[76] They had been evicted from there by Heracles, who had consecrated them to Delphian Apollo, and had been sent to the Argive Akte from Delphi. But this destination did not put an end to their fate of wanderings. The Argives attacked the Dryopian city of Asine, conquered it and expelled its population, who were then rescued by the Spartans, who gave the Asinaeans a new home in the land they had conquered in the First Messenian War. Thus was Messenian Asine founded.

Although this story is attested in its fullness only by rather late sources, it is generally believed that some parts of its last portion reflect, more or less accurately, real events of the early archaic period. The settlement of old Asine in the Argolid has been the focus of archaeological investigations, and the results of the excavations show clear signs of destruction in the late eighth century, which may obviously be connected with the evidence from the written sources.[77] The tally may be less neat than it has often been assumed to be, however, since apparently there is abundant evidence for settlement continuity after the late eighth century.[78] But of course, such evidence cannot be taken as directly contradicting the story of the expulsion of the Dryopians.

In the eighth century, Argolic Asine appears to have been an important settlement, certainly a match for Argos, to judge from the respective

---

[74] See Strab. 7.7.1. The passage goes back to some extent to Hecataeus (early fifth century BC), but it is impossible to tell whether the reference to the Dryopians comes from the Milesian; see Strid 1999: 13–14.

[75] Strid 1999: 12–13.   [76] On the homeland of the Dryopians, see Strid 1999: 51.

[77] Morgan and Whitelaw 1991: 83 with further refs.   [78] See now Wells 2002.

archaeological remains.[79] In terms of material culture, it was markedly different from the other settlements of the Argive plain, which has suggested that its inhabitants might have considered themselves ethnically different from their neighbors.[80] There is of course no way to tell whether they thought of themselves as Dryopians, however, and the origin myths of the Dryopians which are reflected by the sources with varying levels of detail are rather likely to be Argive constructions whose ultimate goal was to justify the conquest of Asine. This would explain the striking parallel between Heracles evicting the Dryopians from the Dorian homelands and the Dorian and Heraclid Argives evicting them from Asine. However, the Dryopian identity was not necessarily an Argive product from the outset, especially since the role of Argos cannot explain the fact that Dryopians were supposed to have settled in a number of other places in Greece, ranging from Euboea to Ionia.[81]

Lack of archaeological investigation on the site of Messenian Asine, today Koroni, makes it impossible to follow the itinerary of the Asinaeans from the Argolid to their new homes. However, later evidence leaves no doubt to the fact that the Asinaeans of Messenia did indeed think of themselves as Dryopians. According to Pausanias, they were in fact the only Dryopians who were not ashamed of being identified as such (4.34.11). They had a peculiar version of their myth of origins, in which their ancestors had migrated to the Peloponnese of their own initiative (4.34.10). More importantly, they worshipped their mythic forebear Dryops with a mystery cult, considering him a child of Apollo. The importance of Dryops and his connection with Apollo are confirmed by coins struck by Asine in the second century BC, showing a seated figure on one side with the legend "Dryops," and the head of Apollo on the other.[82] In more or less the same period, an inscription from Hermione shows the Asinaeans asking to be allowed to take part in the cult of Demeter Chthonia at Hermione on the strength of their ancestral ties with the Hermionaeans.[83] In all likelihood, recognition of the ethnic specificity of

---

[79] Billot 1989–90: 39–40 with further refs.

[80] See Hall 1997: 136–7. On ethnicity and material culture, see below, pp. 135–6.

[81] On the Dryopian identity and its meaning, see Hall 1997: 74–7.

[82] Head 1911: 432. It is tempting to see in the mysteries celebrated for Dryops the influence of the prestigious mysteries of Andania, along the lines of the interpretation suggested for the mysteries of the Syrian Goddess in Thouria, see above, n. 64.

[83] *IG* IV 679, to be dated in the third or second century BC. The Chthonia of Hermione are discussed at length by Perlman 1984: 329–37; on our inscription, see ibid. 333 and Strid 1999: 72. Note that the inscription cannot be connected with Asine in the Argolid, resurrected as a subdivision of the Argive polis, as suggested by Moretti, *ISE* 45; the two proxenies from Mycenae mentioned by

the Asinaeans is to be seen also in a decree from Delphi granting proxeny to two individuals described as "Asinaeans from Messene" or "from Messenia."[84] The decree dates to a period some years after the one for Pankrates of Thouria, and, as that one, is inscribed on the high triangular pillar that carried a famous Messenian dedication from the fifth century (see figure 4). The difference in phrasing between "Messenian from Thouria" and "Asinaean from Messene" almost certainly reflects the perception that an Asinaean could not be properly called a Messenian.

It seems, in sum, that the Dryopian identity of the Asinaeans of Messenia remained a well-known fact throughout antiquity. Interestingly, this peculiarity went together with a number of other peculiarities, which make us wonder about the true nature of the Dryopian identity itself. First of all, Asine does not seem to have taken part in the Messenian uprising in the second quarter of the fifth century. Then, after the liberation of Messenia in 369, Asine remained loyal to Sparta and resisted an onslaught by the Arcadians, during which the commander of the Spartan garrison, the Spartiate Geranor, was killed (Xen. *Hell.* 7.1.25). Only with Philip's intervention did Asine become a part of the Messenian polity, and this situation seems to have lasted for little longer than a century. By 196 BC, the Messenians were reclaiming Asine (Polyb. 18.42.7), which had become a member of the Achaean League. It is tempting to see here a historical context for the renewal of the ties between Asine and Hermione.

Considering what we know of Asine's political history from the fifth century onwards, one would say that the Dryopian identity of the Asinaeans matched perfectly their peculiar political course and provided a ready explanation for their lack of inclination to be Messenian. But in a sense, this conclusion begs the question: after all, even if we believe that Messenian Asine had been colonized by refugees from the Argolid at the time of the First Messenian War (Paus. 4.14.3), one wonders why they had preserved their Dryopian identity ever since, considering that, far from being associated with any prestigious or otherwise desirable trait, their being Dryopian called into question their very Greekness. The Asinaeans could have simply embraced their identity as Lakedaimonian *perioikoi*.

Moretti as parallels, *IG* IV 497 and 498, both explicitly call Mycenae a *kōmē* and refer to its inhabitants as *kōmetai*, while in our inscription (lines 12–13) Asine is called a polis.

[84] *SEG* 12.219, dated 315/14 BC by Sánchez 2001. Unfortunately, the inscription has a lacuna that makes it impossible to tell whether it had the form "Messene," as we would expect, or "Messenia." Grandjean 2002: 550 argues as if "Messenia" were on the stone, even though she indicates the lacuna in her quotation of the inscription.

But in their case, local considerations may have been outweighed by their need to fit the construction of their ethnic identity into the framework of generally accepted notions on the ethnic breakdown of the Peloponnese. The myth of the division of the Peloponnese at the time of the return of the Heraclids, which probably originated in Argos in the early fifth century, problematized the ethnic self-definition of the *perioikoi* living west of the Taygetos, Lakedaimonians in Messene, settled in the land that had been assigned to the Heraclid Kresphontes. In the case of Thouria and of other perioikic towns east of the Pamisos, the problem was probably addressed by retracing the eastern border of Kresphontes' portion. The promotion of the Dryopian identity of the Asinaeans of Messenia may have been, to some extent, an alternative response to the same challenge. It may be significant in this connection that the conflict between Argos and Sparta was inscribed deeply in the story of the wandering of the Asinaeans: according to Pausanias (2.36.4), the Argives had evicted the Asinaeans from the Argolid because the latter had supported a Spartan invasion of the region. Doubts on the historicity of this episode do not make the story less interesting.[85]

In view of the fact that the Dryopian identity seems to have served especially to set off the Asinaeans from the Messenians, it seems surprising that Pausanias goes out of his way to downplay the hostility between Asinaeans and Messenians, first by stating that the Dryopians of Asine had been forced against their will to follow the Spartans in their invasion of Messenia (4.8.3), then by adding that they remained neutral in the Second Messenian War (4.15.8) and for that reason were not expelled from Messenia at the time of the liberation in the fourth century (4.27.8). However, Pausanias' perspective is likely to reflect the situation of Messenia in his own times, when apparently the connection between Asine and Messene was close enough for young Asinaeans to enroll in the epheby at Messene.[86] As long as it had mattered, it seems that the Dryopian identity of the Asinaeans had been a symbolic expression of their unwillingness to be Messenian. It is a striking paradox that one of the earliest documented ethnic groups in Messenia did not define itself as Messenian – nor as Lakedaimonian, for that matter.

* * *

[85] Pausanias' story is mostly considered a retrospective fiction (Kelly 1967, Morgan and Whitelaw 1991: 83–4).
[86] See the unpublished inscription *SEG* 47.386.

The three case studies discussed in this chapter shed light on different ways of constructing ethnic identities in Messenia from the classical period onwards. Taken together, they define the framework for an investigation of the Messenian identity in its historical development. The struggle for the temple of Artemis Limnatis and the changing ethnicity of the Thourians point clearly to a key structural element of the Messenian identity, the oppositional relationship to Sparta, thereby offering one further example of the essentially oppositional nature of ethnicity. On the one hand, we observe the desperate need to draw and enforce a boundary that was inseparably linked to the Messenians' very right to existence. However, ever since the liberation of Messenia in 369 BC, the city at the foot of Mount Ithome seems to have been particularly interested in this process, while a city like Thouria could repeatedly overstep the ethnic border between Messenians and Spartans, rearranging its ethnic definition accordingly. The centrality of the opposition to Sparta becomes even clearer once we observe that the other border of Messenia, the one that separated it from Arcadia to the north, while also the object of heated territorial disputes during the Hellenistic age, never acquired a comparable symbolic meaning.[87] In narratives of the Second Messenian War, one has even the impression that locating the conflict in the area of the river Neda in some sense merged the traditional conflict with Sparta with the troubled relationship between the Messenians and their northern neighbors, Megalopolis and the Achaean League. If this is the case, it is all the more striking that Sparta alone, the symbolic opponent in Messenian memory, could stand for other enemies – ultimately for any enemy.[88]

Because of the historical circumstances in which Messenian ethnicity emerged, drawing a boundary to separate Messenians and Spartans was a primary necessity, but at the same time an extremely delicate operation, given the apparent scarcity of cultural markers such as cults and language to articulate and sustain such a boundary. The fact that the border itself was to some extent inscribed in preexisting mythic traditions, originating probably outside Messenia (below, p. 65), further complicated the situation, introducing a rather rigid parameter that had to be reckoned with. To some extent, the way chosen by the Messenians was to assert an

---

[87] The difference between the ethnic borders Messenians–Arcadians and Messenians–Spartans illustrates impressively Barth's observation that not all ethnic boundaries of a group work in the same way, have the same degree of permeability, and imply the same type and the same level of opposition; see Barth 1969b and Fabietti 1998: 100–4.

[88] On the topography of the Messenian wars, see below, pp. 85–6; on conflicts between the Messenians and the Achaean League, pp. 262–4.

independent identity while at the same time vindicating Spartan cultural traits, such as the cult of Artemis Orthia/Limnatis, as ancestrally Messenian,[89] but this was a delicate balancing act, and it is not surprising that, retrospectively, Pausanias could lament the weakness of Messenian tradition (3.13.2).

The survival of the Dryopian identity across the centuries adds an important dimension to the problem. By choosing early on to understand themselves as neither Messenian nor Lakedaimonian, the Asineans were in a subtle way setting the course for their future political allegiances. Whatever its origin, their ethnic self-definition had a very clear and consistent function. It would be interesting to know how prominent their Dryopian identity had been before the Messenian revolt in the fifth century.

The peculiar situation in which ethnic identities developed in classical and Hellenistic Messenia had clear historical roots and brought about specific ways to construct the past and deal with it. Those constructions will form the focus of the next chapters.

---

[89] This theme will appear again and again in the next chapters. See especially pp. 233–8 on the cult of Artemis Orthia in Messene, and cf. the cult of the Dioscuri and the conflicting traditions on their birth, ibid.

CHAPTER 3

The return of the Heraclids and the mythical birth of Messenia

By the age of Plato at the latest, the Greeks saw the return of the Heraclids to the Peloponnese at the head of a Dorian army as a turning point, not only for the history of that region, but also for Greek history in general. Although the farther mythical past was certainly very important to them, there is no doubt that in the fifth and fourth centuries the Dorian states of the Peloponnese, and especially the Spartans, had a particularly strong feeling of continuity between their present and the Dorian migration. To choose this mythical episode as a starting point for an investigation of the history of the Messenians is therefore peculiarly appropriate. In the pages that follow, the Dorian migration and the return of the Heraclids will not be considered as historical events, but rather as narrative constructs that variously embody different stages of beliefs about the past held by Greeks of the archaic, classical, Hellenistic and early Imperial ages. In other words, ancient narratives of the Dorian migration and the return of the Heraclids will not be considered here as more or less distorted memories of events of the early Iron Age. Their controversial historicity will not be at stake.[1] The focus will be on their function as foundation myths for polities of the Peloponnese and as ethnic charters for their inhabitants, in an attempt at locating their variants in space and time. More specifically, the analysis will be undertaken from a Messenian point of view, in order to explain how and when these myths, which certainly did not originate in Messenia, came to have a meaning for the self-perception and self-representation of the inhabitants of this part of the Peloponnese.

Greek mythology has numerous examples of myths that narrate the arrival of a population in a new land, typically under the guidance of a hero. Leaving aside the attempts by modern scholars to extract history from such narratives, their function in their historical context is obvious: they are

---

[1] For recent attempts at sounding the historical value of the Heraclid–Dorian complex, see e.g. Vanschoonwinkel 1991: 331–66 and Eder 1998.

foundation myths that explain and justify the presence of a certain group in a certain place or region, or its political structure or customs – a kind of cultural product that is widespread in all times and places. However, this function does not in itself suffice to make mythical narratives gain acceptance. Although in most cultures narratives concerning the distant past (that is, among the Greeks, myths[2]) often follow rules of plausibility that are different from those that determine the truthfulness of a normal story, every culture has criteria of form and content that have to be met for a narrative of the distant past to be considered acceptable. In other words, although anthropologists have sometimes been drawn to maintain the opposite, no culture accepts arbitrariness in dealing with the past, and especially not with those parts of the past that have a relevant social function.[3] A corollary of this is the fact that the past, particularly when cast in a fixed chronological structure, is not an inexhaustible resource. It rather offers only a limited number of slots, as it were, and when too many of them are occupied, it becomes difficult to find space for new creations, unless the inventor has the discursive or extra-discursive means to sacrifice old myths to the new ones.

Such dialectic of conservation and construction cannot obviously be subsumed under the seductive but imprecise heading "invention of tradition." It is rather a creative engagement with the past, which allows a group or a polity to have an image of its own history, or myth-history, that is satisfactory in terms of both functionality and plausibility. The implicit tension between these two requirements takes different forms in different cultural contexts. In Greece, where many autonomous polities shared not only the same small land but also the same mythical heritage, made up of stories that with very few exceptions were supposed to have taken place in that land,[4] the tension between plausibility and functionality most often took the form of a dialectic between local and panhellenic myths. The former reflected most directly what a community liked to think about its past, giving expression to the functional side, but at the same time they needed to be acceptable on a panhellenic level in order to

---

[2] From a Greek point of view, the border between myth and history was a rather fuzzy one; see Dowden 1992: 39–53; Gehrke 1994: 239–64; id. 2001.

[3] This applies also to cultures in which the past is transmitted mainly orally; see Vansina 1985: 190–1. On the social rules for constructing the past, see the path breaking studies by Appadurai 1981: 201–19 and Peel 1984: 111–32. A similar point is made by Pohl 2000: 26–8 with regard to early medieval historiography.

[4] On the localization of myths in the Greek landscape, see Buxton 1994.

be plausible, while the panhellenic myths, enshrined in the works of the most illustrious poets and therefore less easy to tamper with and often completely out of date, set parameters for the acceptability of the local myths. The myth of the return of the Heraclids to the Peloponnese offers ample and instructive evidence of these negotiations, all the more obviously so in that it involved the foundation of a number of different polities which stood in complex relationships with each other precisely when the myth was developing.

THE ORIGINS AND MEANING OF THE MYTH OF THE DIVISION

To begin with, it will be useful to summarize the plot of this myth, or rather, of this complex of myths.[5] For various reasons, to which we will turn our attention later on, Heracles harbored claims on three regions of the Peloponnese: Messenia, Laconia and the Argolid. After his death and apotheosis his descendants were expelled from the Peloponnese. Their return was a rather complex enterprise in which the help provided by the Dorians, a tribe of central Greece with whose king Aegimius Heracles himself had established contacts, was decisive. Some sources knew of one or more failed attempts before the Heraclids were finally successful, about two generations after the Trojan War. It is more than likely that the tradition of multiple attempts resulted from a merging of stories that were originally independent.[6] In the final expedition, the Heraclids were represented by Aristomachos' three sons, Temenos, Kresphontes and Aristodemos.[7] They led the Dorian army to the northern shore of the Corinthian gulf, where Aristodemos died and left behind two infant sons, the twins Eurysthenes and Prokles. The ships necessary to cross the gulf were built in Naupaktos – probably a pun on the city's name. Once landed in the Peloponnese, the Dorians defeated the Achaeans, led by Orestes' son Tisamenos, who died on the battlefield or sought refuge in the northwestern part of the peninsula, the future Achaea. After the victory, the conquerors apportioned the land among themselves and their

[5] This summary does not reflect any specific source and its details do not all turn up in all sources. For an exhaustive presentation of the evidence, see Prinz 1979: 206–313, and add the recently published papyrus fragments from the summaries of Euripides' *Temenos* and *Temenids*, on which see below, pp. 49–50.

[6] See Prinz 1979: 284–92.

[7] On the origins of the connection of Heraclids and Dorians in the myth, see Prinz 1979: 252–9 and 293.

allies. Arcadia remained to its original inhabitants, who had not taken part in the war, Elis went to Oxylus, who had helped the expedition, and the rest was divided among the Dorians and their leaders, the Heraclids: Temenos got the Argolid, Kresphontes Messenia, Eurysthenes and Prokles Laconia.

This tripartition constitutes a common foundation myth for three different parts of the Peloponnese which never belonged together. At least two of these polities probably had their own independent Heraclid foundation myths, which obviously did not feature the other two. In a sense, the tripartition, like the whole complex of the returns of the Heraclids, is *a priori* likely to be the result of the merging of independent foundation myths.[8] Although it could also come from some other place, the most logical assumption is that the merging originated in one of the three polities involved. To reconstruct the origin of this myth, it is necessary to scrutinize carefully the sources of all its variants and compare them with what we know of the histories of Laconia, Messenia and the Argolid in the corresponding periods. Such a task is all the more urgent, given that no comprehensive scrutiny of the myth has been undertaken in light of a number of papyri which have significantly enhanced our knowledge of one of the earliest groups of texts in which it featured, Euripides' tragedies on the return of the Heraclids.

The division of the land among the Heraclids is the focal point of the myth. Whenever the process is described explicitly, we learn that the land was divided into three portions and these, or at least two of them, Laconia and Messenia, were assigned by lot. In all but the most cursory versions of the drawing of the lots, it appears that Kresphontes got Messenia by deceit. According to Euripides and Ephorus, it was Oxylus who divided the land into three lots in the first place – appropriately for a three-eyed being.[9] After the division, lots were drawn by Temenos, Kresphontes and Aristodemos' twin sons (to whom one portion was assigned). The agreement was that each party should cast a pebble into a jug full of water; the pebbles would then be randomly extracted, and the one whose pebble came out last would get Messenia, the best portion. Instead of a pebble, the wily Kresphontes threw into the jug a clod of earth that dissolved in the water. This version of the lottery appears first in some rather late

[8] "The product of a cumulative aggregation of accounts" (Hall 1997: 57).

[9] For Euripides' version, see POxy. 2455, fr. 9 = *TrGF* (68)–(69) i, from the *hypothesis* (summary) of the *Temenids* (Harder 1991: 119–23). Ephorus on Oxylus: Strab. 8.3.33 (= Ephorus *FgrHist* 70 F 115). Luppe 1987: 194–5 collects the ancient sources on Oxylus. Oxylus' three eyes reflect a very common mythic motive, on which see the fascinating study of Camassa 1983: 17 and 31–5.

sources, such as the *Bibliothēkē*, a compilation of myths transmitted under the name of Apollodorus and going back to the late first or early second century AD, and Polyaenus' collection of stratagems from the age of Marcus Aurelius.[10] According to other sources, it was agreed beforehand that the Argolid should be assigned to Temenos, because he was the eldest of Aristomachos' sons. This version certainly appeared in Euripides' *Temenos* and was also probably alluded to in his *Temenids*.[11] According to Pausanias, who also follows this version, it was decided to draw lots for Messenia and Laconia after Kresphontes had failed in his attempt at convincing the other Heraclids to give him Messenia, since he was the next-eldest brother after Temenos. In Pausanias' narrative of the deceitful draw Temenos helps Kresphontes to deceive the sons of Aristodemos (Paus. 4.3.3–5). It is unclear whether this detail appeared already in Euripides. In his *Temenos* the drawing of lots for Laconia and Messenia was organized by Temenos and was apparently described in some detail. In the *Temenids* an injustice against Aristodemos' sons was mentioned, which should imply that this tragedy also said something about the lots and the deceit.[12] At any rate, Kresphontes' trick of throwing a clod of earth in the water was already well known in Euripides' time, for Sophocles alludes to it in the *Ajax* (1283–7).[13]

Obviously, at least in the form in which we know it from the fifth century on, the myth of the tripartition was not a charter for friendship and cohesion. Its function seems rather to explain why, although being ethnically related, the three polities founded by the Heraclids were on bad terms – which in fact they were for most of their history from the sixth

[10] Ps.-Apollod. 2.8.4, 177–8 and Polyaen. 1.6 respectively. On Polyaenus' source, probably Ephorus, see Schettino 1998: 99–101 and 157–8. For the dating of the so-called Pseudo-Apollodorus see Henrichs 1987: 243 and n. 6.

[11] POxy. 2455 fr. 9 and 10 = *TrGF* (68)–(69) i–ii, from the summaries of *Temenids* and *Temenos* respectively. The subdivision of the fragments between the summaries of the two tragedies follows Harder 1991: 123–4. On the text of fr. 11 see also Luppe 1995. The fact that in fr. 9 line 9 Temenos is characterized as the eldest brother has to be connected to his receiving the Argolid by common agreement (cf. fr. 10 line 4); cf. Luppe 1987: 196–7; of course, this does not mean that the remaining parts were not assigned by lot.

[12] POxy. 2455 fr. 9 line 12; see Luppe 1987: 197. On how the drawing of the lots was described in *Temenos* see Harder 1991: 123–4. It seems clear that in POxy. 2455 fr. 10, from the summary of *Temenos*, Temenos oversees the procedure (see also Luppe 1987: 199–201), which may suggest that here, too, as in Pausanias, he participated in the deceit. The fact that in Paus. 4.3.5 Messenia corresponds to the first lot and Laconia to the second, unlike what happens in Eur. *TrGF* 727e (in Strab. 8.5.6, probably from *Temenos*, cf. Luppe 1987: 200 and Harder 1991: 134), does not mean that on the whole Pausanias cannot have followed Euripides' version (cf. Harder 1991: 128 and n. 27); Pausanias had his own reasons to change the sequence of the lots, see below, p. 58.

[13] The precise date of Sophocles' *Ajax* is controversial, but the play is generally attributed to an early phase of the playwright's activity, in the 450s or 440s; see Ugolini 1995, in favor of a date c. 446–444 BC.

century BC at the latest to the second century AD. The kinship between the founders stresses the continuous and almost proverbial enmity between the polities they founded.[14]

Kresphontes' casting the deceitful lot has been the starting point of most attempts at clarifying the meaning of the myth. Carl Robert rightly called the tripartition "a legend that serves to justify the hostility of the Spartans towards the Messenians."[15] The trick seems to undercut from the outset the legitimacy of Kresphontes' rule over Messenia, and since Messenia was under Spartan domination from the eighth to the early fourth century BC, it is tempting to see in Kresphontes' deceit a justification of the Spartan conquest of Messenia.[16] If this is really the meaning that our myth is supposed to convey, then it has to originate from Sparta. Accordingly, it has generally been assumed that the myth of the division of the Peloponnese among the Heraclids, in the form in which it has come down to us, is indeed a Spartan myth.

But in fact the remote origin of the myth of the division of the southern Peloponnese cannot be Sparta. After all, why should a Spartan myth introduce a tripartition, instead of simply having the land divided in two parts from the outset (one part including both Laconia and Messenia)? Also, the story of the lots implies that Sparta was the least desirable draw, and although this may reflect the truth, it is somewhat difficult to accept that the Spartans saw it precisely that way. For although the story of the Dorian expedition led by the Heraclids is attested in Sparta very early, and although a fragment of Tyrtaeus shows that the conquest of the Peloponnese by an army of Dorians led by Heraclids was very prominent in the Spartans' views of their past since the seventh century,[17] nevertheless, for the Spartans the main significance of the distinction between Heraclids and Dorians had to do with domestic politics, because the two Spartan royal families were supposed to be descended from Heracles, and their Heraclid genealogy was the base of their special position in Spartan society.[18] The Spartans' claims to their own land were less closely

---

[14] On brotherhood and enmity in Greek myth see Brelich 1958: 274–5. Hdt. 6.52.8 on Eurysthenes and Prokles offers a good example of how natural it was to associate a pair of brothers with rivalry and hostility.

[15] Robert 1921: 662. [16] See e.g. Vitalis 1930: 50–1; Kiechle 1966: 497; Harder 1991: 130 n. 32.

[17] Tyrt. fr. 2,12–15 West². See Malkin 1994: 33–4; Hall 1997: 59–60.

[18] That the Heraclid genealogies of the Spartan kings were meant to separate them from the common Spartiates emerges rather clearly from a number of sources; see e.g. Pind. *Pyth.* 10.1–3, Hdt. 5.72.3. Malkin 1994: 34–6 suggests that in Tyrtaeus, fr. 2 West², the Heraclid myth is invoked to legitimize Spartan domination of Messenia at a time when it was called into question by the Messenian revolt, i.e. the Second Messenian War. However, the revolt did not question Spartan possession of

based on their Heraclid heritage. After all, Laconia, like Messenia, was not Heracles' true homeland; Heracles had conquered it and given it back to its legitimate ruler Tyndareus, who had previously been expelled, and only because Tyndareus' direct heirs, Castor and Polydeuces, had died before their father, Tyndareus decided to leave the kingdom to Heracles.[19]

In the Argolid, things were different. Only here was it justified to speak of a return of the Heraclids, since Heracles himself came from Tiryns and his mythical ties to the Argolid were incomparably closer than to Laconia.[20] All variants of the myth describe Temenos as the eldest of the brothers and most of them explicitly attribute to him a leading role in the expedition.[21] The territorial implications of the myth also point to Argos as a much better candidate for its remote origin. To the Spartans the division assigned only what they controlled anyway, Laconia, and at the same time it implicitly impeached the legitimacy of their domination over Messenia; despite Kresphontes' ploy, the fact remained that the myth depicted Messenia as an originally independent entity.[22] As for Argos, by unifying the whole of the Argolid in Temenos' lot the myth attributed to the city a territorial extension that was otherwise anything but obvious. The so-called Acte, the area of Epidaurus and Troezen, does not seem ever to have been under Argive control, and even the settlements on the eastern border of the Argive plain, Mycenae, Tiryns and Midea, were apparently conquered by the Argives only after the Persian Wars.[23] Far

Laconia, which is what Tyrtaeus talks about; his verses insist on the Heraclid pedigree of the Spartan kings in order to convince the Spartans to obey them, that is, even here the Heraclid genealogy has a preeminently domestic function; cf. van Wees 1999: 2, who summarizes Tyrtaeus' verses as follows: "The Spartans must obey their kings, the Heraclids, since their power is divinely sanctioned."

[19] Isocr. *Archid.* 18 and Diod. 4.33.5; see Malkin 1994: 22–4. As for Messenia, it belonged to the Heraclids as *doriktētos*, because Heracles had conquered it and killed Neleus and all his sons except Nestor, and then entrusted the land to him asking him to guard it for his descendants (Isocr., ibid.). Hall 1997: 61 correctly underlines that the Heraclid claims to Laconia and Messenia were less direct than those to the Argolid.

[20] So already Vitalis 1930: 51 and now Hall 1997: 61–2 and 89–99.

[21] See e.g. Ps.-Apollod. 2.8.2–3, 172–5; Polyaen. 1.9.

[22] So e.g. Kiechle 1966: 496–7. Prinz 1979: 311 rejects the idea that the tripartition latently questioned the Spartans' rights over Messenia, but his own interpretation, according to which the myth simply anchored in the past the balance of power in the Peloponnese in the early archaic period, is not very satisfactory, since the unification of the Argolid before the fifth century seems to have been nothing more than an aspiration of the Argives (see below, p. 59), while Messenia as a unit is clearly a result of the Spartan conquest.

[23] On the political topography of the Argolid see Piérart 1997: 321–4. On the Argive conquest of the plain in the first half of the fifth century, see Moggi 1974: 1249–63 and Hall 1995: 589. Piérart 1997: 325–31 correctly emphasizes that this chronology seems inconsistent with the Argive conquest of Asine in the late eighth century. However, his suggestion that in the archaic period the settlements on the eastern border of the plain were linked to Argos in a relationship similar to that of the

from simply reflecting an existing situation, from an Argive point of view Temenos' lot was an expression of territorial ambitions.[24]

Considering the undisputably Argive imprint on the myth of the division of the land among the Heraclids, most scholars think that this myth originated at Argos rather than Sparta. On this assumption, Kresphontes' trick, which does not seem to make much sense in the framework of an Argive myth, has almost inevitably to be considered a Spartan version of the originally Argive tradition.[25]

And yet, this two-tiered reconstruction, with a primitive Argive myth featuring a fair tripartition followed by a Spartan version including the deceit, is itself not unproblematic. For one thing, there is no preserved version of the tripartition that does not feature the deceiving of Aristodemos' sons. Moreover, it is questionable whether the Spartans would have produced a version of the myth in which they were deceived by their opponent, particularly considering that guile was a highly prized virtue at Sparta and an important component of the Spartans' image of themselves.[26] But there is one further argument that strongly speaks against attributing a Spartan origin to the story of Kresphontes' trick: according to Herodotus (6.52.1), the Spartans maintained that it had been Aristodemos himself who had led them into Laconia and died after the conquest. In affirming this, Herodotus says, the Spartans contradicted all poets. Herodotus' comment suggests that in his time, that is, almost certainly before Euripides' Heraclid tragedies,[27] at least one poetic work

---

perioikoi to Sparta cannot be easily reconciled with the fact that Mycenae and Tiryns participated in the Second Persian War (see e.g. ML 27), while Argos remained neutral. At any rate, even accepting Piérart's hypothesis one would have to admit that Argive control on the plain tightened during the second quarter of the fifth century.

[24] This is shown very clearly by Thuc. 5.69.1 (see below, n. 34), and also by the tradition of the shadowy king Pheidon, the tenth descendant of Temenos, who allegedly succeeded in unifying under his rule the whole of Temenos' lot (Strab. 8.3.33 = Ephorus *FgrHist* 70 F 115); see below.

[25] See e.g. Vitalis. 1930: 50–3, and most explicitly Tigerstedt 1965: 33–5 and Kiechle 1966: 496–7, who postulate the existence of an earlier version which did not feature Kresphontes' trick.

[26] Jordan 1990: 66–7. On the recourse to tricks by Spartan generals, see Powell 1989b; on the function of deceit in the education of the young Spartans, e.g. Xen. *Lac. Resp.* 2.6–9 (with Rebenich 1998: 55) and Vidal-Naquet 1981: 160–3; cf. also Sergent 1978: 7–11. This explains the cliché of the duplicitous Spartan explored by Bradford 1994, which, however, can hardly be considered a free Athenian invention, as Bradford maintains.

[27] *Temenos* and *Temenids* are difficult to date, but they can hardly be earlier than the peace of Nicias in 421; see Harder 1991: 118 n. 5. It is tempting to connect these tragedies, or at least one of them (the *Temenids* could be later, see Poole 1994: 16) with the political relations between Athens and Argos between the peace and the Sicilian expedition (on which see Kagan 1981: 71–142); this would coincide nicely with the popularity of the myth of the division among the Heraclids at Argos in 418 BC suggested by the allusion in Thuc. 5.69.1 (see below, n. 34).

dealt with the division of the Peloponnese among the Heraclids;[28] the allusion seems to fit some poem of panhellenic relevance, probably epic, better than a local Argive myth, let alone a Laconian one.

Most importantly, however, Herodotus' evidence makes it extremely hard to assume that the story of the tripartition among Temenos, Kresphontes and Eurysthenes and Prokles originated in Sparta. The point is reinforced by a passage in Xenophon's *Agesilaus* (8.7), which also seems to imply that the Spartans thought that Aristodemos had lived at Sparta. Therefore, in order to locate at Sparta the origin of the story of the deceit, one would have either to postulate a version of the story in which it was Aristodemos himself who was deceived, a version that would have to have disappeared without leaving any trace, or be ready to assume that, although Kresphontes' deceit of Eurysthenes and Prokles was originally a Spartan myth, in Herodotus' time the Spartans did not find it expedient to recognize it as such; in that case, the myth would owe its survival to the fact that it had already been captured in some poem of panhellenic relevance.[29]

Clearly neither of these two possibilities is entirely satisfactory. On a closer look, Herodotus' "poets' version" presupposes the version of the Spartans, and must therefore be more recent. Aristodemos' twin sons constitute the foundation myth of Sparta's puzzling double monarchy, which distinguished the Spartan constitution from any other in the Greek world.[30] One would expect Spartan memory to locate the birth of this institution in Sparta herself: it would be pointless to make it older than the foundation of the Spartan state through the Heraclid and Dorian conquest of Laconia. This is exactly what the Spartans thought, according to Herodotus: after Aristodemos' death the Delphic oracle advised them

[28] See Robert 1921: 656, who, however, does not propose any precise attribution of such poems. Cf. Vitalis 1930: 53, who thinks of Kinaithon's *Herakleia*, without further arguments. It is not clear whether Kinaithon's fr. 6 and 7 Bernabé are correctly attributed to this poem, since the manuscripts call the author once Kinaithon and once Konon; cf. Jacoby 1957: 499–500, who would rather correct Kinaithon to Konon, and Huxley 1969: 86; on the texts see also Davies 1988: 142. Even if one is ready to attribute to Kinaithon a *Herakleia* based on these fragments, it is still doubtful if such a poem would have dealt also with Heracles' descendants. The composition of genealogical poetry by Kinaithon (seventh or sixth century?) is documented, see Huxley 1969: 86–9. *Pace* Malkin 1994: 35, there is no evidence that Stesichorus mentioned Eurysthenes and Prokles. The fragment Malkin refers to is now attributed to Ibycus, not Stesichorus (Ibycus S 181 Davies; see Barron 1984: 20–1), and furthermore Eurysthenes and Prokles are not mentioned in the poem itself but in a scholion.

[29] This assumption is implied e.g. by Vitalis 1930: 53, who attributes the story of Kresphontes' deceit to the Spartan poet Kinaithon (see previous note).

[30] See e.g. Prinz 1979: 286. On the Spartan double monarchy see e.g. Oliva 1971: 23–8; Clauss 1983: 117–19; Carlier 1984: 306–10.

to regard both sons as kings (Hdt. 6.52.3–7). But if the twins have a crucial function for the explanation of the origin of the Spartan double monarchy, they are absolutely superfluous for the myth of the deceitful division. Even if we assume that the adult Aristodemos would not have been a suitable victim of the trick, one minor son of his would have been enough: there was no reason to have two. In other words, in purely logical terms the version in which Aristodemos arrived in Laconia and his twin sons were born there must be older. And incidentally, if Aristodemos had died before reaching the Peloponnese, his brothers would have been responsible for his children. Thereby the double monarchy would have almost been invented, perhaps as a means of preemptively crippling Sparta,[31] by Temenos and Kresphontes, as the "poets' version" may have implied. Again, one can hardly imagine the Spartans producing such an image of their mythic past.

Further arguments speak against the assumption that Kresphontes' deceit of Eurysthenes and Prokles may come from Sparta. For the Spartans, the legitimacy of their rule over Messenia, a key aspect of the myth, became in the early fourth century at the latest a sensitive issue. One would not expect them to have anything against a mythic foundation for their claims. Although evidence on this point coming directly from Sparta is lacking, it is possible to reconstruct, albeit with some degree of uncertainty, how the Spartans argued on a mythical level to back up their policy. Their arguments apparently made no use of Kresphontes' deceit. In Isocrates' *Archidamos*, a fictive speech of the Spartan Archidamus, son of Agesilaus and future king of Sparta, after the liberation of Messenia by the Thebans, which is certainly based on precise knowledge of contemporaneous controversies, Kresphontes' tricky appropriation of Messenia is not even mentioned.[32] What justifies the Spartan conquest is the murder of Kresphontes by his subjects and the alleged flight of his children to Sparta (*Archid.* 22–3, see below, p. 62). In other words, from a Spartan

---

[31] On the traditional enmity between the kings of the two dynasties see again Hdt. 6.52.8; anyone familiar with fifth- and fourth-century Spartan history could have easily come up with many examples.

[32] It is debated whether Isocrates' *Archidamos* should be seen as a mere rhetorical play or be attributed any serious political meaning; see e.g. Bringmann 1965: 55–6 and Moysey 1982. For us the relevant point is that the speech was written few years after the liberation of Messenia, that is, it comes from the very years in which the Spartans were trying to question the legitimacy of the new polity and to convince the other Greeks to reject it (see Roebuck 1941: 41–5; Hamilton 1982: 82–3). In Athens, one may expect people to have known which arguments the Spartans were using (so Jehne 1994: 11 n. 21). It is even possible that Isocrates was later in personal contact with Archidamus, see Tigerstedt 1965: 485 n. 811.

viewpoint, the deceit in the drawing of the lots was not the best possible argument to defend Spartan claims on Messenia.[33]

Although the Spartans, as Isocrates shows, seem to have devised a justification of their claims in the framework of the myth of the division, one may even doubt whether that myth ever really gained any popularity in Sparta. To begin with, the division presupposed the identification of Nestor's kingdom with Messenia, because the Heraclid claims on Messenia were based on the relations between Heracles and Nestor (see above n. 19). The fact that in the second half of the fifth century the Spartans called Pylos Koryphasion (Thuc. 4.3.2 and cf. 4.118.4; 5.18.7) suggests that they rejected the identification of this place with Homeric Pylos. Moreover, as far as is possible to tell, every time the myth of the division of the Peloponnese among the Heraclids was used as an argument in a territorial controversy, it was used against the Spartans. Two major territorial truncations which the Spartans underwent in the late fourth and late third centuries at the hands of the kings of Macedon were probably carried out under the aegis of that myth.[34]

To sum up, in order to locate in Sparta the origin of any version of the division that included Kresphontes' trick one has to be ready to make a number of complex and unverifiable assumptions, all at the expense of some very strong objections. It is impossible to avoid the conclusion that the only preserved version of this myth, which included the deceit, did not come from Sparta. This conclusion at the same time questions the assumption that an Argive ur-version of the tripartition, different from the transmitted one, ever existed. The reason for postulating an ur-version was that it seemed incredible that an implicitly anti-Messenian element such as the deceit could come from Argos, all the more so since in some sources the Argive Temenos helped Kresphontes arrange the deceit. Therefore, it is necessary to fix our attention on tricky Kresphontes to see how anti-Messenian his story really has to be.

In interpreting this mythical character, one should not forget that common moral standards, even Greek, did not apply to heroes: as a matter of fact, Greek heroes were supposed to indulge in all sorts of

---

[33] Characteristically, the only instance in which this tradition is used against the Messenians, the oracle of Apollo given to the Spartans at the time of the First Messenian War (Diod. 8.13 and Paus. 4.12.1), goes back to a later and rather pro-Messenian source, Myron of Priene; see Parke 1938: 66–72, and below.

[34] See above, p. 18, and contrast Thuc. 5.69.1: before the battle of Mantineia, in 418 BC, the Argives are fired up by their commanders and called to fight to reestablish the original *isomoiria* in the Peloponnese, a patent allusion to the division among the Heraclids. On the possible implications of this appeal, see below, pp. 208 and 214.

crimes and misdemeanors which did not endanger their heroic status; guile, or *mētis* as the Greeks called it, was a perfectly acceptable component of heroic identity.[35] This is especially true in the case of founder heroes, and guile and deceit figure prominently in the foundation stories of Greek colonies, mythical and historical;[36] the fact that in such stories the role of the deceived is played by barbarians does not change their fundamental meaning – it only highlights the positive connotation of deceiving as opposed to being deceived. It is important to emphasize that the use of deceit in charter myths whose function is to justify the conquest of land by the Greeks, precludes the possibility that for them deceit might implicitly have called into question the legitimacy of conquest. The myth of the division of the Peloponnese depicts Kresphontes was a typical *mētis*-hero, a trickster-founder.[37] Although one may speculate that the Messenians, in later ages, would have been happier with some other kind of founder hero, Kresphontes' trick does not have to be taken as an anti-Messenian and pro-Spartan trait of the story.

Besides the characterization of Kresphontes as a trickster, there is one further level of meaning embedded in the story of the deceitful drawing of the lots. Because Kresphontes' lot (the clod of earth) dissolved in the water, only two pebbles could be taken from the jug, or just one in the version in which lots were drawn for Laconia and Messenia only. Since Kresphontes did not use a real lot, he could not draw one. Or, one might say, he did not really take part in the drawing: in a symbolic way, his trick backfired. The (in)solidity of his lot mirrors the (in)solidity of his gain. There could hardly be a clearer sign of the fact that this myth originated in an epoch in which Messenia was not independent. Although it does not justify the Spartan domination, it grounds it and gives it a mythical logic. This interpretation of the hidden meaning of Kresphontes'

[35] The obvious case is Odysseus, see Pratt 1993: 55–94. See in general Brelich 1958: 261–5 (*hubris* as typical of Greek heroes) and 256–9 (deceit). On Greek *mētis*, see the classic Detienne-Vernant 1978. Guile applied also against friends and relatives is a distinctive component of a number of characters, not only of Greek myth, who do not thereby receive any negative connotation. One only has to think of Jakob and Esau or Romulus and Remus; the absence of negative implications in the latter case is emphasized by Cornell 1983: 1117.

[36] Heroic *hubris* associated with founders: Cornell 1983: 1116–17 and Dougherty 1993. Deceit and conquest of the land: Polyb. 12.6.1–15 and Polyaen. 6.22 (Lokroi Epizephyrioi); Strab. 6.1.15 (Metapontion): cf. Cataldi in Nenci-Cataldi 1983: 598–9. Although they did not belong to the mythic past, foundation stories of colonies functioned exactly like foundation myths, both regarding their meaning for the collective identity of the colonists and regarding their sensitivity to later agendas.

[37] This is most clearly visible in a fragment of Ennius' *Cresphontes*, fr. LIII Jocelyn. On this tragedy and its Greek model see below, n. 61. On tricksters in a cross-cultural perspective see Hynes and Doty 1993.

vanishing lot is confirmed indirectly by the pro-Messenian Pausanias
(4.3.5).[38] In his version, Messenia was to go to the one whose lot came out
first, and it was Temenos who prepared the lots, making the one of
Eurysthenes and Prokles of earth dried in the sun and baking the one of
Kresphontes; thereby it was the lot of Eurysthenes and Prokles that was
dissolved in the water.[39]

Incidentally, what makes Pausanias' version of the division really precious is precisely the fact that it comes from a clearly tendentious source.
This makes it all the more telling that even Pausanias mentions the deceit
(4.3.3–5). He does try to justify Kresphontes' course of action by
emphasizing that he was the eldest after Temenos, for he attributes the
active role in the trick to Temenos rather than Kresphontes, but not even
he can deny that Messenia had been acquired by deceit. This means either
that this story was so established by Pausanias' times that even the
Messenians had to put up with it, however unhappily – for we can be sure
that Pausanias would have gladly accepted any local version that might
have been more favorable to the Messenians – or that the myth was not
perceived as irreparably anti-Messenian. But perhaps the two conclusions
should not be seen as mutually exclusive. Pausanias' attempt at white-
washing Kresphontes speaks for the first possibility, but the fact that the
Spartans did not use the myth of the deceitful division to buttress their
claim on Messenia speaks for the second.

If this interpretation of the meaning of the myth and its ramifications is
accepted, the next step is to locate in time its variants and to try and
reconstruct their historical backgrounds. In doing this, one has to venture
onto extremely slippery ground, and conclusions have to be hypothetical
in direct proportion to their specificity. The first source that requires
discussion in this context is a passage from Strabo's *Geography*. In the
course of a short history of Elis, essentially derived from Ephorus, Strabo
says that the Argive Pheidon, tenth descendant of Temenos and the most
powerful man of his age, had unified under his control the whole of
Temenos' lot. Furthermore, he had introduced a new system of weights
and measures and invented coinage. He also tried to conquer all the cities
that had once been conquered by Heracles and to take control of all the
agōnes founded by Heracles. He even succeeded in organizing an

---

[38] On Pausanias' philo-Messenian *Tendenz*, see below, pp. 94–100 and 323–7.
[39] This is the reason for the difference between Pausanias' and Euripides' descriptions of the drawing
of the lots, and so the possibility remains that Pausanias might draw mainly upon Euripides'
version, directly or indirectly.

Olympiad, which the Eleians, however, did not accept in their registers (Strab. 8.3.33 = Ephorus 70 F 115).

The idea of a lot of Temenos appears only in association with the myth of the tripartition and makes no sense without it. Therefore, this passage strongly suggests the possibility that the myth may have functioned as a charter for Pheidon's politics.[40] This does not give us a time frame, since Pheidon, the record holder for *hubris* according to Herodotus (6.127.3), is among the least datable characters in the whole of archaic Greek history, with a chronology that fluctuates happily between the early ninth and the late seventh century BC.[41] The alleged extension of his conquests does not help fix him in time either, but rather makes things more puzzling: as we saw above, in the early fifth century Mycenae and Tiryns were independent of Argos, and there is no strong reason to assume that in the previous two centuries it had been otherwise. No reason, that is, except Strabo's description of Pheidon's conquests. But then one starts wondering to what extent this character and the deeds ascribed to him are to be taken seriously, and to what extent they might themselves reflect later events and project them back into the past. Achievements like inventing coinage and introducing weights and measures make Pheidon dangerously similar to a culture hero, some Argive Lycurgus, and such a resemblance does not bode well for his claim to historicity.[42]

A comprehensive discussion of the evidence for Pheidon would not bring decisive results. On more solid ground, it is possible to observe that at Argos in the first decades of the fifth century the interest in myths connected to Heracles and the Heraclids seems to be increasing. After the democratic reforms that took place in this period, among the names of the *phatrai*, the subdivisions of the four Argive tribes, appear many a Heraclid name: we have *Temenidai, Kleodaidai, Daiphontees.*[43] As noted before, it is in this period that Argos takes control over Mycenae and Tiryns, and the final appropriation by the Argives of the Perseid genealogy, which is

---

[40] This has been often thought in the past; see already Robert 1921: 656 with further references.

[41] On Pheidon's chronology, ancient sources give a number of irreconcilable data; see the lucid summary given by Nafissi in Maddoli–Nafissi–Saladino 1999: 366–7, where the main modern attempts at solving the controversy are discussed. Nafissi wisely opts to leave the question open. Koiv's detailed analysis of the post-Herodotean tradition (2001: 327–47) shows convincingly that it was based on synchronisms with the history of Sparta and Corinth, not on any reliable evidence.

[42] The comparison with Lycurgus has been suggested by Hall 1995: 586–7; see also Piérart 1991: 139–40, who suggests that it was really Ephorus who interpreted Pheidon's foreign policy as an attempt at reconquering Temenos' lot (see now Piérart 1997: 325).

[43] Unfortunately, not all of the relevant material is published. See Piérart 1986: 282–4 and 1991: 139–40, who connects the ascendancy of Heraclid myths at Argos in this period with the emergence of democracy.

presupposed by the story of Temenos, is also likely to belong to these years.[44] Perhaps even the origin of the tradition about Pheidon should be seen as a component of this Heraclid revival in mid-fifth-century Argos.

It is easy to see how well the myth of the division of the Peloponnese would fit into this context. The myth itself is attested for the first time in 462 BC in Pindar's Fifth Pythian.[45] Sophocles' allusion suggests that an Athenian audience of the mid fifth century was familiar with the story of Kresphontes' trick. In the 460s Messenia was shaken by the revolt after the earthquake, when for the first time since the seventh or even the eighth century in the Peloponnese a group emerged whose members called themselves "the Messenians" and considered themselves the descendants of the "old Messenians" from the time before the Spartan conquest (below, pp. 182–8). The fact that this time Argos was for once not on the Messenians' side could explain why the myth does not show a markedly pro-Messenian tendency.[46] Argos in the 470s represents clearly an almost perfect background for a revival of the myth of the Heraclid conquest and division of the Peloponnese, and it is worth considering seriously if the origin itself of the myth has to be earlier.[47] Of course, the insistent association of the Dorians with the tripartite division added to its plausibility from the outset.[48] As has been noted, the Heraclid claim to Messenia presupposes its identification with the kingdom of Pylos, which is attested for the first time in 490 by Pindar's Sixth Pythian, where Nestor is called, retroactively so to speak, "the Messenian elder."[49]

---

[44] See Hall 1997: 98. The 460s and 450s are increasingly seen in current research as a period of ascendancy for Argos, visible in its foreign politics and also in architectural activity in the Heraion; see Leppin 1999: 299–301.

[45] Pind. *Pyth.* 5.69-72, celebrating the victory of Arcesilaus the Fourth of Cyrene in the chariot race. On date and occasion see Angeli Bernardini et al. 1995: 159–60. The Spartan connections of Cyrene probably explain why, in Pindar's version, Sparta is the first lot mentioned.

[46] Temenos' participation in the deceit could then be interpreted as an attempt at weakening this connotation and connected either to the relations between Athens and Argos in the 420s (see above, n. 27), or to the Argives' participation in Epaminondas' liberation of Messene in 369 (see below p. 214), depending on whether or not one believes that already in Euripides Temenos helped Kresphontes.

[47] One should of course not equate automatically the first attestation of a myth with its date of birth, but it is significant that no source before Pindar mentions or even alludes to the division of the Peloponnese among the Heraclids. On Hes. fr. 233 Merkelbach–West, which West 1985: 58–9 connects with this episode, see Huxley 1969: 109–10 and Merkelbach and West in their commentary on the fragment. Bremmer's argument for dating the story of Kresphontes' trick in the sixth century or earlier (Bremmer 1997: 14) depends on the fact that he considers the version in which Aristodemos dies before the division to be earlier than Herodotus' Spartan version (Hdt. 6.52.1). Once one admits that this sequence must be reversed, Bremmer's point, though not conclusive, would speak in favor of dating the story to the fifth century.

[48] See Musti 1986b: 39–41.

[49] For an analogous anachronism, cf. Soph. *OT* 1301, where Argos is called Dorian in an age preceding the Dorian migration.

Homeric epic, by contrast, located Pylos farther north (below, p. 72), so that, whatever the relations between Nestor and Heracles, in the framework of that version of mythic geography they would not have constituted a title of property on Messenia.

KRESPHONTES' FATE AND HIS SUCCESSORS

The myth of the division of the Peloponnese depicted Messenia as an independent entity and thereby implicitly questioned the Spartan rule thereof. It seems that a Spartan reply was not long in coming. Barring a frontal attack on the story of the tripartition, where the Spartans do not seem to have gotten very far, the next sensitive point in the myth was Kresphontes' fate. The oldest source on this is Euripides' tragedy *Kresphontes*, around 430–424 BC, in which the king of Messenia is killed by another Heraclid called Polyphontes, who then becomes king, marries Kresphontes' wife Merope, and tries to eliminate Kresphontes' offspring. Merope hides one of them, Kresphontes junior, in the home of a guest-friend in Aetolia. In proper tragic style, the child comes back as an adult, risks being killed by his mother, who does not recognize him, and finally dispatches the murderer of his father.[50]

Euripides' *Kresphontes* is the earliest source on the fate of the king, and it is difficult to say whether he was freely creating in a mythological vacuum or reporting and perhaps modifying an existing story.[51] One might be inclined to suspect that Euripides was unlikely to have been attracted by the problem of the continuity of Kresphontes' lineage if the problem had not existed already; on the other hand, by introducing Kresphontes junior Euripides devised a sort of zero-sum game, one which does not necessarily presuppose any earlier version – it might well be his own contribution. If, however, an earlier version did exist, it may well have been on the lines of what we find in Isocrates' *Archidamos* (22–23), an obviously pro-Spartan story which must come from Sparta. In this

---

[50] The fragments have been edited by Musso 1974 and Harder 1985. On the plot see Test. 5–6 Harder = *TrGF* (39) ii a–b and Harder 1985: 7–14. On the dating, Musso 1974: xxvii–xxviii (suggesting 423) and Harder 1985: 3–4 and 118–19. According to Lucil. fr. 1169 M., Euripides called Polyphontes the brother of Kresphontes the elder; if Lucilius is accurate (Ps.-Apollod. 2.8.4, 177 = Eur. *Kresph.* Test. 6 Harder = *TrGF* (39) ii d simply calls Polyphontes a Heraclid), one wonders why Polyphontes was excluded from the division of the Peloponnese: one more reason to consider Polyphontes Euripides' own creation.

[51] Both Polyphontes and Kresphontes junior are generally considered Euripidean inventions; see Harder 1985: 9–11, who cautiously admits the possibility that Euripides might have been drawing on some little-known local myth, and Bremmer 1997: 14–15.

version, it is the Dorians of Messenia who killed Kresphontes, thereby violating the oath of loyalty to the Heraclid kings. Kresphontes' children, whose names are not mentioned, fled to Sparta asking for the Spartans to avenge their father and entrusting to them Messenia. The Spartans consulted Apollo, who answered that they should help the suppliants. So they did, and conquered Messenia. Isocrates' Archidamus tells this story to legitimize the Spartans' claim on Messenia, which is obviously the primary function of the story itself, although the motif of the oaths exchanged between Dorians and Heraclids had wider implications, showing even more clearly its ultimate Spartan origin: the Dorians of Sparta were the only ones who had kept their word – witness the fact that only Sparta was still ruled by Heraclid kings.[52] Here we have in all probability the Spartan reply to the Argive or pro-Argive story of the tripartition.

It is easy to show how the various versions of the fate of Kresphontes and of his descendants reflect the political situation from which they emerged. Euripides, with his tragic plot, has a rather pro-Messenian take on the story: Kresphontes junior reconquers his father's kingdom alone, rather than seeking help elsewhere, for instance at Sparta.[53] This attitude is consistent with the relations between Athenians and Messenians in the second half of the fifth century, when the Athenians gave Naupaktos as a new homeland to the Messenian rebels who left the Peloponnese, after which the Messenians from Naupaktos were precious allies for the Athenians throughout the Peloponnesian War.[54] But of course Euripides' version would be more explicitly pro-Messenian if the poet were working on a preexisting story along the lines of the one told by Isocrates – which, however, remains uncertain. At any rate, it is clear that the liberation of Messenia by Epaminondas in 369 BC brought forth further modifications of the myth. Aipytos, the name of Kresphontes' surviving son in some sources, was also the name of an Arcadian hero. In Nicolaus of Damascus (90 F 31), obviously drawing on Ephorus, Aipytos is saved by his grandfather Kypselos of Trapezous, king of Arcadia. The Arcadians' role

---

[52] The motif of the oaths exchanged between the Heraclids and the Dorians recurs in a more complex form in Plato's *Laws* (683c ff.), where the loyalty of Dorians and Heraclids at Sparta is explicitly contrasted with the turmoils that brought an end to the Heraclid kingdoms at Argos and Messene; see Niese 1891: 4. The story must be based on the oaths exchanged between the Spartan kings and the ephors, as Tigerstedt 1965, 325 n. 136 plausibly suggests.

[53] For a recent discussion of the methodological problem of reading political meanings in Attic tragedy, see Pelling 1997: 214–24. On Euripides' attitude towards Sparta, see Poole 1994.

[54] See below, p. 188. *Kresphontes* may have been performed during the Athenian expedition at Pylos, in which the Messenians of Naupaktos had an important part (Treves 1944: 103 n. 4).

in saving Aipytos, which emerges in the sources from the mid fourth century onwards, clearly reflects the Arcadians' participation in the liberation of Messenia and in the foundation of the new city at the foot of Mount Ithome, in which they cooperated with the Argives under Epaminondas' supervision.[55] Incidentally, Pausanias, the author who more than any other emphasizes the role of Arcadians and Argives in the refoundation of the Heraclid kingdom of Messenia, says that Aipytos was reinstated in Messenia not by the Arcadians alone, but also with the help of Isthmius, son of Temenos, who appears only here, and of the kings of Sparta, Eurysthenes and Prokles (Paus. 4.3.8). This shows that Isocrates' version was a rather well-established one and strengthens the suspicion that it might precede Euripides': Pausanias and/or his sources would have certainly avoided giving the Spartans a positive role in this story, if only the tradition that made of them the rescuer had not been too authoritative to be ignored.

The fate of Kresphontes' reestablished dynasty was not bright either. From Diodorus (15.66.2) we learn that the Spartans had finally taken over Messenia after – or because – Kresphontes' descendants had lost the kingship. According to Nicolaus (90 F 34), the reigns of Aipytos and his successors were characterized by uninterrupted conflicts with their subjects, until the Spartans conquered the land. Since it is possible to show that both Diodorus and Nicolaus depend on Ephorus,[56] their evidence can be seen as referring to one and the same story. Unfortunately we cannot tell exactly who, in the version they were drawing on, gave back the kingdom to Aipytos after he had been saved from the murderers of his father (Nicolaus 90 F 31). What is clear is that this story, like the one in Isocrates' *Archidamos*, dated the Spartan conquest of Messenia long before the so-called First Messenian War,[57] which ancient sources locate in the second half of the eighth century. Furthermore, it seems to be a fundamentally pro-Spartan story, in which the conflict between Aipytos and his

---

[55] Noted already by Robert 1921: 672–3; see now Harder 1985: 54 and Bremmer 1997: 15. On the relations between Messenia and Arcadia, see Polyb. 4.33.7-9 and below, p. 215.

[56] See e.g. Stylianou 1998: 437 (on Diod. 15.66) and 49–50 (on Ephorus as source of Diodorus' Greek history in book 15). Nicolaus and Ephorus: Jacoby 1926: 234–5 and 243.

[57] As Jacoby 1930: 424–5 saw. Stylianou 1998: 439 suggests, without further explanation, that on this point Diodorus misunderstood Ephorus, who did not really say that the Spartans had conquered Messenia already before the murder of king Teleklos (the *casus belli* of the First Messenian War); he may be thinking of Ephorus, *FgrHist* 70 F 216, where Messene is conquered at the end of the First Messenian War, but even in that fragment nothing tells us that Ephorus did not describe that war as a revolt. His version of these episodes becomes understandable only if one considers Nicolaus, *FgrHist* 90 F 34, which Stylianou does not do.

descendants on the one side and their subjects on the other all but legitimizes the Spartan takeover. But since Aipytos and his dynasty are probably an Arcadian wedge in Messenian mythology, we should not confine the investigation to an alternative Sparta–Messenia. As usual, Pausanias' version helps sharpen the perspective: Aipytos took revenge on the murderers of his father, but with the rest of the subjects he was so popular that the dynasty ended up being called Aipytidai rather than Kresphontidai (4.3.8). This is on the one hand an answer to the negative depiction of Aipytos in (the source of) Nicolaus; on the other it suggests that Aipytos may function as a connecting element between the Heraclids and an originally independent dynasty. Euripides, who calls Kresphontes' son Kresphontes after his father, and Isocrates, who does not give any names to Kresphontes' children, strengthen this impression. Pausanias' emphasis on Aipytos' popularity could also reflect his attempt at hiding the rather precarious connection between two originally independent genealogemes.[58]

In spite of their general resemblance, Isocrates' and Ephorus' versions are clearly different. Considering the intense reworking of the Peloponnesian past that took place in the central decades of the fourth century,[59] Ephorus' depiction of the fate of the Aipytidai is not surprising, although its precise meaning remains elusive. Isocrates' version rendered any further defense of the Spartan claims over Messenia superfluous, unless some authoritative version on the lines of Euripides' had imposed itself, thereby provoking Ephorus' story. But the possibility should also not be ruled out that the latter might have been the result of a learned attempt at merging mutually inconsistent versions of earlier sources. Ephorus' version was itself very influential. It obviously lies at the base of Pausanias' story of the Aipytidai, as shown by Pausanias' somewhat clumsy attempt at filling the time space between Aipytos and the First Messenian War with the names of a dynasty that originally had a much shorter period to cover.[60]

One further point of interest is the motivation of Kresphontes' murder. This seems to have been unproblematic in the early versions of the story. In Euripides' *Kresphontes* the Heraclid Polyphontes does not appear to have had any particular reason to kill the king, apart from the desire to usurp his place (Eur. *Cresph*. Fr. 66 A line 22), which suffices for a tragic

---

[58] In other words, the sequence Kresphontes–Aipytos looks very much like a fracture point between two independent "genealogemes"; see Hall 1997: 83–9.

[59] See Pearson 1962; Musti, in Musti and Torelli 1994: xii–xxvii and below, pp. 76–83.

[60] The chronological problems which result if one tries to locate in time Pausanias' Aipytid dynasty are lucidly pointed by Musti, in Musti and Torelli 1994: 210–11.

plot. Even in Isocrates' *Archidamos* no special reason for the murder is mentioned except insubordination of the subjects (*Archid.* 22). But by Ephorus' time at the latest, this too had become a controversial issue.[61] Nicolaus (90 F 31) tells in detail how at the beginning Kresphontes had granted to the original inhabitants of the region equality of rights with the Dorian newcomers, but then, realizing that the Dorians were far from enthusiastic, tried – "as it had been done in Lakedaimon"[62] – to withdraw his previous decision, with the result that in the end both the Dorians and the locals became angry at him, and the Dorians decided to eliminate him. After all, he was a Heraclid, no Dorian. This distinction probably assumed a special meaning after Epaminondas' liberation of Messenia. The tribes of the new Messenian polity did not bear the traditional names of the Dorian tribes, but were named after Heracles' descendants. Since Sparta was seen as the quintessence of Dorianism, it would be understandable that the new polity, born under Theban control, would not have been too keen to emphasize its Dorian heritage. Kresphontes' death at the hands of the Dorians of Messenia and the names of the tribes go together in suggesting that the new Messenians wanted to depict themselves as Heraclids rather than Dorians.[63]

* * *

If the reconstruction of the evolution of the myth of Kresphontes suggested above is correct, the guidelines of the mythic past of the Messenians were determined by Spartans, Argives, Athenians, much more than by the Messenians themselves. For a number of reasons it is rather unlikely that the mythic history of Messenia from Kresphontes to Aipytos, as we know it from the sources, originated in Messenia. If the myth of the tripartition really emerged in the first half of the fifth century, then it belongs to an age in which the Messenians would hardly have been in a

---

[61] In this period a further version of Kresphontes' murder could be dated, one that was the model for Ennius' *Cresphontes*. Apparently, in this tragedy the question whether or not Kresphontes' murder had been legitimate was discussed at some length; see Jocelyn 1967: 270–4.

[62] An allusion to the origin of the division between Spartiates and *perioikoi*, see below n. 64.

[63] Pausanias seems to argue against this trend, by describing the relations between Dorians and "old Messenians" in an idyllic way (4.3.6; see Musti in Musti and Torelli 1994: xiv) and emphasizing the Dorian identity of the Messenians (4.27.11). In connection with Kresphontes' death he speaks of a conflict between the wealthy and the demos (4.3.7). But he is less distant from Ephorus than it might seem: in 4.3.6 the "old Messenians" seem to be identified as the demos. The names of the tribes had also to do with Theban and Argive influence, see below, pp. 230–2. Hall's suggestion (2003: 157) that Nicolaus reflects conflicts between newcomers and local inhabitants at the time of the liberation of Messenia is seductive, but not very helpful.

position to assert their own views on their mythical past. As has been observed, the Heraclids were really at home only in the Argolid. Their claim on Messenia was based on the fact that Heracles had killed Neleus, the king of Messenia, and all his sons except Nestor, because they had stolen from him Geryon's cattle. Then Heracles had given Nestor the land, which belonged to him as war booty. As for Kresphontes, all we know about him is his participation in the division and his death. His organization of the kingdom of Messenia, as evidenced by Strabo's quotation of Ephorus (Strab. 8.4.7 = Ephoros 70 F 116), with the foundation of a capital and four cities ruled by kings appointed by Kresphontes, is obviously constructed by analogy to the Dorian conquest and organization of Laconia, which in its turn reflects the situation in fourth-century Laconia, explaining the origins of Helots and *perioikoi* as parts of the Lakedaimonian state.[64] Except for the conflict with the Dorians, which, as noted above, may reflect and retroject historical circumstances of the time of the liberation of Messenia, Kresphontes' policy is clearly a learned construct.

Which role did Kresphontes and the myths centering upon him play for the collective identity of the Messenians after the liberation from Sparta? His son Aipytos shows up only once, in Pausanias' list of the heroes who were evoked in the ceremonies connected to the foundation of the city at the foot of Mount Ithome (4.27.6). Kresphontes seems to have been more popular. He was depicted in the temple of Messene, a hall of fame for Messenian heroes, probably in the late fourth century.[65] Much later, we know from Imperial inscriptions that the college responsible for the cult of Artemis Orthia at Messene was called "the holy elders, descendants of Kresphontes."[66] And of course, one of the Messenian tribes bore his name. The names of the tribes must go back to the liberation in 369, and interestingly they all belong to Heraclid heroes. Three of them

---

[64] In Laconia, Eurysthenes and Prokles founded six cities, ruled by kings and inhabited by Dorians and other colonists on an equal footing. Agis, Eurysthenes' son, abolished equality and compelled the non-Dorians to pay a tribute. The inhabitants of Helos mutined and were enslaved (Strab. 8.5.4 = Ephoros 70 F 117). On the parallelism between the organization of the Dorian kingdoms of Laconia and Messenia according to Ephorus, see Luraghi 2003: 124–6; the early history of the Argive branch of the Heraclids seems to have been reconstructed by Ephorus along similar lines, see Andrewes 1951: 40–1.

[65] Paus. 4.31.11. On the chronology of the painter and the location of the paintings see below, p. 269.

[66] Themelis 1994a: 111 and *SEG* 23.215, 217, second and third centuries A D. Note also the use of the name "Kresphontes" by a prominent Messenian who was eponymous priest of Zeus Ithomatas in 126 A D (*IG* V 1, 1469; the text printed in the *IG* has to be corrected: there is no sign on the stone of the article in genitive after the name in line 1, which means that Kolbe was wrong to supplement the abbreviation indicating that this Kresphontes' father was also called Kresphontes).

were ancestors of Kresphontes: Hyllos, Aristomachos and Kleodaios. The fourth, Daiphontes, was a Heraclid of the Argive branch,[67] which makes it even clearer that the Messenians chose these names to distance themselves from the Spartans.

Although Kresphontes was no product of Messenian mythopoetic, he did play an important role for the Messenian identity. It could hardly have been otherwise. When Messenia finally became a free polity in 369, the myth of the return of the Heraclids and the tripartition of the Peloponnese was established, and there was no chance for the new Messenians to create a mythic past for themselves by ignoring that myth, assuming, that is, that they wanted their past to be acceptable to a panhellenic audience. Even though Kresphontes, marked by the latent ambiguity of the trickster, was perhaps not the most desirable founding hero that a Greek polity might have thought of, the now finally free Messenians could not simply ignore him. Their mythic past had to adapt to the guidelines of entrenched representations, navigating the straits between authoritative stories, which could not simply be discarded. Only a very narrow leeway remained for the Messenians to work on their own past.

---

[67] On the names of the tribes of Messene, see Jones 1987: 146–8; on Daiphontes, see Harder 1991: 126–9 and below, p. 231.

CHAPTER 4

The conquest of Messenia through the ages

Thanks to the fourth book of Pausanias' *Description of Greece*, there is virtually no event or complex of events in archaic Greek history for which the evidence of the ancient literary sources can be said to approach, in terms of comprehensiveness and level of detail, that for the Spartan conquest of Messenia. This is slightly embarrassing. Ephorus said that narratives of the most distant past are the more credible the less detailed they are (*FgrHist* 70 F 9), and a modern reader would concur, albeit with some qualification. However, Pausanias' narrative of the First Messenian War, which he dated to the second quarter of the eighth century, takes some twenty-four pages of Greek. It may help us absorb the implications of this fact if we recall that Pausanias was farther away in time from that war than we are from John Lackland and the battle of Bouvines. Of course, he certainly had recourse to the work of earlier authors, but the fact that his narrative is more than four times longer than all the remaining evidence for that war does not encourage optimism.

In a nutshell, this peculiar situation is at the root of all problems that affect the reconstruction of an archaic history of Messenia, not to mention Sparta. By working their way backwards from Pausanias and pointing out the compatibility between his narrative and the bits and pieces preserved by earlier sources, some scholars have produced extremely detailed histories of the southern Peloponnese in the eighth and seventh centuries. However, other scholars, impressed by the gap of at least two centuries between the latest phase of the Spartan conquest of Messenia and the earliest possible date of a prose narrative of those events, have treated Pausanias' narrative as the untrustworthy result of later stratification, governed by ideological and propagandistic concerns that belong to the periods following the liberation of Messenia by the Thebans in the fourth century BC. Essentially, the argument should have been settled in favor of the skeptics by the mid twentieth century.[1]

---

[1] Jacoby 1943 subsumes decades of work, mostly by German scholars, who scrupulously dissected the historical narrative in Pausanias and compared it with all available ancient sources. In many ways,

Later attempts at salvaging Pausanias by assuming e.g. that the poems of Tyrtaeus or other lost works of archaic poetry included detailed information on the wars cannot be taken seriously, considering both the evidence for historical references in archaic poetry and the way that later Greek prose authors used to draw inferences based on such poetry: Strabo's suggestion (8.4.10) that Tyrtaeus came from Erineos – and that therefore Apollodorus must have been wrong in making him an Athenian – should give pause to anybody who intends to argue along similar lines.

To be sure, the notion, occasionally entertained by scholars, that the memory of the heroic resistance of their ancestors may have been handed down through the centuries, presumably with a healthy dose of embellishment, among the helotized Messenians themselves, is not one to be assessed with the instruments of source criticism. The problem of the possible social contexts for the transmission and creation of ideas about the past in Messenia under the Spartan domination has to be approached in the first place by a scrutiny of contemporary evidence, which is almost exclusively archaeological. Such a scrutiny will form the matter of the next chapter.

However, if ancient notions and narratives of the archaic history of the Messenians and of the Messenian Wars cannot offer a solid basis for a historical reconstruction, they are interesting objects of investigation in themselves. Observing the evolution over time of ancient views of the conquest of Messenia and the fate of its inhabitants under Spartan rule offers fascinating insights into another historical phenomenon: the battle over the Messenian identity that arguably started in the mid fifth century, certainly peaked in the fourth, and continued, with important changes in function and meaning, through the Hellenistic period and all the way to the age of Pausanias. This is the perspective that will be pursued in the present chapter. After a reconsideration of the little textual evidence for the Spartan conquest of Messene that comes from the archaic age, attention will turn to the development and progressive articulation of stories of the Messenian Wars from the fifth century onwards. Finally, the fate of Messenia under Spartan domination will be examined with the same method, pointing out variations and changes over time. While the events dealt with by the sources that will be discussed in this chapter are essentially confined to the archaic age, this chapter will in fact span the whole history of Messenian identity.

the starting point of the process was Schwartz 1899, whose hypercritical positions were then revised by other scholars and by Schwartz himself.

TYRTAEUS AND THE SPARTAN CONQUEST OF MESSENE

Spartan expansion west of the Taygetos is documented by a preciously early piece of evidence. Tyrtaeus, who composed his elegies probably in the mid seventh century or soon afterwards, thought that "spacious Messene, good to plough and good to plant," had been conquered thanks to king Theopompos, dear to the gods, by the "brave fathers of our fathers" after twenty years of fighting (fr. 5 W²). If the "fathers of our fathers" Tyrtaeus refers to are to be taken literally, the conquest had taken place two generations before himself. This assumption, shared by most readers of Tyrtaeus, ancient and modern, forms the backbone of the chronology of the First and Second Messenian Wars in ancient historiography.[2] However, it has been pointed out that in Greek "our fathers" often simply means "our ancestors," so that Tyrtaeus' "fathers of our fathers" could in theory also mean something like "our distant ancestors."[3] Be that as it may, according to Tyrtaeus, after resisting for twenty years the enemies "abandoned their rich fields and fled from the high Ithomaean Mountains"; in other words, the Spartans conquered their land and drove them away. This point is important, in view of later versions that, as we shall see, implied that the defeated Messenians, or at least the majority of them, remained in their region, to be reduced to the status of Helots in due course.[4]

In order to assess the implications of this piece of evidence, it is necessary to determine precisely what Tyrtaeus thought the "fathers of the fathers" led by Theopompos had conquered. Later authors, like Strabo (8.5.8) and Pausanias (4.1.4), explained that before the foundation of Epaminondas' Messene in 369 BC, no city with that name had existed, while "Messene" in olden times had been the name of the whole region which in their own times was called "Messenia." This made it possible for ancient and modern readers to embed Tyrtaeus' verses into a general representation of a First Messenian War, which had brought to the Spartans control of the region.[5] Broadly speaking, Strabo's and Pausanias'

---

[2] See e.g. Jacoby 1943: 114 and cf. Paus. 4.13.6, 15.2–3.

[3] Schwartz 1899: 429; see also Andrewes 1951: 44, Nafissi 1991: 37 and n. 26, Musti, in Musti and Torelli 1994: 224–7, and the discussion in Jacoby 1943: 154.

[4] *Pace* van Wees 2003: 35 n. 6, the οἱ μέν in line 7 means 'they,' not 'some' (if it meant 'some' it would have to refer to some Spartans!), and it must have been connected to something like ἡμεῖς δέ or some other form referring to the victorious Spartans.

[5] With an important difference: as Jacoby 1943: 112 has correctly emphasized, all ancient sources say or imply that Messenia had been completely conquered by the Spartans as a result of what modern scholars call the First Messenian War. The notion that the Spartans conquered only part of Messenia, e.g. the Pamisos valley and the Stenyklaros plain, during this war, and completed the conquest of the region during a second war, appears only in modern research; it has been argued

views were not too far off the mark, at least as far as the classical and Hellenistic ages are concerned. The idea that the portion of Spartan territory west of the Taygetos and south of the river Neda somehow formed a unit underlies the tradition of the division of the Peloponnese among the Heraclids, a tradition that, as we have seen, is attested for the first time by Pindar in 462 and probably originated at Argos, perhaps not much earlier. When Thucydides located Pylos in what had once been the Messenian land (4.3.2; 41.2), he was obviously assuming that more or less everything west of the Taygetos had been Messenian land. Apparently, the name of this regional unit was "Messene."[6] The Messenian state created by Epaminondas was accordingly called "Messene," while its main city's original name was Ithome.[7] During the third century, the name Messene came progressively to indicate only that city, while the regional name Messenia emerged, creating the situation Strabo and Pausanias were familiar with. However, it is not *a priori* clear that for Tyrtaeus, too, "Messene" should have been the name of a region,[8] let alone that that region should have included the whole of later Messenia. The only other archaic source in which the name "Messene" appears is the *Odyssey* (21.13ff.), which relates the encounter of young Odysseus and Iphitos in Lakedaimon (dative), at Messene (ἐv plus dative), in the house of Ortilochos, where Iphitos gave Odysseus the famous bow as a present to establish guest-friendship. Although "Messene" in this passage has sometimes been interpreted as referring to a region rather than to a city, it is clearly more natural to interpret the second place-name as a specification of the first, as indicating something smaller than a region, that is, presumably a city, or at any rate a smaller territorial unit. It would be strange if all the geographic information conveyed in these verses were that Ortilochos' place was somewhere south of the Neda and west of the Taygetos.[9]

---

especially by Franz Kiechle, 1959: esp. 65–70, and accepted e.g. by Clauss 1983: 20 and Cartledge 2002: 103.

[6] The first instance of the use of "Messene" as the name for Messenia is Eur. *TrGF* 727e *ap.* Strab. 8.5.6, from the lost tragedy *Temenos* (see Harder 1991: 133–4 and above, p. 50 n. 12); throughout the passage, Strabo regularly uses "Messenia," except when he introduces line 10 of the fragment, where his "Messene" is highly likely to reflect Euripides' terminology. Fragments of Pherecydes (fr. 117 Fowler = *FgrHist* 3 F 117) and Hellanicus (fr. 124a and 125 Fowler = *FgrHist* 4 F 124 and 323a F 23) suggest that the use might be older by some decades, ultimately coinciding with the emergence of the tradition of the division of the Peloponnese among the Heraclids.

[7] For a discussion of the meaning of the name Messene and of the name of the settlement at Mount Ithome from the liberation of Messenia onwards, see below, pp. 216 and 266.

[8] The epithets associated with it in Tyrt. fr. 5 W² can refer to both cities and regions.

[9] For the identification of this Messene as a place rather than a region, see Visser 1997: 485–6. His further suggestion that this place should be located in Laconia rests on no argument.

In fairness to previous scholars, it must be emphasized that one reason for their readiness to accept Strabo's and Pausanias' views on the original meaning of the name "Messene" was the lack of archaeological evidence for an archaic settlement on the site of later Messene.[10] Now that new excavations have shown that a settlement existed at the foot of Mount Ithome already in the ninth and eighth centuries (below, pp. 112–13), the case should be reconsidered. In the light of the new evidence, it seems preferable to think that Tyrtaeus' Messene was the Geometric settlement at Mount Ithome with its territory, extending perhaps southwards on the western side of the Pamisos, possibly as far as the sea. The later interpretation of the name in fact reflects an attempt at projecting back in the past a regional unity that was really a result of Spartan expansion.

The Homeric geography of the southwestern Peloponnese seems to reflect, and to project back to the age of the heroes, a rather developed stage of the process of Spartan westward expansion. The Messene of the *Odyssey* is a part of Lakedaimon, Menelaus' kingdom, and it probably appears also, thinly disguised, in the mysterious city of Messe, mentioned in the Lakedaimonian portion of the *Catalogue of Ships* (*Il.* 2.582), together with Sparta.[11] Furthermore, the six cities offered by Agamemnon to Achilles in an effort to convince him to return to the fight (*Il.* 9.149–53) were located, insofar as it is possible to pinpoint any of them, along the gulf of Messenia,[12] while Homeric geography does not know of any independent entity between the shadowy kingdom of Pylos, roughly Triphylia, and Lakedaimon.[13] Interestingly, the only thing we learn about the Messenians from the *Odyssey*, apart from the fact that they were supposed to possess ships and have access to the sea (*Od.* 21.19),[14] is that they had a somewhat dubious reputation: Odysseus went to Messene to complain because Messenian raiders had stolen from Ithaca some cattle together with the herdsmen, while Iphitos was there looking for twelve

---

[10] Cf. e.g. Meyer 1978: 137.
[11] Discussed in Visser 1997: 483–6; cf. Shipley 1997: 253. The possibility that Messe should be identified with Messene occurred already to the ancient readers of Homer (mentioned by Strab. 8.5.3). Tellingly, the only author who appears to know a location for Messe is the philo-Messenian Pausanias; his Messe of course is in Laconia (3.25.9).
[12] See Hope Simpson 1966: 113–31, and Visser 1997: 492–501.
[13] On the location of Pylos and the situation of the southwestern Peloponnese in Homeric geography see Giovannini 1969: 28–30 and Visser 1997: 508–31.
[14] Probably for this reason it has sometimes been thought that the Messene of *Od.* 21.15 should be identified with Pherai, where Telemachus met Diocles, son of Orsilochos, on his way from Pylos to Sparta and back (*Od.* 3.486-8 = 15.185–8); however, even if one adheres to a strictly realistic reading of Homer's geography, there is no reason to exclude that Messene could have a harbor, presumably west of the mouth of the Pamisos or in the area of Kyparissia.

mares of his that had been abducted. One wonders whether this should not be seen as the first trace of the Spartans' attempt at justifying in front of a broader audience their violent conquest of Messene. Unfortunately, it is not possible to locate in time these hints in a less than controversial way. However, the widespread view that the poems reached the stage in which we know them sometime between the late eighth and the early seventh centuries would of course have interesting consequences for the chronology of the Spartan expansion in Messenia.[15]

Besides talking about the conquest of Messene, Tyrtaeus may have also mentioned further fights against the Messenians in his own times. The relevant text (fr. 23 W^2) comes from a very fragmentary papyrus, but it clearly mentions the Messenians, fighting, and "us," and the only verb in a finite form is in the future tense.[16] In fact, this would explain why later authors thought that Tyrtaeus had lived at the time of the Second Messenian War and fired up the Spartans with his poems.[17] In assessing the meaning of this fragment, it has to be pointed out that, as we shall see in a moment, fifth-century authors seem to know nothing of a further war between Spartans and Messenians. This is of course not a conclusive argument against reading it in Tyrtaeus, since after all it seems that his elegies had not been used as evidence on the Spartan conquest of Messenia before the fourth century. However, it is worth entertaining the notion that what Tyrtaeus referred to was not an all-out war of regional expansion, all the more so since for him Messene was not the whole region, but probably only a settlement or a portion of the region, and correspondingly "the Messenians" could only be the inhabitants, or former inhabitants, of that settlement or area.

Finally, some verses of Tyrtaeus may be relevant to the problem of the Messenians' fate after the war. However, their interpretation is much less straightforward than in the case of the conquest of Messene. In order to illustrate the fate of the Messenians after the First Messenian War, Pausanias (4.14.5) quotes two couplets, not adjoining but presumably coming from the same poem, that describe the harsh plight of unspecified people who were compelled to give up half of the produce of their fields

---

[15] Dealing with any form of the Homeric question is not germane to the present investigation. For this reason, the implications of the Homeric passages just discussed will not be pressed too far.

[16] For the interpretation of this fragment see West 1974: 188.

[17] Most explicitly Aristot. *Pol.* 1306b37–1307a22; Philochorus *FgrHist* 328 F 216; Diod. 8.27.1; but this is also implied by the story that made of Tyrtaeus an Athenian, see below, n. 31. A further battle against the Messenians may have been mentioned in the passage referred to in Tyrt. fr. 9 W^2; however, the reference is certainly not based on direct reading of Tyrtaeus, so we may have to do with a case of ancient interpretation rather than with real Tyrtaean material (see also below, n. 37).

and to mourn at their masters' funerals (fr. 6 and 7 W²). This has often been taken as a description of the conditions of the Helots, to which the vanquished Messenians would have been reduced.[18] It should be noted, however, that Pausanias thought otherwise, since he quotes the couplets to corroborate his statement that the Messenians had not been reduced to the status of Helots after the Spartan conquest of Messenia (cf. 4.14.4). The same point is made in a passage of the late second-century AD rhetor Aelian (*VH* 6.1), also depending directly or indirectly on Tyrtaeus, where the conditions imposed on the Messenians are clearly not being interpreted as Helotry.[19]

Given the fact that Tyrtaeus' verses were used to buttress a particular position in a very sensitive controversy, one should probably be cautious in reading into them anything that is only in the surrounding sentences of Pausanias and not in the verses themselves. In other words, the assumption that the verses referred to the Messenians at all should not be regarded as a certainty, particularly since the conditions imposed upon the Messenians after the first and second wars respectively were clearly an object of disagreement among later authors (see below), which would be surprising if among Tyrtaeus' verses there had been an unambiguous testimony on this point. The obligation to come to mourn at the masters' funerals finds an interesting parallel in the description of the conditions imposed by the Corinthian Bacchiads on the Megarians,[20] but in their case there is no hint of alienation of resources. Moreover, Tyrtaeus' verses, in which different words for "masters" recur twice,[21] seem to describe people held in a relation of personal dependence rather than a submitted community; they recall to some extent the "shameful slavery" imposed by some Athenians on others according to Solon (fr. 36.13–15 W²). If they do not refer to a condition imposed on some part of the population of Messene, which they might, they should probably be seen as describing the plight of a dependent labor force working for the Spartiates. Be that as it may, in the end the only thing that Tyrtaeus does say explicitly about the Messenians, in the very few verses that we have considered earlier (fr. 5 W²), is that they

[18] See e.g. Lotze 1959: 28 and 32–3; Oliva 1971: 108–12; Link 1994: 1 n. 6; Hodkinson 2000: 126–7; Cartledge 2002: 303; van Wees 2003: 34–5.
[19] For more detailed arguments in support of the interpretation presented here, see Luraghi 2003.
[20] According to the Atthidographer Demon (*FgrHist* 327 F 19), writing probably in the late fourth century, the Megarians were compelled to go to Corinth to mourn at the funerals of the Bacchiads. The parallel with Tyrtaeus has been noticed by Bockisch 1985: 44–5.
[21] Notice particularly δεσπόσυνοι (fr. 6.2 W²), possibly a Doric word, cf. Plut. *Life of Lycurgus* 28.10 and *SGDI* 4334.

fled from their country after twenty years of war. He may have had a lot more to say, for all we know, but this can only be the object of speculation.

MESSENIAN WARS: THE FIFTH AND FOURTH CENTURIES

Fifth-century historians, insofar as their works are preserved, do not seem to have had any specific interest in the Spartan conquest of Messenia: apparently they simply took it for granted. Herodotus (3.47.1) says that, according to the Samians, the Spartans embarked in an expedition against Polycrates around 525 BC in order to reciprocate the Samians' envoy of ships to help the Spartans against the Messenians, at an unspecified point in the past. Antiochus of Syracuse (555 F 13 *ap.* Strab. 6.3.2), narrating the foundation of Taras, says that it occurred "after the Messenian war." Thucydides (1.101.2) simply alludes to the enslavement of the Messenians by the Spartans in the past, in a way that suggests that he expected his readers to know what he was talking about.[22] It is hard to infer anything based on these tantalizing hints. Certainly at least Antiochus' words suggest that for him there had been only one Messenian war, and Thucydides in particular might be taken to concur.

The vagueness of these references has to be set in the context of the general scarcity of references or allusions to Spartan history before the mid sixth century in Herodotus and Thucydides. One wonders if the survival of more fifth-century authors would have changed this general pattern: perhaps not, since both Herodotus and Thucydides, two historians otherwise so different from one another, share a very peculiar view of the early archaic history of Sparta, one characterized by extreme social disorder in its earliest phase, succeeded by Lycurgus' reforms that brought about, still in the very distant past, the whole package of Spartan social and political institutions – from the common messes to the ephorate. This plot, with the sharp sequence disorder–order located far in the past, *de facto* denying any development or change of social and political institutions, is very likely to originate from Sparta itself and to reflect the structure of the Spartans' collective memory: the kind of collective memory that Jan Assmann calls "cold," one that systematically excludes change from the past of the group and confines the emergence of its institutions to the foundational phase, after which nothing is supposed to have changed any more.[23]

---

[22] For the interpretation of this passage see Luraghi 2002c.
[23] Sparta's *kakonomia*: Hdt. 1.65.2 and Thuc. 1.18.1. On "cold" and "warm" collective memories, see Assmann 1992: 66–86, esp. 68–70, and specifically on Sparta Paradiso 1995: 35–45.

Considering these facts, it hardly comes as a surprise that no local history of Sparta is attested for the fifth century, while the first prose works dedicated specifically to Sparta are descriptions of its constitution – some of them composed by prominent Spartans, such as the general Thibron and the exiled king Pausanias.[24] In this framework, lack of interest in the history of Spartan expansion is anything but surprising.

Considering the conquest of Messenia in the framework of the Spartans' perceptions of their past may not seem a very satisfactory approach, but it is the only one the literary evidence admits, as far as the period down to the end of the fifth century is concerned. Signs of heightened interest in the Messenian past in the course of the century almost invariably target the mythic portion of it, in particular the division of the Peloponnese among the Heraclids, and it is rather unclear to what extent any of that reflects ideas about their past held by people who considered themselves Messenians. As we will see more in detail, only very tentatively is it possible to trace elements of the later narratives of the wars back to the period preceding the Spartan rout at Leuktra.[25]

It is a commonplace, but no less true or interesting for this reason, that interest in the Messenian wars began to arise after the liberation of Messenia by Epaminondas. This is typical of the Greek conception of the relationship between sovereignty, tradition and collective identity: a new polity created on the Greek mainland could only be seen as legitimate if it was in some sense the re-creation of something that had existed before – if it could be understood in terms not of discontinuity but of reestablishing continuity. However, it is important to realize that the resurfacing of Messenian ethnicity in connection with the Theban victories was not an isolated occurrence, but rather one instance of a broader process of ethnic redefinition that involved many areas of the Peloponnese in the first half of the fourth century and brought about a correspondingly wide-ranging restructuring of the Peloponnesian past, typically not as dramatic as in the case of the Messenians but similar in many ways. New entities like Pisatis and Triphylia suddenly popped up, usually ushered in by the one or the other of the major powers competing for regional hegemony, and by the second half of the century the past and the present of the Peloponnese had changed, in some cases beyond recognition.[26]

---

[24] On the absence of a local historiography at Sparta see Thommen 2000.

[25] See below on the story of Teleklos' death at Limnai, which may go back to the fifth century, possibly to the years around the Peace of Nicias (see also below, p. 159).

[26] See below, pp. 210–14, and the contributions collected in Luraghi and Funke 2008.

Broadly speaking, it is an advanced stage of the process of rediscovery of the Messenian past that is documented, albeit imperfectly, in the literary evidence. In other words, the modern reader is likely to encounter a rather domesticated version of the revision of the history of the Messenians that started with the liberation of Messenia, a version that had been filtered in works of Panhellenic scope and smoothed sufficiently for it to be compatible with accepted notions of early Peloponnesian history. This version appears to have been quite respectful of the Spartan viewpoint; the opinion, sometimes voiced, that the historiography on the Messenian wars from the fourth century onwards was essentially pro-Messenian is unfounded – it is in fact a consequence of an excessive readiness to take Pausanias as representative for fourth-century historiography.

The only source that seems to reflect an early stage of the battle for the Messenian past is Isocrates' speech *Archidamos*, which has been introduced above (p. 55) in connection with the Heraclid conquest of the Peloponnese. As we have seen, Isocrates' Archidamus had a very clear-cut view of how and why the Spartans had subdued Messenia, always called "Messene" in the speech. The Spartans took control very early, because the Messenians had killed their own Heraclid king, Kresphontes, and exiled his children; these fled to Sparta, also ruled by Heraclid kings, and entrusted their land to the Spartans, begging for revenge. The Spartans, after consulting the oracle of Apollo, accepted the gift and the task and conquered the land (*Archid.* 22–3). In short, their claim to Messenia was founded on the ancestral rights of the Heraclids, on Apollo's will, and on armed conquest, and was therefore as unimpeachable as their claim to Laconia itself (*Archid.* 25). Clearly, this story cancels any Messenian claim to independence based on the division of the Peloponnese among the Heraclids. It is not clear how exactly Isocrates–Archidamus envisioned the Spartan conquest proper. The idea that the final siege of the Messenian stronghold (*Archid.* 23) lasted for twenty years (*Archid.* 57) is obviously taken, directly or indirectly, from Tyrtaeus (fr. 5 W²),[27] while the 400 years of Spartan domination over Messenia (*Archid.* 26) may refer to some accepted chronology for the First Messenian War, but can hardly be reconciled with the notion of an early takeover soon after the return of the Heraclids.[28]

---

[27] Note that because of the shift in meaning of the name "Messene," fourth-century readers were bound to deduce from Tyrtaeus that the Spartans under king Theopompos had conquered Messenia, i.e. the region, rather than a settlement in that region.

[28] See especially Santarelli 1990. One wonders if this figure, thrown in casually by Isocrates-Archidamus, has not been taken at times unduly seriously by scholars.

Isocrates' description of the long war includes a further detail which may correspond to something that later sources would include in their narratives of the first war, the fact that both sides turned to the oracle of Delphi (*Archid.* 31), which recurs, with a different bias, in Pausanias (4.12.1–4).[29] However, the words used by Isocrates suggest the suspicion that he might actually be referring to the alleged oracle that ordered the Spartans to ask for help at Athens and prompted the Athenians to send Tyrtaeus. This story originated most likely in the years between Leuktra and Mantinea,[30] was clearly known to Plato, who considered Tyrtaeus an Athenian (*Laws* 1.629a–b), and is attested explicitly for the first time by Callisthenes (124 F 24).[31] If this suspicion should turn out to be correct, then Isocrates would be mixing together elements which later sources were to divide between the early Spartan takeover and the two Messenian wars. Even if the confusion is more limited, certainly Isocrates' Archidamus is not being particularly careful to distinguish the successive stages of the Spartan expansion in Messenia – which should not be surprising in a political pamphlet. On the whole, it may be more appropriate to look at Isocrates' speech as a witness to an early phase in which claims and counterclaims were being tossed around in a rather unstructured way, before being rationalized and organized in a consistent fashion by historians such as Callisthenes or Ephorus; in other words, Isocrates may not be mixing and merging episodes that were otherwise seen as belonging to different historical contexts, as he seems to be doing if we compare his views with the canonical form of the history of the Messenian wars as it was worked out later in the century. It is a real pity that we understand so little of the Messenian response.[32]

---

[29] According to Isocrates, only the Spartans received instructions from Apollo on how to sacrifice and where to seek help in order to win the war; the Messenians received no answer. Pausanias' story involves an oracle encouraging the Spartans to conquer Messene by deceit (4.12.1, also in Diod. 8.13.2), while the Messenians received an incomprehensible prediction of defeat (4.12.4). A later oracle given to the Messenians promised victory to whoever would be the first to offer 100 tripods to Zeus Ithomatas (4.12.7); unexpectedly, the Messenians were preempted by the Spartan Oebalus (4.12.9). On these oracles, see Parke 1938: 66–72.

[30] When the Spartans asked for help at Athens, mentioning past reciprocal benefactions (Xen. *Hell.* 6.5.33) or reminding the Athenians that they had helped Sparta already in the past (Callisthenes 124 F 8).

[31] For Isocr. *Archid.* 31 as an allusion to Tyrtaeus, see Jacoby 1943: 113. The story is also in Diod. 8.27, on which see Jacoby 1943: 114. The version found in Justin (3.5.5–6) and Pausanias (4.15.6), according to which Tyrtaeus was lame and the Athenians had sent him because they did not want to help the Spartans, obviously intends to excuse Athens and is certainly a later elaboration.

[32] Whatever its context (see below, p. 223 n. 49), the surviving fragments of Alcidamas' *Messenian Speech* do not address the issue of the wars.

Our fragmentary knowledge of fourth-century historiography suggests that by the 330s a canonical version of the wars had emerged, at least in outline. It involved a first war, fought in the age of the Spartan king Theopompos, lasting for twenty years, and ending with the Spartan conquest of the region, and a second war taking place in the age of Tyrtaeus, two generations later.[33] The cornerstone of this reconstruction was obviously the passage of Tyrtaeus discussed at the beginning of this chapter.[34] Some elements of this master-story show clear traces of having originated in the historical context of the liberation of Messenia by the Thebans and their allies. Although no source goes so far as to bring in the Thebans as allies of the Messenians in their ancestral struggle against the Spartans, the distribution of the allies on both sides, especially in connection with the Second Messenian War, bears a suspicious resemblance to the alliances in the Peloponnese immediately after Leuktra, with Argives, Arcadians, Sicyonians and Pisatans on the side of the Messenians and only Corinth on that of Sparta.[35] The suspicion becomes certainty at least in the case of Pisatis, which everyone now agrees never existed as an independent political entity before being created by the Arcadians in 365 B.C.[36] In some cases, we can still recover details of this close correspondence between past and present. The Arcadian king responsible for betraying the Messenians in one of the most important battles of the Second Messenian War, the battle of the Great Trench,[37] happens to be Aristokrates of Orchomenos, and Orchomenos happens to have been the only important Arcadian city that resisted joining the Arcadian League in 370 and remained loyal to Sparta.[38] More generally, it can scarcely be

---

[33] However, this canonical version admitted important variations, such as Ephorus' accepting in a modified form the notion that the Spartans had taken control of Messenia well before the First Messenian War; see above, p. 63, and below, p. 102.

[34] Callisthenes was probably the first historian to make use of Tyrtaeus to reconstruct the history of the wars, in a retrospective excursus of his *Hellenics*, written between 343 and 335 B.C; see Jacoby 1943: 118, 121, 130, and Prandi 1985: 55–8. On the Second Messenian War in Ephorus, see Andrewes 1951: 42–3.

[35] See the brilliant demonstration by Tausend 1992: 145–61. Note that Jacoby 1943: 114 suggested that the depiction of the coalitions in the Second Messenian War might predate Callisthenes and ultimately go back to Theban historiography of the time of Epaminondas.

[36] On Pisatis, see Nafissi 2003, Möller 2004: 254–66, Ruggeri 2004: 178–83, Giangiulio 2008, and below, p. 213.

[37] The battle itself may have been mentioned by Tyrtaeus, or perhaps more likely, given the suspiciously general place-name, spun out of some passage of Tyrtaeus'; cf. Tyrt. fr. 9 W² and see Jacoby 1943: 130, Kiechle 1959: 25–6.

[38] The connection had already been noticed by Schwartz 1899: 448; see also Robertson 1992: 239 and n. 21. On Aristokrates' betrayal at the battle of the Great Trench, see Callisth. *FgrHist* 124 F 23. On Aristokrates being an Orchomenian, Strab. 8.4.10. Orchomenians not joining the Arcadian League: Xen. *Hell.* 6.5.11–14 and Nielsen 2002: 342 (note that Orchomenos was pro-Spartan also in 418,

doubted that the prominent role attributed by Callisthenes to the Arcadians, who received the Messenian exiles after the debacle and gave them citizen rights, reflects the decisive involvement of the Arcadians in the creation of a free Messenian state in 370/69.[39] One even wonders whether the notion that exiled Messenians had been naturalized as Arcadians could not have been used to pass off Arcadian immigrants who joined the new Messenian state as descendants of "old Messenians." By contrast, the Samians, who according to Herodotus helped the Spartans against the Messenians, are not mentioned by any later source on the Messenian wars and seem simply to have fallen out of the picture, clearly because they had no function in early fourth-century Peloponnesian politics.

Apart from the tantalizing references in the fragment of Callisthenes mentioned above, we have very little evidence on aspects of the wars from pre-Hellenistic sources. One interesting exception involves the *casus belli* of the First Messenian War: the murder of the Spartan king Teleklos by the Messenians in the sanctuary of Artemis Limnatis, after he ran to the rescue of a group of Spartan maidens who had been assaulted by the Messenians while they were taking part in a religious festival. Strabo refers twice to the rape of the maidens without mentioning the murder of the king (6.1.6, 8.4.9), and once to the murder of King Teleklos who had come to Messene for a sacrifice (6.3.3) – here it is the rape of the maidens that goes unmentioned. Diodorus briefly alludes to Teleklos' death as the cause of the war (15.66.2), while Iustin's epitome (4.1.1) shows that Pompeius Trogus referred to the rape of the maidens, too. Pausanias (4.4.2) is the only extant author who brings together the death of the king and the rape of the maidens, but it is reasonable to assume that the two episodes originally belonged together and that it is only by accident that extant earlier sources refer to the one or the other but not both – all the

Thuc. 5.61.4–5, 63.2). Pausanias makes Aristokrates a Trapezuntian (4.17.2), that is, he links him to one of the communities that had disappeared in conjunction with the foundation of Megalopolis (see Paus. 8.27.3–4 and Nielsen 2002: 423–5; actually, Trapezus is listed as one of the communities that tried to resist the incorporation); for the reasons for this shift, see Tausend 1992: 151. The invocation of Zeus Basileus in the epigram that alluded to the punishment of Aristokrates, quoted by Callisthenes (and clearly composed after the liberation of Messenia, Prandi 1985: 57), may also be worth noting; according to Diodorus (15.53.4), one of the favorable omens fabricated by Epaminondas before the battle of Leuktra took the form of a response from the oracle of Trophonius in Lebadeia ordering the Thebans to institute competitions in honor of Zeus Basileus after the victory. On the cult of Zeus Basileus at Lebadeia, see Schachter 1994: 110–18. No cult of Zeus Basileus is attested in Arcadia (Jost 1985: 239–40).

[39] See Prandi 1985: 55–8. The flight to Arcadia of the Messenian refugees is described also in Paus. 4.22.2; however, according to Pausanias (4.23.3) only the Messenians who were too old to participate in the colonial expedition remained in Arcadia. On the Arcadians and the liberation of Messenia, see below, p. 215.

more so, since Strabo (6.1.6) does refer to the fact that the Messenians, beside raping the maidens, also killed those who came to their aid. Alternatively, it is also possible to think that some sources took the rape of the maidens and others the murder of the king as the factor that triggered the war.[40]

Ever since the Messenians became a free polity, this story must have been an object of dispute, just as the sanctuary itself; we would expect *a priori* various versions with contrasting orientations. However, only Pausanias offers a pro-Messenian version of the story, in which the Spartan maidens turn out to be Spartan youths disguised as maidens by King Teleklos – all the better to fall upon the most illustrious of the Messenians, who had come to the sanctuary to participate in a religious festival.[41] To explain the situation, Pausanias specifies that the sanctuary was common to Messenians and Spartans, who shared it in virtue of their common Dorian heritage. Interestingly, for the other authors it does not seem to be necessary to explain what the maidens or King Teleklos were doing in a Messenian sanctuary.

Pausanias' Messenian version of the story need not be very old. First of all, it bears a suspicious resemblance to Herodotus' story of the massacre of the Persian embassy by Alexander of Macedon (5.20).[42] Second and more important, according to the Messenian version Teleklos' death had not determined the outbreak of the war,[43] which means that this version cannot be older than the story of Polychares and Euephnos, documented by Pausanias himself and by Diodorus, which offered an alternative narrative for the outbreak of the war, one centered upon a theft of cattle that laid responsibility for the war squarely in the Spartan field.[44] This alternative story can be traced back to the work of Myron of Priene, in

---

[40] In this case, it may be relevant that only the rape is explicitly located in the sanctuary of Artemis, while Teleklos' death seems to take place more generally in Messenia. The connection between the Limnai episode and the foundation of Rhegion is discussed below, pp. 157–9.

[41] Calame 1979: 8–12 and 18–22 offers an illuminating comparison of the two versions, arguing purely from their internal logic that the Spartan version is older; for the implications of Calame's analysis for the date of the Messenian version, see below, n. 43.

[42] See Pearson 1962: 409. Note also that Pausanias' Messenian version, with its implication that the Spartan youths were indeed killed by the Messenians in self-defense, responds to a Spartan one in which the maidens committed suicide after the rape, which does not seem to happen in Strabo, Diodorus, and Justin, and therefore probably also not in their source. This detail may have been added by Myron, see Berg 1998: 42.

[43] And its very narrative logic made it impossible for this story to function as *casus belli*, as shown by Calame 1979: 21.

[44] Diod. 8.7 and Paus 4.4.5–8, the latter actually even more favorable to the Messenians. On Myron of Priene as their common source, see Jacoby 1943: 128 and below, n. 56. The Messenian protagonist of the story, Polychares, has probably been lifted from the list of the Olympionikai, see Moretti no. 4, Ol. 4, 764 BC.

the third century BC. However, it is quite possible that Pausanias really gathered the Messenian version of the Limnai story at Messene, where it may have circulated for some time.[45] Clearly, it did not make much headway into mainstream Greek historiography, since no other ancient author appears to know it.

Beside exculpating the Messenians, the story of Polychares and Euephnos had the additional advantage of detaching the proximate cause of the war from the Spartan king Teleklos. For in fact Teleklos' murder was an acceptable cause for the First Messenian War only until the idea became generalized that Theopompos' Agiad colleague during the war had been king Polydorus, Teleklos' grandson. The synchronism Theopompos–Polydoros is generally thought to have been derived from Tyrtaeus, which is possible but not entirely certain.[46] At any rate, the connection between Teleklos and the beginning of the First Messenian War must have been a problem already for fourth-century historians such as Callisthenes and Ephorus, and a new explanation of the war, which eliminated this chronological conundrum, would have certainly been welcome.

There can be no doubt that the story of Teleklos is older than the alternative explanation of the war. Diodorus, Strabo and Pompeius Trogus all used standard fourth-century sources, especially the *Universal history* of Ephorus of Cumae, and this fact would explain why for them the presence of King Teleklos and/or of the Spartan maidens in a Messenian sanctuary was not particularly noteworthy: as we have seen, Ephorus dated the Spartan takeover of Messenia to well before the First Messenian War. Strabo actually refers to Teleklos' death in his report of Ephorus' version of the foundation of Taras (6.3.3, with *FgrHist* 70 F 216). This brings us back at least to the third quarter of the fourth century, but the story may be older still. While Teleklos could hardly be taken as a contemporary of Theopompos in the revised chronologies of the Spartan kings current from the fourth century onwards, the two of them occupy precisely the same place in Herodotus' genealogies of the Agiads and Eurypontids.[47] On the whole, although certainty is unattainable, the story

---

[45] It may have originated in connection with the last phase of the conflict for the Dentheliatis, see above, pp. 21–3, and below, pp. 299–300.

[46] On the association of Theopompos and Polydorus and its possible origin, see Schneider 1985: 20–3. Its occurrence in Pompeius Trogus fr. 54a 3 Seel strongly suggests that it was present in some fourth-century standard work of reference, most likely Ephorus' *Universal History*, as noted by Kiechle 1959: 96–7, who points to the similarity between Iust. 3.4, from the epitome of Pompeius Trogus, and Ephorus *FgrHist* 70 F 216.

[47] Hdt. 7.204 for the Agiads and 8.131.2 for the Eurypontids. For a clear and comprehensive discussion of the Spartan king lists in their various versions, see Schneider 1985: 17–23.

of the rape of the maidens and of the murder of King Teleklos is likely to have originated quite early, probably already in the fifth century, especially if those scholars are right who maintain that the pattern of the story shows that it served as *aition* for an initiatory ritual performed by Spartan maidens.[48] Considering that the story appears to underpin the legitimacy of Spartan domination of Messenia, it would be tempting to connect its origin with one of the moments during the fifth century when such domination was called into question: either the revolt after the earthquake or the years around the Peace of Nicias, when Pylos was garrisoned by the Messenians from Naupaktos for several years (below, p. 190).

The case of the Limnai affair is the clearest instance of a more general and somewhat surprising phenomenon: throughout the fourth century, which is usually and most likely correctly taken to be the formative phase of the ancient tradition on the Spartan conquest of Messenia, no clear traces are preserved of a Messenian version of the facts that would dramatically challenge the cornerstones of the Spartan reconstruction, which buttressed the legitimacy of the Spartan conquest of Messenia. We have to reach the Hellenistic age to find evidence of histories of the Messenian wars written uncompromisingly from a Messenian point of view – and most probably, for the consumption of a Messenian audience.

HELLENISTIC CONSTRUCTS: A PAST FOR THE MESSENIANS

Clearly, whatever fourth-century authors may have had to say about the Messenian wars, their accounts cannot have been very detailed, for when Pausanias set out to write his own comprehensive history of early Messenia, he had to resort to later authors in order to beef up the story of the wars. As he informs us, the main sources on which his account was based were the prose writer Myron of Priene and the Cretan epic poet Rhianus. According to Pausanias (4.6.1–2), Myron had dealt with the history of the First Messenian War, almost down to its end but not quite, while Rhianus had written about the Second, starting from the battle of the Great Trench, in which Aristokrates' treason had taken place.[49] Myron and

---

[48] Calame 2001: 142–9 and Leitao 1999. In that case, of course, the story would necessarily go back to a time when the sanctuary was in Spartan hands, i.e. certainly before Philip's invasion of Laconia in 338 (above, p. 17). On archaeological evidence for the cult of Artemis Limnatis, see below, p. 123; as noted there, archaic and early classical dedications to Artemis Limnatis offer some support to Calame's interpretation.

[49] Because Rhianus calls the Spartan king under whom the war took place Leotychidas, scholars for a long time entertained the possibility that his poem actually dealt with a Messenian revolt at the

Rhianus are both rather shadowy figures, and their chronology is unclear. There is a slight possibility that Myron might be mentioned in a passage of the Latin grammarian Rutilius Lupus as a contemporary of the Athenian politician Chremonides, who was famously associated with the war against Macedonia in the 260s and went in exile at the court of the Ptolemies, whose fleet he apparently led to defeat against the Rhodians in the battle of Ephesus, sometime in the 250s.[50] A Myron is mentioned as author of an *Encomium of Rhodes* in the Lindian temple chronicle (*FgrHist* 106 F 4–5).[51] It would not be surprising if he were the same man as Pausanias' Myron, who is definitely the kind of writer we would expect to have engaged in the Hellenistic genre of encomiastic local historiography, whose shadowy authors are often documented by honorary inscriptions set up by their grateful patrons.[52] Myron's Messenian work, in at least two books and perhaps not many more, was definitely pro-Messenian and anti-Spartan. If Pausanias' narrative of the First Messenian War is anything to go by, Myron was not exactly a pragmatic historian in the Polybian mold: he seems to have been fond of long-winded rhetorical speeches and his battle narratives appear to be a mixture of adaptations from passages of canonical authors with colorful and implausible details and massive doses of pathos.[53] The taste of Hellenistic tragic historiography is felt particularly strongly in episodes such as the story of the Delphic oracle's order to the Messenians to sacrifice a virgin from the Aipytidai family, which in Pausanias ends in a confrontation between the Aipytid Aristodemos, the Messenian leader in the last part of the war, who offered his own daughter, and an anonymous Messenian to whom the daughter had been betrothed, and finally with Aristodemos' useless murder of the maiden.[54] Myron also shows signs of a rather casual attitude to evidence, witness his claim that King Theopompos had been killed during the First Messenian War – *pace*

beginning of the fifth century. This hypothesis, which was argued extensively for by Jacoby, has, however, been discarded with good arguments, see below, p. 174 n. 2 with references.

[50] Pearson 1962: 411, Mazzarino 1966: 463–4.
[51] On Myron's *Encomium of Rhodes*, and on city encomia in general, see now Higbie 2003: 197–8.
[52] See the evidence collected by Chaniotis 1988: 297–326.
[53] On the character of Myron's work, see Jacoby 1943: 123–7. On his battle descriptions, see also Pearson 1962: 413–14: consider especially the story of the fence around the Messenian camp in the battle of the fourth year of war (Paus. 4.7.3–6). For borrowings from Thucydides, see Jacoby 1943: 125–7 and Pearson 1962: 413.
[54] The story is reported in detail by Pausanias (4.9.3–10). For the attractive suggestion that the sacrifice was intended to atone for the death of the Spartan maidens, who in Pausanias' version of the Limnai affair (4.4.2) had committed suicide after the rape, see Berg 1998: 41–2 and 46. She also notes astutely that the herald who brought back from Delphi the oracle was called Tisis, which in Greek means "retribution."

Tyrtaeus.[55] One further peculiarity of his history of the First Messenian War was that it included the Messenian hero Aristomenes, whom most other authors associated with the second war.[56]

Tellingly, Pausanias' narrative of the operations of the First Messenian War has almost no topographic detail.[57] We learn that the Spartans stormed the Messenian town of Ampheia at the beginning of the war and then used it as their base of operation,[58] but nothing is said as to where the two major battles, in the fourth and fifth year of the war, took place. Interestingly, in the first war Pausanias gives a decentralized impression of the Messenians. The Spartans, operating from Ampheia, are said to have been unable to conquer the cities of Messenia because of their strong fortifications (4.7.2), and only after the undecided battle of the fifth year did the Messenians decide to concentrate at Ithome (4.9.1). Once Ithome had fallen, the Spartans conquered the other cities of Messenia (4.14.2). These short and allusive references suggest that the awareness that Messenia did not consist only of one main central settlement may have been more pronounced in Myron's work than it ends up being in Pausanias, whose vision of early Messenia in general, and of the wars in particular, is in many ways resolutely centripetal. This tantalizing hint of a link between Myron's putative image of Messenia and the political relations between the main settlement of Ithome and the rest of Messenia from the mid fourth to the mid third century (below, pp. 254–64) deserves to be noticed.

In this respect, too, Rhianus' epic poem *Messeniaka*, tentatively dated to the second half of the third century,[59] may have marked a sea change. Pausanias' topography of the Second Messenian War is much clearer but also in a sense much narrower than his topography of the first. Everything

---

[55] Paus. 4.6.4 = Myron *FgrHist* 106 F 3. This idiosyncratic notion makes it possible to discover traces of Myron's Messenian oeuvre in other ancient authors, e.g. Plut. *Life of Agis* 21.2. Myron's attitude is stigmatized by Jacoby 1943: 124 as "indifference towards anything that is really historical and factual."

[56] Paus. 4.6.3 = Myron *FgrHist* 106 T 1. For this reason, Diodorus' account of the First Messenian War in book VIII, preserved only in fragments, is highly likely to come from Myron – Jacoby prints it as an appendix to Myron's fragments, *FgrHist* 106 F 8–14. On Myron and Diodorus see also Pearson 1962: 414.

[57] See Jacoby 1943: 124–5.

[58] The only detail useful for a localization of Ampheia is that the Spartans were able from there to intercept communications between the Messenians and Delphi (Paus. 4.9.3). For the identification of Ampheia with the fortified settlement of Kastro Gardiki, that controlled two passes from Messenia towards the region of Megalopolis, see Pikoulas 1987–88.

[59] See Pfeiffer 1968: 122, 148–9, Castelli 1994b: 73–9 and Cameron 1995: 298–9, the latter two pointing to Callimachus' influence on him. The fragments are collected in Castell 1998.

happens in the northeastern part of the region, and the action revolves around a small number of well-identified foci, Mount Ithome, the plain of Stenykleros, Andania, and the fortress of Eira in the valley of the river Neda, which marked the northern border of Messenia towards Arcadia. In other words, the war is clearly confined to what, from the liberation of Messenia onwards, was the territory of the polis of Ithome – which by the time Rhianus was writing may have been called already Messene. The only other parts of Messenia that are mentioned explicitly by Pausanias are Pylos and Mothone, whose inhabitants migrate to Sicily at the end of the war.[60] It looks as if, in the context of Pausanias' Second Messenian War, "the Messenians" meant essentially the inhabitants of the territory of the future city of Ithome/Messene. On the other hand, raids conducted by the hero of the story, the Messenian Aristomenes, extend to Sparta itself and to some famous landmarks and some lesser-known places in the Spartan territory, such as Karyai, the otherwise unknown town of Aigila, Pharis, and Amyklai.[61]

Rhianus' poem appears to have been focused uncompromisingly on the Messenian hero Aristomenes. In locating him in the Second Messenian War, Rhianus followed earlier authors, such as Callisthenes, who called this war the "Aristomenian war."[62] Pausanias (4.6.3) declared that in Rhianus' *Messeniaka* Aristomenes shone no less splendidly than Achilles in the *Iliad*. Wilamowitz called the poem *Räuberilias*, "a bandits' *Iliad*."[63] We cannot object to Pausanias' judgment, in view of his direct knowledge of the poem, but the kind of stories he associated with Aristomenes does suggest that the latter must have been an epic hero of sorts: wounded in more or less honorable places (4.16.8), captured by the enemy a number of times (4.18.4, 19.4), on occasion saved by women (4.17.1, 19.5–6), engaging with various outcome in mass kidnapping of Spartan maidens and matrons (4.16.9, 17.1), he does not really resemble a Homeric hero.

---

[60] Paus. 4.18.1 and then 23.1. However, there is no positive reason to believe, and some reason to doubt, that this detail came from Rhianus (see below, p. 151).

[61] Both in the case of Aigila and in that of Pharis, one wonders if Aristomenes' feats might not have taken place in Messenia itself. Paus. 4.16.8 may suggest that actually the cattle raid was placed by his sources in Pharai, not Pharis. As for Aigila, the fact that the priestess of Demeter figured in the procession of the mysteries of Andania, at least in the first century AD (*IG* V 1, 1390, line 31; for the date, see below, pp. 298–9), seems more easily explained if the place was in Messenia than if it was in Laconia. However, both places are said by Pausanias to be in the *Lakonikē* (4.16.8 and 17.1 respectively), and further evidence seems to suggest a localization of Aigila in Laconia, see Shipley 1997: 267–8.

[62] This choice would be particularly pointed if he wrote later than Myron, as most scholars now tend to think, *pace* Jacoby (see above, n. 59).

[63] Wilamowitz 1900: 106; cf., however, Jacoby 1943: 165.

Apollonius' Jason is probably a more appropriate comparison.[64] Rhianus was clearly a good representative of the poetic culture of his times. He is known as an author of sophisticated erotic epigrams and of critical editions of both Homeric poems, and his *Messeniaka* will have been just as *à la page*. It is really a pity that so little is documented of his epic works. His longest fragment in hexameters, of unidentified provenance, had long been taken as a polemic against the divinisation of kings, but recent scholarship has doubted that the passage expresses a real political agenda.[65] Other works of his, documented only by lexicographers, include *Achaika* in at least four books, *Eliaka* in at least three, *Thessalika* in at least sixteen, and a *Herakleia* in at least fourteen.[66] Apart perhaps from the last, they all fall in the purview of a genre of Hellenistic poetry in hexameters that Jacoby called "ethnographic epos," whose topic was the sum of the old traditions of a given region or city.[67] This genre was not a pure exercise in erudition without connections to the real world; rather the opposite. As we know from epigraphic evidence, Hellenistic political communities were very keen on having their early history, or rather myth-history, celebrated in verse, and a host of wandering poets catered to this need.[68] We do not know if Rhianus ever left Crete, but the titles of his works link him with this world of celebration of civic pride.[69]

In spite of the fact that they formally belonged to different genres, if we look at them in terms of function and audience the works of Rhianus and Myron were probably much less different from one another than we might have thought. Hellenistic inscriptions honor both poets and, even more frequently, authors of prose works for merits acquired in celebrating the past of a community. It is clear that ethnographic poems could have precisely the same function as encomiastic local historiography. Although formally different, the two genres seem to have been functionally interchangeable.[70] That both Myron's and Rhianus' works in fact belong in this context has not been clearly recognized, most likely because of an

---

[64] See Castelli 1994a: 13–16.
[65] See Cameron 1995: 14–16; in his criticism of earlier overinterpretations of these verses, he might be going too far, cf. Jacoby 1943: 198–9, and see also Castelli 1994b: 81–2 with further references.
[66] Or perhaps four: see Pfeiffer 1968: 148.   [67] Jacoby 1943: 87–9.
[68] See Hardie 1983: 18–21 and the evidence collected in Chaniotis 1988: 322–43. Note e.g. Demoteles of Andros (*IG* IX 4, 544 = *FgrHist* 400 T 1), honored by the Delians in the first half of the third century for having dealt with the sanctuary of Apollo and the polis of the Delians and for having written down the local myths, and Aristodama of Smyrna (*IG* IX 2, 62 = *FgrHist* 483 F 1, around 218 BC), honored by the cities of Lamia and Chaleion for having composed poetry on the *ethnos* of the Aetolians and on the ancestors of the two communities.
[69] See Chaniotis 1988: 371 and n. 1.   [70] See Chaniotis 1988: 362–5 and Cameron 1995: 298.

excessive fixation on their subject matter as opposed to their function. Ethnographic poetry and prose works in praise of cities or *ethnē* seem to have focused normally on the time of the origins, on foundation myths of local cults and mythic relations between communities. Even though there is some evidence that early history could also offer material for celebrations in poetry or prose,[71] the history of one war does not at first sight correspond to the profile of this genre. However, from a Messenian point of view, it could fulfill exactly the same function.

Precisely because it had been part of the Lakedaimonian state for centuries, Messenia did not have much of a mythic heritage that could form the subject matter of a eulogy. The poverty of Messenian archaiologia is still obvious almost six centuries after the liberation, in Pausanias' work. However, scarcity of mythic material was not the only reason that pointed to the Messenian wars as a suitable – if paradoxical – subject matter for an encomiastic reworking of the Messenian past. Polybius (4.32) amply shows that well into the Hellenistic period it was still difficult for the Messenians to shake off a reputation for cowardice, a reputation clearly originating from their supposed incapacity to face the Spartans at the time of the wars and thereafter. The defeat and enslavement at the hands of the Spartans were a stain on the Messenian past, and cried for correction. Narrating the history of the Messenian wars from a resolutely Messenian point of view was an obvious way to try to repair this deficit. Unless Pausanias is seriously misleading, both Myron and Rhianus transformed the wars into a tale of glorious Messenian victories in pitched battles and guerrilla raids. Only treason and trickery brought them down, and no occasion is missed to praise their gallantry in the face of the ruthless Spartans.

In the end, rather than emphasize the fact that their focusing on the history of one single war sets them apart from the rest of works celebrating the local pride of Hellenistic cities, we should probably conclude that the works of Myron and Rhianus show that the Messenian wars were a crucial element of the Messenian past as perceived by the Messenians themselves. Ironically Sparta, the ancestral enemy, remained central to the self-definition of the Messenians well into the Hellenistic period.

A HERO FOR THE MESSENIANS

At this point we, like Pausanias, have to digress in order to deal with the deeds and chronology of one specific Messenian, the gallant Aristomenes.

---

[71] See Chaniotis 1988: 372–7, esp. 372 n. 804.

As we have seen, he was important enough to be included in both Myron's history of the First Messenian War and Rhianus' epic on the Second, and also to be the protagonist of a lost biography by Plutarch.[72] We know from Pausanias that Aristomenes received a heroic cult in Messene (4.32.3). Inscriptions show that the cult dated back at least to the Augustan age,[73] and there is no serious reason to doubt that it was in fact older. The question is, how much older. Pausanias has the Messenians call back Aristomenes at the time of the liberation by Epaminondas (4.27.6), but this is no guarantee that his cult was introduced at that point.[74] If the Messenians really brought Aristomenes' bones back from Rhodes, where the hero was supposed to have died, this may have happened later. Since it is reasonably certain that Aristomenes' death in Rhodes featured in Rhianus' poem (*FgrHist* 265 F 41), one might venture that there was some connection between the poem and the introduction of the cult, on the occasion of the return of the bones, perhaps in the late third century BC.[75]

However, stories about Aristomenes must have been circulating from earlier on. Already for Callisthenes, in the third quarter of the fourth century, the Second Messenian War was the "war of Aristomenes," and there is at least one concrete reason to think that Aristomenes was already prominent at the time of the liberation of Messenia or very soon thereafter. According to Pausanias, after the fall of Eira and the retreat of the Messenians to southern Arcadia, Aristomenes gave his two daughters in marriage to Damothoidas of Lepreon and Theopompos of Heraia, and his sister to Tharyx of Phigaleia.[76] Theopompos and probably also Tharyx come from families that are otherwise attested during the classical period. Two athletes from Heraia, both called Theopompos, won in the pentathlon and wrestling contests at Olympia in the fifth century.[77] An athlete called Narykidas, from Phigaleia, was victorious as a wrestler at Olympia probably in 386 or thereabouts, and since the name is not otherwise attested, it is tempting to correct it to "Tharykidas" in Pausanias' text, all the more so since a Tharykidas from Phigaleia is mentioned in the

---

[72] And to be devoted a book-length study in the early twenty-first century AD: Ogden 2004.
[73] *SEG* 23.207, l. 14; see also *SEG* 35.343 and Themelis 2000: 34.
[74] Pausanias' narrative of what for him is the foundation of Messene is highly distorted to say the least. See below, pp. 151–2.
[75] Such a connection is suggested in C. Castelli's unpublished dissertation, according to Castelli 1994a: 8–9. See also Castelli 1998: 9–10. Note that a priest of Aristomenes is attested in a Rhodian inscription of Imperial date, *IG* XII 1, 8.
[76] Wade-Gery 1966: 292–5 has drawn scholarly attention to Aristomenes' connections.
[77] See Paus. 6.10.4–5 and Nafissi, in Maddoli, Nafissi and Saladino 1999: 245–6.

sympolity treaty between Phigaleia and Messene from around 240 B.C.[78]
Since "Tharykidas" actually means "the son (or descendant) of Tharyx,"
an intended connection between this prominent Phigalean family and
Aristomenes' brother-in-law is more than likely.

Besides the athletic exploits of the descendants of two of them,
Aristomenes' in-laws have something more in common. They all came
from roughly the same area, southwestern Arcadia and Triphylia. This of
course makes sense in purely historical terms: if we want to take these
marriages as historical, than the fact that the grooms came from three
cities close to Eira is reassuring. However, there may be more to this
geographical distribution of marriage connections. While we know next
to nothing about any of these places in the seventh century, their history
in the fifth and fourth centuries has some interesting aspects. Lepreon
seems to have been an independent polis at the time of the Persian wars,
since it sent 200 hoplites to the battle of Plataia (Hdt. 9.28) and its name
appears on the serpent column of Delphi (ML 27). It had entered a
relationship of dependence on Elis some time before the Peloponnesian
War in order to receive protection against the Arcadians – with Phigaleia
in the front line, we would think. During the Peloponnesian War,
Lepreon wrestled its freedom from Elis with the help of the Spartans, who
settled there a garrison formed of freed Helots. Later, Lepreon became
part of the newly formed Triphylian federal state, under the Spartan aegis,
and finally joined the Arcadian League in 370.[79] Heraia may have been
connected to Elis in the early fifth century but was certainly a member of
the Peloponnesian League later during the century, fought on the Spartan
side at the battle of Mantinea in 418, and was forced to join the Arcadian
League after some resistance, presumably in the early 360s.[80] As for
Phigaleia, all we can say is that it was in all likelihood a member of the
Peloponnesian League and then joined the Arcadian League, probably
in 370.[81] It seems safe to conclude that the tradition on the marriages
of Aristomenes' sister and daughters is very unlikely to have originated

---

[78] See Paus. 6.6.1 with Nafissi, in Maddoli, Nafissi and Saladino 1999: 212–13, and *IG* V 2, 419 = Ager
40 = Magnetto 38, line 7. On the sympolity between Messene and Phigaleia see below, p. 257.
[79] On the relations between Lepreon, Elis, and Sparta see now Falkner 1999, who suggests that the
Spartans may have been particularly interested in establishing a presence in that area, just north of
the mouth of the river Neda, because of the threat posed by the Athenian occupation of Pylos (see
below, p. 189). On the emergence of Triphylia as an ethnic and political entity in the early fourth
century, and its final absorption by Arcadia, see Nielsen 1997a.
[80] The relation between Elis and Heraia depends on the reading of *IvO* 9, on which see now Roy
2000: 138 and n. 23. On Heraia, Sparta, and the Arcadian League see Nielsen 2002: 386.
[81] See Nielsen 2002: 588.

before Heraia and Lepreon ceased to be allies of Sparta and became members of the Arcadian League. The years after the liberation of Messenia seem to offer the best context.[82]

This is about as far back into the past as we can get. Aristomenes' adventures have sometimes been interpreted as an expression of a popular tradition that might go back to the centuries of Spartan domination, but the analogies to Hellenistic novel are far more convincing, and point in precisely the opposite direction.[83] If the image of Aristomenes the guerrilla hero that we find in Pausanias has any deeper roots, then one might think of the Messenians who were raiding the *Lakonikē* from Pylos in the years before the Peace of Nicias. Aristomenes would have been a perfect model for them, and the idea that his character may have originated in this connection, either among the Messenians of Naupaktos or among the Helots and *perioikoi* of Messenia, has some attraction. But just as interesting as trying to trace Aristomenes back in time is to observe the stratification in his stories. Some selective explorations of key themes may allow us to get a sense of this process.

Of the many sanctuaries, gods, and heroes that appear in connection with Aristomenes, one is particularly striking because of its location: the oracular sanctuary of Trophonius at Lebadeia. There the hero went, according to Pausanias (4.16.7), following the direction of the oracle of Delphi, to recover his shield, which had been magically stolen by the Dioscuri during a battle. Later, Aristomenes dedicated his shield in the sanctuary, where Pausanias himself saw it. This story makes good sense in the framework of the relations between Thebes and the Messenians, and its origin could be linked either to the liberation of Messenia or to a moment of renewed contact between Messenians and Boeotians which various indices would seem to date to the early second century BC (see below, p. 263). Another passage of Pausanias (4.32.5–6) relates an odd story according to which on the eve of Leuktra the oracle of Trophonius urged Epaminondas to raise a trophy and decorate it with Aristomenes' shield, promising that it would be a guarantee of victory. A Theban

---

[82] Although it cannot be absolutely excluded, it is also less likely that the tradition emerged after the Arcadian League split in 363 (see Nielsen 2002: 490–3); we do not know for sure that Triphylia, Phigaleia, and Heraia did not end all on the same side, but it is not very probable, considering their previous allegiances and later history.

[83] The notion that the quality of the exploits attributed to Aristomenes, especially but not only by Pausanias, suggests the existence of a rich and ancient popular tradition on the Messenian hero has been advanced by Shero 1938: 504 and is now developed by Ogden 2004; however, the adventures of the Messenian hero remind one much more of Hellenistic romance, as rightly pointed out by Auberger 1992a, 1992b.

inscription from the years after Leuktra (*IG* VII 2462 = RO 30) has long been taken as a confirmation of the story,[84] implying that the Thebans indeed knew about the Messenian hero and chose to honor him even before the battle. However, closer analysis of the inscription has shown that, while Pausanias' story seems in some ways to be connected with it, the facts mentioned there are in fact quite different.[85] The story of Aristomenes' shield in the sanctuary of Trophonius is best seen in the context of the peak in his prominence during the third century.

Another sanctuary has a much closer and more important relation to the Messenian hero: the sanctuary of Andania.[86] In Pausanias' narrative, Aristomenes is said to have been born in Andania, and the mystery cult associated with Andania has a big part in the story. Towards the end of the war, once divine signs had made clear that Eira was going to fall, Aristomenes left the city alone at night to go to Mount Ithome and buried there a sacred object that, according to the oracles of one of the founders of the mysteries of Andania, Lycus, guaranteed that the Messenians would win back their freedom in due course – unless, that is, that object were seized by the Spartans (4.20.3–4). At the time of the liberation of Messenia Epiteles, the Argive general in charge of cooperating in what for Pausanias is the foundation of Messene, was guided by a dream to that same object, which turned out to be a bronze box enclosing the texts of the mysteries, inscribed on lead sheets (4.26.7–8). In the dream, Epiteles saw a priest of the mystery cult, allegedly Caucon, the Athenian priest who according to Pausanias had originally instituted it.

The same priest, according to Pausanias' informants, appeared to Epaminondas, too, announcing to him that the time had come to restore to the Messenians their fatherland, since the wrath of the Dioscuri against them had ceased (4.26.7). The wrath of the Dioscuri, Pausanias explains, had been provoked by two young warriors from Andania, called Panormus and Gonippus, who had once massacred a number of Spartans in their

---

[84] See e.g. Jacoby 1943: 175–6. The connection is still accepted by P. A. Hansen in his edition of the inscription in *CEG* 632.

[85] The incompatibility between the events described by Pausanias and those alluded to, rather obscurely, in the inscription has been pointed out by Beister 1973, further refined by Tuplin 1987: 94–107, who also eliminates the implausible idea of a trophy erected before the battle – all the more awkward, since the trophy was an offer to the gods to thank them for the victory. See ibid. 102 for the suggestion that Pausanias' story may be derived in part also from a misinterpretation of the inscription. Tuplin's conclusions are accepted by Rhodes and Osborne, see RO 30.

[86] On the cult of the Karneiasion grove by Andania, apparently one of the most important to post-liberation Messenians, see now the expansive treatment of Deshours 2006, and cf. below, pp. 236–7 and 294–9.

own encampment. The two warriors had arrived at the Spartan camp on horseback, wearing white tunics and red mantles, at a time when the Spartans were celebrating a ritual in honor of the Dioscuri. The Spartans mistook the two for the gods, and Panormus and Gonippus were able to kill many of them (4.27.2–3).

At first sight, the two episodes have little to do with one another. Each taken by its own, the recovery of the sacred box with the text of the mysteries and the end of the wrath of the Dioscuri, fulfills a condition necessary for Messene to be born again; however, the two stories taken together look like a reduplication – all the more so, since the appearance of the priest of the mysteries in Epaminondas' dream links the second story to the cult of Andania, too. The notion that the multiple connections between the mysteries and the rebirth of Messene may be the product of reduplication is reinforced by the peculiar multiple foundations of the mysteries themselves in Pausanias' narrative, involving a sequence of three traveling priests from Attica.[87] In order to make sense of these stories, it is important to be alert to a deformation that somehow obfuscates their consistency: Pausanias' transforming the gods celebrated in the mysteries, from the Great Gods documented by inscriptions at least until the Augustan age, into Great Goddesses. It is not clear if this transformation reflects a real evolution of the cult between the first and second century AD. However, considering Pausanias' tendency to promote the cult of Demeter and Core, the Great Goddesses of Eleusis, to a Panhellenic dimension, it cannot be excluded that the Great Goddesses of Andania are a product of his own bias.[88] As for the Great Gods honored in the mysteries, even though they may originally have been the Boeotian Kabeiroi, by the early first century at the latest they were apparently identified with the Dioscuri.[89]

This of course explains the connection between Epaminondas' dream and the mysteries: the gods whose wrath had to cease for Messene to be liberated were none other than the Great Gods of Andania. It becomes

---

[87] Pausanias (4.1.5–9) has as many as three successive foundations of the mysteries, first by Kaukon, who came from Eleusis to Andania and initiated queen Messene, who gave her name to the region, then by Lykos, also an Athenian, who "enhanced the prestige of the rites" and finally by the Athenian Methapos, who reorganized the mysteries at an unspecified point in time. See Robertson 1988: 240–54 and below, p. 296.

[88] On Pausanias and the cult of Eleusis, see especially Goldmann 1991: 153–4, Piolot 1999: 212–13 and Deshours 2006: 213–18. On his transformation of the Great Gods of Andania into Great Goddesses, see also Robertson 1988: 247–8.

[89] See Pasquali 1912–13: 101 and Deshours 2004: 125 n. 81. Pausanias' religious agenda is discussed below, p. 297. On the Kabeiroi at Andania see below, p. 237.

reasonable and appropriate that the founder of the mysteries should appear to Epaminondas, and it comes as no surprise that the story which according to Pausanias (4.27.1–3) caused the wrath of the Dioscuri turns up in a different source, with Aristomenes as its protagonist (Polyaen. 2.31.4). Pausanias probably wanted to wash his hero of the accusation of impiety.[90] Keeping in mind that the two stories appear amalgamated into a seamless whole in Pausanias' narrative, and may therefore have been modified to fit the context, it is very tempting to attribute them to the two declared sources of Pausanias' history of the Messenian wars. The story of the urn, tied as it is to the context of the second war, would then come from Rhianus' poem, while the story of the wrath of the Dioscuri could come from Myron's work. It may be relevant in this connection that Pausanias does not give a very clear indication as to when the incident occurred,[91] which would be understandable if he took the story from a source that told it in the context of the First Messenian War, according to Myron's date for Aristomenes. In other words, the two stories that link the resurgence of Messene to the cult of Andania probably testify to the importance of this cult for the identity of third-century Messenians.[92] The fact that Pausanias included both stories, as in general his emphasis on the importance of the cult, is certainly a partial consequence of his use of third-century sources, but may also have something to do with a revival of the cult in the first century AD (below, pp. 294–9).

PAUSANIAS' WARS

This brings us finally to confront the richest source for the history of the Messenian Wars, Pausanias' *Description of Greece*. Investigating the

[90] Note that the impious implications of the episode are much less strong in Pausanias' version than in Polyaenus'. The latter depicts the slaughter of the Spartans, caught in the midst of a religious festival, as a planned action, with Aristomenes and his companion disguising themselves as the Dioscuri better to surprise their enemy. In Pausanias, on the contrary, it looks as if Panormus and Gonippus simply exploited a favorable opportunity that had come about accidentally.

[91] He simply says "before the battle at Stenykleros" (4.27.1), which should refer to the battle of Kaprousema, the second great battle of the war, that took place in Stenykleros (4.15.8). The sacrilege would explain why, in that battle, the Dioscuri stole Aristomenes' shield (4.16.5) – which of course makes best sense if Aristomenes had been the perpetrator of the offence. If the battle mentioned in 4.27.1 is really Kaprousema, then it should be noted that it falls in the part of the Second Messenian War that, according to Pausanias himself, had not been dealt with by Rhianus (4.6.2). For the first part of that war, Pausanias presumably used some other source, or indeed adapted episodes from Myron's narrative of the first war.

[92] But it is important to keep in mind that this attribution is rather hypothetical and the stories, or one of them, might actually be even significantly later, connected with the reform of the cult carried out by Mnasistratus possibly in the year 24 AD – after all, it is doubtful that the Dioscuri could have been called Great Gods before the second century BC (see below, p. 237).

development of ancient representations of the Messenian Wars, we have already in various occasions uncovered the internal stratification of Pausanias' text. However, it is important to remind ourselves that we are not dealing with a true stratigraphy, formed of juxtaposed layers with little contamination. The historical excursus in Pausanias' fourth book cannot be regarded as the result of a simple process of cutting and pasting earlier sources. Even though accurate scrutiny may make it possible to recognize, always hypothetically, elements that reflect earlier historical contexts and go back to the works of earlier authors, it is crucial to appreciate that in Pausanias' narrative such elements have been amalgamated to form what reads as a remarkably seamless narrative sequence. The fact that the two authorities mentioned by Pausanias, Myron and Rhianus, not only did not complete each other, but were in some aspects mutually incompatible, suggests significant reworking of their accounts. That the traces of such reworking are not more visible should not mislead us into underestimating the extent of the phenomenon – rather the opposite.[93]

In Pausanias' narrative, the hostility between Spartans and Messenians started in the generation before the First Messenian War, under the reign of Phintas in Messenia and of Teleklos at Sparta, when the Limnai incident took place. The fact that the war did not begin until much later is taken by Pausanias as an argument for the conclusion that the Spartans did not really think that they had been wronged by the Messenians (4.4.3). Then, a generation later, another incident happened, when the Spartan Euaephnus stole some cattle that the Messenian Polychares, winner of the stadium race in the fourth Olympiad (764 BC), had entrusted to him. The story escalated, Euaephnus killed Polychares' son, and finally Polychares started to kill every Spartan he ran into. This, together with the murder of Teleklos and Kresphontes' deceit, was brought forward by the Spartans as their reason to go to war (4.5.1), while the Messenians retorted that the real motive was that the Spartans coveted the fertile land of Messenia – out of their inborn greed and lack of Panhellenic patriotism, of which they would show more examples in subsequent history (4.5.3–4).

Before the war really broke out, a rather surprising turn of events took place in Messenia. For reasons that are not made clear, Phintas was

<hr>

[93] It is difficult to tell with certainty whether such reworking was Pausanias' own work or derived from his direct source, which would then be an anonymous author who in his turn adapted the accounts of Myron and Rhianus, as Jacoby 1943 thought; on a possible historical context for such an author, see below, pp. 299–300. In any case, Pausanias' own contribution should not be underestimated; see Pearson 1962: 414 n. 41.

succeeded by his two sons, Antiochus and Androcles (4.4.4). When the Spartans delivered an ultimatum asking for Polychares to be handed over to them, a controversy broke out among the two brothers, with Antiochus favoring the hard line and Androcles pleading for reconciliation with the Spartans. Finally, two factions coalesced around the two brothers and in the ensuing civil strife the supporters of Androcles were massacred (4.5.6–7).[94]

Antiochus reigned alone for a few months and died, to be succeeded by Euphaes, who led the Messenians in the first part of the war (4.5.8). The war began in the second year of the ninth Olympiad (743/2 BC), fifth year of the archonship of Aesimides at Athens (4.5.10), and lasted for twenty years. The Spartans' first move consisted in seizing Ampheia, a small town on the border between Laconia and Messenia, without any previous declaration of war. From there, they raided Messenia, abducting cattle from the countryside and attacking the cities, but without being able to conquer any of them. As for the Messenians, they responded by plundering the coastal towns of Laconia and the countryside around the Taygetos (4.7.2). Then, after four years, King Euphaes suddenly decided to lead the army against the Spartans. As soon as the latter realized that the Messenian army was on campaign, they also marched out to face them. A rather odd battle followed, in which Euphaes' strategy seems to have consisted of putting his army in a position in which the Spartans could not attack it. A year after this stalemate, the Spartans marched out again, urged on by the reproach of their elders, and a new battle followed. This time the fight was real, both sides took many casualties and the result was again a draw.

At this point, weariness started taking hold of the Messenians, who were also struck by a plague. The king decided to concentrate them all at Ithome, a place easy to defend, and ask Apollo for instructions. The oracle answered requesting the sacrifice of a virgin of the house of Aipytos, selected by lot.[95] The lot fell on the daughter of the Aipytid Lykiskos, but the seer Epebolos prevented her from being sacrificed, saying that she had been in fact adopted as a child. Meanwhile, to be on the safe side,

---

[94] This strange story may have been prompted by the fact that some of Pausanias' sources mentioned the conflict among the Messenians in connection with the Limnai affair, when the Messenian faction that wanted to make reparations to the Spartans was expelled and finally went on to participate in the foundation of Rhegion; see below, pp. 157–9.

[95] Note that built into the oracle is the development of the story: the oracle says that, should the sacrifice prove impossible, the Messenians would be allowed to sacrifice another virgin offered voluntarily.

Lyciscus fled to Sparta with his daughter. To save the situation, the Aipytid Aristodemos, who appears here for the first time, offered his own daughter, but her fiancé tried to save her by alleging that she was not a virgin. The enraged Aristodemos killed his daughter and cut her open to refute the allegation. Epebolos at first pointed out that murder could not satisfy the god, and so it was necessary for another virgin of Aipytid blood to be sacrificed, but then Euphaes managed to persuade him to tell the Messenians that the request of the god had been satisfied, and of course all the Aipytids concurred.

Six years after this episode the Spartans marched against Ithome (4.10.1). Yet another fierce but undecided battle followed, in the course of which Euphaes was fatally wounded. He died childless soon thereafter, and the Messenians chose as his successor the popular Aristodemos, in spite of the sacrilege. In the fifth year of his reign, after years of guerrilla warfare, a large pitched battle took place, with both sides flanked by their allies, and the Spartans were soundly defeated. At this point, Apollo came to their rescue, suggesting that the land of the Messenians, originally acquired by Kresphontes by deceit, would now fall to deceit. Another oracle, given to the Messenians, stated that the war would be won by the party that first dedicated 100 tripods to Zeus Ithomatas. The oracle leaked and a cunning Spartan called Oibalos was able to preempt the Messenians by smuggling into the sanctuary 100 clay tripods hidden in his sack. At this point a number of unfavorable omens happened and Aristodemos lost confidence and committed suicide on the tomb of his daughter. The Messenians elected a general and fought on for some months, while the war turned into a siege. Finally, they abandoned Ithome. Those among them who had guest-friends abroad fled, the others went back to their towns, which were attacked and conquered by the Spartans. So the First Messenian War came to an end, in the first year of the fourteenth Olympiad (724/3 BC), the twentieth year of war, as required by Tyrtaeus' verses.

The period between the two wars is disposed of very quickly. We hear that the Spartans settled in Messenia the Asinaeans, exiled from the Argolid, who founded here a new Asine, and the descendants of Androklos, who received the district of Hyamia.[96] The Messenians who remained at home were subjected to harsh conditions (see below), and as soon as a new generation grew up, especially in Andania, times were ripe for revolt.

---

[96] Probably identical with the Hyamitis mentioned by Ephoros (*FgrHist* 70 F 116 in Strab. 8.4.7) as one of the regions into which Kresphontes divided Messenia.

After establishing clandestine contact with their old allies, the Argives and the Arcadians, the Messenians rose in the thirty-ninth year after the fall of Ithome, fourth year of the twenty-third Olympiad (685/4 BC), in the third generation after the First War – again, Tyrtaeus' chronology is respected. Three major battles were fought in the first three years of the war, interspersed by Aristomenes' incursions into the Spartan territory. Again, the topography of the battles is rather vague, but at least they have names; one of them is said to take place in Stenykleros, and in general one has the impression that they may have had a precise location after all, unlike the battles of the First War. The first battle, fought in a place called Derai by the Messenians and Spartans alone, without allies, was essentially a draw; the second, fought in Stenykleros at the place where Heracles had exchanged oaths with the Neleids on a sacrificed boar, was a Messenian victory, while in the third, the battle of the Great Trench, the treason of the Arcadian king Aristokrates gave the victory to the Spartans.

At this point, rather surprisingly, Aristomenes persuades the Messenians to abandon all their cities, including Andania, and concentrate in a place called Eira, in the valley of the Neda river, at the northern end of the region. Only the inhabitants of Pylos and Mothone stayed home. Eira was besieged for eleven years, while Aristomenes conducted guerrilla actions in the Spartan territory and perhaps in Messenia itself. Finally, it came once again to deceit that brought down the Messenians, framed in a story of adulterous love between a Messenian woman and a renegade Spartan herdsman, who in the end deserted back to the Spartans and showed them the way into the fortress of Eira. After a long and desperate fight, Aristomenes led the Messenians' flight to Arcadia. From there, most of the exiles joined the Messenians from the coastal cities of Mothone and Pylos in a colonial expedition to Sicily. Invited by the Diagorid Damagetos, who married his daughter, Aristomenes went to Rhodes, in hopes of enlisting Ardys king of Lydia and Phraortes king of Media as allies, but died of illness on the island. Eira, says Pausanias, fell in the first year of the twenty-eighth Olympiad (668/7 BC; 4.23.4).

This summary hardly does justice to the variety and the wealth of detail and side-stories of Pausanias' narrative. Its chronological precision is unparalleled in any other extant portion of Greek historical narrative of the archaic age.[97] Considering the deficiencies and inconsistencies in the sources he was using, Pausanias or his immediate source did a very thorough job indeed – from a modern scholar's perspective, one would

---

[97] For one possible inconsistency, see Musti, in Musti and Torelli 1994: 230–1.

have wished that he had been a bit less successful in hiding the traces of his reworking of the sources. It is certainly possible, in general terms, to venture suggestions as to the provenance of one or the other portion of the story, but in the end no single detail that is attested only in Pausanias can be taken to derive from an earlier author. The history of the Messenian wars in book IV of the *Description of Greece* is and remains a text from the second century AD, the product of a very creative engagement with previous works.

Besides being smooth in terms of narrative flow, Pausanias' story of the wars is also absolutely consistent in terms of bias. The Messenians, with few exceptions easily explained by human nature, are constantly acting in the right. They do all they can to avoid the war, and once they have been attacked, they fight with bravery and fairness to defend their fatherland. Only treason and deceit cause their defeat, and at the bottom of their souls they remain unconquered. Their opponents the Spartans are the exact opposite. They have to be scolded by their old people to march into battle (4.7.7) and seem to think that glory consisted in enslaving other Greeks (4.7.9). Their strength is not a result of inborn bravery but of the discipline they have been trained to since childhood (4.8.6). They have no problem in stooping to deceit and corruption in order to gain the upper hand in the conflict, and greed is their only true motive.[98]

The story of the Messenian wars stands out among the historical excursuses of Pausanias for its length and comprehensiveness. The idea, sometimes voiced, that Pausanias devoted so much attention to history because Messenia did not offer monuments to speak of, can hardly be taken seriously. After all, nothing prevented him from cutting Messenia shorter and merging it with some other region. His must clearly be seen as a positive choice, not as a *faute de mieux*. It has been observed that Pausanias' attitude to historical information is quite peculiar, in that he tends to avoid repeating what has already been dealt with in satisfactory detail by those he considers his most prominent predecessors, above all Herodotus. In the case of the history of the Messenian wars he must have felt that his classical predecessors had left a gap that needed to be filled.[99] This he did, synthesizing and amalgamating the detailed but incomplete accounts of Myron and Rhianus or abridging the work of an earlier author who had done just that, absorbing and probably consciously appropriating the bias of his written sources and probably also of his Messenian

---

[98] On Pausanias' contrasting depictions of Messenians and Spartans, see Auberger 2001: 264–74.
[99] On all this, see Moggi 1993 with further references.

informants,[100] and creating a final product whose very quality makes it all but useless as evidence on the events it ostensibly deals with.

ARCHAIC MESSENIA: CONQUEST AND ENSLAVEMENT

As far as the archaic age is concerned, the end of the Second Messenian War represents in the sources the end of the political history of Messenia. What followed was the exile or enslavement of the Messenians, and then the time without events of the Spartan domination. Ancient views of the fate of the Messenians after the Spartan conquest of their land can be showed to have changed over time even more clearly than the history of the wars. The earliest positive evidence comes from Thucydides. Relating the uprising against Sparta that exploded in Messenia after the earthquake in the 460s, Thucydides (1.101.2) noted, as we saw, that the majority of the Helots who revolted were descendants of the "old Messenians," who had been enslaved in the past (Thucydides simply says τότε, probably meaning "on that well-known occasion").[101] It is no accident that the first mention of the enslavement of the Messenians should appear in the context of the fifth-century revolt, given the central importance that their Messenian identity had for the rebels. Thucydides' allusion to the enslavement is rather vague, and he does not explain whose descendants the other Helots were, who also took part in the uprising, nor does he say explicitly whether the revolt was confined to Messenia or raged in Laconia, too. Considering that the few topographic details on the revolt that we find in early sources consistently refer to Messenia, it is perhaps more likely that Thucydides thought that not all the Helots living west of the Taygetos were descendants of the "old Messenians."

With the liberation of most of Messenia by Epaminondas in 369, the fate of the "old Messenians" became a hotly debated issue, tied as it was to conflicting claims, on the one hand the right of Sparta to control the region, on the other the right of the new Messenian polity to be recognized as legitimate.[102] Isocrates' *Archidamos*, our only evidence for the Spartan take on this question, has much more to say on how Messenia had come to form part of the Spartan state than about the fate of the Messenians after their land had been conquered. Besides stating rather

---

[100] On Pausanias and second-century AD Messenians, see below, pp. 323–7.

[101] See Ducat 1990: 132 and Whitby 1994: 116 n. 38, and below, p. 195. The interpretation of this passage is discussed in Luraghi 2002c.

[102] The recognition of Messene as a sovereign state was a stumbling block in attempts at renewing the common peace in the 360s; see Jehne 1994: 80–5 and 96–7 and below, p. 222.

casually that the Spartans expelled those who were guilty of murdering Kresphontes (*Archid.* 32), Isocrates-Archidamus insists strongly on the fact that the citizens of the new polity founded by the Thebans in 369 were not, as he says, "the true Messenians," that is, descendants of the people the Spartans had fought against, but rather Helots, former slaves of the Spartans (*Archid.* 28 and 87–8). In other words, the Messenians were no longer there, and the Helots living in Messenia and forming, in the Spartan perspective, the citizen body of the new Messene were not the descendants of the free Messenians of old, and therefore had no legitimate right to the land the Thebans had given them. Predictably, Archidamus does not feel the need to address the question of who the Helots of Messenia really were. The Spartiates, while devising a set of ritualized practices that construed the Helots as a group,[103] do not seem to have been inclined to entertain the notion that the Helots formed in any sense an ethnic group. At any rate, they consistently refused to recognize the Messenian identity of the fifth-century rebels, even after they allowed them to leave Ithome.[104] Archidamus' position on the identity of the Helots living in Messenia confirms that considering the Helots as an ethnic group was not something the Spartans were inclined to do, and understandably so, if one considers the implicit claim to a fatherland that is intrinsic to any ethnic group.[105]

The Theban-Messenian point of view on this issue can be reconstructed only tentatively and indirectly, using later sources. Rather surprisingly, or perhaps not so surprisingly, the Theban "party line" seems to have agreed with the Spartans' – as identified on the basis of the *Archidamos* – on a crucial point: the assumption that no Messenians were living in Messenia at the time of the liberation by the Thebans. Where the Theban-Messenian version of course sharply disagreed from the Spartan one, was in maintaining that the citizens of the new Messenian polity were indeed Messenians, the descendants of the "old Messenians" who had been exiled to various places at various points in time and returned to their old fatherland, freed by Epaminondas.[106] It seems clear that the Thebans and their allies depicted the foundation of the new independent Messenian polity as a return, not a liberation, of the Messenians. As for

---

[103] On the practices of ritualized contempt, which were supposed to instill in the Helots the sense of their irreparable inferiority, see below, p. 204 and n. 110.

[104] This is shown by the conditions of the truce which allowed the rebels to leave the Peloponnese; see Thuc. 1.103.1, discussed below, p. 198.

[105] On the Spartans' attitude and its logic, see Figueira 1999: 221–2.

[106] Sources and discussion below, pp. 219–23.

the citizens of the new polity, whoever they were, wherever they came from, to be associated with former slaves would not have been very attractive for them. In the dawn of the new Messene, the supposed Messenian origin of the Helots west of the Taygetos seems to have been forgotten by all and everybody.

The problem was bound to resurface, however, in the works of a historian like Ephorus, less directly sensitive to the claims and counter-claims of the parties involved and more interested in producing a con-sistent and reasonable history of the archaic Peloponnese. Like Plato, Ephorus attributed great significance to the early history of Dorian Messenia. Conflicts between the Dorian kings and their subjects had caused an early involvement of the Spartans, who had taken control of the region well before the First Messenian War (above, p. 63). While there is no reason to doubt that for Ephorus the conquered Messenians had been turned into Helots at a certain point, it is not possible to say with cer-tainty at which point this had happened. The excerpt from Nicolaus on the fate of Aipytos' dynasty (*FgrHist* 90 F 34) speaks of enslavement in connection with the Spartan takeover, but one should probably not put too much weight on this, since this information comes in the very last sentence of the excerpt, which may well be telescoping what the original text depicted as a longer process. In a passage of Diodorus, which covers more evenly the whole history of Messenia from Nestor to Epaminondas and is commonly recognized as deriving from Ephorus, a clear distinction is visible between the period when the Spartans were κύριοι of Messenia, after the descendants of Kresphontes lost the kingship (15.66.2), and the situation that obtained after the First Messenian War, when the Messenians became slaves of the Spartans (15.66.3). Furthermore, in Ephorus' version of the story of the foundation of Taras, reported by Strabo (*FgrHist* 70 F 216 *ap.* Strab. 6.3.3), reference is made in passing to the fact that after the first war the Spartans apportioned the Messenian land among themselves. It seems more likely on the whole that in Ephorus' view the Messenians or some of them had been Helotized as a result of the First Messenian War.[107]

Interestingly, Ephorus' version of the Spartan conquest of Messenia bears an important similarity to Isocrates', in that it presupposes a rather early date for the Spartan takeover.[108] Of course, Ephorus had a much more precise reconstruction of the stages of this process, based in part on a more scrupulous use of Tyrtaeus' poems as evidence. One obvious result

---

[107] See Kiechle 1959: 60.   [108] This has been noted already by Niese 1891: 6.

was assigning to the final conquest a significantly lower date than the one implied by Isocrates' rather confused hints. However, it is noteworthy that a work as influential as Ephorus' *Universal History* should have been so respectful of the Spartan viewpoint. At the same time, on the basis of the passage of Diodorus just mentioned (15.66.5), Ephorus may have taken on board one important tenet of the Theban-Messenian version of the liberation of Messenia, that is, the notion that the Messenians had finally deserted their land after the failure of the revolt of the fifth century – but on this point, as we have seen, Spartans and Thebans were in paradoxical agreement.[109]

The other most influential historian of the fourth century alongside Ephorus, Theopompus of Chios, may not have followed him on this last point. In a fragment from his work *Hellenica* (*FgrHist* 115 F 13 *ap*. Athen. 6.272a), describing, perhaps in conjunction with Kinadon's conspiracy,[110] the hard plight of the Helots, Theopompus specifies that they had been subject to the Spartans for a very long time and were in part Heleatai, who had formerly inhabited a place called Helos, in Laconia, and in part from Messene. Since the passage cannot refer to the situation before the revolt in mid fifth century, we have to conclude that Theopompus considered the Helots living in Messenia after the revolt to be descendants of the "old Messenians."[111] In his case, what one would like to know is how he described the refoundation of Messene by Epaminondas. However, both in his case and in Ephorus' we should not forget that all we have are fragments or passages by later authors, which may distort their views.

From the Hellenistic period, which was certainly decisive for the construction of a Messenian past, and saw dramatic transformations in the Spartans' views of their past, too,[112] no direct evidence has survived to document how the fate of the "old Messenians" after the conquest of their land was being conceptualized, and our appreciation of this depends on our willingness to recognize the outlines of third-century authors in Pausanias' work – a delicate operation under the best circumstances. Even though we happen to know that Myron was interested in the hard plight

---

[109] If this reconstruction is correct, one would like to know who were, in Ephorus' view, the Helots who lived in Messenia at the time of the liberation. The idea that not all the Helots living in Messenia were actually descendants of the "old Messenians" is probably also implicit in Thucydides' description of the rebels in the 460s.

[110] As suggested by Jacoby 1930: 357.

[111] For a more detailed discussion of Theopompus' views on Helotry, see Luraghi 2003: 127–9.

[112] Particularly in connection with the reforms of Agis the Fourth and Cleomenes the Third; on the reinvention of Spartan tradition in this period, see most recently Flower 2002: 195–208 with further references.

of the Helots (106 F 1–2), we cannot tell anything for sure about his views of the consequences of the First Messenian War for the vanquished Messenians. The mere fact that he spoke about Helotry at all suggests that, in his view, the Messenians were reduced to this condition already after the first war; admittedly, this suggestion would inspire more confidence if Pausanias did not say that Myron had not narrated the history of the war down to its end. As for Rhianus, only speculation based on Pausanias may lead to the assumption that he dated the reduction of the Messenians to the state of Helots after the second war.[113]

The next explicit evidence on this issue dates to the late first century BC and comes from the works of Diodorus Siculus, Pompeius Trogus, Nicolaus of Damascus, and Strabo. However, these authors mostly reflect – and, as we have seen, often explicitly refer to – the views of mainstream fourth-century historiography, particularly of Ephorus, who clearly enjoyed a very high prestige in their age.[114] Therefore, first-century sources are on the whole more useful in reconstructing the views of earlier historians. To find an identifiably new stage in the development of ancient ideas on what had happened to the Messenians after the Spartans had conquered their land we have to reach the second century AD and, again, the work of Pausanias.

In Pausanias' prodigiously detailed narrative, the fate of the Messenians is described very precisely and step by step. The First Messenian War ended with those Messenians who had guest-friends in other places, mostly in the Peloponnese, leaving their fatherland, and the others surrendering to the Spartans (4.14.1). Pausanias' description of the hard conditions of the surrender imposed upon the Messenians by the Spartans is based on some verses of Tyrtaeus discussed earlier in this chapter (4.14.4–5). One important element mentioned by Pausanias that is not found in Tyrtaeus' verses is the oath not to revolt against Sparta.[115] This hard and humiliating plight was not yet Helotry, and Pausanias uses Tyrtaeus to make this point. On the contrary, the defeated Messenians

---

[113] It is not surprising that Myron's and Rhianus' views on the plight of the Messenians who remained in their land to be enslaved by the Spartans should not emerge very clearly from the sources; as Asheri 1983: 29 points out, a pro-Messenian perspective was bound to focus on the brave who had chosen exile.

[114] For Diodorus' use of Ephorus, particularly for the history of mainland Greece in book 15, see Stylianou 1998: 49–50. For Nicolaus, see Jacoby 1926: 233–4. Strabo explicitly quotes Ephorus on Helotry (8.5.4 = 70 F 117).

[115] It is surprising that Pausanias did not suppress this detail, which made of the Messenian revolt led by Aristomenes an act of perjury. This may be one more example of the force of the Spartan views on early Messenian history, noted above, p. 104.

appear to have preserved some level of political organization of their own.[116] After the defeat of the long revolt two generations after the first war, exile brought the Messenians farther away, to southern Italy and Sicily (4.23.5–10), and those who stayed behind were finally reduced to the condition of Helots, or rather "merged with the Helots," as Pausanias says (4.16.1 and 24.5), while the Spartans divided the land among themselves.[117]

Pausanias separated the conquest of Messenia, resulting from the First Messenian War, from the enslavement of the Messenians and their transformation into Helots, which happened after the Second. In a sense, in so doing he replicated the sequence of the Spartan subjugation that we found in Ephorus, except that Pausanias down-dated the first phase to the First Messenian War and the final enslavement to the Second. He was certainly not the only ancient author to do so, and probably not the first. As we have seen, the idea that after the Spartan victory in the first war the Messenians became dependent without being enslaved is also found in Aelian (*VH* 6.1), in a passage which reflects the same verses of Tyrtaeus quoted by Pausanias, but cannot depend on Pausanias himself. Unfortunately, it is impossible to locate in time the ultimate source of Aelian's passage, nor to say with any certainty if Pausanias depends on the same source. The interesting point is that both in Ephorus and in Pausanias the enslavement seems to have been the result of a revolt of the Messenians, a punishment meted out on them by the Spartans.

*   *   *

In Pausanias' narrative, the Messenian "party line" gains its final victory. The time of the enslavement is made as short as possible, all the Messenians choose the road of exile in due course, and free Messene is populated by their descendants, not by slaves freed by the arms of the Thebans. As for the wars, they become a mixture of victories in non-decisive engagements and defeats brought about by treason, and the reader is left in no doubt as to which party is the most deserving. However, it would be wrong to consider the sparse notices found in earlier sources as if they were stray pieces of the same mosaic. Enough evidence has survived to show positively that views on the Spartan conquest of Messenia and the subsequent fate of the Messenians changed significantly in time and from author to

---

[116] See Paus. 4.18.1 and Kiechle 1959: 58–9.

[117] In another passage (3.20.6), Pausanias says that the enslaved Messenians came to be called Helots, although they were Dorians. This probably does not mean that Pausanias thought that Messenia was inhabited only by Dorians at the time of the Spartan conquest: in book 4, he tells how in Messenia the Dorians did not expel the previous inhabitants, that is, the Achaeans (4.3.6).

author, reflecting to a significant extent, although in ways that are not always clear to us, the agendas of the communities who saw those stories as their own past. This is ultimately the most important result of our survey: ancient views of the fate of the Messenians under Spartan domination were by and large shaped in a recognizable way by the struggles for freedom and identity that raged in Messenia during the fifth and fourth centuries, and by the need of the later Messenians to acquire an early history with which they might identify.

CHAPTER 5

Messenia from the Dark Ages to the Peloponnesian War

From the scrutiny of the literary evidence on Messenia from the return of the Heraclids to the Spartan conquest conducted in the previous two chapters, two broad conclusions should result in a reasonably uncontroversial way. The first and positive one is that such evidence sheds interesting light on the struggles for the Messenian past – in fact, for the Messenian present – that took place from the moment when, in the second quarter of the fifth century, Spartan domination of the land west of the Taygetos started being called into question. The second and negative one is that it will never be possible to reconstruct the history of Messenia from the eighth century to the sixth in any detail and with any degree of confidence based on the literary evidence. No matter how many details of Pausanias' early history of Messenia derive ultimately from oral traditions handed down for centuries among the inhabitants of Messenia, the amount of observable deformation is such that it is simply impossible, in the absence of contemporary evidence, to isolate supposedly genuine bits from the flow of the story.

A different but related question is what sort of ethnic identity and collective memory we should expect among the inhabitants of Messenia under Spartan rule – a legitimate and extremely interesting question, but one that has often been approached from a rather unhelpful angle. In scholarship of the second half of the last century, the problem of collective memory in Spartan-dominated Messenia emerged fundamentally as an outgrowth of the older problem of the sources of Pausanias. Once Jacoby had shown conclusively with the instruments of *Quellenkritik* that only a very small amount of information could be traced back to late fourth-century historiography, and almost none really went back to sources contemporary with the Messenian wars, the case for an archaic history of Messenia based on the literary sources – that is, ultimately on Pausanias – had to be supported with arguments of a different kind, basically evoking the collective memory of the defeated Messenians, transmitted underground through the centuries of Spartan rule and finally resurfacing after the liberation. The skeptics responded by pointing out that the Spartan conquest seemed to have caused a break in memory, visible in the fact that the history of pre-conquest Messenia was to a large extent the product of a bricolage based on the early history of Sparta.[1] The loss of Messenian memory could be explained by the social structure of the surviving Messenians, thrown into slavery by the Spartans.

The use of new critical instruments, provided by a keener awareness of the potential of archaeological evidence for illuminating issues related to the construction and articulation of collective identities, has pointed to a way out of this debate, which risked becoming sterile. The sketchy depiction of the "cadres sociaux" of Messenian memory outlined above triggered a more accurate investigation into the actual social structure that might have supported, or failed to support, the transmission of a Messenian memory under Spartan rule, an investigation that involved scrutinizing patterns of settlement and, to some extent, material evidence in pre-liberation Messenia.[2] Even though in its first incarnations this new avenue of research has remained caught in the ancient "master narrative" that resolved early Messenian history in a dichotomy of Helots and Spartiates,[3] rather than approaching the evidence with an open mind for its meaning, it has to be recognized that it has the important merit of finally turning scholarly attention to contemporary evidence, that is, to the archaeology of Messenia before the fourth century. Such an approach deserves being pursued further. With all its limitations, archaeological evidence from Messenia can tell us a number of extremely interesting things, many of which the literary sources would not have led us to expect.

DARK AGE IN MESSENIA

In the Mycenaean period, Messenia was probably the most densely populated region in Greece, and certainly one of the most prosperous.[4]

---

[1] This view has been expressed forcefully by Domenico Musti, see Musti in Musti and Torelli 1994: xv, the Spartan conquest of Messenia had brought about a kind of "deculturation."

[2] This approach has been pioneered by Susan Alcock; see Alcock 2001 and now especially Alcock 2002b: 140–52. A similar attempt at connecting the problem of Messenian tradition with the archaeological evidence from archaic Messenia has been developed by Boehringer 2001.

[3] This is candidly recognized in Alcock 2002b: 153.

[4] Hope Simpson 1981 lists as many as 242 sites from Bronze Age Messenia, as against 90 from Argolid, Corinthia and Megarid and 85 from Boeotia, Eastern Locris, Phocis, Malis and Northern Euboea.

Figure 2 Archaeological map of Messenia

The number of *tholos* tombs, the monumental burial places of Mycenaean elites, found in Messenia vastly outnumbers any other area of Greece.[5] From the early fourteenth century, Mycenaean Messenia came under the control of its most powerful center, Pylos, located on a long ridge dominating the coastal plain to the north of the Bay of Navarino. The kingdom of Pylos, whose economic structure can be reconstructed in a remarkably detailed way thanks to the Linear B documents found in the palace, was organized in two provinces. The so-called "Hither Province" extended west of a line connecting the Aigaleon ridge with Mounts Maglavas and Lykodimos, and finally reaching the Messenian Gulf possibly north of Longà. This was the core of the Pylian kingdom, and at some early stage the kingdom itself was identical with it. The "Further Province" comprised the Pamisos Valley and the Valley of Soulima, reaching the coast of Western Messenia just north of Kyparissia. Its main center, called Leuktron – re-u-ko-to-ro in the Linear B documents – is generally identified with the Mycenaean settlement that lies under Thouria on the Ellinika ridge (see above, p. 28). It may have originally been the capital of an independent kingdom that was later swallowed up by Pylos. Another important center of the province was Nichoria, overlooking the western corner of the Gulf of Messenia, probably ti-mi-to-a-ke-e in the documents.[6] The Hither Province, especially the terraces overlooking the western coast of Messenia, seems to have been more densely populated than the Further Province, whose most important settlements were concentrated on the hills surrounding the southern Messenian plain and the Soulima Valley.[7]

Around 1200 BC, for causes that are still imperfectly understood, the kingdom of Pylos came abruptly to an end, and with it, it seems, the vast majority of settlements in Messenia. Only about 10 per cent of Late Helladic IIIB sites show traces of human presence in the following phase, Late Helladic IIIC (conventionally c. 1180–1060 BC).[8] In the first phase of the Dark Ages, called DA I and dated c. 1075–975 BC, the same situation predominates.[9] Gaps in the material sequences of most sites might suggest

---

[5] See Pelon 1976: 396–403 and now Zavadil 2001.

[6] On Bronze Age Nichoria, see McDonald and Wilkie 1992. On the organization of the kingdom of Pylos, Bennett 1994. For a brief overview of Mycenaean Messenia, see Davis 1998: 53–144.

[7] For maps showing the distribution of Bronze Age settlements in Messenia, see McDonald and Rapp 1972 (pocket maps) and Hope Simpson 1981: 114.

[8] See Eder 1998: 144–61.

[9] The chronology of Dark Age Messenia is based on the sequence of the pottery from Nichoria, the only site of this period that has been subjected to extensive excavation. For the delimitation of the

a further catastrophic event between Late Helladic IIIC and DA I.[10] At any rate, the dozen or so sites that have produced DA I pottery were all frequented already in the Mycenaean period.[11] Also visible in this early phase are the first signs of what will much later become a characteristic phenomenon in Messenia, interest in Bronze Age tombs, both in the form of deposition of possibly votive objects and in the form of secondary burials.[12]

During the tenth and ninth century, or period DA II, the number of sites seems to have remained more or less the same. The amount of evidence, however, increases significantly, and the only site from this period that has been thoroughly excavated, the hill of Nichoria, shows signs of a remarkable development from the phase DA I, with scarcely any sign of building activity, to the phase DA II, when the settlement became a small village of some 200 souls, centered around a rather large apsidal building that harbored a small altar and storage facilities. This building has been plausibly identified as the residence of the local chief, which apparently also functioned as focus for the religious life of the community.[13] It seems reasonable to suppose that a number of the sites from which DA II pottery has been reported may have been of a similar nature. If the evidence were more abundant, we would probably recognize clusters of small settlements centered around a larger one, of the size of Nichoria, ruled by a local chief whose dwelling also performed a religious function.[14] Since no central place has been discovered where the chiefdoms could enter in contact and competition with each other, it has been plausibly suggested that the sanctuary of Olympia could have had such a function in the ninth century. Some of the monumental bronze Geometric tripods dedicated there in the ninth and early eighth centuries might be the remains of competitive conspicuous consumption practiced by individuals of the rank of the chief who inhabited the big house on the Nichoria ridge.[15]

---

periods, see Coulson 1986: 9–11. Messenian DA I corresponds to the phases more commonly called Sub-Mycenaean and Protogeometric.

[10] Eder 1998: 161–2.

[11] On Messenian DA I pottery, see Coulson 1986: 12–27.

[12] See Antonaccio 1995: 77 (Koukounara, tomb α 1) and 88 (Nichoria, tomb Nikitopoulos 6).

[13] Mazarakis Ainian 1997: 74–9 with further references. On the "altar" in the building, see Antonaccio 1995: 205; on life at Nichoria in the Dark Ages, see Thomas and Conant 1999: 36–59.

[14] For this reconstruction of the political landscape of Iron Age Messenia, see Morgan 1990: 68–78.

[15] Morgan 1990: 89–90 and 93. In support of her argument for the Messenian origin of a significant proportion of the tripods, see the Geometric tripod leg from Ithome published in Maaß 1978: 33–4, n. 57 and pl. 67 (first half of the eighth century).

In spite of evidence pointing to increase in population, in the tenth and ninth centuries Messenia was still a rather peripheral corner of the Greek world. Messenian DA II pottery belongs in the Western Greek *koinē* that embraces much of the western Peloponnese and Laconia, and furthermore Ithaca, Aetolia and Acarnania.[16] Specific signs of influence from Laconia, especially in sites such as Volimos, on the Messenian side of the Taygetos ridge, and on the Messenian Gulf, have attracted scholars' attention in view of the later history of the region.[17] Interestingly, the heaviest concentration of Dark Age sites remains in the Navarino plateau, the area of Mycenaean Pylos.[18] The Mycenaean past was clearly very visible for Dark Age Messenians, who in some cases continued building tombs in the Bronze Age tradition of the *tholos* and more generally seem to have taken inspiration from Bronze Age tombs for the shapes of the more prestigious among their own graves.[19] Burials of DA II date in Bronze Age tombs are definitely attested for Tholos I at Tragana,[20] north of the Bay of Navarino and the Osmanaga Lagoon, and for Tomb 6 of the chamber tomb necropolis on the east side of the Ellinika ridge, the site of later Thouria.[21]

Dark Age settlements in Messenia seem to have followed the Mycenaean pattern, although on a much smaller scale, perching on hilltops and terraces overlooking the coastal plains and the valleys, rather than occupying the fertile plains themselves. In the vast majority of cases, the sites had been frequented already during the Bronze Age. The only probable exception documented so far is a site that was destined to play a major role in Messenian history thereafter: the area of Mount Ithome. Geometric pottery has been found in soundings conducted at various locations at Mavromati, the site of later Ithome/Messene, and the presence of a settlement on the site since the ninth century, or since the first half of the eighth at the latest, must be considered virtually certain.[22] Although so

---

[16] Coldstream 1968: 220–32; Coulson 1986: 68–9.   [17] Coulson 1986: 71, 76; Eder 1998: 173–4.
[18] Coulson 1986: 71–2.   [19] Eder 1998: 172.
[20] See Coulson 1986: 51–2; Antonaccio 1995: 77; Eder 1998: 154–6; Boehringer 2001: 247.
[21] Chatzi-Spiliopoulou 2001: 293–4. These findings make it more probable that the DA II vases from Thouria discussed in Coulson 1986: 31–5 and Eder 1998: 172–3 also came from a Bronze Age tomb, as noted above, p. 35 n. 58. Materials of DA II date have been found also in the *tholos* of Psari, north of Dorion in the Soulima Valley, according to Chatzi-Spiliopoulou 1998: 537 n. 8; cf. Boehringer 2001: 283.
[22] Geometric sherds have come to light in soundings around the later temple of Asklepios (Themelis, *Praktika* 1987: 87), close to the Klepsydra fountain in the modern village of Mavromati (Themelis, *Praktika* 1988: 45) and to the small temple of Artemis Orthia (Themelis, *Praktika* 1991: 95). Unfortunately, the sherds have not been published in detail. The few that are reproduced in Themelis, *Praktika* 1987: 87 fig. 12 and pl. 68 show a decoration in concentric circles that might suggest a date in the DA II phase, although a DA III date cannot be excluded (cf. Coulson 1986: 32; 52; 66). Notice also the fragment from the leg of a bronze tripod, dated to the first half of the

far evidence of Bronze Age presence on the site is almost non-existent,[23] the extremely strong natural position in which this settlement was located still adheres to the Mycenaean pattern outlined above.

In marked contrast to what was happening in the rest of Greece, for Messenia the eighth century seems to have been a period of stagnation. Pottery of the phase DA III, covering roughly the first half of the century, is extremely rare, and its decoration increasingly monotonous – interestingly, still showing Laconian influence.[24] The scarcity of DA III materials from Messenia may reflect simply lack of investigation rather than real decline in settlement numbers, or perhaps a tendency to a stronger concentration of the settlements themselves,[25] but it must be noted that even at Nichoria the phase DA III is very sparsely represented.[26] The same pattern continues in the Late Geometric phase, in the second half of the eighth century, documented only in a handful of sites.[27] In between, in the central years of the eighth century, the settlement of Nichoria was destroyed by fire, and never reoccupied.

However, eighth-century Messenia also presents some interesting novelties. From the Mycenaean chamber tomb necropolis of Volimidia, not far from the village of Chora and from Ano Englianos, ancient Pylos, comes the first reasonably clear evidence of cult attached to Bronze Age tombs, in the form of two dozen Late Geometric vases, including imports from Corinth and Laconia, and of a number of bronze pins deposited in the chamber tombs Angelopoulos 4 and 5. The materials seem to fall around 740–730 BC.[28] Together with some more controversial or unpublished evidence from the *tholos* of Kopanaki and from a cist grave at

---

eighth century, said to come from the mountain itself, mentioned above, n. 15. An Early (?) Geometric ithyphallic statuette is reported by Themelis, *Deltion* 21 (1966), B', 164 (no photo).

[23] For some scanty evidence going back to the Bronze Age, see Themelis, *Praktika* 1987: 88–9.

[24] To the three locations listed in Coulson 1986: 66–9 (Nichoria, Ano Englianos, and Stenosia, near Koukounara), add the Geometric sherds from Akovitika, dated DA III by Morgan 1993: 39 n. 18. Laconian influence has been detected also in Geometric bronze horse statuettes from Messenia, see Zimmermann 1989: 117–18.

[25] As suggested by Morgan 1990: 98, followed by Eder 1998: 176–7.

[26] Notice, however, that in the late ninth century the chief's dwelling, building IV 1, was replaced by an even larger apsidal building, IV 5; see Mazarakis Ainian 1997: 79–80.

[27] For a rather conservative survey of Late Geometric finds from Messenia, see Coulson 1988: 54 n. 5.

[28] Since nothing points to the presence of Late Geometric burials in these tombs, the cultic interpretation seems preferable, *pace* Van der Kamp 1996: 71. Coulson 1988 offers the most detailed publication of the vases; for the pins, see Boehringer 2001: 251–2. A DA II jug found in the tomb Angelopoulos 11 could push the initial date of cultic activities to the late tenth–early ninth century, unless it belongs to a burial; for description and chronology of this vase, see Coulson 1988: 72, and 73–4 for a cautious discussion of its interpretation. A good overview of post-Bronze Age finds in the necropolis of Volimidia is found in Boehringer 2001: 249–58 with further references.

Karpophora, near Nichoria, and two Late Geometric vases, probably
related to a purification ritual, from tomb 6 of Koukounara, they form a
modest but interesting corpus of evidence for the attitude of eighth-
century Messenians to their Bronze Age predecessors.[29]

A second novelty is represented by the probable appearance of sanctuaries. In a place called Lakathela, on the east side of the Ramovouni
ridge, not far from the Bronze Age acropolis of Malthi and from the
medieval castle of Mila, a sounding brought to light, on top of layers that
included Bronze Age pottery and walls, a number of small bronze and clay
statuettes of animals, datable from the second quarter of the eighth
century to the early seventh.[30] The massive buildings that were later
erected on the site seem best explained as the remains of a sanctuary, and
small animals like those found at Lakathela occur regularly in sanctuaries
of Geometric date. A Geometric bronze horse, still unpublished, and a
series of bronze pins ranging from Late Geometric to archaic have been
reported from Volimos, too, suggesting that from around the mid eighth
century the site of the later sanctuary of Artemis Limnatis already had
religious associations.[31] Similar evidence comes from the sanctuary of
Poseidon at Akovitika, where the earliest sherds appear to be DA II in
date and are accompanied by a bronze horse dated to the first half of the
eighth century.[32] Unlike Lakathela and Volimos, the one on the side of a
ridge, the other high in the mountains, Akovitika represents also the first
example of a new pattern of site distribution, located as it is in the middle

---

[29] For Kopanaki, see Boehringer 2001: 284–6; for the group of graves at Karpophora (Akones),
Antonaccio 1995: 89 and Boehringer 2001: 269–70; for Koukounara 6, also known as Akona 1, see
Van der Kamp 1996: 74 and Boehringer 2001: 265–6 and 310–11 with n. 4. On the interpretation cf.
Antonaccio 1995: 77. Note that the impression of widespread cult activity at Bronze Age graves in
Geometric Messenia conveyed by the diagram in Alcock 1991: 452 is somewhat misleading.
Coldstream 1976, from whom the data are taken, lists also finds of later date and takes a rather
ecumenical attitude towards the evidence, cf. e.g. his discussion of the chamber tomb at Nichoria
(usually called Vathirema), 10 and n. 22.

[30] See Karagiorga 1972 and *Deltion* 27 (1972), 258–62. For a more detailed discussion of this
excavation, see below.

[31] The bronze horse, inv. no. 13, is on display in the Benaki Museum at Kalamata, with more small
bronzes from the sanctuary, all later in date. See Zimmermann 1989: 114 n. 1. The site of Volimos,
frequented already in the Bronze Age, has produced DA II sherds, see Coulson 1986: 35–7. The pins
have been published by Kilian-Dirlmeier 1984: nos. 1407, 1453–5 (Late Geometric; see 129 and 131
for the chronology), 1838, 3034, 3342 (Late Geometric or early orientalizing, 201 and 205), 4164,
4434 (archaic, seventh to early sixth century; see 254–8). McDonald and Hope Simpson 1961: 225
suggest that Volimos may have been a refuge site in the Geometric period, and only later become a
shrine; cf. however Mazarakis Ainian 1997: 324 n. 541.

[32] For the excavation of the sanctuary, see Themelis 1969. Date of the horse according to
Zimmermann 1989: 117. Notice, however, that the site was apparently already frequented earlier;
one Submycenean sherd and a few DA II ones are present among the finds (Moritz Kiderlen,
personal communication).

of the coastal plain, just east of the mouth of the river Pamisos and not far from the sea. Finally, the fragmentary tripod leg from Mount Ithome, dated to the first half of the eighth century, is probably to be taken as evidence for the cult of Zeus Ithomatas, who we know was still honored and associated with tripods in the fourth century and later.[33]

In the general scantiness of Late Geometric and Early Archaic evidence, a small group of pithos burials stand out for their assemblages and location. The most famous, and the only one that has been published in detail, was found on the Nichoria ridge, at a high point commanding a broad view to the east and south. The pithos had been covered by a cairn of stones, and enclosed the body of a tall young male, identified as a warrior by the presence of an iron sword and spearhead. Three Late Geometric vases allow dating the burial to the years around 725 BC.[34] When the warrior was buried, the settlement on the hill had already been destroyed and abandoned for some decades, but the grave itself and a further Late Geometric tomb in the Vathirema ravine suggest the presence in the second half of the eighth century of another village somewhere in the vicinity. Close in date to the Nichoria pithos burial is an unpublished one from Viglitsa, near Romanos, north of the Bay of Navarino; a bronze cauldron functioned as its lid.[35] A third pithos, from Pera Kalamitsi, in the vicinity of Kalamata, should go back to the same period. The grave goods consist of a small group of bronzes, four Late Geometric pins and a small bronze horse, the latter showing strong Laconian influence. The assemblage appears to be datable to the third quarter of the eighth century.[36] The horse above all is untypical for graves: it rather seems to belong in the context of a sanctuary, and one wonders if this peculiarity is to be linked in any way to the fact that an archaic sanctuary in this place is documented by an archaic terracotta antefix of Laconian type.[37] Finally, a somewhat later pithos burial from Pyla, east of the Bay of Navarino, contained some small bronzes with parallels from the

---

[33] On the Hellenistic coins of Messene associating Zeus and the tripod, see Zunino 1997: 94–5. A stone base of a tripod can be seen walled in the Monastery on the top of the mountain: Amandry 1987: 127–9.

[34] See Coulson et al. 1983. For the date of the vases, Coldstream 1977: 162.

[35] Notice in *BCH* 86 (1962): 726. The date results from the pottery found in the pithos, see Coulson 1988: 54 n. 5.

[36] Notice of the find in Themelis, *Deltion* 20 (1965), B' 2, 207. Coldstream 1977: 162 dates the assemblage to c. 700 BC. See, however, Heilmeyer 1979: 102, suggesting a date immediately after 750 BC for the horse (similarly Zimmermann 1989: 119, third quarter of the eighth century) and Kilian-Dirlmeier 1984: 131, 139, 152 for the Late Geometric date of the pins.

[37] However, Geometric bronze horses are not completely unheard of in grave contexts; see Kilian-Dirlmeier 1979: 166–7.

sanctuary of Artemis Orthia in Sparta, and fragments of three iron swords.[38]

The use of pithos burials in Messenia is documented only sporadically for the earlier phases of the Dark Ages. The four burials discussed above could be the product of influence from a region where this kind of burial was very common in the eighth century, the Argolid. Clearly these burials belong to rather wealthy people. Two of them have warrior connotations, and one received offerings of a kind that are normally found in sanctuaries. The location of the Nichoria pithos burial has suggested that the survivors wanted to enlist the protection of the dead warrior,[39] and the pithos of Pera Kalamitsi may come from what later became a cult place. This scattered evidence could refer to the emergence of a warrior aristocracy in Late Geometric Messenia, entrusted with the defense of the community and perhaps preserving the religious prerogatives that were visible in the chief's dwelling in Dark Age Nichoria. The militarization of the Messenian elite, if this is what we are seeing here, could have something to do with the communities being exposed to increasing pressure, which in theory could derive from internal strife or from external aggression. Such a reading of the evidence, whose hypothetical nature cannot be sufficiently stressed, would have interesting implications for the history of Messenia in the second half of the eighth century.

In all, eighth-century Messenia stands out negatively rather than positively. If DA II Messenia appeared to be rather isolated, signs of contacts with other regions, which become more frequent in the course of the eighth century, point mostly – and ominously – to Laconia. More generally, the evidence presented so far does not bear comparison with the record from other parts of the Greek world, especially considering that Messenia has been investigated more thoroughly than most other regions. The style of artifacts such as bronzes and pottery shows the region to have been more or less receptive to influences from its neighbors, but definitely not exerting any influence in its turn. In the Late Geometric period, when very characteristic local styles of pottery decoration were emerging across Greece, pottery from Messenia fails to show signs of such a

---

[38] Notice of the find in Themelis, *Deltion* 20 (1965), B' 2, 208; on the grave goods see Coldstream 1977: 162 and Kilian-Dirlmeier 1979: 220 (nos. 311, 1103, 1336–7, 1342, 1359–61), who suggests a date around the end of the eighth century and the first years of the seventh.

[39] McDonald and Coulson 1983: 326. For further speculation see Morgan 1990: 99, who suggests that the warrior could have "achieved prominence in the conflicts that surrounded the end of the settlement," and Mazarakis Ainian 1997: 353, tempted to see him as the last inhabitant of unit IV 5, the chief's dwelling, though admitting that no evidence can confirm this tantalizing suggestion.

development.[40] The early deposits of Lakathela and Akovitika appear negligible compared to the early layers of archaic sanctuaries such as Artemis Orthia, Perachora, Olympia etc. Most strikingly, there is no evidence of the emergence of major settlements.

ARCHAIC AND EARLY CLASSICAL MESSENIA

With the end of the eighth century, the distribution of settlements in Messenia starts to assume the shape that it will preserve for the rest of antiquity. While almost all Dark Age sites had been frequented in the Bronze Age already, this is the case for only about a half of Late Geometric and archaic sites. The main focus of the region shifts from its western portion, the coastal plateaus west of the Aigaleon ridge, to the Gulf of Messenia and the Pamisos Valley.[41] Another change, one that is harder to grasp in detail but visible in outline, is the emergence of coastal settlements, especially on the western side of the Gulf of Messenia. The number of sites that show signs of human presence is slowly growing, too: the list drawn by the *Minnesota Messenia Expedition* in 1972 included seventeen definite and two possible archaic sites, as against eleven definite and three possible in the Geometric period.[42] It should be noted, however, that the true increase seems rather to come with the classical age, for which as many as forty-eight definite and thirteen possible sites have been identified.[43] No archaic settlement has been excavated, only two large and apparently isolated buildings, at Kopanaki and Vasilikò. Most important are a small number of sanctuaries, some already mentioned above, where some rather limited excavations have brought to light reasonably diagnostic assemblages. Attention will first concentrate on them.

The sanctuary of Apollo Korythos at Longà/Ayios Andhreas, on the eastern coast of the Akritas peninsula, between modern Koroni and

---

[40] See Coldstream 1977: 160–2; for Coldstream's interpretation of the local styles in Late Geometric pottery as signals of emerging polities see Coldstream 1983, 1984. In the light of such a thesis, the absence of a strongly characterized LG style in Messenia is all the more significant.

[41] The process is well shown by Eder 1998: 178, who tends to see its roots already in the Geometric age. See also Morgan 1990: 99–100, who connects the alteration of the settlement pattern to the Spartan conquest.

[42] To the list, at least three new sites with archaic materials should be added: Mavromati, where archaic materials turned up in the 1990s (see below, pp. 124–7), Lakathela and Kopanaki.

[43] Even though the growth goes back to some extent to the fifth century, in most cases it is impossible to tell apart with certainty fifth- and fourth-century settlements and consequently, to assess the extent to which the increase was in fact a result of the liberation of Messenia in the fourth century (on whose effect on the density of settlements see below, pp. 132–3). At any rate, with reference to the fifth century Lazenby and Hope Simpson 1972: 94 speak of "a considerable expansion throughout the region."

Petalidi (that is, ancient Asine and Korone respectively), is the best-documented Messenian sanctuary from the time before the liberation of Messene in the fourth century. The site, located just off the modern road that connects the village of Longà with the coastal settlement of Ayios Andhreas, was excavated in 1915 by Friderikos Versakis in a single campaign lasting little longer than three months. Versakis thought he had identified five temples on the site, dating in his opinion from the Dark Ages to Roman times.[44] Although his interpretation of the remains of the buildings is usually regarded with some skepticism, nobody has yet undertaken a thorough reinvestigation of any part of these remains, except for Carl Weickert, who connected some of the architectural remains to a Doric peripteral temple with six columns in the front, dating it to the second half of the sixth century BC on the basis of fragments of a capital and of the entablature.[45] The earlier architecture of the sanctuary is extremely hard to decipher, in the virtual absence of stratigraphic evidence, but the presence of foundations of earlier buildings is reasonably clear. The finds do not seem to go back beyond the seventh century.

The cult is usually thought to associate a warlike aspect with that of Apollo as a healing god. The epithet is attested, in inscriptions and literary sources, in the forms Korithos, Korythos, and Korynthos.[46] Since some heroes named Korythos are known, one of them connected with Paris and Helen, it has sometimes been thought that Korythos might originally have been an independent deity, later to be associated with Apollo.[47] In any case, the epithet Korythos can hardly fail to be connected with the word *korus*, helmet,[48] putting an emphasis on the warlike aspect of this cult. The fact that weapons were abundantly dedicated in the sanctuary in the late archaic and early classical periods further underscores the point, and so does the name of Enyalios, which appears to be associated with the god in a poorly published inscription of the late fifth century.[49] The character

---

[44] Versakis 1916.

[45] Weickert 1929: 151–3; see also Bookidis 1967: 399–403. The southern sector of Versakis' excavation (see his map at p. 71) is currently covered.

[46] To the inscription published by Versakis 1916: 117, add *SEG* 11.994 and 995.

[47] See Weicker 1922: 1466–7, and Hope Simpson 1966: 131 n. 161. The relationship between Apollo and Korythos could resemble that between Apollo and Hyakinthos at Amyklai, on which see Antonaccio 1995: 178.

[48] See Zunino 1997: 168. A hero Korythos, *eromenos* of Heracles and inventor of the *korus*, appeared in the *New History* of Ptolemaeus Chennus (2.15), an Alexandrian erudite of the age of Trajan and Hadrian.

[49] The inscription apparently accompanied the dedication of a helmet, a *korus*, and possibly was also meant as a pun on the god's epithet. See Versakis 1916: 115, and the hardly legible photograph on pl. 7 fig. 63, and cf. Jeffery 1990: 204 and n. 2 for the date.

of Apollo Korythos as a healing deity is documented only by Pausanias (4.34.7), which, considering the rising popularity of healing cults from the late classical period onwards, might suggest a later addition.[50] If one considers only the evidence relevant to the archaic and classical periods, Apollo Korythos seems to be a close relative of the warlike Spartan Apollo who stood on the throne at Amyklai.[51]

The connection with Laconia and Amyklai is strengthened by the nature of the finds from the sanctuary. Versakis recovered a fair number of bronzes from the sixth and early fifth centuries, among them the well-known statuette of a hoplite now in the National Museum in Athens, and an archaic kouros, both of very high quality and decidedly Laconian in style.[52] In addition, there is a small bronze bell with feet, of a type that is usually met in Sparta and almost nowhere else.[53] The pottery is Laconian: six aryballoi span the sixth century, and some further sherds seem to fall in the same time period.[54] But the most interesting piece of this Laconian checklist is a large marble capital, certainly votive and datable to the mid sixth century, with a crown of leaves below the echinus and the same motif on the upper border of the abacus (plate 5). The only close parallels to this very remarkable artifact come from Sparta: the capitals and *geison* of the throne of Amyklai[55] and the capital reused in the church of Ayios Vasilios at Xirokampion, south of Sparta.[56] Although the capital from Longà/Ayios Andhreas is larger than its Spartan counterparts, the similarity is sufficiently close to justify considering it a product of the same

[50] A healing could also conceivably be the reason for the dedication *SEG* 11.994, of late Hellenistic date. One might be tempted to see here the traces of a process similar to the one whereby the cult of Apollo Hyperteleatas in southern Laconia, well documented in inscriptions ranging from the archaic period to the early Empire (*IG* V 1, 980 ff.), had been replaced (or complemented?) by a cult of Asklepios by Pausanias' age (Paus. 3.22.10).

[51] Note also that the association of Apollo Korythos with Enyalios, which can be glimpsed in the dedication mentioned above (n. 49), recalls the connection of Phoibos and Enyalios at Sparta; cf. Paus. 3.14.9 and 20.2.

[52] See Herfort-Koch 1986: 104, k 78, and 117, k 135. Also from Longà are k 88 and k 90 (106–7).

[53] See Versakis 1916: 93, ill. 33 and now Villing 2002: 247–8.

[54] For the aryballoi, see Versakis 1916: 101–2 and pl. 8, fig. 51 at 103, and cf. Stibbe 2000a: 23–4, 33, 39–40 (nos. A 54, F 8, K 11, K 12, L 19, L 26). Furthermore, compare Versakis' no. 9 in pl. 3, fig. 51, with Stibbe 1972: 18–19; no. 5 of the same plate with Stibbe 1994: 234 no. 10.

[55] See Herrmann 1983, Faustoferri 1996: 344–57 and pls. 22–3. Contrary to what Faustoferri says (349; same imprecision in Barletta 1990: 51, who was unable to locate the capital), the capital of Longà/Ayios Andhreas is by no means a simplified version of those of Amyklai, and it does have triangular leaves in the background of the main crown of leaves; indeed, it is the most spectacular piece of the series.

[56] Currently on display in the Archaeological Museum at Sparta. See Barletta 1990: 50–1 and Mertens 1993: pls. 65, 4. Mertens' overview of Doric capitals (pls. 64–5) gives a very clear idea of how similar the capital from Longà/Ayios Andhreas is to those from Laconia and how different from anything else.

Plate 5   The Doric capital from the sanctuary of Apollo Korythos, now in the courtyard of
the Benakeion Archaeological Museum of Kalamata

workshop that produced the entablature of the throne. On different
levels, the warlike character of Apollo Korythos, this small Laconian
inventory of votives, and the fact that all archaic inscriptions from the
sanctuary are in Laconian alphabet and dialect, give this sanctuary as
strong a Spartan flavour as that of any sanctuary in Laconia itself.

Chronologically close to the sanctuary of Apollo Korythos is the
sanctuary of the river-god Pamisos at Ayios Floros, north of Thouria.
Matthias Valmin was able to recover the foundations of the small Hellenistic temple dedicated to the river-god, which had been seen still
standing by nineteenth-century travelers before it was robbed of its fine
poros and limestone blocks.[57] According to Valmin, the temple had been
built over an earlier sacrificial pit, possibly enclosing one of the springs
of the river.[58] The earliest votives go back to the early archaic period,

[57] Valmin 1938: 420–65. On the cult of Pamisos, see Breuillot 1985: 797–9. Salowey 2002: 174 suggests
that Heracles was associated to the healing cult of Ayios Floros, basing his argument on the bronze
discussed below, n. 61.
[58] Valmin 1938: 424 and Van der Kamp 1996: 76.

probably to the first half of the seventh century. The pottery mostly finds parallels among archaic Laconian vessels.[59] Having been submerged in wet soil for centuries, the bronzes are much more corroded than those from the sanctuary of Apollo Korythos, and therefore more difficult to date precisely or to attribute to a particular school. Some small bronze statuettes of bovines, of sub-Geometric appearance, show close similarities to Laconian bronzes.[60] A group which represents in all probability Herakles dressed in a bell-corselet and fighting against the Hydra appears to date from the late sixth century, and might stem from a Laconian or Laconizing workshop.[61] The same is true of the much better-preserved statuette of a spear-thrower, bearing a dedication by Pythodoros to the Pamisos, in Laconian alphabet.[62] It comes from the antiquities market and is now in the Princeton University Art Museum, but it can hardly have been found anywhere else than at Ayios Floros, where Valmin was told that the owner of the field in which the temple lies had not only taken blocks of stone away for reuse, but had also found and sold objects of bronze and terracotta.[63] In her study of archaic Laconian bronzes, Merlene Hertfort-Koch calls the statuette a product of a local workshop that replicated in a simplified way the style of contemporary Laconian bronzes.

The next three sanctuaries appear to go further back in time. In the sanctuary of Poseidon at Akovitika, located not far from the coast west of Kalamata, systematic investigation has started only very recently. After the accidental finding of a hoard of bronze statuettes, a first sounding produced only remains of Hellenistic and Roman buildings.[64] The high level of the ground water prevented the excavators from going any deeper. Ten years later a rescue excavation was carried out, revealing the remains of the foundations of a peristyle (see plate 6), dated to the sixth century and partly built using spoils from earlier buildings, which point to a previous phase

---

[59] Valmin 1938: 454–63.   [60] Schmaltz 1980: 141–2.

[61] Valmin 1938: 440–1 and pl. 33 no. 7; cf. Herfort-Koch 1986: 54–9. Unfortunately, the object was badly damaged during restoration, as can be easily seen comparing the two pictures published by Valmin with each other and with a later one (*LIMC* V.2, *Herakles*, no. 2827), which shows signs of further deterioration.

[62] Already mentioned in the first edition of Jeffery 1990: 202, but first published by Mitten and Doeringer 1967: 62–3. See Herfort-Koch 1986: 52, and k 118 (113). A further inscription from Ayios Floros has been seen by Bernhard Schmaltz on one of the bulls found by Valmin, now in the National Museum in Athens (NM χ 15292); since Valmin had not seen it, it may have become visible after the cleaning. See Schmaltz 1980: 141 n. 316 and Valmin 1938: tav. xxxiv 4. I am very grateful to Prof. Schmaltz for sharing with me his photographs of this inscription, which is, however, illegible and does not present any significant feature in terms of dialect or alphabet.

[63] Valmin 1938: 420.

[64] Notice in *BCH* 83 (1959): 639–40. The bronzes are listed by Leon 1968: 175, who publishes one of them; see also Herfort-Koch 1986: 104 k 80.

Plate 6 The excavations of the sanctuary of Poseidon at Akovitika

of the complex, dating probably to the seventh century.[65] As we have seen above, the oldest finds from the site go back to the first half of the eighth century.[66] A fifth-century inscribed dedication, in Laconian dialect and alphabet, attests that the remains belong to a sanctuary of Poseidon, here called, as in Sparta, Pohoidan.[67] Further evidence relating to this sanctuary may come from the victory-list of Damonon of Sparta, inscribed possibly in the late fifth century, which speaks of chariot races at a festival called Pohoidaia in a place called Theuria which is obviously identical with Thouria in Messenia.[68] If these Pohoidaia were held in Akovitika, then we have interesting evidence for the extension of the territory of Thouria; if not, we have testimony for the existence of a further sanctuary

[65] Themelis 1969: 352–7. Investigations at Themelis' excavation site were started again in the spring of 2005 by a German team led by Dr Moritz Kiderlen. One of the first results of their work has been to dispel the notion of a late seventh-century destruction layer, cautiously advanced by Themelis. I am extremely grateful to Dr Kiderlen for sharing information on the results of this very interesting new project and for his warm welcome when I visited his excavation in March and June of 2005.
[66] DA III sherds and the Geometric bronze horse, above n. 32.
[67] See Themelis 1969: 355 (*SEG* 25.431b) and Themelis 1970: 116–18.
[68] *IG* V 1, 213, lines 18–23. For the date of this inscription, see above, p. 31 n. 47.

of Pohoidan in Messenia, near Thouria. One is tempted to apply Ockham's razor and choose the first option, particularly on account of the name "Gulf of Thouria," attested by Strabo (8.4.5) and presumably indicating a part of the Gulf of Messenia, which should imply that the territory of Thouria in some form and in some period reached the sea.[69]

The sanctuary of Artemis Limnatis, the bone of contention in the long controversy between Spartans and Messenians discussed in chapter 2, is much better known from literary sources than from its archaeological remains. However, sufficient finds come from the area of the chapel of the Panayia Volimiotissa to make certain that this was the location of the sanctuary, in the mountains north-northeast of Kalamata, on an ancient itinerary that connected Laconia and Messenia.[70] The cult, as we have seen, was prominent in Hellenistic and Roman times, as is attested by inscriptions, some of which have been reused in the walls of the chapel together with stones that probably stem from the sanctuary. From the earlier periods only stray finds have been reported, but these are fairly diagnostic. The earliest votives are represented by the Geometric horse and by the Late Geometric pins discussed above, which probably date the origin of the sanctuary. One of the archaic pins is of a type found elsewhere only at Sparta.[71] A bronze siren, originally attached to a fibula, is a Laconian product of the early sixth century.[72] A mirror-handle with the engraving of a standing woman in profile has been found in the area; it also stems from a Laconian workshop and may be dated to the mid sixth century.[73] Another simpler, but complete mirror found in Volimos was given to the Museum of Kalamata in 1973. It has been assigned to the second quarter of the fifth century and bears a dedication to Limnatis, confirming that the sanctuary was already devoted to this goddess in the archaic and classical periods.[74] The alphabet and dialect of the dedication

[69] For the identification of the sanctuary in which the Pohoidaia took place with the one of Akovitika, see Themelis 1970: 118; cf., however, Mylonopoulos 2003: 247, who thinks that the sanctuary of Akovitika should rather have been controlled by Pharai. In any case, the sanctuary of Akovitika was abandoned in the late fifth century, and probably moved elsewhere (see above, p. 36 n. 60).

[70] See above, p. 23 n. 33. For the minimal architectural remains, mostly of Roman times, see E. Papakostantinou, *Deltion* 37 (1982) 2, 136.

[71] Kilian-Dirlmeier 1984: 241 nos. 4164 and 256, mid seventh–early sixth century.

[72] See Herfort-Koch 1986: k 156. For the provenance see *BCH* 83 (1959): 640.

[73] First published by G. P. Papathanasopoulos, *Deltion* 17 (1961–62), 2, 96 fig. 4. For the chronology see Oberländer 1967: 32–5, and Stibbe 1996: 151–2, who favors a slightly higher date, around 570–560.

[74] The mirror is published by L. Parlama, *Deltion* 29 (1973–74), 2, 315 and pl. 198a. The transcription in *SEG* 29.395 should be slightly corrected: given the presence of ανεθεκε, Λιμνατι must be a dative, as in *IG* V 1, 226 and 1497, and O- could be the first part of the dedicant's name. It is extremely tempting to connect some further archaic bronzes with the sanctuary in Volimos: the cymbals *IG* V 1, 225, 226 and 1497, inscribed in Laconic alphabet and dialect and dedicated to

are Laconian. The cult itself has a strong Laconian association: Limnai was the name of the Spartan district where the sanctuary of Artemis Orthia was, and since most of the other cults of Artemis Limnatis in the Peloponnese were connected with Sparta in one way or another, the epithet Limnatis must have simply meant 'the goddess of Limnai,' that is, Orthia. This hypothesis is supported by the fact that a later inscription uses for the Artemis of Volimos the epithet Orthia.[75]

Finally, the sanctuary of Lakathela cannot be associated with any specific deity. The votives start in the Late Geometric period, and the two monumental structures that have been partially brought to light by the excavation should date to the archaic period, judging by the stratigraphy.[76] One of them is a rather puzzling circular building, the other probably a stoa, of which a wall more than 28 meters long has been found. A detailed history of this sanctuary cannot be reconstructed, especially since the pottery found in the soundings is unpublished. According to the excavator, no sherds were found later than the early fifth century.[77] Fragments of black glazed tiles from an archaic Laconian roof have been found immediately above a destruction stratum containing burnt timber and below a stratum containing broken fragments of the wall.[78] This situation suggests a destruction of the building, which could be dated to the early decades of the fifth century. Thereafter, there are no further traces of human presence – which perhaps does not mean too much, given the limited extension of the excavation. It is worth noting that in the archaic period Laconian roofs are found only in or around Sparta.[79]

Further evidence for archaic sanctuaries has been recovered in recent years in Mavromati, in the course of excavations whose main target was the late classical and Hellenistic city. West of the stoai surrounding the

Limnatis, and a mirror now in Munich, also inscribed Λιμνατις (see Oberländer 1967: 44 and Stibbe 1996: additional plate 12), all the more so since a bronze cymbal has been found in Volimos and is now on display in the Benaki Museum at Kalamata (inv. 39, unpublished). Two of the inscribed cymbals were bought in Mistra, the third is unprovenanced, as is also the mirror. *Pace* Jeffery 1990: 194 n. 3, the three cymbals cannot be interpreted as phialai, cf. e.g. the objects held by the small female figures in Herfort-Koch 1986: 97 k 56 and 99 k 61, and 37 for their interpretation (an unpublished example was found in Kalamata, 103 k 74).

[75] See above, p. 24 n. 34.

[76] See Karagiorga 1972: 12–20 and *Deltion* 27 (1972): 258–62 (more detailed as far as stratigraphy and sherds are concerned).

[77] Karagiorga, *Deltion* 27 (1972): 260.

[78] The stratigraphy is described in Karagiorga 1972: 14–16 and *Deltion* 27 (1972): 259–60, with slight differences (e.g. the black glaze of the tiles is mentioned only in *Deltion* 260). On archaic Laconian roofs see Winter 1993: 95 and 309–10. They were apparently used only for temples, and perhaps for public buildings; see Catling 1996: 85

[79] Winter 1993: 95; a couple of probably Laconian-influenced roofs come from southwestern Arcadia.

Hellenistic Asklepieion, three campaigns led by Themelis from 1992 onwards brought to light a fairly complicated building, or rather a complex of buildings unified at a later stage, with phases dating to different periods and materials from the seventh century BC onwards.[80] The architectural history of this complex, the so-called sanctuary omega or omega-omega, is difficult to reconstruct, but there seem to be remains of at least one small building dating back to the archaic period. Some fragments of quite large terracotta relief plaques of remarkably high quality may have been metopes or architectural ornaments of this building, which Themelis tentatively interprets as a small oikos.[81] Whatever their function, the little that remains of the reliefs looks thoroughly Laconian in style, as is shown by a comparison with Spartan hero-reliefs in general and in particular with two large terracotta plaques from the deposit of Ayia Paraskevi, belonging to the sanctuary of Alexandra and Agamemnon at Amyklai.[82] In the sanctuary an enormous number of smaller terracotta votive plaques and statuettes have been found. A few of them date to the archaic period, starting probably in the second half of the seventh century.[83] Particularly striking is a sixth-century terracotta representing a group of three figures sitting on a bench, two of which, dressed, flank and support a third, female and naked, who raises her hands to her head in a gesture of mourning. It has parallels only in the *Lakonikē*, at Sparta, Aigiai, and near Kalamata, and apparently nowhere else; the parallels, however, are extremely close.[84] The same iconography is also represented by a remarkable group, hand-made in the round, dating most probably to the second half of the sixth century and with stylistic

---

[80] On the three campaigns devoted to this complex, see the preliminary reports by Themelis, *Praktika* 1992: 74–9, *Praktika* 1993: 40–55 and *Praktika* 1994: 81–6. On the terracotta plaques see Themelis 1998a: 157–86.

[81] Themelis, *Praktika* 1993: 51 and pl. 26, nos. 2–3.

[82] Both are included in Salapata 1992: plates 38a and 48a. I am very grateful to Gina Salapata for allowing me to make use of her unpublished dissertation. For more accessible reproductions see Salapata 1993: 190–1 and fig. 3, and Stibbe 1991: pls. 28–30.

[83] Themelis 1998a: 162 fig. 3 is the most remarkable example. Themelis tentatively suggests that the mold may have been imported from Corinth, although no close parallel has been found so far. See also Themelis 1998a: 166 and fig. 15, 167 and figs. 15 and 18, 175–6 and fig. 44, 177–9 and figs. 47, 48, 54.

[84] See Papaefthimiou 2001–2: 136–8 (to which add the example from Dimiova, see below). The terracotta from Messene, of which four examples have survived, all from different molds, was originally published by Themelis 1998a: 175 fig. 41. The terracotta from Sparta, from the sanctuary of Alexandra and Agamemnon at Amyklai, is shown in Stibbe 1996: 248 figs. 131–2. Three fragmentary examples recently found in a sanctuary close to the perioikic town of Aigiai (on which see Shipley 1997: 251–2) are published in Bonias 1998: 199–200 and pl. 54. By far the best-preserved example of this type was found in the Dimiova cave, immediately east of Kalamata, and is now on display in the Benaki Museum at Kalamata (P. Themelis, *Deltion* 20 (1965), 2, 207, has a scarcely decipherable picture, plate 217); see also below, n. 91.

affinities with Sparta.[85] On a more general level, it is interesting to observe that Gina Salapata's survey of terracotta votive plaques in the framework of her study of the plaques from the sanctuary of Agamemnon and Alexandra led her to the conclusion that this sort of votive offering should be considered typically Spartan.[86]

It is extremely difficult to say, on the bare evidence of the plaques, which gods or heroes were worshipped in the sanctuary at Mavromati during the archaic age.[87] The offerings on the whole, and in particular the plaques, seem to point rather towards a hero-cult.[88] The only epigraphic evidence coming from the omega-omega complex itself is represented by a late fourth-century shield with a votive inscription to Polydeukes; this may suggest that the Dioscuri were at least among the deities worshipped in the complex already at an earlier date.[89] The recent discovery of two fragments of a limestone relief, reemployed in the theater, representing one of the Dioscuri and datable to the second half of the fifth century, shows that in any case the divine twins were the recipients of cults in this area.[90] The terracotta groups of three figures discussed above, with their peculiar iconography, could also point to the identity of one of the deities worshipped in this area. Combining iconography and provenance of the other examples, the group may be seen as evidence for the worship of a deity with a kourotrophic function: perhaps Eileithyia, who had a sanctuary at Messene in Pausania's times (4.31.9), or perhaps Artemis, whose temple in later times stood nearby.[91]

More evidence for the presence of one or more archaic sanctuaries has been found in soundings in the court of the Hellenistic Asklepieion. In the southwestern part of the court, the remains of earlier buildings have come to light, together with more terracotta plaques and votives predating

---

[85] On this group, see Papaefthimiou 2001–2, esp. 133 (date and style).

[86] See Salapata 1992: 159–86.

[87] For discussions of the deities worshipped in the sanctuary omega-omega, see Themelis 1998a: 182–6 and Torelli 1998: 469–71.

[88] In Laconia, terracotta plaques appear to have been found only in hero shrines, not in sanctuaries dedicated to gods, see Salapata 1993: 194. On plaques as typical offerings for heroes see also Boehringer 2001: 292 n. 5.

[89] See Themelis, *Praktika* 1994: 84–5 and *SEG* 45.302.

[90] The first fragment was published by Themelis, *Praktika* 2002: 30; for the second, see *Ergon* 2006: 41 and pl. 35.

[91] The identification with Artemis is cautiously put forward by Papaefthimiou 2001–2: 139–41. The connection with Eileithyia has been advanced by Stibbe 1996: 247–53 for the terracotta from Sparta, and is independently suggested by Torelli 1998: 468–9 for those found in Messene. According to Bonias 1998: 109–14, in the sanctuary at Aigiai Artemis and the previously unknown hero Timagenes were worshipped. On Artemis and Eileithyia, see Pingiatoglou 1981: 98–119. On the fourth-century temple of Artemis at Messene, see below, p. 234.

the liberation of Messenia.[92] A fragment of a terracotta Laconian acroterion confirms the existence of a sacred building of archaic date in this area.[93] Taken together, this evidence is best explained by supposing the existence of at least one further shrine built in the archaic period.

Scattered evidence of archaic sanctuaries comes also from the surroundings of Kalamata and from the Ellinika ridge, the site of Thouria. In the first case, remains of a Laconian antefix suggest the presence of an archaic temple at Pera Kalamitsi, about a kilometer east of Kalamata.[94] From a cave located between the modern villages of Phare and Eleochori, a group of terracotta figures have been reported, presumably stemming from a small shrine.[95] Closer to Kalamata, on the Tourles hill, opposite the medieval Kastro, archaic terracotta plaques, still unpublished, have been found in an area with significant Mycenaean remains and traces of chamber tombs; in all likelihood, we have here to do with yet another case of cult at Bronze Age tombs.[96] Even more tantalizingly, the Benaki Museum at Kalamata possesses a group of twenty bronze pins said to come from modern Antheia, uniformly distributed in date from the second half of the eighth to the first quarter of the sixth century. In theory, they could come from tombs, but given their chronological spread they seem best interpreted as an assemblage coming from a sanctuary.[97] Antheia is the modern village closest to the Ellinika ridge, so it is reasonable to connect this find with Thouria.

The unpublished plaques from the Tourles hill are not the only evidence for cult activity in connection with Bronze Age tombs during the archaic and early classical periods. One of the *tholoi* at Koukounara has

---

[92]   On the soundings in the southern part of the Asklepieion court, see Themelis, *Praktika* 1993: 57–9; *Praktika* 1994: 86–8; *Praktika* 1995: 60–3. The chronology of the finds is still quite uncertain, but they appear to start between the late seventh and the early sixth century, Themelis, *Praktika* 1995: 62.

[93]   The acroterion has been published in Themelis 1994b: 150. According to Themelis, it was found in the area of the Asklepieion, but it does not seem to feature in any of the excavation reports. Since in this contribution Themelis mentions only the 1987 campaign as having to do with the Asklepieion (1994b: 141 n. 6; cf. *Praktika* 1987: 79–90), it is likely that the acroterion was found in one of the soundings around the Hellenistic temple that were opened in 1987. On the connection between archaic Laconian roofs and sacred buildings, see Winter 1993: 95.

[94]   Themelis, *Deltion* 20 (1965), B′ 2, 207; see Winter 1993: 141 and 107–8 (date: c. 600–530). For the precise location, see the map in Hope Simpson 1966: 117.

[95]   Again Themelis, *Deltion* 20 (1965), B′ 2, 207; note that I misplaced this sanctuary in Luraghi 2002: 56 n. 62.

[96]   I owe this information to the kindness of Gina Salapata; see Salapata 1992. For the site, see Hope Simpson 1955: 241–3.

[97]   The pins are published by Kilian-Dirlmeier 1984, nos. 1484, 1840–1 (Late Geometric), 2600, 2678–9, 2690, 2948, 3035, 3183, 3347, 3436, 3584 (late eighth to first half of the seventh century, see 201, 205, 218), 3945, 3956, 3973, 4169, 4332, 4482–3 (second half of the seventh century to first quarter of the sixth, 253–8).

produced an orientalizing pyxis, rather idiosyncratic in style, with general similarities to Laconian vases of the same period,[98] and probable evidence for a hero-cult in the form of animal bones, which, however, might be related to finds from the end of the fifth century.[99] More clear-cut is the situation in the *tholos* of Papoulia, on the plateau to the west of Mount Maglavas. Fragments of eight drinking cups of different forms, almost all Laconian, and again animal bones strongly suggest cult activity at this site between the late seventh and the early sixth century.[100] The foot of one wine amphora from the *tholos* of Tourliditsa, located between Mount Lykodimos and Mount Maglavas just south of the modern road from Pylos to Kalamata, is said to go back to the archaic age, without any further details, and a similar situation occurs in the case of a group of Mycenaean tombs at Karpophora-Akones near Nichoria. More archaic pottery has been found in *tholoi* at Kopanaki and Vasilikò, although the lack of detail in the publication makes it difficult to define its chronology and provenance. In all four cases, traces of sacrifice have also been found, not necessarily contemporary with the archaic pottery, since in all these tombs later pottery was found, too.[101] Finally, from the necropolis of Volimidia come three very modest black-glazed vases, dated to the archaic period by George Korres.[102]

A somewhat different case, at least from our point of view, is represented by a chamber tomb in the Vathirema ravine, southwest of the Nichoria ridge.[103] It is not clear if the tomb itself was originally Mycenaean,[104] but no Bronze Age remains have been found in it, and the burials it harbored apparently date to the Late Geometric period, accompanied by pottery, in part of very high quality.[105] Then, the scanty notices on the excavation speak of an uninterrupted sequence of pottery

---

[98] Cf. Margreiter 1988: 107.

[99] The tomb is Koukounara 4, alias Gouvalari 1. See Boehringer 2001: 261–5 (261 n. 1 for the nomenclature of the tombs at Koukounara). The pyxis is reproduced in *Praktika* 1959: pl. 148 a and 1960: pl. 153 b.

[100] The best discussion of the finds is offered by Boehringer 2001: 259–60, with references to the Laconian parallels.

[101] See Boehringer 2001: 267–70 (Karpophora and Tourliditsa), 282–6 (Vasilikò and Kopanaki); note the fragments of a crater rim from Kopanaki (Boehringer 2001: 285), to be compared with those from Vathirema. On Tourliditsa, see also Van der Kamp 1996: 74–5, based on autopsy of the materials.

[102] Korres 1981–82: 415–16.   [103] Boehringer 2001: 268–9.

[104] As suggested by Coldstream 1977: 161.

[105] On the pottery from this grave, see Coulson et al. 1983: 270; a pyxis lid with horses appears to be an import from Attica (Coldstream 1977: 162).

from the Late Geometric to the classical period.[106] In the absence of any detail, it is difficult to decide what to do with this information. If it were accurate, then the tomb at Vathirema would be unique – which makes one all the more suspicious.[107] At any rate, no evidence of animal sacrifice is reported.

Turning to the evidence for archaic settlements, everything becomes much more complicated, not only because of the usual lack of systematic investigation, but also because most of the places where important settlements are documented by the literary sources for the classical or Hellenistic periods, with the exception of Thouria, have been inhabited without interruption thereafter and are therefore difficult of access for archaeological investigation. While in most cases stray finds make it possible to reconstruct a rough chronology for human presence at the site, it often remains hard to gauge the size and nature of such presence. For places such as Kalamata, Petalidhi, Koroni, Methoni, we are almost completely in the dark.[108]

Two of the sanctuaries discussed above have been claimed to have been parts of archaic settlements. In the area of Lakathela, the very succinct excavation reports mention surface remains and the excavator proposes to identify Lakathela with Dorion, mentioned by Pausanias and Strabo.[109] However, without further fieldwork this suggestion cannot be assigned much weight. The case for Mavromati is clearly stronger. Although it is not possible to rule out with absolute certainty the possibility that the archaic and early classical finds from this site could belong to a shrine or complex of shrines isolated in the countryside, the assumption that they had to do with a settlement on the site of the later city appears clearly preferable, especially since more finds from the archaic period come from

---

[106] N. Yalouris, *Deltion* 16 (1960): 108, and G. P. Papathanasopoulos, *Deltion* 17 (1961–62): 95. However, Coulson 1983: 332 states that no archaic pottery has been found in the tomb (without further details).

[107] In a showcase of the Benaki Museum at Kalamata that includes finds from Vathirema there is the fragmentary rim of what appears to be a column crater with a decoration of foliage in black on a red background and a small red-figure pelike. Although being of much higher quality than any of the pottery found in Bronze Age tombs (with the partial exception of the pyxis from Koukounara), none of the pottery on display is recognizably archaic; the decoration of the crater finds its best parallel in an olpe found in Kynouria and published in Karouzou 1985: 41–2. On the whole, the vases from the Vathirema tomb on display can be dated to the last quarter of the fifth century, that is, they are contemporary with the classical vases from the Tholos F at Nichoria (see below, p. 241 and n. 106). I am very grateful to Dr. Ulrike Polczyk for advice on the pottery from Vathirema and for pointing me to the olpe published by Karouzou.

[108] Hope Simpson 1957: 242–52, is the best introduction to the scanty evidence.

[109] Karagiorga, *Deltion* 27 (1972), B′, 262. The sources referring to Dorion are collected by Shipley 1997: 255.

the Ithome area.[110] It is not clear whether or not we can speak of settlement continuity from the Geometric to the archaic period,[111] but on the whole it seems difficult to reject the conclusion that a settlement existed here from the second half of the seventh century onwards.

From archaic and early classical Messenia only two sites have been investigated that can certainly be identified as habitation sites. They are rather similar to one another, in terms of shape and chronology, and located in the same area, the Soulima Valley: one on a plateau southeast of the modern village of Vasilikò, the other inside the modern village of Kopanaki.[112] In each case, only one large building has been found, with a number of rooms of different sizes and shapes surrounding a courtyard, abundant fragments of roof tiles, and with external walls of a thickness that clearly suggests the existence of a second storey. The building at Vasilikò measures roughly 23 by 26 meters, the one at Kopanaki, 30 meters by 17.[113] Both buildings are rectangular, with an entrance in the southeastern corner. In both, fragments of fine ware as well as of big storage vessels have been found. Valmin interpreted the building at Vasilikò as a small fort, controlling the Soulima Valley and the Stenykleros Plain.[114] However, if that were the case one would expect the building to have been located farther to the north, closer to the slopes of the Vasilikò hill, whence it would have enjoyed the same breadth of sight from a less exposed position. The general shape of the building is not reminiscent of Greek fortifications, and the close similarity to the building at Kopanaki strongly suggests that they both were habitations, presumably large farmhouses.[115]

---

[110] A small bronze statuette of Hermes, now in the storerooms of the National Museum of Athens (X 7539), is said to come from the area of Mount Ithome. First published in De Ridder 1894: 149 no. 832, pl. IV.1, this small bronze has often been connected with Arcadia; see e.g. Lamb 1925–6: 138 no. 9, and pl. XXIV. But see now the example published by Stibbe 2000b: 121–7, which shows that our Hermes is much closer to Laconian workmanship. I thank the Director of the National Museum of Athens, Ioannis Touratsoglou, for allowing me to study and photograph this object in September 1999, and Anastasia Panayiotopoulou for her help on that occasion.

[111] Judging from the notices published to date, there could be some gap between a Geometric settlement and another (smaller?) one, dating from the second half of the seventh century. At least, the late eighth and early seventh centuries are not as clearly represented as the periods before and after, and Geometric and archaic–early classical materials have not yet been found in the same spots.

[112] See Valmin 1941 and Kaltsas 1983, respectively.

[113] At Vasilikò, Valmin also identified a staircase and the first three steps of a stair; Valmin 1941: 63–4. Second floor at Kopanaki: Kaltsas 1983: 217–19.

[114] See esp. the discussion in Valmin 1941: 72–3, where Valmin considers also the possibility that the building might be interpreted as residential.

[115] See Kiderlen 1995: 26–7 and 108–9 for a typological study of the Kopanaki building, and Catling 2002: 163 for comparison with (typically smaller) possible farm sites individuated by the *Laconia Survey*.

The small finds from Kopanaki have been published in a detailed way. They seem to date the life of the building to the years between the second quarter of the sixth century and the second quarter of the fifth. Since signs of destruction by fire were found, the excavator suggests that the building may have been destroyed in the course of the Messenian revolt after the earthquake, in the 460s.[116] The pottery is generally Laconian. In the case of the Vasilikò building, the small finds have not been published in detail, but some Laconian elements are recognizable nevertheless.[117] Some graffiti on sherds date to the fifth century, and one of them may have been inscribed by an Arcadian.[118]

Finally, evidence for settlements in Messenia comes from the results of the Pylos Regional Archaeological Project (PRAP), an intensive survey conducted from 1992 to 1994 in western Messenia, mostly on the coastal plain north of the Bay of Navarino, on the Englianos Ridge and in a couple of areas to its northeast. The main focus of the survey was the Bronze Age, and the areas surveyed have been selected accordingly. Nevertheless, it is striking that archaic and classical sites appear to be fewer than half the number of Late Bronze Age sites. Most interestingly, the survey has failed to find evidence for the scattered farmsteads that characterize the Greek countryside in this general time span, according to other surveys.[119] On the other hand, the very few settlements that have been identified appear to be rather large.[120] In a sense, the settlement pattern recovered by the PRAP is "Hamlet without the prince," since unfortunately no permission was given to explore the area south of Petrochori, where important finds from the Hellenistic age, accompanied by significant earlier materials, suggest the presence of the main settlements of this region.[121] Nevertheless, and keeping in mind that western Messenia was a rather peripheral district in the archaic and classical

[116] Kaltsas 1983: 220–1 (destruction) and 221–37 (small finds). It is not completely clear why Catling 1996: 34 n. 15 prefers a later date for the destruction of the Kopanaki building. At any rate, Conrad Stibbe in his studies of Laconian black-glazed pottery seems perfectly satisfied with Kaltsas' chronology; see Stibbe 1994: 47 (one-handled mug G 2) and 87, and Stibbe 2000a: 53–4 (Narrow-necked jug C 2, second half of the sixth century = Kaltsas 1983: 228 no. 7), 61 (oinochoe C 12, first quarter of the fifth century = Kaltsas 1983: 227–8 no. 6), 77 (hydriai E 1–3, last quarter of the sixth century-early fifth = Kaltsas 1983: 226 nos. 1, 3, 2).

[117] See e.g. the characteristic knobbed handles in Valmin 1941: 67 pl. 6 and cf. Catling 1996: 268 n. 479.

[118] Valmin 1941: 67–72; cf. Jeffery 1990: 203 n. 2 and Pikoulas 1984: 181–4.

[119] Davis et al. 1997: 456; Alcock et al. 2005: 163–73.

[120] See Alcock et al. 2005: 166 and the comparison with other sites from Laconia in Hodkinson 2003: 260.

[121] See McDonald and Rapp 1972: 264 sites 6–9 and especially 310 site 401.

ages,[122] the peculiar settlement pattern noted by the PRAP deserves attention.

MAKING SENSE OF THE EVIDENCE

On the basis of the archaeological evidence, archaic Messenia gives an undeniable impression of underdevelopment compared to other regions of Greece, in terms of sheer quantity of materials, density of settlement, and size of sites and sanctuaries. The most conspicuous characteristic is the lack of a central settlement that would significantly surpass all the others in magnitude and could function as a center of political aggregation, such as is found in most Greek regions. It cannot be reasonably doubted that this situation was a consequence of the fact that the political center of Messenia happened to be Sparta, and that during the periods commonly associated with the birth and development of the Greek city-state, no independent political entity existed in the territory west of the Taygetos and south of the river Neda. The archaeological evidence from the eighth century does not even show signs of incipient concentration of power in a specific settlement. The fact that "the Messenians" conquered by Tyrtaeus' ancestors had allegedly been able to fight back against the Spartans for as many as twenty years might by itself point to the emergence of such a concentration, but we should beware of taking Tyrtaeus' hortatory poetry as straightforward historical evidence. The fact that, contrary to what was happening in many other regions of the Greek world in the eighth century, the finds from Messenia point to stagnation and possible decrease in population size is more likely to offer us reliable evidence on the historical processes at play in the region. With an eye to the evidence for the fifth and fourth century, in purely archaeological terms it would be fair to say that in Messenia the curve of human presence in the landscape was some three centuries behind the rest of Greece.

If the consequences of the Spartan rule over Messenia seem to be visible in the archeological record, the process by which such rule was established has not left unequivocal traces. The destruction of Nichoria around the mid eighth century has often been connected with Spartan raids west of the Taygetos. The emergence of a warrior elite in the late eighth century,

---

[122] The comparison with the size and density of sites individuated by the Minnesota Messenia Expedition in Alcock et al. 2005: 158–62 should be taken with some caution, *pace* the authors. McDonald and Rapp 1972: 264–321 offer size estimates almost only for Bronze Age settlements, without any indication as to which age the figures refer to, which means that the figures used for the comparison with the size of settlements located by PRAP rest on extremely flimsy ground.

if this is a correct deduction from the four eighth-century pithos burials discussed above, could also have something to do with external pressure on the region, perhaps especially on the southern Pamisos Valley, more directly exposed to Spartan attacks. But the fact that two out of four of these graves come from the Pylos area, which used to be the center of Messenia in the Bronze Age and in the earlier part of the Dark Ages, may point to a more complex explanation. Less controversially, the spread of Spartan influence in the late Dark Ages seems to have taken the obvious route, reaching Volimos and the Makaria first:[123] one more reason to regard with diffidence later accounts, such as Pausanias', in which the Spartans invade Messenia from the northeast and all the fighting seems to take place from Ithome northwards (see above, pp. 85–6). Otherwise, no clear pattern emerges from the evidence. Some sanctuaries, such as Akovitika, Lakathela, Volimos, Mount Ithome, and the sanctuary from which the pins said to come from modern Antheia are likely to originate, go back to the mid eighth century or earlier, that is, probably predate Spartan encroachment on the region. Interestingly, as far as we can tell almost all of them continue into the archaic age. The sanctuary of Zeus on Mount Ithome, documented by one single stray find from the Geometric age and not by excavations of any kind, cannot be regarded as a true exception. Other sanctuaries, such as those in Mavromati, Ayios Floros, and Longà/Ayios Andhreas, are likely to have been established when Messenia was already under Spartan control. Cult at Bronze Age tombs, while becoming much more widespread after the liberation of Messenia, as we will see in more detail, is documented sporadically and at different locations from the Late Geometric period to the fifth century. This practice deserves special attention, because it is not attested in Laconia. Certainly its existence in Messenia was largely a consequence of the incomparably higher density of monumental remains of the Bronze Age in the region. Regardless of how we choose to interpret the attitude of the inhabitants of Messenia to these features, their very presence characterized the Messenian landscape in a distinct way, offering a rigid parameter, with which they had to come to terms in projecting their views of the past onto that landscape.

All in all, Spartan rule, although freezing the development of Messenia by comparison with other parts of Greece, does not seem to be associated

---

[123] The easier route across the Derveni pass, leading directly in to the *Stenykleros* plain from the north, only became available once Sparta took control of the Belminatis and the uppermost part of the Alpheios valley.

with any clear and consistent discontinuity attested throughout the region. Probably the most important phenomenon that becomes visible in the early archaic period, and can therefore be seen most likely as a consequence of the Spartan domination, is the shift of the main focus of settlement from Western Messenia to the Pamisos Valley. If this trend had already started by the mid eighth century, at least Spartan rule consolidated it for centuries to come. The situation that obtained in the Bronze Age, when the Pylos area was the heart of the region, disappeared and was replaced by a new pattern that lasted for the rest of antiquity.

There are two aspects of the evidence from archaic Messenia that are relevant, in a more or less straightforward way, to the inhabitants' perception of their past and of their ethnic identity, and to some extent also to the transmission of such perceptions. They relate in particular to their cults and to the regional character of the material evidence. Starting from the first aspect, for any community of Greeks from the archaic age onwards, sanctuaries constituted an essential place of aggregation, in which collective identities were articulated through ritual practice, and there is no doubt that this function was discharged by Messenian sanctuaries as well. In general, the Greeks took for granted that an ethnic group would be characterized by its own cults, that is, by a particular selection of gods from the pool of the Greek pantheon. Different epithets were normally the marker that allowed associating cults in a specific way to a particular community. As Robert Parker aptly put it, "differentiation by religious practice is as it were the default setting of a Greek's mind when he is thinking casually about ethnic divisions."[124]

From this perspective, the evidence offered by the cults of archaic Messenia is rather diagnostic and surprisingly consistent. Most deities find close parallels at Sparta, and some were seen in antiquity as typically Spartan. The warlike Apollo of Longà/Ayios Andhreas is clearly related to the Spartan Apollo worshipped at Amyklai. The Artemis Limnatis of Volimos appears to be an alter-ego of the quintessentially Spartan Artemis Orthia. The Dioscuri, too, were proverbially Spartan. As for Poseidon at Akovitika, the form of his name, Pohoidan, points again to Spartan parallels, especially the Pohoidan of Tainaron. The quality of the offerings, especially the plaques from the sanctuaries in Mavromati, points to further parallels with Laconia in the field of ritual behavior. Deviations from this rule are very rare. The river-god Pamisos is not a true exception,

---

[124] On religious practice as a sign of a common ethnic identity among the Greeks, see Parker 1998: 16–21; the quotation is from p. 20.

since his cult was obviously anchored in the Messenian landscape. More relevant is the case of Zeus Ithomatas. The scarcity of archaeological evidence from the archaic period invites caution, but it fair to say that, judging by later history, this cult might conceivably have possessed more explicit Messenian associations already during the archaic period, at least potentially.

The material evidence is remarkably consistent in its regional flavor: as noted above, in so far as they can be classified in terms of their shapes and style, pottery and bronzes mostly find parallels in Laconia.[125] The same is true of the very few pieces of monumental architecture and sculpture, including the marble capital from Longà/Ayios Andhreas, the terracotta architectural decorations from Pera Kalamitsi and Mavromati, and the terracotta reliefs from Mavromati. It would appear as though archaic Messenia lacked a material culture of its own. However, assessing the meaning of such evidence for the question of ethnic self-definition is not straightforward. On a basic level, homogeneity in material culture inside the political borders of Lakedaimon is surely a product of the more intense exchange that took place within the region as opposed to contacts with the rest of the Peloponnese. A mechanism of this kind is certainly responsible for the differences in local styles observed across the Greek world, especially in the archaic period, and for their marked tendency to be coextensive with political or ethnic units.[126] The question is, to what extent we should regard regional differentiation as simply reflecting political and/or ethnic borders, and to what extent it may be legitimate to assume that differences in material culture were actually seen as ethnic markers and actively used to construct ethnic borders.

The absence of a constant correspondence between ethnic identity and material culture has been one of the central tenets of archaeological research in the second half of the twentieth century, in reaction to a previous tendency to assume that regularities in material assemblages

---

[125] To the small bronzes mentioned above, some further items may be added, such as the Palladion from Nisi, now in Mariémont (Herfort-Koch 1986: 38 and 91 k 42, dated c. 530), and an unpublished statuette of a cymbal-player from Kalamata, now in the local museum (Herfort-Koch 1986: 103 k 74, c. 550–530), which contribute to the definition of archaic Messenian bronze workmanship as a branch of Laconian bronze workmanship. For a characterization of archaic bronzes from Messenia see Leon 1968: 175–85, Floren 1987: 226.

[126] This minimalist interpretation of the ethnic meaning of material culture in archaic Greece should not conceal the fact that the tendency of borders between styles to correspond with borders of other sorts, be they ethnic or political, is in itself noteworthy and not to be taken for granted; see Jones 1997: 114–15 on the absence of a consistent and necessary correspondence between levels of interaction and homogeneity in material culture. For the concept of regional styles, see especially Raeder 1993: 105–9.

could be automatically translated into ethnic groups.[127] The study of ethnicity has shown that, while it is too schematic to say that the choice of which cultural traits will be perceived and used as ethnic markers in any given context is purely arbitrary,[128] there is no cross-cultural regularity in the connection between cultural traits, including material culture, and ethnic borders. In other words, unless we have direct evidence of the fact that certain cultural traits were loaded with ethnic meaning in a given context, we should not assume that this was the case.[129]

In a recent contribution, Carla Antonaccio has brought together some pieces of evidence, in the form of passages from Herodotus and Thucydides, in support of the notion that some cultural traits, including patterns of dressing and the shapes of objects, could indeed be associated by the Greeks with what she calls "local identities," i.e. they could be associated with ethnic or political borders.[130] Surely her conclusions cannot be generalized, in view of the observations above, but it can be conceded that she has made a plausible case for the interpretation of material culture as a marker of borders between communities of Greeks. In other words, even though the pervasive Laconian associations of material culture in archaic Messenia cannot carry the same weight as the cults and religious practices discussed above, they can certainly be regarded as additional evidence, whose consistency, or lack thereof, with the conclusions based on more solid indicators has to be taken into account.

On a slightly more solid ground, the handful archaic and early classical inscriptions from Messenia, mostly from the sanctuary of Apollo Korythos, are consistent with the use of Laconian dialect and alphabet. In archaic Greece, dialects and local alphabets had much clearer ethnic implications than material culture,[131] but in the case of Messenia, the scarcity of the evidence does not encourage phrasing conclusions in very strong terms. Yet, it is fair to say that inscriptions, material culture and cults paint a remarkably consistent picture of archaic Messenia as a part of the Spartan state, culturally and ethnically almost completely homogeneous with the rest.

---

[127] For a discussion of the problem, see Jones 1997: 15–29.
[128] For a balanced and perceptive discussion, see Eriksen 1991. The question of the arbitrariness of ethnic markers is discussed in a broader framework above, pp. 8–10.
[129] The approach advocated by Jones 1997: esp. 87–92, based on the application of Bourdieu's theory of practice to the expression of cultural difference proposed by Bentley 1987, does not overcome this fundamental problem, see Hall 1998.
[130] Antonaccio 2003: 57–65; the quote is from p. 65.
[131] See Morpurgo Davies 1987 on the dialects and Luraghi forthcoming on the alphabets.

How does the archaeological evidence discussed so far map onto what we know from the literary sources? As the discussion in the previous chapter has shown, in terms of historical background very little can be said about archaic Messenia in a reasonably uncontroversial fashion. According to Tyrtaeus, the Spartans had conquered Messene – that is, a portion of the region later called Messenia, probably corresponding to the area of Mount Ithome – after a very long war, in the second half of the eighth century or in the early seventh. A further war during the seventh century, in Tyrtaeus' times, is possible but not certain. By the fifth century, Messenia had become a part of the *Lakonikē*, that is, of the Spartan territory, and was inhabited, like the rest of the Spartan territory, by *perioikoi* and Helots. The *perioikoi* were citizens of the Spartan state, but without active political rights.[132] Together with the Spartiates, they formed the group called the Lakedaimonians. They lived in small towns scattered all over the *Lakonikē*, with their own sanctuaries and probably their own territory, and formed part of the Spartan army. The Helots tilled land that belonged to the Spartiates, the ruling elite of the Spartan state, and mostly lived close to the fields, although some of them served in the Spartan households.[133] The settlement pattern and social organization of the Helots are extremely poorly documented, and therefore controversial.

Precisely how the situation that we observe at the end of the archaic period had come about is extremely hard to tell, and the intricacies of claims and counterclaims about the "real identity" of inhabitants of Messenia do not make the task easier. As we have seen, by Thucydides' times it was thought that (some of?) the Helots of Messenia were the descendants of the once free Messenians. This notion somehow disappeared in the early fourth century, in connection with the liberation of Messenia, and then resurfaced, in a less qualified way, at the end of the century. At least in the case of those Helots who revolted against Sparta after the earthquake in the 460s, this ethnic ascription seems to have corresponded to what they thought of themselves. However, the notion that Helots working Spartiate lots in Messenia were simply the descendants of the once free Messenians, reduced to slavery at the time of the Spartan conquest, in spite of its almost unanimous acceptance in modern scholarship, is problematic. As we have seen, ancient opinions on this

---

[132] See the definition given by Mertens 2002: 288: "A distinct status-group within the Lakedaimonian citizen-body." On the status of the *perioikoi*, see also Hampl 1937, Shipley 1992, Lotze 1993/4, Cartledge 2002: 153–9 and below, p. 204 and n. 113.

[133] On the inclusion of Helots in the spartan households, see Hodkinson 1997 and Paradiso 1997.

matter were rather more qualified than their modern reception, and most importantly, changed very significantly over time, reflecting conflicts over the Messenian identity in the classical and Hellenistic ages. In order to assess the plausibility of the collective enslavement theory, we cannot really rely on ancient evidence. Comparative research on slavery and regimes of dependent labor suggests that we should regard the idea of mass enslavement as the origin of Helotry with skepticism.[134] Based on the little we know about dependant labor in archaic Greece, it would seem that the Helots are more likely to have been the product of a process of transformation and unification of preexisting forms of dependence, including chattel slavery. The idea that they, or some of them, formed a homogeneous ethnic group is more likely a result than a precondition of their shared predicament.[135]

The relevance of archaeological evidence to the study of the Helots of Messenia is severely undercut by the fact that it is hard to tell exactly which portions of the region were inhabited by them. Most scholars would tend to locate the lots of the Spartiates in the most fertile districts, such as the northern Messenian plain and the Soulima Valley, and perhaps also in the southern Messenian plain, or Makaria, west of the Pamisos.[136] Recently, the settlement pattern identified by the Pylos Regional Archaeological Project has been interpreted as evidence of Helot settlement, suggesting that Helots in Messenia, apparently unlike their counterparts in Laconia, lived in rather large village communities, and not scattered in small farmsteads through the countryside.[137] Such a pattern of settlement would of course have important consequences for the social organization of the Helots, and ultimately for their ability to develop and transmit a collective memory and traditions of their own. The village communities could be expected to have developed, or indeed preserved, a sense of their common identity. Furthermore, they would have had to be administered somehow, and the most reasonable assumption would be

---

[134] The argument is deployed in a more comprehensive fashion in Luraghi 2002b, developing the comparative observations of Patterson 1982: 110–13; see also Raaflaub 2003: 171–2; Patterson 2003: 289–99, who offers further suggestions on the process that brought about Helotry in Laconia and Messenia respectively. The criticism by van Wees 2003 does not seem decisive to me, and I plan to address it fully elsewhere.

[135] On the emergence of ethnicity among the Helots, see the discussion below, pp. 202–4.

[136] On the extension and location of Spartiate land in Messenia see, among others, Roebuck 1945: 151 and 157–8; Lotze 1971: 64–5; Figueira 1984: 100–4, 2003; Hodkinson 2000: 142–5, who in my opinion overestimates the extension of the land directly controlled by the Spartiates.

[137] For a comparison of the patterns individuated by the PRAP and by the *Laconia Survey* respectively, see Hodkinson 2003: 260–1.

that the Helots themselves provided the personnel that ran their communities. This, in turn, would imply a significant amount of social stratification among the Helots.

Since the Spartans were absentee landowners, the suggestion that their estates, especially in Messenia, were managed by overseers taken from the Helots themselves is extremely plausible. Some ancient evidence has been brought to buttress this suggestion.[138] However, the existence of Helotic villages remains much more speculative. It has been stated correctly that there is no overwhelming reason to think that the area investigated by the PRAP was not inhabited by Helots.[139] However, it has to be admitted that, looking at Messenia as a whole, the area selected by the PRAP survey, inasmuch as it is marginal, is really not one of the first we would look at in search for the land owned by the Spartiates. Tellingly, once we look beyond the area investigated by the Laconia Survey, other regions of the southern Peloponnese offer interesting comparisons. The closest parallel to the settlement pattern that surfaced in the Pylos region is apparently met in perioikic districts on the northern and northeastern borderland of the *Lakonikē*, equally characterized by largish nucleated settlements and by the absence of scattered farmsteads.[140]

While unfortunately lacking in the contextual information that could derive from a survey, the buildings at Kopanaki and Vasilikò are much more promising candidates as possible evidence for the form of Spartiate estates and, directly or indirectly, of Helotic settlement. The pattern they seem to suggest is markedly different from the one that can be deduced from the survey data for the Pylos region: rather than to villages, they point to extensive estates, farmed by large groups of Helots gravitating around the main buildings, possibly in a plantation-like pattern.[141]

---

[138] Hodkinson 2003: 258–9. Hodkinson builds especially on a lemma of the Byzantine lexicon that goes under the name of Hesychios. The word of the lemma is most likely corrupted, and it has been restored by Wilamowitz as *mnōionomoi* (ibid. 258, n. 44). It is explained in the lexicon as "leaders of Helots." That these people should be themselves Helots is unsure to say the least; after all, the name *mnōionomoi* recalls the parallel of magistracies attested at Sparta and elsewhere, such as the *gynaikonomoi*, who obviously were not women, and the *paidonomoi*, who were not themselves *paides*. But even so, sources on ancient Sparta mention various categories of uncertain status, which may represent some sort of intermediaries between Spartiates and Helots and could very well have been drawn from the ranks of the Helots themselves; see Lotze 1962, Bruni 1979, Ducat 1990: 166–8 (consider especially the case of the *mothōnes*). Research has generally focused on their potential military role, but clearly they could have had a function in the organization of the Spartan agrarian economy.

[139] Alcock 2002a: 193.   [140] See Sirano 1996–7: 432 and especially Catling 2002: 240–3.

[141] Harrison and Spencer 1998: 162, Luraghi 2002b: 231–2. Note that both sites appear to start during the sixth century, which would fit the chronology for the emergence of the Helotic system suggested in Luraghi 2002b: 233–4.

However, it should be noted that, even in this case, the evidence does not point to dispersal through the countryside in small farmsteads, the pattern that had been most commonly hypothesized.[142]

The *perioikoi* of Messenia are easier to locate on the ground, at least in theory.[143] Perioikic towns were scattered along the coast of the Messenian gulf, from Kalamai, the modern Eleochorion (formerly Yiannitza), at the end of an important route crossing the Taygetos, to Pharai, on the site of modern Kalamata, and Thouria, further inland on a ridge dominating the Pamisos Valley but probably extending its territory to the coast, then Asine to the south along the Akritas peninsula, Mothone on the other side of it, and north of Mothone, Koryphasion[144] and Kyparissiai, on the west coast of Messenia, and finally Aulon, controlling the access to the region from the valley of the Neda.[145] Another important approach from the northeast was guarded by the fortress of Gardiki, most probably ancient Ampheia.[146] As in Laconia itself, the Spartiate land in Messenia was surrounded by a belt of perioikic settlements, which occupied a significant portion of the region.

Some perioikic settlement probably existed on the western coast of the Gulf of Messenia north of Asine. Korone, founded (or refounded) in connection with Messenian independence, may actually have been the successor of a perioikic settlement, which may or may not have had the same name.[147] The archaic settlement at the foot of Mount Ithome, given

---

[142] Alcock et al. 2005: 170. Cf. Catling 2002: 236–7 on the settlement pattern observed in the area of the *Laconia Survey*, and especially his conclusion that apparently Spartan control "was imposed through a system of nucleated settlement, perhaps backed up by a military presence at key points."

[143] On the *perioikoi* of Messenia, see Roebuck 1941: 28–31, and Lazenby and Hope Simpson 1972: 86. The evidence from literary sources and inscriptions has been recently collected by Shipley 1997: 226–81; see the index at pp. 190–1.

[144] The Koryphasion that was stormed by the Arkadians in 365/4 (Diod. 15.77.4) must have been a perioikic settlement. Since Thucydides appears to imply that there was no settlement on Koryphasion (i.e. Paliokastro) when Demosthenes landed there (4.3.2), it is possible that a settlement, perhaps a fortress, was established after the Athenians finally evacuated their stronghold. Archaeological investigations in the castle by S. Marinatos (report in *Ergon* 1958: 149–50) brought to light pottery from roughly the mid fifth century onwards, and a considerable quantity of pottery from the sixth to the fourth century has been collected in the area south of the castle, towards the entrance of Navarino Bay; see McDonald and Hope Simpson 1961: 243.

[145] On the location of Aulon, see Valmin 1930: 107–12, Roebuck 1941: 25–6 n. 95 (Aulon a region), Lazenby and Hope Simpson 1972: 98 n. 101, Cartledge 2002: 234. Strab. 8.3.25 clearly considers Aulon a region. Xen. *Hell.* 3.2.25 suggests the same.

[146] See Pritchett 1985: 39–46 and Pikoulas 1988: 479–85.

[147] Hope Simpson 1957: 249 mentioned five early classical Doric capitals from the site of Petalidi, but later Lazenby (in Lazenby and Hope Simpson 1972: 89) on the basis of on Paus. 4.34.5 called Korone a new foundation of the 360s century. Valmin 1930: 177–9 seems to consider the remains of ancient fortifications to predate the age of Epaminondas and tantalizingly alludes to the richness of ancient remains in Petalidi.

the quality of its material remains and its position, rather removed from the Stenykleros plain but dominating large stretches of the Messenian landscape, can hardly have been anything other than a perioikic settlement. A puzzling question is what this place would have been called during the Spartan domination, since it seems quite unthinkable that it preserved the name of Messene, which might well have been its name before the Spartan conquest. Epaminondas' city, built in same place, was called "Ithome" (see below, p. 228), and the name may have been in use before. A further problem, which could be related to this one, is represented by Aithaia, a settlement of *perioikoi* mentioned by Thucydides in connection with the revolt of the earthquake, and rather difficult to locate.[148] Since the name does not recur in any source from the fourth century onwards, except Philochorus, and especially not in topographical surveys like those of Ps. Skylax, Strabo, and Pausanias, one might be inclined to connect it with a settlement that changed its name at some point, most probably at the time of Epaminondas' liberation of Messenia. This could apply for instance to Korone, which according to Pausanias (4.34.5) was refounded precisely at that time, although Pausanias gives the earlier settlement the name of one of the cities offered to Achilles by Agamemnon, Aipeia.[149] One might also wonder if Aithaia could not have been the early name of the settlement by Mount Ithome, although this would imply that Thucydides' knowledge of Messenian topography was rather vague. However, given our own poor knowledge of important areas of Messenia, such as most of the Pamisos valley, it should not be excluded that Aithaia might not have been identical with any known archaic or early classical site of Messenia.

The identity of the *perioikoi* of Messenia is a rather puzzling problem. The extension of their presence makes it hard to believe that they might all have come from Laconia, in a sort of internal colonization:[150] to a large

---

[148] The manuscripts of Thuc. 1.101.2 give the ethnic name in the (obviously corrupted) forms αιϑεεις or αιϑνεις, generally corrected to Aἰϑαιῆς, based on Steph. s.v. Aἴϑαια, that includes Philoch. 328 F32a and a reference to Thucydides; Philochorus calls Aithaia "a polis of *Lakonikē*, one of the hundred" (on the "hundred poleis" of *Lakonikē* see Strab. 8.4.11). For earlier attempts to locate Aithaia, see Valmin 1930: 62–3 and Lazenby and Hope Simpson 1972: 86 and n. 41. Thucydides does not say that Aithaia was in Messenia, but all modern scholars tacitly assume that this was the case, and indeed it is hard to imagine that a perioikic town east of the Taygetos would dare to revolt against Sparta, even after the earthquake.

[149] See Christien 1992: 33. For different locations of Homeric Aipeia see Strab. 8.4.5.

[150] Pharai is called a *colonia Lacedaemoniorum* in Nep. *Con.* 1.1, but this terminology is much more likely to be the result of an inappropriate rendering of some Greek term that indicated the perioikic status of Pharai, than to reflect the fact that Pharai was thought to have been colonized by the Spartans; see Shipley 1997: 257.

extent, perioikic communities in Messenia are very likely to have been the result of the absorption of preexisting settlements by the expanding Spartan state, in a process not unlike the one that must have taken place in some parts of Laconia itself.[151] On this process, however, ancient sources are totally silent. Only in the cases of Asine and Mothone is any information available, making of the former, as we have seen, a settlement of Dryopians from Asine in the Argolid, expelled by the Argives and resettled by the Spartans, and of the latter ethnically undefined refugees from Nauplion, also expelled by the Argives and settled in Messenia by the Spartans, but later, at the time of the Second Messenian War.[152] The reticence of the sources can be easily explained. From the *a posteriori* perspective of the Messenian vulgata, according to which fighting against the Spartans was the mission of every true Messenian, *perioikoi* who had peacefully coexisted with the hated Spartiates for centuries would have been despicable *collaborateurs*, best forgotten.[153] As we will see in more detail below, this vulgata maintained that all the "ancient Messenians" had either gone into exile after the Second Messenian War or had been enslaved by the Spartiates, and in this case had left their land after the revolt in the fifth century. The presence of indigenous *perioikoi* in Messenia clearly questioned this simple narrative, and was consequently passed over in silence.

As discussed above, the archeological evidence shows that archaic Messenia was to a significant extent inhabited by people who apparently spoke the same language as the Lakedaimonians east of the Taygetos, employed the same alphabet, used and produced the same kind of pottery

[151] As far as the problem of the origin of the perioikic communities is concerned, recent scholarship shows a healthy amount of caution; see Shipley 1997: 203–5. Cartledge 2002: 84–6 charts some possibilities. See now Hall 2000: 82–7. On the Spartiate influence on the emerging and development of perioikic settlements in Laconia, see Catling 2002: 243–8.

[152] According to Paus. 4.24.4, Mothone was assigned to refugees from Nauplia after the Second Messenian War. See also Theop. *FgrHist* 115 F 383 *ap.* Strab. 8.6.11, where it is not clear if the transfer of the Nauplians to Mothone comes from Theopompus or not; doubts on the general reliability of this story are expressed by Hall 1995: 583–4, who reasonably suspects that the story might have been generated on the template of Asine in order to make sense of the "parallel lives" of these two towns. It can hardly be accidental if Asine and Mothone, which remained loyal to Sparta long after the liberation of Messenia (probably until 338/7 BC: see Roebuck 1941: 57 and below, p. 254), are the only perioikic towns of Messenia that have a foundation story, and that both were depicted as founded by people coming from outside the region.

[153] Tellingly, the only perioikic settlements mentioned by Pausanias in Messenia – or rather, the only settlements that he seems to consider to have existed during the Spartan occupation – are Asine and Mothone (4.14.3 and 24.5 respectively). Although he does mention e.g. Thouria in the topographical part of book 4, he does not say anything about it for the period of the Spartan occupation.

and bronzes, mostly worshipped the same gods and offered them the same sort of votives. As originators of most of such evidence, the *perioikoi* are clearly more appealing candidates than the Helots. Whatever one thinks of the status and economic level of the Helots, probably not many scholars would be ready to attribute to them major stone buildings like the ones at Longà/Ayios Andhreas, Lakathela, and Akovitika, or dedications on a monumental scale, like the votive column from Longà/Ayios Andhreas, or objects of the quality of the terracotta and limestone reliefs from Mavromati or the bronzes from Longà/Ayios Andhreas. To reinforce the point, the lists of deities worshipped in Messenian sanctuaries tally nicely with what Robert Parker observed about the cults of the *perioikoi*: although they had their own sanctuaries and festivals, their religion was dominated by the same gods that were also prominent among the Spartiates. Parker's list includes Artemis, the Dioscuri, Poseidon and, above all, Apollo.[154] In other words, shrines in Messenia in the archaic and early classical period correspond closely to the pantheon of the Spartiates, as did also the shrines of Laconian *perioikoi*.

In view of this, it would obviously be very tempting to interpret the evidence as reflecting a polarity between culturally Laconian *perioikoi* and Messenian Helots. After all, this is exactly where the written sources would lead us, with their insistence on exile and enslavement as the fate of the "old Messenians" and their almost absolute silence on the *perioikoi*. The next step would be to locate Messenian tradition among the Helots and to try to understand to what extent such tradition had been handed down from the time before the Spartan conquest, and to what extent it was the product of later times. Although the difference between Helots and normal chattel slaves is often overestimated, there are significant indications of the existence of a certain level of social stratification and organization among the Helots, and the conditions in which they lived, as far as it is possible to reconstruct them, could conceivably have been conducive to the emergence of a group identity, that might have defined itself in ethnic terms. Of course, there would still be the problem of what the *perioikoi* of Messenia thought of how they had come to inhabit their towns. However, a number of reasons speak against accepting the notion of a simple polarity between Laconizing *perioikoi* and Messenian Helots.

To begin with, it is important to stress that some of the places where the *perioikoi* were living or worshipping their gods would later have an

[154] Parker 1989: 145.

enormous importance for the Messenian identity. Mavromati was the cradle of resistance against Sparta in the fifth century, while Thouria revolted on the same occasion and became in the fourth century one of the most important centers of free Messenia. The sanctuary of Apollo Korythos received what is almost certainly a dedication of weapons captured by the rebels in their struggle against the Spartans and their allies. Noteworthy as well is the fact that the Laconian look of the Messenian material culture applies also to areas and places that seem more easily connected with Helots than with *perioikoi*, such as Kopanaki and Vasilikò. But the most powerful argument for blurring the divide between *perioikoi* and Helots comes from a close observation of the evidence of cult at Bronze Age and Early Iron Age tombs.

The idea that archaic and early classical offerings at Bronze Age tombs in Messenia were an expression of anti-Spartan resistance has been voiced many times, in more or less refined ways.[155] Certainly the coincidence between the liberation of Messenia from Sparta and the increase of evidence for cult at Bronze Age tombs can hardly be accidental (see below, pp. 239–44). For the archaic and classical periods we have rather to do with a scattered phenomenon, and in no single case do the offerings appear to span long periods of time without interruption, thereby following, although on a smaller scale, a pattern that is typical of this phenomenon already in the eighth century and also outside Messenia.[156] Most interesting is the fact that offerings at Bronze Age tombs, besides being documented in many places that cannot be assigned with any confidence to either Helots or *perioikoi*, appear both in areas that were certainly perioikic, such as Pharai/Kalamata, and in others that were most likely Helotic, such as the Soulima Valley. The broad range of variation in the quality of the offerings, from the pyxis of Koukounara to the cheap black-glazed pots of Volimidia, concurs in suggesting that interest in old tombs cut across classes, and perhaps across statuses, as well.

The meaning of this practice may well have been less than homogeneous. Broad investigations of cult practices in connection with Bronze Age tombs and hero-cults suggest that offerings at earlier graves probably

---

[155] See especially Alcock 2002b: 149–52, with references to her previous works. In a somewhat less sophisticated form, a "nationalistic" interpretation of cult activity at Bronze Age tombs in Messenia had been circulating for a while before being articulated explicitly, see Marinatos 1955: 154 and cf. Wilkie 1983: 333.

[156] Antonaccio 1995: 246: "With few exceptions ... Iron Age tomb cult is of short duration and very limited scope." Lack of continuity is underlined also by Boehringer 2001: 362–3.

imply the perception of or the aspiration to a genealogical connection with the people buried in those graves on the part of the living.[157] On the other hand, conspicuous disposal of goods is always susceptible to be a way of articulating social superiority, and this possibility should not be excluded in the present case.[158] In any case, acts of commemoration performed at monuments that could not but be perceived as stemming from a distant past offered a focus for the articulation of a common identity. Furthermore, it should be stressed that in Laconia interest in Bronze Age tombs was rare in the eighth century and disappeared thereafter. At the very least, this was a tradition that belonged to the part of *Lakonikē* west of the Taygetos. It may not have had an anti-Spartan connotation all along, but it could have acquired one in time. At the very least, it shows that people living west of the Taygetos, almost certainly both Helots and *perioikoi*, would from time to time engage in a cultic behavior that was different from those of the people of Laconia.

* * *

To conclude, archaeological evidence suggests that eighth-century Messenia was probably not a burgeoning region on its way towards political unity, that might have offered organized and sustained resistance to Spartan aggression. The twenty-year war that Tyrtaeus pointed to as a model to his contemporary Spartans was probably the exception rather than the rule. By and large, Messenia is likely to have become part of the Spartan state in a fashion that is comparable to how Laconia itself did, and Spartan Messenia looked pretty much like Laconia, except that it did not have a central settlement equivalent to Sparta. The bulk of the evidence would lead us to expect the inhabitants of Messenia to have shared the ethnic self-perception of those of Laconia, whatever that might have been. However, in assessing the meaning of the evidence discussed in this chapter we ought not to forget that, whatever cultural traits can function as its markers in any given context, ethnic identity remains essentially a discursive phenomenon, which means that ethnic borders are not always visible on the ground. This said, it is also interesting to observe that traces of local traditions are not completely absent in archaic Messenia. They will have to be kept in mind once we consider the two moments in which Messenians suddenly emerged

---

[157] Antonaccio 1995: 140–3 and 246–9, where the nature of the offerings at Bronze Age tombs and the difference between them and the materials offered at hero-shrines are outlined very clearly.
[158] See Hodkinson 2003: 276–7.

in the landscape west of the Taygetos: first the earthquake revolt in the fifth century and then the liberation of Messenia by Epaminondas. But first we have to consider the emergence of the first polity that called itself "the Messenians": unexpectedly, this community was not in the Peloponnese, but in Messina, Sicily.

CHAPTER 6

The Western Messenians

After the disappearance of their predecessors sometime during the archaic period, the fifth century saw the return of the Messenians to the political landscape of Greece. Unexpectedly, however, they did not reappear at first in the area they were most closely associated with, the southwestern Peloponnese. Instead, the first polity that called itself "the Messenians" arose in Sicily, on the site of the ancient Chalcidian colony of Zankle, which was founded anew around 490 BC by the tyrant of Rhegion Anaxilaos and called Messene. The name of the new colony reflected the fact that the tyrant considered himself to be of Messenian descent. Participation of Messenians coming directly from the Peloponnese to the foundation of Sicilian Messene is controversial and ultimately unlikely, but almost a century later for a short while a large contingent of Messenians from Naupaktos was indeed settled in the city, whence it went on to found the city of Tyndaris, on the northeastern coast of Sicily. In spite of their name and traditions of origin, the nature of the relationship of the Western Messenians to the Messenians of the Peloponnese turns out to be unclear and possibly ambivalent, and a scrutiny of the little we know about the Messenian diaspora on the Strait of Messina may shed interesting light on the development of the Messenian identity as a whole.[1]

THE MESSENIAN STRAIT

The sources for the foundation of Rhegion, a Greek polis on the tip of the toe of the Italian peninsula, refer to it as a colony of the Chalcidians from Euboea. According to the earliest authority, the fifth-century historian Antiochus of Syracuse, they had been summoned by the people of Zankle, another Chalcidian colony in Sicily, who even provided the

[1] The evidence on the Western Messenians is discussed by Asheri 1983: 32–6.

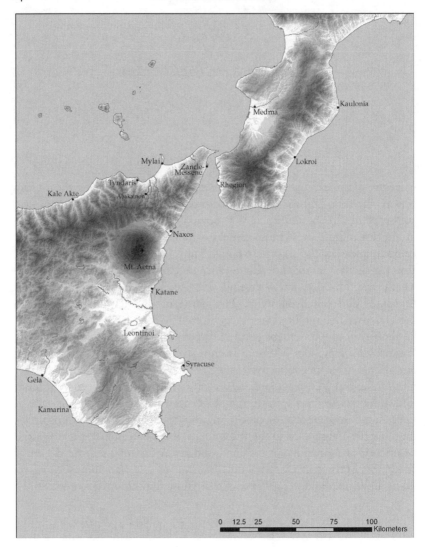

Figure 3 Eastern Sicily and the tip of the Italian Peninsula

oikist.[2] Some authors (Strab. 6.1.6, Her. Lem. 55 Dilts) mention the fact
that the Chalcidians had been joined by a group of Messenians who had

---

[2] Antiochus *FgrHist* 555 F 9, *ap*. Strab. 6.1.6. For a comprehensive discussion of the ancient written
sources on the foundation of Rhegion, see Ducat 1974a. A whole book has been devoted to the
topic by Ganci 1998, whose interpretations of the evidence are, however, mostly highly speculative.

left their country before the outbreak of a war against Sparta, clearly the first one, while Pausanias (4.23.6) has Alkidamidas, an ancestor of the tyrant Anaxilaos, sail to Italy after the fall of Ithome that marked the Messenian defeat in the First Messenian War. It is extremely difficult to tell how seriously such pieces of information should be taken. In spite of Strabo's statement that Rhegion had been ruled by Messenians from its foundation all the way to the early fifth century, from the archaic period no recognizable traces of this Messenian diaspora have survived, which has induced some scholars to doubt the very historicity of the Messenian participation in the foundation of Rhegion in the eighth century. However, even though later events and agendas may have colored the sources that narrate the Messenian migration to Italy (see below), the alternative suggestion that Messenians may have moved to Rhegion only some time after the foundation of the Chalcidian colony, for instance after the failure of their revolt in the seventh century,[3] is even less satisfactory – the later the Messenians arrived at Rhegion, the more we would expect to find their traces in the evidence. On the whole, though, the evidence for the history of Rhegion before the fifth century BC is so scarce that arguments from silence hardly carry any weight. The only element one may be tempted to attribute some relevance to is the absence of non-Euboean traits in the dialect of Rhegion as documented by a handful of inscriptions.[4] This of course could speak in favor of a Messenian presence at the very beginning of the colony, so early that by the time of our earliest documents it had been completely assimilated by the Chalcidian majority, and/or of a very small contingent, formed by just a few families, or finally of the notion that there were no Messenians in archaic Rhegion at all. It seems impossible to decide between these alternatives.

Whether or not Messenians had participated in the foundation of the city, our sources say explicitly that the tyrant of Rhegion Anaxilaos considered Messene his fatherland. Anaxilaos seized power in 494 BC, overthrowing an oligarchy and occupying the acropolis of Rhegion.[5] This is about all we know of his rule in the city, except for the fact that in later sources (Iust. 4.2.4–5) the tyrant ended up being praised for his justice.

---

[3] See e.g. Asheri 1983: 32, but similar hypotheses have been formulated quite frequently.
[4] See Luraghi 1994: 194 and n. 34 with further references. On the characters of Greek dialects in Sicily and Magna Graecia, note especially Salvaneschi 1975.
[5] The date results from the combination of Hdt. 6.23.2 and Diod. 11.48.2 (Anaxilaos dies after 18 years of rule). Further on Anaxilaos, Aristot. *Pol.* 1316a38, Dion. Hal. *RA* 20.7.1 (with an eccentric view on the succession to Anaxilaos: see Luraghi 1994: 216). For a comprehensive investigation of the tyranny on the Strait in the early fifth century, see Luraghi 1994: 187–229.

His involvement in international politics is somewhat better documented. According to Herodotus (6.22–3), when a group of Samians and a few Milesians sailed to Sicily after the defeat of Lade, following an invitation from Zankle to found a colony of Ionians on the northern coast of Sicily, Anaxilaos intercepted them in Lokroi and convinced them to seize Zankle instead. The enterprise was facilitated by the fact that the tyrant of Zankle, Scythes, was campaigning against the Sicels with the Zanklean army at that very time. Anaxilaos' scheme, however, met with mixed results. The Samians were indeed able to take control of Zankle, but when the tyrant Hippocrates of Gela showed up with his army, summoned by his allies the Zankleans, the Samians decided that coming to terms with him was the most expedient line of conduct, especially since Hippocrates turned out to be ready to sacrifice his allies. The agreement left the Samians in control of Zankle, while Hippocrates claimed for himself half of the goods and slaves from the city and all that were to be found in its territory, and sold into slavery the Zanklean army, with the exception of 300 most prominent citizens. These he delivered to the Samians in the expectation that they would execute them, but the Samians spared them.

According to Herodotus, Anaxilaos had originally approached the Samians because he was already hostile to Zankle. The tyrant probably inherited this conflict from the oligarchy that ruled Rhegion before him, as suggested by dedications of weapons in Olympia celebrating a victory of Zankle over Rhegion, dated to the very first years of the fifth century (*IGDS* 2). In all likelihood, the hostility was ignited by the conquest of Zankle by Hippocrates of Gela, who installed Scythes in the city as his vassal. Given the traditionally close ties between the two Chalcidian colonies on the Strait of Messina, it is easy to envision a failed attempt by the Rhegians at freeing Zankle from Geloan hegemony.[6] The failure may conceivably have facilitated Anaxilaos' rise to power. In any case, taking control of the Sicilian side of the Strait remained a top priority for him even after the Samian scheme backfired. Around 490, after Hippocrates' death and probably taking advantage of troubles in his empire associated with the succession of his right-hand-man Gelon, Anaxilaos made his move on Zankle, expelled the Samians and Kadmos of Kos, probably a collaborator of Hippocrates like his father Skythes, and founded the city anew with the name of Messene.[7]

---

[6] On this episode, see Luraghi 1994: 189–92.
[7] Thuc. 6.4.6; see Luraghi 1994: 206–8. The date of Anaxilaos' expulsion of the Samians from Zankle can be reconstructed on the same basis as the coinage of the Samians, bearing a sequence of letters of the

The loss of the tenth book of Diodorus' *Historical Library* and lack of interest on the part of Herodotus mean that Anaxilaos' conquest of Zankle and the foundation of Sicilian Messene are severely underdocumented, but the sources, such as they are, suggest that a more abundant selection of evidence might generate more problems than it would solve. Or at least, this is what seems to emerge from a scrutiny of the most comprehensive ancient narrative of these events, a passage from Pausanias' history of Messenia (4.23.5–10). According to Pausanias, after Eira, the Messenian stronghold in the last part of the Second Messenian War, had been conquered by the Spartans in 668 BC (4.23.4), the survivors led by Aristomenes retreated to Arcadia, where they were approached by other Messenians, from the coastal cities of Pylos and Mothone, who had evacuated their land and were anchored in the Elean harbor of Kyllene. While Aristomenes decided to stay back and pursue an adventurous scheme in order to continue the fight against Sparta, all the Messenian refugees from Arcadia, except those who were too old or too poor, led by Aristomenes' son Gorgos and by Mantiklos, the son of the seer Theoklos, joined the fleet and accepted the invitation of Anaxilaos, tyrant of Rhegion and fourth descendant of Alkidamidas, who had left Messenia after the fall of Ithome in the First Messenian War. With almost the same words Herodotus used to describe his approach to the Samians, Pausanias' Anaxilaos told the Messenians of the hostility between himself and the Zankleans, whose city had a most favorable location and commanded a prosperous territory. So he offered to help the refugees to conquer the city. After his fleet had defeated the fleet of Zankle, the Messenian refugees defeated the army and then stormed the city. Anaxilaos advised the Messenians to put to death the defenders, who had sought refuge on the altars, and sell into slavery the rest of the population, but the pious Messenians, themselves victims of injustice at the hands of fellow Greeks, did not intend to inflict injustice on other Greeks and preferred to share the city with its former inhabitants. The name of the city was changed from Zankle to Messene, and finally Mantiklos founded a sanctuary of Heracles outside the walls of Zankle. The sanctuary came to be known as sanctuary of Heracles Mantiklos.

alphabet that seem to suggest their being minted in subsequent years, starting presumably from 494 BC. Delta is the last letter that appears on tetradrachms, while smaller denominations have a zeta. This would suggest seven years of production, since the Samian alphabet included the digamma, but it should be noted that the smaller denominations minted by the Samians in Zankle have various symbols and not only letters of the alphabet, and in consequence it is not certain that their evidence can be added to that of the tetradrachms. See Luraghi 1994: 207 n. 86, with further references.

Apart from this last piece of information, which may well be an aetiological explanation of a cult that really existed in Sicilian Messene,[8] and from the name of Anaxilaos' ancestor Alkidamidas, virtually every single detail of Pausanias' very promising narrative is demonstrably the product of a distorted adaptation of passages from Herodotus and Thucydides – not to mention the fact that Pausanias dates Anaxilaos to the second quarter of the seventh century. The Messenians take up the role of Herodotus' Samians, and correspondingly the Samian presence in Zankle is projected backwards to the time of the foundation of the city, itself described by cannibalizing Thucydides' passage on the early history of Zankle.[9] Over the years, scholars have disagreed as to the amount of historical information that can legitimately be extracted from Pausanias' narrative. In any case, it is fair to say that it takes a good deal of optimism to use this passage as evidence for the participation of Messenians from the Peloponnese in Anaxilaos' conquest of Zankle.[10] It seems hard to believe that Pausanias or his source, whoever that was, would have taken the trouble to rework Herodotus and Thucydides if he had had available a source that narrated the episode with the Messenians as its protagonists. Even though Pausanias and/or his source(s), apart from their impossibly early chronology for this event, were not alone in connecting Zankle's change of name with an influx of Messenian refugees from the Peloponnese,[11] in the end it seems preferable to follow Thucydides' more sober version, according to which Anaxilaos called the city Messene after his old fatherland, and settled in it colonists of various origin – a mixed bunch of people, as Thucydides puts it.

Weapons dedicated at Olympia from a victory of the Messenians over the *Mylaioi* should refer to mopping-up operations in the territory after

---

[8] See Asheri 1988: 7–8.

[9] A helpful synopsis of the relevant passages is offered by Pareti 1914: 72–5. It should be pointed out that Pausanias' version of the early history of Zankle cannot derive from confusion: its closeness to the texts of Herodotus and Thucydides identifies it as a conscious and intentional historical forgery. This should be kept in mind in assessing the historical value of the portions that have no parallel in other extant sources.

[10] But modern historians are well provided with optimism; see most recently Ganci 1998: 19–24.

[11] According to Strabo (6.2.3), Sicilian Messene took its new name, at an unspecified moment, from the Messenians of the Peloponnese, who founded it, while Diodorus (15.66.5) simply says that the city took its name from the Messenians of the Peloponnese, and it is unclear whether he means that this happened when the exiles from Naupaktos migrated to Sicily or before (which seems the most likely interpretation of the passage). Notice that Diodorus continues to call the city Zankle until the end of the tyranny in 461 (at least); see Diod. 11.48.2, 59.4, 66.1, 76.5 and the discussion below, n. 26.

the takeover.[12] Mylai, a small Greek settlement on the northern side of Cape Pelorus, does not seem to have been an independent polis, but was definitely the kind of place where a group of people expelled from the city could entrench to attempt resistance, which suggests that the *Mylaioi* may be seen as previous inhabitants of Zankle, evicted by Anaxilaos' colonists.[13] Probably soon after its foundation, the new colony started to mint coins with exactly the same types used at Rhegion, but with different weights and the legend "of the Messenians."[14] Anaxilaos, fulfilling his role as founder of the city, apparently moved there, entrusting Rhegion to his son Leophron.[15] Judging from this and from the fact that the output of its mint was significantly larger than that of Rhegion, Messene seems to have become the main center of his "kingdom of the Strait."

Anaxilaos' next initiative, at some point between 490 and 480 BC, was probably a campaign against the south Italian city of Lokroi, with which he seemed to be still on good terms at the time of the Samians' arrival. Once again dedications of weapons at Olympia taken from the Lokrians by Messenians and Rhegians are the only evidence for this episode – unless they stem from the early phases of the war against Lokroi in 477 (see below).[16] Anaxilaos' alliance with the tyrant of Himera Terillos, whose daughter Kydippe he married, must also fall in these years, since at least one son born of this wedding could claim his father's throne as early as 467 BC.[17] Finally, Anaxilaos followed the use of Sicilian tyrants of this age of competing in hippic events in the Panhellenic games. His team won the race of mule carts at the Olympiad of (probably) 484, and the tyrant celebrated by commissioning a victory ode from Simonides and by

[12] *SEG* 24.313–14 = *IGDS* 5, two helmets with the same inscription, apparently engraved by the same hand; see Luraghi 1994: 213.

[13] This episode may explain Strabo's attributing the foundation of Himera to the "Zankleans of Mylai" (6.2.6); as it is, this is nonsense, but it may be a garbled reference to an influx of Zanklean refugees coming from Mylai, who perhaps formed the tribe "Zanklaia" documented in a recently published inscription from Himera, dating to the early fifth century and recording a redistribution of land. On the inscription, see Brugnone 1997: 263 (date), 271–4 (tribe "Zanklaia"), 301–4 (historical context: the tribe was formed by the 300 Zanklaeans spared by the Samians – but their final expulsion from Zankle should be dated after Anaxilaos' conquest).

[14] For the first series minted by Anaxilaos at Rhegion and Messene, see Caccamo Caltabiano 1993: 17–31.

[15] Sources in Luraghi 1994: 215.

[16] *SEG* 24.311–12 = *IGDS* 4, a helmet and a greave, dedicated by the Messenians for a victory over the Lokrians (only the inscription on the greave is complete, but the preserved portions of both are identical, which supports the generally accepted notion that they go back to the same occasion); *SEG* 24.304–5 = *IGDGG* 34a–b, again a helmet and a greave, dedicated by the Rhegians for a victory over the Lokrians. All the four inscriptions look extremely similar. For a discussion of the historical background, see De Sensi Sestito 1981a: 603–4 and n. 23.

[17] The marriage is mentioned in Hdt. 7.165; for a reconstruction of the tyrant's family, see Vallet 1958: 369–70.

changing the types of the coins of both Rhegion and Messene, issuing new coins which showed the mule cart on one side and a hare on the other.[18]

Even though Herodotus (7.165) depicts him as the prime mover behind the scheme that brought a substantial Carthaginian expeditionary corps to Himera in 480, Anaxilaos did not participate directly in the campaign, and seems to have emerged essentially unscathed from the defeat. However, the victory of the Akragantine–Syracusan bloc, under the leadership of the now tyrant of Syracuse Gelon, was a serious setback for him, and probably compelled him, formally or not, to recognize the supremacy of Syracuse. When Gelon died in 478, and his successor Hieron was soon plunged into a conflict with the old ally Theron, tyrant of Akragas, Anaxilaos must have thought that the situation was too favorable to let it go.[19] Around 477, a new Rhegian–Messenian expedition, probably led by Leophron, invaded the territory of the Lokrians. The latter turned to the goddess Aphrodite, pronouncing the famous vow to prostitute their daughters if saved,[20] but it was Hieron who relieved them, sending his right-hand-man Chromius to threaten war if Anaxilaos did not stop the campaign immediately. It may be on this occasion that a daughter of Anaxilaos married Hieron, as a token of submission.[21]

When the flamboyant tyrant died, a year later, his son Leophron may not have been alive any more, or he was excluded from succession for reasons we cannot ascertain. At any rate, Mikythos, a man of Anaxilaos' court, was chosen as regent and tutor for the tyrant's young sons, probably offspring of his marriage with Kydippe.[22] During his regency, Mikythos sent troops to support Taras in a war against the Iapygians, incurring a famously disastrous defeat, and founded a short-lived colony at Pyxous on the Tyrrhenian coast of Bruttium.[23] In spite of the limited success of such initiatives, he may have been too active for Hieron's taste: in 467/6 the tyrant of Syracuse summoned Anaxilaos' sons and suggested that it was time for them to claim their father's power. Mikythos left

---

[18] For a comprehensive discussion of the chronology and iconography of these series and of the date of Anaxilaos' victory, see Millino 2001, who convincingly argues for 484 rather than 480. The famous and possibly witty opening of Simonides' victory ode is Sim. Fr. 515 Page.

[19] See De Sensi Sestito 1981a: 633.

[20] Iust. 21.3.2 with Sourvinou-Inwood 1977; cf., however, Redfield 2003: 411–16.

[21] Schol. Pind. Pyth. 1.112, quoting Philistus, FgrHist 556 F 50, and Timaeus, FgrHist 566 F 97; for the chronology of the marriage, see Vallet 1958: 367–8.

[22] Hdt. 7.170.4; Diod. 11.48.2; Iust. 4.2.4–5. See Luraghi 1994: 224–5 and n. 153.

[23] See respectively Hdt. 7.170.3 and Diod. 11.52 (alliance with Taras and defeat against the Iapygians) and Diod. 11.59.4 and Strab. 6.1.1 (colony at Pyxous). For discussions of Mikythos' initiatives, see De Sensi Sestito 1981a: 639–42 and now Millino 2003, whose suggestion of switching the chronology of the two episodes seems, however, unnecessary and not supported by the sources.

Rhegion and moved to Tegea. From there, in order to thank the gods for curing his son of a serious illness, Mikythos dedicated an extraordinary number of bronze statues, proudly calling himself in the dedicatory inscriptions "Rhegian and Messenian," that is, as comparable examples show, a citizen of Rhegion and Messene – clearly he had been one of Anaxilaos' colonists.[24]

As the tyrannies of Sicily fell one after the other, the island was thrown into turmoil, with exiles and people who had been deported by the tyrants to other cities trying to reinstate the status quo ante against the opposition of tens of thousands of mercenaries settled in various cities by the tyrants themselves.[25] Anaxilaos' sons were among the last to be overthrown, around 461 (Diod. 11.76.5). What happened then in the two cities is unclear, but it is at least possible that Messene was chosen as the place to settle mercenaries evicted from other Sicilian cities.[26] At any rate, while Rhegion immediately abandoned the coin types introduced by Anaxilaos, Messene preserved them essentially unchanged for decades. Their legend, however, which up to that point had been *Messēniōn*, "of the Messenians," was changed around 455 BC to the Doric form, *Messaniōn*.[27]

For the following centuries, we have no further sign of existence of the Messenian component of Rhegion. In Thucydides' narratives of the Athenian expeditions to Sicily during the Peloponnesian War, whenever the ethnic heritage of Rhegion is brought up, the city is always referred to as Chalcidian.[28] In 399, when the Rhegians organized a military expedition against Dionysius the First, tyrant of Syracuse, Diodorus (14.40.1) says that, being a Chalcidian colony, the Rhegians were particularly upset

---

[24] The dedications at Olympia are mentioned by Herodotus, 7.170.3 and Pausanias, 5.26.2–4 and 24.6. The archaeological evidence related to Mikythos' dedications is discussed in detail by Eckstein 1969: 33–42. The fragments of the dedicatory inscriptions are *IvO* 267–9. For the interpretation of the double ethnic, Luraghi 1994: 226.

[25] On these rather complicated events, see Asheri 1980.

[26] See De Sensi Sestito 1981b. Diodorus, who calls Sicilian Messene "Zankle" up to this point (see above, n. 11), says that the mercenaries were settled "in Messenia" by common decision of the Sicilians. Since it seems unthinkable that this might refer to Peloponnesian Messenia, most scholars think that "Messenia" here really means Sicilian Messene. It remains unclear what exactly Diodorus thought about the change of name of Zankle, except for the fact that he refers elsewhere to the fact that Sicilian Messene derived its name from the Messenians of the Peloponnese.

[27] Caccamo Caltabiano 1993: 67–9.

[28] Thuc. 3.86.2 (Rhegion on Leontinoi's side at the time of the first Athenian expedition, in 427/6, because of their ethnic affinity); 6.44.3 (at the beginning of the second expedition, in 416/15, the Athenians ask for help from the Rhegians, arguing that they had come to help their fellow Chalcidians of Leontinoi, but their request is rejected); 6.46.2 (failure to win over the Rhegians in spite of their ethnic affinity to the Leontinians frustrates the Athenians); 6.79.2 (in his speech at Camarina during the winter of 415/14, the Syracusan Hermocrates remarks that not even the Rhegians, in spite of being Chalcidians, were on the Athenians' side).

because the tyrant had enslaved their Chalcidian kinsmen of Naxos and Katane.[29]

Messene on the other hand seems to count as Dorian, at least for Thucydides,[30] and remained consistently on the Syracusan side, except for a short period between the summer of 426 and the summer of 425, after the Athenian general Laches stormed Mylai and then forced the Messenians to join the Athenian alliance (Thuc. 3.90.2–4). In the spring of 425, a joint Syracusan–Lokrian expedition summoned by the Messenians themselves put an end to Athenian control of the city (Thuc. 4.1). Later, after the peace of Gela of 424, Lokrian colonists moved to Messene, brought in by a faction of Messenians during a civil strife, and for a short while the city remained under the control of Lokroi, but two years later the Lokrian colonists were already on their way back home (Thuc. 5.1.1).

Interestingly, Thucydides never explicitly addresses the issue of Messene's ethnic heritage, even though the theme of ethnic solidarity is absolutely central to his depiction of the Athenian expeditions. It may be less than surprising that, when the Rhegians convinced the *stratēgoi* of Messene to join their expedition against Dionysius of Syracuse, the argument they used was that the tyrant had enslaved Greek cities, without any ethnic specification. However, what is really noteworthy is that the question of the ethnic origin of the Sicilian Messenians did not surface, to judge by the only extant source, when finally Messene received the first documented settlement of Messenians in the west, in the first years of the fourth century BC. Some of the Messenians who had been evicted by the Spartans from Naupaktos and Kephallenia after the end of the Peloponnesian War came to Sicily, where the tyrant of Syracuse Dionysius the First enrolled them as mercenaries. After the Carthaginians seized and plundered Sicilian Messene in 397, the tyrant resettled the city with 600 Messenians, together with 1,000 men from Lokroi and 4,000 from the Lokrian colony of Medma (Diod. 14.78.5). The Spartans, however, seem to have protested against this measure, because – according to Diodorus – they resented the Messenian exiles being settled in such a prominent city, whereupon Dionysius gave them territory taken from the Sicel city of Abacaenum, on the northern coast of Cape Pelorus. There, the exiles founded Tyndaris, destined to grow into a full-fledged polis in the

---

[29] On the relations between Messana, Rhegion, and the tyrant of Syracuse, see Raccuia 1981.

[30] This seems to be implicit in Thuc. 3.86.2: in 427/6, all the Dorian cities of Sicily except Camarina were allies of Syracuse, all the Chalcidian cities of Leontinoi. Messene, as it turns out (Thuc. 3.90.2), was indeed allied to Syracuse. The legend "*Messana*" on its coins reinforces the impression; see also below.

following years. This is the last we hear of Messenians in the West, except for Pausanias' isolated statement that Messenians from Rhegion and Sicily moved to the Peloponnese to join Epaminondas' Messene in 369 BC (4.26.2–5).

THE ETHNIC IDENTITY OF THE WESTERN MESSENIANS

Even though Sicilian Messene kept its name for the rest of its history, the most striking aspect of Western Messenicity is its discontinuous nature. As far as we can tell, it was really only under Anaxilaos and his successors that the Messenian identity of the cities of the Strait came to the fore in any guise, and the somewhat ambiguous relationship to the Western Messenian heritage of the Messenian exiles who finally founded Tyndaris reinforces the impression. In order better to grasp this peculiar situation, we will concentrate our attention in the following on the sources mentioning the Messenian migration to Rhegion at the time of the foundation of the colony, and on the ethnic identity of Sicilian Messene. Finally, we will turn to evidence for cults in the cities of the Strait, including Tyndaris, in an attempt at better defining the relationship between the Western Messenians and the Messenian ethnicity in the Peloponnese.

Messenian participation in the foundation of Rhegion is mentioned by two ancient authors, Strabo and Heraclides Lembus' excerpt from the *Constitution of the Rhegians*. The latter, much more brief and sketchy, derives clearly from the same source as the former.[31] Strabo relates how the Messenians who finally settled in Rhegion had been expelled from their country because they were in favor of offering reparations to the Spartans for the rape of the Spartan maidens in the course of a sacred ceremony at Limnai and for the murder of the Spartans who had run to their rescue. As discussed above (pp. 24–5), this episode, which involved also the killing of the Spartan king Teleklos, is often mentioned in the sources as the cause of the First Messenian War. After being defeated by their fellow countrymen, continues Strabo, the Messenians went to Makistos in Triphylia,[32] whence they sent a delegation to Delphi to complain against Apollo and Artemis for having been rewarded so poorly

---

[31] See the synopsis in Ducat 1974a: 94–5.
[32] The choice of Makistos as the place to which the Messenians escaped is not completely obvious in geographical terms, and may have something to do with the presence, not far from the city, at Kombothekra on Mount Lapithos, of a sanctuary of Artemis, possibly with the epithet Limnatis (Sinn 1981 and above, p. 24 n. 34); conceivably, in some fuller version of the story the Messenians may have arrived there as suppliants of the goddess. See Luraghi 1998: 339 and n. 39.

for their piety. Apollo, however, replied that they should rather be grateful to his sister, for the exile effectively saved them from the impending destruction of their fatherland. The god further ordered the Messenians to join the Chalcidians on their way to Rhegion. So they did, and as a consequence the leaders of Rhegion from the foundation up to Anaxilaos were all of Messenian stock.

An alternative version of the Messenian migration to Italy is mentioned by Pausanias, who says that Alkidamidas, fourth ancestor of Anaxilaos, had come to Rhegion after the death of king Aristodemus and the Spartan capture of Ithome, in 724 BC according to Pausanias' own chronology (4.13.7). It may be significant that Pausanias does not say explicitly whether Alkidamidas' relocation coincided with the foundation of Rhegion,[33] and it is a bit puzzling that the incident is not mentioned in the passage where the fate of the Messenians after the end of the war is described (4.14.1). In any case, Strabo's story implied accepting what Pausanias (4.4.2) calls the Spartan version of the Limnai incident, and it is therefore hardly surprising that Pausanias does not follow it.[34] As shown above, his whole narrative of the western adventures of the Messenians is a rather artificial concoction based on passages of other authors referring to different episodes, which cannot be taken seriously. Some early information on Anaxilaos' genealogy may well be part of the mix, but separating in Pausanias' passage original elements from distortions is impossible – unless the original elements are preserved by other sources, that is.

Tracking down the provenance of Strabo's story is extremely difficult. In the text of the geographer, the story of the Messenians is framed by two quotations from the early historian Antiochus of Syracuse, but scholars have mostly been wary to assume that Strabo extracted it from his work, too.[35] The story presupposes a rather precise and detailed narrative of the outbreak of the First Messenian War, such as no other fifth-century historian seems to have been aware of. However, the appearance of the Limnai episode cannot be construed as a clear-cut indication of a later origin of the story. As discussed above, the connection between Teleklos

---

[33] It may be pointed out that, if Strabo's story was compatible with the accepted chronology of the foundation of Rhegion, then Pausanias' version, which implied a date twenty years later – such was the traditionally accepted duration of the First Messenian War – may have been *a priori* not reconcilable with the idea that the Messenian exiles had participated in the foundation of the city.

[34] On the two versions of the incident presented by Pausanias, see above, pp. 80–2.

[35] For a detailed discussion of the sources of Strab. 6.1.6, see Musti 1988: 37–40, who shows that, while it is possible that Antiochus mentioned the participation of Messenians in the foundation of Rhegion (cf. ibid., 18–19), what Strabo has to say about the Chalcidians and Messenians does not derive from Antiochus, but from some later source, possibly Timaeus of Tauromenium.

and the outbreak of the war is unlikely to have originated with the works of historians of the second half of the fourth century, who seem to have synchronized King Theopompos, the conqueror of Messene according to Tyrtaeus, with the Agiad Polydoros, two generations after Teleklos. If one were to venture a guess as to the historical background to the origin of the Limnai story, the final years of the Archidamian War, with a garrison of Messenians from Naupaktos entrenched in Pylos, seem to offer the most promising option, but of course an earlier date, e.g. in connection with the revolt after the earthquake, cannot be excluded.[36]

Even if we could confidently anchor in time the story of Teleklos' death, all we would gain for the present discussion would be a terminus post for the emergence of Strabo's narrative. There is, however, one aspect that may suggest that, for all its wealth in details, this story may not be much later than the first appearance of the Limnai incident itself. According to Strabo, Apollo told the Messenians that their fatherland was going to be conquered by the Spartans shortly thereafter. While of course temporal proximity between the Messenians' escape and the fall of their fatherland may have been included in the story to enhance its dramatic effect, one wonders if this element of the story should not point to a rather early phase of the development of narratives of the Messenian wars, before the notion that the First Messenian War had lasted twenty years became widely recognized.[37]

Only speculation as to the meaning of Strabo's story may open the way to envisioning possible scenarios for its origin. If we imagine a situation in which the only available explanation for the Spartan conquest of Messenia was one that accused the Messenians of sacrilege and murder, the function of our story seems to be to exculpate the Western Messenians – interestingly, without turning the blame against the Spartans. A story that absolved the Messenians of Rhegion and condemned all the others can hardly have originated elsewhere but at Rhegion itself, among those of its citizens who considered themselves of Messenian stock. As for when the story first emerged, it is worth pointing out that in Strabo it is linked with the historically unlikely notion that Rhegion had been ruled by

---

[36] For more on the origins and development of the story, see above, p. 82. On the revolt and the occupation of Pylos, see below, pp. 188–90.

[37] The length of the First Messenian War was derived from Tyrtaeus' verses (fr. 5. W²), whose evidence does not seem to have been used before the mid fourth century; in Isocrates' *Archidamos* (57), a siege of twenty years is set in the context of the Spartan Heraclids' conquest of Messenia. Callisthenes, writing at the beginning of the fourth century, is thought to have been the first ancient historian to make systematic use of Tyrtaeus as a source for the Messenian wars; see Jacoby 1943: 118, 121, 130, and above, p. 79 n. 34.

Messenians until the time of Anaxilaos, and that there are no references, in any source, to the Messenians of Rhegion after the time of Anaxilaos. Moreover, Strabo's story at the same time depicted the Messenians of Rhegion as the descendants of pious Messenians who had been saved by Artemis from the destruction of their fatherland, and eliminated hostility to Sparta from their background. It could therefore be linked to the alliance between the "kingdom of the Strait" and the Spartan colony of Taras and seen as a parallel of sorts to the foundation story of Taras that Strabo extracted from Antiochus of Syracuse, according to which the Tarantines were the descendants of those Spartans who had not participated in the conquest of Messenia.[38]

Such a conclusion, obviously, would posit a much earlier date for the story of the death of Teleklos than fifth-century sources in general tend to suggest, and one wonders if there is really sufficient reason to do so. As we shall see, evidence on the ethnic self-perception of the Western Messenians in the early fifth century does not encourage the assumption that their notions of early Messenian history were particularly developed at that point in time. Even though it stands to reason that Rhegion's "Messenian moment" under the rule of Anaxilaos must have generated or developed narratives that explained the presence of Messenians in the city, the real question is, how similar such narratives were to the story we find in Strabo, and related to it, whether it is possible to envision a convincing alternative scenario for the origin of this story.

Neither question can be answered in a less than tentative way, but a possible line of approach is suggested by Ducat's observation that the sources on the Messenians of Rhegion seem to go back to traditions that explained the origins of a few prominent families, rather than a mixed colonial enterprise:[39] no ancient source, after all, ever calls Rhegion a mixed Chalcidian–Messenian colony, and no source has preserved the name of a Messenian oikist, as we would expect in the case of a mixed colony.[40] If Ducat is right, the absence of evidence for a Messenian component in fifth- and fourth-century Rhegion would be more understandable – and incidentally, the same would be true of the absence of evidence from the archaic period, especially as concerns the dialect and alphabet of Rhegion.

---

[38] Antiochus *FgrHist* 555 F 13 *ap.* Strab. 6.3.2; for a possible connection between the foundation stories of Rhegion and Taras, see Kiechle 1959: 7–8, and Luraghi 2003: 116–17 and n. 31, with further references.

[39] Ducat 1974a: 98–9.

[40] This, however, does not seem to have been a firmly established rule. On mixed colonies and their oikists, see Malkin 1987: 254–60.

If Strabo's story originated or was developed in the late fifth century or later, it would also be easier to explain the suspicious claim that the city had been under Messenian leadership throughout the archaic period: the claim was limited to the age for which it was less easy to refute it. Finally, a story that characterized the Messenians of Rhegion as not hostile to the Spartans, thereby reversing the key feature of the Messenian identity as it came to be defined from the mid-fifth century onwards (see below, p. 334), could conceivably have something to do with political events at the time of the great Athenian expedition to Sicily, when Rhegion, in spite of its Chalcidian heritage, essentially refused to help the Athenians, who were ostensibly defending the Chalcidians of Leontinoi against the Syracusans, allies of Sparta.[41] Let it be noted that on that occasion, if any Rhegians were still defining themselves as Messenian, the question of the meaning of their Messenian identity posed itself in very concrete terms: Messenians from Naupaktos were present in the Athenian expeditionary corps.[42]

In conclusion, the little that can be guessed as regards the Messenian identity in Rhegion, based essentially on Strabo, is that it may have functioned as a way for a – probably rather small – component of the citizen body to differentiate itself from the rest, rather than as the charter myth for a political community. The only detail that it seems possible to establish is that the Messenians of Rhegion did not regard the Spartans as their natural enemies, and thereby probably turned their back on Messenian irredentism as it emerged from the 460s. These observations offer a starting point to consider the most striking product of the Messenian minority of Rhegion, the foundation of Sicilian Messene.

There can be no doubt that, by diverting the Samians towards Zankle, Anaxilaos intended to take control of the city, if only indirectly. Had the Samians not disappointed him, Messene could have been founded a few years earlier. The paradox of having a political community formed mostly by Ionians and calling itself "the Messenians" may not have disturbed the tyrant too much. At any rate, when Sicilian Messene finally came into being, its population, according to Thucydides, was a mix of diverse provenance. Considering the main groups from which people were migrating west in the early fifth century, we would expect the citizens of Messene to have included Greeks from Asia Minor fleeing from the failure of the Ionian Revolt and mercenaries from the Greek mainland,

---

[41] As pointed out by Hermocrates of Syracuse in his speech at Camarina, Thuc. 6.79.2; on the lack of commitment of Rhegion at the time of the expedition see also Thuc. 6.44.3, 46.2.

[42] Thuc. 7.31.2 (Demosthenes embarks Messenian hoplites on his way to Sicily in 413/12), 57.8.

mostly from Arcadia.[43] In itself, this fact did not predetermine the ethnic identity of the city. Normally, in the Greek world, when a new city was founded, its overall ethnic definition was a function of its mother-city, the one from which the oikist came, even though we may suppose that, as a rule, the colonists themselves were of mixed origin. In the case of Messene, however, the connection with the mother city may not have been straightforward: the colony was founded by Rhegion, and should therefore have been Chalcidian like Rhegion, but the founder was himself not of Chalcidian stock, and gave the city the name of his old fatherland. Subsequent evidence shows, as noted above, that Sicilian Messene at any rate was not considered a Chalcidian colony. Were the citizens of Messene in any sense seen as ethnically Messenian?

The kind of evidence that we would normally use to answer a question of this sort does not offer a clear picture in our case. Our knowledge of the cults of Sicilian Messene is not such as to allow any clear conclusion,[44] as we will see more in detail. On the other hand, in the first decades of its life Sicilian Messene used, for all its official manifestations, such as dedications of booty at Olympia and legends on coins, the Ionic dialect and the Chalcidian alphabet, just as Rhegion.[45] This situation can be explained in two different ways: either Messenian ethnicity was not really a central element of the identity of the colony, or Dorianism had not yet been recognized as a necessary component of the Messenian identity, as it later would.[46] Surprising as it may sound, this second conclusion cannot be ruled out. Only the tradition of the division of the Peloponnese among the Heraclids established that being Messenian, in post-mythic times, meant being Dorian, but it is not clear that this tradition existed at all before the early fifth century (see above, pp. 60–1). After all, in the archaic age the kingdom of Pylos was known as the homeland of the Ionians of Asia Minor.[47] On the other hand, Thucydides used, for the name of the tyrant of Rhegion and founder of Sicilian Messene, the Doric form,

[43] It has been occasionally suggested (e.g. by Vallet 1958: 373 n. 4) that Mikythos may have relocated to Tegea because he was Arcadian, possibly a mercenary formerly in the service of Anaxilaos.

[44] For a comprehensive discussion of the evidence for the cults of Rhegion and Sicilian Messene, see Camassa 1993.

[45] See the documents mentioned above, nn. 12 and 16. Mikythos' dedications at Olympia, above n. 24, written in the Chalcidian alphabet, present some dialectal features that may point to lateral influence of Dorian and Western Aeolian dialects according to Salvaneschi 1975: 85–6, but one wonders if they should not be attributed to the Elean stonecutter who inscribed the text and left his mark in the shape of some letters.

[46] As suggested by Hall 2003: 154 n. 62.

[47] For the ancient evidence on the Ionian migration and the provenance of the Ionians, see Prinz 1979: 314–76; for the Pylian origin of the Ionians, esp. 318–40.

calling him "Anaxilas." Now, unlike Herodotus who Ionicized all personal names, Thucydides mostly respected their original dialectal spelling,[48] and this suggests at least the possibility that the tyrant himself used the Doric spelling for his name, thereby subscribing to the notion that a true Messenian ought to be Dorian. Of course, it is also conceivable that Thucydides, for whom the Dorian ethnicity of the Messenians was an accepted fact, restored the Dorian spelling of a name he found in Ionicized form in a written source, but it seems that we have to allow at least for the possibility that Sicilian Messene at its birth was simply not defined as ethnically Messenian.

This unclear background complicates the question of the change from Ionic to Doric spelling on the coins of the city. On the basis purely of the study of the dies, the shift has been dated around 455 BC, that is, not immediately after the end of the tyranny, but quite soon thereafter. Now, a passage in Diodorus can be interpreted in the sense that Sicilian Messene became the homeland of mercenaries who had been expelled from other cities of the island.[49] The event is narrated in the course of 461 BC, but Diodorus is notorious for concentrating in the same year series of events that in fact lasted for a longer period of time, and we cannot confidently exclude that the change in the spelling of the name of the city corresponded to the settlement of the mercenaries. But even if we accept this connection, the shift to a Doric spelling is not easily accounted for. The scarce information we have about the provenance of the mercenaries of the Sicilian tyrants does not point exclusively, indeed not even predominantly, to Dorian areas.[50] Furthermore, the change in spelling did not correspond to a change in types: the coinage of Messene, from now on Messana, retained the types of the mule cart and the hare, whose association with the founder of the city, the tyrant Anaxilaos, was explicit. In other words, the settlement of the mercenaries is not a straightforward explanation for the use of a Dorian dialect in documents that were official expressions of the city, nor for the fact that later in the fifth century Messene–Messana was apparently counted among the Dorian colonies of Sicily. One wonders if this sort of Dorianization *a posteriori* might not be

---

[48] On the spelling of names in Herodotus and Thucydides, see Hornblower 2000b: 138. Note especially the Ionic spelling of Leotychides in Thuc. 1.89, which Hornblower attributes to the influence of Herodotus. If that is the case, one would be more inclined to think that Thucydides would not have Dorianized a name he found in Ionic form in his source(s), but this can be no more than an indication.

[49] See above, n. 26.

[50] All the available evidence refers to mercenaries of the tyrants of Syracuse, and points to Arcadia as their homeland; see Bettalli 1995: 92–9.

a consequence of the revolt in Messenia, which established explicitly Dorianism as a component of the Messenian identity.[51] This, of course, would imply that the Messenians of Sicily did indeed consider themselves Messenian in ethnic terms.

As a matter of fact, it has to be recognized that the sequence of evictions and resettlements that characterizes the history of Zankle–Messene–Messana during the fifth and early fourth centuries was bound to affect the ethnic identity of its inhabitants, creating a situation in which, in terms of self-definition, at different points in time more than one option was available to the individual citizens, and possibly also to the polis as a whole. For instance, Leontiskos and Symmachos, two athletes who won at Olympia in 456 and 452 BC and in 428 and 424 BC respectively, competed as citizens of Sicilian Messene, but were known as being of Zanklean stock.[52] In such a situation, and in view of the recognized situational nature of ethnic identities in general, it may be wrong to assume consistency over time. There is even a precious piece of evidence that seems to suggest that the Messenians of Sicily somehow embraced an open-ended identity. According to a fragment from Callimachus' *Aetia*, in the cult ceremonial dedicated to the founders of the city, they, unlike the citizens of all other Sicilian colonies, invoked their founders without mentioning their name and leaving it open whether there were one, two, or more of them.[53] Even though we cannot anchor in time precisely this piece of information, it offers an intriguing insight in the identity of the city. Uncertainty as to the name and number of the founders could not but imply uncertainty as to the mother city, problematizing the central element of its ethnic definition.

The fate of the Messenians of Naupaktos in Sicily shows that, whatever the ethnic classification of the citizens of Sicilian Messene, they were not automatically seen as homogenous to the Messenians of the Peloponnese. It also opens up an interesting perspective on the relationship of the

---

[51] See below, p. 167 and n. 61, and pp. 189–90.

[52] Paus. 6.2.10 mentions the two athletes as partial exceptions to the surprising fact that no Messenians won at Olympia during the long years of the exile from the Peloponnese; he then adds that the Greeks of Sicily say that these two athletes were actually "old Zanklaeans" and not Messenians (Leontiskos' statue is mentioned in 6.4.3). See Asheri 1983: 33. This piece of information would inspire more confidence if it had been based on epigraphic evidence from Olympia rather than on a reference to Sicilian oral tradition (from Pausanias' age?).

[53] Call. *Aetia* 2.43.58–83 Pfeiffer. As Vallet 1958: 63 n. 1 rightly points out, although the *aition* roots the ceremony in the foundation story of Zankle, it is clear that this peculiar ritual is much more likely to be a product of the troubled story of Zankle–Messene–Messana from the early fifth century to the early fourth. On the ritual described by Callimachus, see Malkin 1987: 198–200.

Western Messenians to the Messenian heritage of the mainland. The sheer fact that the refugees from Naupaktos enrolled as mercenaries under the tyrant of Syracuse Dionysius, rather than peacefully settling in Rhegion or Messene, may already be significant of itself. Moreover, when the Spartans objected to their being settled in Messene by the tyrant, they do not seem to have had problems with the Messenian heritage of the city, but only with the fact that it was too prominent a place for their old enemies to settle in. Apparently, the existence of a whole city whose inhabitants called themselves "the Messenians," and the fact that their ally Dionysius was restoring it, did not disturb the Spartans. As for the refugees from Naupaktos, by calling their new city Tyndaris, the city of the Tyndarids, and displaying the Dioscuri and Helen on their coins,[54] they were in all likelihood voicing a claim we find articulated explicitly in Pausanias, according to whom the Messenians maintained that the Tyndarids were really Messenian, not Spartan.[55] Quite apart from the fact that this way of reclaiming as Messenian a well-known component of the Spartan mythic heritage is otherwise attested as a feature of the Messenian identity, the colonists of Tyndaris were clearly reaffirming hostility to Sparta as a component of their being Messenian.

This said, evidence on the cults of Artemis and Apollo in the area of the Strait may suggest the existence of shared elements in the identity of the Western and Peloponnesian Messenians. A small group of sources, whose preservation we owe to ancient grammarians' attempts at tracing the origins of bucolic poetry, refer to Orestes' wanderings in the area and to cults he supposedly founded.[56] In a passage from Probus' commentary on Virgil, including fragments of Varro and Cato, the hero sails west with his sister Iphigenia, carrying a statue of Artemis from Tauris, and is finally purified from the murder of his mother near Rhegion, in a place marked by the presence of seven rivers. There, Orestes established a sanctuary of Apollo, whence, according to Varro, the Rhegians used ritually to take a laurel wreath before setting sail for Delphi. Both Cato and Varro also mention that Orestes' bronze sword, the one he had used to kill his mother, used to be displayed in the sanctuary, suspended from a tree. The *scholia* to Theocritus add that, once purified, Orestes crossed over to Sicily, in the area of Tyndaris. What he did there we are not told, but it

---

[54] On the coinage of Tyndaris, see Consolo Langher 1965.
[55] Paus. 3.1.4, 26.3, 4.31.9; see Gengler 2005: 324–5.
[56] The following summarizes the results of Luraghi 1998, where the sources and the relevant manuscript evidence are discussed in detail.

seems obvious to assume this to be a variant of the story that sent Orestes to the area of Syracuse, where he founded a temple of Diana Facelina or Facelitis. Such a conclusion is all the more likely, since the existence of at least one temple of Diana Facelitis in the area of Tyndaris is otherwise attested. Altogether, the sources point to an original story in which the hero, following an oracle, had come with his sister and the statue of Artemis to the territory of Rhegion, had been purified there, founded a sanctuary of Apollo and consecrated there his sword, and finally crossed to Sicily and founded another sanctuary, to harbor the statue of Artemis from Tauris, either in the territory of Tyndaris or near Mylai.

This was obviously an aetiological story that connected the foundations of two sanctuaries, one for Apollo in the territory of Rhegion, probably close to the river Metaurus, which marked its border towards the Lokrian colony of Medma, and one for Artemis on the northeastern coast of Sicily. The story probably goes back to a moment when Messene and Rhegion were closely associated, as they were, as far as we can tell, only under Anaxilaos and his successors, while the presence of Apollo and Artemis recalls in a striking way the migration of the Messenians to Rhegion as narrated by Strabo. Furthermore, the epithet of the goddess, present only in Latin sources in the form Fa(s)celina or Fa(s)celitis, and the provenance of the statue from Tauris have been interpreted as linking this cult to the cult of Artemis Orthia/Limnatis.[57] The conclusion, often formulated by scholars, that these two cults have something to do with the Western Messenians and the foundation of Sicilian Messene, seems reasonable.[58] If that is the case, it is interesting to observe that the cult putatively established in Sicilian Messene under Anaxilaos was a Spartan cult attested also in Messenia, and connected to the alleged cause of the outbreak of the First Messenian War, and also that the same cult was apparently established in Tyndaris – unless what actually happened was simply that the preexisting sanctuary, located in the area of Mylai, ended up in the territory of Tyndaris when the city was founded.

All in all, the evidence offers a controversial picture of how the Western Messenians constructed their identity, in itself and in relation to other groups of Messenians and to the Messenian homeland. Much of what has been said so far is admittedly tentative, and it has to be recognized that, quite apart from the possibility of real gaps in the evidence, operating on the basis of few pieces of information scattered over a rather long period of time implies the risk of producing simplified and one-sided pictures of

[57] Camassa 1993: 141–7. [58] See Vallet 1958: 79, Costabile 1979, and Asheri 1988: 8–9.

processes that were much more complex. Keeping this danger in mind, it seems reasonable to look for a conceptual framework that may help our interpretation of the data.

In conceptualizing the place of the Western Messenians in the history of the Messenian identity, comparative research on diasporas may offer a valuable starting point. In contrast to the traditional the concept of diaspora based essentially on the experience of the Jews, focussing on aspects such as their deportation, expulsion, and scattering all over the Mediterranean world and beyond, recent scholarship has advocated the usefulness of a broader concept of diaspora, one that includes non-compulsory migrations and movements of population motivated by trade or conquest. Such a broader definition of the concept, while not uncontroversial in its scholarly as well as political implications, offers an advantage in that it makes it possible to observe shared features between historical processes that were previously seen as incomparable, creating a sociological template on which to map case studies.[59]

Especially in cases in which the homeland of the diaspora group is under some sort of foreign domination, the diaspora itself can take up the leading role in articulating and defining the ethnic identity of the group, over and above any portion of it that may have remained back in the homeland. It is in this sense that Jonathan Hall has recently proposed to attribute a key function to the Messenian diaspora, especially in the definition of Dorianism as a feature of the Messenian identity.[60] As it stands, this conclusion is problematic for two reasons. On the one hand, Hall denies, against the evidence, that the rebels who fought against the Spartans in the 460s identified themselves as Messenian before they left the Peloponnese.[61] On the other, the notion that Dorianism as a

---

[59] For a very promising, if somewhat preliminary, attempt at a comparative sociology and typology of diasporas, see Cohen 1997, with the discussion by Safran 1999. For the change in the definition of diaspora, see e.g. Tölöyan 1996: 12–15. It is important to keep in mind that the field of diaspora studies is very much in flux, and definitions and categories are by no means uncontroversial – especially because of the obvious political implications of diaspora identities in the contemporary world. There is a clear tension in scholarship between the definition of a sociological category of diaspora and recognizing or denying the status of diaspora of this or that group.

[60] See Hall 2003: 148–55.

[61] For the definition of the rebels as Messenians in all sources about the revolt, see below, pp. 195–6. Note that the dedications of weapons by the Methanioi strongly suggest that the idea that the Messenians were actually Dorians was articulated explicitly in Messenia itself in connection with the fifth-century revolt.

component of the Messenian identity was first articulated by the Messenian diaspora sits uneasily alongside the epigraphic evidence discussed above, which shows that in its earliest documents Sicilian Messene used an Ionic dialect. Furthermore, Hall's identification of the Messenians as a diaspora relies on attributing to all Messenians abroad features, such as the determination to return to their homeland, that are documented only for one group, namely the Messenians of Naupaktos (see below, p. 193). However, his proposal to analyze groups of Messenians outside the Peloponnese in the light of comparative research on diasporas can lead to interesting insights – if in a direction somewhat different from that advocated by Hall himself.

Diasporas are a special sort of ethnic group, and the articulation of a diaspora identity should be seen as a special case of ethnicity, understood as the process whereby a group articulates its shared identity in ethnic terms.[62] This specification is important because, even though it is certainly right in empirical terms that a diaspora cannot be defined as such at the very moment of migration and needs a certain period of time to emerge as a diaspora,[63] in sociological terms the collective identity of a diaspora can be analyzed with the same categories applied to ethnicity, and need not be any more based on objective facts and "genuine" historical traditions than ethnicity itself.

A diaspora is identified by a series of features, not all of which need to be present for a group to be defined as a diaspora.[64] Obviously, the fewer the features observed in any single case, the more doubtful the definition of that case as a diaspora, but even a negative conclusion may have interesting historical implications. A diaspora may be provoked by dispersal of a human group from its homeland, either as a consequence of a violent and traumatic event such as a civil war or foreign conquest, or by expansion in pursuit of work, trade, or colonial or imperial ambitions. The diaspora community shares a collective memory of the homeland, its location and history – the amount of creativity involved in generating

---

[62] On ethnicity as a process, see e.g. Fabietti 1998: 21–2 with further references. For discussions of the relationship of diasporas to ethnicity, see Tölöyan 1996: 16–19, Butler 2001: 204–5.

[63] In the sense that it takes some time before it becomes clear whether a group of migrants will be assimilated or preserve a sense of its discrete identity, as emphasized by Marienstras 1985: 225, followed by Cohen 1997: 24, 185–6. See also Butler 2001: 192, who suggests an empirical span of two generations for a migrant community to become a diaspora. It should be noticed, of course, that the alternative between assimilation and creation of a diaspora identity admits all sorts of intermediate possibilities, as pointed out by Safran 1999: 257–8.

[64] The following checklist is based on Cohen 1997: 23–6 and 184–7. See also Butler 2001: 197–209 (with occasional essentialist overtones).

such memory may vary significantly, and idealization is the norm. Such a collective memory is the cornerstone of a strong sense of ethnic distinctness, often involving the shared perception of a common fate. A diaspora is typically united by a collective commitment to the defense and/or prosperity of the homeland, or to its liberation, and tends to develop a return movement. It often lives in a troubled relationship to its host society, and by contrast develops a sense of empathy and solidarity with groups of the same putative ethnic origin in other lands, which are typically construed as other branches of the same diaspora.[65]

It is immediately clear that the little we know about the Messenians of Rhegion and Messene maps rather poorly onto this checklist. The nostalgia for the homeland is expressed in Anaxilaos' decision to call Messene his new foundation on the Strait. Yet, it is controversial what that name really implied for its citizens. If it is true that a collective name is a powerful ethnic symbol,[66] in the case of a Greek colony the situation may be a bit more complicated. We have on the one hand cases of colonies such as Megara Hyblaia or Lokroi Epizephyrioi, whose very name signaled their ethnic heritage, but on the other hand, we have no reason to believe that e.g. the citizens of the Chalcidian colony of Naxos in Sicily perceived any special link to the Aegean island of Naxos. Even though the reference to Peloponnesian Messene certainly determined Anaxilaos' decision, this does not automatically demonstrate that the Messenians of the Strait conceived of themselves as ethnically Messenian, let alone related to any other branch of the Messenian diaspora.

According to Strabo's story, the traumatic event that had determined the migration of the first wave of the Messenian diaspora was a civil war among Messenians. Conflicts within the motherland are omnipresent in the foundation legends of Greek colonies.[67] In the light of diaspora studies, we might speculate that this trait should be connected to the fact that Greek colonies saw themselves, at any rate from as early as we can tell, as a final destination, and did not develop a return movement.[68] In

---

[65] To this list, some scholars, e.g. Butler 2001, would add the simultaneous presence of branches of the diaspora in different places – although here there is some discussion on what exactly constitutes different places.

[66] On the symbolic and performative power of the ethnic name, see especially Ruby 2006: 44. The necessary relationship between ethnonym and ethnicity has been often remarked upon, see Smith 1986: 22–4, Fabietti 1998: 16, Hall 2002: 125 and above, p. 10.

[67] The elaboration of the trauma of leaving the motherland in the foundation stories of Greek colonies has been brilliantly investigated by Carol Dougherty; see Dougherty 1993a, 1993b.

[68] For a preliminary and still rather sketchy attempt at considering Greek colonization from the point of view of diaspora studies, see Sheffer 2003: 46–7.

other words, the fact that the Messenians of Rhegion, to judge by their foundation legend, turned their back on their fellow Messenians of the Peloponnese may have more to do with the specific configuration of Greek colonization than with the nature of the Messenian diaspora in Rhegion. Incidentally, this observation on the specific nature of Greek colonies from the point of view of diaspora studies could also explain the lack of evidence for a return movement in Tyndaris, although in this case the argument from silence should be used with particular caution.[69] In any case, it seems fair to say that the Messenian legend of Rhegion hardly set the foundations for solidarity with other groups of Messenians.

However, it is on the level of ethnic solidarity that the Messenian diaspora of Rhegion and Sicilian Messene most conspicuously fails the test. In extant sources on the Peloponnesian War and the early fourth century, there is no evidence of solidarity between the Western Messenians and the other branch of the Messenian diaspora, the Messenians of Naupaktos, which is especially noteworthy since the latter participated in the second Athenian expedition to Sicily and, as we have seen, a rather large number of them ended up settling in Sicily. Ethnic solidarity seems to have been so far from everybody's mind, that it does not even feature among the reasons for Spartan discontent with the initial settlement of the Messenian mercenaries in Messene.

On the other hand, all the criteria that define a diaspora apply to the Western Messenians in Pausanias' narrative. There, the original nucleus, settled in Rhegion after the First Messenian War, welcomed, under Anaxilaos' leadership, the new wave of exiles generated by the Second Messenian War (4.23.6), then the Messenians expelled from Naupaktos (4.26.2), and finally, when Epaminondas gathered all Messenians to create a free Messenian state in the Peloponnese, the Messenians from Rhegion and Messene duly returned home (4.26.5) – the priest of Heracles Mantiklos in Messene even had a dream announcing the impending rebirth of Messenia (4.26.3). This is rather puzzling. As discussed above, the early portion of Pausanias' history of the Western Messenians contains an alarming amount of historical falsification. What should we make of

---

[69] It is true that Diodorus' description of the growth of the colony immediately after its foundation (14.78.5) does not encourage the hypothesis that a significant number of its founders left it some three decades after the foundation, but the passage is clearly rather laconic and unspecific. Moreover, the absence of Tyndaris among the centers of Messenian diaspora described by Pausanias (4.26.1–5) may depend on the suppression of their eviction from Messana. In any case, the silence of the sources about a possible return of the citizens of Tyndaris to the Peloponnese is not completely trivial.

the rest? In theory, it cannot be excluded that some of the Messenians of Naupaktos settled in Rhegion as well, as Pausanias says, but if that was the case, unless we jettison Diodorus' testimony on the Messenian mercenaries of Dionysius, we have to admit that, when Rhegion waged war on Syracuse in 399, exiles from Naupaktos were fighting on both sides – so much for ethnic solidarity. All in all, it seems unwise to base any argument about the Western Messenians on Pausanias' testimony. There can be no doubt that Pausanias construed the Messenians as a diaspora, in a way that corresponds nicely to the sociology of diasporas discussed above, but such a depiction, consistent as it is and, whenever parallel evidence is available, irreconcilable with all other sources, has to be seen as the product of a reconstruction *a posteriori* of the Messenian identity, either in the Hellenistic age or possibly even later, during the Early Empire. In other words, the narrative we find in Pausanias, which implies that the Messenian diaspora had ceased to exist when Messenia had been liberated by the Thebans, has clearly been created retrospectively from the perspective of a community of Messenians of the Peloponnese, who appropriated early Messenian history and turned it into their own ancestral history.

*   *   *

If one should venture a conclusion based on the evidence discussed so far, it would be that, rather than constituting a Messenian diaspora according to the criteria detailed above, the Western Messenians of Rhegion and Zankle are better understood in the framework of an ethnic movement set in motion by specific historical circumstances, and possibly fueled by the traditions of the origins of some aristocratic families of Rhegion, which in their turn do not have a stronger claim to historicity than classical Geek family traditions in general.[70] The Messenian ethnicity in the cities of the Strait seems to have been rather vaguely linked to the Peloponnese, and in so far as the Western Messenians positioned themselves at all on the map of the Greek world, they did so by canceling their ancestral enmity for the Spartans. The fate of the Messenians of Naupaktos confirms this impression of a lack of connection between the Western and the Peloponnesian Messenians.

And yet, the conclusion that the Western Messenians are of no relevance for a history of the Messenian identity would probably be too radical. If the cult of Artemis in Sicilian Messene really goes back to the

---

[70] See Thomas 1989: 95–195 on the case of Athens, as usual the best documented.

age of Anaxilaos, and if the affinity to Artemis Limnatis noted by scholars is more than unspecific and accidental, then it would seem that the Western Messenians used, in order to articulate their Messenian identity, a strategy that was used, and for good historical reasons, also by their Peloponnesian fellows, turning a recognized element of Spartan myth-history into a component of a Messenian identity. In this sense it may be possible to talk of a broad phenomenon of articulation of a Messenian identity in the early fifth century, that involved the Western Messenians as well as the rebels in the Peloponnese, a phenomenon in which other parts of the Greek world participated as well, if indirectly. This tentative conclusion would to some extent be reinforced if it is indeed correct to regard the Dorianization of Sicilian Messene and its transformation into Messana as the product of an attempt at reinforcing its Messenian identity by bringing it in line with shared perception of the ethnic classification of the Messenians.

Finally, and more speculatively, it may be interesting to reflect on the impact of the birth of a political community that called itself "the Messenians," even though in Ionic dialect, and celebrated its victories by dedicating in Olympia spoils taken from its enemies on the battlefield.[71] The victorious Messenians of Sicily may have offered food for thought to the Helots and *perioikoi* who revolted against Sparta in the 460s: the episode to which our attention has now to turn.

---

[71] And possibly also of the presence in Tegea in Arcadia of a rather prominent individual, who called himself "Rhegian and Messenian" on the inscriptions that accompanied his lavish dedications in the sanctuary. May Mikythos have been at the back of the Spartans' mind when they forced the Tegeans to expel the Messenians from their territory? See below, p. 198 n. 91.

CHAPTER 7

The earthquake and the revolt: from Ithome to Naupaktos

If we look at the written sources, between the so-called Second Messenian War and the *Pentekontaetia* it seems as if nothing was happening in Messenia. The structure of the Messenian vulgata and of Spartan historical memory conspire to make of the sixth century a Dark Age of Messenian history. But in the years after the Persian Wars the Spartans were suddenly compelled to fight for their land west of the Taygetos. Probably around 469 BC, the southern Peloponnese was hit by a devastating earthquake, which destroyed many buildings and claimed a high number of victims. As Sparta was weakened by the catastrophe, a revolt broke out in Messenia. It took the Spartans ten years, hard fighting and the help of their allies, including the Athenians, to recover control of the region and to gain the upper hand on the rebels, who were entrenched on Mount Ithome. What the Spartans could not prevent was the birth of a polity calling itself "the Messenians," a polity *sui generis* formed by the rebels, who left the region under a truce and received from the Athenians Naupaktos on the Gulf of Corinth as their provisional dwelling. The origins of this polity and the identity of its members will form the topic of this chapter. Before addressing it, however, it is necessary to review briefly some sources which seem to refer to an earlier Messenian revolt in the very first decades of the fifth century.

PLATO'S WAR

In the *Laws*, Plato mentions twice a war between Spartans and Messenians at the time of the Persian Wars (*Leg.* 692d and 698e). Since Plato is not a historian, this piece of information would probably not have been taken seriously were it not for some other sources which apparently could be connected to the same events alluded to by Plato. Strabo (8.4.10) lists four Messenian wars prior to the liberation of Messenia by Epaminondas; the suggestion that he might allude to the Pylos campaign sounds like special pleading and can hardly be regarded as satisfactory.[1] It seems more natural to identify Plato's war with Strabo's third war. Furthermore, as we have seen, Pausanias reports a migration of Messenians to Rhegion when Anaxilaos was tyrant (4.23.6). Pausanias' date for this migration, after the Second Messenian War, in the mid seventh century according to his chronology, is hard to reconcile with the fact that Anaxilaos was tyrant of Rhegion in the early fifth century. If a choice has to be made between these conflicting indications, it is obviously possible to ignore the connection with the Second Messenian War and date the migration to 489 BC. Of course, the strongest objection to accepting the historicity of Plato's war is that Herodotus appears to know nothing about it. However, in a conversation between Aristagoras of Miletus and King Cleomenes of Sparta he has the Milesian argue that it did not make sense for Sparta to keep fighting for the control of the Peloponnese against Argives, Arcadians and Messenians rather than join the Ionians and conquer the rich lands of Asia (5.49.8). Although none of these sources alone would seem to carry much weight, taken together they may gain some force. Messene in Sicily was founded by Anaxilaos around 490 BC, Aristagoras came to Greece looking for support at the beginning of the Ionian Revolt, around 499, and Plato connects his war with the battle of Marathon. We might conclude that a revolt had started in Messenia around the turn of the century, lasting for some ten years.[2]

A number of monuments, known mostly from literary tradition only, have been tentatively connected with this revolt: a statue of Zeus, dedicated in Olympia by the Spartans, which Pausanias – or rather his informants – connected with the Second Messenian War;[3] three bronze tripods from Amyklai, which, according to Pausanias, were said to be dedications from

---

[1] This solution has been considered recently by Hunt 1998: 29 n. 12, who, however, accepts the historicity of Plato's war. Beloch 1926: 272–3 proposed identifying the fourth war with the expulsion of the Messenians from Naupaktos at the end of the Peloponnesian War; see Jacoby 1943, 117–18.

[2] In the research of the early twentieth century, this war used to be to a large extent intertwined with the problem of the chronology of Rhianus' war; this is true especially of Jacoby's seminal contribution, his commentary to the fragments of Rhianus. For a helpful and even-handed summary of earlier research up to Jacoby, see Oliva 1971: 139–45. The main argument against Jacoby's thesis is its inability to explain Paus. 4.6.3 = *FGrHist* 265 F 42, see Musti in Musti and Torelli 1991: xviii. With characteristic lucidity, Jacoby 1943: 135–6 had already seen and addressed this argument, but his solution seems too complicated and not very appealing, see the sensible critique by Pearson 1962.

[3] It is not completely clear whether δεύτερα in Paus. 5.24.3 refers to ἀποστᾶσι or to κατέστησαν, depending on whether the impossible ὅτε of the manuscripts is corrected to τότε or simply excised. See Maddoli in Maddoli and Saladino 1995: 332 and Jeffery 1949: 28 n. 21 for earlier bibliography. Depending on which interpretation is chosen, Pausanias might also be referring to the revolt after the earthquake.

the booty taken in the war against the Messenians (Paus. 3.18.7–8);[4] finally, the cult statue of Zeus Ithomatas, a work of the Argive sculptor Ageladas, originally made for the Messenians of Naupaktos, according to Pausanias (4.33.2). However, on closer scrutiny the association of these monuments with a Messenian war or revolt in the early fifth century is hardly compelling.

The Zeus statue from Olympia is the only one for which Pausanias' reference does not stand in isolation: thanks to the fact that he quotes the inscription, it has been possible to identify a hollow cylindrical base of blue-gray marble of Laconian origin, found in the sanctuary and inscribed in Laconian alphabet (*IvO* 252 = ML 22 = *CEG* 367), as its base. The letter-forms seem to exclude a date in the seventh century.[5] However, Lilian H. Jeffery authoritatively stated that the letters do not quite fit a date in the mid fifth century, either, and therefore the dedication cannot be convincingly associated with the revolt after the earthquake. Hence she suggested connecting the statue with a war between Spartans and Messenians in the early fifth century.[6] Yet the inscription cannot be regarded as independent evidence for the historicity of Plato's war, for the letter-forms cannot rule out a date in the 460s, nor in the second half of the sixth century, for that matter. More importantly, the connection with a Messenian revolt results exclusively from lore attached to the monument – if not from Pausanias' own speculation. The inscription itself, offering the statue to Zeus and asking him to be propitious to the Lakedaimonians, does not read as a victory dedication at all.

A scrutiny of the tripods in Amyklai leads to a similar conclusion.[7] In the absence of archaeological finds, the dates of the artists who made them, Kallon of Aegina and Gitiadas of Sparta, are our only point of reference. Only the former can be dated on the basis of contemporary evidence. His signature in an inscription from the Athenian acropolis dates to the late sixth century or to the first decades of the fifth.[8] Gitiadas was credited with the bronze reliefs that adorned the famous temple of Athena Chalkioikos, the poliadic temple of Sparta. His chronology oscillates

---

[4] Pausanias thought of the first war, cf. 4.14.2.   [5] Cf., however, Dillon 1995: 62–3.
[6] Jeffery 1949: 26–30; similarly Jeffery 1961: 196, more explicitly excluding the possibility of a later date, which she had still contemplated in her previous contribution. This date is accepted by Meiggs and Lewis, with words of caution as to the historical context, see ML 22.
[7] The tripods were brought into the discussion about Plato's war by Jeffery 1949: 26–30. On tripods upheld in the middle by statues, see Chamoux 1970 and Steinhart 1997: 40.
[8] The inscription is *IG* I³ 753 = *DAA* 85; cf. also 752 (where perhaps Kallon's name might be restored) and 754 (= *DAA* 86 and 87 respectively), by the same stonecutter. All three were found in the "Perserschutt" on the acropolis. For their chronology see Raubitschek 1949: 91–2 and 508–9.

between the early and the late sixth century.[9] But the decisive point is that, once again, Pausanias clearly did not find the motive for the dedications in inscriptions that accompanied them.[10] Without rejecting the connection between the tripods and military victories, in the sixth and early fifth century the Spartans would have had sufficient occasion to thank the gods.

The statue of Zeus Ithomatas poses a more complex and extremely interesting problem. The works ascribed to Ageladas range over such a long stretch of time that some scholars have suggested there were two artists with the same name, probably grandfather and grandson.[11] Ageladas the Elder was apparently active in the last decades of the sixth century, and his son Argeiadas is documented around 480. Ageladas the Younger, son of Argeiadas, could have made the statue of Zeus for the Messenians of Naupaktos soon after they settled there. However, other scholars prefer to assume that all the sources refer to the same artist, whose activity would have to start in the last decades of the sixth century.[12] In this case, it is of course tempting to push the chronology of the Zeus Ithomatas farther back than Pausanias would allow, dissociating it from the Messenians of Naupaktos and taking it instead as a sign of the Messenians' claim to independence in the early fifth century.[13]

Some skepticism as to the connection between the statue and the Messenians in Naupaktos is not completely unreasonable. It is obviously impossible to exclude that Pausanias might have collected this piece of information at Messene, but it should also be kept in mind that for him the Messenians of Naupaktos were the only independent Messenians that had existed between the Second Messenian War in the seventh century

---

[9] See e.g. Nafissi 1991: 149 and n. 217. The early chronology, based on the archaeological date of the temple of Athena Chalkioikos, has recently been defended by Stibbe 2000c: 65–71, with very strong arguments. Since it is not possible to date Gitiadas' activity in the Chalkioikos temple, scholars increasingly tend to date Gitiadas on the basis of on Kallon's chronology, e.g. Pipili 1987: 80, which of course easily brings about circular arguments, cf. Hunt 1998: 30 (who also confuses Ageladas' Zeus Ithomatas and the Spartans' Zeus from Olympia). Of course, this presupposes that the three dedications were contemporary: see Raubitschek 1949: 508; cf., however, Cartledge 2002: 154 and the next note.

[10] As Kiechle 1959: 117–18 correctly noted. This observation makes it also clear that it is after all not certain that the three tripods were dedicated on the same occasion; if not, Gitiadas' chronology cannot be tied to Kallon's. More generally, one is tempted to follow Jacoby's suggestion (1943: 172) that the connection of the tripods and the Messenian war is Pausanias' own speculation (cf. also Stibbe 2000c: 71); after all, it is striking that Pausanias connects all archaic Spartan dedications to the Messenian wars.

[11] The case for the two Ageladas is set forth in detail by Moreno 2001.

[12] See e.g. Stewart 1990: 247–8.   [13] As suggested by Cartledge 2002: 132.

and the liberation of Messenia in the fourth. If Ageladas was to be credited with a statue of Zeus Ithomatas, from Pausanias' viewpoint the only people who could have commissioned it were the Messenians of Naupaktos; he would not have been any more ready than modern scholars to assume that this role had been performed by the Helotized Messenians of the Peloponnese before the revolt, and after the revolt there were according to him no Messenians left in the Peloponnese. But of course, in this line of thought Pausanias was forgetting the *perioikoi* of Messenia, as modern scholars regularly do, too, and working under the assumption that the sanctuary of Ithome had been in use only during periods of Messenian independence. However, if the sanctuary of Apollo Korythos could harbor a monumental dedication by the same workshop that had built the throne of Apollo at Amyklai, we should perhaps not be too quick in dismissing the possibility that, even without a Messenian uprising at that point, the Zeus of Ageladas could have been commissioned for the sanctuary of Ithome in the early decades of the fifth century or even in the late sixth. It could have been a Spartiate dedication, after all, since, as we will see, the Spartans took Zeus Ithomatas seriously enough to consider the rebels his suppliants; or it could have been dedicated by the *perioikoi*, since there was a perioikic settlement at the foot of Mount Ithome during the archaic and early classical period. Under the assumption that the cult of Zeus Ithomatas had specifically Messenian, as opposed to generally local, connotations at this point, one might even venture that commissioning the statue was a sign of some awakening of Messenian ethnicity, which somehow anticipated the uprising later in the century. But this would be speculation. The important point is that the Zeus of Ageladas is no evidence of a Messenian war in the early fifth century, any more than the tripods of Amyklai or the Zeus of the Spartans in Olympia are. The case for the historicity of the revolt has to rest on the written sources, and most of all on Plato's own testimony.

Plato's *Laws* include many references to past history. His reconstruction of the development of the Spartan constitution (*Leg.* 3.691d ff.) is embedded in the story of the division of the Peloponnese among the Heraclids, with Messene and Argos functioning as examples of bad legislation and offering a foil against which Sparta's good constitution will stand out all the more sharply. Argos and Messene show what Sparta could have become, had it not been saved, in the first place, by divine foresight, that is, by Aristodemus' untimely death, which brought about the dual kingship, sheltering the Spartan constitution from the negative consequences of giving all the power to a single individual (*Leg.* 691d–692c).

The bad constitutions of Argos and Messene brought their fruits in due course, at the time of the Persian Wars (*Leg.* 692d–e). In spite of their splendid victories on land and at sea, the anonymous Athenian who takes part in the dialogue says that the way in which the Greeks repulsed the Persians was in fact disgraceful. This unexpected and paradoxical statement is explained as follows: of the three great cities of the Peloponnese only one, Sparta, fought against the barbarian, while one, Messene, attacked the Spartans, trying[14] to prevent them from joining the Greek cause, and the third, Argos, the most powerful of all at the time of the division of the Peloponnese, rejected the requests of the Greeks and refused to fight against the barbarians.

This first reference to the Spartan–Messenian war has to be kept in mind once we turn to the second, more specific one, which refers to the time of Marathon. Here Plato pays homage to a mainstay of Athenian propaganda, emphasizing that Athens fought alone for the whole of Greece at Marathon.[15] This splendid deed is described by Plato as a result of the old Athenian constitution, still free from the excessive license of full-fledged democracy (*Leg.* 698a–c). Only the Spartans were ready to help the Athenians, but were hindered by the war against the Messenians or perhaps by some other factor: οὐ γὰρ ἴσμεν λεγόμενον, concludes Plato in a suspiciously Herodotean way.

It is hardly necessary to point out that Plato's take on the history of the Persian Wars is highly peculiar in almost every detail. However, Plato himself obviously possessed broad historical knowledge. He certainly knew Herodotus' *Histories*, and expected his readers to know them and to be able to recognize ironic allusions to them, but in all likelihood the father of history was not Plato's only reading on the Persian Wars: he was probably familiar at least with Ctesias' *Persica*.[16] Although for him historical narratives served as arguments, and historical accuracy was not necessarily a priority, his allusions to historical events should not be

---

[14] The imperfect διεκώλυον, that describes the Messenians' behavior in Plat. *Leg.* 692d, has to be taken as conative: after all, the Spartans did take part in the Persian Wars, and the reference to Argos shows that Plato is here speaking of the Persian Wars as a whole (Ducat 1990: 142), not only of the Marathon campaign.

[15] Already Thuc. 1.73.4. The participation of the Plataeans is regularly passed over in silence in this connection; see Walters 1981 and Loraux 1981: 159. On Plato's familiarity with fourth-century Athenian ideology, see e.g. Morgan 1998: 105–6.

[16] See in general Weil 1959: 118–19 and *passim*. Moggi 1968: 213–20 tends to see Herodotus as Plato's only source on the Persian Wars; cf., however, Jacoby 1922: 2067, with strong arguments for Plato's knowledge and use of Ctesias (and cf. Plat. *Leg.* 685c with Diod. 2.22.2). On the connected problem of the depiction of the Persian Wars in the *Menexenus*, see Tsitsiridis 1998: 264–7.

jettisoned without careful scrutiny.[17] According to a basic law of classical philology, that says that whenever a reputable extant Greek author says something odd, he is taking it from some less reputable lost Greek author, it has sometimes been suggested that Plato might have been drawing, at least in part, upon some highly biased source from the second quarter of the fourth century, one which conjured up a Messenian revolt in 490 in order to indict the Messenians for the Spartans' failure to help the Athenians at Marathon.[18] The agenda of this hypothetical source would be transparent. The Theban hegemony had compelled Athens and Sparta to reconciliation, and Messene, Epaminondas' brainchild, was a predestined object of common hatred for Spartans and Laconizing Athenians.[19] However, this hypothesis is almost certainly wrong – which does not mean that Plato's Messenian war is not a product of pro-Spartan bias.

In the first place, it is not clear that in the early fourth-century an excuse was needed for the Spartans' absence from Marathon. The Athenian version of Marathon, as it appears in fourth-century orators, maintained that the Athenians had attacked the Persians without waiting for the Spartans, who did their best but arrived on the battlefield the day after the battle, after a forced march of three days and three nights.[20] This narrative excused the Spartans from the outset, concentrating on the bravery of the Athenians. There was no need for a war to detain the Spartans, and even allowing for propagandistic exaggeration a war was not a particularly fitting explanation for their brief delay. Moreover, Plato does not really say explicitly that the war against the Messenians was the true cause of the Spartans' delay. He first refers, without giving details, to a war between Messenians and Spartans at the time of the Persian Wars, that is, sometime around 490–480. His second reference, if read carefully, is hardly more precise.[21] The Athenian, who leads the discussion in the dialogue, says clearly that the real motive for the Spartans' absence is not recorded, as far as he knows. But since he maintains that the Messenians, rather than join the fight against the barbarian, attacked the Spartans at the time of the

---

[17] Cf. e.g. Weil 1959: 52–4 and Morrow 1993. Plato's general attitude to past history does not, however, inspire much confidence in his accuracy, see most recently Morgan 1998 and Johansen 1998.

[18] E.g. den Boer 1956: 169–70.   [19] Jacoby 1943: 116.

[20] Already Herodotus (6.120) said explicitly that the Spartans had rushed to Marathon, as soon as their religious obligations had been fulfilled. Later authors consistently leave aside the motive given by Herodotus and emphasize the Athenians' eagerness to fight (Lys. *Funeral oration* [2].21–6, Isocr. *Panegyricus* [4].86–7). On the Marathon myth in Athenian tradition, see e.g. Loraux 1981: 157–73, Nouhaud 1982: 149–55. Corcella 1992 presents and discusses a further source, probably later, that gives a version similar to Isocrates'.

[21] My interpretation of this passage is strongly indebted to Ducat 1990: 142.

Persian Wars, it is just a small step for him to suggest that the war against the Messenians could have been the reason for the Spartans' late arrival at Marathon. The vague wording of this passage would be slightly strange if Plato had had a source that made this connection explicitly, or even emphatically, as might be expected from a propagandistic pamphlet. It rather seems as if he had on his desk only Athenian propaganda on Marathon and Herodotus' passage, according to which the Spartans were delayed by religious scruples. It is especially the strange coda, "there were perhaps other obstacles," concluding with the Herodotean giveaway οὐ γὰρ ἴσμεν λεγόμενον, that strongly suggest that Plato was consciously manipulating information.[22]

As a matter of fact, while it is conceivable that Plato at times reflected the political agenda of authors he read, he certainly had a political agenda of his own, as shown prominently by his peculiar presentation of the Cleisthenic democracy.[23] That Plato was rather pro-Spartan is a well-known fact,[24] and his way of presenting the Spartan–Messenian conflict is clearly influenced by this. He seems to speak as if he did not know that at the time of the Persian Wars the region west of the Taygetos was simply a part of the Spartan state. However, later in the *Laws* he mentions the frequent revolts of the Messenians against the Spartans as the main drawback of Helotry (*Leg.* 777b–c), showing that he not only knows perfectly well about the Spartan domination in Messenia, but is also willing to follow the Spartan "party line" in refusing to recognize that, at the time he was writing, Messenia was an independent polity again. The conclusion can hardly be avoided: Plato is not misinformed, he is misleading.[25]

There is one more reason to rule out the possibility that Plato might have found his Messenian war in some previous source. Plato was not the only ancient author to be less than impressed with Herodotus' explanation of the Spartans' absence at Marathon. Plutarch found it suspicious, too, and was all too ready to attribute it to Herodotus' meanness (*De mal.*

---

[22] See the comparison of Herodotus and Plato by Jacoby 1943: 114–16. While Plato here is certainly evoking Herodotus, it is not completely clear how he expects his reader to take this reference. The pseudo-Herodotean passages in *Timaeus* (Luraghi 2001d: 154) might encourage us not to take too seriously Plato's attempt at rewriting history; we may be dealing here with one more case of Platonic irony, as defined by Rowe 1987: 95.

[23] Or should we say, Solonian democracy? See Morgan 1998: 108–13.

[24] See e.g. Morrow 1993: 40–3; Powell 1994.

[25] See Weil 1959: 118 and Moggi 1968: 217. Dušanić 1997 argues that Plato's depiction of early Peloponnesian history in the *Laws* is a political pamphlet, targeted at the political situation of the 350s, but he may be pressing the evidence too far. Note that, by essentially equating Messenians with rebel Helots, Plato is also taking sides in an Athenian debate over the Messenian identity that can be traced in Thucydides and in Alcidamas' *Messenian Speech* (see below, p. 202 and 223).

Her. 26 = *Mor.* 861e–f). Against the father of history, Plutarch fires the guns of Athenian propaganda, giving as a well-known fact the story according to which the Spartans did all they could to be there on time, but were unable to match the eagerness of the Athenians. If one considers the impressive number of sources that Plutarch was able to muster in his indictment of Herodotus, his silence about a Messenian attack on Sparta gains in significance.[26] If the idea that Plato concocted his war out of thin air seems unappealing, it is possible to speculate that he may have found in Herodotus himself hints that could seem to point in the direction of a war between Spartans and Messenians at the time of the Persian Wars. Aristagoras' speech (5.49.8) may be taken to mean just that, and a couple of allusions that in fact refer to the revolt in the 460s (9.35.2 and 9.64.2) could be taken as a sign that hostilities between Spartans and Messenians extended from the early 490s until after Plataea. But one might well feel some uneasiness in branding Plato as a careless reader of Herodotus.

Be that as it may, once Plato's testimony is questioned, it becomes clear that the other sources which are often taken as referring to a Messenian war in the 490s cannot stand independently. Pausanias' passage on the foundation of Sicilian Messene has been shown to be a cut-and-paste product, unlikely to be based on any earlier evidence (above, pp. 151–2). Aristagoras' speech is obviously an anachronism, reflecting the revolt of the 460s.[27] Only Strabo's reference to four wars, of which the first and the second are clearly identical with the canonical First and Second Messenian Wars and the fourth seems to be the revolt in the 460s, remains puzzling. It is hard to believe that Strabo had his fourth war from Plato,[28] but it is equally difficult to think of an alternative, especially since Strabo's usual fourth-century sources have only three wars.

Perhaps not every reader will be satisfied that the arguments so far presented suffice to impose a negative answer to the question of the historicity of Plato's war. To conclude, it may be useful to summarize the respective hermeneutic prices, so to speak, of the two alternatives. Considering Plato's war to be fictive implies: first, admitting that Plato manipulated the narrative(s) of early fifth century history he was drawing upon; second, assuming that some archaic dedications at Olympia and Sparta, whose occasion had been forgotten, were later connected with the Messenian wars, probably because these wars, especially after the emergence of an independent Messenian polity and the corresponding "rediscovery"

---

[26] This has been noted in passing by Pearson 1962: 401 n. 12.   [27] Braun 1994: 42 n. 1.
[28] See Jacoby's discussion, 1943: 117–18.

of archaic Messenian history, were seen as the most important events in the archaic history of Sparta; and third, accepting that we simply do not know what Strabo really meant. However, accepting the historicity of a Messenian war in the 490s implies taking seriously what Plato says about it; it simply will not do to speak of a small or even potential war,[29] a major event has to be envisioned, one that would justify Plato's depiction – and possibly also the prestigious dedications supposedly associated with it. In other words, it is clear that in order to take Plato's war as historical fact one has to be prepared to admit that Herodotus' depiction of Spartan history in the early fifth century is massively distorted – not a very attractive proposition, after all.

THE REVOLT

With the revolt that broke out in Messenia in the 460s, we are finally on more solid ground, even though no extant ancient source offers a comprehensive narrative of the revolt itself. All we have is a small corpus of references and allusions, often contradictory, that make it very difficult to reconstruct in a less than controversial way some of the most central aspects of the revolt. It is clear from all sources that it began after the earthquake, although it is not as clear when this happened: dates found in the sources range from 469/8 to 464/3 BC.[30] Also unclear is whether the revolt involved from the beginning only Messenia, or Laconia too.[31] Plutarch describes the Helots rushing to storm Sparta, which lay in ruins, and falling upon the Spartiates who had survived the earthquake,[32] while other sources more vaguely speak of the rebels attacking Sparta itself. Some skepticism towards the idea that Laconia was involved in the revolt may be suggested by the fact that most of these sources describe the events in a way that presupposes, as we will see more in detail below, a firm distinction between Messenian and Laconian Helots, whereby only the latter are called Helots, the former being simply called Messenians; in

[29] As some scholars have done, who connect the war with Cleomenes' activity in Arcadia (Hdt. 6.74); see e.g. Wallace 1954: 32–3.
[30] For a survey of the chronological problems connected with the revolt, see Luraghi 2001a: 280–5 with further references; Buonocore 1982 offers a detailed discussion with extensive quotations of the sources.
[31] See the discussion of the evidence by Ducat 1990: 132–4.
[32] As the story goes, the Spartiates were saved by the prompt reaction of king Archidamus, who ordered them to seize their arms and drew them up in combat formation, anticipating the danger: Plut. *Cim.* 16.6–7. Diod. 11.64.1 is a less vivid variant of the same story. On these passages as evidence that the revolt raged in Laconia, too, see Whitby 1994: 115–16 n. 38.

other words, for them "Helot" means "Helot of Laconia." Therefore these authors or their sources could have been misled into believing that Laconian Helots had participated in the revolt by earlier authors who, like Thucydides, said that only some of the Helots who revolted were of Messenian descent. However, it is difficult to decide; although it cannot be excluded that Diodorus and Plutarch indirectly preserve genuine, if perhaps dramatized, memories of unrest in Laconia itself,[33] the evidence for the revolt, in so far as it gives hints of topography, consistently refers to Messenia: Thucydides says that the perioikic town of Thouria, located east of the Pamisos, joined the revolt (1.101.2), Herodotus mentions the defeat of a Spartan army in Stenykleros (9.64.2),[34] Aristophanes (*Lys.* 1141) and the Old Oligarch (*Ath. Pol.* 3.11) speak of Messene and Messenians as the Spartans' foe. In sum, it seems reasonable to assume that the revolt, if not from the outset, then very soon thereafter concentrated in the territory west of the Taygetos.

The reactions in Sparta are depicted memorably in Aristophanes' *Lysistrata* (1137ff.), when the protagonist reminds the Spartans of the time when Poseidon and Messene were after them, and their envoy Perikleidas came to Athens, pale in his purple robe, sitting at the altars as a suppliant and asking for a relief army. This depiction of Spartan desperation may be somewhat exaggerated, but it is clear that the revolt was perceived by the Spartans as a very serious threat.[35] Years later, according to Thucydides, the Plataeans could refer to the revolt as the "great scare" (φόβος μέγιστος, 3.54.5), and in fact the Spartans summoned help from everywhere: besides the Athenians, also Plataeans, Aeginetans (Thuc. 2.27.2) and Mantineans (Xen. *Hell.* 5.2.3) sent troops, the latter possibly as members of the Peloponnesian League. As in the case of the Athenians, having sent help on the occasion of the revolt was clearly seen as a special title of merit.

The seriousness of the situation is conveyed also by an episode of the revolt which we know thanks to an isolated reference in Herodotus (9.64.2). Relating the later destiny of the illustrious Spartan Arimnestos,[36] the man who killed Mardonius at Plataea, Herodotus says that he died in Stenyklaros together with a unit of 300 men under his command, having

---

[33] Figueira 1999: 215–16 and n. 18.
[34] Cf. also 9.35.2, where Ithome may be mentioned in conjunction with the revolt, if one accepts Paulmier's emendation of Ἰσθμῷ to Ἰθώμῃ; the rebels, at any rate, are called Messenians.
[35] See Jordan 1990: 48.
[36] The fact that Herodotus calls Arimnestus ἀνὴρ ἐν Σπάρτῃ λόγιμος does not mean that Arimnestus was not a Spartan, as it has sometimes been thought; see De Vido 1996.

clashed against the whole of the Messenians.[37] Herodotus' laconic state-ment does not allow locating this episode at a specific point in the development of the revolt. However, since the Spartans appear to be fighting alone, and perhaps to have been taken by surprise, it seems to fit better an early phase of the revolt. Perhaps Arimnestus marched into Messenia with his troops as soon as the Spartans learned about what was happening. Since the clash happened in Stenyklaros, the Spartans prob-ably came from the Derveni pass, the most convenient way into Messenia. Perhaps the earthquake had damaged the roads through the Taygetos, or, more likely, those roads were closed to the Spartans because Thouria, controlling some of the passes, had sided with the rebels.[38]

A second Herodotean reference to the revolt is much more difficult to pinpoint. It is embedded in the story of the Iamid seer Tisamenus, who had been promised by the oracle of Delphi five victories in the greatest competitions (Hdt. 9.33–5). After he failed as an athlete, the Spartans realized that the Pythia meant wars, not athletic events, and went out of their way to secure Tisamenus' cooperation, granting Spartan citizenship to him and his brother. As a seer for the Spartan army, Tisamenus was involved in a string of five victories beginning with Plataea and ending with Tanagra. The last but one was against the Messenians, but unfor-tunately the Herodotean text that refers to it is damaged, and it is not very easy to restore.[39] Accepting the standard correction, Tisamenus would have been involved in a conflict against the Messenians near Ithome. It remains unclear whether a battle is meant or the conflict as a whole.[40] If the former were the case, it might have been a victory that allowed the Spartans to bottle the rebels on Mount Ithome.

Be this as it may, the sources converge in giving the impression that at some point the war became a siege, with the rebels entrenched on the

[37] On the interpretation of this passage, see Luraghi 2001a: 286 n. 23; Ducat 1990: 141 mistakenly connects πολέμου ὄντος and Μεσσηνίοισι πᾶσι, which leads him to a distorted interpretation of the situation in Messenia before the revolt.

[38] Some sources mention the devastating effects of the earthquake on the Taygetos: Plut. *Cim.* 16.4, *Schol.* Aristoph. *Lys.* 1142b Hangard-Holwerda. On the passes across the Taygetos, see the references at p. 23 n. 33. On the importance of the Derveni pass as a gateway to Messenia, see Hope Simpson 1966: 125–6.

[39] See Lapini 1996: 156–66. His suggestion of restoring in Hdt. 9.35.2 the obviously wrong πρὸς τῷ Ἰσθμῷ to πρὸς τῷ σεισμῷ, instead of following Paulmier's πρὸς τῇ Ἰθώμῃ, is not completely convincing; his objections to Paulmier's solution fail to take into account that Ithome is the name of a mountain (cf. e.g. Polyb. 18.27.7). There is no point in looking for an Isthmus in Messenia, following Wilamowitz and Valmin 1930: 64–5; Paus. 3.11.8 only means that the damage in the text of Hdt. 9.35.2 is old.

[40] Cf. e.g. Oliva 1971: 154 (a battle) and Lapini 1996: 159 (the war).

mountain and the Spartans unable to drive them out from there. At this point, the Spartans asked for help at Athens, perhaps for the second time,[41] and Cimon marched into the Peloponnese in 462/1. However, the Athenians' experience with siege warfare could not bring about the quick victory the Spartans had expected, and so the Athenians were dismissed for reasons that are unclear. According to Thucydides (1.102.3), the Spartans were suspicious because of the Athenians' different ethnic origin and revolutionary character, and feared they would eventually side with the rebels.[42] Whatever its reasons, this was a slap in the face for the Athenians, and the pro-Spartan Cimon, who had convinced the Athenians to help Sparta, had to pay for this with ostracism, according to Plutarch (*Cim.* 17.3).

The reason for the dismissal of the Athenian contingent has often been questioned by modern scholars, and alternatives have been proposed, sometimes with a certain amount of fantasy.[43] Obviously, the fact that the Athenians in the end helped the rebels find a new place to live means that Thucydides' explanation might be anachronistic. This suspicion is confirmed if we consider how the revolt and the Athenian intervention are construed by the so-called Old Oligarch (*Ath. Pol.* 3.11). In order to confirm his theory, according to which Athens, being ruled by the worst citizens, should always side with the worst in any conflict, the author considers cases where the Athenians had chosen the side of the best, that is, of oligarchy, with negative consequences in the long run. For instance, he says, the Athenians chose to side with the Spartans, instead of siding with the Messenians, and as a result the Spartans attacked them as soon as they had got the upper hand in the revolt.[44] Form his viewpoint, that is, the Messenians would have been the natural allies of the Athenian democracy, the regime of the worst. This way of understanding the revolt has obvious points of contact with the one that is presupposed by Thucydides' description of the Spartans' motives for dismissing the Athenians from Ithome, and helps to make sense of it: if the revolt is seen as a conflict between democrats and oligarchs, that is, between the mob and the

---

[41] Plut. *Cim.* 17.3 knows of two Athenian rescue expeditions; however, he may be transforming diverging accounts of the same episode in two different episodes, see Luraghi 2001b: 282–3.

[42] Similarly Diodorus (11.64.2). Plutarch (*Cim.* 17.3) and Pausanias (4.24.6) are less explicit, but presuppose a similar scenario.

[43] For a recent discussion of the main explanations, with some new suggestions, see Bloedow 2000; see also Buonocore 1982: 104–5. Lang 1967: 268 suggests that the Spartans had initially called in the Athenians so that the latter would have fewer troops to employ against Thasos. Thucydides' explanation is accepted with some qualification by Figueira 1999: 233.

[44] The author is clearly referring to the battle of Tanagra in 457 BC, a precious indication for the chronology of the revolt; see Lapini 1997: 286–7 and 1996: 154–6 with further bibliography.

good in the Old Oligarch's terms, then the oligarchic Spartans would have had all the reasons to fear that the democratic Athenians could change sides. But of course, this view reflects Athenian ideas on the natural alliance between democrats, and it is doubtful, to say the least, that the Spartans would have held similar views so early in the fifth century.[45]

After the Athenians went back home, the siege seems to have continued for a while, until it was decided to resolve the situation by compromise. The rebels were not able to hold out any longer, and the Spartans learned, according to Thucydides (1.103.2), that there was an old Delphic oracle enjoining them to leave alone – or let go – the suppliant of Zeus Ithomatas. The rebels were allowed to leave the Peloponnese with their wives and children, under condition that they would never come back; if any one of them were to be caught in the Peloponnese, he would be the slave of his captor.[46] The exiles were received by the Athenians, probably remained in Athens for a while, and finally were settled on the Gulf of Corinth in Naupaktos, which the Athenian general Tolmides had conquered at the end of his naval expedition around the Peloponnese, according to Diodorus (11.84.7–8).[47]

In this sketchy reconstruction of the development of the revolt, two more documents have to be integrated, whose relevance has only recently been recognized: two bronze spear butts with dedicatory inscriptions, coming from Olympia and from the sanctuary of Apollo Korythos in Longà/Ayios Andhreas respectively.[48] The name of the dedicant is the same in both cases: the Methanioi. The spear butt from Olympia, whose inscription is completely legible, was dedicated as booty taken from the Lakedaimonians. The inscription on the spear butt from Longà/Ayios Andhreas is incomplete, because its tip is broken; the preserved part reads μεθαν[—]ανεθε[—]αθαναι[—]λαιδο[—]. Since the dedication comes from a sanctuary of Apollo, it is unlikely that it can have been dedicated to Athena: most probably, the inscription should be interpreted to mean that the spoils dedicated with the spear butt had been taken from

---

[45] Further reasons for regarding Thucydides' explanation of the dismissal of the Athenians with some skepticism are mentioned by Badian 1993: 95. The second motive, the ethnic difference between Ionian Athenians and Dorian Spartans, also reflects political trends that seem to belong to the age of the Peloponnesian War rather than to the *Pentekontaetia*.

[46] Thuc. 1.103.1. On the treaty, see Oliva 1971: 162. The punishment threatened for any of the Messenians who returned, to the Peloponnese expressed clearly the Spartans' views of the social identity of the rebels, just as treating them as suppliants; see also below, p. 198.

[47] See Badian 1993: 163–9.

[48] The inscriptions are published as *IvO* 247 and *SEG* 40.362 respectively. On the sanctuary of Apollo Korythos, see above, pp. 117–20.

the Athenians.[49] To judge from the forms of the letters, the two inscriptions could date from the late sixth century or from the first half of the fifth, and neither has characters that would allow pinpointing its alphabet. The identity of the dedicants is a puzzle. Earlier scholarship had connected the spear butt from Olympia with Methana in the Argolis, whose inhabitants might conceivably have taken part in a battle between Argos and Sparta in the early fifth century.[50] However, the spear butt from Longà/Ayios Andhreas can hardly have been dedicated by them, too. Therefore, it has been suggested that we separate the two dedications and attribute the one from Longà/Ayios Andhreas to the perioikic city of Mothone.[51] This solution however does not work, either. Although it is possible that the name of Mothone had a secondary form "Methone," the ethnic derived from it appears to have been consistently "Mothonaioi," not "Mothanioi" or "Mothonioi," just as the ethnic of Argolic Methana was "Methanaios."[52] Accordingly, it seems preferable to interpret "Methanioi" as a variant of "Mesanioi," as the rebels called themselves once they had left the Peloponnese.[53] Above all the combination of Spartans and Athenians as enemies of these Methanioi speaks strongly in favor of such an interpretation.

If we take the two spear butts as dedications by the rebels, the next question would be where should we locate them in the course of the ten years of war. As in the case of the battle in Stenyklaros mentioned by

---

[49] See Jeffery 1990: 204, *pace* Zunino 1997: 173; the fact that the sanctuary at Longà has not been excavated more thoroughly hardly justifies her assumption that Athena might have been worshipped there, too: all the inscriptions that have been found in the sanctuary refer to Apollo, as does Paus. 4.34.7.

[50] Notice, however, that Methana, like the other small cities of the eastern Argolid, was a natural enemy of Argos (cf. the case of Epidauros, Piérart 2004) and hence more likely an ally than an enemy of Sparta.

[51] Jeffery 1990: 177 and 203–4: Messenian Mothone is called "Methone" e.g. in Thuc. 2.25.1, the first documented occurrence of the name. Jeffery notes that Argolic Methana is also occasionally called "Methone," and suggests that Messenian Mothone could also have been called in Doric Methana. However, differences between Ionic and Doric dialectal forms would not explain the equivalence of Methana and Methone (one would rather expect an Ionic form "Methene"). More importantly, the form "Methone" for Methana in the Argolid is documented only in Thucydides (4.45.2; 5.18.7), and should probably be seen as the consequence of an old damage to the text; see Maurer 1995: 75 and Strab. 8.6.15. In conclusion, there is no reason to assume that Methana has ever been a form of the name of Messenian Mothone.

[52] See Meyer 1932a: 1375 and 1932b: 1382.

[53] This interpretation is advanced by Bauslaugh 1990: 661–8. Hall 2003 has some reasonable objections relating to the phonetic equivalence of "Methanioi" and "Mesanioi"; however, considering that there was probably no traditional orthography for the name "Messenians," some incertitude in its very first appearance should not be given too much weight, especially considering the lack of standardization in orthography that characterizes Laconian inscriptions (Morpurgo Davies 1993: 266–9).

Herodotus, a date close to the beginning of the revolt would seem most likely, at least for the spear butt from Olympia, which, as a matter of fact, could even originate from that very battle. The same cannot be true of the dedication from Longà/Ayios Andhreas, which incidentally would represent a serious argument in favor of Plutarch's two Athenian expeditions, since the victory over the Athenians commemorated by the inscription seems less easy to connect to a phase of the revolt in which apparently the rebels were more or less besieged in their stronghold on Mount Ithome. Both dedications would also encourage resisting the impression which some of the sources, especially Thucydides, give, that is that the revolt almost immediately turned into a siege. Finally, besides testifying to the military successes of the rebels, the dedication from Olympia would also show their attempt at making their existence visible to a Panhellenic audience, an attempt which the prestigious dedications by the exiles from Naupaktos will reveal even more conspicuously.[54]

THE MESSENIANS IN NAUPAKTOS

Naupaktos remained a Messenian stronghold for more than half a century, until after the end of the Peloponnesian War, and for as long as they remained on the Gulf of Corinth the Messenians of Naupaktos were loyal and precious allies for the Athenians. In the *Pentekontaetia* they seem to have been involved in various campaigns in northwestern Greece. Pausanias' elaborate narrative of their temporary conquest of the Akarnanian city of Oiniadai (4.25), an inveterate enemy of the Athenians, has often been dismissed as pure fiction, but might deserve being taken seriously after all.[55] A date before the thirty years' peace would then seem inescapable, and a further victory, against the Aitolians of Kalydon, documented by a dedicatory inscription from Delphi (*SEG* 32.550; see below), should be dated similarly.

At the very beginning of the Peloponnesian War, in 431, the Messenians participated in the Athenian campaign against Mothone and Elis (Thuc. 2.25). During the war, besides securing for the Athenian fleet a friendly harbor on the Gulf of Corinth, they were involved in the repression of the oligarchs on Corcyra in 427 (Thuc. 3.81) and in Demosthenes'

---

[54] More archaeological evidence on the revolt may come from research in Mavromati-Messene. Notice that the destruction horizons at Kopanaki and Lakathela (see above, pp. 131 and 124) seem to fall chronologically within the scope of the revolt.

[55] See Freitag 1996: 78–82, who dates the episode in 454 BC.

unsuccessful campaign in Aetolia in 426 (Thuc. 3.94–8)[56] and then fought with distinction in his victorious campaign in Akarnania in the winter of 426/5 (Thuc. 3.105–13). In the course of that campaign, Demosthenes realized the potential usefulness of having allies who spoke Dorian just like their Peloponnesian enemies and who could potentially be mistaken for them.[57] Later, in 425, the possibility of employing the Messenians for raids against the Spartan territory was, according to Thucydides, one of the assets Demosthenes referred to in his attempt to convince his fellow generals to support his plan to occupy Pylos (Thuc. 4.3.2–3); Demosthenes pointed to the familiarity of the Messenians with what had once been their father-land[58] and to the fact that they could deceive the Spartans because they spoke the same dialect.[59] The Messenians ended up playing an important role in the campaign; it was their commander who surrounded the Spartiates on Sphakteria and compelled them to surrender (Thuc. 4.36). After the Spartiates had surrendered, Pylos was occupied by a garrison of Messenians, who sent there their best troops, because they regarded – says Thucydides – Pylos as a part of their old fatherland, and inflicted heavy damage on the Spartans with their raids (Thuc. 4.41.2; cf. Diod. 12.63.5).

For the first time the Spartans were faced in their own territory with a hostile presence that triggered Helotic desertion, and as a consequence they began to fear massive uprisings (Thuc. 4.41.3).[60] The situation became even more worrying for them the following year, when Nicias

---

[56] As a matter of fact, according to Thucydides the Messenians advised Demosthenes on how to organize the campaign and urged him to undertake it. Their knowledge in the political relations of northwest Greece must have gone back to their campaigns before the thirty years' peace. In Thuc. 3.94.3 the Messenians refer to existing hostility between Naupaktos and the Aetolians, which must have something to with their dedication in Delphi.

[57] Thuc. 3.112.4: the Messenians were to delude the Ambraciots into thinking they were their Peloponnesian allies; on the episode, see Petrocelli 2001: 86–8. It is not completely clear who the Ambraciots were supposed to think the Messenians were: the contingent led by the Spartiate Eurylochos must have included troops from various members of the Peloponnesian league, and the only ones who receive a separate mention are the Mantineians, who did not speak Doric at all. Considering, however, that the Ambraciots, colonists of Corinth, must have themselves spoken a Doric dialect, it is probably justified to assume that in this occasion, as will be explicitly the case later, Thucydides means that the Messenians were taken for Lakedaimonians.

[58] In spite of its superficial plausibility, this argument is a bit strained. Only the younger among the Messenians who had left the Peloponnese in the mid 450s would still have been alive, and one wonders how many of them came from the Pylos area anyway. Demosthenes' insistence on the fact that Pylos was a part of the old fatherland of the Messenians makes one wonder if the whole scheme might not have been put to him by the Messenians in the first place.

[59] Thuc. 4.3.3 and 41.2; see Figueira 1999: 213 and Petrocelli 2001: 88–90.

[60] Cf. the famous and controversial passage on the Spartans' fear of the Helots, Thuc. 4.80.2–5, on which see Hornblower 1996: 264–5.

occupied Kythera and from there launched raids on the coasts of Laconia and Messenia (Thuc. 4.53–5). Fear of unrest among the Helots, and possibly not only among them, was one of the major factors that convinced the Spartans to sue for peace (Thuc. 5.14.3). Tellingly, the alliance between Sparta and Athens concluded right after the peace included a clause that obliged the Athenians to help the Spartans in case of a slave revolt (Thuc. 5.23.3). The Messenians clearly were very much on the Spartans' mind: once the Athenians refused to give back Pylos, the Spartans asked and obtained that they should at least withdraw from there the Messenians and the Helots who had deserted to Pylos (Thuc. 5.35.6–7).[61] The Helots were apparently settled in Krane on the island of Kephallenia, only to return to Pylos in the winter of 419, when the Argives urged the Athenians to bring back there "the Messenians and the Helots" (Thuc. 5.56.2–3). Messenians seem to have returned to Pylos, too.[62]

Information on the role of the Messenians during the rest of the war is thinner. They participated in the Sicilian expedition, summoned again by Demosthenes in 413 (Thuc. 7.31.2), and were involved under Conon's command in the repression of the pro-Lakedaimonian faction in Corcyra in 410 (Diod. 13.48). They also garrisoned Pylos and defended it from the Spartans, probably until 410.[63] Meanwhile, more deserters from the *Lakonikē*, originally assembled in a fort built by the Athenians on

---

[61] Whereas the Spartans describe the people they want to see removed from Pylos as "the Messenians and the Helots" (Thuc. 5.35.6), the way this group is described when it is mentioned for the second time is not completely perspicuous; in the form in which it has been transmitted, the text of Thuc. 5.35.7 may well mean that, beside the Helots, other people from the *Lakonikē* had deserted, who would then have to be *perioikoi* (in B. Jowett's translation, the Athenians withdrew "the Messenians, Helots, and Lakedaimonian deserters"; see also the translations by Blanco, Canfora, and C. F. Smith, but cf. de Romilly, Donini; Classen, Krüger, and Stahl emended the text). The best discussion of this sentence is offered by Steup, App. 262–3, with full references to earlier editors and commentators. It is tempting to see the two sentences that describe the group to be evacuated in 5.35.6 and 5.35.7 respectively as a case of conflicting focalization, with the Spartans perceiving the deserters as Helots only, and the Athenians seeing them as what they were, i.e. Helots and *perioikoi*. The curiously abstract description of the Spartans' fears in 4.41.3 could also point to the fact that the Helots were not the only danger (so Classen). Note, however, that in 5.56.3 the deserters withdrawn from Pylos seem to be described, from an Athenian point of view, as "the Helots of Krane" – but there is no reason to take that sentence as reference to all of them. See also below, p. 201, on Thucydides' views of the Messenian identity.

[62] It is not clear from Thucydides who exactly was brought back to Pylos in 419; Thuc. 5.56.3 refers only to "the Helots from Krane," but 7.57.8 implies presence of Messenians in Pylos. Diod. 13.64.5 refers explicitly to Messenians defending Pylos to the end – and to nobody else. For Xenophon (*Hell.* 1.2.17), Pylos was occupied by "the Helots who had deserted from Malea to Koryphasion." This disagreement probably reflects contrasting biases more than anything else (note also that Xenophon uses the "Spartan" name Koryphasion, cf. Thuc. 4.3.2); from a Messenian perspective, fugitives from Laconia were Messenian by definition.

[63] On the chronology see Lewis 1977: 126 n. 112.

Cape Malea in 413 (Thuc. 7.26.2) and abandoned the following winter (Thuc. 8.4), had also been moved there. After the failure of a relief expedition led by the Athenian Anytos, the Messenians, unable to withstand the siege any longer, once again concluded a treaty with the Spartans and evacuated the stronghold.[64] Nothing more is heard of them in the last years of the war.

Apart from these traces in the record of events, the Messenians of Naupaktos have left behind some very impressive monuments that tell a lot about their concerns and their way of conceptualizing themselves as a political entity (fig. 4). From its very birth, the new polity of the Messenians was clearly anxious to make its existence known among the Greeks.[65] The victory against the Kalydonians was commemorated by an extraordinarily conspicuous offering at Delphi, a triangular pillar of marble, more than eight meters tall, decorated by two rows of bronze shields, which probably supported a bronze tripod upheld by a marble statue.[66] The same urge is expressed by the most famous Panhellenic offering of the Messenians, the Nike of Paionios, erected at Olympia most probably right after the peace of Nicias.[67] Floating in the air more than eight meters above ground, carried by the eagle of Zeus, on top of a triangular pillar, before the temple, slightly removed to its left, the Nike conveyed an explicit message. According to the inscription, the statue was a tithe dedicated to Zeus from the booty taken by Messenians and Naupaktians "from the enemies"; this may be understood as a cumulative reference to victories during the Archidamian war, but other cases of dedication formulated in the same way suggest that a specific occasion, such as the involvement in the Athenian victory at Pylos, should not be ruled out.[68] The row of shields that decorated the upper part of the pillar

---

[64] See Diod. 13.64.5–7, Xen. *Hell.* 1.2.17, Aristot. *Ath. Pol.* 27.5.

[65] Figueira 1999: 215, aptly speaks of "a virtual *blitzkrieg* of self-assertion by the Messenians spanning about a generation from *c.* 460."

[66] On this monument, see Jacquemin and Laroche 1982: 191–207; the inscription is *SEG* 32.550. The name of Kalydon seems to be the only possible supplement. For a date during the *Pentekontaetia* see ibid. 199 and 204.

[67] It is doubtful that the Messenians would have had access to Olympia before the peace and the break between Sparta and Elis (on which see Roy 1998, Hornblower 2000a). For the historical and art-historical interpretation of the monument, see Hölscher 1974; on the statue in particular, 89–92, and Borbein 1973: 165–9. The pillar has been reconstructed by Herrmann 1972. The dedicatory inscription, *IvO* 259 = *IG* IX 1² 3, 656 = ML 74, runs as follows: "The Messenians and the Naupaktians dedicated to Olympian Zeus as a tithe from the enemies." Pausanias (5.26.1) wrongly connects it with the Messenian victory over Oiniadai; see Maddoli and Saladino *ad loc.* A further Messenian dedication in Delphi (*SEG* 19.391), whose chronology is unclear, could date back to the fifth century; see the discussion below, pp. 340–3.

[68] The cumulative reference theory has been advanced by Hölscher 1974: 74–5 and n. 9; see, however, Jacquemin 1999: 93–4 with other cases of dedications "from the enemies."

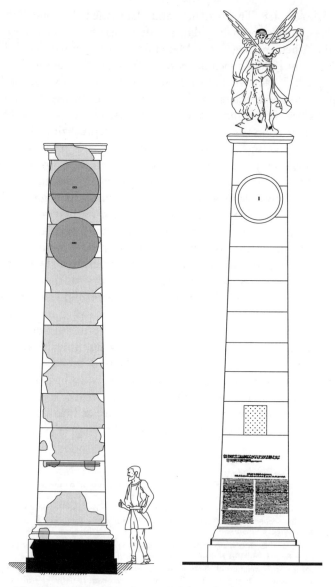

Figure 4 The pillars of the Messenians at Delphi and Olympia (after Jacquemin and Laroche 1982 and Hölscher 1974 respectively)

may have carried some direct evidence as to who exactly the defeated enemies were,[69] but even if they did not, it must have been clear to everybody that the monument was a slap in the Spartans' face; the visual connection with the golden shield dedicated by the Spartans and their allies for their victory over Athens and Argos at Tanagra, located on top of the frontal pediment of the temple of Zeus, could hardly go unnoticed,[70] and the Spartans, for their part, got the message: Lysander is said to have dedicated in Sparta two statues of Nike on an eagle after the Peloponnesian War, as if to expiate the shame with a double reparation.[71]

The Nike of Paionios was dedicated, according to the inscription, by Messenians and Naupaktians, and the name of the Naupaktians is to be supplemented in the inscription on the pillar of Delphi, too.[72] This, together with a mid-fifth century inscription from Naupaktos that records some sort of agreement between Messenians and Naupaktians, shows that the two communities actually lived side by side and cooperated in military enterprises.[73] Beyond this, these inscriptions also make us aware of an important fact relating to the nature of the Messenians as a political entity. Far from becoming Naupaktians or renaming their new place of residence "Messene," the Messenians depicted themselves as a political community

---

[69] For evidence of the presence of the shields on the pillar, see Herrmann 1972: 82–3. Spartan shields would have been recognizable by the letter Lambda (for Λακεδαίμων) they bore, see Grandjean 2003: 74 and n. 102.

[70] The shield of Tanagra is mentioned by Pausanias (5.10.4); see also ML 36. The connection between the shield and the Nike has been observed by Hölscher 1974: 82–3; as Massimo Nafissi points out to me, there might even be a verbal pun emphasizing the link between the two offerings and playing on the double meaning of *aetos*, "eagle" and "pediment": in Greek, both offerings could be said to be sitting on an *aetos*.

[71] Lysander's dedications are mentioned by Pausanias (3.17.4), who connects them to Lysander's victories of Notion and Aigospotamoi. Hölscher 1974: 76–7 convincingly suggests taking them as a response to the Nike of Paionios; his further point, that the statues were dedicated in Sparta because at that point the Spartans were still excluded from Olympia, is more controversial, cf. now Hornblower 2000a. Note the motif of the two-for-one reparation, present also in expiation for the sacrilegous murder of the regent Pausanias (Thuc. 1.134.4); the two statues of the regent in the precinct of Athena Chalkioikos were still seen by Pausanias (3.17.7).

[72] See Jacquemin and Laroche 1982: 196–8.

[73] SEG 51.642, preserving the oaths exchanged by Messenians and Naupaktians to sanction an agreement that must have been laid out in the first part of the document, which is lost. For the chronology, see Matthaiou-Mastrokostas 2000–3: 449–54, suggesting a date around 430–420 BC. However, the technical quality of the inscription, in perfect *stoichēdon* style, and the presence of Ionian traits in the shapes of the letters suggest that this document may have been inscribed by a stonecutter from Athens, in which case the relevant parallels would have to be looked for among Athenian inscriptions, and an earlier date, closer to the migration of the Messenians to Naupaktos, would be more likely. The evidence of the inscriptions contradicts the notion, found in Diod. 14.34.2 and Paus. 10.38.10, that the Naupaktians had not returned to their polis until the Messenians were expelled by the Spartans. On the likely cooperation between Naupaktians and Messenians, see Pomtow 1896: 583–8.

without a land, living alongside the previous inhabitants of the city, which continued in its existence as an independent polis. The official name of the Messenians must have been *hoi Messanioi hoi en Naupaktōi*, occasionally used by Thucydides (2.9.4; see also e.g. Diod. 12.60.1). As it appears, the Messenians conceived of themselves as a polity in exile, obviously in the hope of being able eventually to return to their real fatherland in the Peloponnese.[74]

It is this never-forgotten aspiration, and not only their consistent loyalty to Athens, that explains why, after the end of the Peloponnesian War, and more precisely after the successful conclusion of their campaign against Elis, the Spartans decided to evict the Messenians from Naupaktos and from a fortress they occupied on the island of Kephallenia (Diod. 14.34). The fortress is obviously Krane, where the Athenians had settled Helots and perhaps other fugitives from the Peloponnese who had made their way to Pylos (see above). Interestingly, by 401 they were all Messenians. According to Diodorus, faced by the Spartan onslaught the Messenians took their weapons and left Naupaktos and Kephallenia, some of them moving to Sicily, to fight as mercenaries for Dionysius of Syracuse, and some to Cyrene, where they helped to restore the Cyrenaean aristocrats to the city, from which they had recently been exiled.[75] After some campaigns, Dionysius settled his Messenian mercenaries in Messana, which had been laid waste by the Carthaginians in 397 and after all had the right name to harbor them, but then, afraid of annoying his allies the Spartans, the tyrant decided to relocate the Messenians to another place, in the territory of the indigenous town of Abacaenum, not far from Messana. There they founded the city of Tyndaris, that is, the city of the Tyndarids, a fortress in an important strategic position, defending the approach to Messana along the northern coast of Sicily.[76] But the Messenian diaspora must have spread even wider than this. As we happen to know from the *Hellenica of Oxyrhynchus*, the personal guard of the exiled Athenian admiral Conon in 395 was formed by Messenians, too (*Hell. Ox.* 20.3).[77]

---

[74] See the pertinent observations of Figueira 1999: 220 " . . . a Messenian community was sheltered at Naupaktos, whose colonial status was suppressed conceptually and rhetorically."

[75] On the fate of the Messenians from Naupaktos who went to Sicily, see above, p. 156.

[76] The story of the Messenians in Sicily is in Diod. 14.78.5, where, however, they are said to have come from Naupaktos and Zakynthos, instead of Kephallenia.

[77] See Bruce 1967: 129. Conon had been operating in Naupaktos during the Peloponnesian War (Thuc. 7.31.3), and commanded the Messenians in Corcyra in 410 (Diod. 13.48).

WHO WERE THE REBELS?

At this point, it is necessary to leap back in time to address a question that has been left open, namely, the identity of those who revolted after the earthquake. The rebels are defined in the sources in different ways. Herodotus speaks simply of war between Spartans and Messenians, without explaining in any detail who the latter were.[78] The Old Oligarch does the same, adding by implication that the Messenians were "the worst" and thereby assimilating them to the Athenian *dēmos*. Likewise, for Aristophanes, Perikleidas had come to Athens to ask for help against Messene.[79] Thucydides (1.101.2) describes the rebels in a more detailed way: they were Helots and the *perioikoi* of Thouria and Aithaia, and since the majority of the Helots who revolted were the descendants of the old Messenians, who had been enslaved in the past, all the rebels came now to be called "Messenians."[80] However, later authors offer a different picture. While Xenophon speaks of Sparta being besieged by the Messenians (6.5.33) and calls the revolt "war against Messene" (5.2.3), following fifth-century usage, the Attidographer consulted by the commentator on Aristophanes, presumably Philochorus,[81] spoke apparently of the Messenians revolting against the Spartans after the earthquake, and the Helots fall-ing upon Sparta at the same time (*Schol.* Aristoph. *Lys.* 1142b Hangard-Holwerda). Diodorus describes a common attack by Messenians and Helots, very clearly distinguishing them as two different entities (11.63.4 and 64.4; cf. 15.66.4), and says that under the terms of the truce the Spartans allowed only the Messenians to leave the Peloponnese, while they punished those of the Helots who had been responsible for the revolt and enslaved the others (11.84.8). According to Plutarch (*Cim.* 16.7; cf. *Lyc.* 28.6) the revolt was started by the Helots, who were able to win over also some *perioikoi*, and at the same time the Messenians also attacked the Spartans. Finally, a different view on the revolt is found in Pausanias, according to whom not all the Helots revolted, but only those who were of Messenian descent (3.11.8 and 4.24.6).

In spite of their obvious inconsistencies, it is not too difficult to make sense of these sources. Once again, as in the case of the division of the

---

[78] Herodotus is typically sparing in details on events that fall outside the chronological boundaries of his work (see Vannicelli 1993, esp. 16–18); his sketchy reference cannot be used as evidence for the continuing existence of a free Messenian polity into the early fifth century, as Hammond 1955: 375–9 and Ducat 1990: 142–3 – with qualification – do.

[79] For Aristophanes, as probably for Euripides (*TrGF* 727e *ap.* Strab. 8.5.6, see above, p. 71 n. 6), "Messene" is already the name of the region usually called "Messenia" from Polybius onwards.

[80] For the interpretation of this passage, see Luraghi 2002c.   [81] Jacoby 1954: 455.

Peloponnese among the Heraclids and in that of the conquest of Messenia, the sources reflect rather clearly the historical contexts from which they originate – in fact, in this case even more clearly than in the two previous ones. With different degrees of precision, the early sources are consistent. Thucydides says explicitly that the rebels were called Messenians, and Herodotus and the Old Oligarch simply name them such without explanation. Aristophanes calls "Messene" the entity that attacked the Spartans. By contrast, the later sources clearly regard Helots and Messenians as two distinct entities. Their view should not be confused with Thucydides', which presupposes that both Helots of Messenian origin and other Helots took part in the revolt. Rather, the later sources either describe the revolt as in fact the sum of two different revolts (*scholia* to Aristophanes and Plutarch) or say that Helots and Messenians agreed upon attacking the Spartans together, but were then separated again at the end of the war (Diodorus). In other words, for Thucydides the revolt was started by Helots of Messenian descent, other Helots and *perioikoi*, and during the revolt and after they all came to be called Messenians; for Diodorus, Plutarch and the scholiast two different groups revolted together: the Helotized Messenians of Messenia and the Helots proper of Laconia.[82]

The liberation of Messenia by the Thebans is the pivotal point around which the definitions of the rebels, and hence by implication the interpretation of the revolt, turn.[83] For the free Messenians it was obviously very desirable to separate their own past from that of the Helots of Laconia, who were still enslaved well into the Hellenistic period.[84] Their claim to their ancestral land, as we will see more in detail below, was predicated upon their descent from the rebels and thus, indirectly, from the free Messenians of old. Therefore, it was important for them to state clearly that the Helotized Messenians had remained all along distinct from the "true" Helots. This is why all post-fourth century sources insist upon the distinction between Helots and Messenians. What they mean, of course, is not that at the time of the earthquake in Messenia there were

---

[82] Therefore it is difficult to be certain that the notion that the revolt extended to Laconia v(Diod. 11.64.1 and Plut. *Cim.* 16.7) is not the result of Thucydides, or a source that described the revolt in similar terms, being misinterpreted by later authors for whom Helots living in Messenia were really Messenians, and therefore the Helots of non-Messenian origin to whom Thucydides indirectly alludes had to be in Laconia.

[83] See Oliva 1971: 154 and Figueira 1999: 217–18. Both emphasize Ephorus' role as direct or indirect source of the later authors; see also Ducat 1990: 98. Cf. Vidal-Naquet 1981: 246–7 on the influence of the liberation of Messenia on the perception of Helotry.

[84] On the Helots in Hellenistic Sparta, see now Kennell 2003.

still any free and non-Helotized Messenians: Diodorus, Plutarch and Pausanias all clearly assume that all the Messenians had been evicted from their own land by the Spartans or reduced into slavery by the seventh century at the latest.[85] Although at first sight he may seem to offer a different perspective, Pausanias gives the most characteristic version of this revisionist view of the revolt. For him, not all the Helots revolted, only those who were of Messenian descent. Thereby Helots of non-Messenian origin and the *perioikoi* are completely erased from the record of the revolt. Tellingly, for Pausanias the *perioikoi* of Messenia – in so far as he mentions them at all – all seem to have been refugees from the Argolis.[86] As for Xenophon, writing in the immediate aftermath of the liberation of Messenia, his adherence to fifth-century terminology is not surprising, given that the reformulation of the Messenian past would just have started in his time, and even if he knew about it, he was certainly not willing to endorse it, because it obviously conflicted with his die-hard Spartan agenda.[87]

The fact that the *perioikoi* participating in the revolt all but disappear from the sources – with the exception of Plutarch, who obviously takes them from Thucydides – is not surprising. The Messenian "party line," as it emerged after the liberation, affirmed that the brave Messenians had been enslaved *en masse* after the Second Messenian War – with the exception of those who had left the Peloponnese earlier – then revolted at the time of the earthquake, left the Peloponnese after a long fight and finally came back to found a new, free Messene in the aftermath of Leuktra. This scenario obviously had no role for the *perioikoi*. They could not be seen as Messenians, since all Messenians had been enslaved or evicted by the Spartans. *Perioikoi* of Messenia, rubbing shoulders for centuries with the hated Spartans, would have been despicable *collaborateurs*, not to be associated with the Messenians' struggle for freedom. In other words, the revolt is only one specific case of the almost total silence of post-liberation sources on the *perioikoi* living in Messenia in the previous centuries.[88]

---

[85] It would therefore be a mistake to connect these late sources with Herodotus as evidence for the fact that Messenia had remained free until the time of the earthquake, cf. above, nn. 37 and 78.

[86] See Paus 4.14.3 on Asine and 4.24.4 on Mothone and above, p. 142 n. 152.

[87] On Xenophon's attitude to the newly founded Messenian state see below, p. 222.

[88] Notice also that the participation of *perioikoi* goes unmentioned already in retrospective references to the revolt in Thucydides (2.27.2, 3.54.5); this may have to do with a general unwillingness, on the part of the Spartans, to admit separatist tendencies among them.

MESSENIAN ETHNOGENESIS

It seems clear that the way in which later sources depict the rebels is relevant for the construction of a Messenian identity after the liberation of Messenia, but does not constitute reliable evidence concerning the identity of the rebels themselves. In trying to reconstruct who the rebels thought they were and how they were perceived by others, only the fifth-century sources can be really useful. The Spartan viewpoint on the matter is still clearly recognizable: the Spartans considered the rebels fugitive slaves. According to Thucydides (1.128.1), the Spartans thought that the earthquake had been a punishment meted out to them by Poseidon, because they had dragged from his sanctuary on Tainaron some Helots who had sought asylum there and slaughtered them. Since earthquake and revolt were so closely associated, it seems safe to assume that the Spartans saw a connection between a sacrilegious massacre of slaves and a revolt of slaves.[89] The same view of the revolt is expressed in the conditions of the truce that allowed the rebels to evacuate Ithome, which implicitly treated them as runaway slaves who had placed themselves under the protection of a god but could be enslaved again if they came back to the Peloponnese. The Spartans refused to consider the rebels free human beings,[90] which is particularly interesting considering that *perioikoi* took part in the revolt, too.

However, the Spartans themselves had to recognize that the rest of the Greek world did not share their views. In a treaty with the city of Tegea, probably dating from the aftermath of the revolt, they requested that the Tegeans expel "the Messenians" from their territory.[91] Later, during the Peloponnesian War, the Spartans seem to have come to accept the Messenians of Naupaktos; according to Thucydides, they now called them "Messenians," and in 401 they obviously did not think that trying to enslave

---

[89] See Jordan 1990: 47–9. The connection between the sacrilege and the revolt explains probably why Pausanias (4.24.5) has a different version of the episode, in which the suppliants of Poseidon were not Helots, but criminals who had been sentenced to death; these would have no link with the (for Pausanias) Messenian rebels and, more importantly, would not suggest an association Messenians–Helots; see Luraghi 2005: 184–8.

[90] See Figueira 1999: 234–5.

[91] In all likelihood, the treaty between Tegea and Sparta, which obliged the Tegeans to expel the Messenians from their territory (Plut. *Aet. Gr.* 5 = *Mor.* 292b and *Aet. Rom.* 52 = *Mor.* 277b–c = Aristot. Fr. 609,1 and 609,2 Gigon = *Staatsverträge* II, 112), traditionally dated to the archaic period, dates in fact from immediately after the end of the revolt; see already Moretti 1946: 101–3 and now Cawkwell 1993: 369–70 (connecting the treaty with Plato's war, that Cawkwell considers historical), Braun 1994: 43, and Nielsen 2002: 188–90 and 393–5. Polyaen. 2.10.3, where Kleandridas triggers a *stasis* in Tegea, is decisive for the dating of the treaty.

them again was feasible. Certainly the Spartans were acting cautiously, under the assumption that a community that had lived free for some five decades and had kept fighting on various fronts for most of that time could not easily be reduced to slavery again. However, this change of attitude, dictated by sheer political realism as it may have been, should not be seen as trivial. Some of the "Messenians" whom the Spartans were evicting from Naupaktos and Kephallenia in 401 had been Helots only a few years earlier. In all likelihood, the first stories that justified the Spartan conquest of Messenia emerged in this cultural and political climate.[92]

The self-representation of the rebels was consistent. Thucydides' gloss, according to which they were all called Messenians because the majority of the Helots who revolted were of Messenian descent, diverts attention from a crucial point: the denomination was clearly chosen by the rebels themselves. This is shown by the fact that the political community formed by the rebels in Naupaktos after leaving the Peloponnese was itself called "the Messenians," as we have seen. It is quite unlikely that they would have kept this name if they had not themselves chosen it from the beginning. This would be all the more true in view of the dedications of weapons by the Methanioi discussed above, whose connection with the rebels is not certain, but highly likely. In short, it can confidently be assumed that the rebels regarded themselves as "the Messenians," a name that identified them as an ethnic group.[93] However they might have come to think of themselves as Messenians, it is perfectly clear that they had very strong reasons for sticking to their Messenian identity. Their choice was dictated by the way group identities were perceived in the Greek world. Every polis or ethnos, every political community that had an accepted claim to a territory was perceived and represented by the Greeks in ethnic terms, that is, essentially as an extended kinship group.[94]

In other words, in order to be able to stake a legitimate claim to autonomy the rebels had to define themselves as an ethnic group, and in order to sustain their claim to a territory they needed to devise a charter myth, or even better, to insert themselves into some already existing mythic complex. In the early fifth century, the diffusion of the myth of

---

[92] See above, pp. 83 and 159. Notice also that the fact that the Spartans were now accepting the Messenian identity of the exiles does not mean that they were ready to recognize the existence of Messenians in their own territory; see below, p. 223.

[93] On the meaning of ethnic names as the kernel of ethnic identification, see e.g. Smith 1986: 22–4, Fabietti 1998: 16 and above, p. 10.

[94] See Weber 1972: 235–42, with penetrating observations on the function of ethnicity in ancient Greece.

the division of the Peloponnese among the Heraclids had established, probably for the first time, the idea of a unitary land called Messene, *de facto* identical with the western half of the Lakedaimonian territory. From the point of view of Greek mentality, the rebels had no choice but to define themselves as Messenians.[95] As we have seen, even after the failure of the revolt the rebels were clearly unwilling to give up their Messenian identity and the corresponding claim on the Messenian land. Emphatically, they did not regard themselves as a colony, but rather as an exiled community, temporarily living away from its own territory. Their spectacular dedications in Olympia and Delphi document the attempt of this community to capture the attention of a Panhellenic audience. The Spartans understood perfectly the nature of the Messenian presence in Naupaktos and consequently regarded them as a latent threat, which explains their insistence on evicting the Messenians from the Gulf of Corinth after the end of the Peloponnesian War.

On the whole, then, it is not too difficult to figure out why the rebels would have wanted to depict themselves as Messenians and why the Spartans would have tended to reject their self-ascription as far as they could. If we approached Messenian ethnogenesis from a purely situational or functionalist perspective, nothing more would be necessary to explain this process. But such an approach would be one-sided.[96] What remains to be explained is how concretely the rebels came to see themselves as Messenians. If in fact the people living in the *Lakonikē* west of the Taygetos, Helots and/or *perioikoi*, had always subscribed to the Messenian identity, from before the Spartan conquest, the revolt would not be a surprise, but such an assumption is difficult to reconcile with the evidence discussed in the previous chapters. Clearly, a different approach is needed. For purposes of analysis, the problem of the emergence of Messenian ethnicity in the fifth century should be divided into two separate aspects, its tradition and its sociology. In other words, it can be helpful to separate at first the question of whether and how the rebels, or some of them, were linked by a chain of tradition to the Messenians who had fought against the Spartans in the eighth century, and the question of how concretely an ethnic identity, under whatever name, could emerge and spread among the Helots and *perioikoi* living in the *Lakonikē* west of the Taygetos.

---

[95] In this perspective, the Old Oligarch's take on the revolt (3.11) shows most clearly its pro-Spartan twist, in that it hits the very core of the legitimizing strategy of the rebels, by calling them Messenians but at the same time describing their revolt as a *stasis*.

[96] On ethnicity as a process of drawing of borders and on the problem of the "contents," see above, pp. 8–10.

Here the sources are rather less helpful. Thucydides' deceptively reassuring answer to the second question is all we have, and it can hardly be regarded as satisfactory. As we have seen, the notion that the Messenian identity was attributed to the rebels by someone else is essentially unacceptable. There are certainly many cases in which a marginal group accepts an ethnic ascription that comes from the outside, and often tries to neutralize its connotations,[97] but in the case of the Messenians this scenario is out of the question. Their Messenian ethnicity was the foundation of their claims, and nobody else had any interest in defining them as Messenians, least of all the Spartans, who resisted consistently, even in later times, the notion that people living in their territory west of the Taygetos had a separate ethnic identity (below, pp. 222–3). But there are further reasons for taking a moderately skeptical approach to Thucydides' description of the Messenian ethnogenesis.

On the surface, such a description reminds one of modern models for the emergence of ethnic groups. Research in the history of the barbarian kingdoms in the early Middle Ages has identified a recurrent process whereby a smaller group that carries a particular myth of origin can become the center of aggregation for a larger ethnic entity, functioning as the "kernel of tradition," in Wenksus' helpful definition.[98] Although this model can in fact be profitably applied to explain the emergence of Messenian ethnicity in the fifth century, it should be clear that Thucydides' view does not presuppose a sophisticated appreciation of the mechanics of ethnicity, but is rather an attempt at placing the Messenian identity of the rebels in the framework of accepted views of early Peloponnesian history.[99] An attempt, it may be added, that is perhaps less innocent and even-handed than it might seem. Although Thucydides does say that the rebels came to be called "Messenians," he conspicuously avoids calling them by that name in his narrative of the revolt, using instead the periphrasis *hoi en Ithomēi* (1.101.3, 102.3, 103.1). Elsewhere, he shows more signs of not taking Messenian ethnicity too seriously. His calling the Messenians of Naupaktos who fought in the Sicilian expedition 'those who are now called the Messenians' (Thuc. 7.57.8) is revealing of an attitude that was shared by other prominent Athenians: when Alcibiades' uncle Axiochos, one of the profaners of the Eleusinian mysteries,

---

[97] See Hall 1997: 31.
[98] See Wenskus 1961: 54–82, esp. 75–7, and cf. the discussion above, p. 8.
[99] On the reconstructions of the origins of Helotic slavery in ancient sources, see Vidal-Naquet 1981: 235–42 and above, pp. 137–8.

called one of his slaves "Messenios," he was obviously making a sarcastic statement on the true nature of the Messenians.[100] Thucydides' notion that the Messenian identity essentially came from the Helots may be regarded as an expression of this same view.

If we remain in the framework of the ethnogenesis model, it is clear that the Helots do not make ideal candidates for the function of the "kernel of tradition" in the emergence of Messenian ethnicity. In general terms, it would not be hard to imagine that a group defined by a specific social status or function could have begun, under the pressure of the ruling elite, to understand itself in ethnic terms; parallels for this kind of phenomenon have been observed.[101] However, such a process requires the existence or the formation of an elite inside the group, one that controls the symbolic and communicative means to broadcast and uphold this ethnic identity.[102] It is rather unclear to what extent the Helots controlled the means, mostly of a ritual nature, which normally permitted the perpetuation of group identities among the Greeks. In the field of religion, where alone it is possible to check, the result is clearly negative: there seem to have been no specifically Helotic cults, in either Laconia or Messenia, which might have functioned as foci for the Helots' collective identity. Every time Helots are met in a religious context, the context is that of a Lakedaimonian cult.[103] The case of cult at Bronze Age tombs, which has been evoked as a possible focus for the transmission of a sense of community among the Helots of Messenia,[104] is only partially an exception. While it seems reasonable to regard at least some manifestations of this practice as connected to the articulation of a sense of ethnic distinctness, it should be born in mind that it was not specifically linked with the Helots, and more importantly, that it appears to have been extremely discontinuous in time, especially before the late fifth century.[105]

---

[100] The name of the slave appears in one of the lists of the property confiscated to the profaners, Pritchett 1953: 287–90. Rosivach 1999: 129 n. 3 points out, against Pritchett 1956: 280, that the name does not imply that the slave was a Messenian, or for that matter, a Greek. The same attitude can be noticed in Plato's *Laws* (see above). In the early fourth century, Alcidamas' *Messenian Speech* (see below, p. 223 n. 49) offers one further testimony of the intra-Athenian discourse on Messenian identity, which tended to frame the question as one of freedom or slavery, not of ethnicity.

[101] See e.g. Kohl 1998: 275–9.   [102] See Armstrong 1982: 7–8.

[103] See Parker 1989: 145. Ducat 1990: 177–8 discusses cautiously the existence of a specifically Helotic culture, and notices the absence of any traces of it in the sources. Placido 1994, in spite of its title, is a discussion of Helotic presence in Spartan sanctuaries.

[104] See especially Alcock 2002b: 146–52.

[105] The evidence and its interpretation are discussed above, pp. 127–9, and below, pp. 239–45.

In comparative terms, the conditions of Helotic dependency were not particularly conducive to the emergence of a counter-elite which would be able and willing to challenge the Spartan domination in symbolic terms,[106] and actually the scanty traces of elites among the Helots show them as characterized by a strong drive toward integration in the Lakedaimonian identity.[107] However, the distance between Sparta and Messenia means that some basic conditions are likely to have been different on the two sides of the Taygetos. Even considering that Helotic villages in Messenia are a possibility rather than a certainty, the fact remains that the Spartans were absentee landowners, who must have been rarely present on their estates in general, and even more rarely on those west of the Taygetos. This means that those estates must have been largely run by Helots, so that some level of hierarchy among them must have existed for the system to function.[108]

If it seems sociologically rather unlikely that the Messenian identity could have been created and transmitted by the Helots, it is much less problematic to assume that it could spread among them, for reasons that have to do essentially with the way in which the Spartiates structured and conceptualized their world, their *kosmos*, and the place of the Helots in it. Clearly, the conquest of Laconia by the Heraclids and the Dorians formed the basis of the Spartans' claim to their land. It is much less clear if the Spartans also shared the ethnic interpretation of the groups living in *Lakonikē* that becomes current in Greek historiography since the late fifth century. There is no reason to think that the Spartiates understood the origins of the difference between themselves and the Helots in ethnic terms.[109] However, they seem to have had a very precise view of who the Helots were *hic et nunc*, so to speak: less-than-human beings who embodied all the characteristics that the Spartans despised. The Spartiates devised a

---

[106] See Armstrong 1982: 6–7: "Emergence of such a counterelite is especially difficult in sedentary agricultural societies where dominant elites monopolize communication by symbols and supervise the socialization of all members of the polity by inculcation of myths legitimizing the elite's dominance." Among the factors that can support the emergence of an ethnic identity among an oppressed lower class, Armstrong mentions linguistic difference between the ruling and the ruled, which does not seem to have existed among Spartiates and Messenians, see above.

[107] See Ducat 1990: 162–4; Figueira 1999: 223 (Helots as "understudies"); Hodkinson 2003: 272–4. On the particularly telling case of the alleged plot of the regent Pausanias (Thuc. 1.132.4), see Nafissi 2004: 168–9.

[108] See Hodkinson 2003: 263–78; on the settlement pattern of the Helots in Messenia, see also above, pp. 130–1.

[109] See Figueira 1999: 221: "In the socialization by which the Spartiates endeavored to inculcate into the Helots their inferior status, it is noteworthy that elaborated *ethnic* symbolism was not included."

collective identity for the Helots that was essentially a reversed image of what they thought of themselves, and proceeded to impose such an identity on the Helots by a complex of practices that could be called ritualized contempt and had the goal of humiliating the Helots and instilling in them the sense of their inferiority.[110]

These practices and others, such as the yearly declaration of war on the Helots by the ephors, whatever its origin, which allowed the Spartiates to kill any Helot they wished without ritual impurity,[111] implicitly construed the Helots as a discrete group. The possible effects of these practices on the self-perception of the Helots will have been reinforced by the fact that they probably had more family continuity than was normally the case with slaves in the Greek world: at the very least, the fact that the Spartiates tended not to manumit them made of them a self-reproducing population. The construction of the Helots as a group, in a symbolic and material sense, was of course a function of Spartan domination, but at the same time it conferred upon them a potential for unity of action that was totally absent otherwise among Greek slaves.[112] The revolt in Messenia may be seen as the first documented manifestation of this potential.

Still, it is less easy to admit that the Helots could also have functioned as the catalyst for the emergence of Messenian ethnicity and for the revolt. For general and specific reasons, the *perioikoi* of Messenia would be far better candidates for such a role. The political organization of the perioikic communities is very poorly understood, but it is clear that they must have been something between large villages and small towns in terms of size, with some level of political institutions and with their own territories and sanctuaries, which of course were frequented also by Spartiates.[113] Although they were "second-class citizens" in the Spartan state, they certainly possessed a full social structure with their own local elites. In other

---

[110] The construction of this Helotic identity by way of ritualized practices has been investigated in a path-breaking contribution by Jean Ducat; see Ducat 1974b, 1990: 105–27; see also Figueira 1999: 221–5, with further excellent observations.

[111] Aristot. fr. 538 Rose, *ap.* Plut. *Lyc.* 28.7.

[112] See Vidal-Naquet 1981: 211–21; Ducat 1990: 181–2; Cartledge 1985: 40–6, and see chapter 5 on the settlement pattern of the Helots in Messenia and its possible implications. Note the paradox in the way the Spartiates dealt with the Helots: on the one hand, they were marginalized and ostentatiously mishandled more than normal slaves, on the other they could reach a level of integration in the political community of the Lakedaimonians that other slaves could not reach elsewhere in Greece.

[113] See Lotze 1993/4. The political status of the perioikic communities has been discussed in a number of recent contributions, in part in the framework of the Copenhagen Polis Centre; see Shipley 1997, Hall 2000, and Hansen 2004 for the application of the concept of "dependent polis" to the perioikic settlements (esp. Shipley 1997: 206–11). Cf., however, the criticism formulated by Mertens 2002: 288–91.

words, they had all the social requirements that the Helots seem to have lacked to provide the moving force for Messenian ethnogenesis.

Besides their sociological suitability to function as a "kernel of tradition," there are more specific reasons that point to the necessity of reassessing the role of the *perioikoi* in the revolt. In the first place, the level of their participation seems to have been considerable. Thouria appears to have been the second most important settlement of Messenia throughout its history. Aithaia may not have been as important, unless we know it under a different name in later times – as a matter of fact, perioikic settlements on the northwestern side of the Messenian gulf are unlikely to have opposed the revolt, since the rebels appear to have had access to the sanctuary of Apollo Korythos at Longà/Ayios Andhreas. Another perioikic settlement that presumably joined the revolt is the one located at the foot of Mount Ithome. Furthermore, a concrete point that has to do with the events themselves should be noticed: the rebels were extraordinarily successful in military terms, witness the annihilation of Arimnestos and his 300 and the dedications of weapons discussed above. Now, while the Helots played at best a secondary function in the Spartan army,[114] the *perioikoi*, although they did not receive the intensive military training of the Spartiates, contributed hoplites to the Lakedaimonian phalanx,[115] and the presence of a significant number of these well-trained hoplites in the ranks of the rebels helps account for the fate of Arimnestos and his men. To strengthen this point, one of the spear butts dedicated by the Messenians comes from a perioikic sanctuary, the sanctuary of Apollo Korythos at Longà/Ayios Andhreas.

The presence of a dedication of booty taken by the rebels in one of the most important perioikic sanctuaries of Messenia and of a perioikic settlement in the place where the rebels dug in to resist the Spartan counteroffensive directs our attention to a possibly deeper level of perioikic involvement in the revolt – while at the same time bringing us from the problem of the sociology of Messenian ethnogenesis to the problem of the roots of Messenian ethnicity. Mount Ithome became in time the truest symbol of the Messenian identity. This might to some extent be a consequence of its role in the revolt, but Mount Ithome is used to describe the land of the Messenians already by Tyrtaeus (fr. 5.8 West[2]).

---

[114] The military role of the Helots has possibly been underestimated, see e.g. Welwei 1974: 108–81. Hunt 1997: 129–44, and 1998: 23–78, argues against this reductive view, but seems to fall into the other extreme. For a more balanced appraisal see Ducat 1999: 43.

[115] On the military role of the *perioikoi* see Ducat 1999: 41–2; Lotze 1993/4: 40; Mertens 2002: 288 and n. 19.

The archaic and classical settlement at the foot of the mountain is the best possible candidate as the abode of at least some of the 'kernels of tradition' around which Messenian ethnogenesis precipitated.

The conclusion that a leading role in Messenian ethnogenesis in the fifth century should be assigned to the *perioikoi* of Messenia, or to some of them, might sound like a paradox, considering the evidence about the Lakedaimonian nature of their cults, language, alphabet and material culture, which clearly suggests their participation in a largely homogeneous Lakedaimonian ethnicity east and west of the Taygetos. The paradox is epitomized by the dedication of spoils by the rebels in the sanctuary of Apollo Korythos, possibly the most Lakedaimonian of all sanctuaries in Messenia. However, such evidence does not really question the notion that the *perioikoi* of Messenia could be the prime movers of Messenian ethnogenesis in the fifth century; it rather bears on the problem of the history and function of Messenian identity itself. The Lakedaimonian cultural pattern in late archaic and early classical Messenia corresponds perfectly to a phenomenon that scholars have often noticed, the prevalence of Spartan myths and cults in post-liberation Messenia, and, we may add, among the Messenians of Italy and Sicily. In other words, the evidence strongly suggests that in the Peloponnese Messenian ethnicity emerged as a process of fission within a larger group that perceived itself as ethnically Lakedaimonian.[116]

When this process started is hard to tell. As we have seen, at least one ritual practice, cult at Bronze Age tombs, seems to have set apart Messenia from Laconia during the archaic period. Interestingly, the practice seems to have been shared by *perioikoi* and Helots. Its meaning, however, is not exactly obvious. If it was indeed perceived as a characteristic practice of people inhabiting the western part of *Lakonikē*, it could be considered a potential element of an ethnic identity. Even if we are prepared to stretch the string of hypotheses this far, it would still be rather unlikely that this ritual practice could have been understood by those who engaged in it as a component of their Messenian identity. It seems better to take a cautious approach and regard this old and distinctive ritual practice as one of the elements which may have facilitated Messenian ethnogenesis in the early fifth century. Reversing the perspective, once the ethnic border between

---

[116] For a typology of processes that lead to the emergence or disappearance of ethnic groups, see Horowitz 1975: 111–18; in Horowitz' terms, fifth-century Messenian ethnogenesis would be defined as proliferation, that is, the emergence of ethnic boundaries that create a discrete ethnic group from within a preexisting ethnic group.

Messenians and Spartans was articulated, any practice that could set the former apart from the latter was bound to be interpreted in ethnic terms, but this does not mean that it already had that meaning to those who engaged in it in earlier times.

Messenian identity emerged out of the aspiration to autonomy and independence of some *perioikoi*, who lived quite far from the center of the Spartan state, across the mountains, in a fertile region with well-marked natural borders. It was conceivably triggered by the rigid genealogical separation between Spartiates and *perioikoi*, which – it can be argued in the light of comparative research on ethnic processes – was very likely to produce an ethnic consciousness sooner or later. The whole process was certainly helped by the presence of a large slave population working the Spartiates' land in Messenia, a closed, self-reproducing group, equipped with the prerequisites for developing a group identity which in turn would offer an ideal terrain for an ethnic charter myth.[117]

Three more factors help to account for the emergence of Messenian ethnicity precisely at this point in time and for its plausibility to the rest of the Greek world. First, the "Messenian policy" of the tyrant Anaxilaos of Rhegion, which brought about the foundation of an independent polis called Messene, whose existence was immediately broadcast in the Panhellenic sanctuaries. The presence of Micythus, "Rhegian and Messenian," in Tegea in the late 460s (above, p. 155 n. 24) represents almost an ideal link between the Messenians on the Strait and Messenian ethnogenesis in the Peloponnese. Second, the symbolic creation of a region called Messene by the myth of the division of the Peloponnese among the Heraclids, a myth that seems in its turn to have originated in Argos in the first decades of the fifth century. It was on this concept of Messene, *de facto* corresponding to the western part of *Lakonikē*, that the Messenian identity of the rebels was predicated, as shown by the fact that they considered Pylos part of their fatherland, witness Thucydides. This, incidentally, does not encourage optimistic views of the relatedness of fifth-century Messenians to the Messenians who had fought against the Spartans two generations before Tyrtaeus. The third factor is more general and more speculative. Kurt Raaflaub has argued that the experience of the Persian Wars was decisive in the elaboration in Greek political ideology of the concept of

---

[117] The Messenian identity is acutely characterized by Figueira 1999: 224: "... instead of reflecting genealogy, feeling 'Messenian' or identifying oneself as 'Messenian' appears to be inversely correlated with the degree of compliance with the Spartan government and with the Spartiates as a social class." However, Figueira limits his considerations to the Helots.

political freedom of a community, as opposed to individual freedom.[118] We do not have to speculate that possibly some of the rebels had fought in the large Spartan army that took part in the battle of Plataea, to realize that this new political concept may have been a source of inspiration for them.[119]

* * *

In conclusion, the Messenian experience in the fifth century had shown that Messenian ethnicity could pose a serious threat to Sparta, as underlined both by the expulsion of the Messenians in 401 and, earlier, by the Spartans' insistence after the peace of Nicias on the removal of the Messenians from Pylos, even if the Athenians kept a garrison there. It is not clear to what extent the Athenians themselves realized what kind of weapon the Messenians represented against the Spartans, and to what extent they were willing to make full use of it;[120] at any rate, the lesson was apparently not lost on the Argives, who in the winter of 419 urged the Athenians to bring back the Messenians to Pylos, alleging that the Spartans had violated the terms of the peace (Thuc. 5.56.2). The Argives had been enemies of the Spartans for centuries, and they may have had a better appreciation of the politics of the Peloponnese.[121] But some decades had to pass before favorable conditions made it possible to exploit this weapon against their old enemies.

---

[118] Raaflaub 2004: esp. 59–65.

[119] The Zeus Ithomatas of Ageladas, if it was really commissioned in these years, should also be mentioned in this context, see above, p. 176.

[120] See Lewis 1977: 28. His suggestion, ibid. n. 13, that the Argives did not see the point, either, is less convincing, if one looks at the relations between Argos and Sparta in a long-term perspective, cf. the evidence mentioned here and below, p. 214, and the probable Argive origin of the myth of the division of the Peloponnese among the Heraclids. Thucydides' insistence on the Spartans' irrational fear of a Helot uprising (Ducat 1990: 83) may suggest that the Athenians had evaluated the situation carefully and simply thought, on the basis perhaps of the results of the occupation of Pylos and Kythera, that this was not a realistic option, no matter how much that perspective terrorized the Spartans. Note that Thucydides always talks in terms of Helot revolt and shows clear signs of not taking Messenian ethnicity very seriously – he was not the only one at Athens to think so, as noted above. Also, he seems to turn a blind eye to the problem of unrest among the *perioikoi* and does not think it noteworthy that the *perioikoi* of Kythera became allies of the Athenians and even sent troops to Sicily (Thuc. 7.57.6).

[121] One further piece of the puzzle may be provided by Thuc. 5.69.1: before the battle of Mantinea in 418, the Arive generals incite their soldiers to fight to reestablish the *isomoiria* in the Peloponnese, an allusion to the division among the Heraclids (see above, p. 56 n. 34) which would conceivably imply freeing Messenia from Sparta. More on the Argives' position on Messenia below pp. 214–15.

CHAPTER 8

The liberation of Messene

After 401, the Messenians disappeared again from mainland Greece for three decades. They reappeared as a consequence of that enormously momentous event, the defeat of the Spartans at Leuktra in 371 BC. In the fall of 370/69, Epaminondas led a huge expeditionary corps formed by the army of the Boeotian League and its allies, and the armies of Argos, Elis and Arcadia, in the first invasion of Laconia since the return of the Heraclids.[1] Although vastly outnumbering the Spartans, the army was unable to take Sparta itself, and after ravaging the countryside between Sparta and the sea Epaminondas led his troops north along the Eurotas Valley and then marched out of Laconia into Messenia.[2] The most direct way from Sparta to the Pamisos Valley led, then as now, across the Taygetos by way of the Langadha Pass. However, given the size of the army and the time of the year,[3] it is likely that Epaminondas retraced his way back towards the Alpheios basin and marched into Messenia by way of its natural entrance, the Derveni Pass. The sources do not mention any resistance met by Epaminondas, and it is hardly thinkable that there could have been any. The allied army must have reached Mount Ithome undisturbed. That place was to be the focus of Epaminondas' next action, clearly intended to cripple the Spartans once and for all: the foundation of an independent Messenian state, centered on a large fortified settlement at the foot of the mountain, which functioned as its acropolis.

The choice of the site for this settlement made sense in a number of ways. Mount Ithome has a central position in Messenia, overlooking both

---

[1] Plut. *Ages.* 31.1. The panic among the Spartan women at the approach of the invading army was to become proverbial; see Xen. *Hell.* 6.5.28 and David 1981: 85. For the topos of Sparta *aporthētos* ("never plundered") see also Diod. 15.81.2 and especially *CEG* 819, Lysander's dedication at Delphi for the victory of Aegospotami.

[2] The best modern narrative of the campaign is found in Buckler 1980: 70–90. See also Hamilton 1991: 215–31. On the situation at Sparta in the aftermath of Leuktra and during the Theban invasion, see David 1981: 78–88.

[3] See Buckler 1980: 86. Diod. 15.65.5 suggests that the army entered Messenia from the Derveni pass.

the Stenyklaros plain and the lower Pamisos valley, within easy reach of
Arcadia by way of the Derveni pass, and could easily be defended in case
of a Spartan counterattack, which would definitely have been expected.
Furthermore, the site had important symbolic overtones. Even though
most of the legendary story of the Messenian resistance in the archaic
period probably originated later, Mount Ithome was implicitly referred to
as the Messenians' dwelling by Tyrtaeus and, perhaps more importantly,
it was associated with the revolt against Sparta in the fifth century: there
the Messenians had held on for many years against the Spartans. If there
was a monument of Messenian resistance, it was Mount Ithome. By making
it the center of the resurgent Messenian state, resistance against Spartan
aggression was evoked from the outset as a key point of the identity of the
new Messenians.

THE FOUNDATION OF MESSENE AND ITS REGIONAL CONTEXT

The loss of the land west of Mount Taygetos was a lethal blow that
permanently lamed the hegemonic ambitions of the Spartans. The creation of the new Messenian state has sometimes been seen as one aspect
of a broader strategy pursued by Epaminondas in the years following
the victory of Leuktra: together with Megalopolis, the "Big City" of the
Arcadians founded one year later, the Messenians joined Sparta's old
enemies the Argives as part of a chain of hostile neighbors that would
make it very difficult for the Spartans to look beyond the borders of their
territory.[4] Thebes' insistence on the independence of the Messenians as a
necessary condition for a common peace in the years after 369 underscores
both the importance of Theban patronage for the new polity and the fact
that the Thebans clearly saw Messenian freedom as an important component
in their anti-Spartan strategy.[5] However, in the case of the Messenians as in
the case of Megalopolis, local circumstances are important, too, and in
more than one way. The ultimate success, if not the very birth, of the

---

[4] On the anti-Spartan implications of the foundation of Megalopolis, see Buckler 1980: 107–8, with
helpful comments on the Theban involvement and its true relevance. See also, on the Arcadian
context, Nielsen 2002: 414–42. Like Buckler, Nielsen also tends to attribute a rather secondary role
to Theban initiative in the foundation of the city. For an extended and judicious discussion of
Messene and Megalopolis as parts of a "master plan" by Epaminondas, see Demand 1990: 107–19.
[5] The return of Messene under Spartan control was the clause that pushed the Thebans to refuse the
peace that Philiscus of Abydus was trying to broker in 368 (Xen. *Hell.* 7.1.27); the freedom of
Messene was one of the requests of Pelopidas at Susa and one of the conditions of the peace the
Thebans unsuccesfully tried to have the Greeks agree upon in 367 (Xen. *Hell.* 7.1.36, 39; Diod.
15.81.3). See Ryder 1965: 134–6, Jehne 1994: 79–90.

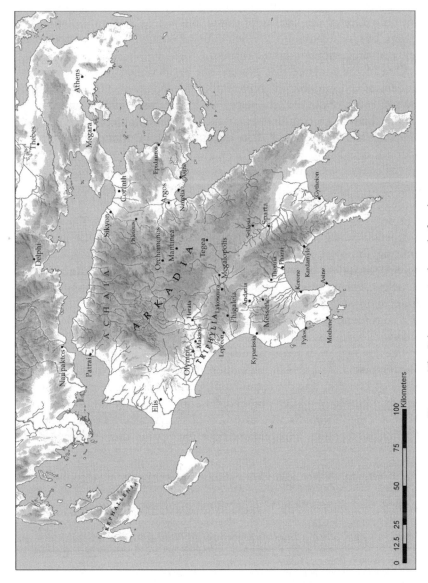

Figure 5 The Peloponnese in the early fourth century

new Messenian polity has to be seen in what can only be termed an extraordinarily favorable regional context. In the Peloponnese, the first decades of the fourth century saw a surprising number of changes, which not only affected the balance of power and the very political map of the region, but included also the redefinition of ethnic borders and the emergence of altogether new ethnic entities.[6]

One of the roots of this process can be identified in the centrifugal tendencies of a number of communities dependent on Elis, especially in the area south of the river Alpheios,[7] which received momentum from the conflict between Sparta and Elis that had been simmering since before the peace of Nicias of 421.[8] After the end of the Peloponnesian War, the Spartans decided to discipline their old allies, whose support had been crucial to the establishment of Spartan power in the Peloponnese. At first, the Spartans presented Elis with an ultimatum, requesting that the Eleans allow their dependent allies[9] to be autonomous. Faced by a refusal, king Agis led two expeditions against Elis. The final result of the war was independence for a number of small poleis, most of which joined in forming Triphylia, a brand-new federal state.[10] The Triphylian cities had never been united before, and indeed the region itself had hitherto been nameless. The creation of the new state had its symbolic counterpart in an eponymous hero Triphylos, almost certainly "discovered" for the occasion as a convenient common ancestor. In other words, the Triphylians seem to have viewed and represented themselves as an ethnic community.[11]

The Triphylian experiment ushered in a new era for ethnicity in the Peloponnese. The political unification of Arcadia, immediately after the battle of Leuktra, was the culminating point in an increasing salience of Arcadian ethnicity that can be traced through the early fourth century.[12] At that time, Triphylia was absorbed in the Arcadian League, and the Triphylians became, and remained for the rest of their history, ethnic

---

[6] In the following, references on the ethnic awakening in early fourth-century Peloponnese are kept to a minimum; for detailed discussions of the various episodes, see Luraghi-Funke 2008.

[7] On the dependant communities and their relationship to Elis, see Roy 1997.

[8] Schepens 2004. The conflict had originated from a controversy over the city of Lepreon, see Thuc. 5.31.2–5 and Falkner 1999.

[9] Xen. *Hell.* 3.2.23; formally, these communities were *symmachoi* of Elis (Roy 1997: 292–3), and it is not clear that the name *perioikoi* used here by Xenophon was actually employed by the Eleans to designate them (Roy 1997: 283).

[10] The conditions of the peace are discussed in Roy 1997: 299–304.

[11] On Triphylia, see especially Thomas Nielsen's brilliant study, Nielsen 1997, revised in a broader framework in Nielsen 2002: 229–69, and now Ruggeri 2004: 73–143. For a possible trace of this first phase of Triphylian ethnicity in the genealogy of Triphylos, see below n. 13.

[12] See especially Pretzler 2008.

Arcadians. A statue of the hero Triphylos, now considered a son of the hero Arkas, appeared together with the ethnic fathers of the Arcadians on the monument dedicated by the Arcadian League at Delphi in 369.[13] The very location of the monument, in front of Lysander's dedication for the victory of Aegospotami, left the ancient viewer in no doubt as to who was the implicit target of this statement of triumphant Arcadian ethnicity, and the dedicatory inscription explicitly mentioned the invasion of Laconia as the occasion for the dedication.[14]

The next novelty in the ethnic map of the Peloponnese came soon after the liberation of Messenia. Out of the conflict between Arcadia and Elis in 365 the new ethnic state of the Pisatans emerged, placed by the Arcadians in control of the sanctuary of Zeus at Olympia. The mythic genealogy of the new ethnic community linked it to Arcadia and Messenia. After running the 104th Olympics in 364, which saw fighting in the sacred precinct when the Eleans tried to interfere, the Pisatans were abandoned by their protectors the Arcadians and then annexed again by Elis in 362. However, Pisatis' brief existence as an independent polity generated a heritage of stories which told of conflicts between Pisatis and Elis over the control of Olympia in the archaic age. Appropriately, Pisatis, which had never existed as an independent political community before 365, appears as an ally of the Messenians in some narratives of the Messenian Wars.[15]

In sum, the Peloponnese in the first decades of the fourth century is characterized by a sort of ethnic fluidity that goes a long way in explaining the ultimate success of the Messenian state. The question of where the political initiative for the liberation of Messenia came from has to be seen in relation to this regional context. The sources on the foundation of

---

[13] On the monument of the Arcadians, see Paus. 10.9.5–6, the dedicatory inscription *CEG* 824, and Bommelaer 1991: 104–6 with further references. Cf. Xen. *Hell.* 7.1.26 (368 BC): the Triphylians claimed to be Arcadian. On the heroes mentioned in the inscription and represented by the statues see Nielsen 2002: 249–50; on Triphylos, Ruggeri 2004: 94–6. In the inscription Triphylos is called son of Arkas and Laodameia, daughter of Amyklas. The latter, obviously connected with Laconian Amyclae, must be a survival of a previous genealogy that connected Triphylos to Laconia, clearly in relation to the Spartan creation of Triphylia around 400 BC; see now Ruggeri 2008.

[14] On Lysander's monument, Bommelaer 1991: 108–10 with further references. Note that the relation between the two monuments was made explicit by the inscription of the Arcadians twice mentioning that the dedication had been made out of spoils taken by plundering Lakedaimon; the epigram of Lysander's monument, *CEG* 819, boasted that Lakedaimon had never been plundered!

[15] On Pisatan ethnicity, see esp. Möller 2004: 257–66 and Giangiulio 2008. On the history of Pisatis, Ruggeri 2004: 178–97. On traditions about conflicts between Pisatis and Elis in the archaic age, see also Nafissi 2003: 29–30 and 33–3 on the genealogy of Pisos, eponymous of the Pisatans. On the end of Pisatan independence, see Ruggeri 2004: 198–200. An inscription from Olympia records an alliance between Pisatans, Sikyonians, and Messenians, see now Ringel, Siewert, and Taeuber 1999 (= *SEG* 49.466b). Pisatan participation in the Second Messenian War: Strab. 8.4.10, see also above, p. 79.

Messene tend to present Epaminondas as the moving force. However, the presence of Arcadians and especially Argives in the army that invaded Laconia and liberated Messenia suggests that the competence in Peloponnesian politics – and especially in the politics of Peloponnesian ethnicities – which was required in order to conceive this plan may have come from them. The decisive role of Epaminondas and Thebes in the birth, and even more in the survival, of Messene can hardly be overestimated, as we shall see, but the roots of his scheme may lie in the Peloponnese. For different reasons, both the Arcadians and the Argives may be suspected of having been more than superficially involved in it.

The Argives' active and enthusiastic participation in the foundation of the free Messenian state is directly referred to by Pausanias. According to him, the Argives had elected Epiteles to lead their army and to found Messene anew (4.26.7). A dream led this Epiteles towards the place on Mount Ithome where Aristomenes had buried a bronze hydria that contained the texts of the mysteries of the Great Goddesses of Andania. The whole complex of stories that Pausanias associates with Andania, as we have seen, is not likely to be older than the third century BC, and some parts of it may be even later,[16] and cannot be unqualifiedly used as evidence for earlier periods. However, some support for Pausanias' depiction of the Argives' participation might be found in the fact that one of the tribes of the new Messenian polity bore the name of the Argive Heraclid Daiphontes, as an Argive *phatra* also did.[17] Moreover, a number of clues seem to suggest that the Argives had for some time been keenly aware of the fact that rule over Messenia was the cornerstone of Spartan supremacy. The tradition about the division of the Peloponnese among the Heraclids, which implicitly questioned this situation, seems to have originated in Argos, and according to Thucydides before the battle of Mantineia in 418 the Argive commanders fired up their troops by reminding them that they were fighting to reestablish *isomoiria*, or equality in the division of the Peloponnese (Thuc. 5.69.1).[18] Although it is impossible to be certain, with Pylos occupied by the Messenians it is at least likely that *isomoiria* did not mean only Argive control over the whole of Temenus' lot, but also the end of Spartan domination over Kresphontes' lot, i.e. Messenia. After all, just a year before the battle the Argives had urged the Athenians to take the

---

[16] See above, pp. 92–5, and below, pp. 294–9. The most obvious case of late addition of course is the transformation of the Great Gods worshipped in the sanctuary of the Karneiasion into Great Goddesses.

[17] On the names of Messenian tribes, see below, pp. 230–1.   [18] See Vannicelli 2004: 289.

Messenians back to Pylos, alleging that Sparta had violated the peace of Nicias.[19] This is as close as we can get to definite proof that the liberation of Messenia was really an Argive idea – quite close, actually.[20]

As for the Arcadians, it is the subsequent history of their relations with the Messenians that prompts consideration of their role in the birth of the new polity. Soon after the liberation, the Arcadians seem to have played a major part in expanding the original territory of the free Messenians. As we know from Xenophon, an Arcadian onslaught on Asine, probably right in the summer of 369/8, was repelled by a Lakedaimonian garrison led by a Spartiate, who lost his life in the battle.[21] It was the Arcadians again who conquered Kyparissia and Koryphasion, on the western coast of Messenia, in 365/4, adding them to the territory of the Messenians.[22] The Messenians, in their turn, took to the field in 368 and again in 364 to defend southern Arcadia against the Spartans.[23] Finally, we happen to know from an inscription from the late first century BC that the citizens of the small Messenian town of Kalamai, west of Pharai towards the Taygetos Range, worshipped a hero Hippothoos as their ancestral god (*patrios theos*), and the only hero Hippothoos otherwise documented was the Arcadian king who had moved the capital of Arcadia from Tegea to Trapezous.[24] Arcadian involvement in the birth of free Messene has also left its traces in the role of the Arcadian king Kypselos of Trapezous in saving Aipytos son of Kresphontes, a tradition which seems to go back to

---

[19] Thuc. 5.56.2 and see above, p. 190.

[20] It should be noted, however, that according to Tausend 1992: 155, Argos' role in the sources on the Messenian Wars seems to emerge only in the second stage of the development of the tradition, that is, not yet with fourth-century authors such as Ephorus and Callisthenes. Coupled with the fact that only Pausanias, and no earlier source, refers explicitly to Argive intervention on the occasion of the liberation of Messenia, Tausend's observation might point to Argos becoming interested in establishing contacts with the Messenians only significantly later than the liberation of the region. However, even though Pausanias' depiction of Argos' eager support for the foundation of the free Messenian polity and the increasing presence of Argos in later sources on the Messenian Wars may reflect a new phase of Argive interest in Messene, for which there is further evidence (see below, p. 295, on the oracle of Apollo Pythaeus), this should not necessarily be construed as a reason to doubt the early involvement of the Argives with Messene, for which after all first-hand evidence can be invoked (see below on the names of the Messenian tribes).

[21] Xen. *Hell.* 7.1.25; see Roebuck 1941: 38.   [22] Diod. 15.77.4; see Roebuck 1941: 29 nn. 9 and 38.

[23] Xen. *Hell.* 7.1.28–9 and 7.4.27. For the alliance between Messenians and Pisatans, see above n. 15. For one further case of the Messenians assisting Megalopolis against Sparta in 352, see below n. 66.

[24] *IG* V 1, 1370, lines 24–5, τοῦ γὰρ Ἱπποθόου τοῦ πατρίου πάντων ἡμῶν θεοῦ σαμεῖον ὁρῶν κατεσκεύασε τὸ ἱρόν. On Hippothoos see Paus. 8.5.4, 8.10.3 (sacrilege and death) and especially 8.45.7 (Hippothoos depicted in the Calydonian hunt on the pediment of the mid-fourth-century temple of Athena Aleia, the most prominent monument of Tegea); there was a tribe Hippothoontis in Tegea, *IG* V 2, 39 and 40, Paus. 8.53.6 and see Jones 1987: 139–42. It should be noted, however, that a Spartan Hippothoos appears in the list of the sons of Hippocoon killed by Heracles given by Apollodorus (3.10.5).

the fourth century. The Arcadian and Triphylian family connections of Aristomenes, and the Arcadians' role in rescuing the refugees from the Second Messenian War also make best sense as originating close to the liberation of Messenia.[25] Although the Arcadians had not spent the last century waiting for the right moment to cut down the Spartan supremacy, as the Argives had, their political activism especially in the years immediately after Leuktra and their close relationship to the new Messenian polity in its first years of life converge in suggesting that they might have had an active role in the plan of crippling Sparta by freeing Messenia.[26]

Defining precisely the role of the Thebans, despite their prominence in the sources, is slightly problematic. Epaminondas is explicitly credited with the foundation of the new polity – variously defined as a refoundation or sometimes even as a *synoikismos* – by a number of authors.[27] More intriguingly, there is evidence suggesting that the liberation of Messenia may have been seen by Epaminondas himself as one of his main achievements.[28] Certainly, stripping Sparta of its land west of the Taygetos was very much in Thebes' interest, but the same can be said of the Arcadians and Argives, as we just saw. The fact that some ancient sources attribute Theban ascendancy almost exclusively to Epaminondas' genius, while others ignore him altogether, makes it difficult to find a convincing balance. Much later, the city at the foot of Mount Ithome – originally called Ithome, but by that time calling itself Messene (see below, p. 268) – seems to have considered Epaminondas its founder,[29] but there is no evidence that Ithome or the

---

[25] See above, pp. 62 (Kypselos) and 89–90 (Aristomenes' in-laws and Callisthenes on Arcadians and Messenians).

[26] The respective nature of the Argive and Arcadian connections with the new Messene might suggest that the Argives were more involved in the planning and foundation of the new polity, and the Arcadians in protecting it in its first years of life – but this conclusion might be accused of reflecting widespread prejudice against the political intelligence of the Arcadians!

[27] Refoundation of Messene by Epaminondas: Diod. 15.66.1, Nep. *Ep.* 8.4, Plut. *Ages.* 34.1. Theban initiative and Epaminondas' role are emphasized throughout Pausanias' narrative, Paus. 4.26.6–28.1, and cf. 9.14.5. See also Plut. *Pel.* 24.9 (verb *synoikizein*, cf. Polyb. 4.33.7, where, however, *synoikismos* might be used by extension, since the passage refers to both Megalopolis and Messene).

[28] The foundation of Messene, the invasion and plunder of Laconia, and the unification of Arcadia were allegedly mentioned by Epaminondas in his defense against the accusation of having retained his power as Boeotarch four months beyond the expiration of his term of office; see Plut. *Mor.* 194b = *Reg. et imp. apophth.* 23 (the same passage recurs literally in Ael. *VH* 13.42), and *Mor.* 540d–e = *De se ips. laud.* 4; in Plut. *Mor.* 817f = *Praec. ger. reip.* 23 and Nep. *Ep.* 8.4 only the invasion of Laconia and the liberation of Messenia are mentioned. On the trial of Epaminondas, see Buckler 1980: 138–42. Cf. also the epigram on Epaminondas' statue in Thebes, discussed below (p. 220), mentioning the return of the Messenians and the foundation of Megalopolis as his two great achievements, beside the humiliation of Sparta. Epaminondas' defense, in the version of Plut. *Reg. et imp. apophth.* 23, is so similar to the text of the epigram, that the two can hardly be independent of one another.

[29] Pausanias mentions two statues of Epaminondas in Messene, one in the stoa of the Asklepieion, built in the first half of the second century BC, the other in the *hierothysion* (Paus. 4.31.10 and 32.1

whole Messenian polity was a colony of Thebes *stricto sensu*. None of the ties that normally existed between Greek colonies and their mother cities is documented in their case: no strong evidence for Theban cults in Messenia, no Boeotian names for the tribes of the new polity,[30] no commonality of dialect. This points to a peculiar feature of the new polity. As the Messenians saw it, the birth of their free state was in reality a restoration of something that was supposed to have existed in the past, not a foundation in the strict sense of the word, and the Thebans clearly concurred: the ancestral rights of the Messenians were the foundation of the legitimacy of the new polity, which correspondingly had a vested interest in playing down its own novelty.[31] However, Epaminondas may perhaps have played in some sense the part of the founder of Ithome, possibly seen as a new city founded in the old Messenian land (see below, p. 228).

Even if we cannot be sure that he acted as a founder in a technical sense, Epaminondas may in all probability be credited with a decision which was to have important consequences both for the initial survival of the new Messenian polity and for the history of Messenia for centuries to come, the decision to fortify the settlement at the foot of Mount Ithome. Still standing today for long stretches, the fortification wall was the most striking component of the city for an ancient visitor (plates 7 and 8).[32] Built in stone up to the top, nine kilometers long, it was a true masterpiece of military architecture which exploited the nature of the terrain to the best effect. The acropolis, high on the summit of the steep mountain, had its own independent fortification, which seems to have included the remains of an earlier fortification wall, dating back in all likelihood to the time of the revolt in the fifth century. Although Pausanias explicitly locates the construction of the wall at the time of the liberation of Messenia (4.27.7), insisting on the extraordinary speed that characterized the building process, scholars have for a long time tended to prefer a significantly later date, in the early Hellenistic era. However, recent studies have shown that in terms of architectural technique a date soon after the liberation of

respectively; see Themelis 2000: 45 and below, p. 278). Especially the position of the former, among the main gods of Messene, suggests that the Theban general was regarded in some sense as the founder of the city. However, *pace* Leschhorn 1984: 164–6, there is no explicit evidence for a cult for Epaminondas in Messene. The facility with which the sentence "By my councils … holy Messene receives at last her children" from the epigram that accompanied Epaminondas' statue in Thebes (Paus. 9.15.6) is paraphrased by Pausanias as "Epaminondas was the founder (*oikistēs*) of Messene" (Paus. 9.15.5; cf. also 9.14.5) is a warning.

[30] On the Messenian tribes see below, p. 231.
[31] If we had more information on Triphylia and Pisatis, we would doubtless find similarities.
[32] As witnessed by its prominence in Pausanias' description of the city, 4.31.5.

Plate 7   The fortification walls of Messene, western sector

Messenia is likely, underlining that the *emplekton* technique that was used to build the wall was apparently an innovation introduced by Theban military architects, first seen in fortifications connected with the Theban hegemony.[33] This suggests a strong Theban initiative in the building of the fortification wall of Messene. For what it is worth, Pausanias has an idyllic description of the walls being built to the accompaniment of Boeotian and Argive flutes (4.27.7). This massive work betrays both a deep understanding of Sparta's strengths and weaknesses and a realistic attitude towards the new polity's chances of survival if faced with a Spartan onslaught and without external help. Epaminondas must have thought that the Messenians simply had to be in a condition to resist long enough for a rescue army to reach them. The permanence of a strong garrison in the city once Epaminondas left confirms this point.[34]

---

[33] See now the comprehensive examination of the fortifications by Müth-Herda 2005. For the development of the *emplekton* technique and the chronology of the fortifications of Messene, see Karlsson 1992: 73–8.

[34] Diod. 15.67.1, Epaminondas leaves a strong garrison in Messene; it is not clear whether these people are Thebans or allies, e.g. Arcadians or Argives. The Spartans were proverbially incapable of dealing with fortifications, see e.g. Thuc. 1.90.1 and 102.1.

Plate 8 The fortification walls of Messene, western sector, seen from the museum at Mavromati

THE NEW MESSENIANS

Ancient sources offer radically divergent definitions of the citizen body of the new Messenian polity, and clearly reflect conflicting views which ultimately originated with the parties involved – Thebans and Messenians on the one side, Spartans on the other.[35] This is not at all surprising, since defining the identity of the Messenians was after all decisive for the question of the legitimacy of the new polity.

From a Theban–Messenian point of view, the birth of the new Messenian state seems to have been described as a *grande rentrée* of the descendants of all the Messenians who had been chased away from their land by the Spartans over the centuries. This is the depiction found in Diodorus (15.66.6), in Plutarch's lives of Pelopidas (24.5) and of Agesilaos (34.1),[36]

---

[35] See the detailed discussion of the evidence by Dipersia 1974: 54–61. An excellent analysis of the Theban and Spartan positions is offered by Asheri 1983: 36–9.

[36] Plutarch's *Pelopidas* depends largely on Callisthenes' *Hellenica*, a work composed in the late 340s and characterized by a strong bias in favor of the Thebans; Georgiadou 1997: 15–24 with further references. On the sources of his *Agesilaos*, see Shipley, D. R. 1997: 47–50.

and, with fuller detail, in Pausanias (4.26.5), who specifies that Epaminondas summoned the Messenians from Italy, Sicily, and Euhesperides,
whither they had fled when the Spartans, after defeating Athens, had
expelled them from Naupaktos. More importantly, the same view is
expressed in the epigram that accompanied the statue of Epaminondas at
Thebes, quoted again by Pausanias (9.15.6): "By my councils Sparta was
shorn of her glory / and holy Messene receives at last her children; / by
the arms of Thebes Megalopolis was encircled with walls / and all Greece
is autonomous in freedom." Unfortunately, the epigram cannot without
some caution be treated as contemporary evidence, because it is impossible
to be sure that the monument that carried it survived the destruction of
Thebes by Alexander the Great, and if it was rebuilt when Cassander
promoted the refoundation of Thebes in 316, or later, there is no guarantee
that the epigram was not concocted at that point.[37] However, it should
be noticed that the *autonomia* mentioned in the last line of the epigram
seems to reflect political slogans and arguments of the first decades of the
fourth century with an accuracy that would be quite surprising in a later
fabrication, originating in a different political climate.[38] In conclusion, it
is a fair surmise that the epigram and other sources reinforce one another
in suggesting that from a Theban perspective the citizen body of the new
Messene was formed by old Messenians returning from overseas.[39] One
point deserves to be emphasized: according to the Theban–Messenian
version of the liberation of Messenia, there were no old Messenians left
in the region itself at the time of Epaminondas' campaign, since all
descendants of the "ancient Messenians" had left the country after the
revolt in the fifth century at the latest. This is made explicit in Pausanias,

[37] Only Asheri 1983: 37 n. 31 notes the problem. See Bearzot 1997 on Cassander's refoundation of
Thebes. According to Pausanias (9.7.1), Messenians and Megalopolitans participated in it, alongside
the Athenians, while Diodorus (19.54.2) mentions only the Athenians and unspecified other Greeks
from Greece proper, Sicily and Italy. Pausanias' list could be fictitious, especially since Messenia,
unlike Megalopolis, was not on Cassander's side at this point (cf. Diod. 19.54.4, 64.1, but see
Roebuck 1941: 60–1) and no Messenians or Megalopolitans appear on a fragmentary inscription
recording financial contributions from various parts of Greece for the rebuilding of Thebes; see
Gullath 1982: 89–97 (still no Messenians or Arcadians appear in a new fragment of the inscription
that is being published by K. Buraselis). The more we believe that Messene and Megalopolis really
participated in the reconstruction of Thebes (as does Bearzot 1997: 267–9), the stronger the suspicion
that their presence in the epigram for Epaminondas might be a product of this age, and *vice versa*. It
should also be noted that some sources depict the destruction as less than total; according to Arr.
1.9.9, the acropolis was spared – the statue might conceivably have been there.
[38] See Rhodes 1999.
[39] Diodorus' addition (15.66.1) that citizenship was also accorded to everyone who wanted it, as often
occurred in the event of a new foundation, adds a touch of realism to this ideologically charged
view, without questioning it.

but is clearly presupposed by Diodorus and Plutarch as well. Strikingly, none of them speaks of the liberation of Messenians living in Messenia.[40] In this, the legitimizing strategy put in place by the Messenians and their protectors the Thebans ended up in paradoxical agreement with the Spartan take on the issue (see below).

This view of the population of the free Messenian polity has been questioned since antiquity, and not only by the Spartans. In his speech against Leocrates, delivered in 330 BC, the Athenian orator Lycurgus quoted two examples of cities which had been deserted by their inhabitants and never recovered from the catastrophe: one is Troy, the other is Messene, which had been repopulated 500 years after its destruction, says Lycurgus, by people assembled randomly (*Leocr.* 62). It is important to note the – somewhat strained – logic of Lycurgus' argument. In order to emphasize the gravity of Leocrates' flight from Athens threatened by the Macedonians after Chaeronea, Lycurgus asserts that for a city the utmost catastrophe is to be deserted by its own citizens; from such an occurrence, no city could recover. In other words, Lycurgus implies that the expulsion of the Messenians by the Spartans represented the end of Messene, which the refoundation by the Thebans could not remedy; by implication, he denies any continuity between the "new Messenians" and the "old." In using Troy and Messene as examples to pillory Leocrates, Lycurgus may be pushing his argument a bit too far, but obviously he trusts that his audience agrees with his interpretation – for otherwise he would have picked different examples.

Lycurgus may certainly reflect a specifically Athenian take on the issue – one that is not necessarily innocent of bias.[41] However, there are further reasons to regard the notion of the "return of the Messenians" with some skepticism. One of them is the fact that there is no evidence for the *grande rentrée* at the other end, so to speak, that is, in sources referring to the history of the cities where the Messenians had sought refuge at the end of the fifth century. Diodorus states bluntly that the Messenians in Cyrenaica were massacred almost to a man during a civil war (14.34.3-6). As for the Messenians of Tyndaris in Sicily, all we know, from Diodorus,

---

[40] If we combine this with Thucydides' description of the rebels at the time of the earthquake, we may come to a very interesting, if somewhat unexpected result: in all probability, neither Thucydides nor the later sources thought that *all* Helots in Messenia at the beginning of the fifth century, before the earthquake, were of Messenian origin, unless of course they also believed that all Helots had left Messenia as a consequence of the revolt – not a very probable assumption.

[41] The Messenians did not take part in the battle of Chaeronea and were on friendly terms with Philip; see Grandjean 2003: 67–70 and below, p. 254 n. 13.

is that this new city prospered and soon reached a population of 5,000 citizens (14.78.5). There is no mention here of a return of any of them to the Peloponnese. None of this amounts to positive evidence against the possibility that some descendants of the Messenians of Naupaktos could have formed a part of the citizen body of the new Messenian state. After all, the group of exiles who according to Pausanias went to Euhesperides is not necessarily one and the same as the one that ended up being slaughtered in the Cyrenaean *stasis*,[42] and Diodorus' statement on the fate of the Messenians in Cyrene could be exaggerated. However, on the whole the sources do suggest some skepticism as to the demographic relevance of the *grande rentrée*.[43]

The Spartan take on the issue is reflected in the most impressive way by Xenophon's complete failure to mention the liberation of Messene – all the more awkward, since later in the *Hellenica* free Messenians turn up a number of times.[44] This attitude tallies with the Spartans' stubborn refusal to recognize the existence of the Messenians as an independent polity, which torpedoed various attempts at concluding a common peace in the 360s.[45] In a more articulate way, the Spartan party-line is elaborated in Isocrates' *Archidamos*, a speech in which the speaker purports to be Archidamus, son of Agesilaus and future king of Sparta, the dramatic setting being the debate on the Theban offer of peace at Sparta in 366.[46] According to this version, the Thebans were not restoring the true Messenians, which – says Archidamus-Isocrates – would still have been an unjust action, but at least a plausible one; rather, they were trying to free the Helots, the slaves of the Spartans, and to settle them on the Spartan

---

[42] See Grandjean 2003: 57 and n. 38.

[43] Asheri's assessment (1983: 39) seems fundamentally correct: "One has the impression that in 369 there must have been very few people scattered in the West and in North Africa who could appear in front of the Theban envoys as 'Messenians' and were personally ready to pack their belongings in order to 'repatriate'."

[44] Xen. *Hell.* 7.1.29, 4.27, 5.5. See David 1981: 81 and Jehne 2004 on the general problem of Xenophon's silence over episodes he must have assumed his reader to know about; Jehne focuses on the Second Athenian League, but his conclusions have implications for the case of the liberation of Messenia, as well.

[45] See Ryder 1965: 79–86; Jehne 1994: 84–90.

[46] The offer of peace is mentioned by Xenophon, *Hell.* 7.4.7–11; see Ryder 1965: 138 and Jehne 1994: 84 n. 217. There is some disagreement among scholars as to whether Isocrates' *Archidamos* should be taken as a mere rhetorical exercise or given a proper political meaning; see e.g. Bringmann 1965: 55–6 and Moysey 1982: 118–27. Regardless of which view is taken of this question, which might ultimately be insoluble, the fact remains that the speech was composed in the years immediately following the liberation of Messenia, when the Spartans were trying to challenge the recognition of Messene by the other Greeks, and certainly an Athenian audience knew which arguments the Spartans were deploying; see the judicious discussion by Jehne 1994: 11 n. 21, with further bibliography, and cf. the passage from Xenophon quoted in the next note.

border, so that the Spartans would see their former slaves made masters of a land that had been bequeathed to the Spartans by their ancestors and belonged to them every bit as sacrosanctly as Laconia itself did[47] – indeed, the Spartans might end up seeing their former slaves bringing to Olympia and to the other Panhellenic festivals first fruits and sacrifices larger than those of the Spartans themselves (*Archid.* 28, 86, 87, 96). As Giulia Dipersia put it, the Spartan view voiced by Isocrates was meant to reduce the "Messenian question" to a conflict between slaves and masters. Clearly, Archidamus-Isocrates tries to play on shared attitudes towards slavery in order to win the sympathy of the other Greeks by insisting on the subversive nature of the Thebans' action.[48] It is important to stress that this putative Spartan version explicitly denies that the Helots living in Messenia were the descendants of the "ancient Messenians," and on this point it agrees with the Theban–Messenian version, in the sense that both maintained that no Messenians were living in the region at the time of Epaminondas' campaign. Needless to say, the two parties upheld this surprising notion for opposite reasons.[49]

Given that both versions of the identity of the new Messenians are so obviously biased, it is somewhat puzzling that modern scholars have generally preferred the Spartan version to the Theban–Messenian one

---

[47] The same attitude is expressed by the Spartans in Xen. *Hell.* 7.4.9 (year 366/5): Messene has been transmitted to them by their ancestors and it would be shameful for them to give it up. The coincidence is noteworthy. Note also that, while denying the Messenian identity of the citizens of the new polity, Archidamus seems to admit that the "old Messenians" had existed at some point in time (see also above, p. 77); this would again reflect the attitude of the Spartans who, after denying the Messenian identity of the rebels during the fifth century (see above, p. 198), according to Xenophon called them retrospectively "Messenians" when they sent for help to Athens during the invasion of Laconia (*Hell.* 6.5.33).

[48] Dipersia 1974: 58. The same view of the citizens of Epaminondas' Messene is reflected in the proverbial expression δουλότερος Μεσσήνης, later misunderstood by the paroemiographers and connected to the harsh conditions imposed on Helotized Messenians (Macarius 3.35, Zenobius 3.39). Cf. the man called Messenian, slave of one of the Hermocopids, above, p. 102 and n. 100.

[49] The contrast between the Spartan and the Theban lines can be seen also in the contrasting descriptions of Pelopidas' requests during the debate at the Persian court in 367 BC; for Xenophon (*Hell.* 7.1.36) Pelopidas wants Messene to be autonomous, for Plutarch (*Pel.* 30.5) he wants it to remain in existence (οἰκεῖσθαι). Compared with these two versions, the line upheld in Alcidamas' *Messenian Speech*, tentatively dated to the early fourth century, reveals itself as the product of an intra-Athenian discourse on the Messenian identity. One of the only two fragments of the speech reads, "God has given all men their freedom; nature has made no man a slave" (fr. 1 Muir), which clearly stems from a defense of the Messenians' right to freedom that was based on general principles rather than on their ancestral rights – a line of argument the Messenians themselves may not have liked too much, judging by the evidence discussed above. On the speech and its implications, see Raaflaub 2003: 162–3. Born in Elaia, on the coast of Mysia, in Asia Minor, Alcidamas was an influential teacher of rhetoric in Athens in the early fourth century; see Muir 2001: v–vi.

rather than simply acknowledging that we have to do with two competing political agendas generating two opposite depictions of reality. Certainly Archidamus' view does not account in a very satisfactory way for the evidence of survey in western Messenia, which suggests an increase in the population of the region at the time of the liberation from Sparta,[50] and therefore, one would suppose, some sort of influx of population from outside. Lycurgus' view of the identity of the Messenians, while not completely unbiased, also suggests that his audience thought that at least a significant part of the population of the new Messenian polity came from elsewhere. This line of thought is reinforced by a recent study of the demography of the Helots, which suggests a rather low figure for the Helot population of Messenia at the time of Epaminondas' invasion.[51] Therefore, while at first sight the notion that the Helots of Messenia formed the main component of the citizen body of Epaminondas' Messenian state might seem a reasonable assumption, on closer inspection it betrays a somewhat simplistic understanding of the attitudes of the Helots towards their masters, and of other inhabitants of *Lakonikē* towards the Spartiates. On the contrary, evidence for the reactions to Epaminondas' invasion within *Lakonikē* points to a complex situation on the ground.

According to Xenophon (*Hell.* 6.5.25), who had no inclination whatsoever to show the Spartan state in a negative light, an embassy of *perioikoi* approached Epaminondas as he still hesitated to march into the Spartan territory, offering themselves as hostages and assuring Epaminondas that, if he so much as dared to march further, all the *perioikoi* would revolt against the Spartiates, and adding that already then they hardly followed the Spartans' calls to arms.[52] At least some *perioikoi* really joined the

---

[50] This is at least the record for the only portion of Messenia for which survey evidence is available, the area investigated by the Pylos Regional Archaeological Project. See Davis et al. 1997: 483: the end of the Spartan domination "is marked by a notable growth in the number and size of settlements"; see also Alcock et al. 2005: 163. Evidence from the Five Rivers Area, along the northwestern corner of the Gulf of Messenia, between Petalidhi and the mouth of the river Pamisos, is compatible with this picture; see Lukermann and Moody 1978 and Coulson 1983: 337. In this connection, it is interesting to observe that, while four of the five tribes in which the citizen body of the new Messenian polity was divided were named after Kresphontes and his three direct ancestors, the fifth was named after the Argive Heraclid Daiphontes (see below, p. 232 and n. 73). This is normally, and surely correctly, connected with the role of the Argives in the foundation, but it is tempting to think that this new tribe might have been composed of settlers from outside Messenia.

[51] Figueira 2003: 227.

[52] According to Plut. *Mor.* 346b = *De glor. Ath.* 2, after Leuktra Epaminondas pillaged the Spartan territory and persuaded the *perioikoi* to revolt against the Spartiates; see also Plut. *Pel.* 24.1 and David 1980: 300–3 and 1981: 86–7. Desertion of the *perioikoi* is also regularly mentioned in passages that refer retrospectively to the situation of the Spartans faced by the invasion: Xen. *Hell.* 7.2.2

invading army and participated in Epaminondas' campaign (*Hell.* 6.5.32) – the collaboration of the Karyans was particularly helpful in opening the way of the Eurotas valley to the Theban army.[53] However, it should also be pointed out that, in spite of the promises that some of them made to Epaminondas, there was no universal revolt of the *perioikoi* at the time of the invasion. For instance, the perioikic harbor town of Gytheion resisted the onslaught of Epaminondas' army for three days (*Hell.* 6.5.32).

We have one intriguing if anecdotal piece of evidence for the attitude of non-Spartiates to the ruling elite of the Spartan state some thirty years before Epaminondas' invasion of Laconia in 369: according to Kinadon, mastermind of a subversive plot in the first year of Agesilaus' reign, every Helot, *neodāmōdēs*, *hypomeiōn*, or *perioikos* passionately hated the Spartiates and would have been glad to eat them raw (Xen. *Hell.* 3.3.6).[54] Equally intriguingly, in Plutarch and Pausanias we read that Epaminondas at Sparta in 371 answered Agesilaus' request of autonomy for the Boeotians by pointing to the situation of *Lakonikē* and requesting that the Spartans grant independence to their *perioikoi*.[55] Epaminondas may simply have been trying to make his point *per absurdum*; however, considering the reactions of the *perioikoi* to the Theban invasion of Laconia, we should perhaps not exclude that his reply to Agesilaus may have built upon recognized discontent towards the Spartiates among the *perioikoi*.

As for the Helots, contrary to what might have been expected, they do not seem to have turned uniformly against their masters at the time of Epaminondas' campaign in Laconia. According again to Xenophon (*Hell.* 6.5.28–9), with the Theban army just across the Eurotas as many as 6,000 Helots were ready to fight for Sparta in return for the promise to be

---

(referring to all the Helots and many *perioikoi*) and *Ages.* 2.24 (the slaves and many perioikic poleis); however, these passages, general as they are, should be taken with some caution, see below n. 58. Desertion of Helots and *perioikoi* from the ranks of the Spartan army is mentioned in Plut. *Ages.* 32.7 and Polyaen. 2.1.15.

[53] See Buckler 1981: 75–7 on the Karyans' role in Epaminondas' campaign; the sources on Karyai are collected in Shipley 1997: 238–9. As Shipley correctly observes, the wording of Xen. *Hell.* 6.5.25 seems to suggest that the Karyans were *not perioikoi*, although it is hard to imagine what else they could have been; Karyai may have been originally an Arcadian town, later absorbed by the Lakedaimonians, see Nielsen 2002: 324.

[54] On Kinadon's conspiracy and its implications, see David 1979 and Lazenby 1997.

[55] On this incident, reported by Plutarch (*Ages.* 28.1–2) and Pausanias (9.13.2), see Keen 1996: 115–17. See also Cartledge 1987: 379–80, Jehne 1994: 71–4, and Rhodes 1999. Note also that according to Pausanias (3.8.3) the Eleans, too, had responded to the Spartan ultimatum in 402 (see above) by challenging the Spartans to grant autonomy to their *perioikoi*. The historicity of the Eleans' reply has been doubted and ultimately cannot be proved; it may be worth pointing out, however, that we are just a couple of years before Kinadon's conspiracy.

liberated if they fought well.[56] This suggests either that they were not certain that by deserting to the Thebans they would gain freedom, or that they preferred to become free Lakedaimonians rather than leave Laconia as free men.[57] On the other hand, desertion among Helots enrolled seems to have been rampant, as also among the *perioikoi*.[58] The Helots were faced in a particularly pressing way with the traditional dilemma between revolt and integration, and their response to this situation does not seem to have been uniform.

On the whole, then, the evidence shows that the rifts in the Spartan state that became conspicuous on the occasion of Epaminondas' invasion were rather less clear-cut than has often been supposed, and did not simply run between Helots on the one side and Spartiates on the other – Kinadon was not completely wrong after all. It is also important to stress that it is not at all clear that attitudes of Helots and *perioikoi* towards the Spartiates depended on where in *Lakonikē* they lived. It is true that the Helots who tried to gain freedom by fighting for their masters happened to *be* in Laconia at the time of the Theban invasion. However, the invasion clearly did not take the Spartans by surprise, and it is therefore rather likely that a proportion of the Helots living in Messenia which we cannot estimate had been mobilized and happened to be east of the Taygetos at that point.[59] As for the *perioikoi*, just as loyalty to Sparta is found on both sides of the Taygetos – Gytheion in Laconia, Asine in Messenia – willingness to revolt can hardly have been concentrated only in one region. Internal dissension within *Lakonikē*, which clearly went well beyond simple separatist aspirations west of the Taygetos, must have been one more factor that facilitated the creation of the Messenian polity.

The evidence does not suggest noticeable differences in the reactions of Helots and *perioikoi* to the invasion of *Lakonikē*: loyalty and disloyalty to

---

[56] Although the measure was exceptional, the practice was not new. Between 425 and 369, the Spartans seem to have recurred rather frequently to the recruitment of large contingents of Helots with the promise of freedom (after the campaign for which they had been recruited?), especially for expeditions abroad; these were the *neodāmōdeis*, on whom see Ducat 1990: 160–1. Cozzoli 1978: 223–4 is probably right to suggest a connection between this phenomenon and Sparta's willingness to allow Dionysius the First to recruit large contingents of mercenaries among the Lakedaimonians (Diod. 14.44.2; 58.1).

[57] The figure mentioned by Xenophon has seemed too high to some scholars for practical reasons (e.g. Cozzoli 1979: 199–200, who prefers to follow Diod. 15.65.6, who spoke of 1,000 freed Helots).

[58] Plut. *Ages.* 32.7; Polyaen. 2.1.15 refers to the same episode. In general, specific references to the reactions of Helots and *perioikoi* to the invasion, such as this one and those discussed above, are to be preferred to Xenophon's generic *a posteriori* allegation (*Hell.* 7.2.2, *Ages.* 2.24) that during Epaminondas' invasion, many *perioikoi* and *all* the Helots had revolted against the Spartiates, as Hamilton 1991: 227 and n. 38, rightly stresses; cf. David 1980: 320 n. 14.

[59] On the use of Helots with support function in the Spartan army, see Ducat 1990: 157–9; 1994.

the Spartiates are equally represented among both categories. In light of these observations, the question of the relationship between Messenian ethnicity and the attitudes of Helots and *perioikoi* to the Spartiates may be in need of a Copernican revolution. Rather than pointing to Messenian ethnicity as a motivating factor in how Helots and *perioikoi* reacted to the Theban-led invasion of *Lakonikē*, the evidence seems to suggest that, at a time when discontent with Spartiate rule was strong on both sides of the Taygetos, the revolt of Helots and *perioikoi* had longer-lasting effects in Messenia because there it could marshal ethnic symbolism – and also, of course, owing to geographic reasons. The existence of Messenian ethnicity was by now accepted by everyone, including the Spartans,[60] who simply refused to recognize the new Messenians as its legitimate carriers. It seems that Messenian ethnicity was as much a cause as an enabling factor in the birth of the new Messenian polity.

Seen against this background, Archidamus' city of slaves does not have as strong a claim as scholars have often allowed, to being considered a fair depiction of how the citizen body of Messene was formed. Beside the archaeological evidence mentioned above, which seems to suggest an influx of population from outside the region, it is probably fair to assume that Laconian *perioikoi* who joined forces with the Thebans must have formed part of the citizen-body of the new city, since they could hardly expect that the Spartans would leave them in peace as soon as the Theban army had left Laconia.[61] And of course, one would expect *a priori* significant participation among the *perioikoi* of Messenia – motivated by Epaminondas' army, if nothing else.

The involvement of *perioikoi* of Messenia in the new Messenian polity is never directly mentioned in the sources,[62] and can only be inferred from general observations on the extension of the new polity. What the evidence does suggest is that the city that was growing at the foot of Mount Ithome, with its state-of-the-art walls, was only a part, if the most impressive, of the new polity. The new Messene was more, perhaps much more, than only that city. This is not immediately clear in the sources, in part for reasons of terminology. At the beginning, the city itself was

---

[60] On the terms of Spartan acceptance of Messenian ethnicity, which of course did not involve acceptance of the claims by any group of people on the Spartan land west of the Taygetos, see above, n. 47 and pp. 198–9.

[61] The *perioikoi* of Karyai, right on the Arcadian border, apparently felt safe enough to remain, but a year later they were massacred to a man by Archidamus, leading an army of Spartans and mercenaries sent by Dionysios of Syracuse (Xen. *Hell.* 7.1.28).

[62] This is perhaps the most striking case of the erasure of the *perioikoi* living in Messenia from the Messenian national legend; see below, p. 336.

almost certainly called "Ithome," while the name "Messene" indicated the new polity, whose citizens were accordingly "the Messenians" and appeared as such on their coins and in international treaties.[63] According to Pausanias (4.26.5), Epaminondas had been told by a dream to give back the Messenians "their fatherland and their poleis," and indeed Pausanias later refers briefly to the reconstruction of the "other poleis" as taking place parallel to the foundation of Ithome, which he anachronistically calls Messene (4.27.7). Plutarch also describes the liberation of Messene, saying that Epaminondas and Pelopidas took away the Messenian land from the Spartans, called back the old Messenians from wherever they were, and founded Ithome (*Pel.* 24.9), possibly suggesting that the foundation of Ithome formed part of a larger process.

Apart from these general statements, in only a few cases is there direct evidence to show how other settlements became part of Messene. Kyparissia and Koryphasion did not join in of their own will, but were compelled to do so by the Arcadians in 365/4 (see above). That this should happen on the western coast of Messenia, a relatively peripheral and isolated area, is perhaps not too surprising. It would be interesting to know what happened in the core area of the region, especially in the lower Pamisos valley. Here only Korone stands out, thanks to Pausanias' saying that the town, formerly called Aipeia, had been founded anew when the Thebans brought the Messenians back to the Peloponnese. Its founder was allegedly the Boeotian Epimelides of Koroneia, who named the new town after his own, but later the name was distorted by the Messenians (Paus. 4.34.5). Although one might suspect this story of being an *a posteriori* explanation of the similarity between the names of the two places, the Arcadian onslaught on Asine in 369/8 or thereabouts strongly suggests that the western coast of the Messenian gulf north of Asine was no longer Lakedaimonian at that time.[64] If Korone was really founded anew, however formally, it might parallel Ithome, which also arose on the site of a former perioikic town that had been the cradle of the revolt in the fifth

---

[63] Roebuck 1941: 37 and n. 54 first realized this. To the sources mentioned by him, add the generally overlooked lemma of Stephanus of Byzantium, s.v. *Ithome*, where Ithome is called a polis of – significantly – Messene, and Plut. *Pel.* 24.5 (the Thebans found Ithome). Note also that the ethnic "Ithomaeans" is by far the most likely supplement for *SEG* 43.135 line 9, see Matthaiou 2001: 223. Recently, Grandjean 2003: 93–8 has contested Roebuck's views, but without considering all the evidence. Consider also the use of "Messene" as name of the region in fifth-century authors such as Pherecydes (fr. 117 Fowler = *FgrHist* 3 F 117) and Hellanicus (fr. 124a and 125 Fowler = *FgrHist* 4 F 124 and 323a F 23), Euripides fr. 1083, Aristophanes, *Lys.* 1141, above, p. 71.

[64] Note also that at Korone Pausanias (4.34.6) saw the tomb of Epimelides, who was obviously worshipped as the founder of the city.

century but seems nevertheless to have been still in existence in the second half of the century. The insistence of Pausanias on the fact that the city at the foot of Mount Ithome had no predecessors in the centuries before could betray an attempt at disguising the continuity between new Messenians and old *perioikoi*, and would parallel the representation of the new polity as formed totally by old Messenians returning from exile, which was the official Theban–Messenian line.

Much more problematic is the fate of the important perioikic settlements east of the Pamisos, Thouria, Pharai and Kalamai. Kalamai, as we have seen, probably worshipped an Arcadian hero as its ancestral god. In the case of Thouria, which had taken part in the revolt after the earthquake, direct evidence shows that it had become Messenian again by 322, but there are strong arguments to suggest making it a part of free Messenia from the outset, especially its fortification wall, built in isodomic ashlar masonry of the early fourth century and using the same *emplekton* technique as was used also at Ithome (above, p. 33 and plates 3 and 4). On balance, the most likely assumption seems to be that at least Thouria and Pharai, and probably also Kalamai, were part of the new Messenian state;[65] especially considering how stubbornly the Spartans refused to recognize its legitimacy, if they had had at their disposition convenient strongholds west of the Taygetos and just across the Pamisos river, it would be really incomprehensible why they did not use them as a jumping-off spot to attack the Messenians, and yet, all Spartan campaigns in the Peloponnesus until the coming of Philip of Macedon pointed to Arcadia,[66] and we do not find in the sources a single piece of evidence for Spartan military activity in southern Messenia. The silence of the sources on any conflict in this area at the time of the Theban invasion or immediately thereafter may be taken to demonstrate that it did not take any drastic measures by the Thebans or their allies for it to join Messene, although given the sparseness of our sources this latter point should not be pressed too far. In short, it seems reasonable to conclude that, by the end of the

---

[65] For what is worth, note that Pelopidas is described by Plutarch, on the occasion of his embassy to Susa in 367, as 'the man who had shut Sparta up between Taygetos and Eurotas' (*Pel.* 30.2), which, even making allowance for the exaggeration of this praise, seems to suggest that in the common perception the Spartans had not kept control of any significant extension of the region west of the Taygetos.

[66] To the Spartan campaigns in southern Arcadia in 368 and 365, on which see n. 23 above, add of course the campaign of Mantinea in 362 and again Spartan attacks on Megalopolis in 352 (Diod. 16.39.1–2; see also Paus. 8.27.10 and Buckler 2003: 425); on both occasions the Messenians intervened on the side of their allies.

360s, west of the Taygetos only Asine and Mothone were certainly still Lakedaimonian.[67]

Clearly, although there may be some truth hidden in each of them, neither the Theban–Messenian nor the Spartan view of the identity of the new Messenians can be taken as a reliable guide to what was happening on the ground. Helots who were in Messenia in the winter of 369 certainly became free Messenians, and so did also *perioikoi* of Messenia – some of their free will, others under compulsion. The majority of the Helots and *perioikoi* who had come from Laconia with Epaminondas' army are also likely to have become citizens of the new polity. Finally, some influx of population from the Peloponnese and beyond is probable, and the presence among these people of old "Messenians of Naupaktos" or their descendants is possible, too, although these latter cannot have been more than a few.[68] The very discrepancy between these inferential conclusions and the generalizing views we found in the sources is a key to the problem of the Messenian identity in the fourth century.

MESSENIAN IDENTITY IN THE FOURTH CENTURY

The most revealing evidence for how the new Messenians articulated their identity comes from the names of their tribes. As a number of inscriptions from Ithome/Messene show, the citizen body was divided into five tribes, called Hyllis, Kleolaia, Aristomachis, Kresphontis and Daiphontis.[69] The presence of two of these tribes at Thouria and possibly of one of them at Korone suggests that they applied to all the free Messenians, as one would expect anyway given the usual association between tribes and ethnic identity.[70] The names of the Messenian tribes are transparent. Hyllos was

---

[67] See Ps.Skyl. 45 Müller and Paus. 4.27.8 with Henning 1996; on Asine, see also above, pp. 42–3. One can only guess where the border between Messenians and Lakedaimonians ran on the western side of the Mani peninsula; considering that Philip's intervention pushed it south beyond Leuktron (see above, p. 32 n. 53), the Choireios river or the steep coastland north of Abia seem plausible candidates.

[68] Note that alleged descent from the "Messenians of Naupaktos" may not have been the only conceivable foundation for a claim of Messenian descent: one of the earliest ancient sources on the Second Messenian War, a passage from Callisthenes quoted by Polybius (4.33.5 = *FGrHist* 124 F 23), speaks of Messenian exiles finding refuge in Arcadia at that time, and it would not be surprising if their "descendants" were among the new Messenians.

[69] On the Messenian tribes, see Jones 1987: 146–8. Their number might be reflected in the tradition according to which Kresphontes had originally divided his reign in five parts; see Ephorus *FGrHist* 70 F 116 *ap.* Strab. 8.4.7, and Nicolaus *FGrHist* 90 F 31, but cf. Jones 1987: 147.

[70] On the tribes at Thouria, see *IG* V 1, 1386, and Jones 1987: 148–9, and above, p. 32. The tribe Kleolaia seems to be mentioned in an inscription from Petalidi, ancient Korone, that has been made known recently, *SEG* 48.514 J. This very fragmentary inscription recalls the proxeny *IG* V 1,

the son of Heracles, Kleolaios Hyllos' son and the father of Aristomachos, who was in his turn Kresphontes' father. Daiphontes was a Heraclid from Argos, who had married Temenos' daughter Hyrnetho. The choice of these heroes as eponymous for the tribes is remarkable. In the Greek world, the names of subdivisions of the citizen body were typically related to ethnic identity, although not in a systematic way: Dorians normally had the three ancestral tribes of the Pamphyloi, Hylleis and Dymanes, and often a fourth one, and Argadeis, Aigikoreis, Geleontes and Hopletes recurred in many Ionian cities, though rarely all together.[71]

Considering that the Messenian revolt in the fifth century and the myth of the Dorian invasion had established the Messenians as members of the Dorian *ethnos*, we might have expected the new Messenians to adopt the names of the Dorian tribes, or at least some of them. Actually, this happened only in the case of the tribe Hyllis. The remaining names delineate a subtle and creative strategy of ethnic self-definition. Exploiting the ambivalence between Heraclids and Dorians in the traditions on the division of the Peloponnese,[72] the Messenians were able to connect themselves to a supposed ancestral Heraclid heritage, which constituted the main mythic charter that provided legitimacy to the new Messenian state, while at the same time diverting attention from the Dorian identity they shared with the Spartans – a component of their ethnicity they could not altogether erase, since it had been emphasized by fifth-century Messenians.

However, the new tribal names went much further in placing the new political community in the mythic-historical map of Greece in a very precise way. Heraclid myths were particularly important at Argos. Daiphontes, eponymous of one of the Messenian tribes, was a very prominent character in Argive myth-history: he was Temenos' son-in-law and successor, *de facto* or only *in pectore* depending on the version of the myth. He was also eponymous of a *phatra* at Argos, while another Argive *phatra*

1425, both in terms of letter forms and in having the tribe's name in the genitive followed by a numeral; cf. also Themelis, *Praktika* 2000: 90 and pl. 56b. More cases of tribal names followed by numerals appear in a new inscription from the agora of Messene mentioned by Themelis, *Praktika* 2004: 41, dated to the fourth century. The chronology of *IG* V 1, 1425, dated to the late fourth or early third century by Kolbe on the basis of the letter forms, has been questioned by Roebuck 1941: 60 n. 10, but his assumption that the numeral following the tribal name should be interpreted as the indication of a month according to the Achaean calendar is proven wrong by the new inscription from the agora of Messene. An image of *IG* V 1, 1425 is available in Bardani 1990–91: pl. 41. Still useful the comments on this inscription by Wilhelm 2000: 373–6 (originally published in 1891).

[71] On Dorian and Ionian tribes, see Roussel 1976: 193–263. [72] See Musti 1986b.

was named after Kleolaios.[73] Moreover, the Heraclid heritage formed a strong bond between the Messenians and their new protectors the Thebans: Heracles was a quintessentially Boeotian and more specifically Theban hero *par excellence*. His cult seems to have played a part in the initiation of the warriors of the Sacred Band, the elite Theban unit that had crushed the Spartan hoplites at Leuktra; right before the battle, the weapons dedicated in the temple of Heracles at Thebes had allegedly disappeared, signifying that the hero himself was preparing to join the fight.[74] It is important to note that in exactly the same years the Argives themselves were emphasizing their Heraclid heritage in order to create a mythic connection with Thebes: in the "hemicycle of the kings," a series of ten bronze statues, dedicated in Delphi in the aftermath of the alliance between Thebes and Argos and the liberation of Messenia, depicted Heracles and his Argive ancestors all the way back to Danaos.[75] This parallel strengthens the idea that the Heraclid names of the Messenian tribes were meant to establish a connection with the mythic heritage of Thebes. The assemblage of eponymous heroes of the tribes showcased the ancestral claim of the Messenians to their fatherland, while at the same time emphasizing their mythic connections with Argos and Thebes. This peculiar mix of tradition and innovation, or rather this innovation disguised as the most ancestral of traits, defines fourth-century Messenian ethnicity in an important way.

The extremely consistent and slightly artificial picture offered by the Messenian tribes becomes more concrete and problematic once we compare it with the deities worshipped in post-liberation Messenia. In Greek culture, cults were associated with ethnicity at least as closely as tribal names were.[76] Messenian cults offer evidence for how the Messenians constructed their identity, and also how their identity may have been perceived by other Greeks. The lack of extensive archaeological investigations somewhat limits the diagnostic value of this evidence, because it is difficult to locate in time cults attested only much later by written

---

[73] On Daiphontes' genealogy, see Paus. 2.19.1. Harder 1991: 126–8 discusses various versions of his role in the succession to Temenos. On the *phatrai* of the Daiphontees and Kleodaidai at Argos see Piérart 1986: 282–4. On the Argive *phatrai*, subdivisions of the tribes, see also Jones 1987: 113.

[74] The "miracle" is reported by Xen. *Hell.* 6.4.7; cf. Kallisth. 124 F 22a, Diod. 15.53.4, the latter crediting Epaminondas with engineering it. On the Theban cult of Heracles see especially Schachter 1986: 1–37. Note that the Theban implications of Heracles at Messene were made explicit in the assemblage of statues in the western stoa of the Hellenistic Asklepieion, where Heracles and the personification of the city of Thebes flanked Epaminondas; see below, p. 278.

[75] See Paus. 10.10.5 and, on the form and political meaning of the monument, Salviat 1965.

[76] On the pervasive connection between cults and ethnicity in Greek culture see Parker 1998: 16–21.

sources – usually by Pausanias. However, a careful sifting of the evidence allows some interesting observations. Among the cults documented in Mavromati itself, only a few can be traced back to the age of the liberation. This is probably the case with the cult of Zeus Ithomatas, which was practiced in a sacred enclosure on the top of the mountain.[77] Archaeological evidence from there is scarce, but the very first coins struck by the Messenians show an image of Zeus Ithomatas, in an old-fashioned style that was probably meant to suggest some traditional pedigree for the new polity.[78] Material evidence going back to the fourth century is not abundant in the urban area, either, since the sanctuary of Asklepios was completely rebuilt at a later date, covering up to a large extent the traces of earlier phases.[79]

The cult in the sanctuary omega-omega continued undisturbed from the archaic period to the late fourth or early third century, when the shrine was totally rebuilt, apparently after being destroyed by a fire. Some of the rather scanty evidence on the early architectural phases of the sanctuary may refer to new buildings erected at the time of the liberation of Messenia.[80] The cult of the Dioscuri is explicitly attested by a votive inscription on a bronze shield dating slightly before the destruction (*SEG* 45.302). As noted above, it is not completely certain how far back their cult goes, but the iconography of the dedications would be consistent with their presence from the fifth century at the latest, and probably from earlier on. In other words, the cult of the Dioscuri may conceivably have been introduced in this sanctuary at the time of the liberation of Messenia, but it is on the whole likelier that it simply continued from the period before. The same can be said of the kourotrophic deity whose cult is suggested by the iconography of archaic terracottas.[81]

In the soundings south of the later temple of Asklepios traces have been found of buildings and of an altar that can be connected with Epaminondas' foundation, but even here it is difficult to say with certainty, on the basis of the votives of classical date, which deity or deities were worshipped in this shrine. Asklepios is extremely likely to have been among them, given his importance in the later history of the sanctuary

[77] See Zunino 1997: 103–7.
[78] On the coins of Messene, see now Ritter 2002: 78–80, and Grandjean 2003: 59–65, both arguing convincingly against seeing in the striding Zeus a depiction of Ageladas' statue (see above, p. 176). Archaeological evidence from the top of Mount Ithome: Amandry 1987: 127–9.
[79] On the Hellenistic Asklepieion see below, pp. 277–85. More evidence will likely come from the new excavations of the agora, see below p. 273.
[80] See Themelis 1998a: 157–61
[81] The evidence for the identification of the deities worshipped in the sanctuary is discussed above, p. 126.

and the fact that anatomic ex-votos have been found among the materials associated with these early buildings.[82] However, other deities were venerated in the rooms surrounding the later temple of Asklepios (see below, pp. 276–7), a few meters away from the early remains, so Asklepios may not have been the only recipient of cult in the earlier phase, either. As in the case of the omega-omega complex, here, too, votive terracotta plaques were found, starting in the archaic age and continuing to the late fourth century, without any noticeable change in iconography, which makes it somewhat difficult to be completely certain that Asklepios' worship in this place started in the second quarter of the fourth century and not earlier.[83] However, considering that Asklepios' cult seems to have been booming from the late fifth century,[84] it is on the whole more likely that it was introduced at Ithome/Messene at the time of the liberation. Also to be dated in the fourth century, probably close to the liberation of Messene, is a small prostyle temple dedicated to Artemis Orthia, brought to light by Themelis' excavations between the sanctuary omega-omega and the western side of the later Asklepieion.[85]

Asklepios was still a new god in the early fourth century. Even though his early temple may not have been as prominent among the sanctuaries of the new city as the later Doric temple would be, it is fair to say that the location of his cult speaks in favor of its importance from the beginning. One of the traditions about Asklepios' birth connected it with Messenia, especially with the eastern coast of the Messenian gulf,[86] and this could explain to some extent why he became part of the pantheon of the new city. However, the presence of anatomic ex-votos and of a bath adjacent to the sanctuary shows that even here Asklepios had his usual status of healing deity, and his cult did not have a purely political significance, as has sometimes been suggested.[87] Besides the popularity of the cult in the

---

[82] On plaques and other findings from the courtyard of the Asklepieion, see Boehringer 2001: 277, with further references, and Themelis 2000: 22–3. Note that the anatomic ex-votos do not go back in time beyond the liberation of Messenia.

[83] Boehringer 2001: 277, who points out that there is no clear difference in terms of overall iconography between the plaques from the courtyard of the Asklepieion and those from the omega-omega sanctuary.

[84] On the diffusion of the cult of Asklepios, see Riethmüller 2005, I: 76–7.

[85] For the identification of this temple as temple of Artemis Orthia, see Themelis 1994a: 101–6 and 2000: 10. Morizot's proposal (1994: 399–405, followed in modified form by Maggi 1996: 260–5) to identify it with the temple of Messene mentioned by Pausanias (4.31.11–12) has been finally ruled out by the discovery of the temple of Messene in the agora, see below, p. 273.

[86] The relevant sources are assembled below, pp. 271–2.

[87] For the interpretation of the cult of Asklepios at Ithome/Messene, see Sineux 1997: 18–23. The political interpretation, that makes of Asklepios in this case an ancestral deity without healing

early fourth century, its relative novelty, and the traditions concerning the Messenian origin of the god, there may be one further reason for its introduction in the pantheon of the Messenians. The center from which the cult of Asklepios spread was Epidaurus, a long-standing object of Argive covetousness and therefore a staunch ally of Sparta, one of the very few that did not desert the Spartans after Leuktra.[88] One version of the myth of the Heraclids in the Argolid attributed the conquest of Epidaurus to Daiphontes. By Pausanias' times at the latest, the Epidaurians had appropriated Daiphontes and his wife Hyrnetho, daughter of Temenos, but the quarrel between Argives and Epidaurians as to which city had Hyrnetho's tomb suggests that Daiphontes, too, was a likely object of dispute, in which case one can see the two sides interpreting in divergent ways Daiphontes' role at Epidaurus: founder for the Epidaurians, conqueror for the Argives.[89] It would be tempting to see in the Messenian cult of Asklepios also the reflection of an attempt by the Argives to hijack the main god of their enemies the Epidaurians. However, given the fragmentary nature of the evidence, this hypothesis has to remain somewhat tentative.

Apart from the strongly Messenian Zeus Ithomatas and the probable newcomer Asklepios, the other cults documented for Ithome/Messene in the early fourth century have a striking point in common: an obvious connection with a Spartan heritage. This is hardly surprising in the case of the cults in the sanctuary omega-omega, which represent an element of continuity from the phase preceding the liberation. Even in this case, it is interesting to observe that the iconography of the terracotta plaques, for what it is worth, shows from the fifth century to the fourth no appreciable change that might suggest changes in the deities worshipped in the sanctuary.[90] If one of them was Artemis in her function of kourotrophic goddess, one may speculate about a connection with the little temple *in antis* dedicated to Artemis Orthia.

---

connotations, has been put forward by Orlandos 1976: 38 and discussed in detail by Felten 1983: 82–93.

[88] On the conflictual relations between Epidaurus and Argos, see now Piérart 2004: 27–30.

[89] On the dispute about Hyrnetho, see Paus. 2.28.3–7. It is also suggestive that Temenos' fate and his troubled relations with his children were treated by Euripides in a tragedy, the *Temenids*, that was apparently written at the time of the Athenian–Argive alliance after the Peace of Nicias; see Harder 1991: 118 n. 4 on the chronology, based on formal arguments regarding the metric of the fragments. According to Nicolaus, *FgrHist* 90 F 30, Daiphontes succeeds Temenos, but then at the end of the fragment he seems to be pushing the Dryopes of Epidauros towards secession from Argos, and it is not clear what is supposed to happen after that (Epidaurus is not mentioned). This is likely to be Ephorus' version (see Harder 1991: 118 and n. 26 with Ephorus, *FGrHist* 70 F 18b, and the genealogy in Diod. 7.17), in which the Argive kings were in the end the descendants of Temenos, not of Daiphontes.

[90] On the iconography of the plaques, which is admittedly not very specific, see Themelis 1998a.

Needless to say, Artemis Orthia had herself, if possible, an even stronger Spartan flavor than the Dioscuri, worshipped in the sanctuary.

The presence of these conspicuous Spartan elements in the pantheon of the Messenians does not seem to have been completely unproblematic. In the cases of both Artemis Orthia and the Dioscuri the same pattern can be seen in the sources, consisting in claiming as ancestrally Messenian what was a famously Spartan cult. According to Pausanias (3.1.4, 26.3 and 4.31.9), the Messenians maintained that the birthplace of the Dioscuri was part of their land, not of Laconia. As noted above, the claim was actually earlier than the liberation of Messene: it was implicit in the name of the city founded in 396/5 by the Messenians in Sicily, Tyndaris or "city of the Tyndarids," whose coins appropriately showed Helen on the obverse and the Dioscuri or their symbols on the reverse.[91] In the same spirit, a board connected with the cult of Artemis Orthia at Messene in the Imperial age was called "the holy elders, descendants of Kresphontes," probably implying the claim that the cult itself went back to the Dorian migration and was therefore as old as its Spartan counterpart.[92]

Evidence for cults in the Messenian territory, scanty and unclear though it is, seems consistent with what we see at Ithome/Messene. The combination of the newcomer Asklepios and the old Spartan gods Artemis Orthia and the Dioscuri may find an interesting parallel in the assemblage of gods that were worshipped in the sanctuary of the Karneiasion, near Andania, at the foot of the hills marking the northwestern border of the plain of Stenykleros.[93] The name of the sanctuary, also attested in the form Karnasion, is connected with Apollo's epithet Karneios, found throughout the Doric world and most prominently in Sparta.[94] However, in the sanctuary Apollo was joined by a number of other deities, among whom the Great Gods take pride of place. Theirs was a mystery cult, which seems in time to have become the most prominent cult in the sanctuary. Even though the Great Gods of Andania were later identified

---

[91] On Tyndaris, the Tyndarids, and the Messenian claim on the Dioscuri, see above, p. 165.

[92] See *SEG* 23.215 and 217 (both dated to the second century AD) and below, p. 282.

[93] On the location of Andania, see Valmin 1930: 89–99. The mystery cult is documented by two inscriptions, *IG* V 1, 1390, a very comprehensive collection of the regulations for the cult inscribed in connection with a reform in the early first century BC or AD (for the date see below, pp. 295–8), originally found in the vicinity of the village of Konstantinoi and currently built into the entrance door of the village church, and *Syll.*³ 735, a response from the oracle of Apollo Pythaeus at Argos relating to the same reform. See now Deshours 2006.

[94] On the strong Laconian association of the cult of Apollo Karneios, see Zunino 1997: 175–6. On its connection with the return of the Heraclids and the Dorian migration, Malkin 1994: 149–57. On the Spartan ancestry of the cult of Apollo Karneios at Andania, see Figueira 1999: 240 n. 58.

with the Dioscuri, at the time of the liberation of Messenia this identification seems to be quite unlikely.[95] As Margherita Guarducci saw,
originally the Great Gods were probably the Kabiroi, almost certainly
imported under the influence of Thebes, and the presence of Demeter in
the sanctuary reinforces this suggestion.[96] However, none of the evidence
on the cult of Andania goes back to the fourth century, so caution is in
order. As for the cults documented archaeologically in archaic and early
classical Messenia, that of Apollo Korythos clearly continued, with possibly a new temple built in connection with the liberation of Messenia,
a small prostyle, dated to the late fourth century at the latest.[97] Votives
continue in the sanctuary of the river-god Pamisos, as well.[98] As for the
cult of Poseidon at Thouria, continuity into the Hellenistic period is
probably attested by an inscription, although the sanctuary itself must
have been moved from Akovitika to some other location.[99]

On the whole, the pattern is clear. The scrutiny of the gods worshipped
in Messenia at the time immediately after the liberation shows predominantly continuity with the period before, with a smaller but significant
number of newcomers. At least in some cases, the continuity regards cults
that were normally seen as typically Spartan. Moreover, we have at least one
case of a Spartan cult actually attested for the first time after 369, the cult of
Artemis Orthia.[100] In general terms, the prominence of Lakedaimonian cults
and myths in the pantheon of the new Messenians has been noted for more
than a century.[101] The precise meaning of this situation, however, may not
have received the attention it deserves. The most common explanation used
to be that the Spartan domination of Messenia had brought about a massive

---

[95] The identification of the Dioscuri with the Great Gods of Samothrace, i.e. the Kabiroi, is not
attested before the second century BC; see Guarducci 1934: 184.

[96] Guarducci 1934: 184; see also Figueira 1999: 240 n. 59, Musti 2001: 147, 149 and Graf 2003: 245.
Hemberg 1950 offers a valuable collection of the evidence on the Kabiroi. On the cult of the
Kabiroi at Thebes, see Schachter 1986: 66–110 and Schachter 2003.

[97] See Versakis 1916: 69.

[98] See Valmin 1938: 464. The small Doric temple *in antis* reconstructed by Valmin was probably
built during the third century, to judge by the fragment of painted sima and the antefixes
published by Valmin 1938: 430–2 and figs. 83–4; cf. Themelis 1994b: 152–3.

[99] *IG* V 1, 1387, from Thouria. In the sanctuary at Akovitika, evidence stops at the end of the fifth
century, when the sanctuary was apparently abandoned in consequence of the rise of the soil level
behind it, which exposed it to floods (Moritz Kiderlen, personal communication).

[100] This novelty is somewhat mitigated by two factors: if it is correct to identify (Artemis) Limnatis
with (Artemis) Orthia, then her cult had been practiced west of the Taygetos for centuries, at
Volimos (see above, p. 123); secondly, the kourotrophic goddess worshipped in the omega-omega
sanctuary may have been identified as Artemis (see above, p. 126). Ultimately, the small prostyle
temple could conceivably have been linked to the cult that was practiced in the omega-omega
complex.

[101] See already Niese 1891: 13–14.

obliteration of Messenian culture, so that the "new Messenians" had no choice but to engage in a sort of *bricolage* with the Spartan cultural heritage in order to create their own identity. Certainly this explanation had an important function in countering the romantic tendency on the part of some modern scholars towards accepting uncritically Pausanias' views of the endurance of Messenian tradition or postulating centuries of continuity of an underground Messenian cultural resistance in the face of Spartan domination.[102] And yet, it hardly makes sense to assume that the Messenians, upon freeing their fatherland from Sparta, would take over Spartan cultural traits to build their own identity. This is certainly not what they did with their tribal names. Is it really plausible that the new polity, which was created as a bulwark against Sparta, should choose to introduce right into its midst the cult of Artemis Orthia, the most Spartan of all cults?

This impasse, as in general the whole debate on the continuity or discontinuity of Messenian tradition, results in part from a schematic view of the development of the Messenian identity, one that tends unwittingly to replicate ancient ideological constructs instead of reading them against the grain, as it were. The debate assumes the existence in the early archaic age of some sort of unitary Messenian culture for which no evidence in fact exists. As far as we can tell, the unification of the land that later became Messenia, which was necessary for the emergence of the very concept of Messenia as a unity, was a result of the Spartan conquest. Although some cults of Messenia are highly likely to go back to the time before the Spartan annexation of the region, this does not automatically mean that they were perceived as Messenian, or as more Messenian than cults introduced later, when Messenia was a part of *Lakonikē*. Certainly in *Lakonikē* there were cults and myths that were more closely connected with the area west of the Taygetos than with the Eurotas Valley, but again, that did not make them *ipso facto* Messenian. Whatever cultural unity Messenia had during the archaic and early classical periods, it was a result of its being part of Lakedaimon. The strong Spartan flavor of so many cults in Messenia, even after the liberation, is consistent with this.

Of course, there can be no serious doubt as to the fact that the new Messenians put in place discursive strategies to explain the situation, and in some cases, such as those of the names of their tribes, the birthplace of the Dioscuri, and possibly the origin of the cult of Artemis Orthia, we even catch a glimpse of those strategies. However, aetiology and myth were much more malleable than actual cult, which is why the cults of

[102] See Asheri 1983: 30.

the new Messenians offer such an intriguing picture. De-Laconizing the landscape must have been one of the highest cultural priorities in free Messenia, and yet, rather than give up the Laconian gods and try to replace them, the new community by and large preferred to cling to them, reinterpreting the origin of their cults when it was necessary and possible. The assemblage of deities worshipped in the earliest times of free Messenia makes sense only if we admit that the new Messenians had a strong reason to regard those cults as theirs. This situation was the result of the combination of two interrelated factors. The first is the fact that Spartan traits were part of the Messenian identity from its earliest manifestation, as can be seen in Rhegion and Sicilian Messene in the early fifth century (above, p. 172). The second is the very strong Lakedaimonian component in the population of the new Messenian polity. The fact that the written sources, ideologically biased as they are, tend to ignore such a component should not surprise or worry us too much.

MESSENIAN ANCESTORS

The idea that, in spite of a myth of foundation based on an exile and return story, the roots of the new Messenian ethnogenesis of the fourth century lay mostly in Messenia itself may receive some support from a very important and characteristically Messenian class of evidence, later materials deposed in Bronze Age tombs (fig. 6). Some thirty Bronze Age tombs from Messenia have been found to hold objects ranging in time from the Geometric to the Hellenistic and Roman periods.[103] Unfortunately, only a small portion of the finds have been published in any detail, and discerning broader patterns in terms of chronology, quality of materials, and ultimately meaning, is extremely difficult. In general terms, it can be said that in Messenia interest in Bronze Age graves peaked in the late classical period, remaining sustained through the following centuries, in marked contrast with what happened elsewhere in Greece.[104]

---

[103] On the Geometric and archaic evidence, see above, pp. 113–14 and 127–8.

[104] On this topic, Alcock 1991 is a landmark; for the subsequent development of her views, which involved a significant shift of emphasis from seeing the evidence as expression of the will to articulate social differentiation to connecting it to the affirmation of ethnic identity, see Alcock 2002b: 146–52, 165–7, and cf. the criticism by Boehringer 2001: 326–8. After Korres 1981–2 brought the evidence together for the fist time, the most comprehensive, thorough, and up-to-date survey is to be found in Boehringer 2001: 243–90, with full references to earlier publications; add Chatzi-Spiliopoulou 2001 on Thouria (see above, p. 35 and n. 59). Van der Kamp 1996 contributes an original perspective, some first-hand knowledge of the finds, and a crisp and helpful survey of scholarship on the topic.

Figure 6 Bronze Age tombs with late classical finds

The tombs can be assigned to four general areas: the bay of Pylos and the plateau overlooking it, the western corner of the gulf of Messenia, i.e. the area of Nichoria and Korone, the highlands that link these two areas, and the Soulima valley with the corridor that connects it to the sea. Thouria seems to represent an isolated case. The first area includes seven locations: the large chamber-tomb necropolis of Volimidia, not far from Chora and Ano Englianos, the Middle Helladic *tholos* tomb close to the modern village of Koryphasio, known in scholarly literature as Osmanaga, the two *tholoi* built in the hill of Tragana, west-northwest of Koryphasio, a number of *tholoi* in the area of Koukounara, at the edge of the hills that overlook the bay of Pylos, the *tholos* on the hill that forms the northern end of the Voidokilia, the two *tholoi* on the Routsi ridge near the village of Myrsinochori, directly south of Chora, and the small *tholos* of Papoulia, a bit farther east. The second area centers around the hill of Nichoria and includes the *tholos* at the western end of the hill, a Bronze Age or Geometric chamber tomb dug into the side of the ravine south of the hill, called Vathirema, the Mycenaean and Geometric necropolis of Karpophora, that belonged to the settlement on the hill, and finally a *tholos* found near the road which connects the villages of Daphni and Daras, three kilometers northwest of Nichoria. The highlands between mounts Lykodimos and Maglavas form a corridor that connects the area of Pylos with the gulf of Messenia.[105] In this corridor two sites have produced relevant finds, one just east-southeast of the village of Kremmydia, the other about a kilometer southeast of Soulinari, in a location known in scholarly literature as Tourliditsa. Finally, from the area of the Soulima valley relevant materials have been found in the *tholos* tombs close to the villages of Vasilikò, Psari, Kopanaki, and Mouriatada, and in a location called Peristeria, overlooking the valley of the stream Peristera, some seven kilometers northeast of Kyparissia.

The Nichoria area is the one for which evidence is the most diagnostic. Black-glazed pottery and cooking ware testify to what was most probably cultic activity going on in the *tholos* F from the last quarter of the fifth century to the mid fourth.[106] The chamber tomb of Vathirema offers similar evidence, although here the quality of the fifth-century pottery is higher than in any other Bronze Age tomb in Messenia, and activity seems

---

[105] See Lukerman and Moody 1978: 78–81 and especially figures 7–2 and 7–3.
[106] Coulson 1983: 334–6, according to whom the activity might have ceased in connection with the liberation of Messenia; but cf. 337, where the pottery is said not to extend beyond the mid fourth century. Obviously, the evidence is not conclusive either way, which is not surprising given its nature.

to continue into the Hellenistic period.[107] The *tholos* tomb from Daphni/ Daras has also produced late classical pottery.[108] Finally, traces of cult activity going back to the Hellenistic period come from the area of two Mycenaean tombs in the Karpophora necropolis.[109]

The highlands that connect the Pylos region with the Messenian gulf seem to show a similar pattern, with evidence for cult and pottery from the second half of the fifth century from the *tholos* of Kremmydia and comparable evidence from that of Tourliditsa.[110] The situation is less clear in northern Messenia. Pottery seems to start in the fifth century in the *tholos* of Kopanaki,[111] while at Peristeria a recent reexamination of the material has shown that it starts around 340 BC, continuing in the third and second centuries.[112]

In the Pylos area, cult at Mycenaean tombs may have started slightly later, and with one important exception the evidence is surprisingly scarce. Late classical and/or Hellenistic pottery comes from the cemetery of Volimidia, from the *tholos* of Routsi and from that of Osmanaga.[113] The Late Helladic *tholos* built into an Early Helladic tumulus at the entrance of the Voidokilia bay became the center of rather intense cultic activity sometime during the fourth century, as documented by over 400 terracotta plaques found around the mound and a small building close by, which seems to have served some sort of function in connection with the cult.[114] Comparison with the plaques dedicated in the omega-omega sanctuary at Ithome, which seem to share some matrices with those of Voidokilia, suggests a date around the mid fourth century for the beginning of the cult.[115] In the Pylos area there seems to be only one

---

[107] Details on the pottery from Vathirema, including a small red-figure *pelikē* and the rim of a black-figure crater, above, p. 129 n. 107.

[108] Boehringer 2001: 272.   [109] Boehringer 2001: 269–70.

[110] Boehringer 2001: 266–8; in both cases, the evidence suggests also animal sacrifice.

[111] Boehringer 2001: 284–6.

[112] Danalis 2001–2. The material is abundant and of rather high quality, mostly imported from centers such as Olympia, Athens, Corinth, and Ionic workshops (378–9). The pottery seems to stop in the early first century BC, but then Roman pottery (*terra sigillata*) attest to renewed interest in this ancient tomb. Danalis (382–3) would prefer to interpret the remains as evidence for later burials in the *tholos*; cf., however, Boehringer 2001: 288.

[113] Boehringer 2001: 258 (Volimidia, tomb Voria I, two or three sherds of fourth-century pottery); 259 (Routsi, *tholos* 2, Hellenistic sherds and possible remains of one animal sacrifice), 248 (Osmanaga, some late classical or early Hellenistic sherds).

[114] Korres 1988; for the iconography of the plaques see also Peppa-Papaioannou 1987–8.

[115] Themelis 1998a: 163 (cf. Peppa-Papaioannou 1987–8: pl. 1), 165–6 and n. 37, 170. Themelis thinks that matrices were brought from Ithome/Messene to Pylos. Korres 1988, writing before the publication of the plaques from Mavromati, dated the plaques from Voidokilia to the end of the fourth century. Based as they are on style and not on stratigraphic evidence, these dates have to be taken with some caution.

Bronze Age tomb that has produced any fifth-century materials, the tomb 4 in the Koukounara necropolis, on the hills overlooking the bay of Navarino, and close to Kremmydia and Tourliditsa.[116] Finally, a large number of terracotta plaques were dedicated around the *tholos* on the western side of the Ellenika ridge at Thouria, but they unfortunately remain unpublished.[117] However, on the other side of the hill one of the chamber tombs has produced evidence that goes back to the very time of the liberation of Messenia.[118]

The interpretation of this corpus of evidence is anything but straightforward. In very general terms, since there can be little doubt that Bronze Age tombs were recognized as such, the cult practiced in them was in all likelihood addressed to previous inhabitants of the region. It may be less than crucial in our perspective to decide if such previous inhabitants were seen by the worshippers as heroes or as ancestors.[119] In either case, they were clearly perceived as a powerful presence that had to be appeased, and one that had a particularly close connection to the territory. Cult created a special relationship between the worshippers and these powers. For an understanding of the meaning of this relationship, the perceptions of the past in whose framework it was embedded are of decisive importance. We cannot be absolutely certain that prior to the liberation of Messenia these ancestral dead were not seen as part of a purely Laconian view of the past of the region, but by the mid fifth century the idea that the region west of the Taygetos was a later addition to the original Spartan lot was widespread enough to suggest that most probably the Bronze Age tombs were seen as pre-Spartan and by implication as Messenian. The absence of comparable evidence of cult at Bronze Age tombs from Laconia somewhat reinforces this conclusion.

In spite of the circumstantial arguments that can be brought to its support, this conclusion is and cannot but be hypothetical. The fact that on the whole the evidence for cult at Bronze Age tombs is much more abundant for the period after 369, and that in some cases the cult seems to start right at the time of the liberation, speak in favor of this hypothesis. The alternative, that the cults may have expressed the attempt of some groups to claim superior status for themselves by hijacking the Bronze

---

[116] On the controversial evidence from this tomb see the extensive discussions by Korres 1981–2: 381–92 and Boehringer 2001: 261–5; the fifth century is represented apparently only by one black-glazed cup, Korres 1981–2: 391. The rest of the post-Bronze Age material seems to be Hellenistic or later.
[117] See above, p. 35 n. 59.   [118] Chatzi-Spiliopoulou 2001 and above, p. 35.
[119] See the discussion in Antonaccio 1995: 245–68. At any rate, the terracotta plaques strongly suggest heroic cult, especially considering the parallels from Laconia; see Boehringer 2001: 291.

Age dead as their own ancestors, cannot be ruled out completely, but the nature of the cultic activities involved, mostly of a rather modest level and apparently discontinuous, does not offer strong support for it.[120] On the whole, it seems more likely that we have to do with a claim of auto-chthony, or, in other words, that worshipping local heroes or ancestors in post-liberation Messenia equaled an expression of Messenian ethnicity. But then, it seems reasonable to assume a similar explanation from the beginning for those cults that started before the liberation and continued into free Messenia.

If this conclusion is acceptable, then the chronological distribution of the materials has striking implications. The relative lateness of the evi-dence from the Pylos region could be connected to the fact that this region had to be won militarily by the Arcadians before it became part of the new Messenian polity (see above). Once it did, the temptation to capitalize on its mythical cachet must have been obvious: in the new situation, being Pylian was obviously much more attractive than being Koryphasian, and the cult around the Bronze Age graves at the Voidokilia is in all likelihood to be interpreted as a claim of Pylian identity.[121] In the area of Nichoria, not far from Korone, the respective timeline of interest for Mycenaean graves and liberation from Sparta is completely different, in what could be a revealing way. It seems as if Messenian ethnicity had been brewing here for some forty to fifty years when finally the area became overtly Messenian. Where the stimuli came from may be indi-cated by the scanty evidence from the hills overlooking the Pylos bay and from the highlands that connect that area and the northwestern corner of the gulf of Messenia, and the chronological coincidence between possible statements of Messenian identity in the form of worship of autoch-thonous heroes or ancestors and the presence of Messenians of Naupaktos at Pylos may not be incidental.[122] The absence of similar evidence from the area immediately around Pylos should not be seen as surprising, if only in view of the strong Spartan military presence in the area in these very years.

[120] See Boehringer 2001: 321–2 on the difference in quality between Late Geometric and Late Classical offerings in Bronze Age tombs.
[121] It might be identified with the tomb of Thrasymedes, son of Nestor, mentioned in Pausanias' description of Pylos (4.36.2), as suggested by Torelli, in Musti and Torelli 1994: 270 and Alcock 2002b: 150. Cf. however Korres 1988: 325, and note that the cult does not seem to continue very long into the Hellenistic period.
[122] See Figueira 1999: 240 n. 56.

This hypothetical reading of the evidence would add in an important way to the reconstruction of Messenian ethnogenesis in the fourth century. It would confirm the predominantly local nature of this phenomenon, showing that, although the liberation did come abruptly and by external intervention, Messenian ethnicity was smoldering in Messenia itself. Affirmations of Messenian identity may well have been an early expression of a disaffection analogous to the one that came to the fore among the *perioikoi* of Laconia at the time of Epaminondas' invasion in 369. Even more than in the case of the earthquake revolt, it is impossible to tell for sure if the carriers of the Messenian identity in late fifth-century Messenia were Helots or *perioikoi*. The latter are likely to be archaeologically more visible. In the case of Nichoria, the cult in the *tholos* F is but one manifestation of renewed human presence on the plateau, and is apparently accompanied by a substantial building whose foundations in large limestone blocks have been tentatively identified by the excavators as belonging to a temple.[123] This might suggest connecting the area with the perioikic town that became Korone. However, it would probably be wrong, especially at this date, to take an either-or approach to this question. In all likelihood, both Helots and *perioikoi* were involved in the claim of Messenian identity as expressed by tomb worship.

MESSENIAN ETHNOGENESIS: THE SECOND WAVE

It is time to sum up our observations and to consider their implications for the problem of how the citizens of the new Messenian polity construed their ethnic identity. We have on the one hand sources describing them either as Messenians returning from the exile, or as former Helots; we have to admit on the other hand, unless we are ready to assume massive movements of population in and out of the region, that in fact the citizen body was formed to a large extent of *perioikoi* and Helots, mostly from Messenia itself but also quite a few coming from Laconia with Epaminondas' army, and furthermore of colonists from abroad, some of whom, probably not very many, were or considered themselves to be descendants of the Messenians of Naupaktos. The evidence of the cults is consistent with these inferences, showing some cults continuing from

---

[123] See Coulson 1983: 337 and plan 7–2. The building is much more substantial than those whose traces have been located in the pre-third-century strata of the omega-omega complex and in the courtyard of the Asklepieion at Mavromati. The pottery associated with the building appears to be contemporary with the pottery found in the *tholos*.

the fifth century, some of them typically Spartan, and others apparently new and possibly bearing associations with the cities that most actively cooperated in the birth of the new polity, that is, Thebes and Argos. Of course, we have to assume that the preexisting cults were now seen as ancestrally Messenian. The way in which the Dorian heritage was disguised and manipulated by the Heraclid names of the Messenian tribes gives a telling example of how this could work.

The process of Messenian ethnogenesis in the fifth century may help to explain, at least in structural terms, what was now happening. At the time of the earthquake, we see Messenians suddenly popping up out of the ground in a region which until then looked thoroughly Laconian in terms of cults, material culture, dialect, alphabet, just about every indicator for which we can test. Besides the mythic *bricolage* that certainly took place then, facilitated by the emergence of the myth of the division of the Peloponnese among the Heraclids and perhaps also by the Messenian 'revival' on the Strait of Messina, it seems clear that ultimately the foundation of the Messenian identity of the rebels, what really kept them together, was their hatred for Sparta. This is confirmed by the absorption of renegades from all over the *Lakonikē* during the Peloponnesian War. At first sight, this looks like a perfect illustration of Fredrik Barth's thesis that the essential constitutive element of ethnicity is the boundary, a sheer mechanism of inclusion and exclusion that can exist regardless of the nature and importance of the differences between any two groups. A radically instrumentalist approach to fifth-century Messenian ethnogenesis, one that defines it in terms of function and goals rather than tradition and genealogy, is certainly very tempting.[124] In the fifth century, becoming Messenian essentially meant rebelling against Sparta. Is there any serious reason to reject the idea that the same option of becoming Messenian existed in the early fourth century?

Although this interpretation does seem to have a certain explanatory power, it shares the drawbacks of radically instrumentalist theories in general, the total lack of an emic perspective: it looks at Messenian ethnicity purely from the outside, thereby eschewing the problems that emerge when one tries to figure out how the process developed on the ground. The result is a rather abstract reconstruction: we are confronted with a group of people who had mostly lived in Messenia or Laconia as members of the Spartan state until 369, when they suddenly began to regard

---

[124] See e.g. Sharp 1988, developing Barth's approach and defining ethnicity as the pursuit of political goals through the idiom of cultural commonness and difference.

themselves as the original inhabitants of the region coming back from exile. Even though it is the case that the sense of ethnic identity is often based on the repression of historical truth,[125] one has to admit that, formulated in this way, the reconstruction sounds slightly absurd.

Perhaps, after all, the theory of the *grande rentrée* was promoted only by Theban propaganda, and the Messenians themselves had different ideas on this point. However, there would be no real argument supporting this hypothesis apart from our natural resistance to admitting large-scale invention of tradition taking place in a very short period of time. True, it is only in Pausanias that we find reasonably consistent and straightforward evidence to confirm that the Messenians saw themselves as descendants of "old Messenians" exiled at different points in time between the eighth and the mid fifth century. However, it should be noted that the "Messenian diaspora" story was widely enough accepted to influence retrospectively fourth-century sources on the earthquake revolt, and also that there is not a single source that mentions the liberation of the Messenians in Messenia in 369. If the citizens of the new polity had other views about their identity, these views have left no trace in the sources; this is not unthinkable, but it is on the whole rather unlikely. On the contrary, it would be in complete conformity with a pattern observed in many other cases for a people whose very existence has just been affirmed against strong opposition to shape its narratives on its own past in accordance with the already existing narratives of the neighboring peoples, friends or enemies.[126] In other words, if the Thebans promoted the story of the return of the exiles, one would expect *a priori* the new Messenians to go along with this, whether or not the story fitted empirical reality particularly well. After all, the citizens of the new polity were first and foremost an imagined community, like any political community larger than a village. It was not imperative for all of them to have personally been in exile for the story of the *grande rentrée* to become the dominant narrative on the Messenian past, as long as every former *perioikos* or Helot could think that that story applied to a notionally significant number of his fellow citizens.

One factor must have greatly facilitated this new process of Messenian ethnogenesis. Although Messenian ethnicity certainly included cultural and religious traits that could be seen as specific, such as probably the cult

---

[125] E.g. Fabietti 1998: 23.
[126] On the more comprehensive memory of one ethnic group functioning as a pace-setter for the less comprehensive memory of another, see Smith 1986: 178.

of Zeus Ithomatas, the first wave of Messenian ethnogenesis in the fifth century was based on a concept of Messenian ethnicity that was flexible enough to accommodate the essentially Lakedaimonian cultural pattern that we find in late archaic and early classical Messenia. This Messenian ethnicity, forged in the fifth century, offered a structural template for the second wave of Messenian ethnogenesis in the fourth. In other words, for Messenians of the 360s, integrating Spartan cults and myths cannot have been much of a problem, just as it had not been a problem for the Messenians on the Strait of Messina or for the rebels at the time of the earthquake.

However, massive external influence on the shape of Messenian ethnicity should not completely divert our attention from a very important fact. Cultic activity at Bronze Age tombs may point to the articulation from the last decades of the fifth century of claims of Messenian identity in parts of the region that would become free Messene in 369. If that is correct, upon gaining their freedom thanks to the Theban victory, these Messenians probably sacrificed their own constructions of their past to the Messenian master narrative that was to survive in the written sources, without any contrasting voice but the – equally self-interested, equally implausible – Spartan image of the city of slaves.

* * *

To conclude, the birth of a free Messenian polity was finally made possible by an extraordinary convergence of favorable conditions. It could not have happened without the Theban victory at Leuktra and subsequent invasion of *Lakonikē*. Arcadian and Argive involvement were clearly very important, and a peculiar ethnic dynamic in the Peloponnese must have made it easier for the new ethnic entity to be accepted as such. However, the preexistence of Messenian ethnicity was a necessary precondition for success of the new polity carved out of the Lakedaimonian state.

CHAPTER 9

Being Messenian from Philip to Augustus

The birth of a free Messenian polity in 369 BC did not put an end to the Messenian anomaly: it rather added new facets to it. Latecomers that they were, the Messenians were destined to be haunted for the rest of their existence by their problematic absence from the shared record of the Greek past. Especially during the third century, they seem to have been quite active in their efforts to obviate this situation, as witnessed by the efflorescence of works on the Messenian Wars in this period (above, pp. 83–8). In other ways, though, it was the little history they had, fragmentary as it was, that created problems for the new Messenians. Unlike other new polities that emerged around the same time, such as Triphylia and Pisatis, Messene had existed in Panhellenic consciousness as the lost fatherland of the Messenians for almost a century before it became a political reality. Without underestimating the impact of power relations in the Peloponnese and beyond, this widespread consciousness certainly goes a long way in explaining why the legitimacy of the new political entity found acceptance so quickly. However, the preexistence of an imaginary Messene was something the Messenians now had to come to terms with. The accepted features of what we could call the Messenian prehistory set a framework, especially in geographic terms, for the creation of the new Messene.

Originally conceived of, probably in the early fifth century, as the lot of the Heraclid Kresphontes, Messene had been vaguely identified with the Spartan territory west of the Taygetos range: it embraced not only the area of Mount Ithome and the valley of the Pamisos river, but it also stretched all the way to Koryphasion, called Pylos and identified as the residence of king Nestor by the Messenians and other Greeks (see above, p. 60). A look at a map is sufficient to show that the new Messene that emerged in the years after 369 was based on this same conception. Otherwise, there would have been no reason for perioikic settlements on the western coast of Messenia, for example Kyparissia, conquered by the Arcadians in 365/4 (see above, p. 215), to be added to Messene rather than to Triphylia, and in general for perioikic settlements to be part of the Messenian polity rather than just become independent. The fact that perioikic settlements such as Kyparissia, Koryphasion, and Asine initially resisted incorporation demonstrates that the transformation of this imaginary Messene into a real political entity was controversial. If the Messenian identity in the Peloponnese had consisted essentially of the readiness to fight against the Spartans, once the struggle was finally concluded victory could become a paradoxical threat for the cohesion of the new Messenians. Their passionate insistence on their border conflict with Sparta long after that conflict had lost any real political or economic significance eloquently illustrates this point (see above, pp. 22–4).

The imaginary Messene created by those who had identified themselves as Messenians from the fifth century onwards, and by other Greeks,[1] was certainly not an undifferentiated landscape. Just like any other region of the Greek world, it must have had its own mythic and historical geography. Of the latter, we can identify only a few points, such as Mount Ithome, the bulwark of resistance against Sparta, and Pylos, a place marked out by its Homeric clout but also by having been in the hands of free Messenians for more than a decade during the Peloponnesian War, but there must have been more, some perhaps linked also to the incipient history of the Messenian Wars, whose outlines were being defined in the central decades of the fourth century. However, as far as we can tell Messene had never been unitarily structured as a political space – except as a part of Lakedaimon. In this sense as in others, the needs of the real Messene were different from those of the imaginary Messene that had preceded it.

The creation of the new Messenian polity not only involved changes for the individual settlements that comprised it, it also required putting into place some sort of political structure across the region. Up to that point, the political center had been Sparta itself, and the settlement pattern west of the Taygetos reflected this situation in its lack of an obvious focus and a clear hierarchy. This of course was bound to change. Depending on the constitutional form assumed by the new political structure, in theory all or most of the major settlements in the territory of Messene could have been strengthened to form relatively self-sufficient and equally ranking components of the new polity. For various reasons, events took a rather different turn.

---

[1] See above, pp. 59–60, on the probably Argive origins of the myth of the return of the Heraclids.

As we have seen, free Messene ended up including a number of former perioikic settlements, such as Thouria, Kyparissia, Pharai, Abia, and Pylos. Ithome and Korone, possibly both founded anew, seem originally to have been perioikic settlements, too. In the present state of our knowledge, with the exception of Ithome, it is impossible to tell what difference inclusion in Messene made for the shape or size of any of these settlements. Influx of population from other parts of Greece or simply movement across the region is likely but not directly documented, except for the area of the Pylos survey (above, p. 224). What is perfectly clear, however, is that at Ithome big changes were under way, which would influence the future history of Messenia for centuries to come. The need for a pivotal point that could sustain the new polity, and probably also the location of Spartiate land in the region, that now became free and had no preexisting ties to other perioikic settlements, must have combined to project Ithome into a completely new dimension. There is a vast portion of territory, comprising the Stenykleros plain, the Soulima valley and probably the southern Messenian plain west of the Pamisos, where the absence of any other significant settlement and all that we know of historical events in the following centuries concur in suggesting that what we are looking at is the territory of Ithome. It was incomparably larger than the territory of any other settlement of the region. With its massive wall circuit, almost certainly the most formidable in Greece at that time, and its vast territory, Ithome simply belonged to a higher order than all the other cities of free Messene.[2] For the inhabitants of these settlements, to be Messenian suddenly meant to be subordinated, in whatever form, to a large and powerful city. That it was not Sparta any more may not have made the situation much more appealing to them. Considering these premises, it comes as no surprise that the unity of the Messenian polity turned out to be the key issue for the history of the region ever since its independence. In the Hellenistic period, articulating a Messenian identity became a way, especially for the citizens of Ithome, of promoting cohesion across the region. Ultimately, though, the centripetal force emanating from the city was incapable of keeping the whole region together. Tellingly, Messene ended up being the name of Ithome.

This chapter tries to bring together in a meaningful way the bits and pieces of Messenian history in the more than three centuries from the creation of a free Messenian polity in the Peloponnese to its last participation

---

[2] Roebuck 1941: 109.

in a war, the civil war between Augustus and Antony.[3] After an overview
of the Messenians' role in the political history of the Hellenistic world,
the scanty evidence for the political organization of Messenia will be
scrutinized. Two case studies on religious cults will help to shed light on
the evolution and transformation of the way in which Messenian ethnicity was conceived and articulated during these centuries. The observations gathered from these case studies will then be integrated with the
rest of the relevant evidence, discussed in previous chapters, in an
attempt at reconstructing the outlines of a history of the Messenian
identity from the fourth century BC to the end of the first.

THE MESSENIANS AND THE GREEK WORLD,
FROM MANTINEA TO ACTIUM

The history of the Messenians after the liberation from Sparta is a
complex puzzle, of which the ancient sources have preserved only a few
pieces.[4] In spite of the size and presumable manpower of Messenia, it is
clear that the Messenians never became major players in Peloponnesian
power politics: no significant initiative, in terms of war, peace, or alliance,
was spearheaded by them. Perhaps if we knew more about the political
structure of the region, the reasons for this low-profile foreign policy
would be obvious, but the available evidence permits only speculation.
With their cautious restraint, the Messenians resemble very much Elis,
another middle-sized Peloponnesian power, which quite often ended up
in the same field as the Messenians in the framework of international
alliances and wars. As we will see more in detail, it is possible that the
resemblance extended to the relationship in both regions between a large
dominant polis and a number of minor settlements whose political status
vis-à-vis the main polis is not always clear.[5]

   In terms of their positioning in the Greek arena, in hindsight the
Messenians seem to have tried again and again to replicate the situation
that had brought them freedom in the first place, by seeking the protection of strong allies from outside the Peloponnese – a potentially
dangerous choice in the large-scale international conflicts of the third and

---

[3] For the advent of the Augustan age as a turning point in the history of the Greek polis, marked by
the final loss of their military role, see Millar 2001.
[4] Two excellent reconstructions of the political history of Messenia from the fourth century are
offered by Roebuck 1941, who stops at 146 BC, and more recently by Grandjean 2003, especially
helpful on the numismatic evidence.
[5] On the structure of the Elean state and Elean politics in the Hellenistic age, see Roy 1999.

second centuries BC, in which choosing the wrong side could have devastating consequences. Their resistance to aligning themselves with the most powerful states of the Peloponnese is also a long-term trend, one that was destined to elicit little sympathy in the region.[6] The Messenians' troubled relationship to the Achaean League in the late third and early second centuries is a case in point. But this is a rather late phase of the story, and we have now to start at its beginning.

One of the results of the Spartan defeat at Mantinea in 362 was that the Spartans remained alone in rejecting the legitimacy of the Messenian state, a decision that effectively isolated them in the Peloponnese, bringing to completion the process that had started with the dissolution of the Peloponnesian League.[7] It would take well over a century for the Spartans to reach again a comparable position of prominence in the peninsula. However, involvement in the Sacred War must have seriously curtailed the Thebans' ability to protect their allies in the Peloponnese, and stirred their worries. The Athenians, presumably not particularly popular with the Messenians because of their alliance with Sparta, were only moderately successful in their attempt at capitalizing on the situation. In spite of a head start in concluding a defensive alliance with the Messenians probably around 356,[8] in part because of their own inability to set aside their hatred for the Thebans and their ambiguous position towards Sparta, the Athenians were not able to create a solid network in the Peloponnese and contain Philip's diplomacy.[9] Already in 348 Aeschines was helpless against Macedonian ambassadors in Megalopolis.[10] After the conclusion of the Sacred War, Philip decidedly followed in Epaminondas' footsteps and became the recognized protector of the former allies of the Thebans, especially Messenians and Megalopolitans.[11] The Athenians did not give up, and Messene concluded a new alliance with Athens in 343/2,[12] but ultimately Thebans and Athenians stood alone to face the Macedonians at Chaeronea.

---

[6] See Polybius' comments on this (4.32), and cf. Polyb. 5.20.3.

[7] Buckler 2003: 349–50. The Messenians took part in the battle, Xen. *Hell.* 7.5.4–5, Diod. 15.85.2

[8] References in Dem. *For the Megalopolitans* [18].9, of 353 BC; see Roebuck 1941: 47 and n. 93. The alliance may be referred to in Paus. 4.28.1.

[9] See Dem. *On the Peace* [5].18, from 346 BC. [10] Dem. *On the Treacherous Embassy* [19].10–12.

[11] That Philip, as early as 346 BC, was depicting himself as the protector of the Messenians, obviously against the Spartans, is clear from Isocr. *Letter to Philip* [5].74. For an overview of Philip's politics in the Peloponnese in the late 340s, see Hamilton 1982: 70–80.

[12] See the fragmentary inscription *IG* II–III² 225, where the name of the Messenians is clearly legible. The date derives from *Schol. Aesch.* 3.83, that refers specifically to an alliance of Athens with Messenians, Argives, the Arcadian League led by Mantinea, and Megalopolis in that year.

In retrospect, the battle of Chaeronea came to be seen as a turning point for the freedom of the Greeks, and not having joined the Athenians and Thebans in their last stand may have become something of an embarrassment for the Messenians.[13] At that time, however, siding with Philip turned out to be one of the best moves the Messenians could have undertaken. As we have seen, after Chaeronea the Macedonian king invaded Laconia and curtailed Spartan territory to the advantage of Messenians, Arcadians and Argives. It was presumably now that Mothone and Asine finally became Messenian, together with the Dentheliatis and the western coast of the Mani peninsula as far south as Leuktron.[14]

Philip's support is often invoked in connection with the attempt by Messene and Megalopolis to be admitted to the Delphic Amphiktyony, documented by the purported text of an Amphiktyonic decree cited in Didymus' commentary on Demosthenes.[15] No date emerges from the text itself, but the episode seems to fit the context of the reorganization of the Amphiktyony in 346/5 after the end of the Sacred War.[16] At that point, Philip took over the two seats of the Phocians, and there may have been pressure to exclude the Spartans from the Amphiktyony, since they had been allied to the sacrilegious Phocians. Messenians and Megalopolitans may have thought that there was space for them.[17] The decree grants them the title of benefactors of the Amphiktyony[18] and refers their request to be admitted to the Amphiktyony to the several members. However, since no documents attest their membership in the Amphiktyony in the following

---

[13] See Paus. 4.28.2 and his comments on Chaeronea at 1.25.3; 5.4.9; 7.15.6; 8.6.2. On Pausanias' view of Chaeronea as one of the "black days" of Greek freedom, see Akujärvi 2005: 247–52; in general, on the turning points of the history of Greek freedom as seen by Pausanias, see Habicht 1998a: 105–7. Notice however that as late as the second century BC, the issue of the impact of Macedonian power on Greek freedom was still controversial, see the debate at Sparta in 210 reported in Polyb. 9.28–39.

[14] On the events linked to the acquisition of Dentheliatis, see above, p. 17. For an estimate of the territorial growth of Messene thanks to Philip, see Grandjean 2003: 69 (whose calculation assumes that the territory of the perioikic towns east of the Pamisos became Messenian only now; *contra* see above, pp. 32–3 and 229). On Asine and Mothone in particular see Henning 1996: 21–2.

[15] Didymus *In Demosth.* 4.2–13 Pearson-Stephens. The text has normally been accepted as the genuine, if perhaps slightly doctored, transcription of an inscription, and is therefore present in collections of inscriptions, *Syll.*[3] 221 and *CID* IV 7, with extensive commentary. See also Harding 2006: 117–21 with further references.

[16] See Sánchez 2001: 199–219 and 259–61.

[17] But hardly as replacement for the Spartans, who shared their seat in the Amphiktyony with the Dorians of central Greece (Lefèvre 1998: 53–4). The Messenians may have hoped to be attached to the group of the Dorian cities of the Peloponnese (Corinth, Sikyon, Phleious, Argos, Epidauros, and Troizen); it is more difficult to figure out how the Megalopolitans could have been integrated. See *CID* IV 7 and Lefèvre's commentary.

[18] The only example of this title being granted to cities; otherwise, the title of benefactor of the Amphiktyony was attributed only once, to an individual, in the first century BC. See Lefèvre 1998: 233.

centuries, the request of Messene and Megalopolis must have been rejected.[19]

Certainly this diplomatic maneuver had something to do with a climate in which, in part because of the propaganda associated with the Sacred War, the Panhellenic dimension of the Amphiktyony had received a new emphasis. The Arcadians had lived happily for centuries without being members of the Amphiktyony, but for the new city of Megalopolis, planted in a partially hostile environment, recognition at that level may have seemed especially desirable. The same is true of Messene, whose legitimacy had been contested for a good decade after its foundation. Both may have seen access to the Amphiktyony as a way to make the fact of their existence irreversible.

The pro-Macedonian stance, in spite of its fruitfulness, seems to have been less than uncontroversial among the Messenians. From an aside in a spurious speech transmitted in the corpus of Demosthenes we learn that the main promoters of the pro-Macedonian line, Neon and Thrasylochos, sons of Philiadas, were exiled at some point, presumably after Philip's death, and returned thanks to Alexander.[20] Even though it is impossible to tell for sure why they were exiled, the Messenians' inconsistent attitude to Macedonians and Athenians in the years before Chaeronea seems to offer a plausible scenario for civil strife tied to diverging orientations in foreign politics. Although the Messenians, like Megalopolitans and Argives, did not join the anti-Macedonian uprising of their old enemies the Spartans in 331, immediately after Alexander's death we find them on the side of the rebels in the Lamian War (Diod. 18.11.2; Paus. 1.25.4, 4.28.3). As a result of the defeat, we may suppose that a pro-Macedonian oligarchy was imposed on them, especially since a later inscription seems to refer to the return of exiles.

Antipater's death in 319 and the conflict between his son Cassander and Polyperchon, to whom Antipater bequeathed his position, brought about

---

[19] Sánchez 2001: 259–61 is probably right in seeing in the rejection evidence of the fact that Philip had not transformed the Amphiktyony into an executor of his orders.

[20] Ps.-Dem. *On the Treaty with Alexander* [17].4 and 7, with the commentary of Culasso Gastaldi 1984: 37–8 and 42–3. In the speech, probably originating in Athens in the early third century and based on solid information (see Culasso Gastaldi 1984: 159–83), Neon and Thrasylochos are called tyrants, but this, more than their actual position in Messene, is likely to reflect Demosthenes' tendency to call tyrants all those who were in favor of the Macedonians, and of course Philip himself (see e.g. *Fourth Philippic* [10].4); cf. also Berve 1967: 308. These Messenian politicians and their father were the target of Demosthenes' outrage, *On the Crown* [18].295, a passage famous enough to provoke Polybius' reply, 18.13–15. The accusation of bribery leveled at them is likely to derive from Demosthenes' bias, but see Cargill 1985. On Demosthenes' personal involvement in the attempt at bringing the Messenians on Athens' side, see Habicht 1997: 126.

a new situation, internal and international. Polyperchon's decree proclaiming the freedom of the Greeks (Diod. 18.56) also granted the right of return to exiles, and one of Polyperchon's goals was to overthrow the oligarchies set up by Antipater, and now potential allies of Cassander. An inscription from Ithome, referring to an agreement between the Ithomaeans and two kings, and probably to measures to ensure the return of exiles, is likely to date to this moment and to refer to an alliance with Polyperchon.[21] Ithome seems to have remained firmly on Polyperchon's side, and Cassander failed twice in the attempt at taking control of it, in 316 and in 315 (Diod. 19.54.4, 64.1); in the second case, a garrison of Polyperchon in the city is mentioned. However, in 316 Cassander was able to win over all the other poleis of Messene.[22] Whatever the political structure that united the Messenians at this time, it was obviously breaking apart.

Ithome seems to have remained faithful to Polyperchon until his death, probably in the very last years of the fourth century.[23] There is no evidence that the Messenians joined the Hellenic League created by Antigonos and Demetrios in 302. Demetrios besieged Messene in 295 and was almost killed by a bolt. It is not clear whether he had the better of the powerful fortifications.[24] Probably in this period an alliance was concluded with king Lysimachos, Demetrios' enemy.[25] This time, the party that concludes the treaty is called "the Messenians," which may imply renewed unity in Messene. Again, exiles are mentioned, but this time the treaty seems to include clauses against their return.

For most of the third century, we hear about the Messenians only insofar as they were involved in broader conflicts, mostly for control of the Peloponnese. The loss of the Dentheliatis to Sparta could go back to

---

[21] *SEG* 43.135. See now the detailed study of this inscription by Matthaiou 2001: 221–7; the date suggested is between Polyperchon's proclamation late in 319 and the death of Philip the Third Arrhydaios in 317. Diod. 18.69.3–4 mentions Polyperchon's appeal to the cities of the Peloponnese to conclude an alliance with him and eliminate the oligarchies installed by Antipater, followed by massacres and exiles in the cities. On Polyperchon's activity after Antipater's death, see Heckel 1992: 192–204.

[22] In view of these events, it seems hard to believe Pausanias' passage (9.7.1) according to which the Messenians had participated in the reconstruction of Thebes by Cassander in 316 (see above, p. 220 n. 37), unless it refers to Messenians from the minor cities, not from Ithome – an interesting possibility which cannot be explored further for lack of evidence.

[23] See Heckel 1992: 204. A relief with a royal hunt from Ithome, now in the Louvre, almost certainly inspired by the famous statuary group dedicated by Craterus at Delphi (Jacquemin 1999: 204–5 and 341 no. 350), may come from Polyperchon's funerary monument, according to the attractive suggestion of Palagia 2000: 202–6.

[24] On Demetrios' attack, see Plut. *Demetr.* 33.3–4; on the result of the siege, see Roebuck 1941: 61 and n. 13 and cf. Plut. *Dem.* 13.4.

[25] *SEG* 41.322; on the chronology and the historical circumstances, see Matthaiou 2001: 231.

the early 270s.[26] The Messenians' attitude to Pyrrhus, who invaded the Peloponnese in 272 BC, is ultimately unclear.[27] A successful expedition in support of the anti-Spartan faction of Elis may fall in these years, and a list of Messenians who died in Makistos in Triphylia, dated to the third century and possibly connected to a monument erected above the stadium of Messene, could belong in the same context.[28] The following decades must have seen the Messenians entering the sphere of influence of Aetolia, possibly with a view to finding a new protector against the encroachment of other Peloponnesian powers, such as Sparta but also the nascent Achaean League. It is in this framework that, probably around 240 BC, a treaty of *isopoliteia* and *epigamia* was concluded between the Messenians and Phigaleia, under the auspices of the Aetolian League, putting an end to border disputes between the two parties.[29] It is probably in this framework that the Aetolian cult of Artemis Laphria was introduced in Messene (Paus. 4.31.7).[30] This cautious line seems to have secured peace for the Messenians for a few decades. There is no evidence of their direct involvement in the conflicts between the Aetolians, the Achaeans, and Sparta, nor in the war against Demetrios the Second.

Uninterested as they were in intruding in Peloponnesian affairs beyond what was necessary to avoid the emergence of a serious threat, the Aetolians were ideal allies for the Messenians – as for any other mid-size power with no hegemonic aspirations, such as for instance the Eleans, who significantly often ended up on the same side as the Messenians during the third and second centuries. The alliance between Aetolians and Achaeans posed a first threat to the policy of splendid isolation pursued by

---

[26] See Roebuck 1941: 62.

[27] Iust. 25.4.4 speaks of Messenian ambassadors to Pyrrhos, Paus. 4.29.6 of Messenian support for the Spartans against Pyrrhos; see Grandjean 2003: 74.

[28] The Messenian expedition to Elis is mentioned in Paus. 4.28.4–6; on its possible historical context, see Roebuck 1941: 63–4 and Grandjean 2003: 74. The inscription, *SEG* 47.406, and the monument it may belong to are discussed in Themelis 2001: 199–201. An early third-century date for the inscription is made more likely by the fact that Makistos seems to have disappeared during the century – or at least, it is not mentioned by any other source as existing after the fourth century: see Nielsen 2002: 456–8.

[29] *IG* V 2, 419 = Ager 40 (where the inscription is connected to two others relating to border controversies, *IG* V 1, 1429 and 1430; see Harter-Uibopuu 1998: 46–52) = Magnetto 38. On the relations between Messenians and Aetolians during the first half of the second century, see Grandjean 2003: 75. Two different interpretations of Aetolian politics in the Peloponnese are offered by Grainger 1999: 159–63 (who suggests a date late in 240 for the treaty between Phigaleia and the Messenians) and Scholten 2000: 118–23.

[30] Pausanias says that the cult was first imported by the Messenians in Naupaktos in the fifth century, but this is extremely unlikely, especially in view of their hostile relations to Kalydon, the main center of the cult, on which see above, p. 188. On the sanctuary of Artemis Laphria at Kalydon, which functioned as one of the centers of the Aetolian League, see Antonetti 1990: 243.

the Messenians. It was probably during the war against Demetrios the Second that Pylos became a member of the Achaean League.[31] The Messenians were drawn closer and closer to the Achaeans, and even though they were still able to remain aloof from the Cleomenic War, while at the same time apparently profiting from it, for the peace they had so successfully pursued the days were numbered.[32] Antigonos Doson's involvement in the Cleomenic War resulted in reestablishing Macedonian power in central Greece and the Peloponnese, while at the same time the alliance with Macedonia and the victory over Cleomenes strengthened the Achaean League. The Aetolians felt threatened. It was probably in an attempt at reining in their few remaining Peloponnesian allies (Polyb. 4.5.8) that, immediately after the death of Antigonos Doson, the Aetolians launched pillage expeditions against Messene – as Ithome was by now called – from their base in Phigaleia, thereby setting in motion the mechanism that would finally bring about the Social War.

The situation in Messene may have been complicated by internal conflict between factions, which are likely to have pursued divergent options in foreign policy. When Cleomenes conquered Megalopolis in 223, he was allegedly let into the city by Messenian exiles, but it was to Messene that the Megalopolitans themselves fled once their city fell.[33] When the Aetolian Dorimachos organized unofficial attacks on Messene from Phigaleia, in the summer of 221, using mercenaries rather than Aetolian troops (Polyb. 4.3.5–11), he may have been trying to deter the pro-Achaean faction in the city and reinforce the pro-Aetolian. However, the only result of his maneuvers was to push the Messenians towards Achaea. When renewed raids were launched from Phigaleia the following year, this time by forces of the Aetolian League (Polyb. 4.6.7–12), the Messenians reacted by turning for help to the Achean League, then under the leadership of Aratus of Sikyon (Polyb. 4.7.2).[34] The Messenians'

[31] See Polyb. 4.25.4. Marasco 1980: 120–1 thinks that the Messenians themselves had given over Pylos to the Achaean League, in search for protection against the raids of Illyrian pirates (see in general Polyb. 2.5.2, and Paus. 4.35.6–7 on an Illyrian raid against Mothone, apparently around 230 BC); however, even though the threat of the pirates may well have been the key factor that brought Pylos into the League, it seems difficult to believe that this might have happened with the Messenians' consent, especially considering that in the following years they repeatedly asked for Pylos to be returned to them, see below n. 40.

[32] On the relations between Achaeans and Messenians in the third quarter of the third century, see Grandjean 2003: 77. It was probably after the battle of Sellasia in 222 BC that the Dentheliatis became Messenian again, see above, p. 18.

[33] See Grandjean 2003: 77, Grainger 1999: 233–4.

[34] See Grainger 1999: 254–61, Scholten 2000: 203–5. It is likely that the Messenians concluded an alliance with the Achaean League at this point, see Roebuck 1941: 74–5. According to Pausanias,

request to be admitted to the Hellenic League created by Doson could not be granted by the Achaeans themselves, but they promised support for the Messenians' request and military help against the Aetolians. It is certainly indicative of how the Achaeans estimated the Messenians' commitment on this occasion that they also asked for Messenian hostages to be sent to Sparta, in order to guarantee against the risk that the Messenians themselves might return to the Aetolian side (Polyb. 4.9.5).

The Social War ended up being an inconclusive power struggle between Macedonians, Achaeans, and Aetolians, from which the Messenians derived neither significant advantages nor serious damage. After Philip the Fifth, fresh on the Macedonian throne, admitted the Messenians to the Hellenic League, they at first refused to take part in military operations as long as the Aetolian threat from Phigaleia was not neutralized (Polyb. 4.31.1). Their fleet participated in Philip's campaign against Kephallenia in 218 (Polyb. 5.3.3, 4.4), and in the same year the Spartan king Lycurgus, the new ally of the Aetolians, made an expedition into Messenia (Polyb. 5.5.1). Later in the year, when Philip marched into the Peloponnese, a Messenian army of 2,000 infantrymen and 200 horsemen got underway to join him, but was defeated rather ingloriously, if without too much damage, by Lycurgus at Glympeis, on the border between Laconia and the Argolid on Mount Parnon (Polyb. 5.20.1–10). The following year, Spartans and Aetolians organized a converging offensive, but the Aetolian contingent, which invaded Messenia marching along the coast from Elis, was stopped at Kyparissia. Lycurgus succeeded in conquering Kalamai, but the following course of his campaign cannot be reconstructed with certainty; in any case, once he realized that the Aetolians had been stopped, he himself left Messenia.[35] It is unclear

the Messenians were members of the Achaean League already before Cleomenes' conquest of Megalopolis in 223 (4.29.7), and they took part in the Sellasia campaign and in the conquest of Sparta the following year (4.29.9). Neither of these notices appears in any other source, and Messenian membership in the Achaean League during the Cleomenic War makes nonsense of Polybius' detailed narrative of the outbreak of the Social War. Pausanias' testimony is accordingly mostly rejected by scholars – often silently. Messenian participation in the Sellasia campaign is more often taken seriously, see e.g. Seeliger 1897: 8; Fine 1940: 155–6 and recently Le Bohec 1993: 414–5; see, however, the arguments against this view in Roebuck 1941: 70–1, Grandjean 2003: 77. Fine mentions Doson's decision in favor of the Messenians as supporting Pausanias on the Messenians at Sellasia; however, if one looks at the strife for the Dentheliatis in its entirety, the argument is not very strong. For a partial cautiously optimistic approach to Pausanias' testimony, see Grandjean 2003: 71. For an explanation of the origin of Pausanias' ideas on the relationship of the Messenians with the Achaean League see below, pp. 325–6.

[35] The only source on this campaign is Polyb. 5.91.3 and 92.2–7. After conquering Kalamai, Lycurgus is said to have attacked another place, whose name is preserved in corrupted form and has been emended to either Andania or Antheia (see Walbank 1957: 623–4); in spite of Valmin 1930: 55–6,

whether Kalamai remained in Spartan hands after the peace of Naupaktos in 217.[36]

The years between the peace of Naupaktos and the First Macedonian War were extremely troubled for the Messenians. Hints of constitutional change may suggest civil strife as early as 219. In any case, by 215 times were ripe: *stasis* seems to have erupted even before Philip reached the city. The king, whose very presence in the Peloponnese may have had to do with his plan to turn civil strife in Messene to his own advantage, is made responsible by Plutarch for the actual outbreak of violence, culminating in a massacre of magistrates and prominent citizens and a democratic reform of the constitution.[37] The oligarchs who had ruled the city at the time of the Social War were finally ousted. The Polybian tradition claims that it was Aratus who dissuaded Philip from taking control in this occasion, against the advice of Demetrios of Pharos, the king's evil right-hand-man,[38] and clearly the fortress of Messene was an attractive goal for the king. In 214, Demetrios of Pharos was killed during an attack on Messene, and the following year the king himself led an expedition which ravaged the countryside, but the massive fortifications of the city successfully defied him.[39]

Philip's aggression, and probably also the Achaeans' attempts at dismembering Messenia,[40] pushed the Messenians back towards the Aetolians. It is not clear exactly when an alliance with Aetolia was concluded, but the Messenians were on the Roman–Aetolian side during the

the former seems more likely, see Roebuck 1941: 7 n. 16; the spelling Ἐνδανία for Andania in a new inscription from Messene reinforces this conclusion, see Themelis, *Praktika* 2004: 44 n. 30.

[36] See Grandjean 2003: 79 n. 121.

[37] The relevant evidence, Polyb. 7.10.1 and 12 and Plut. *Arat.* 49.3–50, is difficult to reduce to a consistent narrative. See Roebuck 1941: 81–2. Walbank (1967: 57) is probably right to maintain that Polyb. 7.10.1 describes the situation after the upheaval mentioned by Plutarch rather than an earlier outbreak of civil strife, *pace* Mendels 1980; the fact that the property of exiled citizens had been distributed to the victorious faction can hardly amount to the establishment of a timocracy, as Mendels would have it. On the appearance of *stratēgoi* as leading magistrates in the city at the time the conflict erupted, in contrast to the ephors mentioned at the beginning of the Social War, see Grandjean 2003: 78–9.

[38] According to Polyb. 7.12.2–3, Demetrios urged the king to seize both horns in order to subdue the bull, that is, as Polybius explains, to occupy the fortresses of Corinth and Messene if he wanted to control the Peloponnese.

[39] See Polyb. 3.19.11 (Demetrios' attack, presumably the same mentioned in Paus. 4.29.1–7, who mistakenly attributes it to Philip's son Demetrios) and 8.8.1–4 (Philip's attack).

[40] Pylos had joined the Achaean League before the Social War (see above, n. 31) and in 209 the Aetolians were claiming it back for the Messenians (Liv. 27.30.10). Asine became Achaean before 196 (Polyb. 18.42.7), almost certainly before the Second Macedonian War, when the Messenians were on the Roman side, and possibly during the First Macedonian War: see Walbank 1967: 606–7 and Henning 1996: 24.

First Macedonian War;[41] Messenia appears to have been invaded by the Achaeans in 210/9,[42] troops sent by the Messenians, probably consisting of mercenaries, garrisoned Delphi possibly in 209/8,[43] and finally the Messenians turn up as *adscripti*, together with Sparta and Elis, to the Peace of Phoinike between Rome and Philip in 205 (Liv. 29.12.8–16).[44] Soon after the peace, the tyrant king of Sparta Nabis attacked Messene by surprise, captured the city, could not take the fortifications of the acropolis, and was finally chased away by Philopoimen who rushed in from Megalopolis.[45] Factions in Messene itself, favoring respectively the Spartans and the Achaeans, have been postulated, perhaps unnecessarily, as a background for this episode.[46] Allied to the Romans during the Second Macedonian War, in which they do not seem to have taken part actively, after the war the Messenians saw their request for being given back Asine and Pylos frustrated.[47] All they could get was the possibility of retrieving from Sparta the booty taken by Nabis at Messene in 201 once Flamininus finally decided to discipline the Spartan king in 195 and mounted a campaign against him, in which Messenian troops participated.[48]

It is not completely certain that the Messenians followed the Aetolians in siding with Antiochus the Third when the latter invaded Greece in 192.[49]

---

[41] Almost certainly before the Aetolian embassy to Sparta, in the spring of 210; see Grainger 1999: 316–17.

[42] Liv. 27.33.5 refers to an Achaean victory over Aetolians and Eleans "not far from Messene." See Errington 1969: 59.

[43] The evidence consists of four decrees voted by the Delphians, *FD* III iv, 21–4 = *Syll.*³ 555–6, two bestowing honors on the "polis of the Messenians," and two on the Messenian generals who had led the garrison troops (at least in one case, clearly mercenaries). On only one of the inscriptions has the dating formula been preserved completely: *FD* III iv, 23 is dated to the year of the Delphic archon Alexeas, probably 209/8; see Lefèvre 1998: 312. The decrees were inscribed, appropriately, on the triangular pillar dedicated by the Messenians during the fifth century, see above, p. 191 and figure 4.

[44] On the implications of this, see Roebuck 1941: 86–7.

[45] On this episode, see Roebuck 1941: 88–9 with full discussion of the sources.

[46] Errington 1969: 78–80; on his hypothesis of factions in Messene, cf. Grandjean 2003: 81.

[47] Territorial claims against the Achaean League presented to the Senate by Messenians and Eleans are mentioned in Polyb. 18.42.7. The Senate deferred the claims to the commission of ten senators operating with Flamininus, which at least in the case of Elis, but probably also in that of the Messenians, decided in favor of the Achaean League; see Roebuck 1941: 90 and n. 109.

[48] Liv. 34.35.6; see Roebuck 1941: 91. On Flamininus' campaign against Nabis, see Ferrary 1988: 88–95.

[49] Roebuck 1941: 91 and n. 113 suggests that, like the Eleans, the Messenians also sided with the Aetolians, for otherwise their preexisting alliance with Rome would have protected them against retaliation by the Achaeans; see also Errington 1969: 123. However, actual Messenian participation in the war is mentioned only in a retrospective and rather confused passage of Livy (42.37.8, where Messenians and Eleans are also said to have been *hostes* of the Romans in the war against Philip), and one wonders how far Livy's *cum Aetoliis sentiebant* ("sympathized for the Aetolians," 36.31.2) can be pressed. Flamininus' decision (see below), which was not explicitly unfavorable to the Messenians, may have been dictated by Realpolitik after all; for divergent evaluations of Flamininus' intervention, see Errington 1969: 123–4 and Ferrary 1988: 122–3.

In any case, once the Seleucid army evacuated Greece the Achaeans, now allies of Rome, felt the time had come finally to come to grips with them. In 191, the Messenians refused to join the Achaean League and prepared for war. With an Achaean army led by Diophanes of Megalopolis laying waste to the countryside and besieging Messene, they sent for help to Flamininus at Chalcis, offering their *deditio* to Rome. Flamininus intimated to Diophanes to lift the siege and summoned him to Andania, where he announced his decision: the Messenians were ordered to take back the exiles and join the Achaean League (Liv. 36.31.1–10). Probably in this occasion some more of the Messenian cities became independent members of the Achaean League.[50]

The expansion of the Achaean League to the whole of the Peloponnese caused widespread discontent. At Messene, the main reason must have been the loss of control over the minor cities of the region. The Achaean League did not normally accept federal states of whatever sort as members. Based on the measures taken later in 182 (see below), a partial exception appears to have been made for the Messenians at this stage: it seems that the cities of the lower Pamisos valley and possibly Kyparissia remained tied in some ways to Messene instead of becoming independent members of the League.[51] Still, the loss of the whole Akritas Peninsula represented a massive curtailment. Local party strife in Messene may have further complicated the situation, although this is far from certain.[52]

[50] Roebuck 1941: 94 and n. 124 considers the cases of Korone, Kolonides, Kyparissia, and Mothone. Korone is the best candidate, since a decade later, when they revolted against the Achaean League, the Messenians were planning to attack it (Liv. 39.49.1). For Mothone there is actually no direct evidence, but isolated as it was in the southwestern corner of the Akritas Peninsula, it is not very likely to have remained linked to Messene. The case of Kyparissia is more controversial: Roebuck wonders if it may have been autonomous since 220 or 213, but note that Messene sent ships to Philip during the Social War, and once Kyparissia was gone Messene had no access to the sea. Kyparissia appears as the harbor of Messene in *IG* IX 1², 1475 line 29, the decree of Leucas for Damophon, probably from the early second century. Note that Polyb. 28.16.3 says that Eleans and Messenians expected a Roman attack from the sea in 146, which again suggests some Messenian control of the western shore of the region.

[51] Roebuck 1941: 93 suggests that this may have been due to Flamininus' personal intervention. However, splitting members to their smallest components was by no means a consistently followed policy for the League; other cases of cities which joined the League but retained control of smaller towns in their territory are discussed by Niccolini 1914: 245–6. The most interesting case is Philopoimen's attempt at detaching Arcadian towns from Megalopolis in 194 or thereabouts, see Plut. *Phil.* 13.5 and Errington 1969: 90–1.

[52] See the discussion in Roebuck 1941: 94–5 and nn. 126 and 127. Diophanes' protests against Philopoimen's actions with regard to the Messenian exiles, presented to Caecilius Metellus at Isthmia in 185 (Polyb. 22.10.4–6), are linked to the internal power struggle among the leadership of the Achaean League, and do not necessarily reflect accurately the reasons for the Messenians' discontent with the League itself.

Already in the winter of 184/3, the Messenian politician Dinocrates, trusting his personal ties to Flamininus that went back to the campaign against Sparta in 196/5, came to Rome in search for support. He does not seem to have appeared in front of the Senate, but may have been able to arrange for supplies to be shipped from Italy to Messene to prepare for war.[53] Then he returned to Greece in the fall of 183 with Flamininus, who had been appointed as a legate to Prusias of Bithynia. Flamininus tried to have a meeting of the Achaean League arranged in order to plead the cause of the Messenians, but Philopoimen, then *stratēgos* of the League, realizing that Flamininus was not acting under explicit instructions of the Senate, refused. The Messenians prepared for revolt. Probably on this occasion, a new series of tetradrachms was minted, with the traditional types of Zeus Ithomatas striding and the head of Demeter, and the legend Μεσσανίων Ἰθωμ(αίων). The message was clear: in the attempt at recovering control of the whole region, the city recalled its original status as only one part, if the largest, of a broader polity whose citizens were collectively called "the Messenians." The only recorded measure taken by the rebels, an attack on the city of Korone (Liv. 39.49.1), confirms that regaining control of the region was at least one of the main items on the agenda.[54]

The revolt was curbed by the army of the Achaean League, led by Polybius' father Lykortas, but not before the Messenians were able to capture Philopoimen, who rather rashly rode into Messenia with a small contingent of troops to rescue Korone. The aged Achaean general died in captivity in Messene, possibly poisoned.[55] Boeotian ambassadors, who had reached Messene earlier to mediate between Messenians and Achaeans, appear to have had some role in the peace agreement (Polyb. 23.16.4–5). Even though Polybius goes out of his way to characterize the conditions imposed by the Achaeans as mild (23.17.1), in fact the treatment meted out to the Messenians was rather harsh: a significant portion of the ruling elite of Messene was wiped out (Polyb. 24.9.13), Messenian prisoners were stoned to death on Philopoimen's tomb (Plut. *Phil.* 21.5), the few cities

---

[53] See Errington 1969: 244, based on Polyb. 23.9.12.

[54] Plutarch, referring to the same events, speaks of a planned attack on Kolonides (*Phil.* 18.5); see Roebuck 1941: 99 and n. 146 and Errington 1969: 190 and n. 2. The two towns being located a few kilometers apart on the western coast of the Messenian Gulf, Livy and Plutarch may well refer to the same operation, involving attacking both.

[55] Reasonable doubts on the story of the poisoning of Philopoimen are expressed by Errington 1969: 192–3. For the chronology of the war, see id.: 241–5, dating Philopoimen's death to May or June 182 and the surrender of the Messenians shortly thereafter, before the meeting of the Achaean League in July 182.

that had remained under Messene's control, Abia, Thouria, and Pharai, became independent members of the League, and probably the territory of Messene itself was curtailed to the advantage of Megalopolis.[56]

After the defeat at the hands of the Achaean League in 182, the Messenians all but disappear from the political scene for more than a century. In spite of being members of the League, they do not seem to have supplied any federal magistrates or to have ever hosted a meeting of the federal assembly. At the time of the war of the Achaean League against Rome, there is no trace of direct involvement on their part, nor of Roman retaliation against them. On the contrary, they were confirmed in control of the Dentheliatis soon after 146 BC in the face of Spartan encroachment on the region (above, p. 19). This may also have been the moment when Andania, and with it presumably the plain of Stenykleros, was given back to the Messenians.[57] It is extremely difficult to tell whether, with the fall of the Achaean League, the Messenian cities that had been independent members of the League returned to some sort of closer relationship to Messene. The fact that after 146 some of them had their own distinct coinage and political structures, which could produce their own decrees, suggests at least that, if such a relationship came about at all, it cannot have been very close, and in any case there is no reason to speak of dependence.[58]

Little is known of the history of the Messenians after the Achaean War. A large monument from the agora of Messene, recently excavated, that carried at least three statues of prominent Romans, Sulla, L. Licinius Murena, and the legate Cn. Manlius Agrippa, was erected between 83 and 81 BC and must be linked in some way to the First Mithridatic War. There is no clear evidence that Messenians were directly involved in the

---

[56] On the measures taken by the Achaeans see Roebuck 1941: 102 and n. 167 and Grandjean 2003: 228. The suggestion that Strabo's calling Andania "an Arcadian town" (8.3.6, quoting Demetrius of Skepsis, mid second century BC) reflects the situation that obtained after the war with the Achaean League is confirmed by a new inscription from the agora of Messene, detailing the curtailment of the territory of Messene probably in consequence of the war; see Themelis, *Praktika* 2004: 45–6.

[57] Grandjean 2003: 230. Messenian control of Andania is of course attested by the inscription of the mysteries, *IG* V 1, 1390, currently dated to 91/90 BC, on the assumption that the 55 year in line 52 is to be counted according to the era of the province of Achaea; see now, however, now Themelis, *Praktika* 2001: 75–9, proposing to refer the year to the Actian era and thereby dating the inscription to 24 AD, and the discussion below, pp. 292–9.

[58] See Grandjean 2003: 153–5 on the silver coinage with civic types minted by Korone and 222–4 on the bronze coinage of Thouria, both dated by her between the second half of the second century and the early first. The possible restoration of some sort of federal structure in Messenia must be seen in the framework of the wider problem of the meaning of Paus. 7.16.9–10 on the Romans allowing the restoration of the *synedria kata ethnos* in Greece "not many years" after the Achaean War; see Kallet-Marx 1995: 57–96, esp. 76–82.

war, and therefore it has been suggested that they may have had reasons to be grateful to these Roman magistrates having to do e.g. with being spared on the occasion of collections of funds, food, or forage for the Roman army.[59]

However, there may be reason to think that some fighting did indeed take place in Messenia in connection with the Mithridatic War. A rather puzzling passage in Polyaenus (2.35) refers to a pirate Nikon who used Pharai as his base to plunder the Messenians, was ambushed and captured by the Messenian general Agemachos, and agreed to help the Messenians to penetrate inside the city, which they were thereby able to conquer. If he was the same pirate who was captured by Servilius Vatia Isauricus, the episode should predate the latter's campaign in Cilicia between 77 and 75 BCE.[60] Now, there is evidence that the Laconians, that is, the former *perioikoi* of Sparta who had been made independent by Flamininus in 195 BC after the war against Nabis, supported Archelaos, Mithridates' general, in 87 BC,[61] and Mithridates is supposed to have unleashed pirates in the eastern Mediterranean during the 80s.[62] These events seem to offer a promising historical context for the presence of a – presumably – Cilician pirate at Pharai on the coast of Messenia. If that is the case, the Messenians may have been involved more directly in the war, and correspondingly, the monument for Sulla, Murena, and Agrippa may have to do with such involvement. As a further corollary, if the Messenian conquest of Pharai narrated by Polyaenus does indeed belong in this historical context, then of course the episode offers no evidence on the position of Pharai vis-à-vis Messene in the years before the war.

During the civil wars, the Messenians seem to have failed to choose the right side with remarkable consistency.[63] There is no explicit evidence that they supported Pompey against Caesar, but that seems to have been the general attitude among the Greeks. Then their old enemies the Spartans were quicker in siding with Octavian and Antony against Brutus and

---

[59] The chronology of this monument and possible occasions for its dedication are discussed in Dohnicht and Heil 2004.

[60] The capture and recapture of the "famous pirate" Nico by Servilius is mentioned in Cic. *II Verr.* 5.79. On Servilius' campaign against the Cilician pirates, see de Souza 1999: 128–31.

[61] Laconian cities on Mithridates' side: App. *Mithr.* 29; see Spawforth, in Cartledge and Spawforth 2002: 94–5. On the separation of the Laconian *perioikoi* from Sparta, see Kennell 1999: 190–3.

[62] App. *Mithr.* 92–3. The collaboration between Mithridates and Cilician pirates is regarded with some skepticism by de Souza 1999: esp. 116–18, who sees in the sources reflections of Roman propaganda; cf. however Pohl 1993: 140 and n. 234, who puts the cooperation between Mithridates and the pirates in the broader framework of opposition to the Roman domination.

[63] See Grandjean 2003: 248–9.

Cassius and with Augustus against Antony, while the Messenians apparently supported Antony. As a result, the Dentheliatis, Thouria, and Kardamyle were assigned to Sparta, and Pharai and Gerenia to the league of the Eleutherolaconians. Only under Tiberius the Dentheliatis was finally recovered – but that is part of another story (see above, pp. 21–2).

THE MESSENIAN POLITY, OR PLAYING WITH NAMES

In the foregoing section, the word "Messenian" has mostly been used in a consciously inconsistent way, reflecting the usage of the sources themselves. For indeed, in the majority of cases it is unclear whether by speaking of "Messenians" our sources refer to the citizens of the city sometimes called Ithome or to the inhabitants of the region, whatever their political ties to the dominant city. On close scrutiny, this lack of precision may turn out to reflect an objectively ambiguous and volatile situation, in which the political structure that connected the minor Messenian towns to the city at Mount Ithome may have changed in form and function depending on the power relations that obtained in any given period.

The nature of the new Messenian state created in 369 BC and the way the relations between Ithome and the other Messenians were structured are difficult to grasp.[64] To some scholars the position of Ithome in the Messenian polity recalls the position of Thebes in the Boeotian League at the time of Epaminondas,[65] which would not be a surprise in general terms, but the sources give not the faintest hint as to how far this similarity might have gone. The Arcadian League is also a possible model, although it was less obviously centripetal than Messene. In an anonymous Periplus whose author is usually called the Pseudo-Skylax, apparently dating to the last quarter of the fourth century, Messene is described as an *ethnos*, and Ithome is one of its poleis. However, a few lines later Lacedaemon is described as an *ethnos*, too.[66] Documents from the second half of the fourth century suggest that Messene may have been a federal state of some sort: in two proxeny decrees from Delphi, inscribed on the pillar dedicated by the Messenians of Naupaktos in the fifth century, the beneficiaries are called respectively a "Messenian from Thouria" and a

---

[64] See Roebuck 1941: 109–17, Meyer 1978: 282–4 and now especially Grandjean 2003: 99–101.
[65] See Buckler 1980: 21–33 and Beck 1997: 100–6.
[66] Ps.-Skyl. 45 with the comments of Grandjean 2002: 545. For a dating of this work to the years 338–335 BCE, see Marcotte 1986: 170–2.

"Messenian from Ithome," with the pairing of city ethnic and regional ethnic that is commonly found for citizens of federal states.[67] Another proxeny decree, a few years later, inscribed in the same place, refers to two individuals as "Asinaeans from Messene" or "from Messenia," with a formulation that might reflect conceptions on the ethnic origin of the Asinaeans more than any aspect of the political structure of the Messenian state.[68]

In the following century, evidence for a Messenian federal state is very scarce and unclear. The embassy from Magnesia that came to announce the new Panhellenic competition for Artemis Leukophryene in 208 BC is said to have brought back a decree by the *koinon* of the Messenians, and in spite of authoritative doubts as to the specificity of this designation, it may not be prudent to exclude that this may be a *bona fide* description of the Messenian state at the end of the third century.[69] It should be noted, however, that well before then, in a sympolity treaty concluded with the Arcadian city of Phigaleia around 240 BC,[70] we find the "polis of the Messenians," whose citizens are simply called "the Messenians." The same terminology appears in the decree with which the Messenians recognized the asylia for the temple of Asklepios in Kos, answering to an embassy from Kos in the summer of 242 BC,[71] and in four decrees of the Delphians from the end of the third century (see above, p. 261 n. 43).

On the other hand, evidence discussed above shows that in the late third and early second centuries ties of some sort did exist between the Messenians, understood as the citizens of Messene, and the other cities of the region, or at least, some of them. So much is implied by the

---

[67] *FD* III iv, 5–6, 322/1 and 321/20 BC respectively according to Sánchez 2001: 519. Notice however that the use of city ethnic and regional ethnic is sometimes found also in the absence of a real federal organization; see the example of fifth-century Achaea discussed in Freitag 2008.

[68] *SEG* 12.219, dated 315/14 BC by Sánchez 2001; see above, p. 42.

[69] *IvM* 43 = Rigsby 93, lines 6 and 16–17. Holleaux 1917: 344–5 points out correctly that in Hellenistic inscriptions κοινόν is sometimes used as a synonym of πόλις. Along the same lines, see also Grandjean 2003: 97–8 and n. 30, with further references. However, in the asylia decrees from Magnesia the word κοινόν seems to be used consistently in its normal meaning, see *Syll.*³ 923 = Rigsby 67, lines 8–9 (Aetolians); *IvM* 25 = Rigsby 73, lines 1–2 (Boeotians); *IvM* 34 = Rigsby 84, lines 1, 28 (Phocians); *IvM* 39 = Rigsby 89, lines 3–4 (Achaeans); *IvM* 46 = Rigsby 96, line 11 (Cretans). Cities are called either πόλις or δῆμος.

[70] *IG* V 2, 419 = Ager 40 = Magnetto 38; for the date, see above, n. 29.

[71] *SEG* 12.371, lines 6–19 = Rigsby 15. The asylia is approved by οἱ Μεσσάνιοι in name of οἱ Μεσσάνιοι καί οἱ ἐν Μεσσάναι κατοικεῦντες; the same formulation is found in *SEG* 12.371, lines 32–40 = Rigsby 17, a decree of the Eleans. The second formula must include residents without full citizenship (see *IG* V 1, 1433, line 11, which is, however, much later in date), or is perhaps "Messana" still used as the name of the whole region (and state?) and "Messenians" refers only to the citizens of the main city? This second possibility seems less likely, *pace* Grandjean 2003: 102–3 (I gratefully acknowledge J. Roy's advice on this point).

Messenians' claiming back Pylos and Asine, and if the evidence for cities of Messenia joining the Achaean League on their own in 191 is circumstantial, Polybius is very explicit in saying that in 182 Thouria, Abia, and Pharai were detached from Messene and allowed to "set up a stele of their own" and become members of the League (23.17.2). This of course means that previously they were somehow politically attached to Messene. Pausanias, referring to the war against the Achaeans, speaks of the Messenian leader Dinocrates mustering "the Messenians from the city and as many of the *perioikoi* as came to help" (4.29.11). This description certainly supports the notion that the Messenian cities that had remained in the orbit of Messene were in some sense under its control, but it is difficult to interpret Pausanias in a technical sense. In conclusion, there is no way to tell for sure how the relationship between Messene and the other Messenian cities was structured: our sources could be reconciled with a federal state dominated by a powerful city just as well as with a perioikic system, perhaps along the lines of the situation in and around Elis.[72]

The fact that, since the mid third century, the name "Messenians" could function in official documents alternatively as collective name for the citizens of the capital city or, probably, for the citizens of Messenia as a whole, would confirm the impression given by the literary sources, where almost without exception the group active in political and military affairs is called "the Messenians," even though it is highly likely that in some cases at least not only people from Ithome/Messene were involved, but also Messenians from the other towns of the region.[73] This of course is more than a terminological problem. The lack of precision in the use of the term "Messenians" points to the leading role of the capital city and its tendency to stand for the whole of Messenia. The other face of this leading position is the potential for Ithome/Messene to be isolated and separated from the rest of Messenia, which becomes clearly visible in the late third and early second centuries BC, but can be observed from earlier on.[74] This tension between the centripetal impulse coming from Messene and the centrifugal tendencies of the other cities constitutes an important

---

[72] On which see Roy 1997, 1999: esp. 164–71.

[73] E.g. it stands to reason that the troops from Thouria, Pharai, Kalamai, Korone participated in some of the wars that involved Messenians in the late third and early second centuries BC, before the towns became independent members of the Achaean League, and yet, their participation is never mentioned in the sources. The only exception is Polyb. 5.92.5, where the people of Kyparissia are mentioned for stopping the Aetolian attack in 217.

[74] E.g. in 316 only Ithome remained on Polyperchon's side, while all the other cities of Messenia went over to Cassander, see Diod. 19.54.4 discussed above.

background for any understanding of the development of the Messenian identity in the Hellenistic age.

CENTRALIZING RELIGION AND MEMORY: THE TEMPLE OF MESSENE AND OTHER REGIONAL CULTS

The dialectic between Messene and Messenia, between the large fortified city by Mount Ithome and the region, is reflected in an interesting way by some Messenian cults and sanctuaries. Perhaps the most intriguing case is that of the temple dedicated to the heroine Messene at Messene, described by Pausanias (4.31.11–12). As Pausanias himself explains in another passage (4.1.1–2), Messene was the daughter of the Argive king Triopas and the wife of the first king of Messenia, Polykaon. She had played a decisive role in her husband's decision to abandon Lakonia, where his elder brother Myles had succeeded their father Lelex, and to create his own kingdom in Messenia, where they founded, among other unspecified cities, their capital Andania. Nadine Deshours has rightly emphasized that Messene seems to have been a full-fledged mythic character, not a bare personification of the city as commonly found in Hellenistic Greece.[75] As a matter of fact, a closer scrutiny will show that originally Messene may not have been a personification of the city at all. But first, let us take a look at what Pausanias has to say about her temple.

Inside the temple there was a statue of Messene made of Parian marble and gold. At the back of the temple, Pausanias saw a cycle of paintings by Omphalion, a pupil of the Athenian painter Nicias, which represented a number of mythic characters. Nicias was active in the second half of the fourth century,[76] and Omphalion cannot have been more than a couple of decades younger, which implies a tentative dating of the paintings in the late fourth or early third century BC. Pausanias calls the heroes depicted by Omphalion "those who had reigned over Messene," thereby suggesting a dynastic succession and inviting his reader to put the heroes in a chronological sequence. However, it becomes immediately clear that such an interpretation of the cycle, albeit saying something about Pausanias' own take on the monument, is fundamentally wrong. Pausanias lists Aphareus and his sons, Idas and Lynkeus, then Kresphontes, the leader of the Dorian invaders, then Nestor and his sons, Thrasymedes and Antilochos, then Aphareus' brother Leukippos with his daughters Phoibe and Hilaeira, and finally Arsinoe, perhaps also seen as daughter of

---

[75] Deshours 1993: esp. 37–46.   [76] See Gengler 2000: 144.

Leukippos, with her son Asklepios accompanied by his own sons Machaon and Podaleirios. Leaving aside Kresphontes, who came much later in terms of mythic chronology, we have thirteen heroes spread over only four generations;[77] this would be a rather uneconomical way of depicting a dynastic succession. Obviously, the iconographic program of these paintings followed other principles than those that Pausanias indicates.

All these heroes have one point in common: they were all known already before the liberation of Messenia by the Thebans, and apparently all or at least most of them were already associated with the region west of the Taygetos. Nestor and his sons were prominent in the Homeric epics and since the early fifth century at the latest their kingdom was identified with Messenia[78] and Pylos with Koryphasion.[79] Asklepios, Machaon and Podaleirios are Homeric heroes, too, and the healing demigod was called the son of Arsinoe in a late archaic catalogue poem, either the Hesiodic *Catalogue of Women* or the *Megalai Ehoiai*. In all likelihood this genealogy, which later became known as the Messenian version of the origin of Asklepios, implied already that he hailed from west of the Taygetos.[80] Kresphontes appears for the first time in the second half of the fifth century, but the myth of the division of the Peloponnese among the Heraclids must be a little earlier, dating probably to the first half of the century (see above, p. 60). Leukippidai and Apharetidai belonged to the Spartan mythic heritage and were closely connected to the Dioscuri.[81] Stesichorus (fr. 227) considered Leukippos and Aphareus brothers of the

---

[77] From the generation of Leukippos and Aphareus, through that of their children, then that of Leukippos' grandson Asklepios (if we assume that Arsinoe was indeed seen as the daughter of Leukippos in this genealogy), ending with the generation of the Trojan War, represented by Machaon and Podaleirios on the one side and by Nestor's sons on the other.

[78] Pindar calls Nestor "the Messenian elder" in *Pyth.* 6.32–6 (490 BC, for Xenocrates of Akragas) and Messenia "holy Pylos" in *Pyth.* 5.69–72 (462 BC, written for Arcesilaus the Fourth of Cyrene), the first text to mention the division of the Peloponnese among the Heraclids (see above, p. 60). In Homeric geography, Pylos was located further north, see Visser 1997: 522–30.

[79] For the equivalence Pylos-Koryphasion see Thuc. 4.3.2 and above, p. 56 n. 34.

[80] Hes. fr. 50 M.-W. It is possible that the *Catalogue* reported two different versions of Asklepios' genealogy; see Solimano 1976: 17–23. West 1985: 69–72 maintains that only the "Messenian" version was present in the *Catalogue*. See, however, D'Alessio 2005: 208–10, who argues convincingly in favor of attributing the "Messenian" genealogy to the *Megalai Ehoiai* and notes correctly that in the sixth century this genealogy would have been perceived as Laconian rather than Messenian, in accordance with the general Laconian perspective that seems to characterize the *Megalai Ehoiai*.

[81] The ancient sources on the relations between Dioscuri, Apharetidai, and Leukippidai are collected by Gantz 1993: 324–7. On the cult of the Leukippidai in Sparta, documented by Paus. 3.16.1, see Calame 2001: 185–7. The rape of the Leukippidai was depicted on the throne of Amyklai and in the temple of Athena Chalkioikos, Paus. 3.18.11 and 3.17.3 respectively; for the chronology of these two monuments, both dating back to the late archaic period, see above, p. 119 and 176 respectively.

Spartan king Tyndareos.[82] It is difficult to tell where exactly Leukippos and Aphareus were located in the mythic topography of *Lakonikē*. Since in the *Catalogue* or in the *Megalai Ehoiai* Arsinoe was called daughter of Leukippos, it seems reasonable to think that also Leukippos and the Leukippidai were at home west of the Taygetos. The earliest preserved version of the story of the combat between the Apharetidai and the Dioscuri, in which Lynkeus climbs Mount Taygetos to see the enemy,[83] suggests that also the Apharetidai were thought to hail from that area from early on. After all, every single source from the third century onwards locates them in Messenia.[84]

The fact that all these heroes were known to a Panhellenic audience since before the fourth century and probably all thought of as coming from west of the Taygetos made it very attractive for the Messenians, who suffered under chronic deprivation of tradition, to appropriate them – Kresphontes, associated with the Messenians from the outset, is of course a different case. Apart from this, however, this assemblage of heroes and heroines has another important aspect, which has to do with their topographical distribution within Messenia. Kresphontes had had his capital in Stenykleros, that is, in the northern Messenian plain.[85] Nestor and his sons hailed from the western coast of Messenia, across the Aigaleos ridge.

Asklepios' birthplace in Messenia is not identified, but cults of Asklepios and tellingly also cults for his sons are attested in southeastern Messenia more densely than anywhere else in the Peloponnese. A late fifth or early fourth-century inscription from Thalamai offers the earliest piece of evidence.[86] According to Pausanias (3.26.4), the inhabitants of

---

[82] On the variants of this genealogy see Gantz 1993: 180–1.

[83] *Cypria* fr. 15 Bernabé = 13 Davies; see also Pind. *Nem.* 10.61. For a late sixth-century date for the *Cypria*, see Davies 1989: 93–4.

[84] See e.g. Theocr. 22.208, and cf. Apollod. 3.11.2. The earliest depiction of the combat appears on a late fifth-century Attic *pelike*, see Tiberios 1990, with intriguing speculations on a possible political interpretation of the scene (in which the Dioscuri seem to be succumbing to their adversaries). Calame 1987: 172–4 sees in the combat of Dioscuri and Apharetidai a mythic transposition of the Spartan conquest of Messenia. The notion that this myth had a place in the Spartan mythic heritage would be strengthened by Gengler's suggestion that it appeared in Alcman's *Partheneion*, see Gengler 1995 on Alcm. Fr. 3.30–6, emphasizing verbal parallels with Pindar's *Tenth Nemean*. For the various versions of the myth, see Gengler 2003 and Sbardella 2003. In Sparta in the age of Pausanias there were tombs of Aphareus (3.11.11) and Idas and Lynkeus (3.13.1), probably a consequence of the redeployment of myths after Sparta lost Messenia.

[85] For the location of Kresphontes' capital see Ephorus, *FgrHist* 70 F 116 *ap.* Strab. 8.4.7 and Paus. 4.3.7.

[86] *IG* V 1, 1313, where the name of the god is spelled in the Doric form "Aglapios," documented in the Spartan decree recognizing the *asylia* for the sanctuary of Asklepios in Kos, *SEG* 12.371, line 5. On this form of the god's name see Tsaravopoulos 2002–3: 209. On the provenance of the inscription see Riethmüller 2005, II: 135.

Leuktron worshipped Asklepios above all other gods.[87] In Gerenia, Pausanias mentions a tomb and a sanctuary of Machaon (3.26.9 and 4.3.2), and archaeological and epigraphic evidence points to a Mycenaean *tholos* as the complex Pausanias refers to;[88] near the town Strabo (8.4.4) mentions yet another temple of Asklepios. A further temple of Asklepios was in Abia (Paus. 4.30.1), while at Pharai the sons of Machaon, Nicomachos and Gorgasos, had their own temple (Paus. 4.30.3 and 4.3.2).[89]

Leukippidai and Apharetidai are more difficult to locate, since the sources do not associate them explicitly with any part of Messenia in particular. Arene, founded by Aphareus according to Pausanias (4.2.4), could be identical with the Pylian city of the same name, which does not help since Arene in antiquity had two different locations, both in the northwestern part of Nestor's kingdom.[90] On the other hand, there is some reason to think that the Apharetidai were connected with Pharai.[91] In spite of this uncertainty, one point is clear: if we put all these heroes on a map of Messenia, they cover almost the whole region with minimal overlaps. This suggests the possibility that the heroes depicted by Omphalion may have been chosen with an eye to representing as comprehensively as possible the various parts of Messenia: as a sort of summary of the mythic heritage of the Messenians.

It is clearly no accident that this cycle was in the temple of the heroine Messene. However, the precise meaning of the association of the paintings and the heroine to whom the temple was dedicated depends on the chronology of the temple itself. As discussed above, unlike the usage we find in Polybius and in later authors, who call the region "Messenia" and its main city "Messene," inscriptions and literary sources show clearly that at least until the late fourth century "Messene" was the name of the region, and from 369 onwards of the Messenian polity, not of the city at the foot of Mount Ithome, itself originally called Ithome.[92] Therefore, if

---

[87] For a possible localization of the sanctuary of Asklepios at Leuktron, see Riethmüller 2005, II: 134.

[88] For the location of the heroic sanctuary, see Riethmüller 2005, II: 153. On the *tholos*, Hope Simpson 1957: 236–9. The importance of the sanctuary is documented by the fact that decrees of Gerenia were displayed in it from the second century B C; see *SEG* 11.949 and *IG* V 1, 1336, lines 18–19 (the latter of imperial age). A funerary inscription in Laconian dialect and alphabet, *IG* V 1, 1338, dated to the early fifth century, also appears to have been found in the *dromos* of the *tholos*.

[89] On the topography of myths and cults of Asklepios in Messenia see Solimano 1976: 12–13 and 69–72.

[90] *Il.* 2.591. See Visser 1997: 509–11: there was a northern Arene, later Samikon, in Triphylia, which seems to correspond better to Homeric Arene (*Il.* 11.722–3), and a southern one, between Messenian Pylos and Kyparissia. This reduplication is clearly a consequence of the different localizations of Pylos itself. Idas and Lynkeus are said to hail from Arene also in Ap. Rhod. *Arg.* 1.151–2.

[91] Lykophr. *Alex.* 552 and Steph. Byz., s.v. Φαραί.

[92] On Ithome as the original name of the city, see also above, p. 228.

the cult of the heroine Messene was introduced by the early third century, at that point the heroine would have to have been understood not as representing the city alone, but the whole region.

Strictly speaking, Omphalion's date does not give an unimpeachable *terminus ante* for the temple, since his paintings may have been panels rather than frescoes, and therefore it cannot be excluded with absolute certainty that they might have formerly been displayed in a different building – although this is perhaps not very likely.[93] Until recently, epigraphic evidence in the form of a decree from around 181 BC that was to be displayed in the sanctuary of Messene offered the only solid *terminus ante*.[94] However, recent excavations and new epigraphic finds from the agora of Messene have brought us much closer to an identification of the temple (figure 7). During the 2002 campaign, the foundations and part of the stylobate of a temple built in the Doric order, about two-thirds the size of the Asklepios temple, have been brought to light in the southern part of the agora.[95] The following year, a number of inscribed stelae were found, aligned along the northern side of the temple, with their bases still in situ. The texts of two of them include the provision that they be set in the sanctuary of Messene, offering evidence for the identification of the temple.[96] The published material does not yet offer any definitive indication as to the chronology of this building, but a date in the early third century, or possibly even earlier, seems extremely likely.[97]

---

[93] For a general discussion of paintings in Greek sanctuaries, see Scheibler 1994: 138–49. For what it is worth, no other case of a cycle of paintings moved from one sanctuary to another is known.

[94] See *SEG* 41.323. The inscription includes two documents, the second of which is a decree in honor of ambassadors from Kephallenia, while the first relates to the Messenians' recognizing the institution of a competition which seems to be identifiable with the Nikephoria of Pergamon, instituted in 182/1 (details in Luraghi 2006: 185 and n. 79). Note that *SEG* 41.323 is not on the same stone as *SEG* 41.322, the alliance between the Messenians and Lysimachos, as wrongly stated in Deshours 1993: 58 n. 96 and Sineux 1997: 6 n. 27.

[95] For a preliminary report, see Themelis, *Praktika* 2002: 42–6. On the following campaigns, see *Praktika* 2003: 34–8, *Praktika* 2004: 38 and pl. 4.

[96] Themelis, *Praktika* 2003: 37–8 mentions two inscriptions from the middle of the second century with decrees of Demetrias and Smyrna in honor of judges from Messene. The same provision is included in the great inscription of the monumental "Base of the *hippeis*," located in front of the temple; see Themelis, *Praktika* 2004: 46. For earlier attempts at locating the temple, see Luraghi 2006: 184–5.

[97] The presence of at least seven inscribed stelae from the fourth or early third century (Themelis, *Praktika* 2004: 41), found in their original location along the northern side of the temple, offers some preliminary indication for its chronology. Note that a late fourth-century date for the temple would seem particularly appropriate in view of the fact that some sources suggest that Philip's intervention in the Peloponnese, which allowed the Messenian state to reach its maximum extension, was seen by the Messenians as a second foundation of their city; see Strab. 8.4.8 and Polyb. 18.14.7, with Roebuck 1941: 56–7 and Grandjean 2003: 69. A burst of monumental building activity in the agora would make good sense in such a framework. The presence of one further temple in the agora, opposite the one found in 2002, is announced in *Ergon* 2005: 47.

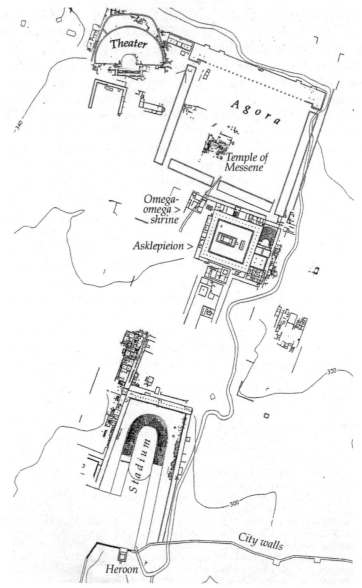

Figure 7 Messene: the area of the excavations (courtesy of Petros Themelis)

Based on the evidence available, it seems possible to suggest an interpretation of the temple of Messene and of the paintings it hosted along the following lines. At some point, perhaps in the fourth century, or in the early third at the latest, a temple was dedicated to the heroine Messene in Ithome. At that point, she was seen as a common ancestor of all the Messenians and a personification of the Messenian state. In the temple paintings were displayed, which depicted a hall of fame of Messenian heroes of a Panhellenic caliber, selected so as to represent the various districts of the region. The temple and the paintings were obviously meant to inspire a sense of common belonging among the Messenians, beyond the borders of Ithome. By Pausanias' time, the pan-Messenian meaning of the sanctuary had faded away. Pausanias, who depicts the history of the Messenians as essentially identical with the history of the city Messene, failed to grasp the meaning of the regional distribution of the heroes in Omphalion's paintings, and interpreted them as a dynastic sequence.

The temple of Messene, with its iconographic program, may not be the only evidence for the attempt, by Ithome/Messene, to function as a focus for the shared mythic memory of the Messenians and ultimately as their religious center. The same urge may be manifested by two further cults, documented by complexes of archaeological evidence from the city. The first complex is constituted by a group of inscriptions recording catalogues of religious magistrates called κιστιοκόσμοι καὶ προστάται of the goddess Athena Kyparissia. Dating mostly to the third century, but some possibly to the fourth, they clearly point to the existence of a temple for this goddess, possibly in the area to the west or northwest of the omega-omega sanctuary, from which a few votive statuettes representing Athena have also been recovered.[98] The second complex is represented by the remains of a small temple located on the southern slopes of Mount Ithome, between the village of Mavromati and the summit. Excavated for the first time by the Expédition Scientifique de Morée in the 1940s; it was identified on the basis of an inscription as a temple of Artemis Limnatis. To judge from architectural elements, it is generally thought to have been built in the second half of the third century BC, but a recent reconsideration of some elements of the roofing seems to point to an earlier date, in the second half of the fourth.[99]

---

[98] The most comprehensive list of these inscriptions includes six items: Müth 2007: 136 and n. 790. For the statuettes, see ibid.: 136 and n. 787.

[99] For the third-century date, see Themelis 1994b: 153 and Müth 2007: 211–16; Badie and Billot 2001: 127 offer parallels that point to a date in the second half of the fourth century for antefixes and portions of sima thought to be pertinent to this temple. The site of the temple has been recently revisited by Petros Themelis, see the notice in *Ergon* 2006: 41–2. The inscription identifying the temple is *IG* V 1, 1442.

In both cases, we find in the urban center a reduplication of sorts of a cult whose main location was elsewhere in Messenia. In the case of Athena Kyparissia, already the epithet signals the primacy of the sanctuary located in Kyparissia, documented by Pausanias.[100] In the case of Artemis Limnatis, the prestige of the old and venerable sanctuary in the Dentheliatis is beyond question. The meaning of such reduplications is less obvious. Depending on when exactly the temple of Artemis Limnatis was built, or more accurately, on when the cult was introduced in the city, its introduction could have been a way of vindicating the cult for the Messenians at a time when the sanctuary on the Taygetos was still or again in Spartan hands,[101] and in this case it would not constitute a real parallel to the cult of Athena Kyparissia.

In trying to interpret the meaning of the introduction of an established cult of regional importance in a city of recent foundation, it may be helpful to look at the rather better-documented case of Megalopolis. Here, Madeleine Jost has pointed out that the creation within the city of sanctuaries that reduplicated famous Arkadian shrines, such as that of Zeus on Mount Lykaion, was not intended to replace the original sanctuaries, but rather seems to have been a way to extend to the city the protection of the gods worshipped in them, and also to create a unified religious landscape that corresponded to the newly acquired unity of the region.[102] It is easy to see how this model could apply at least to the case of Athena Kyparissia, and, if the date in the second half of the fourth century were confirmed, also to the one of Artemis Limnatis. The likely temporal proximity between the introduction of these two cults at Messene and the temple of Messene would reinforce the point. Even though the temple of Messene, with its prominent position in the center of the agora, doubtlessly constituted its centerpiece, the attempt at turning Ithome/Messene into a symbolic center for all the Messenians, where cults and myths from all over the region were represented, was probably rather more comprehensive.

---

[100] Paus. 4.36.7; see also Steph. Byz. s.v. Κυπαρισσία. On the cult of Athena Kyparissia at Kyparissia and Messene and on the connection of epithet and place-name, see Zunino 1997: 163–4.

[101] For a possible date for the Spartan conquest of Dentheliatis during the third century, see above, p. 19 n. 16.

[102] See Jost 1992: 228–32. Of course, the parallel between Ithome/Messene and Megalopolis should not obscure the fact that, in the latter case, it was mostly sanctuaries in what had become the territory of Megalopolis that were reduplicated inside the city. I thankfully acknowledge the advice of Robert Parker on this problem.

THE ASKLEPIEION

The Asklepieion is the most prominent building complex so far brought to light by the excavations of Messene, and one of the most striking Hellenistic architectural complexes anywhere in Greece. It consists of a square courtyard surrounded by stoas, with a big Doric temple and a monumental altar in the center and rooms of various forms and sizes accessible in various ways from the stoas along three sides (see figure 8). Along the western side in particular, a series of rectangular rooms that opened onto the south side of the stoa have been found to contain bases

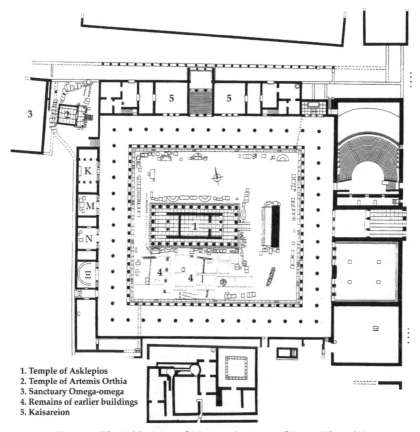

1. Temple of Asklepios
2. Temple of Artemis Orthia
3. Sanctuary Omega-omega
4. Remains of earlier buildings
5. Kaisareion

Figure 8 The Asklepieion of Messene (courtesy of Petros Themelis)

for statues.[103] Combining an early Imperial inscription, which mentions the four halls of the Asklepieion, and Pausanias' description of the sanctuary of Asklepios, Giorgos Despinis in 1966 was able to identify the complex excavated by Orlandos with the Asklepieion.[104]

Although Pausanias, as he does very often,[105] only lists the statues he saw in the sanctuary and not the buildings that harbored them (4.31.10), his short remarks make it possible to make sense of most of the complex. The statues of Asklepios, Machaon and Podaleirios were presumably inside the Doric temple.[106] After mentioning them, Pausanias lists more statues, which he probably saw as he walked under the west stoa from south to north; the statues were in the rooms adjacent to the stoa.[107] It is not certain whether Apollo had a room for himself or shared room Ξ with the Muses, whose statues were on the large semicircular base that was unearthed in the room.[108] Room N was divided into three parts, a central one opening towards the stoa and two smaller ones on its sides, accessible from it. It hosted probably the statues of Heracles, Epaminondas and of the city of Thebes. Since Epaminondas was honored as the founder of Messene, his statue was probably in the slightly larger central part, with Heracles in the northern part and Thebes in the southern.[109] The statue of the Tyche of Messene was in room M. The last and largest room, K, has provided the decisive evidence for the identification of all the others. On the basis of the inscriptions found in it, it has been recognized as the *naos* of Artemis Orthia, and it obviously corresponds to the statue of Artemis

---

[103] The first comprehensive reconstruction was offered by Orlandos 1976; see also Felten 1983: 84–93 and Riethmüller 2005, II: 156–67. For a discussion of the structure of the Asklepieion of Messene in comparison with other similar Hellenistic complexes, see Cain 1995: 123–5.

[104] Depinis 1966: 382–5 and cf. Paus. 4.31.10 and *IG* V 1, 1462; on the identification of the Asklepieion, see also Habicht 1998a: 40–2.

[105] Further examples in Riethmüller 2005, II: 165 and n. 97, and more could be mentioned.

[106] The temple itself must have been dedicated to Asklepios, for otherwise the name of the complex would be odd; see now Riethmüller 2005, II: 163–5 with references to earlier bibliography.

[107] The foundations of the stoa and of the rooms were brought to light by Orlandos, who identified the rooms with letters of the Greek alphabet; see the map in Orlandos 1976: 17 and now Chlepa 2001: 73–89. For the position of the statues, displayed for the viewer almost in a museum setting, see Cain 1995: 125 and the discussion of Müth 2007: 195–7.

[108] On room Ξ, see Chlepa 2001: 82–4. As an alternative, the statue of Apollo could have been located in the southernmost room, room ν, symmetric to the room occupied by his sister Artemis.

[109] This interpretation involves slightly altering Pausanias' sequence, which goes Heracles–Thebes–Epaminondas (whose statue, made of iron according to Pausanias, was the only one that he does not attribute to Damophon). See Themelis 2000: 42–5 and the detailed description of the architecture in Chlepa 2001: 79–80. Torelli 1998: 472–3 prefers to locate Heracles together with the Muses in room Ξ; however, room N is tripartite and therefore unlikely to have contained two statues, as presupposed by Torelli's reconstruction. On Heracles' Theban connections and their function in forging bonds between Thebes and cities of the Peloponnese at the time of Epaminondas, see above pp. 231–2.

Phosphoros mentioned by Pausanias.[110] According to him, with the exception of the statue of Epaminondas all the others were works of the Messenian sculptor Damophon.[111]

Behind the northern stoa, two symmetrical sets of rooms were located on a higher level and accessible by a monumental staircase. This complex has been identified with the sanctuary dedicated to the imperial cult, mentioned as Kaisareion or Sebasteion in various inscriptions.[112] At the eastern end of the stoa, on the ground level of the courtyard, the small room ε contained a fountain that must have had some function in the cult of Asklepios.[113] The eastern side of the complex comprised a few larger buildings of uncertain function: a small *odeion* and a large meeting room. It has generally been assumed that these were public buildings rather than parts of the sanctuary proper, and the further consequence has been drawn that the complex functioned as center of political life, too.[114] However, more recently a general investigation of sanctuaries of Asklepios has made it possible to interpret these two buildings in a convincing way in connection with the cult of the god.[115]

Even though we may be confident that the excavations in Messene, especially but not only in the agora, have still quite a few surprises in store in terms of public architecture, it is reasonable to admit, on the basis also of Pausanias' impression of it (4.31.10), that the Asklepieion must have been the most prominent complex in the city. The series of statues it harbored, with their sometimes very direct references to the past of the Messenians, invites one to read the whole project as a coherent ideological statement that requires careful deciphering.

Starting with the main deity of the complex, it is worth noting that Asklepios rarely took the place of the main god of a Greek city, and his sanctuaries, even when they were not extramural, as they often were,

---

[110] On the cult room of Artemis Orthia, see Themelis 1994a: 107–22 and now especially Chlepa 2001: 10–69. The room is designated as *naos* in an inscription from 42 AD, *SEG* 23.208; see Deshours 2004a: 118–20. On the epithet of the goddess, see below.

[111] On Damophon, see below, n. 130. Themelis 1996: 155–66 lists and describes fragments of sculpture from the area that may belong to Damophon's statues.

[112] See Riethmüller 2005, II: 161.

[113] See Themelis 1993a: 31 and n. 31 and Sineux 1997: 7–8 and 18–19; on the function of this room, see also Torelli 1998: 471–2 and Riethmüller 2005, II: 164.

[114] Torelli 1998: 474. New finds from the agora, however, may suggest that at least some of the public buildings used for political purposes may have been located there.

[115] Riethmüller 2005, II: 164–5: the *odeion* was probably used for cultic performances and for musical competitions in the framework of the festival of the *Asklepieia*, while the meeting room could have been used for incubation.

clearly show a tendency to be located in a marginal position.[116] The prominence assigned to his cult at Messene by the construction of the new sanctuary adjacent to the agora is all the more striking. As noted above (p. 234), the cult of Asklepios was spreading all over Greece precisely at the time of the liberation of Messenia, and it is easy to imagine that the new polity, desperately poor of traditions, could be inclined to adopt this new god, especially since it was possible to claim him in some sense as an indigenous god of the Messenians. Archaeological evidence from earlier strata underneath the courtyard, including anatomic ex-votos and the foundations of a temple and an altar dated to the second quarter of the fourth century (see above, pp. 233–4 n. 82), confirms that already by then a healing god, which it seems reasonable to identify with Asklepios, was worshipped in the area where the Doric temple was later built. Still, comparison with the rather modest architectural remains of the earlier phase suggests that the construction of the new complex involved an increasing prominence for this god, who now took a central place in the Pantheon of the city and even harbored in his sanctuary so many deities important for the definition of the religious and cultural heritage of the Messenians.

The striking centrality of the new Asklepieion has invited scholars in the past to interpret the cult of the god as a purely political one, symbolizing a claim and a statement by the Messenians,[117] but against this it is important to point out that the anatomic ex-votos in the earlier strata, the presence of a bath just behind the southern stoa of the Asklepieion, and the recent reinterpretation of parts of the complex in connection with rituals of purification and incubation typical of the cult of Asklepios, show that even here this deity was venerated in his normal capacity as a healing god.[118] But then, the very choice of Asklepios, a god linked to the private sphere of healing and health, as the main beneficiary of this ambitious architectural project and the recipient and host for the display of Messenian identity embodied by the statues may of itself be indicative of the ideological context in which the complex was conceived.

For indeed, the deities worshipped in the rooms on the western side of the sanctuary seem to form a consistent whole, with a complex but very clear meaning. Apollo's presence was *de rigueur*, since he was the father of

---

[116] Riethmüller 2005, I: 360–3.
[117] For the purely political interpretation of the cult of Asklepion in Messene, see Orlandos 1976: 38 and the more detailed discussion of Felten 1983: 82–93.
[118] Sineux 1997: 18–23. Anatomic ex-votos: Themelis 2000: 22–3. Bath: Themelis, *Praktika* 1989: 77–88 and Sineux 1997: 9 and 20. Buildings on the eastern side of the complex: above, n. 115.

Asklepios. The cult of Apollo in Messenia probably went back to the Spartan era, as suggested also by the frequent occurrence of the epithet of Karneios across the region, and especially in a third-century inscription from Messene.[119] In the Asklepieion, however, his possible association with the Muses would suggest that he appeared under the guise of Apollo *mousagetēs*. The emphasis on this side of Apollo could constitute a novelty in the sacred landscape of Messene, and one might wonder if the Messenians, by emphasizing the god's connection to the sphere of artistic creation and performance, may not have intended to gloss over the Spartan ancestry of their cult of Apollo.

As for Heracles, the hero could be associated with the southwestern Peloponnese in various ways, but to judge from the statues that accompanied his, here he seems to have appeared essentially as a Theban hero. Together with the statue of Thebes he symbolized the mother city of Messene, and appropriately flanked the statue of Epaminondas, depicted as the founder of the city. As discussed above (p. 217), this may not have corresponded to historical reality, in the sense that it is unclear whether Epaminondas had acted as a founder in Messene in a technical sense, and even more doubtful that Thebes could be seen as a *metropolis* of the free Messenians. In other words, by putting together this group of statues in such a prominent position, the Messenians were in some sense redefining their identity, not simply restating it.

Similar considerations could be advanced for the next statue, the statue of Tyche. In Hellenistic iconographic tradition, Tyche represented the city itself,[120] and an early Imperial coin of Messene showing a representation of Tyche wearing a mural crown seems to confirm that in this case, too, Tyche was essentially a personification of the city.[121] Again, the Tyche of Messene can be seen as in some sense modifying the message conveyed by the temple of Messene discussed above, refocusing Messenian identity from the region to the city.

The cult room of Artemis Orthia was the only one that clearly functioned as a temple, as shown also by the altar located in front of it. It was larger than all the others and packed with statues, whose inscribed bases refer to priestesses of Artemis or Messenian maidens connected to her

---

[119] On Apollo Karneios in Messenia, see Zunino 1997: 178 and Paus. 4.31.1, and above, p. 236 on his presence at Andania. For recent epigraphic evidence possibly or certainly connected to the cult of Apollo Karneios in Messene, see Themelis, *Praktika* 1999: 88–9 (= *SEG* 51.474) and especially *Praktika* 2001: 70–1 (= *SEG* 52.412), both dating to the early third century, discussed in Müth 2007: 209.

[120] See in general Christof 2001.   [121] See T. Ganschow in *LIMC*, s.v. "Messene."

cult. It was obviously one of the most important sanctuaries of the city.[122] Since it is hardly plausible that the Messenians might have introduced a Spartan cult after 369, the cult of Artemis Orthia has to be considered, even more certainly than Apollo Karnéios, a remnant of the time when Messenia was a part of the *Lakonikē*. As noted above (p. 236), the Messenians seem to have been uncomfortable with this link to their Lakedaimonian past, and tried to neutralize it by claiming that their cult of Artemis Orthia was, if not older, at least not more recent than the Spartan one, and therefore did not necessarily come from Sparta. The college of priests responsible for this cult is called "the holy elders, descendants of Kresphontes" in two inscriptions of the second or third century AD (*SEG* 23.215 and 217), a designation that implies that the cult was supposed to date back to the time of the Dorian invasion. The fact that Pausanias refers to this Artemis with the epithet Phosphoros could have to do with the iconography of the statue,[123] but we should not exclude that he intentionally avoided the epithet Orthia, which was displayed on various inscriptions in the sanctuary itself,[124] because in his age the cult of Artemis Orthia with its bloody rituals had become the hallmark of Sparta, hardly his favorite corner of the Greek world.[125]

In the present state of our knowledge, it is fair to say that the new Asklepieion became the center of the religious life of the Messenians. More than any other sanctuary, it can be seen as the place where Messenian identity was consciously articulated and displayed. If it is correct to regard it as an organic whole, then it is interesting to observe both what was present in it and what was absent. In the conception of the new sanctuary, the pan-Messenian inspiration of Omphalion's paintings had all but disappeared. There is no trace of the Pylian heroes, in spite of their Panhellenic prestige, and in general almost no reference to cults or heroes associated with parts of Messenia other than the city of Messene. On the other hand, strong emphasis is now placed on the city itself. As noted above, the personification of the political community, the Tyche of

---

[122] Statues and inscriptions are discussed in Themelis 1994a: 110–22. See also Piolot 2005: 123–5. As Themelis' excavations have shown, the temple replaced an earlier small prostyle temple built in the fourth century, probably at the time of the foundation of the city (see above, p. 234); see Themelis 1994a: 101–7.

[123] See Piolot 2005: 132–5.

[124] Of the inscriptions preserved in the sanctuary and carrying the epithet, *SEG* 23.217 could be later than Pausanias, but *SEG* 23.220 is certainly earlier; see Themelis 1994a: 115–16.

[125] On the rituals for Artemis Orthia in Roman Sparta, see e.g. Spawforth, in Cartledge and Spawforth 2002: 205. On Pausanias' attitude to the Spartans, Auberger 2001: 264–8 with reference to the narrative of the Messenian Wars.

Messene, refers clearly to the city, not to Messenia as a whole, a point reinforced by showcasing the role, respectively, of Epaminondas as the founder and of Thebes as the *metropolis* of Messene. Only Apollo and Artemis, with her implicit link to Kresphontes, kept alive the ties to the earlier Messenian heritage that went back beyond the Theban liberation of Messenia in 369. Asklepios retained some of his local flavor, as shown by the fact that in the temple he was apparently flanked by his sons Machaon and Podaleirios, not by his wife Hygieia as usual in other Asklepieia.[126] On the whole, references to the history or myth-history of Messenia before 369 BC are surprisingly scarce, and the most striking absence is that of Aristomenes, the hero of the Messenian Wars.[127]

Unfortunately, it is at the moment rather difficult to locate this extremely interesting complex in a precise historical context. To be sure, recent excavations have solved a number of chronological problems. In the past, some scholars had thought that the Doric temple, with its old-fashioned architecture, had to be earlier than the stoas,[128] but the soundings in the courtyard of the temple have shown that the whole complex was the result of a unitary project, whose construction cannot have started before the late third or early second century BC.[129] Since Pausanias attributes the statues in the Asklepieion to the Messenian sculptor Damophon, and it is clear that the whole series was the product of one single commission specifically destined for this sanctuary, Damophon's chronology has been regarded as a possible way of working out a more precise date for the sanctuary itself. Damophon was obviously a very wealthy and highly regarded citizen,[130] and his activity extended well beyond Messene itself. Statues by him stood in sanctuaries in Lykosura, Aigion and Megalopolis,[131] and his reputation was so high that the Eleans entrusted him with the repair of Phidias' chryselephantine statue of Zeus

---

[126] Hygieia was, however, present in the sanctuary; a dedication to her and Asklepios figured on the upper moulding of a large exedra located in the courtyard in front of Room H and carrying a series of bronze statues, see Themelis 1993a: 31–2 and *SEG* 38.339.

[127] Of course, if the cult for Aristomenes epigraphically attested in the Augustan age (see above, p. 89 n. 73) already existed when the Asklepieion was built, as it seems reasonable to assume, it probably continued to be practiced in connection with the hero's tomb or cenotaph, wherever that was; however, given also the prominence of Aristomenes in narratives of the Messenian Wars, his total absence from the new complex is noteworthy.

[128] As still maintained by Torelli 1998: 470–1.

[129] For this chronology, based on coins and small finds from the earlier layers, see Themelis 2000: 24.

[130] On Damophon's social status, see Themelis 1996: 184–5. A new document to be added to the dossier has been recently found in the excavations of the agora, *Ergon* 2003: 37–9; it is inscribed on what looks like the capstone of a pediment and records the dedication of *akrōtēria* by Damophon and his children.

[131] Paus. 7.23.5–8; 8.31.6; 37.2–7; see Themelis 1993b and 1996: 166–7.

and then granted him honors for his work (Paus. 4.31.6). The citizens of Lykosura even honored him with a statue, because he had remitted them a large sum of money they owed him for his work, as we learn from a decree of Lykosura that was inscribed, together with others coming from six more cities, on a fluted column found near the Asklepieion, which may have been part of some sort of monument for Damophon.[132]

In spite of this significant amount of evidence, unparalleled for any other Greek sculptor, Damophon's chronology is not fixed with sufficient certainty to offer a precise cornerstone for the Asklepieion. Abundant as it is, the evidence on Damophon does not seem to warrant any more precise dating than a general collocation in the first half of the second century for the sculptor's activity.[133] If we turn to the political events involving the Messenians between the Peace of Naupaktos and the destruction of Corinth, it seems immediately possible to exclude that the construction of the Asklepieion may have started in the troubled years between 191 and 182 BC. The years immediately after the end of the Social War, when Messene was torn by civil strife and twice attacked by the Macedonians, in 214 and 213, do not look very promising, either. On the other hand, Messenian involvement in the Second Macedonian War was rather low-profile, so the years from 205 to 195 could offer a plausible background. This is essentially the chronology favored by Petros Themelis, who sees in the Asklepieion a statement of national pride by the Messenian democracy that had emerged from the civil strife that followed the Social War.

Themelis' chronology has been further developed by Mario Torelli, in an attempt at locating the Asklepieion in a precise historical and ideological context. Observing that Damophon seems to have been active mainly in cities that belonged to the Achaean League, Torelli suggested that the Messenian sculptor, who given his high social status can hardly not have been active in politics, was actually an exponent of the pro-Achaean faction in the city; he furthermore advanced an interpretation of the whole complex as reflecting ideological allegiance to the Achaean

---

[132] The decree of Lykosura is *SEG* 41.332. Of the remaining six decrees, four have been recently published: Kythnos, Themelis 1998b (= *SEG* 49.423), Krane on Kephallenia, *IG* IX[2] 1.4, 1583 (= *SEG* 51.467), Leukas, *IG* IX[2] 1.4, 1475 (= *SEG* 51.466), and Oiantheia, Themelis 2003. Two further decrees, by Melos and Gerenia, remain unpublished. Themelis 2000: 88–95 interprets a monumental grave immediately to the south of the southern stoa of the Asklepieion, the so-called Heroon Delta, as a funerary monument for Damophon and his descendants; cf. however Boehringer 2001: 278, and see now Fröhlich 2007: 208–10.

[133] See Themelis 1996: 167–71, based on a reference to a debt in tetradrachms that Damophon had remitted to the city of Lykosura (*SEG* 41.332), and cf. Habicht 1998a: xiv–xv and the discussion of Müth 2007: 180–3.

League in the late third century.[134] Against this conclusion, however, it has to be pointed out that two of the cities that honored Damophon, Oiantheia and Krane on the island of Kephallenia, were members of the Aetolian League, and furthermore, even though Asklepios was a prominent deity in some cities of the Achaean League, and Aratus of Sikyon after his death was worshipped as a son of Asklepios (Paus. 2.10.3), it has to be recognized that Asklepios was hardly one of the most prominent gods of the Achaeans and did not have any immediate connection with the League as such.[135]

More recently, Silke Müth has proposed what appears to be a more promising historical collocation, in the years between the final forced inclusion of Messene in the Achaean League in 182 and the Achaean War.[136] There is definitely something to be said for this proposal. Surely if Damophon's activity points to any political background, it points to a period in which hostility between the Achaean and Aetolian Leagues was not politically relevant.[137] Furthermore, all the previous chronological windows are rather short to accommodate a project of this scale – considering also that Damophon's statues are most likely to have been commissioned when the project was approaching completion. If the years immediately after 182, when the Achaean League curtailed the territory of Messene and granted the city a three-years exemption from federal dues to allow it to recover from the devastations of the war (Polyb. 24.2.3), can probably be excluded, a date between the second half of the 170s and the 160s–150s seems quite reasonable, and would point to a historical context in which the refocusing of the Messenian identity from the region to the city would make perfect sense. The absence of any reference to the Messenian Wars, which seem to have been the object of intense attention during the third century, would offer food for thought regarding the meaning of that portion of the Messenian past to Hellenistic Messenians. But in order further to develop these observations, it is necessary to move to a comprehensive discussion of Messenian identity in the Hellenistic age.

---

[134] Torelli 1998: 478–9. It would not be unparalleled for a sculptor to have been also a prominent politician; cf. the case of the Spartan sculptor Ainetidas, *SEG* 45.341.

[135] See Osanna 1996.

[136] Müth 2007: 183–5, with comprehensive discussion and further bibliography.

[137] It is interesting to note that one of the statues of Damophon seen by Pausanias in Messene, though not in the Asklepieion, was a statue of Artemis Laphria, a typically Aetolian cult that was probably introduced in Messene in connection with the alliance with the Aetolians, *pace* Pausanias; see above, n. 30, and Müth 2007: 69–72.

During the third century BC, the wars against the Spartans supposedly fought by their ancestors in the archaic age seem to have been very much on the Messenians' mind. As discussed above (pp. 83–8), the prose narrative of the First Messenian War written by Myron of Priene, possibly in the central years of the century, and the epic on the Second Messenian War composed by Rhianus during its second half, are best understood as commissioned by the Messenians themselves, in an attempt at boosting and celebrating local identity that is comparable to the pursuits of other Greeks who commissioned works in prose and poetry devoted to their mythic past. In different ways, both works implied a highly centralized view of archaic Messenia, depicted as a unified political space, ruled by the Aipytid kings until the First War, and then essentially again during the second, when the hero Aristomenes, of royal blood, refused to be proclaimed king but, as plenipotentiary general, single-handedly led the Messenians in the revolt against the Spartans. However, there seems to be one important difference between Myron's and Rhianus' Messenia. The former was a land of fortified cities, each capable of resisting the Spartan aggression, and even though Ithome became during the war the main focus of resistance, once it fell the Spartans still had to conquer all the other cities one by one. Rhianus on the contrary makes Andania the crucible of the revolt and concentrates all the action in the northern Messenian plain and, interestingly, in the valley of the river Neda.[138]

In general terms, it is clear that the celebration of resistance to past aggressions embedded in the history of the Messenian Wars could function as a call to unity for third-century Messenians, but the call seems to have been articulated in significantly different ways by the two works. If Myron's transmitted confidence about the strength and cohesion of a unified and somewhat undifferentiated Messenia, Rhianus apparently foregrounded a part of the region that actually coincided with the territory of the polis Messene. In his perspective, this was where the Messenians who had fought for freedom from Sparta came from. Rhianus' perspective could have a twofold implication: on the one hand, the memory of the heroic war against the Spartans was *de facto* claimed exclusively by the polis of Messene, while on the other, the sacrifice of the Messenians from the northern

---

[138] The concentration of the action on the northern border of Messenia during the second half of the war (Paus. 4.17.10–11) suggestively reminds us of the fact that precisely that border, across which lay the Aetolian stronghold of Phigaleia, was a crisis zone for much of the second half of the third century, when Rhianus most likely composed his poem.

Messenian plain, who had faced war and exile for the freedom of the whole region, could function as a charter myth for the supremacy of the polis of Messene and for its leading role within Messenia.

It is immediately clear how the trajectory from Myron's to Rhianus' image of the Messenian Wars can map onto the political history of the region in the course of the third century, and the interpretations of the temple of Messene with its paintings and of the Asklepieion with its statues and shrines nicely complete the picture and provide further evidence for what emerges as an essentially consistent development. It is particularly unfortunate that we know next to nothing about the political structure that connected the various parts of the region at different points in time, and there can be no doubt that, if we were able to sketch a constitutional history of Messenia, many of the developments observed above would acquire a much clearer meaning. But even in the present state of the evidence, it is clear that, as soon as the Messenian identity came to be anchored in a real space, new issues arose that changed it in radical ways. Some of them derived from the balance of power created in the region by the foundation of Ithome, others simply reflected the difficulty of transforming into a political entity an ethnic unity that had existed so far only in theory.

Unlike other areas of Greece that had come to be seen as ethnically homogeneous during the archaic and classical ages, such as Boeotia, Arcadia, Phocis, to name but a few, Hellenistic Messenia provides scarcely any evidence for sanctuaries and cults of regional relevance. The only possible exception, interestingly, seems to be the temple of Artemis Limnatis at Volimos, and it is an exception of sorts. While it is difficult to believe that the temple belonged directly to the polis of Ithome/Messene ever since the Dentheliatis first became Messenian in 337 BC, and still rather unlikely that it did when it was returned to the Messenians after Sellasia, in 222 BC, it appears that after the Achaean War the temple of Volimos was an extra-urban sanctuary of the polis of Messene, as shown by the text of the Milesian arbitration from the early 130s BC. It is not possible to say since when this was so, but the sheer fact that this situation came about at all speaks volumes. If it is correct to regard the sanctuary of Artemis Limnatis as originally in some sense pan-Messenian, it confirms strikingly that hostility to Sparta was ultimately the only banner under which the Messenians could be unified. However, it appears that from the mid second century BC at the latest it was the polis of Messene that carried on the war of memory against Sparta, keeping alive what had been the cornerstone of the Messenian identity. Half a century or so after

Rhianus, poem, the dispute over the Dentheliatis confirms the emergence of an exclusive claim to the heroic history of the resistance against Sparta on the part of the polis of Messene.

Such dynamics have to be linked to objective transformations in the political landscape of Messenia, set in motion by the liberation of the region and accentuated by broader political developments in Hellenistic Greece. While the very foundation of the new, big city at Ithome had consequences for the internal balance of the region, the existence of a new, mighty fortress in the Peloponnese changed the potential relevance of Messenia for Peloponnesian politics. Originally, the imposing fortification walls had been built to contain the Spartans, whose diffidence against fortifications was proverbial. However, in a situation in which the Macedonian rulers repeatedly tried to control the Peloponnese by means of a few impregnable fortresses, Ithome/Messene became an attractive prey – and the mind goes to Demetrios Poliorcetes, retreating beaten and wounded from the walls of Messene, and later on to Demetrios of Pharos telling Philip the Fifth to seize the bull by the horns, and then being killed in the attempt at implementing his suggestion. In other words, pressures from without the region converged with internal dynamics in separating Ithome/Messene from the rest of Messenia, culminating in the progressive dismemberment of Messenia by the Achaean League.

It has to be pointed out, of course, that all the developments we have been observing conspire, for different reasons, in creating a strongly centripetal perspective. We simply cannot tell how Messenian identity was perceived and articulated in any of the cities of Messenia but Ithome/Messene. Keeping in mind that our perspective is skewed in this way, it seems possible to suggest a reconstruction along the following lines. As soon as Messenia became independent, under the name of Messene, cohesion seems to have been its main problem. Some time in the late fourth or early third century, the temple of Messene at Ithome faced this issue by bringing together under the aegis of the heroine Messene heroes standing for the various parts of the region. The cases of Artemis Limnatis and Athena Kyparissia suggest that this policy of bringing together myths and cults from the whole region may have had a broader scope. That the pan-Messenian charter implicit in Omphalion's paintings was articulated in Ithome means that we cannot tell to what extent the message was received across the region, but the very fact that it was articulated at all, and in such an explicit way, is significant.

During the third century, the story of the wars against Sparta, clearly the main charter of Messenian unity, of which the sanctuary of Artemis

Limnatis at Volimos was a permanent icon, was rehearsed repeatedly, in ways that may suggest an increasingly exclusive claim on it by what was by now called the polis of Messene – and ultimately, the shift in the use of the place-name is itself an indicator of the same process. At the same time, settlements on the periphery seem more and more to have gone their own way, until what remained of Epaminondas' free Messene was finally taken apart by the Achaeans. In their last-ditch attempt against the Achaeans, the Messenians from the polis of Messene apparently struck coins with the legend "Messenians of Ithome," a reminder that Messene had once been a larger whole, of which the polis of Messene, formerly Ithome, used to be but a part. The attitude of the Messenians from the other Messenian cities is impossible to gauge. The little evidence we have shows at least no signs of rebellion against the polis of Messene, and the fact that, when Messene seceded from the Achaean League in 182, the cities that had been detached in 192 had to be reconquered with force could simply mean that they harbored Achaean garrisons. But on the whole, it would probably not be wise to assume the same attitude in every Messenian city.

The iconographical program of the Asklepieion probably shows us how being Messenian was articulated at Messene after the defeat. The complex is built around a healing god, and the Messenian heritage is refocused in a much narrower way on the city itself. Epaminondas' role as founder of the city is emphasized, the Tyche of the polis of Messene replaces the "regional" heroine Messene, while Kresphontes, the symbol of the unity of Dorian Messenia, is only alluded to in a very indirect way, if at all, and there is no reference at all to the wars against Sparta. Of course, the new sanctuary did not obliterate the other cults already practiced in the city, but its very addition to the blend must have deeply impacted the whole, and more importantly, it offers very explicit evidence for the concerns of the Messenians at that time.

The defeat of the Achaean League at the hands of the Romans may have brought about some sort of renewed unity in Messenia. However, it is striking that the party that opposed Sparta in the controversy over the Dentheliatis in the years following the Achaean War was the polis of Messene. The sanctuary, with all it meant for the Messenian identity, was now under its direct control. Furthermore, although this new phase of the controversy was probably initiated by the Spartans, it is noteworthy that, by insisting on their claim to the sanctuary of Artemis Limnatis, the Messenians were reaffirming the centrality of the wars against Sparta for their identity.

At the same time, Sparta continued to be the ultimate source of symbols and ritual behavior for the Messenians. Cults, epithets of gods, names of magistracies, all bear evidence of this phenomenon, and it seems as if it did not involve only elements that simply went back to the age of the Spartan domination. Even the most characteristic aspect of the urban landscape of Hellenistic Messene, the proliferation of monumental graves within the city walls, should almost certainly be explained along these lines. The excavations have brought to light so far a total of seven monumental graves, ranging in date from the late third to the second century BC, located around the Asklepieion and in a row to the west of the western side of the gymnasium. Some, like the one designated as K 3, are absolutely spectacular. All of them, as far as we can tell, were set up for multiple depositions, and most seem to have received new depositions long after they had been built. Even though inscriptions make it possible to identify some of the dead, it is on the whole quite unclear who the people were who were buried in these monumental tombs.[139]

Intramural burial in monumental graves for citizens who had acquired extraordinary merits on behalf of their communities is otherwise attested across Hellenistic Greece, but it was clearly an exceptional measure.[140] With one significant exception to be discussed in a moment, no other Hellenistic city offers a density of intramural burials that comes even close to Messene, so much so that Pierre Fröhlich has interpreted the situation in relation to the fact that the still relatively new city, besides lacking a history of its own, also lacked famous figures of old to serve as models, and therefore was more prone emphatically to honor its prominent citizens, as if to create a repertory of examples for others to imitate.[141] But a different explanation is possible. There was actually one other Greek city in which intramural burials were very common: that city was Sparta. To be sure, at Sparta this situation was a result of the very peculiar urban development of the city, which had been constituted for a long period of time by five separate villages, with their own cemeteries close by, and then, when in the third century BC the city was finally encircled with fortifications, the old cemeteries ended up being enclosed in them.[142]

---

[139] For an overview, see Themelis 2000: 88–102 and 114–36 and Fröhlich 2007: 204–17. Even though the development of Messene towards a de facto oligarchy, dominated by few families (the situation we observe in the first centuries AD, see below, pp. 327–8), is most likely to have started in the Hellenistic age, it is not at all clear that the monumental tombs under discussion were in any sense family monuments, and their connection with prominent families, suggested by Fröhlich, remains therefore undefined.

[140] See the evidence collected by Habicht 1995: 90–2; for a case of honorific intramural burial at Messene, see *IG* V 1, 1427, first century BC, and see below, pp. 310–14.

[141] Fröhlich 2007: 221.

[142] See Kourinou 2000: 215–19 (cemeteries) and 35–62 (Hellenistic fortifications).

But the new situation did not bring about a complete relocation of the burial practices: graves, occasionally on a monumental scale, continued to be built within the walls circuit during the Hellenistic period and the early Empire, and the Spartans even interpreted their odd custom as instituted by Lycurgus, in order for the living to familiarize themselves with death and overcome fear.[143] It seems obvious to explain the existence of this custom at Messene, where it started in the late third century, that is, probably at the very time when the Spartans began noticing the peculiarity of their own custom and linked it to Lycurgus, as modeled on Sparta. In all likelihood, the Messenians were once more borrowing an aspect of their ritual behavior from their hated neighbors. As in all other cases, they surely thought that they were reinstating an ancestrally Messenian custom.[144]

*　*　*

If the history of the Messenian identity until the liberation of Messenia offers a case study in ethnicity and ethnogenesis, the most striking phenomena observable in the Hellenistic period have more to do with the transformation of an ethnic group into a polity. As it is often the case with processes of nation building, the central perspective, the one of the core group that tries to aggregate a larger body around itself, ends up being over-represented in the evidence, and it is very difficult to gain a sense of any other perspective. The history of Thouria and Asine, discussed above (pp. 27–43), shows that on the borders allegiance to a shared Messenian past was much more controversial and unstable. From the fourth century to the second, the Messenian identity seems to have become essentially the charter that underpinned the claim to regional leadership of Ithome/ Messene, until it ended up imploding. By the age of Augustus, it seems that Messene had become almost the only depositary of the Messenian heritage.

---

[143] Plut. *Lyc.* 27.1. In this case, the invention of tradition is transparent: in Lycurgus' age, the burials were not within the settlement, as the passage implies; they only became intramural when the circuit of walls turned the five villages of Sparta into an urban unit. On monumental tombs within the Hellenistic walls of Sparta, ranging in date from the archaic to the Hellenistic ages, see Raftopoulou 1998: 133–7.

[144] For further examples of the same phenomenon from the second century AD, see below, pp. 301–3, on the *agōn aristopoliteias* and on the title of *hestia tēs poleōs*.

CHAPTER 10

Messenians in the Empire

The end of the civil wars, the advent of the *pax Augusta*, and the transformation of mainland Greece into the Roman province of Achaea marked an important turning point in the history of the Greeks. Occasional disturbances are documented in certain areas until the Flavian age, but by and large peace enforced by Roman domination became a fact of life.[1] With the loss of political independence, the military role of the polis, which had survived, if in an increasingly curtailed fashion, in the face of the rise of the Hellenistic monarchies and of the Roman conquest, finally came to an end. Even though poleis remained alive as political communities,[2] in various relationships of dependence on Rome but with their own functioning political institutions, one of the main raisons d'être of the polis had disappeared, and with it the main characteristic of the Greek world, internecine conflict. In the first centuries of the Roman Empire, being Athenian, Spartan, Theban, or Messenian could not mean what it used to. Attachment to the *patris* became just one layer in a tiered identity,[3] at the top of which a unified Hellenic identity, based on shared cultural practices and underpinned by the assumption of a shared genealogy, became increasingly important.[4] In parallel to this process, the ruling elites of Greece, consolidated and stabilized by the Roman domination, came to constitute one of the pools from which the imperial elite was recruited.[5]

---

[1] On sporadic episodes of violent strife, internal and/or with possible anti-Roman ramifications, in the province of Achaea, see Bowersock 1965: 101–8, Jones 1971: 17–18.

[2] On politics within the Greek poleis in the age of Plutarch, see Foxhall 2002; for the second century, Kennell 1997.

[3] See the thoughtful remarks of Jones 2004: esp. 13–14.

[4] This development culminated under Hadrian in the creation of the Panhellenion, a general league of the Greeks; see Jones 1996, and especially on the development of Greek ethnicity in the Panhellenion, Romeo 2002.

[5] The progressive integration of the elites of Greece in the empire can be observed by charting the diffusion of Roman citizen rights; especially on the Peloponnese, see Rizakis 2001, and on Laconia and Messenia, Hoët-van Cauwenberghe 1996.

How the Greeks reacted to this new situation is a hotly debated question in current scholarship, but a consensus seems to be slowly emerging, to the effect that attitudes ranging from assimilation into the fabric of the Empire to grudging recognition of Roman domination coexisted, within a general framework in which alternatives to the current political situation were not realistically imaginable. At the same time, the world of the Greek poleis became an integral part of the Empire, in a complex relation of synergy with the rest. For reasons that had to do with how the Romans themselves constructed their identity and their role in the Mediterranean world, Greek culture, especially in the form of a strong connection to the past, formed an important source of symbolic capital whose value was recognized throughout the Empire.[6] This situation in due course opened up various possibilities of personal promotion for the provincial elites of Achaea, ranging from cooptation into the ruling elite of the Empire to participation in the international circuit of intellectuals that goes by the name of Second Sophistic.

The changing world of Imperial Greece is accessible to the modern historian in a surprisingly detailed way. More than is the case for any previous epoch of Greek history, sources available make it possible to observe the articulation of collective identities at various levels, posing questions relating to the different fields in which such identities were affirmed, and ultimately to agency. All of a sudden, we have at our disposal a significant amount of evidence that sheds light on single individuals and families, their dealings with their own political communities and the broader world of the Empire, and their way of perceiving and constructing their present and their past. Needless to say, concentration on these individuals can potentially result in a one-sided perspective on much more complex phenomena. However, even though it may go too far to say that the collective memory of the Greeks in the Early Empire was constituted essentially by the celebration of the local elites, it is clear that their role in the process, in a dialectic relationship with their respective communities, must have been very significant.[7] For a change, Messenia offers abundant evidence for these processes, and to this evidence we will finally turn, as we approach the last stage of the history of the Messenian identity.

---

[6] See Woolf 1994: esp. 131–5.

[7] On this, see Alcock 2002: 40–1, Pretzler 2005: 239, and especially the illuminating works of Lafond 2001, 2005, where epigraphic evidence is profitably compared to Pausanias, whose work functions as a helpful *tertium comparationis*. Compare also the famous case of Salutaris' foundation in Ephesus investigated in Rogers 1991.

MNASISTRATOS, THE MYSTERIES, AND MESSENIAN
HISTORIOGRAPHY

Owing to their consistently unlucky decisions during the civil wars, the
Messenians had entered the *pax Augusta* from a rather disadvantaged position. Their arch enemies the Spartans had fought on the side of Octavian
and Antony at Philippi, gaining the Dentheliatis, and after Actium they had
become the *princeps'* favourites, thanks to Eurykles' role in the battle.[8] The
Messenians had to account for their choosing the wrong side. Augustus'
measures punished them heavily: essentially, the border between Laconian
and Messenian territory became the river Pamisos, as in Euripides' Heraclid
tragedies.[9] Understandably, when Augustus died the Messenians greeted the
new *princeps* enthusiastically.

Their decree in his honor (*SEG* 41.328) includes the sending of an
embassy which, besides expressing grief for the disappearance of the Divus
Augustus and congratulating Tiberius, also had the task of complaining
about the bad situation currently oppressing the city and asking for com-
passion. It is not completely clear what this last sentence refers to. Territorial curtailments ordered by Augustus may be alluded to,[10] but we should
not exclude some other sort of problem. In any case, within ten years of
Augustus' death the Dentheliatis was returned to the Messenians, and, in
the face of Spartan complaints, this measure was confirmed by the Senate,
certainly with Tiberius' approval, in AD 25 (above, pp. 21–3).

The background for this decision cannot be reconstructed with certainty.
Strictly speaking, even the fact that the arbitration of Atidius Geminus in
favour of the Messenians happened under Tiberius and not already under
Augustus is not beyond doubt, although it seems more reasonable to assume
that the Spartans did not wait too long to protest against this decision in
the Senate. In any case, what is clear from Tacitus' narrative is that the
dispute before the Senate, if not already its reopening that brought about
Geminus' arbitration, was fought to a large extent with claims and counterclaims based on extensive use of the works of poets and historians referring
to the age before the liberation of Messenia by Epaminondas. In other
words, the dispute must have involved a significant amount of work on

---

[8] On Sparta in the civil wars, see Spawforth, in Cartledge and Spawforth 2002: 95–100. For evidence
of influence of the Euryclid family at Messene, possibly during the life of Eurykles' son C. Iulius
Laco, see above, p. 22 n. 30.

[9] For archaeological evidence of the Messenians' attempt to realign along the lines of Augustan
ideology, see Badie and Billot 2001: 80–5.

[10] As suggested by Themelis, *Praktika* 1988: 57–8.

the Messenian past. It may be interesting to mention in this connection that scholars at the turn of the century thought that Pausanias' direct source for the Messenian history in book IV was a Messenian local historian of the first century AD, and actually Eduard Schwartz suggested that his work had originated in connection with the last phase of the territorial dispute.[11] Admittedly, Schwartz' hypothesis can hardly be verified. As noted above (see chapter 4), Pausanias' narrative of the Messenian Wars involves extensive tampering with the main sources, the works of Rhianus and Myron, but it seems impossible to exclude with certainty that such a creative engagement with the sources should be credited to Pausanias himself. However, the notion that early Messenian history may have been the focus of renewed attention at Messene precisely in the years in which the dispute around the Dentheliatis flared up again may receive support from an unexpected corner.

One of the most famous ancient inscriptions from Messenia, and certainly the longest, was found in 1858 not far from the village of Konstantinoi, on the eastern side of the hills that divide the northern part of the Stenykleros plain from the Soulima valley. It preserves in painstaking detail the regulations for the mystery cult of the Great Gods that took place in the sanctuary of the Karneiasion,[12] not far from ancient Andania. Especially because of the importance assigned to this place in Pausanias' history of this cult, the document is commonly known as the law of the mysteries of Andania.[13] It includes detailed regulations relating to the organizational and financial aspects of the ritual, the selection of the personnel, and various other aspects, including the repair of the buildings in the sanctuary. A key role in the proceedings is played by a man by the name of Mnasistratos, the only individual mentioned in the inscription.

At the very least, our text must refer to some sort of reform of the cult, but a closer look makes it possible to grasp in more detail the situation it emanates from. The task is highly facilitated by another inscription (*Syll.*³ 735), from Argos, comprising a response of the oracle of Apollo Pythaeus to the Messenians following a consultation by a hierophant Mnasistratos, clearly the same man found in the Andania inscription. Putting together the two inscriptions, we can glean the following scenario. The cult in the Karneiasion had been suspended for some time, and the buildings of the

[11] Schwartz 1899: 457–8.   [12] On the name of the sanctuary, see Deshours 2006: 52 and n. 16.

[13] *IG* V 1, 1390 = *Syll.*³ 736. A book-length treatment of this document and of the cult has been provided by Deshours 2006. For a comprehensive survey of the previous editions of the inscription, see ibid.: 18–20.

sanctuary, a temple of the Great Gods and possibly another building referred to as "*oikos* within the sanctuary," were in need of repairs.[14] Mnasistratos was in all likelihood the descendant of a family that had been linked to the cult in the past, which would explain the fact that he turns out to be in possession of books, kept in some sort of container called a *kamptra*,[15] that seem to have had an important function in the mysteries. Correspondingly, the oracle at Argos calls him a hierophant. He consulted Apollo on behalf of the Messenians, and while it is difficult to tell precisely how his question was formulated, the god replied that the Messenians were to worship the Karneian Great Gods according to the ancestral custom and celebrate the mysteries.[16] Accordingly, the Messenians agreed on the regulations that we find in the inscription. Mnasistratos turned the books and the *kamptra* over to the *hieroi* for the year, who would then do the same with the *hieroi* of the following year, and so on. Among the privileges Mnasistratos secured for himself was a golden crown valued at 6,000 drachmas, and the leading position in the sacred procession. Furthermore, he remained in charge of the statue of the goddess Hagna and of the sacred spring nearby.[17]

As noted above, the mysteries of the Karneiasion feature almost obsessively in Pausanias' history of Messenia from the origins to Epaminondas. At first, queen Messene had been initiated by Caucon, coming from Eleusis (4.1.5, 9). Later, in what looks suspiciously like a reduplication, Lykos came from Attica and initiated Aphareus, his wife, and his children (4.1.6–8, 2.6). During the Second Messenian War, once it became clear that the Messenians were going to be defeated, Aristomenes buried on Mount Ithome a container with the sacred objects and texts of the mysteries, whose preservation guaranteed the future rebirth of free Messene (4.20.3–4), and finally, at the time of the liberation, a prophetic dream

---

[14] See lines 54–6, 59–60 and 63 of the inscription and Deshours 2006: 88–9.

[15] On the meaning of this word, see Henrichs 2003: 249 n. 149, Deshours 2006: 73–4.

[16] The text of the oracle in *Syll.*³ 735, 17–28 has been discussed recently by Deshours 1999. For a close parallel, not used in research so far, cf. LSAM 72 = *Syll.*³ 1044, 5–11, from Halikarnassos, dating to the third century BC and citing an oracle of Apollo from Telmessos. The syntax is exactly the same in both texts, and the comparison allows a number of conclusions concerning the Argive oracle. In both cases, the god advises the consultant to engage in one or more cult practices according to ancestral custom (LSAM 72, 6–8 and *Syll.*³ 735, 24–6), and then in what seems to be a new cultic activity (LSAM 72, 9–10 and *Syll.*³ 735, 26–7). Since the Argive oracle is in direct speech, the god's λέγω δέ corresponds to ἔχρησεν ὁ θεός in the text from Halikarnassos, and *pace* Deshours p. 478 n. 89, the dative plural is the correct restoration for line 27 of the Argive oracle. One consequence of this comparison is that, on the basis of the oracle itself, we cannot tell whether the mysteries existed already or were instituted at this time, as thinks Piolot 1999: 201 n. 35.

[17] On Mnasistratos' role and attributions, see Deshours 2006: 72–7.

told the Argive general Epiteles to dig out the container buried by Aristomenes (4.26.7–8). Furthermore, the priests of the mysteries appear
again and again in the narrative of the wars. The transformation of the
Great Gods into Great Goddesses may reflect another reform of the cult,
at some point in the second century AD, or just be a product of Pausanias'
own agenda, possibly influenced by the Athenian priestly family of the
Lykomidai.[18] For the rest, there are striking correspondences between his
narrative and the rituals and events documented by the two inscriptions,
especially as concerns the sacred objects and the books that Mnasistratos
entrusted to the *hieroi*, which are clearly identical with the books referred
to by Pausanias, those in which allegedly the mysteries were copied when
Aristomenes' cache was found.[19]

The total absence so far of direct evidence on the mysteries earlier than
the Mnasistratos dossier means that we cannot tell with certainty that
Pausanias' own insistence on the crucial importance of this cult is not a
result of precisely this reform.[20] However, such an extreme conclusion
seems rather unlikely, especially considering the clear evidence for stratification in Pausanias' text. Surely if the cult of Andania had been inscribed
into the history of the Messenian Wars all at once, by Pausanias himself or
by his immediate source, we would not expect the reduplications found in
Pausanias' account of the foundation of the mysteries, and the double
prophetic dreams of Epaminondas and Epiteles (see above, chapter 4)
would also be a bit surprising – not to mention Pausanias' insistence on
Andania as the place where the mysteries were celebrated (4.33.4–6), in
spite of the fact that in his own time at any rate the town of Andania was
in ruins and the sanctuary of the Karneiasion was still in operation. Still,
the notion that the cultic reform associated with Mnasistratos impacted
retrospectively the ancient history of Messenia narrated by Pausanias has

---

[18] For the Great Goddesses as Pausanias' contribution, see Robertson 1988: 253–4 and Piolot 1999:
212–13. The second reform has been suggested by Deshours 2006: 213–29, basing her argument also
on the reappearance of a hierophant from Messene in *IvO* 459, approximately dated to the second
half of the second century. In any case, the Athenian priestly family of the Lykomidai, linked to a
cult of Demeter called "Great Goddess" and attested as loosely belonging to the circle of Plutarch's
acquaintances (Robertson 1988: 253), must have something to do with Pausanias' views of the Attic
origin of the mysteries of Andania, or with the second reform, if it ever happened. This explains the
curious figure of Methapus in Paus. 4.1.7–9, and the transformation of Caucon into an Athenian
(Robertson 1988: 240–1).

[19] See Deshours 2006: 71. Of course, this identification is most likely to be *a posteriori*; in any case,
papyrus rolls in Greece are unlikely to have survived four centuries, see Henrichs 2003: 248.

[20] Note, however, the *hieroi* of Karneios and the *Karneiastas* in *SEG* 52.412, third century BC
(Themelis, *Praktika* 2001: 70–1).

some attraction.[21] But in order to assess the possibility of a more specific connection, we first need to discuss the chronology of Mnasistratos' reform.

The inscription of the mysteries includes no explicit dating formula, and the eponymous secretary of the council at the beginning of the oracular response from Argos cannot be dated either. However, the regulations refer repeatedly to the first year in which the mysteries are going to be celebrated, and call it "the fifty-fifth year." On the assumption that this indication was based on the so-called "Achaean era," that counted years starting from 145/4 BC, the inscription has been dated to the year 91/90 BC.[22] For an inscription of this period, aspects such as letter forms and dialectal spelling offer only very general indications, but in our case they can be said to be broadly consistent with the date obtained based on the Achaean era. In recent years, however, an alternative chronology has been advanced. Observing that no other inscription from Messenia seems to be dated according to the Achaean era, whereas many carry dates based on the so-called "Actian era," in which years were counted starting from the year of the battle of Actium in 31 BC, Petros Themelis has suggested to lower the date of the inscription of the mysteries to 24 AD. According to this new date, Mnasistratos would be one and the same with the Messenian honored by the sacred *gerousia* of Artemis in 42 AD (*SEG* 23.208), and most likely also with a further Mnasistratos, a very wealthy man who appears in a list of contributions found not far from Andania (*SEG* 11.979).[23]

At present, it is difficult to assess the likelihood of this new chronology. The number of inscriptions from Messene has more than doubled since Kolbe's volume of the *Inscriptiones Graecae*, and while it can be expected that this increase will offer a much better starting point for chronology based on formal criteria such as letter forms, for the time being such

---

[21] In this perspective, the fact that it was the Argive general Epiteles who received the prophetic dream that allowed the texts of the mysteries to be found could be related to the function of the Argive oracle of Apollo Pythaeus in promoting the reform; see above, p. 214 on Argive involvement in the liberation of Messenia in 369 BC.

[22] On the starting point of the Achaean era, 145/4 rather than 146/5 as often assumed, see Ferrary 1988: 189 n. 228.

[23] Themelis, *Praktika* 2001: 75–8. For a detailed discussion of the evidence, see Deshours 2004a: 115–20, who tentatively accepts the identification of the hierophant and the contributor, but keeps separate the man honored by the *gerousia*, whom she considers probably a descendant of the previous. Whether or not the identification of the three is accepted, Mnasistratos and his family appear to have had extensive connections with the area around ancient Andania. *SEG* 11.979 comes from the vicinity of the modern village of Andania, in the Stenykleros plain, immediately to the east of Konstantinoi and the most likely location of ancient Andania, and is apparently a list of contributions from that area; and from the modern village of Stenyklaros, in the same area, comes another inscription (*SEG* 11.982), dated to the first century AD, in honor of Asklepiades, son of Mnasistratos.

criteria cannot be applied with any confidence. Adolf Wilhelm's observations on the orthography and dialectal spelling of the mysteries inscription[24] remain valid, to be sure, but especially if this document intended to present itself as the reinstatement of an ancestral custom, archaism is precisely what we would expect. After all, Pausanias famously credits the Messenians with preserving their Doric dialect in the purest form (4.27.11). Therefore, keeping in mind that we are moving on shaky and potentially mobile ground, it seems preferable to reflect on whether the lower chronology would offer a convincing historical context for our document.

Whatever form the cult in the Karneiasion grove took during the Hellenistic period, it was almost certainly interrupted, at least from a Messenian point of view, when Andania was assigned to Megalopolis in 182 after the Messenian revolt against the Achaean League (above, p. 264). One possible occasion for the cultic reform attested by the Argive oracle and by the mysteries inscription could indeed be the return of the Stenykleros plain to Messene, which, however, cannot be dated with any confidence based on the evidence currently at our disposal.[25] On the other hand, the lower chronology would bring the reform in close proximity to the final recovery of the Dentheliatis by the Messenians and to the supposed date of Pausanias' immediate local source, and offer an interesting and consistent historical context to Mnasistratos' initiatives.

The first years of Tiberius' reign would then represent a moment of powerful revival for Messenian tradition. On the one hand, the link between the mysteries and Messenian freedom must have endowed Mnasistratos' reform with a powerful symbolic meaning. No matter how much invention was involved, there can be no doubt that the reinstatement of the cult in the Karneiasion was perceived, at least in part, as a recovery of ancestral rites and traditions, and references to books and old writings in the inscription emphasize the point.[26] Possibly at this point a revised version of the early history of Messenia was also produced, one in which the mysteries featured in an even more prominent and systematic way than before. Pausanias' Messenian version of the Limnai incident probably goes back to this phase, and the hypothetical local historian could be

---

[24] Wilhelm 1914: 72–3.

[25] On the assumption that Messene regained the land it had lost to Megalopolis after the Achaean War of 146 BC, Mnasistratos' reform would have come more than fifty years later, according to the traditional dating of the mysteries inscription, or well over a century according to the new date.

[26] In line 84 of the inscription there is a reference to "the spring called Hagna in the old writings"; Henrichs 2003: 248 aptly speaks of "a treasure trove of sacred texts – whether real or imagined."

responsible also for the pervasive imitation of Herodotus found in Pausanias' *Messeniaka*, and possibly even for Herodotean pastiches like the story of the Messenians in Rhegion and Zankle.[27] The dispute over the Dentheliatis, fought precisely with the weapons of ancestral lore and hoary traditions, was at the same time a result and a component of this revival, in so far as regaining control of the mountain district and of the sanctuary of Artemis Limnatis had little practical advantage, but again, a deep symbolic meaning for the Messenians.

In the new world of the Empire, the past was the main source of symbolic capital for the Greeks. The Messenians seem to have been quick to understand the value of this resource. At the same time, the leading role assumed in this process by the hierophant Mnasistratos points forward to a kind of phenomenon that will appear with increasing intensity in the decades to come, that of wealthy and influential individuals who acquired a leading role in the shaping of a community's views of its past and ultimately of its very identity. This was certainly not a completely new phenomenon in Greek history, but the evidence points to a vastly increased scope for influential individuals' impact on the community. It is in this historical context, in the sunset of Messenian history, that Messenians for the first time become visible as individual historical actors.

THE BEST OF THE MESSENIANS

For members of the ruling elites of Greece, striving for prestige and prominence, the new world of the Province of Achaea progressively changed the rules of the game in important ways. If the Hellenistic kingdoms had already created a sort of parallel universe to the world of the polis, with powerful individuals moving back and forth between the two, bringing connections and resources from the large new world of the kingdoms to bear on the life and well-being of their native cities, the Roman province, with its local administration seamlessly integrated into the great fabric of the Empire, brought about a new situation. Again, as in the Hellenistic period, a larger arena was provided for powerful and ambitious citizens, but it was a much more stable one, and one that did

---

[27] On the Herodotean models for the Messenian version of the Limnai episode and for the Messenian migration to Sicily, see above, pp. 81 and 151. Further Herodotean traits include Manticlus' proposal for the Messenians to occupy Sardinia (Paus. 4.23.5) and Aristomenes' project to seek help from Ardys king of Lydia and Phraortes king of Media (Paus. 4.24.2). Note also turns of phrases such as νησιώτας ἀντὶ ἠπειρωτῶν in Paus. 4.23.5 and Hdt. 7.170.2.

not tend to strain as much their ties to their cities. The province offered a new forum for interaction and competition, one in which antagonism between poleis seems to have tapered away, while members of the wealthiest families increasingly formed an estate overstepping the borders of their several cities.[28] Most of the evidence on these individuals has been preserved in the form of decrees granting them honors of various kinds in reward for acts of benefaction. Besides documenting the social transaction that constitutes the actual core of these documents, they preserve a wealth of information on the careers of those honored and ultimately also on their self-representation. It is to this kind of evidence that we will now turn, in the attempt to gauge through these prominent individuals what it meant to be Messenian in the second century AD.

A group of seven statue bases from Olympia, dating to the second century AD, carry inscriptions referring to Messenians honored for having been excellent citizens.[29] Three of them are not otherwise known, one has been identified only tentatively, but the remaining three were highly prominent politicians within the Achaean *koinon*, who had been granted a second statue by the *koinon* itself.[30] As shown by the fact that some of the inscriptions mention the grant of a crown,[31] the seemingly general reference to these men having been excellent citizens, or "the best" citizens, actually points to a formalized procedure. A long inscription from the theater of Messene, honoring Tiberius Claudius Saethida Caelianus, a prominent Messenian whose career we will turn to in a moment, spells out more explicitly the procedure, decreeing that he be granted the statue for the *aristopoliteia* in that year (*SEG* 51.458, col. B l.36–7). The fact that this inscription refers to one statue, in the singular, and the presence of the six bases in Olympia strongly suggest that year after year the Messenians

---

[28] See Jones 1971: 39–47. The families of this elite show a remarkably high level of intermarriage across the boundaries of the cities, see the evidence collected by Spawforth 1985 for Sparta and Epidaurus.

[29] *IvO* 445, for Philonidas son of Diogenes; *IvO* 446, for Publius Aelius Harmoneikos; *IvO* 447, for Tiberius Claudius Crispianus; *IvO* 449, for Titus Flavius Polybios; *IvO* 465, for Iulius Athenaios; *SEG* 31.372, for Tiberius Claudius Kalligenes; *SEG* 49.469, for Marcus Tadius Lykortas. *IvO* 445, 446, and 449 use the formula ἄριστα πολιτευσάμενος, *IvO* 447 has the verb in the present, πολιτευόμενος (for a tentative explanation of the use of the present, see below, n. 32).

[30] See *IvO* 448 (?Tib. Claudius Crispianus); *IvO* 450 (T. Flavius Polybios); *IvO* 458 (Tib. Claudius Kalligenes). The Achaean *koinon* included a portion of the Peloponnese whose extension varied in time during the first two centuries of the Empire, see Kahrstedt 1950b: 70–5; Deininger 1965: 88–91; Sartre 1991: 207–11; for the function of Olympia in it, Bowersock 1965: 92.

[31] According to *IvO* 465 and *SEG* 49.469, the honored had been "crowned with the crown of *aristopoliteia*" by the city of the Messenians, while *SEG* 31.372 has a different formula, "on account of the crown of *aristopoliteia*." A crown appears also in *SEG* 47.402, from Messene, on which see the next footnote.

dedicated there the statue of their fellow citizen who was deemed most worthy.[32] The honors apparently included the granting of a crown.

The kind of competition these texts refer to is documented in somewhat more detail at Sparta. There, an inscription from the age of Trajan records that Titus Flavius Charixenos had been the first to win the *agōn aristopoliteias* after its renewal and to receive the corresponding honors, clearly including a statue, in accordance with the law.[33] In the absence of earlier evidence, we may wonder to what extent the Spartans' claim of having reinstated some preexisting custom should be taken seriously, although there seems no reason to doubt that they thought that was what they were doing.[34] How exactly the *agōn* functioned we do not know, but engagement on behalf of the community must have been what was rewarded. Based on what we know of the careers of the honored, we may presume that euergetism and involvement in local and provincial politics counted towards a citizen's score.[35]

So far, the *aristopoliteia* is attested only at Sparta and Messene,[36] in documents starting from the age of Trajan and continuing into the third century. It is generally assumed that the custom originated at Sparta, in part perhaps also on the strength of the text of the inscription for Titus Flavius Charixenos.[37] In any case, none of the Messenian texts is obviously pre-Hadrianic. The competition for *aristopoliteia* is best understood in parallel with the honorific title of *hēstia tēs poleōs*, also attested mostly at Sparta and so far only once at Messene.[38] In both cases, the Messenians

---

[32] On the basis of the evidence available at present, this seems the most likely hypothesis; it should be noted, however, that the decree for Saethida Caelianus does not refer to the fact that the statue was to be dedicated at Olympia, while the fragmentary inscription *SEG* 47.402 from Messene, where only mention of the crown of *aristopoliteia* is legible, could refer to a statue dedicated at Messene. From the wording of the inscription for Caelianus, *SEG* 51.458, col. B l.36–7, it seems that the honor was granted to him before the end of the year; this might conceivably explain the use of the present in *IvO* 447. For the title of "*aristopolitēs* for life," see below.

[33] *IG* V 1, 467; see Schwertfeger 1981: 253. The formula "receive the honors of *aristopoliteia* in accordance with the law" is standard at Sparta; see *IG* V 1, 65, l. 6–7; 485, l. 5–6; 498, l. 5–6; 536, l. 8–9; 553 l. 12.

[34] On the historical context in which the competition was instituted, or reintroduced, see Spawforth, in Cartledge and Spawforth 2002: 106.

[35] See Spawforth, in Cartledge and Spawforth 2002: 159; Lafond 2001: 403–4.

[36] It is unclear whether an *aristopolitēs* documented in a honorary inscription from Hermione, *IG* IV 714, should be taken as evidence of the existence of the custom there, as well; the inscription uses the adjective as a term of praise, but includes no reference to a competition or to specific honors associated. See Schwertfeger 1981: 254 and n. 22.

[37] See Spawforth, in Cartledge and Spawforth 2002: 198–9.

[38] On this honorific title, attested in inscriptions of the Antonine age, almost exclusively from Sparta, and possibly influenced by the cult of Vesta at Rome, see Kajava 2004: 8–17; on its probable Spartan origin, esp. 17. Beside the new case from Messene, *SEG* 51.458 B, l. 25 (see below), not yet known to Kajava, the only other non-Spartan example is *IvO* 473 = *Syll.*³ 882, from the early third

may have adopted a Spartan custom,[39] confirming the curious porosity of the border between themselves and the Spartans when it came to rituals and cults. From their point of view, they may have simply acted according to traditional practices: there was a grey zone in their past where what was ancestrally Spartan could be, or be claimed to be, ancestrally Messenian.[40] After all, they all witnessed in their city the existence of the cult of Artemis Orthia, the recognized trademark of early imperial Sparta.

However, even if it was ultimately derived from a Spartan practice, the Messenian version of the *aristopoliteia* had one important peculiarity. As far as we can tell, all the evidence points to the Spartans honoring their "best citizens" at Sparta – at any rate, all the evidence, consisting of statue bases, comes from Sparta itself. By displaying the statues of the winners at least also at Olympia, and possibly only there, the Messenians chose as the addressee for the celebration of their best fellow citizens the Achaean *koinon* as a whole. This choice corresponds to a peculiar orientation of the Messenian elite, as demonstrated by the prominence that some of the honored reached within the *koinon*. While two of them, Philonidas (*IvO* 445) and Julius Athenaios (*IvO* 465), are not otherwise known,[41] another, Publius Aelius Harmoneikos, may have been the brother of a *stratēgos* of the Achaean *koinon*.[42] The remaining three had even more distinguished careers. Titus Flavius Polybios was *agoranomos* and then *stratēgos* of the Achaean *koinon*, and *agōnothetēs* of games in honor of Antinoos, probably

---

century AD, for Claudia Tyche, called Eleian and Kleitorian, who was *hestia* for life of the *koinon* of the Arcadians.

[39] As a further parallel, note the honorific title of "*aristopolitēs* for life," apparently attested at Messene by a fragmentary inscription from the second or third century AD (*SEG* 52.407; see Themelis, *Praktika* 2002: 36–7), and common at Sparta, sometimes in the form *aristopoliteutēs*, from the early second century (see *IG* V 1, 468; 504; 681; 685).

[40] Compare the case of the monumental tombs within the city walls, above p. 290.

[41] Note, however, that ancestors of Philonidas, son of Diogenes, are probably represented in the subscription for the repair of monuments *SEG* 23.207, of Augustan age (see Migeotte 1985); at line 29 we find a Diogenes, son of Diogenes, offering 150 *denarii* on behalf of Diogenes, Philonidas, and Philoxenos (on their possible kinship relations see Migeotte 1985: 604). Furthermore, a Philonidas was honored at Messene with a statue as benefactor of the city, sometime in the first century BC, *SEG* 47.395.

[42] He is probably identical with Harmoneikos, son of Ariston, honored by Messene in *IG* V 1, 1399 (Spawforth 1985: 214; the absence of Roman names in this inscription is due to the fact that it is in verse); his mother was the Spartan Ageta, and he claimed to be descended from Heracles and the Dioscuri, possibly through Ageta, who seems to have belonged to one of the most prominent families of the Spartan aristocracy (Spawforth 1985: 213–15). The Messenian P. Aelius Ariston, son of Ariston, honored by the Achaean *koinon* with a statue for having been *stratēgos* of the Hellenes (*IvO* 459), may be his relative, possibly his brother. The strategy was the eponymous magistracy of the *koinon*, see *IvO* 487; on the use of the term Hellenes in official documents of the Achaean *koinon*, see Puech 1983: 24.

also organized in the framework of the *koinon* (*IvO* 450).[43] His career should fall during the reigns of Hadrian and Pius. Tiberius Claudius Crispianus, *archiereus* of the Imperial cult in Messene for life and a man with a distinguished career in the Roman army, was Helladarch under Marcus Aurelius or Commodus.[44] Tiberius Claudius Kalligenes, possibly the last of them in time, was *archiereus* of the imperial cult in Messene for life, and then became *stratēgos* of the Achaean *koinon* and Helladarch, in the late second century AD[45]. Although no monument in his honor was found at Olympia, Tiberius Claudius Saethida Caelianus, whose career will be discussed more in detail below, should be added to this group, having been Helladarch for life, probably in the early years of Pius.

One thing that these documents demonstrate is the perfect integration of the Messenian elite in the world of the province of Achaea. In the first place, our men engage in competition for honor at the civic level. The winners are as it were promoted to a higher league, competing at the regional level of the Achaean *koinon*. Finally, a minority ends up being coopted into the Imperial ruling elite. These levels of competition, city, province, and Empire, correspond perfectly to the layers of identity, *patris*, Greece, and Roman Empire, identifiable in the culture of second-century Greece.[46] This new way of articulating a tiered identity is exemplified in the most striking way by the monuments for Titus Flavius Polybios. As mentioned above, two statue bases from Olympia carry dedications in his honor, one by the Messenians (*IvO* 449) and one by the Achaean *koinon* (*IvO* 450). In both cases, the texts of the decrees in his honor are accompanied by an elegiac couplet that refers to the dedication of a statue of the historian Polybius, the very couplet that made it possible to identify the famous Hellenistic relief from Kleitor as representing Polybius.[47] Clearly, Titus Flavius Polybios thereby claimed his namesake as his ancestor.

---

[43] The Titus Flavius Polybios honored in 257 AD (*IvO* 486 and 487), Messenian and Lakedaimonian, priest of the goddess Roma and winner of the *aristopoliteia*, is probably a descendant from his; on this man, see below. The family seems to have owned one of the two monumental tombs erected probably in the late second century AD outside the Arcadian gate, see Themelis, *Praktika* 1997: 80–2, and the gravestone *SEG* 47.414 (third century AD).

[44] Possibly instituted by Hadrian, the Helladarch was the supreme magistrate of the Achaean *koinon*, and may have been in charge of administering justice for the region according to Greek law, thereby offering an alternative to the Roman provincial courts; see Oliver 1978. On Crispianus' career, Puech 1983: 30. On Greek and Roman law courts in the Province of Achaea, see above, p. 38 n. 67.

[45] Against Schwertfeger 1981: 250–1, Puech 1983: 30–1 shows that *IvO* 458 and *SEG* 31.372 probably refer to the same person, who was first honored by Messene with reference to his activities on a local level (*SEG* 31.372), and later by the Achaean *koinon* (*IvO* 458).

[46] See Jones 2004.

[47] The epigram reads "The city erected this beautiful statue for Polybios, the son of Lykortas, in exchange for his good deeds." See Habicht 1998a: 50; the inscription is *IG* V 2, 370.

In terms of politics of memory and identity, for a Messenian to claim Polybius as an ancestor was an interesting move. As we have seen, the Achaean *koinon* now offered a highly attractive forum for the Messenian elite to engage in competition for honor and power. An ancestor who had been one of the most prominent politicians of the old Achaean League was an excellent way to reinforce one's claims in front of the Achaean *koinon*, which clearly regarded itself as the continuation of the League. For a Messenian, this genealogical connection had the additional advantage of diverting attention from the rather conflictual relationship of the Messenians to the League in the early second century, culminating in the death of Philopoemen and the invasion of Messenia by the army of the League, led by Polybius' father Lykortas.[48] Finally, Polybius was the man who mediated between the Romans and the Achaean League, saving the Greeks from a harsher punishment after the Achaean War:[49] a perfect model for a Greek politician living in the Roman Empire. The fact that the members of his family from the second half of the second century were buried in one of the monumental graves outside the Arcadian Gate, where the road for Megalopolis started (Paus. 4.33.3), symbolically reinforced the statement.

The careers of the prominent Messenians honored as best citizens bring to the fore a reorientation and restructuring of social transactions and political practice: the borders of the polis are no longer the ultimate boundary for political action and competition for honor. These changes cannot but correspond to changes in the sense of what it meant to be Messenian. Even though we cannot obviously tell to what extent the self-perception of these wealthy men was shared by their fellow citizens, we can at least be confident that the choice of Olympia as the forum where the excellence of citizens of Messene was celebrated was a function of the aspiration of the Messenian elite. In the case of Titus Flavius Polybios, we can go one step further and observe that the city, understood as the corporate body that granted honors in exchange for benefactions, accepted and underwrote his claims of ancestry and, implicitly, their associations. In other words, at least in its official incarnation, the demos of the Messenians oriented its honorary and commemorative practices according to the ambitions and self-perception of the elite, and thereby adjusted itself to

---

[48] On these events, see above, pp. 263–4. See also below on possible traces of second-century Messenians' attitude to the Achaean *koinon* in Pausanias' narrative of the war between Messene and the League.

[49] On the honors granted to Polybius by various cities of the Achaean League for placating the fury of the Romans, see below n. 85.

the new way in which members of this elite construed the meaning of being Messenians, within the province of Achaea, within the Roman Empire.[50] Surely this adjustment had an influence on how the Messenians in general perceived and experienced their Messenicity, if only because the celebration of the Messenian elite impacted their landscape in a durable way, as shown in the case of Titus Flavius Polybios, and even more clearly in that of another prominent Messenian who was probably his contemporary, Tiberius Claudius Saethida Caelianus.

THE CLAUDII SAETHIDAE AND MESSENIAN MEMORY

During the Antonine age, only very few men in the province of Achaea could match the prestige and wealth of the Messenian Tiberius Claudius Saethida Caelianus.[51] As we know from various inscriptions in his honor, he was High Priest of the Imperial cult for the province and Helladarch of the Achaean *koinon*, both honors he held for life,[52] besides of course being a lavish benefactor of his hometown. His son, Tiberius Claudius Frontinus, reached the consulate, as *suffectus* to be sure, sometime in the central years of the second century,[53] and his two grandsons, Tiberius Claudius Saethida Caelianus the Younger and Tiberius Claudius Frontinus Niceratus, also had very respectable senatorial careers under Marcus Aurelius.[54] His mother, Claudia Frontina, received the honorific title of *hestia tēs poleōs*, a sort of symbolic mother of the political community.[55]

---

[50] The impact of the local elites on the construction and articulation of memory is a phenomenon well documented in Antonine Greece in general, see above, n. 7.

[51] See Habicht 1998a: 58–9, Themelis 2000: 112–13.

[52] Puech 1983: 27–8 on Saethida's titles. On the high priesthood of the imperial cult of Achaea, celebrated at Corinth, see also Spawforth 1994: 218–24.

[53] His complete nomenclature appears now to have been Tib. Claudius Frontinus Macer Campanus (which must have something to do with the land owned by the family around Abellinum, of which Frontinus' sons were *patroni*), as shown by the dedication of a statue of Hadrian from the theater of Messene. From the photograph published in *Ergon* 2005: 46, it seems that also Tib. Claudius Saethida was mentioned, probably as Frontinus' father. Unfortunately, the final part of the text has been left out of the published image.

[54] Prosopographic evidence in Halfmann 1979: nos. 93, 93a, 126 and 127. The family tree of the Saethidae is laid out in *IG* V 1, 1455, an inscription in honor of Caelianus. Saethida Caelianus the Younger and Frontinus Niceratus are also noteworthy for dedicating statues of the Imperial family accompanied by the two only Latin inscriptions found in Messene so far, *CIL* III, 495, for a statue of Lucius Verus dedicated in 164 AD, and a newly found base for Faustina the Younger, Themelis, *Praktika* 2002: 45–6 and pl. 39a (text also in *SEG* 52.405), to be dated between 161 and 176 AD and carrying the names of the dedicators in the same form as *CIL* III, 495.

[55] *SEG* 51.458 B, l. 25. On the title, see above n. 38. The formula applied to Claudia Frontina seems indeed to suggest that it involved assimilation to the goddess Hestia, as supposed by Kajava 2004.

At least one earlier member of the family was already a prominent citizen of Messene, a Tiberius Claudius Saithidas who dedicated a statue of Nero, probably in 55 AD, and may have financed the renovation of the monumental Arsinoe fountain on the northern side of the agora of Messene.[56] Given the rarity of the name, it can scarcely be doubted that he was an ancestor of Caelianus the Elder, possibly but not necessarily his grandfather. An inscription from the baths on the southern side of the Asklepieion carries the name of an *agōnothetēs* Saithidas, possibly the dedicator of whatever was on the inscribed stone plinth, and seems to date to the first century BC.[57] Again, the rarity of the name suggests that we have to do with one more ancestor of Caelianus the Elder. Clearly, this had been a very prominent family in the city well before his time, as shown also by the fact that his son Frontinus seems to have married a lady from one of the wealthiest families of Messene.[58]

Caelianus' life and career seem to have spanned the reigns of Trajan, Hadrian, and Antoninus Pius. The latest document that can be associated

---

[56] The inscription on the statue base is *SEG* 41.353; for its date, see Habicht 1998b: 493 n. 35. On the fountain and its various phases, see Felten and Reinholdt 2001: 307–23. The inscription referring to the renovation of the fountain in the age of Nero is *SEG* 46.418, and it mentions also the dedication of statues of the Imperial family; the funding may have come from more than one donor, see especially l. 6. The *praenomen* Tiberius is the only portion of the name of the dedicant (s) that is preserved. The identification with the Tiberius Claudius Saethida who dedicated the statue of Nero has been proposed independently by Baldassarra 1999: 148 and by Felten and Reinholdt 2001: 319. Themelis, *Praktika* 1995: 56–7 thought of another prominent citizen of Messene, Tiberius Claudius Aristomenes the son of Dionysius, priest of the Imperial cult in Messene and dedicant of another statue of Nero, *IG* V 1, 1450; on this man and his family, see below.

[57] *SEG* 39.383. See Themelis, *Praktika* 1988: 64–5. The stone seems much too small to have carried a statue, and Themelis speaks generally of a dedication. The inscription itself reads rather like a list of magistrates (cf. e.g. *IG* V 1, 1467). A likely date in the second half of the century would result if the eponymous priest Dionysios who appears in this inscription is indeed the father of Pleistarchia, mother of Dionysios and wife of Aristomenes, documented in *SEG* 23.207, l. 27; see below, p. 319 and n. 100.

[58] The name Frontinus Niceratus of one of Frontinus' sons suggests a link, most probably through Frontinus' wife, with the family of Nikeratos son of Theon, who offered an unlimited amount of money for the restoration of the *bouleion* and the adjoining stoa (*SEG* 23.207, l. 19, Augustan; see above, n. 41) and was *epimelētēs* of the Oupesia in 42 AD (*SEG* 23.208, l.4), and whose son, Tib. Claudius Theon, son of Nikeratos, was honored with a statue in room IX of the gymnasium complex. For the archaeological context, the statue and its base, see Themelis, *Praktika* 1996: 158–62 and id. 2000: 153–58. for the inscription, see *SEG* 47.400a (note also that the now famous Hermes statue came from that same room, and stood on a base that had been reemployed, like the one for Tib. Claudius Theon; unfortunately, the new dedication is lost, but the old one, that ended up on the side of the base that faced the wall, was for another Theon, *SEG* 47.397, dated by Themelis to the first century BC, not AD as in the lemma of *SEG*). An earlier member of this family, Theon the Elder son of Nikeratos, was buried in the monumental mausoleum K 3, behind room IX (or is he identical with the donor of *SEG* 23.207?). On this family, see Fröhlich 2007: 214–16. Cf. also Habicht 1998b: 491–2.

with him is the dedication of a statue of Marcus Aelius Aurelius Verus Caesar, that is, of Marcus Aurelius after he had been elevated to Caesar by Pius in 139 AD. The dedication had been vowed, probably in 139, by "the Greeks" according to Caelianus' proposal, and then realized at his expense.[59] Another base, found recently in the agora of Messene and carrying an almost identical inscription, referred to a statue of Antoninus Pius, dedicated and financed in the same way.[60] It is reasonable, though perhaps not necessary, to assume that this dedication was close in time to Antoninus Pius' rise to the imperial throne in July 138. Considering that Cornelius Pulcher of Epidaurus, who also was Helladarch of the Achaean *koinon* and High Priest for life,[61] seems to have been still alive in 137, while since February 138 the position of Helladarch for the Achaean *koinon* was held, probably *pro tempore*, by the *stratēgos* of the *koinon* Lucius Gellius Areton,[62] Caelianus may well have become Helladarch and High Priest in Antoninus' accession year: what better occasion to initiate the dedication of statues of the emperor and his designated successor?[63]

Another document, still imperfectly known, coming from the theater of Messene, may associate Caelianus with Trajan.[64] The text, inscribed on two large bases of marble, originally located in a niche on the left side of the *proscaenium* of the theater, reports a long decree emanating from the city of Messene and including, after an expansive praise of Caelianus' virtues and benefactions, the most detailed statement of the honors granted to him by his fellow citizens. Apparently, Caelianus had shown his generosity to the city in various ways, and especially by financing a lavish

---

[59] *IG* V 1, 1451. According to the nomenclature used in this inscription, Marcus Aurelius has already been nominated Caesar, but is not yet referred to with the corresponding name, which would be Aurelius Caesar Aug. Pii filius; this seems to suggest that the statue was dedicated immediately after he had become Caesar. For Marcus Aurelius' nomenclature, see Kienast 1990: 137. It is not completely clear if "the Greeks" who dedicated the statue are to be understood as the members of the Achaean *koinon* or the whole province of Achaea; see Puech 1983: 24 and Spawforth 1994: 222, and cf. *IvO* 459, discussed in n. 42 above.

[60] *SEG* 52.405. The text is essentially identical to that of *IG*, V 1, 1451, except of course for the name of the emperor.

[61] On his career, see Puech 1983: 17–21.   [62] See again Puech 1983: 26–7.

[63] While both the statue of Marcus Aurelius and the statue of Antoninus Pius could in theory have been dedicated at a later date, the fact that Saethida the Elder's son dedicated a statue of Hadrian, and his grandchildren were dedicating statues of the imperial family as early as 164 AD does not encourage one to put the date of Caelianus the Elder's dedications too late into Pius' reign.

[64] *SEG* 51.458; Trajan appears in col. B, l. 6, but his name is the only word that can be read in that line, so it is not possible to know why he is mentioned. Since Saethida appears in col. A, l. 3–4 as Helladarch and priest of the Imperial cult, the inscription should be dated to 138 AD at the earliest. Two fragmentary inscriptions coming from the theater, a marble revetment slab and the upper left corner of another base, also seem to refer to Caelianus the Elder; see *SEG* 51.459–60 and the legible photographs published by Themelis, *Praktika* 2000: pl. 46.

renovation of the theater, whose *scaenae frons* and *proscaenium* were now rebuilt on a monumental scale, with precious materials and a profusion of statues, in the best Roman style. Among other things, the decree refers to the dedication of statues of Caelianus *kata phylēn*, to be displayed in the *proscaenium*,[65] of a consecrated statue (*agalma kathierōthēn*) of his mother as *hestia tēs poleōs*, and of statues of his son and his whole *genos*. The text does not say explicitly where the statues of Caelianus' family were to be set up; if they were destined for the theater, then this building became a sort of family monument of the Saethidae. Moreover, Caelianus was also proclaimed the winner of the *agōn aristopoliteias* for the year, and one further statue of him was to be dedicated for that reason.[66] Yet another, equestrian, statue of Caelianus the Elder stood on a large base at the bottom of the steps that led from the eastern side into the *cavea* of the *ōdeion* in the northeastern corner of the Asklepieion (see plate 9).[67]

It is probably because he was so prominent in the landscape of Antonine Messene, that Caelianus ends up being one of the few Greeks of the Imperial age to be recorded by Pausanias. After mentioning statues of the gods and of Epaminondas kept in the *hierothysion*, and the statues of Hermes, Heracles, and Theseus located in the gymnasium, Pausanias writes (4.32.2):

As for Aithidas,[68] I learnt that he was a man older than myself, who gained influence through his wealth and is honored by the Messenians as a hero. There are certain Messenians, who, while admitting that Aithidas was a man of great wealth, maintain that it is not he who is represented on the stele but an ancestor and namesake of his. The elder Aithidas was their leader, when Demetrius the son of Philip and his force surprised them in the night and succeeded in penetrating into the town by surprise.

Given his prominence attested by the monuments we have just considered, and given Pausanias' chronological indication, the wealthy (S)aithidas he

---

[65] That is, five statues, since there were five tribes in Messene. For another case of statues *kata phylēn*, see the dossier of documents regarding another prominent Messenian of the Antonine age, Tiberius Claudius Dionysius Crispianus, discussed below. For more examples of statues dedicated by tribes, see *SEG* 52.408, *SEG* 45.312–13, *SEG* 48.497 and 499.

[66] In theory, *IG* V 1, 1455, copied by Cyriac of Ancona and then lost, might have been inscribed on the base of the statue of Caelianus as winner of the *agōn aristopoliteias* (unless, that is, that statue was dedicated in Olympia, as suggested above); otherwise, we might have to assume one more statue of Caelianus, associated with the inscription.

[67] See Themelis 2000: 112 and pls. 97–8, and *IG* V 1, 1455a.

[68] The problem of Pausanias' spelling of the name should not detain us here. In the following, it will simply be assumed that, however this situation is to be explained, our passage does indeed refer to Saethida; see Habicht 1998a: 38 n. 35.

Plate 9 The *odeion* of the Asklepieion. On the right, the base of the equestrian statue of
Tib. Claudius Saethida

refers to must be Caelianus the Elder. The way his monument is introduced, abruptly starting from the dedicatee before having even mentioned
it, is characteristic of Pausanias' style. In this case, though, his brevity
makes for some obscurity. The heroic cult for Saithidas should presuppose some sort of building, which Pausanias does not bother to mention.
The stele he refers to may have been part of such a building, although it
does not have to have been. No reason is given for the doubt regarding
the identification of the person represented on the stele. The alternative
version of "some Messenians" is not explicitly rejected, but it should be
noticed that Pausanias states his identification of the hero Saithidas as a
fact, in his own authorial voice, while in his detailed narrative of the
Macedonian attack on Messene (4.29.1–5), which took place in 214 BC
and was led by Demetrius of Pharos, not by Demetrius the son of
Philip,[69] Saithidas "the Elder" is not mentioned at all. This may suggest
that Pausanias intended implicitly to question his role.[70]

---

[69] See Grandjean 2003: 80 and n. 123.
[70] On the possible implications of this point for Pausanias' stance vis-à-vis the Saethidae, see below.

If Saithidas received heroic honors, it seems resonable to assume that some sort of building was dedicated to his cult. As we have seen, monumental graves were exceptionally frequent in the center of Messene, and heroic honors and burial in the center of the city are actually mentioned in a late Hellenistic inscription from the city.[71] Some sort of monumental grave or *hērōon* seems to be what we should be looking for. If we assume that Pausanias is mentioning monuments more or less in the order in which he saw them, as he often does, this may help to identify at least the general area where Saithidas' monumental grave may have been located. It is mentioned at the end of a sequence that touches the Asklepieion (4.31.10), the temple of Messene (4.31.11–12), recently uncovered by Themelis in the center of the agora (above, p. 273), then the *hierothysion*, of uncertain location, and finally the gymnasium (4.32.1; see figure 7). It is roughly a north–south itinerary, if slightly circuitous, which may suggest that Pausanias should have met the *hērōon* of Saithidas in the area of the stadium. None of the various documents on the Saethidae family found at Messene, with the possible exception of the inscription with Saethida's genealogy copied by Cyriac (*IG* V 1, 1455), can be connected in any way with this monument. However, a fragment from the top of a large base, found among the debris that covered the track of the stadium and carrying the inscription *Saithidan*,[72] could well belong to whatever monument Pausanias is alluding to, and somewhat reinforces the conclusion that it might have been located in this area.

In this area, there is one natural candidate. Right at the end of the track of the stadium, abundant remains of a small temple-like building have been found (see plate 10). It was a prostyle building with four columns on the front, and it seems almost obvious to interpret it as a *hērōon*.[73] Its location was as prominent as it could possibly be, in the focal point of the whole stadium-gymnasia complex, and this offers a first indication of its chronology. The stadium of Messene was built during the third century BC, on a large landfill that occupied a glen to the south of the Asklepieion complex. Waters coming down from the southwestern side of Mount Ithome tend to find here their natural outlet, and even in modern times channeling has been necessary to prevent the fill from being washed away. The city walls, cutting across the glen, ended up functioning as a sort of

---

[71] *IG* V 1, 1427. On the funerary monuments *intra muros* at Messene, see above, p. 290 and Fröhlich 2007.

[72] *SEG* 48.491; see Themelis 2000: 109.

[73] The most detailed publication of this monument is Cooper 1999; see also Themelis 2000: 102–13, and Müth 2007: 119–24.

Plate 10   The stadium of Messene. At the far end, in the center, the podium of the *hērōon*,
currently being rebuilt

analēmma for the stadium.[74] The *hērōon* stood on a podium more than
seven meters high, built against the outer face of the walls in order to fill
the difference in elevation between the ground outside the walls and the
level of the stadium track. The outer faces of the podium were covered by
layers of slabs, alternating reddish limestone and thinner slabs of light grey
limestone. In order to build it, it was necessary to demolish a portion of the
city walls.[75]

The *hērōon* was built with extraordinary care for details, ranging from
the decorative elements to the use of optic refinements. Frederick Cooper,
who has studied the remains in detail in order to prepare a reconstruction,
favors a mid-Hellenistic chronology, close in date to the Asklepieion
complex, currently dated to the first half of the second century BC (above,
chapter 9). However, it seems *a priori* difficult to believe that the podium
might have been built in an age in which the city wall still retained its
defensive function.[76] Moreover, according to Themelis some of the grey

---

[74] On the stadium of Messene, see now Müth 2007: 91–4 and 216–8.
[75] See Müth 2007: 119.   [76] See Camp 2000: 50.

limestone slabs of the podium are actually reemployed grave stelae, and some of them seem to carry inscriptions coming down in date to the first century AD,[77] while recent stratigraphic investigations conducted by Pieter Broucke around the base of the podium have resulted in a *terminus post* of 68–69 AD for the construction of the little temple.[78] A date in the early Empire for the *hērōon* seems inescapable. The question is rather how much later than the *terminus post* offered by the stratigraphy we should go. Fragments of marble sculpture found among the ruins of the *hērōon* all seem to date around the mid second century AD, and include a headless *imago clipeata* with a gorgoneion on the cuirass, which may have adorned the pediment of the building, and a number of fragments that can be put together to form the figure of a man reclining on the lid of a sarcophagus.[79] At the present, the second century AD seems the most likely date for the building.

In theory, and keeping in mind the possibility that he did not mention it at all, Pausanias' text offers two possible candidates for the identification of this *hērōon*. Right after mentioning Saithidas, he refers to Aristomenes' tomb (4.32.3), suggesting that it was probably located roughly in the same area. Considering Aristomenes' importance in Messenian tradition, it may seem natural to refer to him this prestigious little building, as Cooper and Broucke do. However, the fragments of sculpture found among the ruins of the building do not offer any support to this interpretation, and the shape of the building itself does not agree well with the sacrificial ritual performed in connection with it. According to Pausanias, the bull that was going to be sacrificed to the hero was first tied to a column that was above the grave, and if the animal was able to move the column, this was seen as a favorable omen (4.32.3).[80] It is difficult to see how such a ritual may have been performed in connection with the *hērōon* of the stadium. Furthermore, given Aristomenes' prominence in Messene ever since the time of the liberation in the fourth century, we would rather expect his *hērōon* to be much older than the second century AD, or at least to show evidence of earlier phases.[81] It seems more reasonable to admit that Aristomenes' grave has not yet been found.

---

[77] Themelis 2000: 107.

[78] Broucke forthcoming. I am extremely grateful to Pieter Broucke for sharing with me the text of his very important paper.

[79] See Torelli 1998: 477 (where the recumbent on the sarcophagus is still wrongly identified as a woman), Themelis 2000: 160 and pls. 91–3, and Müth 2007: 121.

[80] The yearly sacrifice of a bull to Aristomenes is mentioned also in an inscription dating to the Augustan age, *SEG* 23.207, l. 13-14.

[81] On stories about Aristomenes and their possible date, see above, pp. 88–91.

On the other hand, the *hērōon* makes for a perfect candidate for the focus of the heroic honors paid to Saithidas by the Messenians. For one thing, its chronology agrees with this interpretation. But there may be more to it. Beside the fact that the location of the *hērōon* oriented towards it the whole stadium complex,[82] its very position almost straddling the city walls, which still in Pausanias' time were seen as the most imposing and most prestigious architectural feature of the city,[83] could have a very specific meaning. According to the Messenian version reported by Pausanias, during the Macedonian attack in 214 BC Saithidas the Elder had led his fellow citizens in fighting off the enemies, who had penetrated inside the city walls. How appropriate, then, that his descendant should be celebrated in a building located right on top of the city wall, as if to claim an ancestral function as defender of the city. In other words, the monument was probably related in a symbolic way to the family history of the Saithidai, in a similar way to the graves of the family of Titus Flavius Polybios right outside the Arcadian Gate being related to that family's claims of ancestry (see above). This, of course, would imply that the monument, even though erected for Caelianus the Elder, in some sense connected him to his ancestor. If we return to Pausanias' text with this in mind, it becomes clear that the divergence in the interpretation of the identity of the man represented on the stele could point precisely to some sort of conflation between Saithidas the Elder and Caelianus.

The hypothesis that, at least as far as the stele is concerned, something about it made possible the double reading that Pausanias refers to, that is, that for some reason it might have been plausible to take its subject as either Saethida Caelianus the Elder, or as his ancestor, Saithidas the Elder, may perhaps receive some illumination from two documents related to another illustrius Messenian of the late second century AD, Titus Flavius Polybios. As discussed above, the statue bases that mention him carry each two texts, a prose dedication referring to him and an elegiac couplet referring to the historian Polybius. The appearance of these two pairs of inscriptions on the bases has perhaps received less attention than it deserved. Formally, all the four texts are dedications of statues, which means that on each base we have two texts with the same function. The association of a dedicatory epigram with a dedication in prose would not

---

[82] See the observations of Torelli 1998: 477, who aptly compares this situation to the complex formed by the stadium of Athens and the funerary monument of Herodes Atticus.

[83] See Paus. 4.31.5 and the detailed analysis of the fortifications by Müth-Herda 2005.

be exceptional in itself,[84] but in this case, the puzzling fact is that the two texts referred to two different people. Dittenberger, in his edition of the inscriptions from Olympia, assumed without discussion that the actual statues represented Titus Flavius Polybios, which may seem reasonable enough, but on second thoughts, one wonders what was the ancient viewer supposed to think: was he or she supposed to identify the man represented by the statues as the historian, clearly mentioned by the epigram, or as his putative descendant? And ultimately, how can we be sure that the statues represented Titus Flavius and the couplet was just meant allusively to evoke his ancestor? Can we really exclude that Titus Flavius was being honored precisely by emphasizing his ancestral tie to the historian by way of a statue of the latter? Statues and reliefs representing the historian Polybius were to be seen in a number of places in Pausanias' Greece,[85] one even in Olympia (*IvO* 302), creating an iconographic context that should have made it possible to recognize a representation of him, if such stood on the bases.

Even though such questions may not be answered with certainty, the very ambiguity they point to is interesting. Clearly, in honoring Titus Flavius Polybios the Messenians and the Achaeans proceeded, in a way that we cannot precisely reconstruct, to conflate him with his famous putative ancestor the historian Polybius, thereby transferring on him in the most emphatic way the prestige of his glorious ancestor. It seems clear that some sort of similar monument could bring about precisely the contrast in interpretation that Pausanias refers to in connection to the stele of Saithidas in Messene: an implicit conflation between the wealthy Helladarch and his brave ancestor, who had saved the city from the Macedonians, potentially resulting in a visually ambiguous monument. The conflation would have been reinforced in light of the interpretation suggested above for the location of the *hērōon* on the city walls.

An even closer parallel to the case of the Saithidai in Messene is the *hērōon* of Podares at Mantinea. According to Pausanias (8.9.9–10), Podares

---

[84] For another example, see *IvO* 445, the statue of the Messenian Philonidas son of Diogenes, including a dedicatory formula in prose and an epigram of two couplets mentioning the statue and comparing Philonidas to Nestor.

[85] See Paus. 8.9.1 (stele with portrait from Mantinea; note that a fragmentary stele from Mantinea, *IG* V 2, 304, dated to the second century BC, carries the beginning of the two verses of the epigram for Polybius that appears, in complete form, in the statue bases for Titus Flavius Polybios), 8.37.2 (stele from Akakesion with inscription referring to Polybius' rescuing the Greeks after 146 BC), 8.30.8 (stele from Megalopolis with elegiac distichs including biographical details on Polybius and again references to his role as mediator between Romans and Greeks after the Achaean war), 8.44.5 (statue from Pallantion). Polybius himself mentions honors he received from the Greeks for placating the Romans, Polyb. 39.5 and 8.1.

had died fighting against the Thebans, led by Epaminondas, at the battle of Mantinea in 362 BC. His fellow-citizens had buried him in a *hērōon* in the agora of their city. However, Pausanias continues, three generations before his time the inscription on Podares' tomb had been modified to refer to a much later Podares, who had lived recently enough to become a Roman citizen. In this case, Pausanias accepts the claim of the people of Mantinea that the heroic honors were paid to the earlier Podares. There is no way to know why Pausanias reacted differently to the local versions of some Messenians and of the Mantineans, but it is difficult to resist the impression that the cases of Saethida and Podares may have been object-ively quite similar, if not identical, associating a prominent citizen of the Early Empire with a more or less putative ancestor, whose glory was enshrined in the very history of the city.[86]

The monuments of Flavius Polybios, Podares, and Claudius Saethida offer us a striking material counterpart to a phenomenon that is well attested among the upper classes of Imperial Greece, their interest in claiming descent from prominent historical figures of classical and Hel-lenistic Greece. To limit ourselves to the best-known examples, Plutarch counted among his friends a Themistocles, descendant of the fifth-century Athenian (*Them.* 32.5); Herodes Atticus claimed to be a descendant of Miltiades and Cimon (Philostr., *VS*, 2.1.1 [546]); the Spartan family of the Voluseni counted among their ancestors, besides an impressive number of mythic characters, the Spartan Lysander;[87] the Claudii Brasidae were one of the most prominent families in Sparta in the Antonine age;[88] Polykrates, the dedicatee of Plutarch's *Life of Aratos*, was supposedly a descendant of Aratos of Sikyon, and incidentally, Tiberius Claudius Polykrates, High Priest and Helladarch most probably after Caelianus,[89]

---

[86] The *hērōon* of Podares has been identified in the excavations of the agora of Mantinea, see Fougères 1898: 190–3 and Jost 1985: 131. Fougères, followed by Jost, takes for granted that the building had been erected for the fourth-century Podares, but it is not clear on what this dating is based; note that, of the three graves found in it, the one in the middle, that is, in the most prominent position, contained grave goods that Fougères dated to Roman times and was covered with the reused base of an equestrian statue, which also points to a rather late date, while the roof tiles with inscriptions referring to Podares, *IG* V 2, 321a and b, are dated by the editor, Hiller von Gaertringen, to the first century AD. On the family of Podares at Mantinea in Pausanias' time, see Pretzler 2005: 240.

[87] On this family, see Spawforth 1985: 215–24; Lysander is mentioned in *IG* IV² 1, 86, 14, an inscription for their relative, the Epidaurian Titus Statilius Lamprias, whose pedigree included the Kerykes of Athens, the Echinades of Epidaurus, Phoroneus, Perseus and Heracles.

[88] On their family tree, see Spawforth 1985: 224–44; the Spartan Brasidas who lived in the age of Augustus and claimed descent from the famous fifth-century Spartan general (Plut. *Mor.* 207f; see Bowersock 1965: 105 and n. 5) was presumably their ancestor, see Spawforth 1985: 226.

[89] Plut. *Arat.* 1 and Puech 1983: 28–9.

was almost certainly his son. This appears to be a relative novelty in Greek social history.[90] Claiming descent from gods and heroes of Greek myth had been a traditional way for Greek aristocrats to articulate their social superiority, at least in the archaic and early classical ages, and the ruling elites of Imperial Greece revived this practice in a grand style.[91] However, tracing their ancestry back to famous characters of Greek history as an additional way to affirm their social status does not seem to have been a common practice of Greek aristocrats of the Hellenistic age. The emergence of this practice, starting in the Julio-Claudian age, is likely to reflect precisely that increasing symbolic value of the history of classical and Hellenistic Greece in the early Empire noted above.[92] Quite possibly, descent from famous politicians of the past reinforced the claims to a leading political role of the ruling elites of Roman Greece.[93]

The way that the Saethidae related themselves to the past by emphasizing their descent from Saithidas the Elder has interesting implications from the point of view of Messenian memory. The last stage of the dispute with Sparta for the Dentheliatis was not too far in the past, and Pausanias and Plutarch concur in showing that in their age the Messenian Wars of the archaic age were still seen as the focal point of Messenian history.[94] The Saethidae, however, preferred to focus on the Messenians' successful defence of their freedom against the Macedonians, and by monumentalizing in a highly emphatic way their relation to the hero of that story, they also promoted the centrality of it for the Messenians as a whole. In doing so, they linked themselves and the Messenians to a theme that was widespread in Greek culture of the early Empire, that is, the notion that

---

[90] See Habicht 1998a: 127, and cf. Jones 1971: 40–1, on the claims to illustrious ancestors, mythic and historical, by the elites of Plutarch's Greece.

[91] See now Lafond 2005: esp. 332–7.

[92] See in general Bowie 1974: esp. 171–2, and Habicht 1998a: 129 on the case of the famous sophist Polemon, a contemporary and close acquaintance of the emperor Hadrian, who gave public speeches at Athens on Demosthenes and the Peloponnesian War, demanding the enormous honorarium of 25 talents.

[93] Ameling 1983: 3–4. One also wonders whether the fact that leading families of Greece started to care about their distant ancestors, a trait that is rather foreign to traditional Greek political mentality but very typical of the mentality of the Roman ruling elite, might not be seen as one result of the Romanization of Greece: after all, most of the men who were staking such ancestral claims were Roman citizens pursuing equestrian or senatorial careers. On the crucial importance of ancestors for defining the status of the members of the Roman ruling elite, see Flower 1996. Compare especially aristocrats of the late Republic claiming famous characters of early republican history as their ancestors, e.g. ibid: 88–9 and pl. 3d for the case of Marcus Brutus putting the faces of Lucius Brutus and Servilius Ahala on his coins.

[94] On Pausanias and the Messenian Wars, see above, pp. 94–100, and this chapter. Plutarch is credited with a (lost) biography of Aristomenes, the hero of the Messenian Wars; see Ogden 2004: 193–5.

the responsibility for the end of Greek freedom lay mainly with the Macedonians.[95] Such a notion had interesting ramifications, the most obvious being exculpating the Romans from the same charge. But no less important, in the case of the Messenians, was probably the redirection of conflict from the inter-polis level, on which the freedom of the Messenians could not but be associated with their wars against Sparta, to a Panhellenic conflict against an external aggressor, a much more adequate charter myth for a city of the province of Achaea, dominated by an aristocracy that was seeking integration in the provincial and Imperial ruling class.[96] To what extent this reorientation of the past did impact the Messenians' perception of themselves is difficult to tell, but certainly the monumental presence of the Saethidae in Messene, officially sanctioned by the political community,[97] and the anchoring of their commemoration in the religious practices of the city through the heroic cult for Saithidas show that their way of articulating a Messenian identity in the framework of the province of Achaea must have been authoritative and influential. On the other hand, the epic story of the wars against Sparta was such a temping source of symbolic capital, that it would be surprising if it had been given up completely within Messene, and there is indeed reason to think that this was not the case. Other major players in the shaping of Messenian memory seem to have had a different approach from that of the Saethidae.

THE NEW EPAMINONDAS, SON OF ARISTOMENES

Of the "best citizens" of Messene honored with statues in Olympia, the most distinguished was Tiberius Claudius Crispianus, called in the decree voted in his honor by the Messenians "The new Epaminondas," former *praefectus* of the First Bosporan Cohort and *tribunus* of the Legio XII Fulminata.[98] He was the scion of one of the most prominent families of

---

[95] See Palm 1959: 64, with references to Plutarch, Pausanias, Aelius Aristides and other authors of the second century; see also Arafat 1996: 89; Habicht 1998a: 105–7; especially on Chaeronea as the end of Greek freedom, Akujärvi 2005: 247–52.

[96] It is probably not irrelevant in this perspective that the Saethidae appear to have had strong connections with Sparta: Caelianus the Elder was honored there with a statue (*IG* V 1, 512), as was his grandson Frontinus Niceratus (*IG* V 1, 533); all the less surprising that hostility to Sparta did not figure in their construction of Messenicity.

[97] See esp. *SEG* 51.458, listing honors granted by the *demos* of Messene to Caelianus the Elder.

[98] In this period, the units seem to have been deployed in Cappadocia, see Hüttl 1936: 240 n. 49. Crispianus' was a typical equestrian *cursus*, covering two of the three *militiae*.

Messene, one that has left behind an impressive paper trail, or rather a stone trail, in Messenia and at Olympia.

The first attested member of the family seems to be Aristomenes, eponymous priest of Zeus Ithomatas soon after the battle of Actium, possibly in 19 BC.[99] He must be the father of the wealthy Dionysios son of Aristomenes, who offered the sum of 500 *denarii* for the restoration of the temple of Demeter and the "so-called stoa of Nikaios," sometime in the first years of the first century AD. The offer was made in his own name and in the name of his mother Pleistarchia, evidently Aristomenes' wife.[100] This Dionysios is presumably none other than the Dionysios, son of Aristomenes, listed among the *trietirenes* of the tribe Hyllis in the ephebic catalogue of the year 3 AD,[101] and the Dionysios, son of Aristomenes, whose statue, portraying him in the idealized form of the Hermes of Andros and accompanied by an inscription calling him *heros*, was dedicated by the polis in room XI, behind the western stoa of the gymnasium and facing the mausoleum K 3.[102]

In all likelihood, we can also reconstruct a portion of his maternal ancestry. A Dionysios was buried together with his daughter Pleistarchia in the mausoleum K 3, the most striking of the burial monuments of the gymnasium of Messene.[103] He may be Aristomenes' father-in-law, which would explain nicely the name of Dionysios, son of Aristomenes, and

---

[99] In the list of magistrates *SEG* 41.335, the reference to the eponymous priest is coupled with the number of the year according to the Actian era. Aristomenes appears in l. 17–18, and his year is indicated with the peculiar form "the fifth and fourth and third year," which might be a circular way of referring to the twelfth year, or 19 BC, unless perhaps Aristomenes was eponymous for three years in a row. Baldassarra 1999: 46 speculates that the same man may appear in the very lacunose decree *SEG* 23.203, dated generally to the first century BC, and be identical with the Aristomenes who erected a funerary stele for his son Damokles and his daughter Menestrata, *IG* V 1, 1479, from the late first century BC or the early first AD according to Kolbe.

[100] *SEG* 23.207, l. 27–8; on the text of these lines, see Migeotte 1985: 600 and *SEG* 35.343. Dionysios is one of the most generous donors, together with Teisarchos son of Dionysios (his uncle?), who also offered 500 *denarii* for the old gymnasium, and after Lucius Bennius Glykon, who offered 1,000 *denarii*, and possibly Nikeratos, son of Theon (member of another well-known family, likely related to that of Dionysios), whose offer is only defined in its goal, while the amount is left open. They are followed at a distance by Kraton, son of Archedamos, who offered a total of 370 *denarii* (l. 12–14, according to Migeotte's reading, *SEG* 35.343).

[101] *SEG* 41.333, see Themelis, *Praktika* 1992: 71.

[102] The inscription on the basis is *SEG* 47.399. For the fragments of the statue see Themelis, *Praktika* 1997: 97–9 and id. 2000: 137–42. A further inscription honoring Diosysios as hero was on the architrave of the room, *SEG* 52.404, see Themelis, *Praktika* 2001: 90–1. On the use of the type of the Hermes of Andros for young aristocrats see Zanker 1995: 255. Notice that the mausoleum K 3 may have been the grave of a member of the family, Eisokrateia daughter of Aristomenes; see *SEG* 47.411 and cf. Themelis 2000: 132 for the correct reading of the man's name.

[103] *SEG* 47.412. On this monument, its shape and chronology, see Themelis 2000: 124–36, and Fröhlich 2007: 212–13.

could conceivably be identical with another Dionysios, eponymous priest of Zeus Ithomatas, in whose year of tenure of the priesthood the first Saithidas epigraphically documented in Messene had been *agōnothetēs* (*SEG* 39.388).

The family obtained Roman citizenship in the next generation, and we find a Tiberius Claudius Aristomenes, son of Dionysios, priest of the Imperial cult, dedicating a statue of Nero, and possibly funding the restoration of the Arsinoe fountain in the agora of Messene.[104] A Tiberius Claudius Dionysius Crispianus, presumably the son of Aristomenes, apparently won the Rhomaia of Aigion, in Achaea, towards the end of the first century A D.[105] An inscription engraved on an epistyle, dated to the 157th year of the Actian era or 126 AD, records as *agōnothetēs* Tiberius Claudius Aristomenes, son of Crispianus.[106] Then comes Tiberius Claudius Crispianus, the new Epaminondas, who was *agoranomos* of Messene in 139 AD.[107]

Of all the members of the family, Tiberius Claudius Crispianus seems to have been the one whose presence was most conspicuous in Messene.

---

[104] The dedication of the statue is *IG* V 1, 1450, where Tib. Claudius Aristomenes is joined by a woman by the name of Gemonia, possibly his wife. As in *SEG* 41.353 (the dedication of a statue of Nero by Tib. Claudius Saithidas), Nero's *tribunicia potestas* is mentioned without a number, pointing to 55 A D, the first year of his reign; see Habicht 1998b: 493 n. 35. On the inscription of the fountain, see above, p. 307 n. 56.

[105] See Rizakis 1995: 382 no. 708; note, however, that Rizakis refers to personal communication from Themelis, and from what he says it is unclear whether the unpublished inscription he refers to is actually *SEG* 48.500, which seems to refer to Crispianus "new Epaminondas."

[106] *IG* V 1, 1469. For the whereabouts of this inscription, see Luraghi 2005: 190 n. 2.

[107] According to the new inscription published by Themelis, *Praktika* 2003: 34. In the inscription, Tib. Claudius Crispianus appears to have the additional *cognomen* Geminianus, possibly related to Gemonia, the name of the presumed wife of Tib. Claudius Aristomenes the Elder (see n. 104). In all likelihood, we have documented a complete or almost complete sequence of five generations of this family. Its first member, Aristomenes, eponymous priest at the end of the first century B C, may have been born around 50 B C. Adding 30 years, we have a possible date of birth around 20 B C for his son Dionysius, compatible with his being among the *trietirenes* in 3 A D. Tiberius Claudius Aristomenes the Elder could have been his son: priest of Nero probably in 55, he could have been born around 10 AD or a few years later. He may have had a son sometime around 40 AD, or a few years later, and this son (unless this member of the family is actually a reduplication, see above n. 105) could have been a successful athlete in his twenties, between 60 and 80 AD. Tib. Claudius Aristomenes the Younger, the *agōnothetēs* of 126 A D, could have been his son, and the father of the "new Epaminondas," who could have been born around 110 AD. This calculation implies rather long generations in this family, which would be consistent with the tendency of Greek men to marry rather late in life (see Spawforth 1985: 192). Considering the alternation of names between generations of the family, the alternative would be to admit that at some point, perhaps before Tib. Claudius Aristomenes the Younger, we miss two generations. Those two generations would have to have been rather short, although not impossibly short by comparison e.g. with the distance between Saethida Caelianus the Elder and his grandson Saethida Caelianus the Younger, see above.

Two statue bases, only partially published, refer to statues dedicated in his honor by the tribes Hyllis, his own, and Kresphontis, and apparently the text, which otherwise follows closely the one that accompanied the statue of Crispianus dedicated at Olympia by the Messenians, refers to the fact that statues of Crispianus had been dedicated *kata phylēn*, as in the case of Saethida Caelianus the Elder, which means that there were all in all five of them.[108] These statues seem to have been erected after Crispianus left the Roman army and before he was elected Helladarch of the *koinon* of Achaea, a position that apparently had meanwhile become yearly.[109] The *koinon* dedicated one statue of Crispianus at Olympia and another possibly in the Karneiasion, or at any rate thereabouts; this second statue was dedicated in connection with his involvement with the cult of the Great Gods.[110]

The epithet "new Epaminondas," appearing on all the statues of Crispianus dedicated by the Messenians, both at Olympia and at Messene, had probably been granted to him by them, following some sort of formal collective decision. The practice of honoring prominent individuals by depicting them as the reembodiment of some glorious character of the mythic or historical past was rather common in first- and second-century Greece. From Messene itself a "new Plato" has recently emerged, and we have a "new Homer and new Themistocles" from Augustan Athens, a "new Lycurgus" and a "new Penelope" from Sparta, and so on.[111] In Crispianus' case, the reference to Epaminondas clearly meant that he was honored as a new founder of the city.[112] We cannot tell exactly why he was granted this title, and he may not have chosen it himself, but it certainly resonated with his family's tradition.

In spite of its illustrious associations, the name Aristomenes, born by Crispianus' father and by at least two of his ancestors, is otherwise very

[108] All that is currently known about these two inscriptions can be found in *SEG* 48.498 and 500, dedicated by the tribes Hyllis and Cresphontis respectively; the words *kata phylēn* are mostly the result of an integration in the former, which should be based on the latter, itself essentially unpublished. *Pace* the editor, the second cognomen of this man can hardly be Hispanos, cf. *IvO* 447.

[109] See Puech 1983: 30.

[110] The inscription, *SEG* 11.984, is currently outside the church of Hagios Atanasios in the village of Kalliroi, immediately south of Kostantinoi. For its interpretation, see Deshours 2006: 29–20, who thinks Crispianus was one of the *hieroi*, the group on charge of the mysteries for the year.

[111] "New Plato": *SEG* 52.406; "new Homer and new Themistocles": Nikanor the Athenian, *IG* II–III² 3788 (see Robert 1980: 15–16, Bowersock 1984: 175–6, Jones 2005); "new Lycurgus": *SEG* 11.810; "new Penelope": *IG* V 1, 598, *SEG* 30.407, 409. See also Lafond 2001: 398 for a "new Athamas" from Teos (Athamas being the mythic founder of the city) and the Emperor Lucius Verus "new Erythros" in Erythae.

[112] On Epaminondas as founder of Messene, see above, pp. 216–17 and 278.

rare in Messene.[113] The reason is probably the very fact that it was the name of the main hero of Messenian resistance against Sparta, a hero also in the religious sense, since he received heroic cult at Messene from the Augustan age at the latest. In general, Greeks did not often use the names of heroes as normal personal names, religious restraint being the most obvious reason. In view of this, the use of the name Aristomenes in Crispianus' family is very likely to have involved an explicit statement: this family in all probability considered the hero Aristomenes its ancestor. We have already observed the numerous cases of Greeks of the early Empire who numbered prominent historical characters or indeed heroes among their ancestors. The Messenian Aristomenes are probably one more case in point.

If this is the case, we are never likely to find any monument for this family comparable to the *hērōon* of Saethida: notionally, the very *hērōon* of Aristomenes was probably the ancestral shrine of this family, and again, tantalizing hints in the sources may point to the politics of memory associated with this monument. In his description of the *hērōon*, Pausanias appends a short historical digression observing that Aristomenes' hate for Sparta endured even after his death, for according to the Messenians he had been present at the battle of Leuktra and his help had been the main cause of the victory of the Thebans (4.32.4). It is rather tempting to connect this way of bringing together Aristomenes and Epaminondas to the family of Crispianus, son of Aristomenes and new Epaminondas.

Unlike the Saithidai, the Aristomenes family seems to have chosen to articulate its own past around the cornerstones of Messenian tradition, from the hero Aristomenes to Epaminondas, and it may be significant that Tiberius Claudius Crispianus was also linked to what seems to have been perceived, in the age of Pausanias, as the most ancestral of all Messenian cults, the mysteries of the Karneiasion. One would be tempted to see here a contraposition, comparable to the contrast in Augustan Sparta between the traditional families of the Spartan aristocracy, with Brasidas in the front line, and the family of the parvenu Eurykles.[114] But this reading may go too far, considering that the record of the Saithidai

---

[113] The only Aristomenes from Messene whose connection with Crispianus' family is doubtful is a sculptor from the late second century B C, son of Agias, and presumably father of another sculptor called Agias, documented in Olympia, *IvO* 397–9, and now also in Messene itself, Themelis, *Praktika* 2004: 35–6. Given the distance in time, it cannot be excluded that he also was an ancestor of Crispianus, but there is no specific reason to assume he was. A gymnasiarch Aristomenes may be documented in a new ephebic catalogue for the year 91 A D, *SEG* 51.473, but the name is damaged and no photograph of the inscription has been published. Outside Messene, the name is fairly common, reflecting the local dimension of the hero Aristomenes.

[114] See Bowersock 1965: 105, Spawforth, in Cartledge and Spawforth 2002: 101.

attested in inscriptions goes as far back as that of the Aristomenes family. The striking fact is that the ways both families anchored theselves in the past corresponded precisely to their trajectories, in so far as we can follow them. While the family of Aristomenes seems to have reached prominence first within Messene, and then within the Achaean *koinon*, but no further, the Saithidai became integrated in the senatorial elite, to the point that the great-grandson of Caelianus the Elder, Tiberius Claudius Saethida Cethegus Frontinus, is documented only in Italy; in all likelihood, the family had moved permanently away from Greece.[115] But apart from this, if it is correct to assume that the family of Crispianus regarded Aristomenes as its ancestor, we have here another example of how a prominent family of Messene merged its own past with that of the Messenians, at the same time promoting specific aspects of it.

PAUSANIAS' MESSENIANS

A cultivated Greek from Asia Minor, probably from Magnesia ad Sipylum, Pausanias travelled Greece in the ages of Antoninus Pius and Marcus Aurelius. Hadrian's creation of the Panhellenion belonged to his youth.[116] In his *Description of Greece*, a survey of the main monuments of continental Greece accompanied by substantial historical excursuses, he regularly gave preference to the period before the Roman conquest, but the cultural climate in which he lived has left clear traces in his work.[117] One of the most obvious is his enthusiasm for the Eleusinian cult, which clearly reflects the emphasis on Eleusis in Hadrian's Panhellenion.[118] His whole concept of Greece as repository of a unified cultural and religious heritage would have been inconceivable before the Roman conquest.[119]

Pausanias' description of Messenia is the product of his coming to terms with structural aspects of Messenian memory and of the Messenian landscape itself, as they had been taking shape over the centuries. The region could not offer the richness in myths that was found in other parts of Greece, a fact Pausanias notes, commenting on the intrinsic weakness

---

[115] See *CIL* VI 16440 (grave stele for Cornelia Quetula, Cethegus' nurse) and *CIL* X 1124 (a dedication of Abellinum to Cethegus as *patronus coloniae*).

[116] For recent discussions of Pausanias' chronology, see Bowie 2001: 21–4 and Hutton 2005: 9–11.

[117] See Lafond 2001. Pausanias' preference for monuments and events from the archaic age to roughly 150 BC and his tendency to ignore later monuments has been observed many times, see e.g Habicht 1998a: 117–40.

[118] On Hadrian and Eleusis, see e.g. Antonetti 1995; on Pausanias and the Eleusinian mysteries, Goldmann 1991. Both problems are discussed in Deshours 2006: 213–16.

[119] See e.g. Pausanias' discussion of the benefactors of Greece (8.52.1–5) with Lafond 2001: 388–9.

of Messenian tradition, which he regards as a consequence of the long exile of the Messenians from the Peloponnese (3.13.2). The polis of Messene seems to be almost the only repository of the Messenian heritage, while most other cities of the region appear to prefer alternative ways of construing their past. Pylos presents itself as the land of Nestor, Mothone as a settlement of refugees from Nauplia in the Argolis, Asine as a settlement of Dryopians, Kolonides as an Athenian colony. Even Korone seems to cherish the memory of its Boeotian founder. Tellingly, where Messenian ethnicity figures most prominently and without alternatives is in the region east of the Pamisos and in the contested borderland with Laconia on the western side of the Mani peninsula.

For better or for worse, Pausanias' detailed overview of the Messenian past reflects choices made to a large extent by the Messenians themselves, especially in the Hellenistic period, and then reiterated on various occasions. Accordingly, most of the space is reserved for the two wars supposedly fought by the Messenians against Sparta during the archaic period, following what was probably a trend in Messenian politics of memory from the third century BC (see above, chapter 4). Beyond the wars themselves, however, reciprocal hatred between Messenians and Spartans is elevated to a general explanation for the whole history of the Messenians, from its very origins to the most recent past. It allegedly caused their alliance with Philip the Second and their absence from Chaeronea (4.28.2), their failure to participate in fending off the Gaulish invasion (4.28.3), finally their taking Antony's side against Octavian (4.31.1). On the other hand, the Messenians' initially circumspect attitude to the Achaean League is justified by their desire not to jeopardize the friendly disposition of the Spartans resulting from the Messenians helping them against Pyrrhos (4.29.6–7).[120] In a word, ever since the first king of Messenia Polycaon took possession of the region because his elder brother Myles came first in the line of succession to their father Lelex, king of Laconia, Messenian history had been in a dialectical relation to Sparta.

In concentrating on the Messenian Wars, Pausanias was probably also pursuing another pervasive goal of his work, that is, to supplement the works of the great historians of the classical age, especially Herodotus and Thucydides, offering narratives of those periods or episodes that they had neglected.[121] The fluent narrative produced, integrating and reworking the

---

[120] It is impressive to observe how Pausanias' assessment of the historical destiny of the Messenians resonated with Polybius' views, expressed some three centuries earlier (4.32.3–10).
[121] On this aspect of Pausanias' work, see e.g. Moggi 1993: 403–4.

material offered by Rhianos and Myron, may be Pausanias' own achieve-
ment, or he may have derived it more or less closely from an author of the
early first century BC, as seems more likely on the whole. Be that as it may,
the insistence on the role of the mystery cult of the Karneiasion reflected
both the agenda of third-century sources and that of the cult reform
carried out by Mnasistratos probably under Tiberius – and it resonated
with Pausanias' personal admiration for the mysteries of Demeter. The
transformation of the gods of the mysteries into goddesses, which makes
possible to draw a close parallel with the cult of Eleusis and ultimately to
declare the Attic origin of the Messenian mysteries, may be again Pausanias'
own contribution, but it cannot be excluded with certainty that his
immediate sources, learned Messenians who perhaps had lived through
the reign of Hadrian or in any case preserved a strong impression of his
panhellenic programme, may have reinterpreted their own cult in this
way. On a minor scale, Pausanias' hand might be recognized in the specific
references to the less-known mysteries of Demeter at Phlya in Attica, a cult
controlled by a family with which he seems to have been in contact.[122]

   The social landscape of Antonine Greece is the background against
which Pausanias' *Messeniaka* should be read. The local elites whose
impact on Roman Messenia has been discussed above formed the upper
end of the social group with which Pausanias mingled during his travels in
Greece, the people he consulted as sources of local knowledge, and occasionally contradicted on the basis of on his own superior competence.[123]
His own interpretations of monuments and reconstructions of the mythic
and historical past originated from a mixture of information he had
collected from written sources and from his interactions with these people.
Viewed against this background, many aspects of his work make much
better sense. To limit ourselves to a particularly obvious example, it has
often been noticed that Pausanias' view of the relationship of Messene to
the Achaean League in the late third century BC is utterly incompatible
with what we know of that complex of events from Polybius, Livy and
Plutarch. For Pausanias, the Messenians had joined the League before the
conquest of Megalopolis by Cleomenes and participated in the battle of
Sellasia, while the conflict between Messene and the League in his account
is toned down as much as possible. The abundant evidence for the
engagement of prominent Messenians in the direction of the Achaean

---

[122] See the astute discussion of Deshours 2006: 213–22.
[123] On Pausanias' references to learned locals and the social background of the latter, see now Jones
    2001; in general, on Pausanias and local traditions, Pretzler 2005.

koinon in the second century AD seems to offer a much better explanation for this peculiar view than just the inaccuracy and carelessness of Pausanias or his sources. As noted above, the politics of memory practiced by the Messenian Titus Flavius Polybios involved in all likelihood a revision of the history of Hellenistic Messene along the same lines.

This last observation points to an aspect of Pausanias' work that tends to escape notice. Much as he makes clear to the reader that his goal is to preserve the memory of events, cults, and rituals of the Greeks from the danger of oblivion, Pausanias' work was in a sense very closely tied to the present. In his description of monuments and in his narratives of the deeds of famous Greeks of the past, Pausanias was continuously intruding with his own authoritative voice in the politics of memory practiced by the elite families who must have constituted both a part of his intended audience[124] and his acquaintances. Form their point of view, he was dealing with extremely sensitive material, the material that constituted the foundation of their claims to social and cultural superiority. If we reconsider Pausanias' discussion of Saithidas in this light, it acquires a completely new meaning. His skepticism towards what "some Messenians" said implicitly questioned the image of the family's past that the Saethidae themselves intended to promote. We cannot tell why Pausanias decided to give such an unflattering assessment of Caelianus, but his descendants, who were certainly around when Pausanias visited Messene, must have been rather unimpressed by the treatment reserved to their claims of ancestry.[125] But there may be more to it than that. While he seems to oppose his authorial voice to a local version, Pausanias at the same time suggests that not all Messenians agreed on the identity of the Saithidas depicted on the stele. Rather than just setting things straight, he may be taking sides in a latent conflict for memory at Messene. If we want to proceed along this line, it does not take a lot of fantasy to identify possible candidates for the opposition to the Saethidae Pausanias seems to be alluding to. The family of Tiberius Claudius Crispianus must have been

---

[124] On Pausanias' intended audience, see the discussion in Habicht 1998a: 24–6 with further references.

[125] Given Pausanias' rather mixed attitude to Roman domination over Greece (see Habicht 1998a: 119–25, Moggi 2002, Hutton 2005: 47), one might speculate that the Saethidae had embraced Romanization too enthusiastically for his taste – note that Caelianus the Younger and Frontinus Niceratus accompanied their dedications of statues of the imperial family with inscriptions in Latin (see above, n. 54), a poignant statement in an epigraphic landscape that was still almost exclusively Greek, in Messene and in the Peloponnese in general. But this can be no more than speculation.

rather pleased with the glorification of the Messenian hero Aristomenes in Pausanias' *Messeniaka*.

Surely the *Periegesis* must include many more cases like this, some of which we may never be able to recognize. Far from being a text of purely antiquarian interest, it impacted very directly concerns that were quite important to the elite families of Antonine Achaea. The past Pausanias dealt with was far from being dead, and its relevance to the world he lived in is a necessary starting point if we want to understand the way he dealt with it.

* * *

Early Imperial Messene offers a striking case study of a phenomenon that is widespread in the Greek cities of this age. Increasingly, the public space is dominated by the physical presence of benefactors and their families, immortalized by statues and – as we know from inscriptions – painted portraits, accompanied by texts recording the acts of generosity by which they showed their excellence and their love for the community. The competitive logic that regulated the social transaction whereby honors were granted in exchange for benefactions possessed its own internal dynamic, which tended to increase the emphasis of the honors.[126] In many cases, it is possible to observe a tendency for monuments of successive generations of the same family to be located adjacent to each other or at any rate in clusters, so that certain corners of the city ended up being veritable complexes that monumentalised one particular family. In the case of Messene, the theatre must have become a sort of family monument of the Saethidae, while monuments in the rooms behind the western porch of the gymnasium were probably meant to create a link to the monumental mausoleum K 3, where members of the same families were buried.

Surely once the agora of Messene is better known, more examples of the phenomenon will emerge. Meanwhile, it is possible to observe that the elite of imperial Messene had predecessors in the late Hellenistic age, like the family of the sculptor Damophon, whose monumental presence in the Asklepieion must have been very conspicuous.[127] The changes to the urban landscape brought about by the practice of honoring

---

[126] On this snowball effect, see e.g. Raeck 1995: 238. In general, for an introduction to honorary practices in Hellenistic and Roman Greece see Wörrle 1995.

[127] See Themelis 2000: 88–95, Fröhlich 2007: 208–10. Besides the column with the decrees in honor of Damophon (above, p. 284 n. 132), there were at least three statues of members of the family in the area.

benefactors with public monuments had an equivalent at the level of social and economic structure in the emergence of a narrow elite that more or less dominated the life of the community. The process that progressively singled out wealthy and influential families can be seen in full swing from the Augustan age to the age of the Antonines, although traces of it are visible already in the last centuries BC.[128]

Such changes in social structure and in the use of public space have a number of consequences for the sense of community and for the ways of articulating a shared past, in terms both of structure and of content. The celebration of benefactors transformed the political community essentially into a corporate body that bestowed honors in exchange for engagement on its behalf – almost a team of umpires assessing the competitors, who, to be sure, were at the same time members of the team.[129] Furthermore, the celebration mostly assumed a dynastic character, in the sense that generations of the family directly connected to the benefactor, and even his more distant ancestors, were involved in various ways in the honors, while the temporal dimension was further reinforced by the anchoring of the honors in the religious life of the city: from Mnasistratos, who was to be crowned every year during the Ithomaia festival (*SEG* 23.208, lines 21–5), to Saethida Caelianus, who received post-mortem heroic honors from the Messenians. In this way, the celebration of the best citizens and their ancestors joined the more traditional celebration of civic cults and festivals, adding a new dimension to the ritual expression of belonging to the community of the Messenians. Furthermore, the way that leading families construed their distant roots, as we have seen, had very specific implications from the point of view of how the shared past of the Messenians was conceived. The history of the relations of Hellenistic Messene to Macedonia and to the Achaean League offers fascinating insights in this process. If we compare the little we know about the Julio-Claudian age, it seems possible to trace a trajectory. The renewal of the cult of the Karneiasion by Mnasistratos, possibly connected to a similar revival of the cult of Artemis Limnatis, seems to coincide temporally with a rewriting of the history of the Messenians. Here, the benefactor Mnasistratos vanishes behind "traditional" rituals and stories that receive a new lease of life. On the contrary, the elite families of the Antonine age seem to appropriate much more directly the past of the community, rearranging specific aspects of it.

In the face of these deep-reaching changes, what did it mean to be Messenian from Augustus to the Antonines? Can we still speak of a

---

[128] See now Shipley 2005: 329–30.   [129] As noted by Wörrle 1995: 242.

Messenian identity, and in what sense? The power of the ritual continuity of the civic cults and the myths and stories tied to them should not be overestimated. We really do not know what the cult of the Karneiasion was like before Mnasistratos' reform, and there is no guarantee that a cult practiced over a very long period of time remains stable in the interpretation of those who practice it. Certainly, at the regional level Messene functioned as a focal point. Youths from Messenia participated in the epheby at Messene, where their names were apparently listed in ephebic catalogues under the heading of their city – but not divided according to the five Messenian tribes, it seems, as were those of the youths of Messene (*SEG* 47.386). One has the sense that the regional dynamic that we see operating here had more to do with the pyramidal structure of the province than with a shared Messenian identity within Messenia. As far as Messene is concerned, the history of the wars against Sparta, the *epos* of the Messenians in Tullio-Altan's terminology,[130] still had much of its prestige, but Pausanias' insistence on it may distort our perspective. Again, the ways elite families of Messene chose to position themselves in the past of the Messenians suggest that the traditional enmity towards Sparta was only one of a number of options: the shared past of the Achaean League and resistance to Macedonian aggression offered viable alternatives.

Because it is a discursive construct, an ethnic identity can never be really pronounced dead. In our case, though, the transition from the second to the third century AD signals a turning point. If Pausanias stated emphatically that, still in his time, the Messenians spoke Doric in its purest form, inscriptions from the central years of the century show the final disappearance even of the few decorative Doric forms that had been intentionally preserved so far. A descendant and namesake of Titus Flavius Polybios, himself a prominent politician of the Achaean *koinon*, who was crowned "best citizen" in 257 AD, is called in one of the two inscriptions in his honor "a true Heraclid," but more interestingly, both the inscription on the statue base dedicated by the Achaean *koinon* and the one on the base dedicated by the Messenians call him "a Messenian and a Spartan." The most important borderline, the one against which the Messenian identity had been first articulated, had finally ceased to be insuperable. If one could be legitimately called a Messenian and a Spartan at the same time, then his Messenian identity must have been something substantially different from what it had been hitherto.

---

[130] Tullio-Altan 1995: 22–4.

CHAPTER II

Conclusions

Diverse and controversial as it is, the evidence discussed in this book converges in delineating a consistent picture of the Messenian identity and makes it possible to reconstruct a reasonably intelligible trajectory for its historical development over the centuries. It is now time to draw the threads together, summarizing briefly in an integrated way the conclusions formulated in the chapters of the book. This will be done first in the form of comparing traditional narratives of the history of the Messenians with what would result from the arguments presented here. Then two rather peculiar monuments will offer starting points for discussions of the structural aspects of the Messenian identity.

STORIES OF THE MESSENIAN IDENTITY

According to Pausanias, the only ancient author who offers a comprehensive account of it, the history of the Messenians could be summarized as follows. Messenia had existed as a unified kingdom ever since queen Messene and her husband Polykaon migrated to the region from the Argolid and Laconia respectively. Various short-lived dynasties ruled Messenia, until the Heraclid Kresphontes conquered it with his army of Dorians, establishing a dynastic line that was destined to occupy the throne until the conquest of the region by the Spartans. In the second half of the eighth century, the First Messenian War brought the whole of Messenia under Spartan control. Some of its inhabitants fled to neighboring regions in the Peloponnese and to Southern Italy, and those who remained rose against the Spartans around the mid seventh century, led by the gallant Aristomenes of Andania. The revolt was unsuccessful and caused a new wave of exiles. Those Messenians who did not leave the region at this point were finally thrown into slavery by the Spartans, becoming Helots, and lived in that condition until their final uprising in the first half of the fifth century, after the earthquake that devastated

Laconia. As a result of this revolt, all remaining Messenians abandoned Messenia and migrated to Naupaktos. Thence they were expelled by the Spartans after the Peloponnesian War. In 369 BC, thanks to Epaminondas, the Messenian diaspora returned to its fatherland from its various places of exile and established, or rather, in Pausanias' perspective, reestablished a free Messenian polity, which from then on became a member of the community of the Greeks.

Modern reconstructions vary in the degree to which they accept this master narrative. Not many scholars take seriously its early portions, although some still believe that even those parts preserve memories of historical events, if in a somewhat distorted fashion. As concerns the Dorian invasion of the Peloponnese, in the last decades the balance has been swinging in favor of the skeptics, but it may be too early to declare the question settled. The Messenian Wars feature as historical events in most overviews of archaic Greek history, and here the extent to which details from Pausanias' narrative are taken seriously varies a great deal. No scholar really accepts the exile and return story. The vast majority think that the previous inhabitants of the region were turned into Helots at the time of the Spartan conquest, and formed the bulk of the citizen body of the free Messenian polity established by Epaminondas. To what extent such Helotized Messenians had been able to preserve a memory of their past as free Messenians and of their wars against the Spartans is controversial, and therefore scholars vary in the confidence with which they create historical narratives based on Pausanias' history of the wars. In any case, the liberation of Messenia by the Thebans finally turned the Messenians into a normal component of the Greek world, with a normal political and cultural life and a normal history. For this reason, and also because scholarship tends to respect borders between epochs, the history of the free Messenians has usually been excluded from discussions of the history of the Messenians before Epaminondas, and vice versa.

Put in rather stark terms, modern reconstructions of Messenian history result from relying exclusively on ancient literary sources, overlooking almost completely all other sorts of evidence, especially archaeological, and from not devoting much attention to the historical contexts from which the literary sources themselves originate, concentrating rather on the likelihood that ancient authors may have had access to reliable information from earlier periods. Only under such premises is it possible to separate, say, the history of archaic Messenia from the history of the Messenians in the Hellenistic age and under the Roman Empire, the periods from which the overwhelming bulk of the literary evidence for

archaic Messenia derives. To be sure, both approaches have their reasons.
If contemporary sources were accepted as the only legitimate evidence,
not much would remain of the history of archaic Greece, and the kinds of
history that can be written based on archaeological remains are not those
in which ancient historians have traditionally been interested. Still, this
book has tried to show that a different approach is feasible. The kind
of story of the Messenians that results from such an approach can be
summarized as follows.

Messene and the Messenians turn up for the first time in the Homeric
poems, to be sure not as participants in the expedition against Troy, and
again in scattered but highly suggestive verses of the Spartan poet Tyrtaeus (chapter 4). They appear to have inhabited the central part of the
region, around Mount Ithome, in the early archaic period, and to have
been engaged in at least one conflict against the Spartans, who prided
themselves on having defeated and chased them away and on having
conquered their land. The Spartan conquest of Messene was projected
back to the mythic age in the *Odyssey*, where Messene is mentioned as a
part of Lakedaimon.

In the wake of the "Greek renaissance" of the eighth century, material
evidence from the region we call Messenia is rather unspectacular,
pointing to its lagging far behind the most developed areas of the Greek
world in terms of size of settlements and sanctuaries, of contacts with
other regions, and probably also of general development of political
structures – a striking situation for a region that had been at the forefront
of Bronze Age Greece (chapter 5). Meanwhile, by the eighth century the
main focus of settlement in the region seems to have shifted from the
western coastal area, which had been the heart of Bronze Age Messenia,
towards the rich agricultural basins of the interior, inaugurating a pattern
that was destined to last until the Middle Ages, when finally the coastal
settlements regained their primacy. The new inland-oriented settlement
pattern points to a decreased relevance of maritime trade, dovetailing
with the limited extent of outside influence shown by the archaeological
evidence.

The low profile of early archaic Messenia has left clear traces in the
almost complete absence of the region from early Greek myth. Even
though the details of any given narrative are not always easy to establish, it
is fair to say that, as far as the mythic age is concerned, that corner of the
Peloponnese features most conspicuously as an area from which people
migrated, to go to Asia Minor or later to Attica – a trend continued, in
the early classical age, by the story of the Western Messenians (chapter 6).

In the course of the seventh and sixth centuries, settlements and sanctuaries increase in size and assemblages grow in quality (chapter 5). Now Messenia appears to be a perfectly integrated part of the Spartan state, as witnessed by material culture and religious cults. To what extent the free *perioikoi* who inhabited the towns of Spartan Messenia and/or the Helots who tilled the land of the Spartiates in the region cultivated and transmitted any sense of their ethnic distinctness within the broader unit of Lakedaimon is extremely difficult to tell, and we have no way to know whether any of them felt related to the Messenians mentioned in the verses of Tyrtaeus and in the *Odyssey*. At any rate, as far as the evidence goes, Spartan Messenia turns out to be remarkably homogeneous. The inclusion of the area south of the river Neda and west of the Taygetos in the Lakedaimonian polity created the base for the perception of this region as a unity.

The notion that the western part of the Spartan territory had actually existed earlier as an entity unto itself, independent and unified under the name of Messene, emerged probably as a by-product of the power struggle between Argos and Sparta (chapter 3). Even though the myth of the division of the Peloponnese among the descendants of Heracles does not show any particular sympathy for the Messenians, it clearly, if implicitly, questioned Spartan control over the region. There is no certainty that this myth, which probably originated shortly before the Persian Wars, in any way reflected or reacted to developments within the region itself, but this is not unlikely, considering what happened soon thereafter. The foundation, on the site of the Chalcidian colony of Zancle, on the Sicilian side of the Strait of Messina, of a city called Messene by the tyrant Anaxilaos of Rhegion around 488 BC (chapter 6), while apparently still based on rather vague notions of the Messenian identity, must have further contributed to the creation of a favorable context for Messenian irredentism. In such context, the first wave of Messenian ethnicity in the Peloponnese took place.

Revolt broke out in Messenia in the early 460s (chapter 7). The rebels, including both Helots and *perioikoi*, chose to identify themselves as Messenians, understood as the original inhabitants of the region. Even though the *epos* of Messenian ethnicity, the master narrative that underpinned the Messenian identity, probably involved a story of Spartan conquest that may have been derived ultimately from Tyrtaeus, the *topos* of the fifth-century Messenians, their ancestral land, which they called Messene, was not confined to the area around Mount Ithome, but included apparently the whole western part of Lakedaimon, all the way to Pylos – a geographic concept derived from the myth of the division of the

Peloponnese among the Heraclids. We cannot say much about the *ethos* of the Messenians of the fifth century, about their cults and institutions, except that they seem mostly to have been derived from Spartan cults and institutions.[1]

As noted above, it is impossible to tell to what extent Messenian ethnogenesis built upon notions and traditions that had been present in the region before the revolt. Offerings at Bronze Age tombs, documented sparsely throughout the archaic and early classical periods (chapter 5), may point to a kind of ritual behavior that differentiated Messenia from Laconia, but the amount of the evidence does not encourage attributing it too much relevance, let alone suggest a specific interpretation in ethnic terms. In any case, the preexistence of a Messenian ethnic identity in Messenia is not necessary in order to explain the revolt. The Spartan oligarchy, as we know it from the fifth and fourth centuries, enforced strict genealogical separation between the ruling elite of the Spartiates and the free *perioikoi*, and granted the Spartiates privileged access to the main resource, landed property. Under such circumstances, tensions and conflicts between the ruling elite and the rest of the free population are precisely what we would expect. At the same time, the Spartiates availed themselves of a self-perpetuating unfree workforce, the Helots, who, because of the higher complexity of their social structure and in part also in consequence of the way their identity was symbolically construed by the Spartiates themselves, were more susceptible than the slaves of other Greeks to perceive themselves as a group and to be mobilized. Discontent with Spartan rule was probably present across the *Lakonikē*, or at least, such turns out to have been the case in the early fourth century, when we finally have some evidence. However, the very geography of the Peloponnese created specific conditions that predestined the western part of the *Lakonikē* to be the focus of revolt. Archaeological evidence for increased settlement density in the region from the early fifth century may point to one further factor.

As for the way in which the revolt was discursively articulated, again, there is no need to postulate a preexisting Messenian tradition in order to make sense of it. Even though the Spartiates conspicuously avoided ethnic symbolism in the way they defined the boundary between themselves and *perioikoi* and Helots, it has to be recognized that the very structure of the Lakedaimonian polity made it logical for revolt against the Spartiates to be

---

[1] For a definition of *epos*, *topos*, and *ethos*, see above, p. 10 and n. 20; the terms are borrowed from Tullio-Altan 1995: 21–30.

construed in ethnic terms.[2] The myth of the division of the Peloponnese offered a convenient framework, one that guaranteed some level of plausibility to the claims of the rebels: if the land west of the Taygetos was Messene, then they had to be the Messenians. However, if we shift attention from the ethnic boundary between Messenians and Spartans evoked by the rebels and look at the cultural contents of Messenian ethnicity, it is immediately clear that what we are observing looks much more like a process of ethnic fission than like the reawakening of an ancient and oppressed ethnic group.[3]

In retrospect, the revolt was a failure, at least for the Messenians. They were first expelled from the Peloponnese, and later, after the end of the Peloponnesian War, scattered across the Mediterranean. The Athenians wavered all along between supporting Messenian ethnicity and siding with Sparta against what the Spartans described as a slave revolt – an ambivalent attitude that characterized the Athenians' dealings with the Messenians still in the fourth century BC. Unlike the Athenians, the Argives had a much more straightforward attitude, obviously reflecting their much clearer-cut relationship to Sparta, and possibly their better knowledge of their old enemies.

Even though, at the end of the Peloponnesian War, the Peloponnese appeared pacified and firmly under Spartan control, the presence of free Messenians at Pylos for many years during the war is unlikely to have been obliterated from memory. When Epaminondas, in 369 BC, led his army into the region, Messenian ethnicity was sufficiently established to become the cornerstone of a new polity carved out of the *Lakonikē* (chapter 8). This new wave of Messenian ethnogenesis was supported by an extraordinarily favorable historical context, one in which the crisis and dissolution of the Peloponnesian League made the renegotiation of ethnic and political borders within the Peloponnese both possible and desirable. In spite of the fact that the roots of fourth-century Messenian ethnicity were to a significant extent local, the dominant way in which the Messenians articulated the birth of their new polity seems to have been the story of exile and return, along the lines that we find in Pausanias. Such a story was unique among the Greeks, and was a product of the unique conditions in which Messenian ethnicity had emerged. Even though other

[2] Cf. Cohen 1974 on the structure of ethnic conflicts and on conflicts for resources construed in ethnic terms.
[3] In the terms of Horowitz 1975: 115–16, this process would be one of ethnic proliferation, i.e. one in which "a new group comes into existence without its 'parent group' (or groups) losing its (or their) identity."

Greeks may have regarded this story with some skepticism, the opposing interpretation of Messenian ethnogenesis held by the Spartans, according to which the new Messenians were really former slaves, does not seem to have been widely accepted in the rest of the Greek world. Rather ironically, it has been revived in a sustained way only by modern scholarship, captivated by its emancipatory implications. The dominance of these two stories obscures the details of the process by which the Messenians articulated their identity. Reinterpretation of Lakedaimonian tradition was clearly at play, but there are hints of a different kind, pointing possibly to Argive influence on cults and rituals, which could conceivably be connected to the influx of population from the Argolis. Archaeological evidence reinforces the notion that the population of the new Messenian polity in part came from outside the region.

The early history of the Messenians, as we know it from later sources, mostly originated among the free Messenians of the Hellenistic period, and reflects their concerns (see chapters 4 and 9). The components of the Messenian identity that had developed over time were now refunctionalized and redefined to become the cultural heritage of free Messene. This process involved specific problems. So far, the Messenians had existed essentially as an ethnic group without a polity, and as soon as they acquired one, the structure and meaning of the Messenian identity was bound to change in response to the structure of that polity. The dominance of the large city at Mount Ithome, itself initially called Ithome, which was probably necessary for the very survival of new Messene, must have created a hybrid situation, fraught with latent tension: while in theory the Messenians seem to have been envisioned as an *ethnos* divided in poleis pretty much like the Arcadians or the Achaeans, the power relations on the ground much more closely resembled those observed in Sparta or Elis. Cohesion turned out to be the main problem for new Messene, and the way the Messenian past was articulated during the late classical and early Hellenistic periods seems to reflect most clearly the attempt on the part of the dominant polis to express and justify its dominance. Even though most of the trouble for Hellenistic Messenians came from their Arcadian neighbors, in part as members of the Achaean League, opposition to Sparta remained the main charter of the Messenian identity, as shown by the importance of the Messenian Wars for third-century Messenians and, even more impressively, by the persistent symbolic meaning associated with the border conflict over the Dentheliatis.

It is clear that this conflict was now kept alive in the specific interest of Ithome, soon to be called Messene, for whose inhabitants it embodied the unity of the Messenians under their leadership (chapter 2). In other parts of the region, ethnic definitions and attitudes to the past seem to have offered a more varied picture. The Dryopian identity cherished by the Asineans may originally have been a response to Messenian ethnogenesis in the fifth century, and remained a genealogical charter for political independence until the Roman conquest (chapter 2). Pylos seems to have bypassed the Messenian portion of its past, playing on myths that connected it directly to the heroic age preceding the return of the Heraclids. In the southern Messenian plain east of the Pamisos, the case of Thouria shows that reviving the Lakedaimonian identity could also offer a viable option for a community that wanted to break loose from the central dominance of Messene. Roman rule, after a first phase in which the *epos* of the Messenians experienced a renewed moment of saliency, slowly changed the function and even the very social surface of the Messenian identity. In the age of Pausanias (chapter 10), the traditional Messenian *epos* was only one of a number of ways for leading families to claim for themselves a central role in the past of the community, in order to underpin their social superiority and their belonging to the ruling elite of the province of Achaea and of the Empire. This last phase in the long history of the Messenian identity is the one that has left the clearest traces in the literary sources.

One of the most striking aspects of this long trajectory is the consistency that characterizes certain structural aspects of the Messenian identity. We will now turn to the two most conspicuous such aspects, the Messenian–Spartan polarity and the construction of the past by the Messenians, and finally consider once again their historical roots.

DAMOSTRATOS AND THE OPPOSITIONAL NATURE OF ETHNICITY

During the 1997 campaign, a rather unconspicuous monument was found close to the north colonnade of the gymnasium of Messene, not far from its monumental gate. It originally consisted of a small pillar supporting a rectangular capital, the only part that now survives, with a cutting in the top surface which signals the presence of a small stele, presumably decorated in painting or relief.[4] The front of the capital preserves the dedicatory inscription of the monument in the form of two elegiac couplets that run as follows (SEG 47.390): "You, o Damostratos, leave behind an immortal memorial of your worthiness / because you have transformed an old hatred into friendship. / To bring about a reconciliation between your

---

[4] See Themelis 2001a: 201–3.

fatherland Sparta and Messene, / something many had wished would happen, has been allotted by fate to you." The general shape of the monument and the letter forms appear to point to a date in the third century BC. Clearly, the Spartan Damostratos, whom we cannot otherwise identify, had been instrumental in achieving some sort of agreement between Spartans and Messenians, perhaps even an alliance.

In spite of the celebratory tone of the epigram, the agreement may not have been all that decisive, for it does not seem to have left conspicuous traces in the sources, and scholars are uncertain as to its historical context.[5] All the more interesting is the contrast between the rather modest monument and the rhetorical emphasis of the dedication. It looks as if, for the Messenians, any sort of agreement with Sparta was not, and could not be, just an episode of international relations like any other; it immediately conjured up the whole historical destiny of the Messenians and correspondingly needed to be conceptualized in that framework, as a turning point that changed centuries of enmity. Even in the third century hostility to Sparta remained a sort of default setting for the Messenians.

And yet, an outsider's view of this phenomenon reveals unexpected facets. Polybius' famous discussion of the historical destinies of Messenians, Spartans, and Arcadians (4.32.3–10) finds fault with the Messenians precisely for their failure to act consistently upon their predicament. From Polybius' point of view, throughout their history the Messenians had been confronted with the hostility of the Spartans and the friendly disposition of the Arcadians, and had themselves been incapable of loyally standing by the latter against the former, in spite of all the ills they had suffered from the Spartans and all the benefits they had received from the Arcadians. Surely in this passage Polybius is manipulating the past, as shown by the fact that he makes the Megalopolitans stand for the Arcadians and the citizens of Messene for all Messenians. His whole argument has a very explicit political agenda, namely to preach solidarity between Messene and the Achaean League. Still, seeing the Messenians accused of inconsistency in their attitude to Sparta is striking. On second thoughts, Polybius' pragmatic take on the issue may shed light on the true nature of anti-Spartan feelings in Hellenistic Messene, revealing that, for all their historical roots, at least in this period they were not a function of political relations. Polybius' views suggest that, in Hellenistic

---

[5] The best candidate seems to be the First Macedonian War, when both Messenians and Spartans were allied with the Aetolians, and apparently also with each other; see Polyb. 16.3.3 – almost ironically, a reference to king Nabis attacking the Messenians in spite of the alliance.

Messenia, opposition to Sparta was not the product of political circumstances or objective conditions and did not have visible consequences in the Messenians' foreign policy.

The centrality of resistance and hostility to Sparta as the main component of the Messenian identity throughout its history is a peculiar phenomenon. Its importance and pervasiveness is visible in many instances, especially in the *epos* of the Messenians. The overarching imperative to cancel from their past any hint of pacific coexistence with the Spartans had paradoxical consequences, such as their accepting the notion of temporary enslavement of their ancestors, maintaining that between the Second Messenian War and the revolt of the fifth century all the Messenians who remained in the region had been turned into Helots. It is true that in the Greek world polities sharing a common boundary were very often hostile to each other, but not even traditional and long-lasting enmities such as that between Athens and Thebes were carried on with a consistency and charged with a symbolic meaning comparable to what we observe in this case. Hostility to Sparta was the *mythomoteur* of Messenian ethnicity.

Its oppositional nature is one of the few aspects of ethnicity on which all scholars agree. Ethnicity cannot exist in a vacuum, and any ethnic group articulates its identity by distinguishing itself from other ethnic groups. Of such dynamics, Greek history offers ample evidence. The Greek world was crossed by multiple ethnic borders, which separated polities or larger groups from one another – surely less fundamental than the main ethnic boundary between Greeks and non-Greeks, but nevertheless symbolically construed in ethnic terms. Greek political communities typically defined membership based on a mixture of legal criteria and ethnic symbolism, expressed by the pervasive kinship terminology used to designate the subdivisions of the citizen body and by the use of typical markers of ethnic boundaries, such as speech patterns and myths of common descent. Ethnic stereotyping, e.g. in Aristophanes' comedies, shows that, in the Athenians' perception, what separated them from Megarians, Spartans, Boeotians etc. was not just the political border of their polis, but a full-fledged ethnic boundary, as articulated most clearly in communal religious practice. In many ways, this situation recalls the one created by the spread of nationalism, with a part of the world constituted by a sort of club of nations, defining themselves against each other but at the same time recognizing each other as units of the same order. Much as they spent most of their time fighting each other, they constituted a broadly homogeneous area opposed to the world of the non-nations – or rather, not-yet-nations.

Against the background of the Greek polis system, the single-minded binary structure of the Messenian identity and the all-important role of the Spartan enemy in it appear as an anomaly. This anomaly can be explained only by the specific historical circumstances in which Messenian ethnicity first emerged, out of a process of ethnic proliferation from within Lakedaimon. For this reason, the ethnic boundary between Messenians and Spartans could not be comparable to any other border for the Messenians. Once Messene finally became independent, it was the inherent centrifugal dynamic of the region that ensured that the memory of the old struggles against Sparta was kept alive, this time as a charter for cohesion and unity. No other war of the archaic or classical periods remained as important and actual during the Hellenistic age as the Messenian Wars.

A MONUMENT FROM DELPHI AND THE CONSTRUCTION OF THE PAST

The painstaking inventory of ancient stones conducted by the French archaeologists in Delphi has allowed them to recognize 46 blocks of gray limestone found out of their original context, but mostly in the northern part of the sanctuary, as parts of a lavish dedication, a base some eight meters long and more than two meters deep, which carried a number of bronze statues. Two inscriptions, only very fragmentarily preserved (SEG 19.391), were carved on the front face of the uppermost of the three layers that constituted the base. They identify the monument as an offering of the Messenians to Pythian Apollo. The distribution of the blocks on the ground has allowed Jean Pouilloux to conclude with reasonable certainty that the base was originally located on a terrace to the left of the ramp that rises to the Lesche of the Cnidians, right above the so-called horse-shoe monument and in view of the east face of the temple of Apollo.[6] One of the inscriptions runs immediately below the upper rim of the blocks, with letters around twelve centimeters high, the other is just below the first, and its letters are much smaller, around five centimeters. On the basis of the few letters preserved, the first inscription has been restored as

[Μεσσάν]ιο[ι Ἀπό]λλω[νι Πυ]θίωι

i.e. "the Messenians to Pythian Apollo," and the second as

[Ἀπόλλονι] Πυ[θίοι] ἀνέθεν [Μεσ]σάνιοι

---

[6] See Pouilloux 1960: 142–51. For the location of the monument, see also Bommelaer 1991: 204.

i.e. "the Messenians dedicated to Pythian Apollo." It is essentially the same text, except that the word order is different and the first inscription does not seem to include a verb. The few letters that are preserved point to a date for the first inscription in the second century BC. The shapes of some letters suggest that the second, smaller one must be significantly older, late archaic or early classical.[7] This would make the base earlier than the pillar dedicated by Messenians and Naupaktians for their victory over Kalydon. In other words, our monument would be the most ancient Messenian dedication at Delphi, and actually the oldest monument of the Messenians altogether.

On the evidence of the inscriptions, the dedication of the Messenians would seem to be a case of recutting of an earlier text, a phenomenon well attested at Delphi, especially on the bases of monumental dedications.[8] This happened for a variety of reasons: in some cases, the earlier text had been cut on the upper face of the base, and could not be easily seen from afar,[9] in others, the monument had been modified and the old inscription ended up being replaced and erased.[10] There is even one instance in which the new inscription ran directly below the old one, which, however, was written right to left.[11] At a closer look, though, the conclusion that the base of the Messenians offers just another case of an inscription recut at a later time turns out to be rather less certain. First of all, at Delphi the practice of calling Apollo "Pythian Apollo" in inscriptions is not attested before the fourth century BC, and becomes really widespread only in the third.[12] Moreover, according to epigraphists, the second and apparently older inscription, for all its archaic letter-forms, was in fact also cut in the Hellenistic period. Tell-tale elements include the shorter central bar of the epsilons and the triangular endings of the strokes of the letters, which form small apices.[13] It seems hard to resist the conclusion that both inscriptions, as we see them, were cut at the same time, with the intention of making one of them look older than the other.

---

[7] The inscription has epsilons with diagonal bars, nus with a shorter right leg, oblique iotas, and the theta is a square encircling a cross; see the drawing in Pouilloux 1960: 143. Such shapes would suggest a date between the last decades of the sixth century and the first half of the fifth.

[8] See the overview by Jacquemin 1999: 216–20.

[9] This seems to be the most frequent case: see the "lower Tarentines" (Bommelaer 1991: 117–18) and the two offerings of the Lipareans (Jacquemin 1999: 81, 122).

[10] As happened in the late third century BC to the base of Marathon, Bommelaer 1991: 134, 136–8 with further references.

[11] The "upper Tarentines," see Bommelaer 1991: 163–4 with further references.

[12] Jacquemin-Laroche 1982: 198–9, Jacquemin 1999: 75–6.

[13] See Pouilloux 1960: 150, reporting also the observations of the first editor, G. Daux (cf. Daux 1937).

This combination of features makes of the base of the Messenians a unique case. The Greeks were clearly aware that the shape of the letters could point to an inscription's antiquity, and imitation of older letter forms when an inscription was recut was not at all unknown at Delphi.[14] This, however, would not explain the situation observed on the base of the Messenians. If we assume that the second, smaller inscription had been cut with an eye to preserving the look of an older inscription that was present somewhere else on the monument, then there was no need for the first, larger one, which is also Hellenistic in date. In other words, if the Messenians had wanted to preserve the archaic appearance of their dedication, there was no reason for them to cut two inscriptions, one archaic-looking and one modern, so to speak. Not to mention the fact that there is no other trace of an inscription on the blocks of the monument, so that the very existence of an earlier text is doubtful – all the more so, since both extant inscriptions, as noted above, refer to Apollo in a form that is not attested before the fourth century.

Scholars have defended an early chronology for this monument, pointing to some of its architectural features, such as the fact that its blocks were not cut perpendicularly on the sides, but joined one another along oblique lines that gave an impression somewhat similar to that of polygonal masonry.[15] While this shape is found in walls well into the Hellenistic age, it is surprising to see it used for the steps of a base. Also, the blocks were held together by dovetail clamps, which occur more frequently in the archaic period. However, neither of these features is really decisive: blocks of similar shape appear – of all places – in the retaining walls of the Hellenistic theater of Messene, where they seem to have been used to give an impression of antiquity, and dovetail clamps are also found on Hellenistic monuments.[16] On the whole, it seems easier to make sense of all the aspects of this monument under the assumption that it was really built in the Hellenistic period, in which case we are dealing with a "patriotic forgery," as Jean Pouilloux put it.

The base of the Messenians at Delphi symbolizes a structural aspect of the Messenian identity. Because of the omnipresence of primordial rhetoric in ethnicity, antiquity is crucial to any ethnic group, and ancient Greece was no exception. Having participated in the Trojan War remained

---

[14] It occurs for instance on the base of Marathon. However, in that case, while the new inscription imitated the letter-forms of the old one, the old inscription was erased.

[15] Jacquemin 1999: 219–20; for a description of the shapes of the blocks, see Pouilloux 1960: 145.

[16] On the retaining wall of the theater of Messene, see Müth 2007: 80–6; on the clamps, Pouilloux 1960: 150.

an important title of nobility for communities of Greeks as long as Greeks waged wars. For the Messenians, because they had gained access to the stage of history so late, the primordial imperative of ethnicity was particularly difficult to satisfy, and at the same time particularly pressing, especially as long as their very right to existence was disputed. Their attempt at making up for the lack of a glorious past can be seen at work in a number of instances, ranging from the paintings in the temple of Messene (chapter 9) to the works of Myron and Rhianus on the Messenian Wars (chapter 4), to Mnasistratos' reform of the cult of Andania and related phenomena (chapter 10). The base of the Messenians at Delphi, however, offers the clearest and most striking example of their conscious endeavor at creating a past: it is at the same time a typical expression of the Messenian identity and a metaphor of it. It is also, to be sure, a cautionary tale for the modern scholar: maintaining a early chronology for the origin of the monument in spite of the paradoxes it involves nicely parallels belief in the reliability of Pausanias' history of archaic Messenia or in the high antiquity of the cult of Andania.

In articulating their vision of their own past, ethnic groups do not typically show what scholars would characterize as selfless respect for historical accuracy. The Messenians were no more prone than other Greeks to manipulating memory and generating patriotic versions of their history, and not more obsessed with the past than average. However, they had to face a peculiarly difficult situation. They had essentially not been there throughout the archaic age, and correspondingly the historical record of that age, as it took shape by the fifth century, had almost no traces of them. Therefore, in their attempt at creating and transmitting narratives of the past they could live with, the Messenians were in the position of having to catch up with their fellow Greeks, while at the same time facing particularly rigid constraints in the form of preexisting and widely accepted narratives of the mythic and post-mythic past. Moreover, the fact that the Messenians came to this game later than almost everybody else in Greece means that their creative engagement with tradition has left traces that are often more visible for the modern observer than is the case with other communities of Greeks – which makes of them such an intriguing case study.

* * *

If at times it looks as though for the Messenians the past was more important than for any other community of Greeks, this is precisely because they had so little of it, and their attempts at dealing with such an unfavorable situation and filling the voids provide fascinating insights. Messenian ethnicity emerged later than almost all other ethnic identities within the family of the Greeks, under very peculiar circumstances that marked it throughout its history. This book has attempted to offer a reconstruction of that history, taking as broad an approach to the evidence as seemed possible, and making use of all the methods that appeared to be appropriate, within the limited competence of the author. The reader will judge whether the author has carried his taste for experiment too far, or not far enough. Certainly, because of the nature and sheer scarcity of the evidence the level of detail that could be achieved may not be very high, especially as concerns potential counter-narratives and alternate constructions of collective identities and memories, on the margins of our visual field. Of course, many conclusions cannot but be tentative. Such limitations are inevitable in an investigation that tries to reconstruct rather volatile social phenomena in the distant past. In spite of this, if the reader may be convinced that such phenomena are worth investigating also in the distant field of classical antiquity, this book will have served its purpose.

Bibliography

Accame, S. (1946) *Il dominio romano in Grecia dalla Guerra Acaica ad Augusto*. Rome.

Akujärvi, J. (2005) *Researcher, Traveller, Narrator: Studies in Pausanias' Periegesis*. Studia Graeca et Latina Lundensia 12. Lund.

Alcock, S. E. (1991) "Tomb cult and the post-classical polis," *AJA* 95: 447–67.

(1999) "The pseudo-history of Messenia unplugged," *TAPhA* 129: 333–41.

(2001) "The peculiar Book IV and the problem of the Messenian past," in Alcock, Cherry and Elsner 2001: 142–53.

(2002a) "A simple case of exploitation? The helots of Messenia," in *Money, Labour and Land*, ed. P. Cartledge, E. E. Cohen and L. Foxhall. London and New York: 185–99.

(2002b) *Archaeologies of the Greek Past: Landscape, Monuments, and Memory*. Cambridge.

Alcock, S. E., et al. (2005) "Pylos Regional Archaeological Project. Part VII: historical Messenia, Geometric through Late Roman," *Hesperia* 74: 147–209.

Alcock, S. E., Cherry, J. F., and Elsner, J., eds. (2001) *Pausanias: Travel and Memory in Roman Greece*. Oxford.

Amandry, P. (1987) "Trépieds de Delphes et du Péloponnèse," *BCH* 111: 79–131.

Ameling, W. (1983) *Herodes Atticus, I: Biographie*. Hildesheim.

Anderson, B. (1991) *Imagined Communities: Reflections on the Origin and Spread of Nationalism*. 2nd, revised edn. London and New York.

Andrewes, A. (1951) "Ephoros' Book I and the kings of Argos," *CQ* 1: 39–45.

Angeli Bernardini, P., ed. (2004) *La città di Argo: mito, storia, tradizioni poetiche. Atti del Convegno Internazionale (Urbino, 13–15 giugno 2002)*. Rome.

Angeli Bernardini, P., Cingano, E., Gentili, B., and Giannini, P. (1995) *Pindaro: le Pitiche*. Introduzione, testo critico e traduzione a cura di B. Gentili. Commento a cura di P. Angeli Bernardini, E. Cingano e P. Giannini. Milan.

Annequin, J., and Garrido-Hory, M., eds. (1994) *Religion et anthropologie de l'esclavage et des formes de dependance. Actes du XXème colloque du GIREA – Besançon, 4–6 novembre 1993*. Annales Littéraires de l'Université de Besancon, 534. Paris.

Antonaccio, C. M. (1995), *An Archaeology of Ancestors: Tomb Cult and Hero Cult in Early Greece*. Lanham, MD.

(2003) "Hybridity and the cultures within Greek culture," in *The Cultures within Greek Culture: Contact, Conflict, Collaboration*, ed. C. Dougherty and L. Kurke. Cambridge: 57–74.

Antonetti, C. (1990) *Les Étoliens: image et religion*. Annales littéraires de l'Université de Besançon, 405. Paris.

(1995) "La centralità di Eleusi nell'ideologia panellenica adrianea," *Ostraka* 4: 149–56.

Appadurai, A. (1981) "The past as a scarce resource," *Man* 16: 201–19.

Arafat, K. (1996) *Pausanias' Greece: Ancient Artists and Roman Rulers*. Cambridge.

Armstrong, J. A. (1982) *Nations before Nationalism*. Chapel Hill.

Asheri, D. (1980) "Rimpatrio di esuli e ridistribuzione di terre nelle città siceliote, ca. 466–461 a.c.," in Φιλίας χάριν: *Miscellanea di studi classici in onore di Eugenio Manni*, Rome: 143–58.

(1983) "La diaspora e il ritorno dei Messeni," in *Tria corda: scritti in onore di Arnaldo Momigliano*, ed. E. Gabba. Como: 27–42.

(1988) "À propos des sanctuaires extraurbains en Sicile et Grande Grèce: théories et témoignages," *Mélanges Pierre Lévêque*, ed. M.-M. Mactoux and E. Geny, vol. I. Annales littéraires de l'Université de Besançon, 367. Paris: 1–15.

Assmann, J. (1992) *Das kulturelle Gedächtnis: Schrift, Erinnerung und politische Identität in frühen Hochkulturen*. Munich.

Auberger, J. (1992a) "Pausanias et les Messéniens: une histoire d'amour!" *REA* 94: 187–97.

(1992b) "Pausanias romancier? Le Témoignage du livre IV," *DHA* 18.1: 257–80.

(2000) "Pausanias et le livre 4: une leçon pour l'empire?" *Phoenix* 54: 255–81.

(2001) "D'un héros à l'autre: Pausanias au pied de l'Ithôme," in Knoepfler and Piérart 2001: 261–73.

Badian, E. (1993) *From Plataea to Potidaea: Studies in the History and Historiography of the Pentecontaetia*. Baltimore and London.

Badie, A., and Billot, M.-F. (2001) "Le Décor des toits de Grèce du IIe s. av. au Ier s. ap. J.-C.," in Marc and Moretti 2001: 61–134.

Baldassarra, D. (1999) *Famiglie aristocratiche di Messene in epoca imperiale*. Tesi di Laurea, Università di Venezia, 1998/99.

Bardani, V. N. (1990–1991) "Ἀπόντος τοῦ λίθου," *Horos* 8–9: 199–200.

Barletta, B. A. (1990) "An 'Ionian Sea' style in archaic Doric architecture," *AJA* 94: 45–72.

Barron, J. P. (1984) "Ibycus: Gorgias and other poems," *BICS* 31: 13–24.

Barth, F. (1969a) *Ethnic Groups and Boundaries: The Social Organization of Culture Difference*. Bergen.

(1969b) "Introduction," in Barth 1969a: 9–38.

(1994) "Enduring and emerging issues in the analysis of ethnicity," in *Rethinking Ethnicity: Beyond "Ethnic Groups and Boundaries*," ed. H. Vermeulen and C. Govers. Amsterdam: 11–32.

Bauslaugh, R. A. (1990) "Messenian dialect and dedications of the 'Methanioi,'" *Hesperia* 59: 661–8.

Bearzot, C. (1997) "Cassandro e la ricostruzione di Tebe: propaganda filellenica e interessi peloponnesiaci," in *Recent Developments in the History and Archaeology of Central Greece*, ed. J. Bintliff. BAR International Series 666. Oxford: 265–76.

Beck, H. (1997) *Polis und Koinon: Untersuchungen zur Geschichte und Struktur der griechischen Bundesstaaten im 4. Jahrhundert v. Chr.* Historia Einzelschrift 114. Stuttgart.

Beister, H. (1973) "Ein thebanisches Tropaion bereits vor Beginn der Schlacht bei Leuktra. Zur Interpretation von IG VII 2462 und Paus. 4,32,5f.," *Chiron* 3: 65–84.

Beloch, K.-J. (1926) *Griechische Geschichte.* 2nd edn., vol. I, part 2. Strasbourg.

Bennet, J. (1994) "Space through time: diachronic perspectives on the spatial organization of the Pylian state," in *Politeia: Society and state in the Aegean Bronze Age. Proceedings of the 5th International Aegean Conference, University of Heidelberg, Archäologisches Institut, 10–13 April, 1994,* ed. R. Laffineur and W.-D. Niemeier. Brussels and Austin: 587–601.

Bentley, G. C. (1987) "Ethnicity and practice," *CSSH* 29: 24–55.

Berg, B. (1998) "Wronged maidens in Myron's Messenian History and the ancient novel," *GRBS* 39: 39–61.

Bernhardt, R. (1985) *Polis und römische Herrschaft in der späten Republik (149-31 v. Chr.).* Berlin and New York.

Berve, H. (1967) *Die Tyrannis bei den Griechen.* Munich.

Bettalli, M. (1995) *I mercenari nel mondo greco, I: dalle origini alla fine del V sec. a. C.* Pisa.

Billot, M.-F. (1989–90) "Apollon Pythéen et l'Argolide archaïque," *Archaiognosia* 6: 35–100.

Bloedow, E. F. (2000) "Why did Sparta rebuff the Athenians at Ithome in 462 BC?" *AHB* 14.3: 89–101.

Bockisch, G. (1985) "Die Helotisierung der Messenier. Ein Interpretationsversuch zu Pausanias IV 14, 4f.," in *Antike Abhängigkeitsformen in den griechischen Gebieten ohne Polisstruktur und den römischen Provinzen. Actes du colloque sur l'esclavage (Iéna 29 septembre–2 octobre 1981),* ed. H. Kreißig und F. Kühnert. Berlin: 29–48.

Boehringer, D. (2001) *Heroenkulte in Griechenland von der geometrischen bis zur klassischen Zeit: Attika, Argolis, Messenien.* Klio Beihefte, Neue Folge, vol. 3. Berlin.

Bölte, F. (1936), "Thuria," in *Paulys Realencyclopädie der classischen Altertumswissenschaft.* VI.1. Munich: 633–8.

(1949) "Pamisos 2," in *Paulys Realencyclopädie der classischen Altertumswissenschaft.* XVIII.3. Munich: 293–5.

Bommelaer, J.-F. (1991) *Guide de Delphes: le site.* Paris.

Bonias, Z. (1998) Ένα αγροτικό ιερό στις Αιγιές Λακωνίας. Athens.

Bookidis, N. (1967) *A Study of the Use and Geographical Distribution of Architectural Sculpture in the Archaic Period (Greece, East Greece and Magna Graecia).* Dissertation. Bryn Mawr.

Borbein, A. (1973) "Die griechische Statue des 4. Jahrhunderts v. Chr.," *JDAI* 88: 43–212.

Bowersock, G. W. (1961) "Eurycles of Sparta," *JRS* 51: 111–18.

(1965) *Augustus and the Greek World.* Oxford.

(1985) "Augustus and the East: the problem of the succession," in *Caesar Augustus: Seven Aspects*, ed. F. Millar and E. Segal. Oxford: 169–88.

Bowie, E. L. (1974) "The Greeks and their past in the Second Sophistic," in *Studies in Ancient Society*, ed. M. I. Finley. London and Boston: 166–209.

(2001) "Inspiration and aspiration: date, genre, and readership," in Alcock, Cherry and Elsner 2001: 21–32.

Bowra, C. M. (1963) "Two lines of Eumelus," *CQ* 13: 145–53.

Bradford, A. S. (1994) "The duplicitous Spartan," in Powell and Hodkinson 1994: 59–85.

Braun, T. (1994) "χρηστοὺς ποιεῖν," *CQ* 44: 40–45.

Brelich, A. (1958) *Gli eroi greci: un problema storico-religioso*. Rome.

Bremmer, J., ed. (1987) *Interpretations of Greek Mythology*. London and Sidney.

(1997) "Myth as propaganda: Athens and Sparta," *ZPE* 117: 9–17.

Breuillot, M. (1985) "L'Eau et les dieux de Messénie," *DHA* 11: 789–804.

Bringmann, K. (1965) *Studien zu den politischen Ideen des Isokrates*. Göttingen.

Broucke, P. (forthcoming) "The heroon at Messene: new observations on order, style, and date," paper delivered at the 107th Annual Meeting of the Archaeological Institute of America, Montreal, January 5–8, 2006.

Broughton, T. R. S. (1984) *The Magistrates of the Roman Republic*, I: *509 BC–100 BC*. Chico, CA.

Bruce, I. A. F. (1967) *An Historical Commentary on the "Hellenica Oxyrhynchia."* Cambridge.

Brugnone, A. (1997) "Legge di Himera sulla ridistribuzione della terra," *PP* 52: 262–305.

Brulé, P., and Oulhen, J., eds. (1997) *Esclavage, guerre, économie en Grèce ancienne: hommage à Yvon Garlan*. Rennes.

Bruni, G. B. (1979) "Mothakes, neodamodeis, brasideioi," in Capozza 1979: 21–31.

Buckler, J. (1980) *The Theban Hegemony, 371–362 BC* Cambridge, MA.

(2003) *Aegean Greece in the Fourth Century BC*. Leiden and Boston.

Bultrighini, U. (2001) "Ricupero dell'identità: Andania, i Dori e la rifondazione di Messene," in *Identità e valori: fattori di aggregazione e fattori di crisi nell'esperienza politica antica*, ed. A. Barzanò et al. Rome: 39–61.

Buonocore, M. (1982) "Ricerche sulla terza guerra messenica," *MGR* 8: 57–123.

Burkert, W. (1979) *Structure and History in Greek Mythology and Ritual*. Berkeley, Los Angeles and London.

Butler, K. D. (2001) "Defining diaspora, refining a discourse, *Diaspora* 10: 189–219.

Buxton, R. (1994) *Imaginary Greece: The Contexts of Mythology*. Cambridge.

Caccamo Caltabiano, M. (1993) *La monetazione di Messana: Con le emissioni di Rhegion dell'età della tirannide*. AMGS XIII. Berlin and New York.

Cain, H.-U. (1995) "Hellenistische Kultbilder. Religiöse Präsenz und museale Präsentation der Götter im Heiligtum und beim Fest," in Wörrle and Zanker 1995: 115–30.

Calame, C. (1979) "Discours mythique et discours historique dans trois textes de Pausanias," *Degrès* 17: 1–30.

(1987) "Spartan genealogies: the mythological representation of a spacial organisation," in Bremmer 1987: 153–86.

(2001) *Choruses of Young Women in Ancient Greece: Their Morphology, Religious Role, and Social Functions.* 2nd, revised edn. Lanham, MD.

Camassa, G. (1983) *L'occhio e il metallo: un mitologema greco a Roma?* Genova.

(1993) "I culti dell'area dello Stretto," in *Lo Stretto, crocevia di culture. Atti del XXVI convegno internazionale di studi sulla Magna Grecia (Taranto 1986).* Naples: 133–62.

Cameron, A. (1995) *Callimachus and his Critics.* Princeton.

Camp, J. McK. II (2000) "Walls and the polis," in Flensted-Jensen, Nielsen and Rubinstein 2000: 41–57.

Capozza, M., ed. (1979) *Schiavitù, manomissione e classi dipendenti nel mondo antico.* Rome.

Cargill, J. (1985) "Demosthenes, Aischines, and the crop of traitors," *AW* 11: 75–85.

Carlier, P. (1984) *La Royauté en Grèce avant Alexandre.* Strasbourg.

Cartledge, P. (1985) "Rebels and Sambos in classical Greece: a comparative view," in *Crux: Essays in Greek History presented to G.E.M. de Ste. Croix on his 75th Birthday,* ed. P. Cartledge and F. D. Harvey. London: 16–46.

(1987) *Agesilaos and the Crisis of Sparta.* Baltimore and London.

(2002) *Sparta and Lakonia: A Regional History, 1300 to 362 BC.* 2nd edn. London and New York.

Cartledge, P., and Spawforth, A. (2002) *Hellenistic and Roman Sparta: A Tale of Two Cities.* 2nd edn. London and New York.

Castelli, C. (1994a) "Riano e Omero: i Messeniaka tra imitazione e innovazione," *Acme* 49: 5–24.

(1994b) "Riano di Creta: ipotesi cronologiche e biografiche," *RIL* 128: 73–87.

(1995) "Poeti ellenistici in Pausania," in *Studia classica Iohanni Tarditi oblata,* ed. L. Belloni, G. Milanese, and A. Porro. Milan: 711–25.

(1998) "I *Messeniaca* di Riano: testo ed esegesi dei frammenti," *Acme* 51: 3–50.

Catling, R. W. V. (1996) "The archaic and classical pottery," in *The Laconia Survey: Continuity and Change in a Greek Rural Landscape,* II: *Archaeological Data,* ed. W. Cavanagh, J. Crouwel, R. W. V. Catling, and G. Shipley. Annual of the British School at Athens, Supplementary Volume 27. London: 33–89.

(2002) "The survey area from the Early Iron Age to the Classical period," in *The Laconia Survey: Continuity and Change in a Greek Rural Landscape,* I: *Methodology and Interpretation,* ed. W. Cavanagh, J. Crouwel, R. W. V. Catling, and G. Shipley. Annual of the British School at Athens, Supplementary Volume 26. London: 151–256.

Cawkwell, G. (1993) "Sparta and her allies in the fifth century," *CQ* 43: 364–76.

Chamoux, F. (1970) "Trépieds votifs à caryatides," *BCH* 94: 319–26.

Chaniotis, A. (1988) *Historie und Historiker in den griechischen Inschriften: Epigraphische Beiträge zur griechischen Historiographie.* Stuttgart.

(1999) "Empfängerformular und Urkundenfälschung: Bemerkungen zum Urkundendossier von Magnesia am Mäander," in *Urkunden und Urkundenformulare im klassischen Altertum und in den orientalischen Kulturen,* ed. R. G. Khoury. Heidelberg: 51–69.

Chatzi-Spiliopoulou, G. (1998) "Μυκηναϊκὴ Μεσσηνία. Τὸ πρόσφατο ἔργο τῆς Ζ' Ἀρχαϊολογικῆς Ἐφορείας," in Πρακτικὰ τοῦ Ε' διεθνοῦς συνεδρίου Πελοποννησιακῶν σπουδῶν (Ἄργος-Ναύπλιον, 6–10 Σεπτεμβρίου 1995), Athens: 534–56.

(2001) "Ὁ 6ος θαλαμοτὸς τάφος τῶν Ἑλληνικῶν Ἀνθείας στὴ Μεσσηνία," in Mitsopoulos-Leon 2001: 285–98.

Chlepa, E.-A. (2001) *Μεσσήνη. Τὸ Ἀρτεμίσιο καὶ οἱ οἶκοι τῆς δυτικῆς πτέρυγας τοῦ Ἀσκληπιείου*. Athens.

Christien, J. (1989) "Les Liaisons entre Sparte et son territoire malgré l'encadrement montagneux," *Montagnes, fleuves, forêts dans l'histoire: barrières ou lignes de convergence? XVI Congrès International de Sciences Historiques (Stuttgart 1985)*, ed. J.-F. Bergier. St. Katharinen: 18–44.

(1992) "L'Étranger à Lacédémone," in *L'Étranger dans le monde grec*, II, ed. R. Lonis. Nancy: 147–67.

Christof, E. (2001) *Das Glück der Stadt*. Frankfurt am Main.

Clauss, M. (1983) *Sparta: Eine Einführung in seine Geschichte und Zivilisation*. Munich.

Cohen, A. (1974) *Two-dimensional Man: An Essay on the Anthropology of Power and Symbolism in Complex Society*. Berkeley.

Cohen, R. (1997) *Global Diasporas: An Introduction*. London.

Coldstream, J. N. (1968) *Greek Geometric Pottery: A Survey of Ten Regional Styles and their Chronology*. London.

(1976) "Hero-cults in the age of Homer," *JHS* 96: 8–17.

(1977) *Geometric Greece*. London.

(1983) "The meaning of the regional styles in the eighth century BC," in *The Greek Renaissance of the Eighth Century BC: Tradition and Innovation. Proceedings of the Second International Symposium at the Swedish Institute in Athens, 1–5 June, 1981*, ed. R. Hägg. Acta Instituti Atheniensis Regni Sueciae, series in 4°, XXX. Stockholm: 17–25.

(1984) *The Formation of the Greek Polis: Aristotle and Archaeology*. Rheinisch-Westfaelische Akademie der Wissenschaften, Vorträge: Geisteswissenschaften G 272. Opladen.

Consolo Langher, S. N. (1965) "Documentazione numismatica e storia di Tyndaris nel sec. IV a.C.," *Helikon* 5: 63–96.

Cooper, F. A. (1999) "Curvature and other architectural refinements in a Hellenistic heroon at Messene," in *Appearance and Essence: Refinement of Classical Architecture: Curvature*, ed. L. Haselberger. Philadelphia: 185–97.

(2000) "The fortifications of Epaminondas and the rise of the monumental Greek city," in *City Walls: The Urban Enceinte in Global Perspective*, ed. J. D. Tracy. Cambridge: 155–91.

Corbetta, C. (1978) "A proposito di due frammenti di Riano," *Aegyptus* 58: 137–50.

Corcella, A. (1992) "Una polemica su Maratona. PMed 71.76, 71.78, 71.79," *RFIC* 120: 422–30.

Cornell, T. (1983) "Gründer," in *Reallexikon für Antike und Christentum*, XII. Suttgart: 1107–45.

Cosmopoulos, M. B., ed. (2003) *Greek Mysteries: The Archaeology and Ritual of Ancient Greek Secret Cults.* London and New York.

Costabile, F. (1979) "Il culto di Apollo quale testimonianza della tradizione corale e religiosa di Reggio e Messana," *MEFRA* 91: 525–43.

Coulson, W. D. E. (1983) "Archaic to Roman times: the site and environs. With a contribution by Nancy C. Wilkie," in McDonald, Coulson and Rosser 1983: 332–50.

(1986) *The Dark Age Pottery of Messenia.* Studies in Mediterranean Archaeology, Pocket-book 43. Göteborg.

(1988) "Geometric pottery from Volimidia," *AJA* 92: 53–74.

Coulson, W. D. E. et al. (1983) "The burials," in McDonald, Coulson and Rosser 1983: 260–72.

Cozzoli, U. (1978) "Sparta e la liberazione degli iloti nel V e nel IV secolo," *MGR* 6: 213–32.

(1979) *Proprietà fondiaria ed esercito nello stato spartano di età classica.* Rome.

Culasso Gastaldi, E. (1984) *Sul trattato con Alessandro: polis, monarchia macedone e memoria demostenica.* Padova.

Curty, O. (1989) "L'Historiographie hellénistique et l'inscription n. 37 des Inschriften von Priene," in *Historia testis: mélanges d'épigraphie, d'histoire ancienne et de philologie offerts à Tadeusz Zawadzki*, ed. M. Pirart and O. Curty. Fribourg: 21–35.

Daim, F. (1982) "Gedanken zum Ethnosbegriff," *Mitteilungen der anthropologischen Gesellschaft in Wien* 112: 58–71.

D'Alessio, G. B. (2005) "The Megalai Ehoiai: a survey of the fragments," in *The Hesiodic Catalogue of Women: Constructions and Reconstructions*, ed. R. Hunter. Cambridge: 176–216.

Danalis, K. (2001–2002) "Ἑλληνιστικὴ κεραμικὴ ἀπὸ τὴν Περιστεριὰ Μεσσηνίας-Τριφυλίας," in Πρακτικὰ τοῦ 5′ διεθνοῦς συνεδρίου Πελοποννησιακῶν σπουδῶν (Τρίπολις, 24–29 Σεπτεμβρίου 2000), Athens: 369–98.

Daux, G. (1937) "Inscriptions et monuments archaïques de Delphes," *BCH* 61: 57–78.

David, E. (1979) "The conspiracy of Cinadon," *Athenaeum* 57: 239–59.

(1980) "Revolutionary agitation in Sparta after Leuctra," *Athenaeum* 58: 299–308.

(1981) *Sparta between Empire and Revolution (404–234 BC): Internal Problems and their Impact on Contemporary Greek Consciousness.* New York.

Davies, M. (1989) "The date of the Epic Cycle," *Glotta* 67: 89–100.

Davis, J. L., ed. (1998) *Sandy Pylos: An Archaeological History from Nestor to Navarino.* Austin.

Davis, J. L., et al. (1997) "The Pylos Regional Archaeological Project. Part I: overview and the archaeological survey," *Hesperia* 66: 391–494.

De Ridder, A. (1894) *Catalogue des bronzes de la société archéologique d'Athènes.* Paris.

De Sensi Sestito, G. (1981a) "I Dinomenidi nel basso e medio Tirreno tra Imera e Cuma," *MEFRA* 93: 617–42.

(1981b) "Contrasti etnici e lotte politiche a Zancle-Messene e Reggio alla caduta della tirannide," *Athenaeum* 69: 38–55.

de Souza, P. (1999) *Piracy in the Graeco-Roman World.* Cambridge.

De Vido, S. (1996) "Ἀνὴρ δόκιμος in Erodoto," *AAT* 130: 255–76.

Deininger, J. (1965) *Die Provinziallandtage der römischen Kaiserzeit: Von Augustus bis zum Ende des dritten Jahrhunderts n. Chr.* Munich.

Demand, N. H. (1990) *Urban Relocation in Archaic and Classical Greece: Flight and Consolidation.* London.

den Boer, W. (1956) "Political propaganda in Greek chronology," *Historia* 5: 162–77.

Descœudres, J.-P., ed. (1990) Εὐμουσία: *Ceramic and Iconographic Studies in Honour of Alexander Cambitoglou.* Sidney.

Deshours, N. (1993) "La Légende et le culte de Messène ou comme forger l'identité d'une cité," *REG* 106: 39–60.

(1999) "Les Messéniens, le règlement des mystères et la consultation de l'oracle d'Apollon Pythéen à Argos," *REG* 112: 463–84.

(2004a) "Cultes de Déméter, d'Artémis Ortheia et culte impérial à Messène (Ier s. av. notre ère – Ier s. de notre ère)," *ZPE* 146: 115–27.

(2004b) "Les Institutions civiques de Messène à l'époque hellénistique tardive," *ZPE* 150: 134–46.

(2006) *Les Mystères d'Andania: étude d'épigraphie et d'histoire religieuse.* Paris.

Despinis, G. J. (1966) "Ein neues Werk des Damophon," *AA*: 378–85.

Detienne, M., and Vernant, J.-P. (1978) *Les Ruses de l'intelligence: la métis des Grecs.* Paris.

Dillon, M. P. J. (1995) "The Lakedaimonian dedication to Olympian Zeus: the date of Meiggs & Lewis 22 (SEG 11, 1203A)," *ZPE* 107: 60–8.

Dipersia, G. (1974) "La nuova popolazione di Messene al tempo di Epaminonda," in *Propaganda e persuasione occulta nell'antichità,* ed. M. Sordi. CISA II. Milan: 54–61.

Dohnicht, M., and Heil, M. (2004) "Ein Legat Sullas in Messenien," *ZPE* 147: 235–42.

Dougherty, C. (1993a) *The Poetics of Colonization: From City to Text in Archaic Greece.* New York.

(1993b) "It's murder to found a colony," in *Cultural Poetics in Archaic Greece: Cult, Performance, Politics,* ed. C. Dougherty and L. Kurke. Cambridge: 178–98.

Dowden, K. (1992) *The Uses of Greek Mythology.* London.

Ducat, J. (1974a) "Les Thèmes des récits de la fondation de Rhégion," in *Mélanges helléniques offerts à P. Daux,* Paris: 93–114.

(1974b) "Le Mépris des Hilotes," *Annales (ESC)* 30: 1451–64.

(1990) *Les Hilotes. Bulletin de correspondance hellénique.* Supplément XX. Athens and Paris.

(1994) "Les Conduites et les idéologies intégratrices concernant les esclaves de type hilotique," in Annequin and Garrido-Hory 1994: 17–28.

(1999) "La Société spartiate et la guerre," in *Armées et sociétés de la Grèce classique: aspects sociaux et politiques de la guerre aux Ve et IVe s. av. J.C.,* ed. F. Prost. Paris: 35–50.

Dušanić, S. (1997) "Platon, la question messénienne et les guerres contre les Barbares," in Brulé and Oulhen 1997: 75–86.

Eckstein, F. (1969) Ἀναθήματα. *Studien zu den Weihgeschenken strengen Stils im Heiligtum von Olympia*. Berlin.

Eder, B. (1998) *Argolis, Lakonien, Messenien: Vom Ende der mykenischen Palastzeit bis zur Einwanderung der Dorier*. Vienna.

Ehrenberg, V. (1929) "Sparta. D. Geschichte," in *Paulys Realencyclopädie der classischen Altertumswissenschaft*, III. 2. Munich: 1373–1453.

Eide, T. (1992) "Pausanias and Thucydides," *SO* 67: 124–37.

Eriksen, T. H. (1991) "The cultural contexts of ethnic differences," *Man* 26: 127–44.

Errington, R. M. (1969) *Philopoemen*. Oxford.

Fabietti, U. (1998) *L'identità etnica*. 2nd edn. Rome.

Falkner, C. (1999) "Sparta and Lepreon in the Archidamian War (Thuc. 5.31.2–5)," *Historia* 48: 385–94.

Faustoferri, A. (1996) *Il trono di Amyklai a Sparta: Bathykles al servizio del potere*. Naples.

Felten, F. (1983) "Heiligtümer oder Märkte?" *AK* 26: 84–104.

Felten, F., and Reinholdt, C. (2001) "Das Brunnenhaus der Arsinoe in Messene," in Mitsopoulos-Leon 2001: 307–23.

Ferrary, J.-L. (1988) *Philhellénisme et impérialisme: aspects idéologiques de la conquête romaine du monde hellénistique*. Rome.

Figueira, T. J. (1984) "Mess contributions and subsistence at Sparta," *TAPhA* 114: 87–129.

  (1999) "The evolution of the Messenian identity," in Hodkinson and Powell 1999: 211–44.

  (2003) "The demography of the Spartan Helots," in Luraghi and Alcock 2003: 193–239.

Flensted-Jensen, P., Nielsen, T. H., and Rubinstein, L., eds. (2000) *Polis and Politics: Studies in Ancient Greek History Presented to Mogens Herman Hansen on his 60th birthday*. Copenhagen.

Floren, J. (1987) *Die griechische Plastik*, I: *Die geometrische und archaische Plastik*. Munich.

Flower, H. I. (1996) *Ancestor Masks and Aristocratic Power in Roman Culture*. Oxford.

Flower, M. A. (2002) "The invention of tradition in classical and Hellenistic Sparta," in Powell and Hodkinson 2002: 191–217.

Fougères, G. (1898) *Mantinée et l'Arcadie Orientale*. Bibliothèque des écoles françaises d'Athènes et de Rome, vol. 78. Paris.

Fournier, J. (2005) "Sparte et la justice romaine sous l'Haut-Empire. À propos de IG V I, 21," *REG* 118: 117–37.

Foxhall, L. (2002) "Social control, Roman power and Greek politics in the world of Plutarch," in *Demokratie, Recht und soziale Kontrolle im klassischen Athen*, ed. D. Cohen. Schriften des Historischen Kollegs – Kolloquien 49. Munich: 173–88.

Frei-Stolba, R., and Gex, K., eds. (2001) *Recherches récentes sur le monde hellé-nistique. Actes du colloque international organisé à l'occasion du 60e anniversaire de Pierre Ducrey, Lausanne, 20–21 novembre 1998.* Bern.

Freitag, K. (1996) "Der Akarnanische Bund im 5. Jh. v. Chr.," in *Akarnanien: Eine Landschaft im antiken Griechenland*, ed. P. Berktold, J. Schmid and C. Wacker. Würzburg: 75–86.

(2008) "Achaia and the Peloponnese in the late fifth–early fourth centuries," in Luraghi and Funke 2008.

Fröhlich, P. (1999) "Les Institutions des cités de Messénie à la basse époque hellénistique," in Renard 1999: 229–42.

(2007) "Les Tombeaux de la ville de Messène et les grandes familles de la cité à l'époque hellénistique," in *Le Péloponnèse d'Épaminondas à Hadrien: unité et diversité*, ed. C. Grandjean, Bordeaux: 203–27.

Ganci, R. (1998) *Uno ktisma, tre memorie storiche: il caso di Reggio.* Rome.

Gantz, T. (1993) *Early Greek Myth: A Guide to Literary and Artistic Sources.* Baltimore and London.

Gehrke, H.-J. (1994) "Mythos, Geschichte, Politik – antik und modern," *Saeculum* 45: 239–64.

(2001) "Myth, history and collective identity: uses of the past in ancient Greece," in Luraghi 2001a: 286–313.

(forthcoming) "Kulte und Akkulturation. Zur Rolle von religiösen Vorstellungen und Ritualen in kulturellen Austauschprozessen," in *Roma e l'Oriente nel I secolo a.C.*, ed. A. Mastrocinque.

Gengler, O. (1995) "Les Dioscures et les Apharétides dans le Parthénée d'Alcman (Frgt 3 Calame)," *LEC* 63: 3–21.

(2000) "Le Peintre Nikias chez Pausanias et IG II2 3055," *ZPE* 130: 143–6.

(2003) "Héritage épique et lyrique dans la poésie alexandrine: les Dioscures et les Apharétides d'Homère à Lycophron," in *Forme di comunicazione nel mondo antico e metamorfosi del mito: dal teatro al romanzo*, ed. M. Guglielmo and E. Bona. Alessandria: 135–47.

(2005) "Héraclès, Tyndare et Hippocoon dans la description de Sparte par Pausanias. Mise en espace d'une tradition mythique," *Kernos* 18: 311–28.

Georgiadou, A. (1997) *Plutarch's Pelopidas: A Historical and Philological Commentary.* Stuttgart and Leipzig.

Giangiulio, M. (2008) "The emergence of Pisatis," in Luraghi and Funke 2008.

Giovannini, A. (1969) *Étude historique sur les origines du Catalogue des vaisseaux.* Bern.

Glazer, N., and Moynihan, D. P. (1975) *Ethnicity: Theory and Experience.* Cambridge, MA.

Goldmann, S. (1991) "Topoi des Gedenkens. Pausanias' Reise durch die griechische Gedächtnislandschaft," in *Gedächtniskunst: Raum – Bild – Schrift*, ed. A. Haverkamp and R. Lachmann. Frankfurt am Main: 145–64.

Goody, J., and Watt, I. (1963) "The consequences of literacy," *CSSH* 5: 304–45.

Graf, F. (2003) "Lesser Mysteries – no less mysterious," in Cosmopoulos 2003: 241–62.

Grainger, J. D. (1999) *The League of the Aitolians*. Mnemosyne Supplement 200. Leiden and Boston.

Grandjean, C. (1997) "Monnaies et circulation monétaire à Messène du second siècle av. J.-C. au premier siècle ap. J.-C.," *Topoi* 7: 115–22.

(2002) "La Question de l'état Messénien, *REG* 115: 538–60.

(2003) *Les Messéniens de 370/369 au 1er siècle de notre ère: monnayages et histoire.* Bulletin de correspondance hellénique, Supplement XLIV. Paris.

Gruen, E. S. (1984) *The Hellenistic World and the Coming of Rome*. Berkeley, Los Angeles and London.

Guarducci, M. (1934) "I culti di Andania," *SMSR* 10: 174–204.

Gullath, B. (1982) *Untersuchungen zur Geschichte Boiotiens in der Zeit Alexanders und der Diadochen*. Frankfurt am Main.

Habicht, C. (1995) "Ist ein 'Honoratiorenregime' das Kennzeichen der Stadt im späteren Hellenismus?" in Wörrle and Zanker 1995: 87–92.

(1997) "Zwei Familien aus Messene," *ZPE* 115: 125–27.

(1998a) *Pausanias' Guide to Ancient Greece*. 2nd edn. Berkeley, Los Angeles and London.

(1998b) "Kleine Beiträge zur altgriechischen Personenkunde," *REA* 100: 387–494.

(2000) "Neues aus Messene," *ZPE* 130: 121–6.

Halfmann, H. (1979) *Die Senatoren aus dem östlichen Teil des Imperium Romanum bis zum Ende des 2. Jh. n. Chr.* Göttingen.

Hall, J. M. (1995) "How Argive was the 'Argive' Heraion: the political and cultic geography of the Argive plain, 900–400 BC," *AJA* 99: 577–613.

(1997) *Ethnic Identity in Greek Antiquity*. Cambridge.

(1998) "Discourse and praxis: ethnicity and culture in ancient Greece," *CAJ* 8.2: 266–69.

(2000) "Sparta, Lakedaimon and the nature of perioikic dependency," in *Further Studies in the Ancient Greek Polis*, ed. P. Flensted-Jensen. Papers from the Copenhagen Polis Centre, 5. Stuttgart: 73–89.

(2002) *Hellenicity: Between Ethnicity and Culture*. Chicago.

(2003) "The Dorianization of the Messenians," in Luraghi and Alcock 2003: 142–68.

Hamilton, C. D. (1982) "Philip II and Archidamus," in *Philip II, Alexander the Great and the Macedonian heritage*, ed. W. L. Adams and E. N. Borza. Lanham, MD: 61–83.

(1991) *Agesilaus and the Failure of Spartan Hegemony*. Ithaca and London.

Hammond, N. G. L. (1955) "Studies in Greek Chronology of the Sixth and Fifth Centuries BC," *Historia* 4: 371–411.

Hampl, F. (1937) "Die lakedaemonischen Perioken," *Hermes* 72: 1–49.

Hansen, M. H., ed. (1997) *The Polis as an Urban Centre and as a Political Community: Symposium August 29–31, 1996*. Acts of the Copenhagen Polis Centre, 4. Copenhagen.

(2004) "The perioikic poleis of Lakedaimon," in *Once Again: Studies in the Ancient Greek Polis*, ed. T. H. Nielsen. Historia Einzelschrift 180 = Papers from the CPC 7. Stuttgart: 149–64.

Harder, A. (1985) *Euripides' Kresphontes and Archelaos: Introduction, Text and Commentary.* Leiden.

(1991) "Euripides' Temenos and Temenidai," in *Fragmenta dramatica: Beiträge zur Interpretation der griechischen Tragikerfragmente und ihrer Wirkungsgeschichte,* ed. H. Hofmann and A. Harder. Göttingen: 117–35.

Hardie, A. (1983) *Statius and the Silvae: Poets, Patrons and Epideixis in the Graeco-Roman World.* Liverpool.

Harding, P (1973) "The purpose of Isokrates, Archidamos and On the Peace," *CSCA* 6: 137–49.

(2006) *Didymos on Demosthenes: Introduction, Text, Translation, and Commentary.* Oxford.

Harrison, A. B., and Spencer, N. (1988) "After the palace: the early 'history' of Messenia," in Davis 1998: 147–62.

Harter-Uibopuu, K. (1998) *Das zwischenstaatliche Schiedsverfahren im achäischen Koinon: Zur friedlichen Streitbeilegung nach den epigraphischen Quellen.* Cologne.

Head, B. V. (1911) *Historia numorum: A Manual of Greek Numismatics.* New and enlarged edn., by Barclay V. Head, assisted by G. F. Hill, George Macdonald, and W. Wroth. Oxford.

Heather, P. (1998) "Disappearing and reappearing tribes," in Pohl and Reimitz 1998: 95–111.

Heckel, W. (1992) *The Marshals of Alexander's Empire.* London and New York.

Heilmeyer, W.-D. (1979) *Frühe olympische Bronzefiguren: Die Tiervotive.* Olympische Forschungen, 12. Berlin.

Hemberg, B. (1950) *Die Kabiren.* Uppsala.

Henning, D. (1996) "Asine und Mothone. Stadtentwicklung und Wirtschaft in südlichen Messenien seit dem 3./2. Jh. v. Chr.," *Laverna* 7: 17–41.

Henningsen, B. (2000) "Die nordischen Demokratien: Regionale Elemente einer europäischen Kostruktionsgeschichte," in *Regionale und nationale Identitäten,* ed. P. Haslinger, Würzburg: 169–81.

Henrichs, A. (1987) "Three approaches to Greek mythography," in Bremmer 1987: 242–77.

(2003) "*Hieroi logoi and hierai bibloi*: the (un)written margins of the sacred in ancient Greece," *HSCPh* 101: 207–66.

Herfort-Koch, M. (1986) *Archaische Bronzeplastik Lakoniens.* Boreas Beiheft 4. Münster.

Herrmann, K. (1972) "Der Pfeiler der Paionios-Nike in Olympia," *JDAI* 87: 232–57.
(1983) "Zum Dekor dorischer Kapitelle," *Architectura* 13: 1–12.

Herrmann, P. (1995) "Γέρας Θανόντων. Totenruhm und Totenehrung im städtischen Leben der hellenistischen Zeit," in Wörrle and Zanker 1995: 189–97.

Higbie, C. (2003) *The Lindian Chronicle and the Greek Creation of their Past.* Oxford.

Hiller von Gaertringen, F., and Lattermann, H. (1911) *Hira und Andania.* Berlin.

Hobsbawm, E., and Ranger, T., eds. (1983) *The Invention of Tradition.* Cambridge.

Hodkinson, S. (1992) "Sharecropping and Sparta's economic exploitation of the helots," in Sanders 1992: 123–34.

(1997) "Servile and free dependants of the classical Spartan 'oikos,'" in Moggi and Cordiano 1997: 45–71.

(2000) *Property and Wealth in Classical Sparta*. London.

(2003) "Spartiates, helots and the direction of the agrarian economy: towards an understanding of helotage in comparative perspective," in Luraghi and Alcock 2003: 248–85.

Hodkinson, S., and Powell, A., eds. (1999) *Sparta: New Perspectives*. London.

Hoët-van Cauwenberghe, C. (1996) "Diffusion de la citoyenneté romaine: notes sur les gentilices impériaux en Laconie et en Messenie," in *Splendidissima civitas: études d'histoire romaine en hommage à François Jacques*, ed. A. Chastagnol, S. Demougin, and C. Lepelley. Paris: 133–49.

(1999) "Notes sur le culte impérial dans le Péloponnèse," *ZPE* 125: 177–81.

Hölscher, T. (1974) "Die Nike der Messenier und Naupaktier in Olympia," *JDAI* 89: 70–111.

Hope Simpson, R. (1957) "Identifying a Mycenaean state," *ABSA* 52: 231–59.

(1966) "The seven cities offered by Agamemnon to Achilles," *ABSA* 61: 113–31.

(1981) *Mycenaean Greece*. Park Ridge, NJ.

Hörig, M. (1984) "Dea Syria – Atargatis," in *Aufstieg und Niedergang der Römischen Welt*, II: *Principat*, 17.3, ed. W. Haase. Berlin and New York: 1536–81.

Hornblower, S. (1996) *A Commentary on Thucydides*, II: *Books IV–V.24*. Oxford.

(2000a) "Thucydides, Xenophon, and Lichas: were the Spartans excluded from the Olympic Games from 420 to 400 BC?" *Phoenix* 54: 212–25.

(2000b) "Personal names and the study of the ancient Greek historians," in *Greek Personal Names: Their Value as Evidence*, ed. S. Hornblower and E. Matthews. Proceedings of the British Academy, 104. Oxford: 129–43.

Horowitz, D. L. (1975) "Ethnic identity," in Glazer and Moynihan 1975: 111–40.

(1985) *Ethnic Groups in Conflict*. Berkeley, Los Angeles, and London.

Horstkotte, H. (1999) "Die Strafrechtspflege in den Provinzen der römischen Kaiserzeit zwischen hegemonialen Ordnungsmacht und lokaler Autonomie," in *Lokale Autonomie und römische Ordnungsmacht in den kaiserzeitlichen Provinzen vom 1. bis 3. Jahrhundert*, ed. W. Eck. Munich: 303–18.

Hunt, P. (1997) "Helots at the battle of Plataea," *Historia* 46: 129–44.

(1998) *Slaves, Warfare, and Ideology in the Greek Historians*. Cambridge.

Hüttl, W. (1936) *Antoninus Pius*, I: *Historisch-politische Darstellung*. Prague.

Hutton, W. (2005) *Describing Greece: Landscape and Literature in the Periegesis of Pausanias*. Cambridge.

Huxley, G. L. (1969) *Greek Epic Poetry from Eumelos to Panyassis*. London.

Hynes, W. J., and Doty, W. G., eds. (1993) *Mythical Trickster Figures: Contours, Contexts, and Criticism*. Tuscaloosa and London.

Jacoby, F. (1922) "Ktesias," in *Paulys Realencyclopädie der classischen Altertumswissenschaft*, XI.2. Munich: 2032–73.

(1926) *Fragmente der griechischen Historiker*, II c: *Kommentar*. Berlin.

(1930) *Fragmente der griechischen Historiker*, II b: *Kommentar*. Berlin.

(1943) "265 Rhianos von Bene (Kreta)," in *Fragmente der griechischen Historiker*, III a: 87–200.

(1954) *Fragmente der griechischen Historiker*, III b: *Supplement: A Commentary on the Ancient Historians of Athens*. Leiden.

(1956) *Abhandlungen zur griechischen Geschichtsschreibung*, ed. H. Bloch. Leiden.

(1957) *Fragmente der griechischen Historiker*, I a: *Kommentar*. 2nd edn. Leiden.

Jacquemin, A. (1999) *Offrandes monumentales à Delphes*. Bibliothèque des écoles françaises d'Athènes et de Rome, vol. 304. Paris.

Jacquemin, A., and Laroche, D. (1982) "Notes sur trois piliers delphiques," *BCH* 106: 191–218.

Jeffery, L. H. (1949) "Comments on some archaic Greek inscriptions," *JHS* 69: 25–38.

(1988) "The development of Laconian lettering: a reconsideration," *ABSA* 33: 179–81.

(1990) *The Local Scripts of Archaic Greece: A Study of the Origin of the Greek Alphabet and its Development from the Eighth to the Fifth Centuries B C*. Revised edn. with a supplement by Alan W. Johnston. Oxford.

Jehne, M. (1994) *Koine Eirene: Untersuchungen zu den Befriedungs- und Stabilisierungsbemühungen in der griechischen Poliswelt des 4. Jhs. v. Chr.* Stuttgart.

(2004) "Überlegungen zu den Auslassungen in Xenophons Hellenika am Beispiel der Gründung des Zweiten Athenischen Seebunds," in *Xenophon and his World: Papers from a conference held in Liverpool in July 1999*. Stuttgart: 463–80.

Jocelyn, H. D., ed. (1967) *The Tragedies of Ennius*. Edited with an Introduction and Commentary. Cambridge.

Johansen, T. K. (1998) "Truth, lies and history in Plato's *Timaeus-Critias*," *Histos* 2.

Jones, C. P. (1971) *Plutarch and Rome*. Oxford.

(1996) "The Panhellenion," *Chiron* 26: 29–56.

(2001) "Pausanias and his guides," in Alcock, Cherry and Elsner 2001: 33–9.

(2004) "Multiple identities in the age of the Second Sophistic," in *Paideia: The World of the Second Sophistic*, ed. B. E. Borg. Berlin and New York: 13–21.

(2005) "An Athenian document mentioning Julius Nicanor, *ZPE* 154: 161–72.

Jones, N. F. (1987) *Public Organization in Ancient Greece: A Documentary Study*. Memoirs of the American Philosophical Society, vol. 176. Philadelphia.

Jones, S. (1997) *The Archaeology of Ethnicity*. London and New York.

Jordan, B. (1990) "The ceremony of the Helots in Thucydides, IV, 80," *AC* 59: 37–69.

Jost, M. (1985) *Sanctuaires et cultes d'Arcadie*. Paris.

(1992) "Sanctuaires ruraux et sanctuaries urbains d'Arcadie," in *Le Sanctuaire grec*, ed. A. Schachter and J. Bingen. Entretiens sur l'antiquité classique, XXXVII. Geneva: 205–38.

Kader, I. (1995) "Heroa und Memorialbauten," in Wörrle and Zanker 1995: 199–229.

Kagan, D. (1981) *The Peace of Nicias and the Sicilian Expedition*. Ithaca and London.

Kahrstedt, U. (1950a) "Zwei Geographica im Peloponnes," *RhM* 93: 227–42.
(1950b) "Zwei Probleme im kaiserzeitlichen Griechenland," *SO* 28: 66–75.
Kajava, M. (2004) "Hestia: hearth, goddess, and cult," *HSCPh* 102: 1–20.
Kallet-Marx, R. M. (1995) *Hegemony to Empire: The Development of the Roman Imperium in the East from 148 to 62 BC*, Berkeley, Los Angeles, and London.
Kaltsas, N. (1983) "Ἡ ἀρχαϊκὴ οἰκία στὸ Κοπανάκι τῆς Μεσσηνίας," *AE*: 207–37.
Karagiorga, T. G. (1972) "Ἀνασκαφὴ περιοχῆς ἀρχαίου Δωρίου," *AE*: 12–20.
Karlsson, L. (1992) *Fortification Towers and Masonry Techniques in the Hegemony of Syracuse, 405–211 BC*. Acta Instituti Romani Regnis Sueciae, series in 4°, XLIX. Stockholm.
Karouzou, S. (1985) "Ἡ Ἑλένη τῆς Σπάρτης. Ἡ μεγάλη πρόχους ἀπὸ τὴν Ἀναλήψη τῆς Κινουρίας," *AE*: 33–44.
Keen, A. G. (1996) "Were the Boeotian poleis autonomoi?" in *More Studies in the Ancient Greek Polis*, ed. M. H. Hansen and K. Raaflaub. Historia Einzelschrift 108 = Papers from the Copenhagen Polis Centre, 3. Stuttgart: 113–25.
Kelly, T. (1967) "The Argive destruction of Asine," *Historia* 16: 422–31.
Kennell, N. M. (1991) "The size of the Spartan patronomate," *ZPE* 85: 131–7.
(1995) *The Gymnasium of Virtue: Education and Culture in Ancient Sparta*. Chapel Hill.
(1997) "Herodes Atticus and the rhetoric of tyranny," *CPh* 92: 346–62.
(1999) "From *perioikoi* to *poleis*," in Hodkinson and Powell 1999: 189–210.
(2003) "*Agreste genus*: Helots in Hellenistic Laconia," in Luraghi and Alcock 2003: 81–105.
Kiderlen, M. (1994) *Megale oikia: Untersuchungen zur Entwicklung aufwendiger griechischer Stadthausarchitektur von der Früharchaik bis ins 3. Jh. v. Chr.* Dissertation. Bonn.
Kiechle, F. (1959) *Messenische Studien: Untersuchungen zur Geschichte der Messenischen Kriege und zur Auswanderung der Messenier*. Kallmünz.
(1966) "Die Ausprägung der Sage von der Rückkehr der Herakliden. Ein Beitrag zur Bestimmung des ethnischen Standorts der Messenier," *Helikon* 6: 493–517.
Kienast, D. (1990) *Römische Kaisertabelle: Grundzüge einer römischen Kaiserchronologie*. Darmstadt.
Kilian-Dirlmeier, I. (1979) *Anhänger in Griechenland von den mykenischen bis zur spätgeometrischen Zeit*. Prähistorische Bronzefunde, XI, 2. Munich.
(1984) *Nadeln der frühhelladischen bis archaischen Zeit von der Peloponnes*. Prähistorische Bronzefunde, XIII, 8. Munich.
Knoepfler, D., and Piérart, M. (2001) *Éditer, traduire, commenter Pausanias en l'an 2000. Actes du colloque de Neuchâtel et de Fribourg (18–22 septembre 1998)*. Geneva.
Kohl, K.-H (1998) "*Ethnizität und Tradition aus ethnologischer Sicht,*" in *Identitäten*, ed. A. Assmann and H. Friese. Frankfurt am Main: 269–87.

Koiv, M. (2001) "The dating of Pheidon in antiquity," *Klio* 83: 327–47.

Kolbe, W. (1904) "Die Grenzen Messeniens in der ersten Kaiserzeit," *MDAIA* 29: 367–78.

Korres, G. S. (1981–2) "Ἡ προβληματικὴ διὰ τὴν μεταγενεστέραν χρῆσιν τῶν Μυκηναϊκῶν τάφων Μεσσηνίας," in *Πρακτικὰ τοῦ Β' διεθνοῦς συνεδρίου Πελοποννησιακῶν σπουδῶν (Πάτραι, 25–31 Μαῖου 1980)*, Athens: 363–450.

(1988) "Evidence for a Hellenistic chthonian cult in the prehistoric cemetery of Voïdokoiliá in Pylos (Messenia)," *Klio* 70: 311–28.

(1990) "Excavations in the region of Pylos," in Descœudres 1990: 1–11.

Koumouzelis, M. (1996) "A monumental chamber tomb at Ellinika, Messenia," in *Atti e memorie del secondo congresso internazionale di miceneologia, Roma–Napoli, 14–20 ottobre 1991*, ed. E. De Miro, L. Godart and A. Sacconi. Rome: 1221–8.

Kourinou, E. (2000) *Σπάρτη. Συμβολὴ στὴ μνημειακὴ τοπογραφία της*. Athens.

Krieckhaus, A. (2001) "Roma communis nostra patria est? Zum Einfluss des römischen Staates auf die Beziehungen zwischen Senatoren und ihren Heimatstädten in der hohen Kaiserzeit," in *Administration, Prosopography and Appointment Policies in the Roman Empire: Proceedings of the First Workshop of the International Network Impact of Empire (Roman Empire, 27 BC–AD 406), Leiden, June 28–July 1*, ed. L. de Blois. Amsterdam 230–45.

Kroymann, J. (1937) *Sparta und Messenien: Untersuchungen zur Überlieferung der messenischen Kriege*. Neue philologische Untersuchungen, 11. Berlin.

Lafond, Y. (1996) "Pausanias et l'histoire du Péloponnèse depuis la conquête romaine," in *Pausanias Historien*, ed. J. Bingen. Entretiens de la Fondation Hardt, vol XLI. Geneva: 167–98.

(2001) "Lire Pausanias à l'époque des Antonins. Réflexions sur la place de la Périégèse dans l'histoire culturelle, religieuse er sociale de la Grèce romaine," in Knoepfler and Piérart 2001: 387–406.

(2005) "Le Mythe, référence identitaire pour les cités grecques d'époque impériale. L'exemple du Péloponnèse," *Kernos* 18: 329–46.

Lamb, W. (1925–6) "Arcadian bronze statuettes," *ABSA* 27: 133–48.

Lambrechts, P., and Noyen, P. (1954) "Recherches sur le culte d'Atargatis dans le monde grec," *La Nouvelle Clio* 6: 258–77.

Lang, M. (1967) "A note on Ithome," *GRBS* 8: 267–73.

Lapini, W. (1996) "Tisameno di Elide (Herod. 9.35.2)," *SIFC* 14: 152–68.

(1997) *Commento all'Athenaion politeia dello Pseudo-Senofonte*. Florence.

Lazenby, J. F. (1997) "The conspiracy of Kinadon reconsidered," *Athenaeum* 85: 437–47.

Lazenby, J. F., and Hope Simpson, R. (1972) "Greco-Roman times: literary tradition and topographical commentary," in *The Minnesota Messenia Expedition: Reconstructing a Bronze Age Environment*, ed. W. A. McDonald and G. R. Rapp, Jr. Minneapolis: 81–99.

Le Bohec, S. (1993) *Antigone Dôsôn, roi de Macédoine*. Nancy.

Le Roy, C. (2001) "Pausanias et la Laconie ou la recherche d'un équilibre," in Knoepfler and Piérart 2001: 223–37.

Lefèvre, F. (1988) *L'Amphictionie pyléo-delphique: histoire et institutions.* Bibliothèque des Écoles Françaises d'Athènes et Rome, Vol. 298. Paris.

Leitao, D. D. (1999) "Solon on the beach: some pragmatic functions of the limen in initiatory myth and ritual," in *Rites of Passage in Ancient Greece: Literature, Religion, Society,* ed. M. W. Padilla. Bucknell Review, 43, 1. Lewisburg: 247–77.

Leon, C. (1968) "Statuette eines Kouros aus Messenien," *MDAIA* 83: 175–85.

Leppin, H. (1999) "Argos: eine griechische Demokratie des 6. Jhs. v. Chr.," *Ktema* 24: 297–312.

Leschhorn, W. (1984) *"Gründer der Stadt": Studien zu einem politisch-religiösen Phänomen der griechischen Geschichte.* Stuttgart.

Lewis, D. M. (1977) *Sparta and Persia.* Leiden.

Link, S. (1994) *Des Kosmos Sparta.* Darmstadt.

Loraux, N. (1981) *L'Invention d'Athènes: histoire de l'oraison funèbre dans la "cité classique."* Paris, The Hague, and New York.

Lotze, D. (1959) Μεταξὺ ἐλευθέρων καί δούλων: *Studien zur Rechtsstellung unfreier Landbevölkerungen in Griechenland bis zum 4. Jahrhundert v. Chr.* Berlin.

(1962) "Μόθακες," *Historia* 11: 427–35, republished in Lotze 2000: 185–94.

(1971) "Zu einigen Aspekten des spartanischen Agrarsystems," *Jahrbuch für Wirtschaftsgeschichte* 2: 63–76, republished in Lotze 2000: 151–70.

(1993/4) "Bürger zweiter Klasse: Spartas Periöken. Ihre Stellung und Funktion im Staat der Lakedaimonier," *Sitzungsberichte der Akademie der Wissenschaften zu Erfurt. Geisteswissenschaftliche Klasse* 2: 37–51, republished in Lotze 2000: 171–84.

(2000) *Bürger und Unfreie im vorhellenistischen Griechenland: Ausgewählte Aufsätze,* ed. W. Ameling and K. Zimmermann. Stuttgart.

Lukermann, F. E., and Moody, J. (1978) "Nichoria and its vicinity: settlements and circulation," in *Excavations at Nichoria in south-west Greece,* I: *Site, Environs, and Techniques,* ed. G. Rapp, Jr. and S. E. Aschenbrenner. Minneapolis: 78–112.

Luppe, W. (1987) "Zwei Hypotheseis zu Euripides-Dramen der Temenos-Sage (P. Oxy. 2455 fr. 9 und fr. 10)," *Prometheus* 13: 193–203.

(1995) "P. Oxy. XXVII 2455 fr.11. Eine Hypothesis aus der Temenos- bzw. Temeniden-Sage," *APF* 41: 25–33.

Luraghi, N. (1994) *Tirannidi arcaiche in Sicilia e Magna Grecia: da Panezio di Leontini alla caduta dei Dinomenidi.* Florence.

(1998) "Il mito di Oreste nel Regno dello Stretto," in *Mito e storia in Magna Grecia. Atti del XXXVI convegno internazionale di studi sulla Magna Grecia (Taranto 1996).* Naples: 333–46.

Luraghi, N. ed. (2001a) *The Historian's Craft in the Age of Herodotus.* Oxford.

(2001b) "Der Erdbebenaufstand und die Entstehung der messenischen Identität," in *Gab es das griechische Wunder? Griechenland zwischen dem*

Ende des 6. und der Mitte des 5. Jahrhunderts v. Chr., ed. D. Papenfuß and V.-M. Strocka. Mainz: 281–301.

(2001c) "Die Dreiteilung der Peloponnes. Wandlungen eines Gründungsmythos," in *Geschichtsbilder und Gründungsmythen*, ed. H.-J. Gehrke. Würzburg: 37–63.

(2001d) "Local knowledge in Herodotus' *Histories*," in Luraghi 2001: 138–60.

(2002a) "Becoming Messenian," *JHS* 122: 45–69.

(2002b) "Helotic slavery reconsidered," in Powell and Hodkinson 2002: 229–50.

(2002c) "Helots called Messenians? A note on Thuc. 1.101.2," *CQ* 52: 588–92.

(2003) "The imaginary conquest of the Helots," in Luraghi and Alcock 2003: 109–41.

(2005) "Pausania e i Messenii: interpretazioni minime," *RFIC* 133: 177–201.

(2006) "Messenische Kulte und messenische Identität in Hellenistischer Zeit," in *Kult – Politik – Ethnos, Überregionale Heiligtümer im Spannungsfeld von Kult und Politik. Kolloquium, Münster, 23.–24. November 2001*, ed. K. Freitag, P. Funke, and M. Haake. Historia Einzelschrift 189. Stuttgart: 169–96.

(forthcoming) "The local scripts from nature to culture," in *Alphabetic Responses to Western Semitic Writing*, ed. P. Haarer. Oxford.

Luraghi, N., and Alcock, S. E., eds. (2003) *Helots and their Masters in Laconia and Messenia: Histories, Ideologies, Structures*. Cambridge, MA.

Luraghi, N., and Funke, P., eds. (2008) *The Politics of Ethnicity and the Crisis of the Peloponnesian League*. Cambridge, MA.

Maaß, M. (1978) *Die geometrischen Dreifüße von Olympia*. Olympische Forschungen, Vol. 10. Berlin.

Maddoli, G., Nafissi, M., and Saladino, V. (1999) *Pausania: Guida della Grecia, VI: L'Elide e Olimpia*. Testo e tradizione a cura di G. Maddoli e M. Nafissi. Commento a cura di G. Maddoli, M. Nafissi e V. Saladino. Milan.

Maddoli, G. and Saladino, V. (1995) *Pausania: Guida della Grecia, V: L'Elide e Olimpia*. Testo e tradizione a cura di G. Maddoli. Commento a cura di G. Maddoli e V. Saladino. Milan.

Maggi, S. (1996) "Sul tempio di Messene a Messene," *Athenaeum* 84: 260–5.

Magnetto, A. (1994) "L'intervento di Filippo II nel Peloponneso e l'iscrizione Syll.³, 665," in Ίστορίη: *Studi offerti dagli allievi a Giuseppe Nenci in occasione del suo settantesimo compleanno*, ed. S. Alessandrì. Galatina: 283–308.

Malkin, I. (1987) *Religion and Colonization in Ancient Greece*. Leiden.

(1994) *Myth and Territory in the Spartan Mediterranean*. Cambridge.

(2001) "Introduction," in *Ancient Perceptions of Greek Ethnicity*, ed. I. Malkin. Cambridge, MA: 1–28.

Marasco, G. (1980) "La politica achea nel Peloponneso durante la guerra demetriaca," *A&R* 25: 113–22.

Marc, J.-Y, and Moretti, J.-C., eds. (2001) *Constructions publiques et programmes édilitaires en Grèce entre le IIᵉ siècle av. J.-C. et le Iᵉʳ siècle ap. J.-C. Actes du colloque organisé par l'École Française d'Athènes et le CNRS, Athènes, 14–17 mai 1995*. Bulletin de correspondance hellénique. Supplément XXXIX. Paris.

Marcotte, D. (1986) "Le Périple dit de Scylax. Esquisse d'un commentaire épigraphique et archéologique," *BollClass* 7: 166–82.

Margreiter, I. (1988) *Frühe lakonische Keramik der geometrischen bis archaischen Zeit (10. bis 6. Jahrhundert v. Chr.).* Waldsassen.

Marienstras, R. (1985) "Sur la notion de Diaspora," in *Les Minorités à l'âge de l'État-nation*, ed. G. Chaliand. Paris: 215–26.

Marinatos, S. (1955) "Παλαίπυλος," *Das Altertum* 1: 140–63.

Matthaiou, A. (2001) "Δύο ἱστορικὲς ἐπιγραφὲς τῆς Μεσσήνης," in Mitsopoulos-Leon 2001: 221–31.

Matthaiou, A., and Mastrokostas, E. (2000–3) "Συνθήκη Μεσσηνίων καὶ Ναυπακτίων," *Horos* 14–16: 433–54.

Maurer, K. (1995) *Interpolation in Thucydides.* Mnemosyne Supplement. 150. Leiden, New York, and Cologne.

Mazarakis Ainian, A. (1997) *From Rulers' Dwellings to Temples: Architecture, Religion and Society in Early Iron Age Greece (1100–700 BC).* Jonsered.

Mazzarino, S. (1966) *Il pensiero storico classico.* vol. I. Rome and Bari.

McDonald, W. A., and Coulson, W. D. E. (1983) "The Dark Age at Nichoria: a perspective," in McDonald, Coulson and Rosser 1983: 316–31.

McDonald, W. A., Coulson, W. D. E., and Rosser, J., eds. (1983) *Excavations at Nichoria in Southwest Greece, III: Dark Age and Byzantine Occupation.* Minneapolis.

McDonald, W. A., and Hope Simpson, R. (1961) "Prehistoric habitation in southwestern Peloponnese," *AJA* 65: 221–60.

McDonald, W. A., and Rapp, G. R., Jr., eds. (1972) *The Minnesota Messenia Expedition: Reconstructing a Bronze Age Environment.* Minneapolis.

McDonald, W. A., and Wilkie, N. C., eds. (1992) *Excavations at Nichoria in Southwest Greece, II: The Bronze Age Occupation.* Minneapolis.

Mendels, D. (1980) "Messene 215 BC: an enigmatic revolution," *Historia* 29: 246–50.

Mertens, D. (1993) *Der alte Heratempel in Paestum und die archaische Baukunst in Unteritalien.* Mainz.

Mertens, N. (2002) "οὐκ ὅμοιοι, ἀγαθοὶ δέ: the perioikoi in the classical Lakedaimonian polis," in Powell and Hodkinson 2002: 285–303.

Meyer, E. (1932a) "Methana," in *Paulys Realencyclopädie der classischen Altertumswissenschaft*, XV.2. Munich: 1375–9.

(1932b) "Methone," in *Paulys Realencyclopädie der classischen Altertumswissenschaft*, XV.2. Munich: 1382–4.

(1978), "Messene/Messenien,' in *Paulys Realencyclopädie der classischen Altertumswissenschaft*, Suppl. XV. Munich: 136–289.

Migeotte, L. (1985) "Réparation de monuments publics à Messène au temps d'Auguste," *BCH* 109: 597–607.

(1997) "La Date de l'oktôbolos eisphora de Messène," *Topoi* 7: 51–61.

Millar, F. (2001) "Greece and Rome from Mummius Achaicus to St Paul: reflections on a changing world," in Marc and Moretti 2001: 1–11.

Millino, G. (2001) "Considerazioni sulla monetazione di Anassilao," in *Hesperìa: studi sulla Grecità d'Occidente*, 14: 105–40.

(2003) "Micito di Reggio e la symmachia con Taranto," in *Hesperìa. studi sulla Grecità d'Occidente*, 17: 207–21.

Misgeld, W. R. (1968) *Rhianos von Bene und das historische Epos im Hellenismus.* Cologne.

Mitsopoulos-Leon, V., ed. (2001) *Forschungen in der Peloponnes. Akten des Symposions anlüßlich der Feier "100 Jahre des Österreichisches Archäologisches Institut Athen," Athen 5.3.–7.3.1998.* Österreichisches Archäologisches Institut. Sonderschriften, Band 38. Athens.

Mitten, D. and Doeringer, S. F. (1967) *Master Bronzes from the Classical World.* Mainz.

Moggi, M. (1968) "La tradizione sulle guerre persiane in Platone," *SCO* 17: 213–26.

(1974) "I sinecismi e le annessioni territoriali di Argo nel V secolo a.c.," *ASNP* 4: 1249–63.

(1993) "Scrittura e riscrittura della storia in Pausania," *RFIC* 121: 396–418.

(2002) "Pausania e Roma," *Gerión* 20: 435–49.

Moggi, M., and Cordiano, G. (1997) *Schiavi e dipendenti nell'ambito dell' "oikos" e della "familia." Atti del XXII Colloquio GIREA. Pontignano (Siena) 19–20 novembre 1995.* Pisa.

Möller, A. (2004) "Elis, Olympia und das Jahr 580 v. Chr. Zur Frage der Eroberung der Pisatis," in *Griechische Archaik: Interne Entwicklungen – externe Impulse*, ed. R. Rollinger and C. Ulf. Berlin: 249–70.

Moreno, P. (2001) "Hageladas (1)" and "Hageladas (2)," in *Künstlerlexikon der Antike*, ed. R. Vollkommer, Vol. I. Munich: 275–80.

Moretti, L. (1946) "Sparta alla metà del VI secolo, I. La guerra contro Tegea," *RFIC* 24: 87–103.

Morgan, C. (1990) *Athletes and Oracles: The Transformation of Olympia and Delphi in the Eight Century BC.* Cambridge.

(1993) "The origins of pan-Hellenism," in *Greek Sanctuaries: New Approaches*, ed. N. Marinatos and R. Hägg. London and New York: 18–44.

Morgan, C. and Whitelaw, T. (1991) "Pots and politics: ceramic evidence for the rise of the Argive state," *AJA* 95: 79–108

Morgan, K. A. (1998) "Designer history: Plato's Atlantis story and fourth-century ideology," *JHS* 118: 101–18.

Morizot, Y. (1994) "Le Hiéron de Messène," *BCH* 118: 399–405.

Morpurgo Davies, A. (1987) "The Greek notion of dialect," *Verbum* 10: 7–28.

(1993) "Geography, history and dialect: the case of Oropos," in *Dialectologica Graeca. Actas del II Coloquio Internacional de Dialectología Griega (Miraflores de la Sierra [Madrid]), 19–21 de junio de 1991*, ed. E. Crespo, J. L. García Ramón, and A. Striano. Madrid: 261–79.

Morrow, G. R. (1993) *Plato's Cretan City: A Historical Interpretation of the Laws.* 2nd edn. Princeton.

Moysey, R. A. (1982) "Isokrates' On the Peace: rhetorical exercise or political advice?" *AJAH* 7: 118–27.

Muir, J. V., ed. (2001) *Alcidamas: The Works and Fragments, Edited with Introduction, Translation and Commentary.* Bristol.

Müller, R. J. (1993) "Tradierung religiösen Wissens in den Mysterienkulten am Beispiel von Andania," in *Vermittlung und Tradierung von Wissen in der griechischen Kultur,* ed. W. Kullmann and J. Althoff. Tübingen: 307–16.

Musso, O., ed. (1974) *Euripide: Cresfonte. Introduzione, testo critico dei frammenti e commento.* Milan.

Musti, D., ed. (1986a) *Le origini dei Greci: Dori e mondo egeo.* Bari.

(1986b) "Continuità e discontinuità tra Achei e Dori nelle tradizioni storiche," in Musti 1986a: 37–71.

(1988) *Strabone e la Magna Grecia: città e popoli dell'Italia antica.* Padua.

(2001) "Aspetti della religione dei Cabiri," in *La questione delle influenze vicino-orientali sulla religione greca: stato degli studi e prospettive di ricerca. Atti del colloquio internazionale, Roma, 20–22 maggio 1999,* ed. S. Ribichini, M. Rocchi and P. Xella. Rome: 141–54.

Musti, D., and Torelli, M. (1991) *Pausania: Guida della Grecia,* IV: *La Messenia.* Testo e traduzione a cura di D. Musti. Commento a cura di D. Musti e M. Torelli. Milan.

(1994) *Pausania: Guida della Grecia,* III: *La Laconia.* Testo e traduzione a cura di D. Musti. Commento a cura di D. Musti e M. Torelli. Milan.

Müth, S. (2007) *Eigene Wege: Topographie und Stadtplan von Messene in spätklassisch-hellenistischer Zeit.* Rahden.

Müth-Herda, S. (2005) *Messene: Topographie und Stadtplan in spätklassischer und hellenistischer Zeit.* PhD dissertation, Berlin.

Mylonopoulos, J. (2003) Πελοπόννησος οἰκητήριον Ποσειδῶνος: *Heiligtümer und Kulte des Poseidon auf der Peloponnes.* Kernos Supplément 13. Liège.

Nafissi, M. (1991) *La nascita del kosmos: studi sulla storia e la società di Sparta.* Naples.

(1999) "From Sparta to Taras: nomima, ktiseis and relationships between colony and mother city," in Hodkinson and Powell 1999: 245–72.

(2001) "La prospettiva di Pausania sulla storia dell'Elide: la questione pisate," in Knoepfler and Piérart 2001: 301–21.

(2003) "Elei e Pisati. Geografia, storia e istituzioni politiche della regione di Olimpia," *Geographia antiqua* 12: 23–55.

(2004) "Tucidide, Erodoto e la tradizione su Pausania nel V secolo," *RSA* 34: 147–80.

Nenci, G., and Cataldi, S. (1983) "Strumenti e procedure nei rapporti tra Greci e indigeni," in *Modes de contacts et processus de transformation dans les sociétés anciennes/Forme di contatto e processi di trasformazione nelle società antiche. Actes du colloque de Cortone (24–30 mai 1981),* ed. G. Nenci and G. Vallet. Rome: 581–604.

Niccolini, G. (1914) *La confederazione achea.* Pavia.

Nielsen, T. H. (1997) "Triphylia: an experiment in ethnic construction and political organisation," in *Yet More Studies in the Ancient Greek Polis,* ed. T. H. Nielsen. Historia Einzelschrift 117 = Papers from the CPC 4. Stuttgart: 129–62.

(2002) *Arkadia and its Poleis in the Archaic and Classical Periods.* Göttingen.

Niese, B. (1891) "Die ältere Geschichte Messeniens," *Hermes* 26: 1–32.

(1906) "Die lakedämonischen Perioken," *Nachrichten von der Königl. Gesellschaft der Wissenschaften in Göttingen, philologische-historische Klasse.* 1906: 101–42.

Nörr, D. (1969) *Imperium und Polis in der hohen Prinzipatszeit.* 2nd edn. Munich.

Nouhaud, M. (1982) *L'Utilisation de l'histoire par les orateurs attiques.* Paris.

Oberländer, P. (1967) *Griechische Handspiegel.* Dissertation, Hamburg.

Ogden, D. (2004) *Aristomenes of Messene: Legends of Sparta's Nemesis.* Swansea.

Oliva, P. (1971) *Sparta and her Social Problems.* Prague.

Oliver, J. H. (1978) "The Helladarch," *RSA* 8: 1–6.

Orlandos, A. K. (1976) "Νεώτεραι ἐρευναὶ ἐν Μεσσήνῃ," in *Neue Forschungen in griechischen Heiligtümern,* ed. U. Jantzen, Tübingen: 9–38.

Orywal, E., and Hackstein, K. (1993) "Ethnizität: Die Konstruktion ethnischer Wirklichkeit," in *Handbuch der Ethnologie: Festschrift für Ulla Johansen,* ed. T. Schweizer, M. Schweizer, and W. Kokot. Berlin: 593–609.

Osanna, M. (1996) *Santuari e culti dell'Acaia antica.* Naples.

Østergård, U. (1992) "What is national and ethnic identity?" in *Ethnicity in Hellenistic Egypt,* ed. P. Bilde, T. Engberg-Pedersen, L. Hannestad, and J. Zahle. Aarhus: 16–38.

Palagia, O. (2000) "Hephaestion's pyre and the royal hunt of Alexandria," in *Alexander the Great in Fact and Fiction,* ed. A. B. Bosworth and E. Baynham. Oxford: 167–206.

Palagia, O., and Coulson, W., eds. (1993) *Sculpture from Arcadia and Laconia. Proceedings of an International Conference Held at the American School of Classical Studies at Athens, April 10–14, 1992.* Oxford.

Palm, J. (1959) *Rom, Römertum und Imperium in der griechischen Literatur der Kaiserzeit.* Acta regiae societatis humaniorum litterarum Lundensis, LVII. Lund.

Papaefthymiou, V. (2001–2002) "Σύμπλεγμα τριῶν εἰδωλίων ἀπὸ τὸ ἱερὸ τῆς Δήμητρος καὶ τῶν Διοσκούρων τῆς ἀρχαΐας Μεσσήνης," in *Πρακτικὰ τοῦ 5´ διεθνοῦς συνεδρίου Πελοποννησιακῶν σπουδῶν (Τρίπολις, 24–29 Σεπτεμβρίου 2000).* Athens: 129–46.

Paradiso, A. (1995) "Tempo della tradizione, tempo dello storico," *StorStor* 28: 35–45.

(1997) "Gli iloti e l'"oikos,'" in Mauro, Moggi and Giuseppe, Cordiano eds., *Schiavi e dipendenti nell'ambito dell'"oikos" e della "familia,"* Pisa: 1 73–90.

Pareti, L. (1914) *Studi siciliani ed italioti.* Florence.

Parke, H. W. (1938) "Notes on some Delphic oracles," *Hermathena* 52: 57–78.

Parker, R. (1989) "Spartan religion," in Powell 1989a: 142–72.

(1998) *Cleomenes on the Acropolis: An Inaugural Lecture delivered before the University of Oxford on 12 May 1997.* Oxford.

Pasquali, G. (1912–13) "Per la storia del culto di Andania," *AAT* 48: 94–104.

Patterson, O. (1975) "Context and choice in ethnic allegiance: a theoretical framework and a Caribbean case study," in Glazer and Moynihan 1975: 305–49.

(1982) *Slavery and Social Death: A Comparative Study*. Cambridge, MA.

(2003) "Reflections on helotic slavery and freedom," in Luraghi and Alcock 2003: 289–309.

Pearson, L. (1962) "The pseudo-history of Messenia and its authors," *Historia* 11: 397–426.

Peel, J. D. Y. (1984) "Making history. The past in the Ijesha present," *Man* 19: 111–32.

Pelling, C. (1997) "Conclusion," in *Greek Tragedy and the Historian*, ed. C. Pelling. Oxford: 213–35.

Pelon, O. (1976) *Tholoi, tumuli et cercles funéraires: recherches sur les monuments funéraires de plan circulaire dans l'Égée de l'âge du Bronze (IIIe et IIe millénaires av. J. C.)*. Bibliothèque des écoles françaises d'Athènes et de Rome, Vol. 229. Paris.

Peppa-Papaioannou, I. (1987–8) "Πήλινα ἀναθηματικὰ ἀνάγλυφα πλακίδια ἀπὸ τὴ Βοϊδοκολιὰ Μεσσηνίας," in *Πρακτικὰ τοῦ Γ΄ διεθνοῦς συνεδρίου Πελοποννησιακῶν σπουδῶν (Καλαμάτα, 8–15 Σεπτεμβρίου 1985)*. Athens: 257–72.

Perlman, P. J. (1984) *The Theorodokia in the Peloponnese*. PhD dissertation, University of Pennsylvania.

Petrocelli, C. (2001) "Le parole e le armi. Omofonia/omoglossia in guerra," *QS* 54: 69–97.

Pfeiffer, R. (1968) *History of Classical Scholarship from the Beginnings to the End of the Hellenistic Age*. Oxford.

Piérart, M. (1986) "Le tradizioni epiche e il loro rapporto con la questione dorica: Argo e l'Argolide," in Musti 1986a: 277–92.

(1991) "Aspects de la transition en Argolide," in *La transizione dal miceneo all'alto arcaismo: dal palazzo alla città. Atti del Convegno Internazionale, Roma, 14–19 marzo 1988*, ed. D. Musti. Rome: 133–44.

(1997) "L'Attitude d'Argos à l'égard des autres cités de l'Argolide," in Hansen 1997: 321–51.

(2001) "Philippe et la Cynourie (Thyréatide): les frontières du partage des Héraclides," in Frei-Stolba and Gex 2001: 27–41.

(2004) "Deux voisins: Argos et Épidaure (mythes, société, histoire)," in Angeli Bernardini 2004: 19–34.

Pingiatoglou, S. (1981) *Eileithyia*. Würzburg.

Pikoulas, Y. A. (1984) "Τὸ φυλακεῖον στὸ Βασιλικὸ καὶ ἡ σημασία του γιὰ τὴν ἱστορικὴ τοπογραφία τῆς περιοχῆς," in *Πρακτικὰ τοῦ Β΄ τοπικοῦ συνεδρίου Μεσσηνιακῶν σπουδῶν (Κυπαρισσία, 27–29 Νοεμβρίου 1982)*. Athens: 177–84.

(1987–88) "Το πόλισμα Ἄμφεια (Παυς. IV 5,9)," in *Πρακτικὰ τοῦ Γ΄ διεθνοῦς συνεδρίου Πελοποννησιακῶν σπουδῶν (Καλαμάτα, 8–15 Σεπτεμβρίου 1985)*. Athens: 479–85.

(1991) "Ἡ Δενθελιᾶτις καὶ τὸ ὁδικό της δίκτυο (Σχόλια στὴν IG V 1, 1431)," in *Πρακτικὰ τοῦ Γ΄ τοπικοῦ συνεδρίου Μεσσηνιακῶν σπουδῶν (Φιλιατρά-Γαργαλιᾶνοι, 24–26 Νοεμβρίου 1989)*. Athens: 279–88.

Piolot, L. (1999) "Pausanias et les Mystères d'Andanie. Histoire d'une aporie," in Renard 1999: 195–228.

(2005) "Nom d'une Artémis! A propos de l'Artémis Phôsphoros de Messène," *Kernos* 18: 113–40.

Pipili, M. (1987) *Laconian Iconography of the Sixth Century BC*. Oxford.

Placido, D. (1994) "Los lugares sagrados de los hilotas," in Annequin and Garrido-Hory 1994: 127–35.

Pohl, H. (1993) *Die römische Politik und die Piraterie im östlichen Mittelmeer vom 3. bis zum 1. Jh. v. Chr.* Berlin.

Pohl, W. (1994) "Tradition, Ethnogenese und literarische Gestaltung: eine Zwischenbilanz," in *Ethnogenese und Überlieferung: Angewandte Methode der Frühmittelalterforschung*, ed. K. Brunner and B. Merta. Vienna and Munich: 9–26.

(1998) "Telling the difference: signs of ethnic identity," in Pohl and Reimitz 1998: 18–69.

(2000) "Memory, identity and power in Lombard Italy," in *The Uses of the Past in the Early Middle Ages*, ed. Y. Hen and M. Innes. Cambridge: 9–28.

Pohl, W., and Reimitz, H., eds. (1998) *Strategies of Distinction: The Construction of Ethnic Communities, 300–800*. Leiden.

Pomtow, H. (1896) "Die dreiseitige Basis der Messenier und Naupactier zu Delphi," *Neue Jahrbücher für Philologie und Pädagogik* 153: 505–36; 577–639; 754–69.

Poole, W. (1994) "Euripides and Sparta," in Powell and Hodkinson 1994: 1–33.

Pouilloux, J. (1960) *La Région nord du sanctuaire. Fouilles de Delphes*, II: *Topographie et architecture*. Paris.

Powell, A. (ed.) (1989a) *Classical Sparta: Techniques behind her Success*. London.

(1989b) "Mendacity and Sparta's use of the visual," in Powell 1989a: 173–92.

(1994) "Plato and Sparta: modes of rule and non-rational persuasion in the *Laws*," in Powell and Hodkinson 1994: 273–321.

Powell, A., and Hodkinson, S., eds. (1994) *The Shadow of Sparta*. London and New York.

(2002) *Sparta: Beyond the Mirage*. London.

Prandi, L. (1985) *Callistene: uno storico tra Aristotele e i re macedoni*. Milan.

Pratt, L. (1993) *Lying and Poetry from Homer to Pindar*. Ann Arbor.

Pretzler, M. (2005) "Pausanias and oral tradition," *CQ* 55: 235–49.

(2008) "Arkadia: ethnicity and politics in the fifth and fourth centuries BC," in Luraghi and Funke 2008.

Prinz, F. (1979) *Gründungsmythen und Sagenchronologie*. Munich.

Pritchett, W. K. (1953) "The Attic Stelai, part I," *Hesperia* 22: 225–99.

(1956) "The Attic Stelai, part II," *Hesperia* 25: 178–328.

(1985) *Studies in Ancient Greek topography*, vol. V. Berkeley, Los Angeles and London.

(1995) *Thucydides' Pentekontaetia and Other Essays*. Amsterdam.

Puech, B. (1983) "Grands-prêtres et helladarques d'Achaïe," *REA* 85: 5–43.

Raaflaub, K. A. (2003) "Freedom for the Messenians? A note on the impact of slavery and helotage on the Greek concept of freedom," in Luraghi and Alcock 2003: 169–90.

(2004) *The Discovery of Freedom in Ancient Greece.* Chicago [translation of *Die Entdeckung der Freiheit: Zur historischen Semantik und Gesellschaftsgeschichte eines politischen Grundbegriffes der Griechen*, Munich 1985].

Raccuia, C. (1981) "Messana, Rhegion e Dionysios I dal 404 al 398 a.C.," *RSA* 11: 15–30.

Raeck, W. (1995) "Der mehrfache Apollodoros. Zur Präsenz des Bürgers im hellenistischen Stadtbild am Beispiel von Priene," in Wörrle and Zanker 1995: 231–40.

Raeder, J. (1993) "Kunstlandschaft und Lanschaftsstil. Begriffe, Anschauungen und deren methodische Grundlagen," in *Der Stilbegriff in den Altertumswissenschaften*, ed. K. Zimmermann. Rostock: 105–9.

Raftopoulou, S. (1998) "New finds from Sparta," in *Sparta in Laconia: Proceedings of the 19th British Museum Classical Colloquium*, ed. W. G. Cavanagh and S. E. C. Walker. London: 123–40.

Raubitschek, A. (1949) *Dedications from the Athenian Akropolis: A Catalogue of the Inscriptions of the Sixth and Fifth Centuries BC.* Cambridge, MA.

Rebenich, S. (1998) *Xenophon, Die Verfassung der Spartaner: Herausgegeben, übersetzt und erläutert.* Darmstadt.

Redfield, J. M. (2003) *The Locrian Maidens: Love and Death in Greek Italy.* Princeton.

Renard, J., ed. (1999) *Le Péloponnèse: archéologie et histoire. Actes de la rencontre internationale de Lorient (12–15 mai 1998).* Rennes.

Reynolds, J. (2000) "New letters from Hadrian to Aphrodisias," *JRA* 13: 5–20.

Rhodes, P. J. (1999) "Sparta, Thebes and autonomia," *Eirene* 35: 33–40.

Riethmüller, J. W. (2005) *Asklepios: Heiligtümer und Kulte.* 2 vols. Heidelberg.

Rigsby, K. (1986) "Notes sur la Crète hellénistique," *REG* 99: 350–60.

Ringel, E., Siewert, P., and Taeuber, H. (1999) "Die Symmachien Pisas mit den Arkadern, Akroreia, Messenien und Sikyon. Ein neues Fragment der 'arkadischen Bündnisstele' von 365 v. Chr.," in *11. Bericht über die Ausgrabungen in Olympia*, ed. A. Mallwitz with K. Herrmann. Berlin: 413–20.

Ritter, S. (2002) *Bildkontakte: Götter und Heroen in der Bildsprache griechischer Münzen des 4. Jahrhunderts v. Chr.* Berlin.

Rizakis, A. (1995) *Achaie, I: Sources textuelles et histoire régionale.* Athens and Paris.

(2001) "Ἡγετικὴ τάξη καὶ κοινωνικὴ διαστρωμάτωση στὶς πόλεις τῆς Πελοποννήσου κατὰ τὴν αὐτοκρατορικὴ ἐποχή," in Mitsopoulos-Leon 2001: 181–97.

Robert, C. (1921) *Die griechische Heldensage*, II: *Die Nationalheroen.* 4th edn. Berlin.

Robert, L. (1980) "Deux poètes grecs à l'époque impériale," in Στήλη. Τομὸς εἰς μνήμην Νικολάου Κοντολέοντος. Athens: 1–20.

Robertson, N. (1988) "Melanthus, Codrus, Neleus, Caucon: ritual myth as Athenian history," *GRBS* 29: 201–61.

(1992) *Festivals and Legends: The Formation of the Greek Cities in the Light of Public Ritual.* Phoenix Supplement 31. Toronto, Buffalo and London.

Roebuck, C. A. (1941) *A History of Messenia from 369 to 146 BC.* Chicago.

(1945) "A note on Messenian economy and population," *CPh* 40: 149–65.

Rogers, G. M. (1991) *The Sacred Identity of Ephesos: Foundation Myths of a Roman City.* London and New York.

Romeo, I. (2002) "The Panhellenion and ethnic identity in Hadrianic Greece," *CPh* 97: 21–40.

Rosivach, V. J. (1999) "Enslaving *barbaroi* and the Athenian ideology of slavery," *Historia* 48: 129–57.

Roussel, D. (1976) *Tribu et cité: études sur les groupes sociaux dans les cités grecques aux époques archaïque et classique.* Annales littéraires de l'Université de Besançon, 193. Paris.

Rowe, C. J. (1987) "Platonic Irony," *Nova tellus* 5: 83–101.

Roy, J. (1997) "The perioikoi of Elis," in Hansen 1997: 282–320.

(1998) "Thucydides 5.49.1–50.4: the quarrel between Elis and Sparta in 420 BC and Elis' exploitation of Olympia," *Klio* 80: 360–8.

(1999) "Les Cités d'Élide," in Renard 1999: 151–76.

(2000) "The frontier between Arkadia and Elis in classical antiquity," in Flensted-Jensen, Nielsen and Rubinstein 2000: 133–56.

Ruby, P. (2006) "Peuples, fictions? Ethnicité, identité ethnique et sociétés anciennes," *REA* 2006: 25–60.

Ruggeri, C. (2004) *Gli stati intorno a Olimpia: storia e costituzione dell'Elide e degli stati formati dai perieci elei (400–362 a.C.).* Historia Einzelschrift 170. Stuttgart.

(2008) "Triphylia from Elis to Arkadia," in Luraghi and Funke 2008.

Ryder, T. T. B. (1965) *Koine Eirene: General Peace and Local Independence in Ancient Greece.* Oxford.

(1994) "The diplomatic skills of Philip II," in *Ventures into Greek History*, ed. I. Worthington. Oxford: 228–57.

Safran, W. (1999) "Comparing diasporas: a review essay," *Diaspora* 8: 255–91.

Sahlins, P. (1989) *Boundaries: The Making of France and Spain in the Pyrenees.* Berkeley.

(1995) "Centering the periphery: the Cerdanya between France and Spain," in *Spain, Europe, and the Atlantic World: Essays in Honour of John H. Elliott*, ed. R. L. Kagan and G. Parker. Cambridge: 227–42.

Salapata, G. (1992) *Lakonian Votive Plaques with Particular Reference to the Sanctuary of Alexandra at Amyklai.* PhD dissertation, University of Pennsylvania.

(1993) "The Laconian hero reliefs in the light of the terracotta plaques," in Palagia and Coulson 1993: 189–97.

Salowey, C. A. (2002) "Herakles and healing cult in the Peloponnesos," in *Peloponnesian Sanctuaries and Cults: Proceedings of the Ninth International Symposium at the Swedish Institute in Athens, 11–13 June, 1994*, ed. R. Hägg. Acta Instituti Atheniensis Regni Sueciae, series in 4°, XLVIII. Stockholm: 171–7.

Salvaneschi, E. (1975) "Filiazione e contatto nel greco italiota e siceliota," *SILTA* 4: 67–112.

Salviat, F. (1965) "L'Offrande argienne de l''hémicycle des rois' à Delphes et l'Héraclès béotien," *BCH* 89: 307–14.

Sánchez, P. (2001) *L'Amphictionie des Pyles et de Delphes: recherches sur son rôle historique, des origines au IIe siècle de notre ère.* Stuttgart.

Sanders, J. M. (1992) Φιλολάχων: *Lakonian Studies in Honour of Hector Catling.* London.

Santarelli, A. (1990) "Isocrate Archidamo 47 e Mirone di Priene sulla cronologia della prima guerra messenica," *RCCM* 32: 29–37.

Sartre, M. (1991) *L'Orient romain: provinces et sociétés provinciales en Méditerranée orientale d'Auguste aux Sévères (31 avant J.-C.–235 après J.-C.).* Paris.

Sbardella, L. (2003) "Mogli o buoi? Lo scontro tra Tindaridi e Afaretidi da Pindaro ai poeti alessandrini," in Ρυσμός: *studi di poesia, metrica e musica greca offerti dagli allievi a Luigi Enrico Rossi per i suoi settant'anni*, ed. R. Nicolai. Rome: 133–50.

Schachter, A. (1986) *Cults of Boiotia*, II: *Herakles to Poseidon.* BICS Supplement 38.2. London.

 (1994) *Cults of Boeotia*, III: *Potnia to Zeus.* BICS Supplement 38.3. London.

 (2003) "Evolutions of a mystery cult: the Theban Kabiroi," in Cosmopoulos 2003: 112–42.

Scheibler, I. (1994) *Griechische Malerei der Antike.* Munich.

Schepens, G. (2004) "La guerra di Sparta contro Elide," in *Ricerche di antichità e tradizione classica*, ed. E. Lanzillotta. Tivoli: 1–89.

Schettino, M. T. (1998) *Introduzione a Polieno.* Pisa.

Schmaltz, B. (1980) *Metallfiguren aus dem Kabirenheiligtum bei Theben. Das Kabirenheiligtum bei Theben*, vol. 6. Berlin.

Schneider, J. (1985) "La Chronologie d'Alcman," *REG* 98: 1–64.

Scholten, J. B. (2000) *The Politics of Plunder: Aitolians and Their Koinon in the Early Hellenistic Era, 279–217 BC.* Berkeley, Los Angeles, and London.

Schwartz, E. (1899) "Tyrtaeos," *Hermes* 34: 428–68.

Schwertfeger, T. (1974) *Der Achaiische Bund von 146 bis 27 v. Chr.* Munich.

 (1981) "Die Basis des Tiberius Claudius Calligenes," in *10. Bericht über die Ausgrabungen in Olympia*, ed. A. Mallwitz. Berlin: 249–55.

Seeliger, K. (1897) *Messenien und der achäische Bund.* Jahresbericht des Gymnasiums in Zittau 567, 1896/7: 3–32.

Sergent, B. (1977) "Le Partage du Péloponnèse entre les Héraklides, I," *RHR* 192: 121–36.

 (1978) "Le Partage du Péloponnèse entre les Héraklides, II," *RHR* 193: 1–25.

Sharp, J. (1988) "Ethnic group and nation," in *South African Keywords*, ed. E. Boonzaier and J. Sharp. Capetown: 79–99.

Sheffer, G. (2003) *Diaspora Politics: At Home Abroad.* Cambridge.

Shero, L. R. (1938) "Aristomenes the Messenian," *TAPhA* 69: 500–31.

Shipley, D. R. (1997) *A Commentary on Plutarch's Life of Agesilaos: Response to Sources in the Presentation of Character.* Oxford.

Shipley, G. (1992) "Perioikos: the discovery of classical Laconia," in Sanders 1992: 211–26.

(1997) "'The Other Lakedaimonians': the dependent perioikic poleis of Laconia and Messenia," in Hansen 1997: 189–281.

(2000) "The extent of Spartan territory in the Late Classical and Hellenistic Periods," *ABSA* 95: 367–90.

(2004) "Messenia," in *An Inventory of Archaic and Classical Poleis*, ed. M. H. Hansen and T. H. Nielsen. Oxford: 547–68.

(2005) "Between Macedonia and Rome: political landscapes and social change in southern Greece in the early Hellenistic period," *ABSA* 100: 315–30.

Simpson, C. J. (1988) "Imp. Caesar Divi Filius: his second imperatorial acclamation and the evolution of an allegedly 'exorbitant' name," *Athenaeum* 86: 420–37.

Sineux, P. (1997) "À propos de l'Asclépieion de Messène: Asclépios poliade et guérisseur," *REG* 110: 1–24.

Sinn, U. (1978) "Das Heiligtum der Artemis Limnatis bei Kombothekra, I," *MDAIA* 93: 45–82.

(1981) "Das Heiligtum der Artemis Limnatis bei Kombothekra, II," *MDAIA* 96: 25–71.

Sirano, F. (1996–7) "Fuori da Sparta. Note di topografia lacone: recenti studi e nuovi dati dal territorio," *ASAA* 74–5: 397–465.

Smith, A. D. (1986) *The Ethnic Origins of Nations*. Oxford.

Solimano, G. (1976) *Asclepio: le aree del mito*. Genova.

Sourvinou-Inwood, C. (1974) "The votum of 477/6 and the foundation legend of Locri Epizephyrii," *CQ* 24: 186–98.

Spawforth, A. J. S. (1985) "Families at Roman Sparta and Epidaurus: some prosopographical notes," *ABSA* 80: 191–258.

(1994) "Corinth, Argos, and the imperial cult: Pseudo-Julian, *Letters* 198," *Hesperia* 63: 211–32.

Steinhart, M. (1997) "Bemerkungen zu Rekonstruktion, Ikonographie und Inschrift des platäischen Weihgeschenkes," *BCH* 121: 33–69.

Stewart, A. (1990) *Greek Sculpture: An Exploration*. New Haven and London.

Stibbe, C. M. (1972) *Lakonische Vasenmaler des 6. Jahrhunderts v. Chr.* Amsterdam and London.

(1991) "Dionysos in Sparta," *BABesch* 66: 1–44.

(1994) *Laconian Drinking Vessels and Other Open Shapes. Laconian Black-Glazed Pottery*, Part 2. Amsterdam.

(1996) *Das andere Sparta*. Mainz.

(2000a) *Laconian Oil Flasks and Other Closed Shapes. Laconian Black-Glazed Pottery*, Part 3. Amsterdam.

(2000b) *The Sons of Ephaistos: Aspects of the Archaic Greek Bronze Industry*. Rome.

(2000c) "Gitiadas und der Krater von Vix," *BABesch* 75: 65–114.

Strid, O. (1999) *Die Dryoper: Eine Untersuchung der Überlieferung*. Uppsala.

Stylianou, P. J. (1998) *A Historical Commentary on Diodorus Siculus, Book 15*. Oxford.

Taita, J. (2001) "Confini naturali e topografia sacra: i santuari di Kombothékras, Samikon e Olimpia," *Orbis Terrarum* 7: 107–42.

Tausend, K. (1992) *Amphiktyonie und Symmachie. Formen zwischenstaatlicher Beziehungen im archaischen Griechenland.* Historia Einzelschrift 73. Stuttgart.

(1993) "Argos und der Tyrtaiospapyrus P.Oxy. XLVII 3316," *Tyche* 8: 197–201.

Themelis, P. G. (1969) "Ἱερὸν Ποσειδῶνος εἰς Ἀκοβίτικα Καλαμάτας," *AAA* 2: 352–56.

(1970) "Ἀρχαϊκὴ ἐπιγραφὴ ἐκ τοῦ ἱεροῦ τοῦ Ποσειδῶνος εἰς Ἀκοβίτικα," *AD* 25: 109–25.

(1993a) "Damophon von Messene. Sein Werk im Lichte der neuen Ausgrabungen," *AK* 36: 24–40.

(1993b) "Ὁ Δαμοφῶν καὶ ἡ δραστηριότητά του στὴν Ἀρκαδία," in Palagia and Coulson 1993: 99–109.

(1994a) "Artemis Ortheia at Messene: the epigraphical and archaeological evidence," in *Ancient Greek Cult Practice from the Epigraphical Evidence. Proceedings of the Second International Seminar on Ancient Greek Cult, Organized by the Swedish Institute at Athens, 22–24 November 1991*, ed. R. Hägg. Acta Instituti Atheniensis Regni Sueciae, series in 8°, XIII. Stockholm: 101–22.

(1994b) "Hellenistic architectural terracottas from Messene," in *Proceedings of the International Conference on Greek architectural terracottas of the Classical and Hellenistic Periods*, ed. N. A. Winter. Hesperia Supplement 27. Princeton: 141–69.

(1996) "Damophon," *YCS* 30: 154–85.

(1998a) "The sanctuary of Demeter and the Dioscouri at Messene," in *Ancient Greek Cult Practice from the Archaeological Evidence: Proceedings of the Fourth International Seminar on Ancient Greek Cult, Organized by the Swedish Institute at Athens, 22–24 October 1993*, ed. R. Hägg. Acta Instituti Atheniensis Regni Sueciae, series in 8°, XV. Stockholm: 157–86.

(1998b) "Ὁ Δαμοφῶν στὴν Κύθνο," in *Kea–Kythnos: History and Archaeology. Proceedings of an International Symposium, Kea–Kythnos, 22–25 June 1994*, ed. L. G. Mendoni and A. J. Mazarakis Ainian. Meletemata 27. Athens: 437–42.

(2000) Ἥρωες καὶ ἡρῶα στὴ Μεσσήνη, Athens.

(2001) "Monuments guerriers de Messène," in Frei-Stolba and Gex 2001: 199–215.

(2003) "Ὁ Δαμοφῶν στὴν Οἰάνθεια," in Τὸ Γαλαξείδι ἀπὸ τὴν ἀρχαιότητα ἑως σήμερα. Πρακτικὰ τοῦ πρώτου ἐπιστημονικοῦ συνεδρίου (Γαλαξείδι, 29–30 Σεπτεμβρίου 2000), Athens: 27–33.

(2004) "Cults on Mount Ithome," *Kernos* 17: 143–54.

Thomas, C. G., and Conant, C. (1999) *Citadel to City-State: The Transformation of Greece, 1200–700 BCE.* Bloomington.

Thomas, R. (1989) *Oral Tradition and Written Record in Classical Athens.* Cambridge.

Thommen, L. (2000) "Spartas fehlende Lokalgeschichte," *Gymnasium* 107: 399–408.

Tiberios, M. (1990) "Apharetides-Tyndarides," in Descœudres 1990: 119–24.

Tigerstedt, E. N. (1965) *The Legend of Sparta in Classical Antiquity*. Vol. I. Stockholm.

Tölöyan, K. (1996) "Rethinking diaspora(s): stateless power in the transnational moment," *Diaspora* 5: 3–36.

Torelli, M. (1998) "L'Asklepieion di Messene, lo scultore Damofonte e Pausania," in *In memoria di Enrico Paribeni*, ed. G. Capecchi. Rome: 465–83.

Treves, P. (1944) "The problem of a history of Messenia," *JHS* 54: 102–6.

Tsaravopoulos, A. N. (2000–3), "Κυθηραϊκά," *Horos* 14–16: 207–11.

Tsitsiridis, S. (1998) *Platons Menexenos: Einleitung, Text und Kommentar*. Stuttgart and Leipzig.

Tullio-Altan, C. (1995) *Ethnos e civiltà: identità etniche e valori democratici*. Milan.

Tuplin, C. (1987) "The Leuctra campaign: some outstanding problems," *Klio* 69: 72–107.

Ugolini, G. (1995) "Aspetti politici dell'*Aiace* sofocleo," *QS* 21: 5–33.

Vallet, G. (1958) *Rhégion et Zancle: histoire, commerce et civilisation des cités chalcidiennes du détroit de Messine*. Paris.

Valmin, N. S. (1928–9) "Inscriptions de la Messénie," *BullLund*: 108–155.

(1930) *Études topographiques sur la Messénie ancienne*. Lund.

(1938) *The Swedish Messenia Expedition*. Lund.

(1941) "Ein messenisches Kastell und die arkadische Grenzfrage," *Opuscula archaeologica* 2: 59–76.

van der Kamp, J. S. (1996) "Anonymous tomb cults in Western Messenia: the search for a historical explanation," *Pharos* 4: 53–88.

van Wees, H. (1999) "Tyrtaios' Eunomia: nothing to do with the Great Rhetra," in Hodkinson and Powell 1999: 1–41.

(2003) "Conquerors and serfs: wars of conquest and forced labour in archaic Greece," in Luraghi and Alcock 2003: 33–80.

Vannicelli, P. (1993) *Erodoto e la storia dell'alto e medio arcaismo (Sparta–Tessaglia–Cirene)*. Rome.

(2004) "Eraclidi e Perseidi. Aspetti del conflitto tra Sparta e Argo nel V sec. a. C.," in Angeli Bernardini 2004: 279–94.

Vanschoonwinkel, J. (1991) *L'Egée et la Méditerranée orientale à la fin du deuxième millénaire: Témoignages archéologiques et sources écrites*. Louvain-la-Neuve.

Vansina, J. (1985) *Oral Tradition as History*. Madison.

Versakis, F. (1916) "Τὸ ἱερὸν τοῦ Κορύνθου Ἀπόλλονος," *AD* 2: 65–118.

Vidal-Naquet, P. (1981) *Le Chasseur noir: formes de pensée et formes de société dans le monde grec*. Paris.

Villing, A. (2002), "For whom did the bell toll in ancient Greece? Archaic and Classical Greek bells at Sparta and beyond," *ABSA* 27: 223–95.

Visser, E. (1997) *Homers Katalog der Schiffe*. Stuttgart and Leipzig.

Vitalis, G. (1930) *Die Entwicklung der Sage von der Rückkehr der Herakliden: Untersucht im Zusammenhang mit der politischen Geschichte des Peloponnes bis auf den 1. Messenischen Krieg.* Dissertation, Greifswald.

Wade-Gery, H. T. (1966) "The 'Rhianos-hypothesis,'" in *Ancient Society and Institutions: Studies Presented to Victor Ehrenberg on his 75th Birthday*, ed. E. Badian. Oxford: 289–302.

Walbank, F. W. (1957) *A Historical Commentary on Polybius*, vol. I. Oxford.

(1967) *A Historical Commentary on Polybius*, vol. II. Oxford.

Wallace, W. P. (1954) "Kleomenes, Marathon, the Helots and Arkadia," *JHS* 74: 32–5.

Walters, K. R. (1981) "'We fought alone at Marathon': historical falsification in the Attic funeral oration," *RhM* 124: 204–11.

Weber, M. (1972) *Wirtschaft und Gesellschaft: Grundriß der verstehenden Soziologie.* 5th edn. Tübingen.

Weicker, G. (1922) "Korythos," in *Paulys Realencyclopädie der classischen Altertumswissenschaft*, XI. 2. Munich: 1466–7.

Weickert, C. (1929) *Typen der archaischen Architectur in Griechenland und Kleinasien.* Augsburg.

Weil, R. (1959) *L'"Archéologie" de Platon.* Paris.

Wells, B. (2002) "Evidence for cult at the acropolis of Asine from Late Geometric through Archaic and Classical times," in *New Research on Old Material from Asine and Berbati in Celebration of the Fiftieth Anniversary of the Swedish Institute at Athens*, ed. B. Wells. Acta Instituti Atheniensis Regni Sueciae, series in 8°, XVII. Stockholm: 95–133.

Welwei, K.-W. (1974) *Unfreie im antiken Kriegsdienst, I: Athen und Sparta.* Wiesbaden.

Wenskus, R. (1961) *Stammesbildung und Verfassung: Das Werden der frühmittelalterlichen gentes.* Cologne.

West, M. L. (1974) *Studies in Greek Elegy and Iambus.* Berlin and New York.

(1985) *The Hesiodic Catalogue of Women: Its Nature, Structure and Origins.* Oxford.

Whitby, M. (1994) "Two shadows: images of Spartans and helots," in Powell and Hodkinson 1994: 87–126.

Wilamowitz-Möllendorff, U. von (1900) *Die Textgeschichte der griechischen Lyriker.* Abhandlungen der Königlichen Gesellschaft der Wissenschaften zu Göttingen. Philologisch-Historische Klasse. n.F., Bd. 4, Nr. 3. Berlin.

Wilhelm, A. (1914) "Urkunden aus Messene," *JÖAI* 17: 467–586.

(2000) *Kleine Schriften, II: Abhandlungen und Beiträge zur griechischen Inschriftenkunde.* Teil III. Österreichische Akademie der Wissenschaften, Philosophisch-historische Klasse, Sitzungsberichte, 679. Vienna.

Wilkie, N. C. (1983) "The hero cult in the tholos," in McDonald, Coulson and Rosser 1983: 332–4.

Winter, N. A. (1993) *Greek Architectural Terracottas from the Prehistoric to the End of the Archaic Period.* Oxford.

Woolf, G. (1994) "Becoming Roman, staying Greek: culture, identity and the civilizing process in the Roman East," *PCPhS* 40: 116–43.

Wörrle, M. (1995) "Von tugendhaften Jüngling zum 'gestreßten' Euergeten. Überlegungen zum Bürgerbild hellenistischer Ehrendekrete," in Wörrle and Zanker 1995: 241–50.

Wörrle, M., and Zanker, P., eds. (1995) *Stadtbild und Bürgerbild im Hellenismus. Kolloquium, München, 24. bis 26. Juni 1993.* Munich.

Zanker, P. (1995) "Brüche im Bürgerbild? Zur bürgerlichen Selbstdartellung in den hellenistischen Städten," in Wörrle and Zanker 1995: 251–73.

Zavadil, M. (2001) *Monumenta: Studien zu mykenischen Gräbern in Messenien.* Dissertation, Vienna.

Zimmermann, J.-L. (1989) *Les Chevaux de bronze dans l'art géométrique grec.* Mainz.

Zunino, M. L. (1997) *Hiera Messeniaka: la storia religiosa della Messenia dall'età micenea all'età ellenistica.* Udine.

Index locorum

Index of inscriptions

Archaeological sites

General index

Abia, 264
Achaea, Roman province, 300
Achaean *koinon*, 303
Achaean League, 19, 26, 36, 42, 44, 257—64
 Messenian membership of, 258
 relationship with Messene, 325, 336
Aetolia, Aetolians, 257—9, 260—1
Ageladas, 176
Agis, king of Sparta in the late fifth century, 212
Aglapios, Doric spelling of Asklepios, 271
Aigila, 86
Aigimios, 48
Aipytos, 62—3, 63—4, 66
Aithaia, 141, 205
Aithidas, 309
Alcidamas, *Messenian speech*, 180, 202, 223
Alkidamidas, ancestor of Anaxilaos, 149, 158
Ampheia, 96
Amyklai, 86
Anaxilaos, 147—54
 Doric spelling of his name in Thucydides, 163
Andania, 92—4, 264
 possibly assigned to Megalopolis after the
  defeat of the Messenians in 182 BCE,
  264, 299
 see also Karneiasion
Androklos, 96, 97
Antigonus the Third Doson, 18, 258
Antiochos, king of Messenia, 96
Aphareus, 296
Apharetidai, 270, 272
Apollo, Korythos, 118, 134, 237
 of Amyklai, 119
 in the Asklepieion, 278
 dedication of the Methanioi to, 186, 205
 Hyperteleatas, 113
 Karneios, 236, 281
 Mousagetes, 281
 Pythaeus, 295
Aratus of Sicyon, 260
Arcadia, Arcadians, 44, 79, 80, 98, 336

dedication at Delphi, 213
involvement in the liberation of Messenia,
 215—16
political unification of, 212
and the return of the Heraclids, 63
Argolid, 49, 50, 52—3
Argos, Argives, 43, 59—60, 79, 98, 208, 335
 their involvement in the foundation of free
  Messene, 214—15, 231
Arimnestos, 183
Aristokrates of Orchomenos, 79
Aristodemos, brother of Temenos and
 Kresphontes, 48
Aristodemos, Aipytid, 84, 97
Aristokrates of Orchomenos, 80
Aristomachos, father of Temenos, Kresphontes
 and Aristodemos, 50
Aristomenes, 85, 86, 88—92, 286, 296, 322
 absent from the Asklepieion, 283, 289
 hero cult for, in Messene, 89
 his tomb, 313
Aristomenes, Messenian of the Augustan age, 319
aristopoliteia, 301
 at Sparta, 302
Arkas, eponymous hero of the Arcadians, 213
Artemis, at Ithome/Messene, 126
 and Artemis Orthia, 24
 at Kombothekra, 157
 Laphria, 257
 Limnatis, 16, 23, 134, 166
 Limnatis, at Ithome/Messene, 275
 Orthia at Ithome/Messene, 234, 236, 278, 281
 her sanctuary at Volimos, 80, 114, 287
Artemis Orthia, 23
Asine in Messenia, Asinaeans, 38—43, 45, 97, 142,
 215, 230, 250, 254, 261
Asklepieion of Messene, chronology of, 283—5
Asklepios, 234—5
 in fourth-century Ithome/Messene, 233
 and Epidaurus, 235
 in Messenia, 270, 271

384